Un-American Activities

Un-American Activities

The Trials of William Remington

The Trials of William Remington

Gary May

New York   Oxford
OXFORD UNIVERSITY PRESS
1994

Oxford University Press

Oxford New York Toronto
Delhi Bombay Calcutta Madras Karachi
Kuala Lumpur Singapore Hong Kong Tokyo
Nairobi Dar es Salaam Cape Town
Melbourne Auckland Madrid
and associated companies in
Berlin Ibadan

Published by Oxford University Press, Inc.
198 Madison Avenue, New York, New York 10016-4314

Library of Congress Cataloging-in-Publication Data
May, Gary, 1944–
Un-American activities : the trials of William Remington / Gary May.
p. cm.
Includes bibliographic references and index.
ISBN 0-19-504980-2
1. Remington, William Walter, b. 1917—Trials, litigation, etc. 2. Trials (Perjury)—United
States. 3. Trials (Espionage)—United States. 4. Communists—United States—Biography.
5. Communist trials—United States. I. Title.
KF224.R46M39 1994
345.73'0231—dc20
[347.305231]   93-25321
                                                                      CIP

4689753
Printed in the United States of America
on acid-free paper

Preface

Alger Hiss. The Rosenbergs. Owen Lattimore. John Carter Vincent and the old China hands. Dalton Trumbo and the Hollywood Ten. To students of the post–World War II Red Scare, all familiar names, their cases still clouded by controversy. But the name of another—today almost forgotten—deserves to be elevated among these: William Walter Remington. "Never a brighter light appeared on the horizon," recalled a boyhood friend.

Born in New York City in 1917, educated at Dartmouth College and Columbia University, Bill Remington seemed to have it all—as handsome as a matinee idol, brilliant and ambitious, he appeared destined for a distinguished government career under Harry Truman. College friends even thought for a time that he might become President. Then, in 1948, came the accusations that destroyed Remington's career. Charged with being a Communist and a Soviet spy during World War II by ex-Communist Elizabeth Bentley, Remington spent the rest of his life fighting to clear his name. His days became an endless series of appearances before congressional committees, government loyalty boards, grand juries, and, after being indicted for perjury in 1950, judges and jurors during two trials in federal court.

The Remington case is important because it touches on many of the important questions that divided America during the Cold War: why were some of the best and the brightest of the New Deal generation attracted to Communism? what was the nature of membership in the American Communist Party and its ties to Soviet espionage? and how did the American political and judicial systems function during a time of acute crisis?

It is also the fascinating story of one man's journey from a conventional middle-class home in affluent Ridgewood, New Jersey, into Communist circles when in college and while working with the Tennessee Valley Authority in the 1930s; marrying a troubled young woman whose Communist connections brought him into contact with Soviet spies; and, finally, being pursued by a vengeful FBI and Justice Department bent on his destruction. Remington's life ended in a way not even his worst enemy could have imagined.

My examination of thousands of government records (most never seen before by a historian) and interviews with Remington's family, friends, and enemies suggests that the Remington story is not a simple morality play, reassuring neither those on the left who believed him the innocent victim of government repression or those on the right who were convinced that he was a Soviet agent brought to justice fairly and honorably. This book, I hope, will rescue Remington from historical anonymity and encourage others to explore this complex and intriguing case, to determine who truly was guilty of un-American activities: William Remington or the government of the United States.

Newark, Delaware   G. M.
January 1994

Acknowledgments

When I began to research the William Remington case, I expected, in my youthful arrogance, that it would be a relatively easy task. Now, eight years later, I am no longer young or arrogant, and the completion of this book proved to be the most complex, frustrating, and demanding work of my life.

First, locating documents was difficult. By accident or design, many of the records of the case were mislaid, misfiled, or reported destroyed. Repeatedly, I was told by rude and impatient government bureaucrats that the files were gone and that I, too, should go, as quickly as possible. Such treatment only intensified my determination to keep digging, and eventually, with persistence, stubbornness, and no small degree of luck, I uncovered the missing documents.

There were also legal obstacles to my gaining access to important records. Questions of illegality surrounded Remington's indictment for perjury by a grand jury in June 1950, so I was naturally interested in how that jury had reached its decision and requested the records. A Justice Department official happily informed me that the *Federal Rules of Criminal Procedure* protected grand jury minutes from public scrutiny—forever; only a federal judge could break the seal that kept them secret. I refused to accept this restriction; what possible reason could there be to deny scholars documents almost forty years old? Fortunately, I found members of the legal community who shared that view and agreed to help me win access, despite the absence of legal precedent and unlikelihood of success. With the indispensable help of the Public Citizen Litigation Group's Patti A. Goldman, a petition was drafted, marshaling legal and historical reasons to support the opening of the records, and filed with the United States District

Court for the Southern District of New York, where the grand jury had held session. Unfortunately, U.S. attorney Rudolph Giuliani opposed our request and a two-year struggle ensued, until the Honorable Whitman Knapp, a courageous federal judge with a reverence for history, rejected the government's call for continued secrecy and ordered the records released. Thus, my first and greatest debt is to Public Citizen, and especially to Patti Goldman, whose brilliant counsel won me the transcripts and, more important, established a partial precedent that other scholars can use to obtain similar records pertaining to other controversial cases of the McCarthy era. New York attorney Andrew Levander also worked with us, and I thank him for his efforts on my behalf.

There were others whose help was essential in reconstructing Remington's life and times. Chief among them were Remington's two wives—Dr. Ann M. Remington and Mrs. Jane Abramson, who kindly and frankly shared their memories of the man and the case. Mrs. Abramson also gave me access to records she had retained and the permission to quote from them. I am forever in her debt.

Many of Remington's high-school and college friends (and enemies) also agreed to be interviewed. I am grateful to Mr. John R. Scotford, Jr., Dartmouth '38, who volunteered to be my "man in Hanover," locating records and men who knew Remington at Dartmouth. These included L. P. Baldwin, Stephen Bradley, Dr. David Bradley, William Bronk, Colonel (retired) Robert Davidson, Samuel Dix, W. Atherton Fuller, William Goodman, Nicholas Jacobson, Asher Lans, Charles Livermore, Dexter Martin, William A. Martin, Donald H. Miller, Jr., John Parke, Irving Paul, Professor Jack Preiss, Alan Rader, Richard Sherwin, Professor Page Smith, and Budd Schulberg. Others, cited in footnotes, corresponded with me.

This book would not exist without the assistance of Remington's principal attorney, the late Joseph L. Rauh, Jr. He gave me unrestricted access to his legal files, which also contained correspondence with Remington's other lawyers— Bethuel Webster, William Chanler, and John M. Minton, whose own records were destroyed after their deaths. While he may not have agreed with my ultimate conclusions about Remington, I hope this work does justice to his brilliance, compassion, and generosity. He was truly a great man, and I deeply regret that he did not live to see the completion of this work. My thanks also to Richard G. Green, Esq., who permitted me to examine his records on the case.

A number of archivists and librarians were also extremely helpful: Kenneth Cramer and his staff at Dartmouth College's Baker Library; Howard Gottlieb at Boston University's Mugar Memorial Library; Mrs. Erica Chadbourn at the Harvard University Law School Library; and Tony Fantozzi and Michael Goldman, of the National Archives and Records Service. Dr. Susan R. Falb, Mary Profitt, and Roger Cronden at the Federal Bureau of Investigation helped me obtain the Bureau's voluminous records on Remington, Elizabeth Bentley, and others involved in the Silvermaster case. Mrs. Patricia Hatfield of Grundy,

Virginia, located obscure records on George McCoy. Professor Gerald Gunther, of the Stanford University Law School, took time away from his own research to locate important records in the papers of Learned Hand. And there were government officials who *did* go out of their way to help: John W. Jackson, David Essig, C. B. Faulkner, and Gary Roberts of the Federal Bureau of Prisons; Adele Fry, clerk of the U.S. district court in Scranton, Pennsylvania; Mel Hoover, Ed Kosheba, and Hank Sadowski of the United States Parole Commission; Charles S. Webb, chief probation officer of the Eastern District of Kentucky; the Honorable William J. Nealon, chief judge for the United States District Court for the Middle District of Pennsylvania; and the Honorable Eugene Siler, Jr., chief judge of the United States District Court for the Eastern District of Kentucky.

I am also happy to acknowledge the financial aid given to me by the University of Delaware General Research Fund and an award from the Delaware Humanities Forum.

At Oxford University Press, Sheldon Meyer, Brice Hammack, and Scott Lenz helped transform this work from a long, unwieldy manuscript, into a better organized, more readable book. Steve Matlack, computer genius, came to my rescue a number of times, and I am grateful for his help.

Finally, to my family—who endured my absences and frequent bouts of discouragement and depression—I offer my thanks and love. This book belongs to them.

Contents

Un-American
Activities

1

Present in the Flesh

"In delicate balance" was the way one official described life at the federal penitentiary at Lewisburg, Pennsylvania, in the fall of 1954. Perched atop a hill overlooking the Susquehannah River, Lewisburg was undergoing a transition from a minimum-security facility that originally housed Prohibition violators to a maximum-security facility for men found guilty of rape, assault, murder, and lesser crimes. Guarding an overcrowded prison population of twelve hundred was a custodial staff of just a hundred eighty-seven men, who considered themselves underpaid, overworked, and physically at risk.[1]

Events beyond the walls also affected the institutional climate. The Supreme Court's recent *Brown* decision ordering the desegregation of public schools seemed to many of Lewisburg's southern inmates a threat to the prison's segregated housing system.[2] Another problem bedeviled prison officials—the Communist issue. In the eating hall, at daily chapel, or exercising in the yard, were men whose names were notorious to Lewisburg's killers, rapists, and thieves. Daily they saw David Greenglass and Harry Gold, associates of Julius and Ethel Rosenberg who were convicted of atomic espionage and executed in June 1953. Most infamous was Alger Hiss, whose imminent release on November 27 enraged some who faced longer sentences than the three and a half years Hiss served for perjury. Also, there was 37-year-old William Walter Remington. "Brilliant of mind, handsome in appearance, engaging in manner," noted the *New York Herald-Tribune*. "Remington was a rising young government economist of outstanding promise in 1948 . . . when Communist accusations against him blasted his career and started him on his road to prison. . . ."[3] Men like

Remington and Hiss "weren't merely newspaper headlines or academic figures," said James V. Bennett, director of the Federal Bureau of Prisons, "they were constantly present in the flesh," a dangerous irritant to the more unstable inmates.[4]

No one was more aware of the tense atmosphere at Lewisburg than William Remington. Committed to Lewisburg in April 1953, Remington's first year and a half was uneventful. A blast from the boiler-house whistle routinely awakened him in his fifty-man dormitory quarters at 6:45 A.M. Countdown was at 7:00, so he quickly washed, shaved, and dressed in the standard prison uniform of blue shirt and slacks. By twos, the prisoners were then marched to the mess hall for a breakfast of cereal and pancakes plus sweet rolls and coffee. Then, Remington reported to the chief clerk's office, where he worked—typing, tabulating, proofreading, and doing "all the little things which take so much meticulous care— and some intelligence." Midday dinner was at 11:30 A.M.: meat, vegetables, salad, and dessert. "Food really excellent, for an institution," Remington thought. Afterwards, there was an hour and a half of leisure time. This he spent reading or playing handball in the yard (the outside recreation area). He returned to the office at 4:30 p.m. Supper was followed by more free time until 10:00 p.m., when his day ended.[5]

He was a model prisoner, reliable, quiet, industrious. He readily admitted to the warden that he had made serious mistakes in the past and hoped that he could begin a new life; so, he shunned Communist inmates like Greenglass, Gold, and, especially, Hiss.[6] Remington was also cool toward others because of a desire to avoid potentially dangerous relationships. He once told his wife,

> . . . I never ask a question . . . that shows any curiosity. . . . What I'm guarding against is a reputation for being too curious (though no one could ever regard me as an FBIer in disguise after what has happened to me). . . . If a fellow were to get into trouble over a fact or a incident, and remembers he told me, my position would be embarrassing. So I'm guarding carefully against excessive confidences.[7]

Remington's strict adherence to prison regulations was rewarded in August 1954, when he received a desired transfer to the hospital night shift (midnight to 8:00 A.M.) and assignment to honor quarters in I Dormitory—four- to six-man rooms, without locks, designed for the more stable, well-adjusted inmate, as well as those who worked at night. He found the patients more interesting than the men he had met in the clerk's office. "New experience for me to see genuine psychos . . . ," he wrote his wife on November 14. "I'm now seeing for the first time how an addict bluffs for drugs, etc. Give me horses, cows, pigs, even chickens, any day! None of them capable of human degradation."[8] Others suffered from more normal illnesses or injuries—accidental or planned. Admitted in late October was seventeen-year-old Lewis Cagle, Jr., who, according to his medical chart, had fallen down a flight of stairs, receiving a severe scalp laceration. Officials were unaware that Cagle's wound was actually caused by his roommate

George McCoy, an illiterate Virginia mountaineer, who had struck Cagle with a steel bed rod.[9]

Both men were familiar to Remington; they were quartered in I-39—the room located across the hall from his own. They, too, worked the night shift, in the power house, where they fired the great boilers that provided heat for the prison. But they were hardly the type of inmate for whom the honor system had been created.

George McCoy was thirty-four years old, short and stocky with receding brown hair and dull blue eyes so closely set that they gave his face a perpetual scowl. On his left biceps was a tattoo of a naked woman named Rosie Kidd. His right biceps bore another tattoo, his social security number; with an I.Q. of 61, he found it necessary to burn it permanently into his flesh in order to remember it. He was "a real McCoy" and proud of it, a member of that large and violent family, which, in the decades after the Civil War, feuded with the Hatfields of Kentucky and Virginia. Beginning in 1947, he ran afoul of the law and began to serve time in a number of state and federal institutions on charges ranging from public intoxication to car theft.[10] Sent to Lewisburg in February 1954, he managed to stay out of trouble. One reward for his good behavior (and the fact that he worked at night) was assignment to honor quarters; in August he moved to I-39.[11] McCoy was perceived by prison officials as quiet and passive, a mild-mannered little moron. Only one report noted a quality of viciousness in McCoy's character; it was this for which the prisoners knew him. While administrators were extolling his virtues, it was well known inside the walls that McCoy regularly carried a knife, and he had the reputation of being a killer.[12]

Lewis Cagle, Jr., was so afraid of McCoy that he armed himself with a brickbat, a one and a half pound brick stuffed in a white sock. Being a victim of violence was a new experience for young Cagle; he was accustomed to being the man who sent others to the hospital. Born in Chattanooga, Tennessee, in December 1936, Cagle was a runaway and car thief by the time he was fourteen. He was incarcerated first at the National Training School, a reformatory for juvenile delinquents in Washington, D.C., from where, in July 1953, he was sent to the Federal Reformatory at Chillicothe, Ohio, for terrorizing younger or weaker delinquents and trying to escape. At "Chilli," Cagle quickly became known as one who intimidated other inmates, and he almost caused a serious disturbance when a gang of angry toughs, tired of such treatment, sought revenge. After "a real bad fight with another prisoner" in June 1954, Cagle was sent to Lewisburg.[13]

Within days of his arrival, he was caught stealing milk, then was found brawling with another prisoner and was put in punitive segregation. In September, he was sent to the power plant, where he would work from midnight to 8:00 A.M. Because he was required to work the night shift, he was moved to honor quarters—I-39.[14]

When Cagle had lived alone at the National Training School and

Chillicothe, he had been relatively well behaved; however, records indicated that problems had occurred when he had been exposed to other prisoners. Now, bureaucratic negligence had put Cagle in the one place where, given his personality, trouble was almost inevitable. His roommates, in addition to McCoy, were Robert Hoosier, a young car thief and escapee from the Indiana State Farm; Robert Carl Parker, twenty-one, car thief and escapee from the State Penitentiary at Richmond, Virginia; and Frederick Nichols, a criminal since the age of thirteen.[15] Cagle and his roommates had much in common. All were products of broken homes; all were illiterate or almost so; all had records of juvenile delinquency; all had stolen cars or trucks and were prone to violence—a dangerous group on the lookout for a victim. It was not long before they found one—living just across the hall in I-32—William Remington.

To the men of I-39, Remington seemed a person both to envy and despise. Cagle and McCoy were short, dark, and unattractive. Remington, at six feet two inches, was almost a foot taller than the little Virginian and also towered over Cagle. He was blond and handsome, even in his dull prison garb. Cagle and McCoy had received only the most primitive of educations and could barely read and write. Remington was a Phi Beta Kappa graduate of Dartmouth College with a master's degree from Columbia University. He acted "high hat," McCoy, Cagle, and Parker later said. They, the most coarse and ill-mannered of men, thought Remington's walk awkward and claimed that he "ate like a pig in the mess hall. He put his elbows on the table and just shoveled the food in his mouth. That offended them," one official was later told.[16]

Then there was the question of Remington's politics. Some months earlier, McCoy had learned from another inmate that Remington was "a Communist—one of the Big Shots in the Party." "I hate Communists," McCoy said later. " . . . I would like to line up a bunch of Communists and shoot them down with a machine gun just like cutting wheat."[17] These feelings were shared, with varying degrees of intensity, by the others. Remington's roommates were also called obscene names and accused of being Communists themselves or Communist lovers because they lived with him.[18]

Such hatred for Remington led to a war of nerves. One late October day, while I-32 was empty, Parker and Hoosier rummaged around, opening lockers and stealing anything that interested them: candy, cigarettes, matches, razor blades. At this point, Remington did not feel personally threatened and dismissed the likelihood of violence as "99 percent hokum." Later, Lewisburg's warden would characterize Remington's attitude as naive.[19]

The thieves struck again on Monday, November 8, while Remington and his roommates were having supper. Pipes and candy were taken and, this time, two pens belonging to Remington. Harry Guthrie, a convicted murderer, called the raids "spite jobs" and was glad that Remington had been victimized. Two nights later, Parker sneaked into an empty I-32 and set fire to the bed of Andrew

Danton, Remington's closest friend. When they returned to their room, they found "the sheets and mattress . . . blazing merrily away." Again, Remington appeared curiously detached from the event, calling it, in a letter home, interesting. That night, he

> tuned in on the [prison] grapevine . . . and discovered that the whole floor is irritated at the fire incident. It "puts on the heat." . . . the officers will be more apt to discover and crack down on the various illicit activities normally in process. . . . Some fellows have a good idea of who's doing the stealing and who tossed the match, but naturally they won't say. However, they are emphatic that no one is in any physical danger. . . . If the situation doesn't improve I'll apply for separate room honor quarters as two roommates already have.[20]

During the next few days tensions lessened, after Remington's roommates were moved out. He interpreted this as a good sign, continuing to believe that the others were the real sources of irritation. "The shocking thing is that the Administration has either so little knowledge or such inadequate means of control that such 'bad' cliques take over effective sway even in 'honor' quarters," he observed. "Ordinarily any man detests [the idea] of being under surveillance. Here, in many quarters, the relatively decent element often wishes to goodness there were more."[21]

On November 21, Remington wrote his wife, "Things have quieted down nicely in our dormitory."[22] In part, his analysis may have been designed to comfort her, for while he was writing such words, he was still trying to mend the rift with the men of I-39. His ally was a sympathetic inmate who had roomed briefly with his adversaries. "During our conversation Remington expressed concern for his personal safety because Hoosier and Parker were always making threats against [Danton] and him . . . ," the inmate later said.[23]

That night, as Remington was writing his letter, McCoy, Cagle, and Hoosier left I-39, walked to the power plant, and began their midnight shift. Hoosier and another inmate quarreled and were removed to segregation. Around 4:00 A.M., McCoy began to complain to Cagle about Remington. "He seemed to be beside himself with anger . . . ," Cagle later noted. "Remington is a no good bum," McCoy told him, "a spy, [a] traitor." McCoy wanted to "mess up his head, straighten him out," and he invited Cagle to join him.[24] At first, Cagle thought McCoy was joking; he was accustomed to hearing McCoy talk about his hatred for Communists, but his actions had never gone further than making obscene remarks and petty theft; however, McCoy was deadly serious. "Let's see if you're a man or a chicken," McCoy taunted. If Cagle would hit Remington with his brick-bat, McCoy would slug him, too. Cagle later claimed that he had refused to join McCoy. His sentence was due to expire in just fifteen days, and he desperately wanted to go home. But "to be called 'chicken' was . . . the worst thing

that could happen to me. . . . I would do most anything to display my courage."
Finally, Cagle said, "O.K."

"I believe that you will do it," McCoy replied.[25]

At around eight o'clock the next morning, Monday, November 22, Robert
Parker crossed the hall into I-32. He searched until he found hidden commissary
items, which he carried away: five packs of cigarettes, several bars of Nestles
chocolate, and packages of peanuts that had been hidden in the sleeves of the
mens' bathrobes. He stole the bathrobes, too. Returning to his room, he placed
his booty proudly on display atop a table and hung up the bathrobes. McCoy,
Cagle, and Nichols soon returned after a quick breakfast in the mess hall.
Nichols, a solitary man, went directly to sleep. McCoy asked Parker where he
got the candy and cigarettes.

From Remington's room, Parker said.

Shouldn't we return the bathrobes? Cagle asked.

"Just let them hang where they are," Parker replied. The men were silent for
a while—outside the room they could hear the janitor sweeping the corridor; the
only sound, the swish of his broom. Then they discussed returning to I-32. If
Remington awoke during their burglary, McCoy and Cagle agreed "to hit [him]
in the head with the brick." (Parker was unaware that they had earlier agreed to
strike Remington whether he awoke or not.) Parker said he would check to see
if anyone was there. " . . . I don't give a damn if [Remington] is in the room,"
McCoy said. "He is nothing but a damn Communist and he tried to sell us all
out. Let's go and get Remington!" The men armed themselves—Parker with a
knife he had stolen from the mess hall, McCoy with his bed rod and Cagle with
the brick-bat.[26]

They moved swiftly across the hall and rushed into I-32. Remington was
alone, sleeping. As Parker moved toward the bathroom, he heard a sound " . . .
like a thump on a hollow drum and saw Cagle swinging the sock. . . . I saw blood
on the side of Remington's head and face and saw him put up his left arm to
ward off the blow. Cagle was hitting him fast." Cagle struck Remington four
times; "blood spurted from his head and flew everywhere."

"That's enough," McCoy said, taking the sock from Cagle; "You're a man. I'll
finish the job." McCoy hit Remington once, "a good blow," Cagle thought—
Remington kicked "like a hog." Cagle went into the bathroom to wash the
blood off his hands, then the three started to leave the room. They saw
Remington struggle to rise and heard him snort. Remington's nose was filled
with blood.[27]

Back in their quarters, Cagle and McCoy burst out laughing. "I think I did
him pretty good," Cagle said.

"I think I killed him," McCoy boasted. Next they disposed of the evidence
of their crime. Parker cut the bloody sock away from the brick, and McCoy
flushed it down the toilet. Disgusted, Parker dropped his knife and said "to hell

with it." McCoy told him to get rid of the brick, so Parker left the room with it, walked down to the end of the corridor, and threw it out the window. He returned to find Cagle and McCoy still joking. "Knock it off," he yelled, probably angry that what he thought would be a search for more cigarettes and candy had turned into an assault, possibly with the most serious consequences for all of them.

"What are you so sore about?" McCoy asked him. "He was no good anyway." "Go to bed and shut up," Parker said.[28]

A short time later, Hoosier, released from segregation, returned to his room. He chatted with the men for a while and then left to go to the control room, two floors below. As he started downstairs, he discovered Remington, bleeding profusely and clinging to the railing. "I can't figure it out," he was mumbling to himself. Horrified, Hoosier turned and ran for help. Two flights above, McCoy, Cagle, and Parker could hear his screams echoing through the stairwell.[29]

"A spy," "a traitor," "a damn Communist [who] tried to sell us all out," McCoy had said of Remington. Such accusations were commonplace in America in 1954, but were they justified in Remington's case? To Fred J. Cook, a journalist who has written extensively about him, Remington was an innocent man sent to prison because of "a betrayal of justice at the highest levels. . . ."[30]

Innocent or guilty? Spy or victim of government repression in a time of national hysteria? Who was William Remington, and what brought him to that stairwell in Lewisburg Prison, his skull shattered and dripping blood?

◆ ◆ ◆

In the spring of 1934, the graduating class of New Jersey's Ridgewood High School selected certain seniors to be memorialized in *The Arrow*, the campus yearbook. Surely no one would forget Chester Newkirk's "Bulldog Look" or Helen Martin's "Sophistication." Unforgettable, too, was sixteen-year-old Bill Remington. His Characteristic: "Incongruity"; Favorite Occupation: "Impressing People"; Saving Grace: "Cerebrum"; Aspiration: "Union Soap Boxer"—this was a remarkably accurate description of William Remington, unconventional and ambitious, brilliant and politically outspoken.[31]

Remington was born in New York City on October 25, 1917, the only child of Frederick and Lillian Sutherland Remington. Fred was almost forty-eight years old; Lillian, twenty-nine. The difference in their ages was not the only thing that separated them. Lillian was born in Granville Ferry, a small village in Nova Scotia and was by temperament and training an artist and intellectual. She grew to be tall and red-headed and was charming, intelligent, and a very impressive and forceful personality. The Sutherlands had once been very wealthy, having earned their fortune in the ship-building trade. But when Lillian and her younger sister, Nan, were growing up, the age of the great clipper ships had passed, so their parents lived frugally on the remnant of the family fortune and whatever small salary their father, an Episcopal minister, could earn.

It was during a visit to New York that Lillian met Fred Remington, a handsome and polished man. Born in 1870 in Massachusetts, the eldest of three children of a middle-class family, he grew up and was educated in Brooklyn, New York. Not long after graduating high school, he went to work for the Metropolitan Life Insurance Company, where he would spend the next forty years of his professional life. Fred is remembered as cautious and conservative. The cause of his conservatism may be partly explained by an incident that his daughter-in-law believed had a profound impact on his personality. When Fred was young, his best friend contracted syphilis and committed suicide. As a result, Fred became obsessive about protecting his health (he would rub his skin daily with salt in the hope of toughening it) and also avoided physical intimacy with women, to the point that the first time he made love was on his wedding night in 1914, when he was forty-four years old.

It was not the happiest of marriages. Lillian felt little respect for Fred, according to her daughter-in-law. She thought that she had been misled about Fred's social standing and finances. Since he was always extremely well dressed and associated with wealthy people, she was later shocked to learn that he had no money. Furthermore, Lillian had wanted more children and believed that, somehow, Fred prevented her from conceiving again and felt quite bitter about it. Fred was untruthful and deceitful, Lillian believed, and she treated his efforts at physical fitness with scorn. Bill came to share her views, telling friends later that he was ashamed of his mediocre father.

Fred also experienced disappointments, especially with his career at Metropolitan Life. At corporate headquarters in Manhattan, he frequently seemed on the verge of becoming a top executive but time after time was passed over for promotion. His failure was intensified by the success of his younger brother, Will, who became quite wealthy as vice president of the American Woolen Company. While Fred seemed cowed by Will, Bill would later openly clash with his rich, ultra-conservative uncle.[32]

Home for the Remington family was Ridgewood, New Jersey, where Fred first settled in 1889. Rural and provincial in the late nineteenth century, Ridgewood, when Bill was born in 1917, was fast becoming an affluent, conservative community, a bedroom town for people on the rise in the New York City area. Executives, bankers, and Wall Street brokers lived there as did millionaire J. J. Newberry. Every morning, a rattletrap bus, nicknamed the "Toonerville Trolley" drove around the town, picking up commuters for the local station, from which the Erie train would take them into Manhattan.[33]

William Remington grew up in a modest Victorian house on East Ridgewood Avenue, the "poor relations in the very rich community of Ridgewood. . . . " "Birth normal," his mother later wrote. "Breast fed. Perfectly healthy." Everyone who knew young Bill, from the old German woman who helped out around the house to the librarian who gave him his first job, considered him an honest and obedient child. If he was peculiar, his mother thought, "it was in general goodness. Never a showy boy nor a leader but always in the top rank picked for dependability." When Lillian was not teaching art to supplement the family income, she and her son would spend their days at Christ Church, where Bill sang in the choir, often served as acolyte, and was baptized and confirmed.[34] His mother also introduced him to the Oxford Group, an affiliate of the Episcopal church committed to social and economic reform. "Through the Oxford Group I developed a complete dedication to a personal God," Remington once said. "I tried to place all my thoughts and acts at God's service, and I became more than usually concerned in that way to helping the underdog as part of my religious philosophy."[35]

His parents also expected that he become physically strong. When he was just four, his mother ordered him to climb a tree in their backyard, and when he refused, she pushed him up, "switching his legs as he cried and resisted."[36] His father would frequently take him hiking on Mount Torin and taught him how to shoot in the small shooting range he had built in his cellar and in the New Jersey mountains. Hiking, camping, and boating on the Bay of Fundy near his mother's birthplace in Granville Ferry would also remain lifelong hobbies for Bill.[37]

Years later, when Bill married, his wife formed "the impression that he never had much fun in his life—that he'd always been under these family strictures: 'be the ideal Christian'; 'work hard'; 'do without.'"[38] Eventually, as many children do, Bill Remington began to rebel against these family rules, but in his case, the rebellion would outlast childhood and adolescence and continue into adulthood. Indeed, one close friend later claimed that Bill's interest in radical politics was, in part, a rebellion against "the rigid discipline of the Remingtons."[39]

Intellectually, he was precocious. He entered Kenilworth Elementary School in September 1922, a month before his fifth birthday. He did well and a few years later was allowed to skip the fourth grade.[40] For Remington, learning was always a serious responsibility; his friends dubbed him "Gloomy Gus." Although he tried to relax, the nickname followed him to junior high at the Beech Street School. At thirteen, he became a Boy Scout but unhappily remained a choir boy—"the oldest and biggest in Christ Church."[41] He was still obedient but was growing increasingly restless as he prepared to enter Ridgewood High School.

His years at Ridgewood, from 1931 to 1934, were among the most important of his life. Coinciding with his adolescence (he was not quite fourteen when school began), it was a time when Remington's rebelliousness would bring him into conflict with his family and many of his peers. Although Ridgewood was considered one of the most rigorous schools in the state, Remington's academic record was superior—he made the "High Honor" role in his sophomore, junior, and senior years. He was also a member of the track team (he ran cross country and threw the javelin) and belonged to the fencing and glee clubs.[42]

With his friend Betsy Hunt, he organized the "inner circle of higher thought," a group of students who explored religious and cultural topics. "The 'inner circle of higher thought' . . . is getting into good order now," he wrote his aunt in October 1933. "People love to argue . . . , and the more they gas, . . . the more practice and delight I have in trying to refute them." Of particular interest was evolution, which clashed dramatically with his religion's doctrine of divine creation. After listening to one fundamentalist minister preach on the subject, Remington "accosted him and talked (mostly argued I'm ashamed to say) for 55 minutes in the shadow of a stately pulpit." Unwilling to accept the minister's sermon, he visited the Museum of Natural History in New York City, seeking a scientist's more learned advice. "I had a marvelous time," he told his aunt. "Evolution is all I ever thought it was and more; and I can prove it, so my religion can be what I damn well please!"[43]

As the nation sank deeper into Depression, politics and economics became unavoidable topics for Remington and his friends. During the presidential campaign of 1932, they traveled to Patterson, New Jersey, to hear socialist Norman Thomas address an audience of the unemployed.[44] Remington was fascinated and returned home a committed radical. He studied the *Communist Manifesto* and soon afterwards announced, while playing football, that he was a Communist. "There was silence," Ralph Bergstrom later recalled. "Then someone asked what does THAT mean? He then said he'd joined the Communist Party. . . . I had the impression Bill did it more to shock or watch reactions," Bergstrom concluded.[45]

Remington's political views did not endear him to his classmates. The ravages of the Depression were never fully felt in Ridgewood; to be sure, some men lost their jobs or, like Fred Remington, had their salaries reduced, but Norman Thomas won no votes there and Franklin Roosevelt very few. The community remained staunchly conservative and hostile toward those, like Bill Remington, who espoused liberal or even radical ideas. His peers called him exotic and weird, the boy who never fit in.[46]

Physically, he also stood out from his classmates. At thirteen, he was five foot nine; a year later, he was six foot one and a half inches tall and still growing to his eventual height of six foot two. His favorite outfit consisted of green slacks, a plaid shirt covered by a Kelly-green sweater, and, atop his head, a beret. "He was tall with a shock of sandy reddish hair, with an almost gangly spareness," recalled one classmate. "He often seemed to be listening or considering with a slight forward tilt of his head. Withal . . . there was [an] air of abstraction . . . leading to an impression of remoteness." Some, in an attempt to break through what they thought was Remington's icy reserve, started calling him "the Golden Haired Canary," but the nickname did not last long.[47]

It was not just his political or intellectual views that many found obnoxious but also the manner in which he expressed them. Many considered him argumentative and supercilious. "Bill did make other people feel demeaned," said one friend, "because they just weren't up to his abilities." Another remembered Remington's "quizzical expression—I was never sure whether he was making fun of me or taking what I said with a grain of salt."[48]

His teachers also found him interesting and even mysterious. Newell Gillem, Remington's English teacher, remembered a strange incident that still astonished him fifty years later:

> We were standing in the main hall one day, . . . talking—when suddenly I thought Bill had lost his balance. One foot came up and I grabbed it—to steady him. He said that he had boasted that he could kick me in the stomach! It sounds like he didn't have much respect for me but I'm inclined to think that he liked to be the bold fellow who defied convention . . . "To Heck with you and your customs, I'll do what I please!"

Gillem liked Remington but thought him "too smart for his own good. He tended to be boastful, superior to those around him."[49] Alice Wharton, chairwoman of the English Department, also thought Remington unusual. "He was . . . shy and often ill at ease and, like many adolescents, he covered up his feelings of insecurity . . . with a show of superiority," she wrote in 1948. "He was known as an intellectual snob, and perhaps he was one, for the world of the mind was the only one in which he received satisfaction and attention. He was called a 'radical' because he thought deeply about subjects which other boys of his years were not concerned with."[50]

Remington's unpopularity did not seem to bother him. On the contrary, to be unconventional was Remington's way of winning notoriety and status in the rigidly status-conscious community of Ridgewood. If he was not the wealthiest student or the most distinguished because of eminent parentage, at least he could be recognized as the most bizarre.

His closest friend at school was also his first love—a brilliant and lovely young woman named Helen Martin. They had much in common; both were very intelligent and outspokenly radical and had conservative fathers and intellectual mothers. They fell in love and spent almost every hour together, going often into Manhattan either to enjoy a Broadway show or to attend meetings of the American Civil Liberties Union, where they listened raptly to its founder, Roger Baldwin.[51]

Remington's courtship created a serious family rift. Fred and Lillian thought that at sixteen Bill and Helen were too young for such a serious relationship and feared that it might lead to an accidental pregnancy, followed by an inevitable marriage that would wreck his plans for college. And, although the Martins were financially comfortable, Lillian, a bit of a snob, hoped that Bill might make a match with the daughter of one of her wealthier friends.[52]

Bill's love life was not his parents' sole concern in 1934. Fred was ill. At sixty-three, despite his lifelong effort to keep himself physically fit, he suffered a serious heart attack and began to prepare for retirement on a pension that could not adequately support a family with a son in college.[53] This meant that Lillian would have to increase her own teaching schedule, and no doubt she felt all the old resentments intensify. Friends of Bill's began to observe hostility developing between parents and son. "There was something lacking in that house," Bill's friend Bob Davidson recalled. "Bill would be the first one to talk and he would be running along on something and his father didn't have too many good things to say to Bill. You could tell there was trouble there all the time." "I don't think Bill ever took up anything that his father recommended," Don Hammond thought. "Bill ignored his mother too. I never saw any real affection crop up anywhere in that family." Bill's relationship with his father had never been good, but now he found himself more and more at odds with his mother. "He had rather conflicting attitudes towards his mother," said a woman who knew them well. "He liked being with her, admired her, but he had to protect himself against her attempts to manage and control him."[54]

Despite his parents' objections, Bill continued to see Helen secretly, but like many a high school romance, theirs began to fade during 1934, their senior year. They were both extremely busy. Helen was managing *The Arrow* and preparing to enter Smith College, while Remington was still an active member of the track team and singing with the glee club and a cappella choir.[55] He, too, had selected a college—Dartmouth, in Hanover, New Hampshire. Although he would receive a partial scholarship, his education would be expensive, and he would have to bear most of the financial burden. His father had decided definitely to retire in September, just as Bill's freshman year began, and Fred's pension was (as Lillian put it) small. But she was confident that through thrift and hard work (Bill would seek part-time employment in Hanover), the family would manage. Bill apparently decided against seeking help from his wealthy uncle Will, who had no children to support; the two frequently argued about the New Deal—the elder William Remington hated FDR, while the younger was a passionate admirer.[56]

Remington graduated in June with "Highest Honors." In *The Arrow*, under a photograph in which he was neatly dressed and looked typically stern, he listed his achievements while at Ridgewood and his "Class Prophesy":

ASPIRATIONS IN 1934: TO DIE, A GENIUS OF THE FIRST WATER, UNRECOG-
NIZED.
REGRETS IN 1954: THAT HIS AMBITION WAS BEING FULFILLED.[57]

2

The New Student—
Dartmouth, 1934–1936

"There was nothing outstanding about Bill Remington when he arrived in Hanover during September 1934, with the other 700 Pea Greens that composed the class of '38," noted the college's newspaper, *The Dartmouth*, in 1954:

> The Greenbook showed he compiled an average record at his hometown high school . . . and above his activities there was a picture of a skinny-faced youngster with unruly blond hair and a sheepish grin. If anyone had bothered to check the birth date of the tall, lanky freshman, they might have been surprised to find that he was only 16, but other than that there was nothing out of the ordinary about Bill Remington.[1]

This was probably the only time that *The Dartmouth* described Remington as ordinary. By the time he was a senior, he was perhaps the most controversial man on campus—liked by a few, disliked by many, and a source of irritation, confusion, and, frequently admiration to faculty and administrators. Political scientist Hugh Elsbree thought him "one of the most unusual undergraduates I have encountered in ten years of teaching," while economist Malcolm Kier confessed that, for a time, he "wasn't certain whether this man was crazy or a genius."[2]

At first, he was just one of 708 men who composed the largest freshman class in the history of the college. He arrived in Hanover on September 15, 1934, when dormitories were opened and orientation week began. President Ernest M. Hopkins distributed certificates of registration, while Green Key, the junior

honor society, gave each man a Bible (Dartmouth was founded in 1769 by mis-
sionaries hoping to Christianize the Indians). The class also received a set of
rules that was supposed to govern behavior during the days ahead. Freshman
beanies were always to be worn outdoors; they must walk around—never
across—the college green; when visiting the Nugget, Hanover's sole movie the-
ater, they were required to sit in side seats; and all rallies and football games were
to be enthusiastically attended.[3] Remington's quarters were in Hitchcock Hall,
an old, four-story brick building, whose suites looked extremely comfortable—a
large living room with fireplace and two bedrooms. Climbing the stairs to his
assigned room—408—he learned that he was not as lucky as others. His single
room on the fourth floor was furnished with two beds, two desks, and little else.
He also found that he had a roommate, Richard Sherwin, a tall, husky eighteen-
year-old from Worcester, Massachusetts.

Sherwin was also very bright but was quickly dazzled by Bill Remington. He
just sat there dumbfounded the whole year while Bill tried to open his eyes to
art, literature, politics, and history.[4] Sherwin, a devout Catholic, also became
the object of Remington's caustic wit. W. Atherton ("Athy") Fuller, who lived
across the hall, later recalled the mischievous look in Remington's eye when he
would needle Sherwin about holding so staunchly to religious beliefs that
Remington thought were antiquated. As a result, Remington and Sherwin spent
little time together, and except for Fuller, Remington had no close friends in the
dorm. "He was not very popular," Fuller said, "because of his supercilious, almost
superior way he had of downing people."[5]

After settling in, Remington quickly sought a way to supplement his income;
his scholarship and aid from home were not enough to finance his education.
Before September ended, he had secured a number of jobs: clerking in the
Sanborn Library, selling stationery and books of football tickets to his classmates,
and managing a student laundry. That year he also carried a full academic
schedule, which included courses in English, French, mathematics, and sociology. His final grade point average for the freshman year would be 3.1, good
enough to earn him a place on the "Third Honor Roll."[6]

He also pursued those activities that had won him success at Ridgewood
High. He joined the freshman track team and the debating squad, which elected
him captain. "He could debate person-to-person on any subject better than anyone I ever heard," recalled Athy Fuller, the team's researcher.[7] He was also an
energetic but often difficult athlete. Arising early in the morning, he would don
green track shorts and a Class of '38 sweatshirt, and, with his javelin resting on
his shoulder, would pedal his bicycle through town to the athletic field.
Remington was not the easiest man to coach. "He would cock his head and
appear to be paying close attention, but I always had an uneasy feeling that his
mind was a thousand miles away . . . ," one of the teachers remembered.[8] Budd

Schulberg, a senior, recalled Remington frequently arguing with his coach about his practice schedule:

> He told the Coach he didn't think throwing the javelin was that important that he should practice every day. "It doesn't work that way," the Coach told Remington. "If you're on the track team you practice when the Coach tells you to practice." And Remington said: "To Hell with it. I won't throw the javelin," and stalked off the field.

But he eventually returned and won his letter. "I remember arguing with him that it would be good for the social movement to be an athlete," Schulberg said, "that you could throw the javelin and still take a stand on social issues, . . . but not Bill—once he'd decided it was a waste of time, nothing would change him. It was both admirable and maddening. He was one of the most stubborn people I've ever known."[9]

Despite his heavy workload—in the classroom, on the athletic field, in the library and laundry—these were lonely days for Remington. Never one to make friends easily, he was uncomfortable among his classmates, especially the many smug, conservative prep-school graduates turned juvenile pranksters who loved to torture freshmen. To junior Donald Miller, who befriended Remington, he seemed "terribly withdrawn, very quiet, lost in that environment."[10] So, Remington set out to find the college's equivalent of the "inner circle of higher thought." Such a group was difficult to find on the Dartmouth campus, a tranquil island in a national sea of student activism.

The Great Depression and the New Deal, the rise of fascism abroad, the example of the Soviet Union as the great socialist experiment of the day—all created great excitement on America's college campuses. "The rah-rah days of the twenties are gone," wrote the editor of the University of Texas's *Daily Texan*. "[The] increased interest of students in politics, . . . and the de-emphasis on fraternities and athletics, show the college man is thinking more and playing less." At U.C.L.A., the editor of the *Daily Bruin* argued that "the Depression killed Joe College. Economic necessity has forced thought into the life of college students." The University of Chicago's *Daily Maroon* noticed "more political and international discussion by students," while the Columbia *Spectator* had fewer articles on "athletic do-or-die spirit" and more "logical criticism . . . which past generations of undergraduates might have resisted."[11]

Sociologists who studied student attitudes in the mid-1930s discovered that a majority now considered themselves liberals. At Purdue, students were more supportive of government aid for farmers, national ownership of railroads, and taxation of large fortunes. A study at the University of Maryland revealed that 75 percent of the students believed it was government's job to regulate hours and wages, while 90 percent felt that relief should be administered from Washington.[12]

Above all, students were opposed to American participation in any future war. From Rhode Island to California, students called war unjustifiable and urged that it no longer be used as an instrument of national policy. In 1934, the socialist Student League for Industrial Democracy and the Communist National Student League organized a national "Student Strike Against War" and suddenly found thousands of students flocking to their banners. On April 13, 1934, twenty-five thousand students—the majority from New York colleges—left their classrooms to cheer speakers "who denounced war, paraded for peace, and adopted resolutions . . . against war." A year later, on April 12, 1935, more than a hundred fifty thousand undergraduates on a hundred thirty campuses demonstrated during the second Student Strike Against War.[13] "A New Student has arisen," concluded *The Student Review* early in the decade. " . . . His school-fed illusions are fading away. He is beginning to realize that his life is inextricably bound up with the social system under which he lives."[14]

Such intense ferment, Remington discovered, was almost nonexistent on the Dartmouth campus. During the 1932 presidential campaign, 90 percent of the Dartmouth student body voted in a mock election to return Herbert Hoover to the White House, while just 5 percent chose Franklin D. Roosevelt. In protest, freshmen Donald Miller and Francis Bartlett organized a Dartmouth chapter of the socialist Student League for Industrial Democracy, but it failed to attract the support of even the few radicals on campus and quickly expired. The handful who considered themselves Communists established an affiliate of the National Student League, but it, too, remained tiny and ineffectual.[15]

Not even the peace issue—which usually appealed to conservatives as well as radicals—had much appeal at Dartmouth. The Green International, a pacifist organization was founded in the spring of 1932 with a hundred members, but within a year, membership dwindled to a dozen students, and the group disbanded.[16] (In contrast, 1933 saw antiwar conferences held at Cornell and Columbia and Berkeley and U.C.L.A.)[17] "Joe College" was alive and well at Dartmouth.

Still, there did exist on campus a group of self-professed Communists, and it was this group that captured Remington's attention during his freshman and sophomore years. It included Francis Bartlett, a quiet, studious intellectual from a wealthy Westchester County family, and Donald Miller, called by one friend a little fireball, as gregarious as Bartlett was withdrawn. Alan Rader, converted to Communism by his boyhood friend Fran Bartlett, was an activist who established Dartmouth's Young Communist League and, in 1936, flunked out of college because of his preoccupation with radical causes. Robert Boehm was, like Bartlett and Rader, a wealthy New Yorker who spent the summer of 1935 touring the Soviet Union. Finally, there was an extraordinary young man from California, Budd Schulberg, son of Hollywood mogul B. P. Schulberg. Brilliant and charming, he was said to be the only man ever to live with a Hollywood starlet while still a student at Dartmouth. Bartlett and Schulberg would later become members of the Communist Party.[18]

Remington's attraction to these men is easily understood. Like him, they were brilliant and unconventional, personifications of the "New Student" of the 1930s. Their lives did not revolve around football games, fraternity pranks, or Winter Carnival (when special trains brought young women up to Dartmouth). Theirs was a world of ideas and causes. These were passionately expressed in *Steeplejack*, "Dartmouth's Journal of Controversy," which they founded and ran. "*Steeplejack* declares for a New Deal at Dartmouth College," the editors wrote in the premier issue in September 1933, "a birth of opinion and literary creativity, a comprehension of the purposes of the College, an integration of undergraduate life with the activities and culture of the outside world." While *The Dartmouth* remained preoccupied with football, tennis, and crew, *Steeplejack* focused its attention on economics and foreign affairs. One issue featured Robert Boehm's exposé of international arms merchants, debates between socialists and Communists, and a front-page editorial entitled WE HAVE HAD TOO MUCH TALK! WHAT CAN WE DO ABOUT WAR?[19] This was the intellectual world that influenced William Remington's own thinking during his first two years at Dartmouth. He later testified:

> During the course of my freshman year my political views moved left quite rapidly. I came to believe in very extensive government ownership and control of industry . . . [,] breaking up big business concerns . . . [,] highly progressive income taxes . . . and I became convinced that labor unions were the answer to a great deal that was unchristian about society.

He was also sympathetic toward the Soviet Union. "I thought Russia a great experiment: they were making great progress toward improvement of living standards and I liked what the Russians were proposing for collective security against Nazism and Fascism." He considered himself a philosophical Communist and made no secret of it.[20]

He also tried to look and act like a radical. "He was a wild man," one friend said, "unkempt, [his] red hair sticking up all the time." He also went around half-dressed, without a coat, and instead of boots wore low-cut tennis shoes, even during the worst Hanover blizzards.[21] Classmate Stephen Bradley remembered "a red-eyed fanatic's look" on Remington's face that reminded him of the abolitionist John Brown. One conservative student later recalled spending

> many hours arguing with Bill in my room. I seldom went to his because it always smelled like rotten apples and was cluttered with Communist books. One time . . . he said that there would come a time during the revolution when he would shoot me down in cold blood.

Others took Remington less seriously—"Oh come off it, Remington," they would cry, when he said something especially outrageous.[22] Unfortunately, Remington's corrosive personality would not be forgotten by those who had been its target, and his careless, insensitive remarks would later contribute to his downfall.

There was another side to Bill Remington, not fully discernible to his classmates. The man who openly called himself a Communist and frequently acted like a bohemian, also wanted to be a part of the world he and his fellow radicals scorned. For example, he seriously considered joining a fraternity—but only Alpha Delta Tau, because he considered it the most aristocratic. "They go after the football players," he wrote his family in 1935. "Down at the house there was no one without a Big 'D'. But of course I'll have one too."[23] Unfortunately, the expenses of fraternity life made it impossible for him to join. Bohemian or aristocrat—which was the real Bill Remington? His life at Dartmouth and later in Washington would reveal what one friend called "a constant tension between his political beliefs and his worldly ambitions."[24] For now, he chose to live on the periphery of campus life, among those the Alpha Delts would have called the outcasts.

His closest friends among the radicals were Donald Miller and Alan Rader. Miller, whose family was devastated by the Depression, also had to work his way through Dartmouth; like Remington, he sold freshman yearbooks and football tickets and scrubbed dishes in the freshman commons, where they first met. Miller was a veteran of *Steeplejack* and unafraid to express openly his radical views. (After graduating, Miller repeatedly tried to join the Communist Party but was rejected because he was considered too boisterous.) Given their common economic difficulties and similar views, Remington and Miller established a close and congenial relationship.[25]

Alan Rader, the son of an affluent General Mills executive, also moved sharply to the left after entering Dartmouth in 1932. He was one of the first to join Dartmouth's antiwar Green Shirts and the National Student League but found their members, ideas, and methods shallow and disappointing. One day, in 1934, he turned to Miller and said, "We ought to have a Young Communist League, don't you think . . . ?"[26] This casual proposal, and what followed, would eventually have disastrous consequences for Bill Remington.

Not long after his talk with Miller, Rader took the train into Boston and met with YCL organizers to establish a Dartmouth chapter. A charter was drafted and arrangements made for the distribution of membership cards and the collection of dues. Meetings began sometime in the fall of 1934; the original group, according to Rader, consisted of most of the campus Communists, excluding Miller, denied membership because of garrulousness. Its youngest participant was Bill Remington. "Bill was one of the central core people," Rader recalled. "Soft spoken, thoughtful, sincerely concerned with important questions, very good at thinking out loud and saying what he believed." It was an informal group, but most applied for membership, received cards, and paid dues. Was

Remington an official member of the group or just an enthusiastic visitor? No one knows for certain. If he was not a formal member, he did "attend meetings," Rader is certain, "and expressed his being in favor of what we were trying to do. I remember him as being one of the activists. . . . "[27]

Although the Young Communist League was considered a Party training ground, it often existed independently (especially in rural New Hampshire where Party leaders left it pretty much on its own). According to the YCL handbook, a member was expected "to develop . . . both [an] understanding of the Communist movement and an ability to take part in the class struggle, so that when [he or she] becomes of age [they] will qualify to enter the Party." Those who were eventually admitted to these exalted ranks were expected "to accept in full the Communist program and the discipline of the Party. . . . " Party goals included opposing imperialist war, defending the Soviet Union, abolishing ROTC, and ending racial injustice.[28]

In practice, Rader's YCL (and its successor) was, as one who was familiar with the chapter notes, "a study group." Members would read Marx, articles from the *Daily Worker*, and pamphlets that the Communist Party put out, but that is as much as they did. Occasionally, they would pass out leaflets urging people not to buy toys made in Germany and Japan. It was all very harmless; no one was plotting to blow up the U.S. Capitol.[29]

Although it was an innocuous organization that had little impact on campus, YCL meetings were kept strictly secret. Those involved feared that public exposure might damage their reputations with administrators. Such fears were not groundless. In 1936, when Donald Miller, who knew nothing about the YCL, briefly left Dartmouth to work for the *New York Times*, Dean Neidlinger told the paper that Miller was a dangerous Communist who should not be employed; the editors hired him anyway. And when Alan Rader's academic record began to suffer because of his political activities and he flunked out, the dean refused his request for readmission.[30] Therefore, the Communists tried to establish public forums approved by the faculty. Stearns Morse, a member of the English Department known to be politically sympathetic, and political scientist Hugh Elsbree sponsored a Marxist study group in 1935. Morse later remembered Dero Saunders's brilliant analysis of *Das Kapital*, but Elsbree thought "the whole thing was a lot of horsefeathers" and quit; the group dissolved after just a few meetings.[31] Remington later admitted attending meetings of a second Marxist study group in 1935, established by Barney Davis, a chemistry instructor. Approximately twenty students gathered in Davis's room on Sunday mornings to discuss current events. Jack Preiss, Class of '40, remembered that Remington also participated in a third group that met during 1937 and 1938.[32]

Remington was joined in these activities by his boyhood friend William Alonzo Martin, Jr., who arrived at Dartmouth as a freshman in September 1935. Although they had not seen one another for years, they discovered that they still had much in common. Martin also considered himself a Communist and his views, said his older brother, Dexter, "drove our parents nuts."[33] Each had qualities that attracted and repelled classmates. Those few who genuinely admired Remington, like Athy Fuller, disliked Martin, whom he called "a serious Marxist [with] no fun and games about him."[34] Martin's friends tended to hate Remington and found it puzzling that the two were such close friends. "They were totally incompatible in every way," their friend Page Smith noted. "Martin was short with a very pale face and a quality of exuberance, vitality, and openness. Remington was tall, cool, calculating—constantly expressing the sense of a secret, private life. . . . "[35] Eventually, these differences would destroy their friendship, but in the beginning, they got along splendidly.

Remington and Martin moved into Crosby Hall, the oldest, smallest, and cheapest dorm on campus—home of the poorest students as well as football players, members of the ski team, and others who did not mind battling cockroaches. Remington was busy with his various part-time jobs, demanding courses, and new extracurricular activities—working for the Junto (an organization that brought political and literary figures to the campus) and writing for *The Dartmouth* now that the *Steeplejack* had expired. "If I didn't have to sleep I could easily find things to occupy me 40 hours a day," he told his family in October 1935.[36] Two professors were especially influential—Allan MacDonald and Sidney Cox, both members of the English Department and popular with most of the campus Communists. MacDonald, a dapper little man with a carefully trimmed mustache, broke the canons of literary orthodoxy by praising the works of D. H. Lawrence and T. S. Eliot. He was also a practitioner of the "New Politics," encouraging his students to participate in liberal activities, because he thought that "if the average Dartmouth undergraduate does not have enough social responsibility to be an active liberal while in college, he will be so hopelessly conservative in later life that he can in no way contribute to the solution of the world's problems."[37]

"Sensitive and defiantly independent" was how one colleague described Sidney Cox, who gave aspiring writers a supportive atmosphere at his Sunday evening literary gatherings. "All the interesting people on the campus came to Sidney Cox's Sunday nights," William Bronk recalled. "Sidney would read something that one of us had written or something he'd been reading—then we'd all quarrel about it." If Bronk thought the conversation dull or too much dominated by Remington, he would chat with Cox's charming wife, Alice, and eat her delicious cakes. Cox was particularly popular with the Communists (although he was basically apolitical). Over the years, Fran Bartlett, Budd Schulberg, Bill Martin, Page Smith, and Remington gathered at Sidney's. After a particularly stimulating evening, Schulberg recalled, he would run home to "try to practice what Sidney had been preaching."[38]

So did Remington. While his interests had once been exclusively political, he now became fascinated by literature and even told college officials in 1935 that his career would be a literary one.[39] His first published work appeared in *The Dartmouth* in the fall of 1935 and reflected his interest in art inherited from his mother. Daily, he spent hours at the Carpenter Art Gallery conferring with Gobin Stair, the assistant curator. They talked endlessly about everything from traditional and avant-garde art to the works of James Joyce, Sigmund Freud, and Karl Marx. Stair thought that Bill's articles on Thomas Hart Benton and Vincent Van Gogh were excellent, while his instructor in Renaissance art, Churchill Lathrop, was "impressed with [his] original insights, observation, and graceful writing"—more typical of a senior than an eighteen-year-old sophomore.[40]

Despite his new interests in literature and art, he was drawn back to politics, as both reporter and participant, when a bitter labor dispute erupted in nearby Rutland, Vermont. It began in November 1935, when some six hundred quarry and marble workers went on strike against the Vermont Marble Company and its owner, the Proctor family. Budd Schulberg, formerly of *Steeplejack* and now editor of *The Dartmouth*, was one of the first outsiders to visit the scene. At strike headquarters in West Rutland, he talked with officials of the International Quarry Workers' Union and the strikers themselves. He found their fury directed against the Proctors. One angry miner said:

> The family are the most reactionary in Vermont. They have a vast estate. . . . For generations they have controlled the politics of our state, the state university, the public utilities and the marble industry throughout North America. They pay the lowest wages in the state and employ the most workers. [They] . . . live like feudal barons, and rule many Vermont towns in such a way that the workers and farmers live like serfs.[41]

If such reports sounded to Schulberg like wild fantasies, he soon discovered that they were close to the truth. In the tiny marble towns of Rutland, Proctor, Florence, and Danby, he found families trying to survive on five dollars a week— and less. He saw children kept out of school because they lacked clothing to protect them from the cruel winter cold. Workers' homes were little more than rotten barns; their daily diet, a bowl of cooked potatoes. Wanting *The Dartmouth* to become truly relevant, Schulberg published his observations on the front page of the newspaper, where once articles about football and fraternities had been predominant. "Here at Dartmouth too many college radicals have attacked campus-lack-of-interest only to withdraw into their own red-ivory tower of social theory," he told his readers on December 3, 1935. "Too many conservatives have been equally guilty, armed with idealistic theories, blind to actual social conditions. Starvation in the quarry area is not a theory but a fact. Members of the Hanover community interested should demonstrate their interest not with theories—radical or conservative—but with actual aid." Schulberg's story electrified both the campus and the town, and the next day, a committee of prominent college officials and townspeople was established to help the miners. *The Dartmouth* staff volunteered to collect contributions of food, clothing, and money and to deliver them to Vermont.[42]

Remington helped, too. With members of the Dartmouth Union and the National Student League, he organized a campus-wide canvass held on Friday night, December 6. The group met first at *The Dartmouth* office in Robinson Hall, where they received their instructions; then, they piled into cars and drove to every dormitory and fraternity house in Hanover. They encountered some minor resistance—a few students complained that they were *wearing* their old clothes, while others admitted that they had never heard of the strike—but most gave generously. At the end of the evening, their collection included camel-hair coats and suede leather jackets, an assortment of shoes and ice skates, a roast chicken, coffee, and a bottle of cod liver oil pills. Late that night, Remington returned to his room, exhausted but exhilarated.[43]

On Saturday afternoon, cars and a truck filled with clothing, food, and other articles arrived in West Rutland. As Remington and other students unloaded the goods, the workers "danced around . . . like small children at Christmas." "Thank God, my children can go back to school now," one man remarked.[44]

The struggle was far from over. Fur coats and suede jackets could clothe but could not feed the workers and their families, and Rutland's Overseer of the Poor, an employee of the Vermont Marble Company, refused to provide relief to the starving strikers. In January 1936, they sued him, and Remington covered the events for *The Dartmouth*. The courtroom was packed with spectators, many of them strikers who hoped that if the jury convicted Overseer John F. Dwyer of neglecting his duties, they would then be assured of receiving state and local aid. Remington, standing in the back of the room, listened closely and took notes as the union's attorney questioned Mrs. Bujak, mother of six and wife of a mill worker earning three dollars a week. She had no shoes, coats, or warm clothes for her children and nothing to eat but potatoes, cabbage, milk, and sauerkraut, she testified. Six times she had asked Dwyer for help, and each time he had refused. Dwyer's attorney, who was also counsel to the Vermont Marble Company, rejected the union's charges, but after an hour and twenty minutes, the jury found Dwyer guilty.[45]

"The quarry workers are fine," Remington wrote his family following the trial. "Cold, hungry and a little miserable. But quite confident now that they'll win." Dwyer's conviction meant that "now the towns are having to support the strikers' families according to the state and federal laws. So everything is really great."[46]

Remington was too optimistic. The strike dragged on for six more months until a tentative settlement was reached through federal arbitration. In late September 1936, workers returned to the marble quarries, their hourly wage now increased two and a half cents. In the case of Mrs. Bujak, relief was a long time coming, and when she opened the envelope, she found a check for four dollars.[47]

By the time Remington learned the ultimate fate of the marble workers, he was a thousand miles away—in Knoxville, Tennessee, working for the Tennessee Valley Authority (TVA) and involved in another struggle between labor and industry. Taking a leave of absence from Dartmouth after his sophomore year was a difficult decision, dictated by financial necessity and a desire to "work and get knocked about a little." His fascination with politics and economics led him to reject his earlier plan for a literary career in favor of a life in public administration. At Dartmouth he had studied the operations of the newly created TVA and hoped to work with it for a year before returning to college. "My life and study in Hanover," he wrote Dean Neidlinger, "would have more far-reaching purpose and direction if I had a foundation of practical experience on which to base my major studies, centering around applied sociology and regional planning." Working for TVA would help him to evaluate what he had already learned and "make my last two years at Dartmouth more valuable."[48]

He arrived in Knoxville in August 1936 and contacted a college friend named Davis Jackson, a messenger at TVA, who offered him a place to live and an introduction to officials in personnel. "Seems to be a fine young chap, mature, very intelligent," his TVA interviewer noted. He thought Remington would make a good messenger and recommended that he be hired.[49]

The bureaucracy moved slowly and hearing nothing from TVA's personnel department, Remington concluded that he had been rejected and returned to Ridgewood. In September, he was back on campus when he received a telegram from TVA, offering him the position of messenger at a salary of $1,080 a year. He immediately sought out the dean (who assured him that he would be re-admitted the next year) and a number of his favorite professors. Nearly everyone with whom he spoke approved of the move—feeling, Remington later noted, "that a year's practical experience would be particularly good for me." He telegraphed his acceptance, rushed home to gather some clothes and books, and, instead of hitch-hiking, took the train to Knoxville "because I was trying to get there in a hurry."[50]

3

Enfant Terrible—
Knoxville, 1936–1937

On an unseasonably warm morning in early October 1936, Nellie Ogle—the owner of a boarding house at 920 Temple Avenue, Knoxville—was visited by two young men seeking a room to rent. One she knew fairly well—Henry Hart, Jr., a graduate of Vanderbilt University. Hart introduced his companion Bill Remington, down from Dartmouth College to spend the year working for TVA. The tall young man with reddish blond hair seemed very nice, Mrs. Ogle thought, although he did look a bit strange, wearing an overcoat and heavy clothing. Mrs. Ogle showed them a downstairs furnished apartment, consisting of a living room, sleeping porch, and bath; the rent (which included meals) was sixty dollars a month. 920 Temple was home to a number of TVA employees, she told them; they would fit right in. The two men agreed and said they would move in that very day.[1]

Remington had arrived in Knoxville a few days earlier, had taken a room at the local YMCA, and had joined TVA's messenger service. It was there that he met Hart, who was looking for a roommate. They discovered that they both enjoyed art, literature, and music and possessed a similar outlook on politics. "Bill was the most seriously committed individual I've ever been close to," Hart later recalled. "He wanted to get results and achieve his goals and he would let no obstacle stand in his way."[2] Remington was equally impressed with Hart, the son of a Methodist minister. He called him the southern aristocrat and was happy with his new friend and his new life. He wrote his parents in October:

Am very comfortable here and immensely pleased with the sensibility of my decision. Job is fine—a bit monotonous before long probably, . . . but I'm right in the
spot to learn what I wanted to learn. . . . When I finish Dartmouth it'll be a little
different from being "just another college boy."[3]

His work, carrying the mail from office to office, quickly proved to be as dull
as he had expected, and he looked elsewhere for stimulation. He joined the
American Federation of Government Employees—a union associated with the
old, conservative AF of L—but decided to work with a group of other young
employees who wished to see the local break away and join the new, dynamic
CIO. Volunteering "to do any kind of leg work that the union could give me,"
Remington pinned notices on bulletin boards, collected dues from his fellow
messengers, and became a member of the Workers Education Committee, which
helped to organize workers in the Knoxville area. Not long after his arrival in
the city, employees at the Holston Hosiery Plant left their sewing machines and
set up a picket around the building, protesting low wages and inhuman working
conditions. Remington and other members of the committee went immediately
to the scene—advising strikers of their rights under current labor law, raising
funds, and trying to boost morale by teaching strikers' children how to play
touch football.[4]

At union meetings and on the Holston picket line, Remington encountered
Remington also visited all-black Knoxville College, where he organized a
program in adult education. "It is going like a house on fire and good things will
come of it," he told his family. " . . . I have written speeches, outlined programs,
done an awful lot of work and made a speech that brought . . . the crowd forward
in their seats. Never have I had to shake so many hands."[5]

At union meetings and on the Holston picket line, Remington encountered
a group of like-minded men and women who would become close friends during
his year in Knoxville. First there was Katherine "Kit" Buckles, an attractive and
intense political radical of twenty-nine who had recently been executive secretary of the League of American Writers—an organization of Communist literary
lights. Remington enjoyed being with Kit, talking about Waldo Frank and
Theodore Dreiser, only names to Remington but friends of Kit's in New York.
Although Kit was ten years older than Bill and presently having an affair with a
socialist, Bill apparently hoped for a romance with her but was rebuffed. More
accessible was Mabel Abercrombie, an exuberant young woman from Georgia,
who also lived at Temple Avenue. Mabel, whose parents were political reactionaries, was a Russophile. She kept scrapbooks filled with news clippings about
the Soviet Union, played Russian songs on the Ogles' piano and taught friends
Russian folk dances. She also enjoyed antagonizing the conservative Mrs. Ogle,
who hated TVA, which, she believed, was ruining the country. Bill also thought
Nellie peculiar (she would often steal candy from his room) and loved to annoy
her by imitating Mabel's more outrageous remarks: "Our economic system has
been on trial for 2,000 years and has never worked properly," he said one night.

Nellie also claimed that Bill insulted her by stating that "she was being exploited by capitalism. . . . "[6]

Mabel introduced him to another young employee of TVA, Muriel Speare, in her mid-twenties, who went hiking with Bill in the Great Smoky Mountains and, when it was necessary, darned his socks. Speare, the daughter of a wealthy financial analyst employed by Wall Street firms, was a graduate of Mount Holyoke College, who drifted south in 1936, eager for new experiences. Despite an excellent education and travel abroad, she felt insulated from life, and after starting work as a junior typist, she joined the union, filled with curiosity. Speare became an active supporter of the CIO faction in its struggle with the AF of L and joined Remington, Abercrombie, and others on the Workers Education Committee.[7]

While Speare was basically an amateur unionist, her friend Christine Eversole, also in her mid-twenties, was a professional. The daughter of a poor Swedish immigrant farmer, Eversole was educated at the University of Colorado, where she had known Kit Buckles. Following graduation in 1932, she taught school in a small Colorado town, but the problems of the underprivileged remained her constant preoccupation. So, in 1936, she enrolled at the Highlander Folk School in Monteagle, Tennessee, to become a union organizer. It was Kit Buckles who urged her to apply for a job with TVA, and after being hired that July as a typist-stenographer, she joined Lodge #136, actively campaigned to shift the union to the CIO, and taught law and labor practices to strikers at the Holston Hosiery Plant. In September, after a whirlwind courtship, she married Forrest Benson, a fellow TVA employee. "I saw [Christine] all the time," Remington later said, " . . . at dinner parties . . . ,[and] square dances. She and I were engaged in a great many things which brought us into overlapping orbits."[8]

Howard Bridgman and Merwin "Pat" Todd were also good friends and fellow activists. Bridgman was twenty-five, a graduate of Amherst College, who was involved in labor activities in New York and North Carolina before joining TVA's messenger service. Everyone liked Bridgman, but they also found him stiff and humorless. More flamboyant was Pat Todd, also twenty-five, a New Yorker educated at the University of Wisconsin and the Sorbonne. Short and stocky, with dirty-blond hair, Todd was a dedicated radical. "He would be prepared to move into any situation, regardless of how great the threat of violence," Hart later recalled. "Like Bill, only further along and . . . a considerable tug on Bill to follow where Pat led."[9]

To conservative TVA officials and the townspeople they met, Remington and his friends were oddities. They were called "radicals" and "the young intelligentsia." One TVA employee thought they were a "closely knit clique . . . who exhibited a certain clannishness, who constantly associated with each other and appeared to have strong secret ties."[10] All tended to date or just socialize within the group. When it came to union activities, workers education, or support for the Spanish Loyalists, they thought and spoke as one.

Bill Remington was the most unusual member of the group. Howard Bridgman dubbed him "the ENFANT TERRIBLE," remembering one early meeting "in which [Remington] said that he had . . . sized up what was wrong with TVA . . . and started telling them how they should change it." Jerome Allen, Bill's boss, thought him possessed by a crusader's zeal to help the stricken South, while to veteran labor activist Horace Bryan, Remington was "a wild young boy who wanted to . . . get into fights in labor organizing activities."

"Everyone knew him as a character," said an acquaintance, David Stone Martin. "He was . . . fanatical in his political beliefs. I won't deny that he was a Communist . . . , that was well known because he approached everyone and asked them to join the Communist Party."[11]

Was there really a Communist Party unit in Knoxville, and was Remington actually a member? Or did he simply associate with those who were?

Building a Communist Party branch at TVA was the principal responsibility of Ted Wellman, the secretary of the Tennessee Communist Party from 1935 to 1939. Wellman, a New Yorker, was " . . . witty and ultra sophisticated," wrote Paul Crouch, who succeeded him as Party secretary. "Plays, movies, and current literature were his main fields of study; drinking and female companionship his favorite hobbies."[12] Given his interests, Wellman must have found his assignment to provincial Tennessee disappointing, and lacking the energy of a dedicated organizer, he delegated his work to Pat Todd and Kit Buckles.

Todd arrived at TVA in May 1935 and quickly invited his roommate to join the Party, but he refused.[13] Kit Buckles, who came to Knoxville in 1936, recruited Henry Hart during a luncheon at the Terrace Tea Room in October. Hart hesitated; still deeply religious, he held back until August 1937, when he finally joined and received a Communist membership book.[14] Buckles also encouraged Remington to join during a luncheon date, but whether he actually received a membership book is unknown, although Muriel Speare, who joined the Party in the summer of 1937, believed that Remington did become an official member.[15] Buckles's first definite success probably occurred shortly before she left TVA in December 1936, when she invited Christine Benson to join the Party and Christine accepted. Benson later testified that she received a membership book from Ted Wellman and attended a few meetings with Buckles and Todd.[16]

Todd was also successful that December. He was able to persuade Howard Bridgman to join. "The manner of joining was very informal," Bridgman later said. "I was asked, I accepted, and then I started to attend Party meetings." Just how informally Communist Party affairs were conducted under Wellman's leadership is revealed by the fact that Bridgman did not receive his membership book until 1938, over a year after he left Knoxville.[17]

It was Bridgman's later recollection that he joined a Party unit that consisted of three members: Todd, Remington, and a woman he initially was unable to remember. (It was probably Christine Benson.) They met fairly regularly, read the *Daily Worker*, and discussed current issues—from union organizing to the Spanish Civil War. They also attempted to enlarge the branch through personal recruitment. For example, Muriel Speare later recalled that Christine Benson approached her in the spring of 1937 and invited her to be a member of the Communist Party. Christine identified the other members of the group, which, Muriel Speare later thought, included Remington. During the next few weeks, she discussed her prospective membership with others in the unit, attended one meeting as a visitor, then joined in June. "The act was clear cut and not one likely to be forgotten," she later said.[18]

Remington also participated in recruitment efforts, according to Rudolph F. Bertram, a labor relations official with TVA. Sometime in May or early June 1937, Bertram received a telephone call from Remington, who asked for a private interview. Bertram told him to come to his office at noon, when they could talk alone. "Remington opened the conversation by talking about workers' education," Bertram later testified, "and after . . . beating around the bush . . . invited me to join the Communist Party, saying my interests and aims in the labor movement were in line with those of the Communist Party." Bertram, a veteran trade unionist, born and educated in Germany, was shocked and angered by Remington's invitation and proceeded to lecture him on the evils of Communism. A bitter discussion ensued that lasted almost an hour. "Remington was not apologetic," Bertram said, and after one last defense of Communist principles, he departed. "He did not say he was a member of the Communist Party, nor did I ask him, although I assumed he was. If not, he was certainly close to it."[19] Remington later claimed that Bertram was mistaken about the subject of their debate: it was the CIO that he had encouraged Bertram to join. But Bertram was adamant that his was the correct version of the story. Circumstantial evidence would seem to favor Bertram. First, their meeting occurred at a time of active recruiting for the Party, when Speare and others were becoming members. Also, given Remington's arrogance, it seems likely that he would try to recruit the one man working with TVA who was the least likely to join and therefore the most prized—Bertram, the German social democrat, who despised the Communists.[20]

Despite all the effort, Party membership at TVA remained small. Muriel Speare later said that the unit numbered no more than ten, while Howard Bridgman put the number between twelve and twenty.[21] Communist Party records for the same period claim only seven members in the clerical and technical branches and thirteen in the industrial branch. (In the city of Knoxville, with a population of a hundred fifty thousand, there were only thirty-three members, according to one Party official.)[22] Whatever the exact number, no member of the Communist Party ever held an important position in the Authority—most were messengers, clerks, secretaries, or stenographers.

It is also important to understand that TVA's Party Branch #1 existed during the era of the Popular Front, that period when official Communist Party doctrine shifted from confrontation to cooperation with the New Deal. "Members . . . looked upon the CP as a kind of advanced guard . . . for extending and improving the New Deal," Paul Crouch later noted. " . . . Wellman signally failed to carry on their 'education' step by step as was done elsewhere throughout the Party, which generally taught its members that support of the Roosevelt Administration was merely a temporary expediency and that the Capitalist state must be overthrown through armed insurrection and a Soviet dictatorship established."[23] Such goals were foreign to the TVA group. "To me, [the Communist Party] was a spearhead for bringing about certain reforms . . . ," Christine Benson said later. " . . . We really wanted America to be what it says it is."[24] This was certainly Remington's view, too, whether he was a member of the Party or just close to it.

Whatever his actual affiliation, Remington tried to look like a member of the revolutionary proletariat. He wore old, dirty clothes and let his hair grow long and rarely combed it. He bought a red motorcycle and, wearing a leather jacket and muddy boots, would leave his boarding house and ride away mysteriously in the early morning hours. "Not long after these rides," the suspicious Mrs. Ogle claimed, "there would be labor strikes at various places around Knoxville"—all, according to Nellie, caused by the boy in the black leather jacket.[25]

By March 1937, Mrs. Ogle had lost all patience with Remington and Hart. Tired of being teased and distrustful of their visitors who she was convinced were Communists, Mrs. Ogle finally asked them to move. Hart was somewhat relieved. He, too, had grown weary of Remington's intensity and volunteered to work in Dayton, Tennessee. Remington learned that Pat Todd was looking for a roommate, so together they took a room at Ruby Cox's old, rambling boarding house at 933 North Broadway. (A short time later, they were joined by Horace Bryan, a 28-year-old labor organizer and, perhaps unknown to his roommates, a member of the Arkansas Communist Party, who was hired by the Workers Education Committee to promote the union at TVA.)[26]

They did not remain long at their new apartment, having again run afoul of a cantankerous landlady. Mrs. Cox did not like the looks of her boarders or their activities. Their conversations were "Communist talk," so she contacted Roy N. Lotspeich, the president of the Appalachian Textile Mills and a rich and powerful figure in Knoxville. Lotspeich directed Sheriff J. C. Cates to hire private detectives to keep watch on Remington and Todd and also to gather information about CIO activities in the city. To lead the team, Cates selected 57-year-old Josephus Remine, a real-estate agent and farmer who, with two aides, was permitted to enter the Cox residence to spy on the "dangerous" young men.

Standing in a dark hallway or secreted in an adjacent room, Remine could hear everything that was discussed. One night, Remine said he heard Remington bragging that "me [sic] and Horace Bryan has [sic] put more people in the Communist Party than all the rest of you put together."[27]

Remine also followed "radicals" to Reeve's Roost, a picnic ground in Dutch Valley, five miles from Knoxville. There, he saw "Communists" dancing in the nude:

> It was eleven couples on a stage back of this fellow's house up under a little mountain and it was out where the police force didn't have jurisdiction, and these eleven were dancing and they were just like they were born in the world; they didn't have anything on.

Among those who visited the "nudist camp," according to Remine, were Remington, Todd, and Bryan.[28] Remington later denied ever going to Reeve's Roost. "From what I have heard of those meetings, they did not invite kids in their teens," he said in 1950. Ultimately, Remine's colorful and not always accurate reports went to Roy Lotspeich, who decided to keep them secret when he discovered a relative of his among Remine's suspects.[29]

Remine's investigation did cost Remington and his friends a place to live. Apprehensive about their midnight meetings, Mrs. Cox asked them to leave, and they moved out on May 13, 1937. Remington and the others took a room at Mrs. Watson's boarding house, but when she learned that they were union organizers and therefore undesirable tenants, they were evicted. Remington finally found a room in a home owned by the aunt of a TVA colleague and lived there for the rest of his stay in Knoxville.[30]

While Remington was moving from room to room that month, the CIO launched a major organizing drive in the South, and Bill and his friends quickly became involved. Pat Todd resigned from TVA to become a full-time organizer for the Textile Workers Union, and Remington soon followed, taking a job with the Workers Education Committee. But most of his time was spent with the Workers Alliance, a union of WPA workers, which, in many places, perhaps including Tennessee, was dominated by members of the Communist Party. In nearby Mascot, he helped a group of workers threatened with lay-offs. A petition was drafted, and Remington arranged for a delegation to march to Knoxville to present the workers' grievances to WPA officials. His next project took him to La Follette, forty miles from the city, where he organized a Workers Alliance of unemployed construction workers. Flushed with success, he agreed immediately when Pat Todd invited him to go to Cookeville, where the Amalgamated Clothing Workers Union was experiencing difficulty organizing workers at the Washington Manufacturing Company. Two organizers had recently been arrested and driven out of town; Todd was asked to take their place. "He told me that he thought it might be . . . interesting," Remington later said, "and as I had nothing else to do . . . I went."[31]

They drove the hundred-thirty-odd miles to Cookeville on a muggy Thursday afternoon in early June. After taking a room at the Arlington Hotel, they met with Maggie Randolph and other union officials. Their adversary, they learned, was formidable. The Washington Manufacturing Company owned factories throughout the state and had so far been successful in keeping the CIO from organizing its plants in Nashville and Cookeville. When earlier conflicts had arisen, the Lion's Club and the mayor negotiated settlements with the workers. Establishing one union controlled by the CIO would be a difficult, even dangerous task.[32]

On Thursday night and Friday morning, Remington and Todd met with sympathetic workers and described the benefits of union membership: higher wages, an end to discrimination against blacks, and elimination of discharge without cause. Some, who had not previously attended such meetings, now signed pledge cards indicating their intention to join the union movement. All agreed to meet late that afternoon at the Arcade Building in the office of J. O. Paris, a CIO supporter. Remington and Todd wanted to meet more workers, so they attached a placard to their car announcing the time and place of the scheduled meeting and drove to the plant. They arrived at three o'clock, a half hour before the first shift ended, and parked in front of the factory so that anyone leaving could see the sign. Bill and Maggie gathered leaflets and waited to greet those first out of the gate. It was not long before the whistle blew, and a few women approached Remington and Randolph, who offered them handbills and explained why they were there. Suddenly a group of men rushed toward Remington, tore the leaflets from his hand, and began hitting and kicking him. When Todd tried to help, they turned on him, cursing and throwing rocks. He managed to escape and ran with Maggie to a nearby flour mill. Inside, they found a phone and called the sheriff, who sent a squad of deputies to disperse the crowd. As Pat and Maggie helped a bruised and shaken Remington into the car, Todd asked a deputy for additional protection. "The best thing you could do is get out of town," he said, but, instead, they returned to Paris's office, determined to hold their meeting despite the incident.[33]

As evening approached, a few workers arrived at Paris's office. From the upstairs window, Todd looked down on the town square, where the men who had attacked them now sat, watching and waiting. Before the meeting could begin, they needed to go to their car for leaflets and pledge cards; surely it would be safe to go—deputies were around, and townspeople had also gathered—no one would dare assault them in the face of the law and in front of so many witnesses. So Pat and Bill went downstairs to the car but never reached it. A group of men grabbed Remington, threw him to the ground and stomped on him. An officer appeared and rescued Todd, who had also been beaten and had a broken arm.

After taking Todd to Paris's office, he returned for Remington, whom he found lying unconscious. He threw him over his shoulder and carried him up the stairs; Paris said a doctor was on the way. Remington's injuries were found to be minor—cuts, bruises, and a slight concussion. The doctor recommended that they leave Cookeville as soon as possible. "Hell no," Todd said, not before those "goons" are arrested. So Paris took them to see Judge Oscar Dowell, and they swore out warrants for fifteen men the workers identified as enemies of the CIO. Then, to ensure their protection, they were moved to the Cookeville jail, where they rested a while and decided to take a late train to Nashville to confer with CIO officials; compatriots would deliver their car and other belongings. "We'll be back!" Remington and Todd told a tiny group of supporters who followed them to the station.[34]

They kept their promise. On Monday, June 8, they returned to Cookeville, along with a CIO motorcade of twenty cars. Honking and shouting, they drove around the plant and twice around the town square—the scene of the beating. Then they departed, their union-organizing mission a failure. The *Putnam County Herald*, spokesman for the Washington Manufacturing Company, fired a final editorial salvo the next morning. Cookeville, it claimed, "had never had any serious labor trouble" before the visit of Remington and Todd and their fellow demonstrators who were characterized as "disgruntled and discharged employees. The attempt to hold a mass meeting . . . failed because of the determination of the reception committee of leading citizens of the town and 90 . . . of the employees of the plant."[35]

When news of the assault reached Remington's parents (through an exaggerated story in a New Jersey paper that described Bill lying unconscious in a Cookeville hospital), they telephoned immediately and urged him to return home at once. Bill calmed them down, reassuring Fred and Lillian that his wounds were minor and that he was feeling fine but explaining that he could not yet leave—there was still important work to be completed before he left Knoxville. They should expect him in Ridgewood around July 4.[36]

His last few weeks were spent saying good-bye to friends in Mascot, La Follette, and Norris and making one final trip through the Great Smoky Mountains to view new TVA dams under construction. But his final days in Knoxville are also shrouded in controversy. Later, Kenneth McConnell, a Communist Party organizer who had arrived in June, claimed that Bill had considered staying on in Knoxville and that he and his wife, Betty, and Pat Todd encouraged him to return to Dartmouth because the Party needed educated Communists. He also testified about being with Remington on other occasions: at a Communist Party meeting in Knoxville; on a trip to Mascot where Remington allegedly pointed out people who might make good Party members; and for an evening when he criticized Remington's appearance, telling him that it "was not necessary to look like a tramp to be a Communist."[37]

Remington would deny that these events occurred, but it seems more likely that McConnell's story, while not without contradictions, is probably closer to the truth than Remington's. Muriel Speare, for example, later recalled that it was her "impression that in his last weeks [Remington] became so filled with enthusiasm for his Party and union work that he began to lose his desire to return to college, preferring to stay in Knoxville where his real destiny lay." She therefore thought it quite likely that McConnell did urge Remington to return to Dartmouth. (It is, of course, just as likely that Remington, relishing the role of Party activist, recently bloodied in the great war between capital and labor, feigned resistance to returning to student life.) Speare also thought the Remington–McConnell relationship closer than Remington later claimed. Some weeks prior to his arrival, she later said, Remington had told her that "a new man was coming to town who would be very helpful" to those in the Communist unit.[38] And Remington's intimate association with those in the Party during 1936 and 1937 makes it almost certain that he must have had some contact with McConnell. Indeed, he would later brag to his classmates at Dartmouth of his close connection with Communist Party officials in Tennessee.[39]

None of this was anything to worry about in July 1937, as Remington prepared to leave. Remington's time in Tennessee had been exciting beyond his expectations. He had been part of one of the New Deal's great economic experiments, had met interesting people, and had been wounded on labor's barricades. How many nineteen-year-olds could make such claims?

In early July, he boarded a train that could have taken him directly home but rode only as far as Virginia. To save money and prolong his experience of American life in 1937, he hitch-hiked the rest of the way north.[40]

4

A Square Character— Dartmouth, 1937–1938

"I'm glad to be back," Remington wrote his Aunt Nan after returning to Dartmouth. " . . . After being away for a year I have changed. . . . Never again will I get mixed up in so much extra truck as I did before." To other relatives and friends, Remington claimed that his TVA experience was a watershed—that after TVA there occurred an authentic change in his philosophy, friendships, and activities. In part, this appears to be true. In his junior year he seemed more politically moderate, less intolerant of opinions different from his own, and more respectful of his teachers and college administrators. But others intimate with Remington at this time offer a different view: that the transformation—if it had occurred—was seriously incomplete—was, in fact, only a tactical move calculated to promote his career. Earlier, he had shown a Communist's angry face to the world; now a new face appeared—the eyes watchful, the smile careful, the voice quiet. His manner, said one observer, "was rather like that of an archdeacon who was a con man on the side."[1]

His first move was to resign from *The Dartmouth*, telling his editor that his goal now was to become the most important man on campus—next to Dartmouth's president, Ernest Hopkins.[2] Specifically, his objectives included winning all the awards the college could give: a Phi Beta Kappa key, a Senior Fellowship, and a nomination for a Rhodes Scholarship.

Success had to come first in the classroom. During his freshman and sophomore years, his grades had been erratic. Each fall semester he earned high marks—a 3.4 and 3.6, respectively; than, come spring, his grades had dropped dramatically—to 2.8 and 3.0. So he entered his junior year with slightly better than a B average, not good enough to qualify for the awards he hoped to win. Now, focusing nearly all his attention on his courses in public administration and sociology, he earned consistently superior marks—3.8 and 3.4—making his junior year his most outstanding scholastically. But his achievement did not occur without one episode of deception. Taking a sociology honors course with professor Wentworth Eldridge, Bill persuaded him to turn in his final grade before he completed the required term paper, promising to finish it in the near future. Wentworth trusted Remington and gave him an A but never received the paper. Embarrassed by his gullibility, Eldridge let the matter drop.[3]

His other professors were also impressed with his classroom performance and demeanor. While before he often "spoke up in class . . . to put down the professor," he now listened respectfully. Sociologist George F. Theriault remembered him as "an extremely able and prodigious worker. It's not very often we get a student who reports back that he looked up the footnotes and outside readings, but Remington did that every day—that's the kind of guy he was." Professor Elmer Snead, who taught Remington political science, noted that he had "a pleasant smile and was rather shy. He almost never opened his mouth in class although . . . he received an A in the course."[4] His Knoxville friends would not have recognized him.

Those who knew him during his earlier radical days at Dartmouth were even more aware of the new Remington. To Professor Allan MacDonald, who was close to the campus Communists, Remington now seemed more disciplined, more ambitious, no longer a bohemian. But no one was more shocked than Bill Martin, his oldest friend. Martin later said that when he first came to Dartmouth in September 1935, Remington was "a nice fellow. He did not comb his hair and went around half dressed. When he came back [from Knoxville] he . . . had his hair combed all the time, dressed up constantly and tried to get all A's."[5] This was certainly not the man Martin had long known and admired.

If Remington had changed during the year 1936–37, so had Martin. The gentle poet had become the leader of the campus Communist movement, as the president of Dartmouth's chapter of the American Student Union and leader of the Young Communist League.

The American Student Union was born in December 1935, when the socialist Student League for Industrial Democracy merged with the Communist National Student League to form a broader student alliance. It condemned discrimination against young people because of race, color, politics, and religion, urged the protection of academic freedom from red-baiting vigilantes, and, most important, called for resistance against war.[6]

The Dartmouth chapter was established early in January 1936 and was led first by an executive committee consisting of Budd Schulberg and other campus activists, including freshman Bill Martin. Under their leadership, the ASU opened a cooperative eating club in the basement of Brock and Stone's barber shop, sponsored a series of foreign films, and brought to campus public speakers, including Mary Van Kleeck and national ASU officials Serril Gerber and the Reverend Jeffrey Campbell, to discuss "The Students' Peace Strike" and "Will Students Fight?"[7]

In late February, a permanent slate of officers was elected. Instead of turning to one of the more prominent radicals, like Budd Schulberg, Dartmouth's students chose Martin to be the new ASU president. His term of office lasted more than eighteen months, another sign of his popularity among those who joined the organization. During Martin's presidency, the ASU continued to be active on campus. In addition to bringing exotic films and speakers to Hanover, the ASU called for support of the Spanish Loyalists and urged the creation of a non-credit course on the causes of war. The group also took their crusade for economic justice off campus, visiting the Rutland Marble fields to see how the workers were faring.[8]

Martin probably expected Remington to become his ally in the ASU upon his return to Dartmouth and was encouraged when Remington became a member of the Executive Board (under new president, Charles Livermore). But to Martin's surprise, Remington began to oppose almost every issue Martin supported. In early November, for example, he and a group (that included Remington) met with Boone Schirmer—the regional organizer of both the ASU and the YCL—to discuss how to commemorate Armistice Day. Schirmer called for a "Peace Strike, during which the students would march out of their classes" and, according to Remington, "raise as much ruckus as possible." Remington fought him and, at the end of a long and contentious evening, won majority support. When the ASU wanted to sponsor a Spanish Relief Committee, Remington thought it unwise and recommended forming a group that represented many campus organizations of all political shades. Throughout the year—whenever Livermore and Martin tried to build up the ASU, Remington would constantly say, "The ASU shouldn't mess around with things like that." Others also recall that Remington balked at participating in ASU affairs; President Chuck Livermore thought Remington inactive, while D. Clark Norris, another officer, noted that "Remington was always hedging and declining . . . pleading a lack of time."[9]

The two Bills also clashed over Remington's involvement with the ASU Co-op Eating Club, which, in Martin's view, was more practical than ideological. Remington began working there first as janitor and dishwasher in return for free lunch and dinner, but when the restaurant—which served around fifty students daily—began to flounder financially, the ASU Executive Board asked him to manage it. He accepted the offer, and Remington's club, now run for profit, was a success. A disgusted Bill Martin called Remington a reactionary and fought with him the entire year about club policies. The two argued so bitterly that the next year Remington refused to be the manager; Martin reestablished it as a co-op ("for himself and his own friends," Remington claimed), but the club quickly went bankrupt.[10]

Remington and Martin also disagreed strongly about members of the faculty and fellow students. "I became a defender of the dean and an admirer of [sociology] professor [Russell] Larmon," Remington later noted. "Martin despised them both. . . . I began to be impatient with many of his friends . . . and he was often more impatient with mine. . . . " Remington's relationships with the college's administrators was now so intimate that they often asked him to keep them informed of campus political developments. Albert Dickerson, Hopkins's chief assistant, valued Remington's report on the Dartmouth peace movement written at his request early in 1938. Remington criticized the extreme leftists and complained about their "hysterical and irresponsible errors," views that were almost identical to those of Hopkins and Dickerson.[11]

He also had a special, secret relationship with President Hopkins, which may partly explain his opposition to so many ASU activities. Hopkins hated the ASU and its members. To him, it was an organization of "psychopathic cases," whose only purpose was to indoctrinate students with left-wing propaganda.[12] Hopkins also expressed his fears to Remington and Samuel Dix (another student affiliated with the ASU) during a meeting in his office. According to Dix, "Hopkins was concerned lest this organization give the college bad publicity and he asked Bill and I [sic] to keep him informed as to what . . . they were trying to do and if we could be a moderating influence, to do it." Remington was more than happy to act as the president's mole inside the ASU—giving rise to the charge that circulated among the radicals that he was "a snitch for the Administration . . . [,] allowing them to keep their finger on the pulse of the radical movement at Dartmouth."[13]

Remington's opposition to ASU policies was shared by a number of students, including two new friends, Charles Davis and William Goodman. Both characterized themselves (and Remington) as political moderates who felt that the ASU's leaders—both nationally and on campus—were too close to the Communist Party. "We wanted a club on campus which would freely discuss political and social ideas," Goodman later stated, "which would not be hampered by Communist party thinking, and therefore we broke away. . . . " Remington shared that view, according to Davis.[14]

At a noisy meeting held in May 1937, the moderates won control of the ASU and decided to close the chapter and create a new organization, which they called the Liberal Union. Instead of an organization that focused its attention on the plight of the Vermont marble workers or the Spanish Loyalists, the Liberal Union would work almost exclusively on educational issues. At a meeting on May 19, the group chose officers. President Bob White was the antithesis of Bill Martin—he was a member of Alpha Delta Phi (considered by Remington the most aristocratic of Dartmouth's fraternities) and of the varsity swim team. Arnold Childs, of Phi Sigma Kappa, was elected vice president, and Bill Remington became executive secretary. Thus, Remington helped to destroy the organization once led by his closest friend.[15]

The struggle between Remington and Martin was also carried on in the Dartmouth chapter of the Young Communist League. But this time, Martin emerged victorious. By September 1937, the composition of the YCL had changed completely—gone were the seniors who had established and led the group during its first period. Leadership fell to Bill Martin, who seemed to relish the job. Asked once by a fellow student what his religion was, Martin replied: "Why, Communism, of course." He was able to attract a new generation of students, including Page Smith, a tall, courtly young man from Baltimore who supported Alf Landon for President in 1936, then, a few weeks, later joined the YCL; Walter Bernstein, an abrasive New Yorker with literary talent; Richard Storey Smith, the son of New Dealer Edwin Smith; Irving Paul, a wealthy New Englander; and a few others who would come and go. The group operated rather informally; occasionally, an official organizer from Boston or New York would visit to collect dues or issue cards, but it was never very clear to Martin who were authentic members.[16]

Men joined in a variety of ways. Chuck Livermore was at one meeting at which cards were distributed, but those in attendance were ordered not to sign their real names. Robert Harvey was given a green YCL card by his recruiter, Walter Bernstein, who asked him for five cents, one month's dues. Page Smith recalled paying an initiation fee, then receiving a card on which he signed his real name. However they may have joined, or if they actually did, Martin's "minute" group of "tried and true thinkers," as he liked to call it, all had the same YCL outlook.[17]

No one was ever certain whether Bill Remington possessed a card, but he attended meetings regularly during 1937 and 1938 and usually challenged Martin, who presided over the discussions. "Most of our talks would revolve around the two Bills. . . . They represented opposites in a great sense," recalled one student. "Bill Martin was exceedingly idealistic, a dreamer. . . . Remington seemed more practical, more realistic. . . . He was a provocative thinker and talker . . . [who] defended his views of Communism with zeal and deep conviction."[18] Remington was not always so persuasive. He tried to recruit his friend John Parke in 1938, urging him to attend a special session at which he could meet Boone Schirmer, the Boston organizer with whom Remington had earlier quarreled but was now, according to Parke's later recollection, a very good friend. Parke refused.[19]

Remington's arguments with Martin and others eventually led to his expulsion from the group because of "deviationist tendencies." Martin assumed responsibility for ejecting Remington, after holding a rump court, but accounts differ as to how Remington left the group. YCL member Robert Harvey later recalled that during one meeting in 1938 "there was a terrible fight between Remington and Bernstein, and Remington never came again. . . . [He] wanted nothing to do with the group." So, by the end of his junior year, Remington was no longer closely associated with the YCL.[20]

The ASU and YCL battles also ruined Martin and Remington's friendship. Remington, since his return from Knoxville, was "a changed [man]," Martin later said, " . . . very circumspect in all his associations with the 'radical' group. Personal career meant more to him than his former friends." "A Reactionary," "a bourgeois materialist," " a natural capitalist"—these were the epithets Martin hurled at Remington. Remington retaliated with equal venom and told Martin that he no longer wished to live with him. He invited Page Smith, a radical and a good friend of Martin's, to room with him in Hitchcock Hall.[21]

In the end, however, 1938 was a year of triumphs for Remington. He published two literary efforts that won awards. His "New Myths in the Southland," an eloquent defense of the TVA, appeared in *The Dart*, a magazine published by Sidney Cox, and was judged "Best Essay." A short story, "If It's Good Enough for Pappy," was accepted for publication in *Pace* and would later receive "Honorable Mention" in a college literary competition.[22]

His two most important prizes came late in the spring; he was elected to Phi Beta Kappa (with a 3.3 grade point average) and received a Senior Fellowship, the highest honor the college could bestow. The program, established by President Hopkins in 1929, was designed to give a few outstanding students the opportunity to devote their senior year to any intellectual pursuit of their own choosing. The seven Senior Fellows selected in 1938 were not required to pay tuition, attend class, or take examinations, and at the end of the year, they would be automatically graduated. Those men who were most successful, or at least satisfied with their lives, Hopkins wrote Remington, were those "who have sought to find out what is actually the truth rather than . . . to substantiate preconceived opinions and to ally themselves with the extremists in either wing of conservatism or radicalism."[23] Hopkins's letter suggests that he hoped that the award might further help Remington to reject those radical notions he had once held but now appeared to be renouncing.

If Remington won his Senior Fellowship because of, rather than despite, his radical history, it is one of the more striking ironies of his career at Dartmouth. The testimonies of Page Smith and John Parke suggest that Remington saw it as a reward for what he considered a clever and successful campaign to persuade the administration that he was now—in Smith's words—"a square character." Remington, Smith said, "preened himself on the notion that somehow he had pulled this off—presenting himself as a reformed radical, the respectable and appropriate person for this fellowship." Smith later learned from a member of the committee involved in the selection process that they were well aware that Remington had very strong Communist convictions but gave him the fellowship anyway because they thought him intellectually deserving. "It was a farce," Smith concluded. "Remington had . . . convinced himself that he was successful but it didn't fool anybody. He was always playing games that didn't fool anybody. That was the thing that was most unfortunate about his character." Parke agreed:

> His tendency to disavow affiliation with the Communist Party, after coming back from Tennessee, and after getting the Senior Fellowship, was probably another Remington tactic. And those of us who had said confidently and enthusiastically . . . the year before—someday this man would be President—began to say . . . that he was wrecking his own chances because of his deviousness.[24]

So, as Remington would have it, he became a new man after TVA. No longer a believer in Communism or an associate of men who held such beliefs, he was now an honored scholar, respected by his teachers and admired by the dean and president of the college. Even his former radical friends, who had fought him in the ASU and the YCL, were forced to agree. And new friends like Charles Davis and Bill Goodman would later insist, based on their experiences with him in 1938, that he could never have been a Communist.

Other events in 1938 and 1939 suggest that no real conversion had occurred and that Remington's behavior was mostly a charade designed to win the benefits of respectability. Bill Goodman and Charles Davis would have been astonished to learn that the man who rejected his earlier radicalism was at that very moment lecturing other students on the virtues of Communism and establishing new relationships that would take him deeper into the Communist orbit.

5

Flirting with Danger—
Dartmouth, 1938–1939

Robbins Barstow was almost eighteen when he came to Dartmouth in September 1937. A senior remembered him "as the darnedest freshman I'd ever seen. A real Joe Intellectual. He used to wander around the campus with a little notebook, listening in on discussions that students were having. He'd tell us to go right on talking—that he just wanted to take notes on what he called Food for Reflection." One of Barstow's friends was a German exchange student and an admirer of the Nazis—his views found a home in Barstow's notebook. So did Bill Remington's thoughts on Communism, which Bill was happy to share with the freshman even though he was working so hard to convince the administration that he was no longer committed to that cause.[1]

During the winter and spring of 1938, Barstow often visited Remington in his room in Crosby Hall. "I was deeply impressed by the brilliance of his mind," he later said, "and by the quiet, earnest sincerity of his expression of the Communist beliefs which he then held. . . . My impression was . . . that he looked down on me a little for not readily accepting them myself, as if the rightness of Communism was pretty obvious."[2]

There was scarcely a question about Soviet affairs for which Bill did not have an answer. What about the trials and executions then occurring in Moscow's season of purges? Barstow asked. The men "who were scuttled really were traitors who had been planted . . . by the enemies of Communism and it was a good thing that they were rooted out . . . ," he remembered Remington saying.

43

"Russia had gone further in the last 20 years than any other country," Remington also said, while capitalism produced only unemployment and misery.[3] When Barstow would later return to his room in Ripley Hall, he would add Remington's remarks to his notebook. "Discussions with Bill Remington. . . . Bright and astute, but I wonder if not more one sided than he admits, . . . Are all his statements . . . true?" Perhaps not even Remington knew, but Barstow was convinced that Bill was most definitely a Communist.[4]

Robb Kelley, a senior, thought so too, and, as with Barstow, Remington encouraged such a view. Kelley had seen Remington in action at meetings of the Marxist study group and concluded that he was the star of the show. Rumor also had it that Remington was already a full-fledged member of the Communist Party. Curious about his colorful classmate, Kelley asked him directly in the spring of 1938 why he was a Communist. Because "his father had always been a stooge for the Capitalists," while he "hoped to contribute something toward improving the lives of common people," Kelley remembered Bill saying.[5] He was certain that all the rumors about Remington were true.

There was, of course, nothing subversive about Remington's conversations with Barstow and Kelley, but they do indicate that he was not telling the truth when he insisted that he was no longer a radical during his junior and senior years. More important than these episodes as evidence of Remington's contin-ued interest in Communism was his relationship with Ann Moos, a 21-year-old Bennington College senior. They first met in February 1938, in Hanover, at a conference of the United Student Peace Committee. She was a slim, attractive brunette, with large brown eyes and a shy, quiet manner. Eight months later, in a ceremony kept secret from both their families, they would wed.

Ann Moos had "the look of a solid, steady person," said one acquaintance, but in fact, she was a woman of fragile emotional health, whose life was filled with bitterness, repressed anger, and hatred.[6] She was born in Chicago, Illinois, on September 5, 1916, the first child of Raymond Redheffer and his wife, Elizabeth Moos Redheffer. Elizabeth was an exceptional person, bright and charming, but subservient to her parents' wishes. She later told Ann that she had wanted to be a physician and had enrolled at Smith College to pursue that career. However, after graduating in 1911, her parents persuaded her to seek a master's degree in physical education at Wellesley, where she attended for only one academic year and received no degree. Instead, she had decided to teach and spent the next two years at the Parker School, until her marriage.

It was Elizabeth's parents who selected Raymond Redheffer to be her hus-band, although he was almost ten years older than she was. According to Ann, she did not love Redheffer but decided to marry him in 1915 anyway; he may not have been exciting, but he was rich and could satisfy her financial demands. At first, Elizabeth wanted a farm, and, although Raymond could well afford it, it was her parents who bought her the house and land in Deerfield, Illinois. But she was no farmer and eventually became bored, so in 1921 she decided to open a nursery school; her five-year-old daughter was its first pupil. Ann was later joined by only a handful of students, and the school never prospered.[7]

By this time, Ann had two younger brothers, but the life of mother, housewife, and teacher held little appeal for Elizabeth. She became attracted to Robert Imandt, a young, handsome, French violinist, whom Redheffer had hired to instruct him in the violin. As part of the arrangement, Imandt was permitted to live in a tent on the family property. In establishing a liaison, Elizabeth used Ann as a go-between; Ann became friendly with Imandt first, then later her mother would visit him. Robert and Elizabeth fell in love, and she asked Raymond for a divorce.[8] Redheffer agreed but exacted a cruel revenge. In return for the divorce, he would be given custody of his two sons while Ann would live with her mother. For six-year-old Ann, this was a stunning psychological blow. Years later, she could still recall the hatred she felt for her parents. Her father was a milksop, who had been dominated by his mother; Elizabeth—she had attacked with her fists. "I was angry about leaving my father. I . . . saw him just twice . . . after that. He had no interest in me." Elizabeth's parents were also furious and refused to help support her attempt to create a new life.[9]

Elizabeth married Imandt in 1923, and with young Ann, the couple moved to the East Side of New York. Elizabeth taught at a private high school in Manhattan, while Imandt tried to become a concert violinist, touring with various orchestras but never becoming successful. He earned a more stable income as a photographer but was unable to give Elizabeth the kind of life she had previously enjoyed. Their tiny apartment was located in the slums of Beekman Place, so Ann was not allowed to play in the streets; she spent most of her days alone. New York was horrible, she remembered.[10]

Elizabeth was reconciled with her parents in 1926, and the Imandts moved to Croton-on-Hudson, where Joseph and Katherine Moos built them a large, handsome home and, for the rest of their lives, assumed financial responsibility for the family. Croton had its beginnings as a small colony of summer shacks populated by artists, novelists, and political radicals. By the mid-1920s, it had become a fashionable area but still populated by those who had originally discovered its charms. Artists like George Biddle and William Gropper lived there, as did such writers as Max Eastman, Floyd Dell, and Heywood Broun.

To educate their children, Elizabeth established the Hessian Hills School, a co-educational institution run on a progressive philosophy that emphasized art, music, and dance. This time, Elizabeth's venture succeeded; enrollment grew, and among Ann's classmates were the children of Heywood Broun, Stuart Chase, and Jerome Frank—as well as others she later characterized as neurotic, rich kids.[11]

After Beekman Place, Croton was heaven, but Ann remained an intensely unhappy child. "I was my mother's puppet," she recalled. " . . . She told me who

I was, who my friends were, what I thought and liked. . . . " Her relationship
with Robert Imandt was neither happy nor healthy. As she entered her teenage
years, she felt a sexual attraction toward him, which Imandt shared. "At fourteen, he tried to dry me off after baths. I remember I thought I was too old for
that kind of stuff. . . . I liked him fine, but he wasn't a father figure. . . ."[12]

She yearned desperately to be free of her mother's control and hoped that
college would provide the means of escape. Radcliffe was her first and only
choice, and she took special exams that she hoped would win her admission.
But her mother had different plans. Elizabeth decided that Ann should attend
Bennington College, educationally as free-spirited as all the schools she had ever
tried to establish. It was, therefore, Elizabeth who sent away for applications,
filled them out in Ann's name, and selected her course of study. "I never had
any choice," Ann later said. "She ran my life the way she wanted and I accepted
it. . . . She always insisted she 'loved' me and wanted to do what was best for me
but what it really amounted to was what was . . . most convenient for her. So I
went to Bennington. I hated the place from day one." To annoy her mother,
she intentionally dropped the name Moos (which she had used since her parents'
divorce) and was known at Bennington as Ann Imandt. Her mother had also
selected her major—social studies (then a mixture of sociology and psychology);
Ann, in a rare show of rebellion, studied art and textile design but eventually
switched to the field chosen by Elizabeth.

She remained a very lonely, young woman, who considered herself neurotic
and inhibited. Her relationships with men were few and unsatisfactory. At college, she briefly dated a local boy but shied away from college men. She recalled
going alone to one dance during her years at Bennington and knew no males at
nearby Williams College. "I just didn't think much of myself," she explained
and blamed Elizabeth. "My mother did her best not to help me become a
woman—give me pointers on how to dress or look, wear my hair. . . . I'd have
been a rival. . . . She just didn't want me to be pretty, [or] popular. . . ."[13]
Elizabeth also had problems. In 1937, Robert Imandt left her suddenly for a
younger woman and they divorced. Both mother and daughter were greatly
affected by this event; Ann thought it was what led Elizabeth and herself deeper
into radical causes. Society was flawed, they reasoned, not themselves. The
Communist Party provided a coherent ideology to believe in, friendships, activities, and, above all, an acceptance they could find nowhere else. That winter, a
neighbor of Elizabeth's took Ann to her first Party function in New York, and
when she returned to campus, she became involved in the American Student
Union and the Bennington Peace Committee. It was the latter group that
brought her to Dartmouth in late February 1938 and to her fateful meeting with
Bill Remington.[14]

Ann and Bill spent the day talking about the issues exciting college radicals—opposition to ROTC and military appropriations and sanctions against

aggressor nations. But it was not all political—something had passed between them. Bill offered to help her with ASU activities at Bennington and promised to write. He did; she answered; and they began to see one another.

A few weeks later, Ann asked him to accompany her to an ASU meeting at Harvard; he agreed, and she offered to drive to Hanover to pick him and Chuck Livermore up—together they would ride to Cambridge. At Harvard, Bill ran into Boone Schirmer and introduced him to Ann. They discussed establishing a YCL chapter at Bennington, and Schirmer promised to visit her. (Soon, Bennington had its first YCL; Ann and a friend were its charter members.)[15]

While driving back to Hanover the following evening, Remington and Livermore bragged to Ann about their activities as labor organizers. "We made ourselves out to be real radicals," Bill later said, in contrast to the sedentary students who they thought were just dilettantes. Bill felt he had won the competition with the tale of his being beaten at Cookeville. After arriving at Hitchcock Hall, Livermore said good night and left Bill and Ann alone in her car. What ensued is a matter of controversy. Bill would later claim that he and Ann did little talking; for once, romance took precedence over politics.[16] But Ann recalled this moment quite differently. Bill, she said, continued to boast about his adventures in Knoxville; then, swearing her to secrecy, he told her that he had joined the Communist Party while with TVA. None of his friends at Dartmouth knew, and he considered it a privilege for her to know his secret.[17]

Bill's revelation, exaggerated or true, did impress Ann, and by June they were engaged. Bill kept the news from his parents, who felt that Ann, like Helen Martin, was unsuitable for their son. His parents' displeasure no doubt intensified his own belief that at last he had found a woman who fulfilled his every desire—bright and attractive, politically committed, and affluent. Bill wanted to marry Ann quickly, but she was uncertain about her feelings. In June, she surprised him by announcing that she planned to spend the summer in North Carolina working at the Ashville Normal School, where radicals helped to educate southern textile workers. Ann hoped that their three-month separation would dampen Bill's ardor and resolve her own doubts.[18]

Her sojourn in Ashland only complicated matters. To her delight, she was reunited with a childhood friend, Leon Goodelman, who was also working there and, as the summer progressed, found herself strongly attracted to him. So intense was her attachment that she later followed him to Columbia University, where he was studying. Ann took graduate courses in economics and spent every moment with him. Together, Ann later claimed, they attended YCL meetings; then she was invited to join the local unit of the Communist Party. Unfortunately, it soon became apparent to Ann that, despite their political affinity, Goodelman did not love her, and the relationship ended. At the same time, Ann left the CP unit at Columbia and joined a branch in Croton.[19]

Bill continued to write her passionate letters, but she held him off until after she stopped seeing Goodelman; their first date, after the summer's separation, was not until October 29, 1938, at the annual Yale–Dartmouth football game. "I really didn't love him or want to marry him," Ann later explained, but her rejection made Remington even more eager to have her. Bill was infatuated, she claimed. "I was the one thing he had to have. . . . He gave me an ultimatum, either I marry him now or he'd never see me again." Realizing that her recent romance was over and desiring to distance herself further from her mother, she finally concluded, "Well, why not? It's something to try. I told him—maybe I'll grow to love you. . . . He was confident he could . . . make me love him. . . ."[20]

Ann had her own demands, which, like Bill's confession of Communist Party membership, later became a subject of dispute. Before she would agree to the marriage, she later testified, "I asked specifically, would he continue to be a member of the Communist Party and . . . believe in Communist principles, and he said, 'Yes . . . ,' that I need not worry on that score. . . ."[21] Bill remembered the incident but denied that he had ever discussed CP membership as a condition of marriage. "We talked about whether we should get married or not," he said. "She was worried [about] my ambition, [and] asked me if I . . . could promise her that I would not become dominated by the desire to be a successful businessman. . . . I promised her that . . . I would never become so anxious to get ahead that I would give up my concern for the underprivileged."[22]

Whether his promised commitment was to principles or Party, Ann accepted it, and they were married on November 23, 1938. Both agreed not to tell family or friends, but this added to their pleasure. "It made it all kind of exciting," Ann thought, "we were doing something secret. [Bill] loved secret things. . . . He loved putting things over on people—planning stuff, getting away with things. Getting married was all a kind of game." After a brief honeymoon in New York, Bill returned to Dartmouth; his bride, to Columbia.[23]

That Bill did truly love putting things over on people and getting away with it was again apparent just a few weeks later, when he attempted to win a Rhodes Scholarship. He had applied months before and, given his recent awards, was confident that the Dartmouth committee would choose him as a candidate. In early November, four nominees, including Remington, were selected, and during his appearance before the state committee in Manchester on December 13, he performed so well that he went on to compete at the district level against men from six northeastern states. At Boston, in the final round, he was eliminated, but it was some consolation to learn later that he had done better than any Dartmouth man in more than a decade.[24]

Actually, he should have been more relieved than disappointed, because his marriage would have disqualified him from receiving the fellowship even if he had won. The Rhodes committee required that the scholarship's recipients be unmarried, but despite his knowledge of this stipulation, Remington had gone ahead and sought an award he was ineligible to hold. Such behavior was highly improper, potentially embarrassing to the college, and a threat to his future ambitions.

Why did he do it? Remington never commented on this incident, but perhaps fellow student John Kelleher came closest to an explanation. "One of the unfortunate elements of his makeup," he noted, "was a need to flirt with danger, to enjoy the thrill of wandering over the line and the satisfaction of escaping once again uncaught." [25]

Having emerged from the difficult Rhodes competition with distinction, Remington next set his sights on winning a fellowship that would allow him to continue his education after graduation in June. Given the precarious state of his family's finances, such assistance was essential; without it, he would have to seek a job at a time when millions were unemployed. He was pessimistic and bitter about his chances. "There's more brilliant men in the class of 1939 than in many years," he wrote his parents. "All are after fellowships. . . . My mathematical chance of getting one is one in 250. . . . There's no point in being hopeful or in worrying. If I get one, I get one, if I don't—I don't—and so what." [26]

Despite this fatalistic outlook, he worked hard on his application (no mention was made of his recent marriage into an affluent family) and also enlisted the support of faculty and administrators who wrote glowing letters on his behalf; many thought Remington deserving because of his recent political conversion. [27] He was successful. On March 16, 1939, Remington learned that he had won the Elijah Parker Fellowship for graduate study in economics at Columbia University. "I accept the award [which carried with it a $1,900 stipend] with the deepest gratitude . . . ," he wrote Albert Dickerson a few days later. [28]

The award of the Parker Fellowship did little to offset the distressing news Fred and Lillian received that same month. Bill and Ann were now officially engaged and planned to marry in June. Bill's parents were not happy. Bill was too young, they thought, to take such an irrevocable step. They were also disappointed that Ann, so different from the daughters of their Ridgewood friends, was to become Bill's wife. Ann was sent to Ridgewood to get to know her future in-laws and was somewhat successful in bringing them around; by mid-April, Bill was feeling better about the future. "It really isn't such a terrible step," he told them, "risky, yes, but neither murderous nor certain death." [29]

Remington's final months at Dartmouth were especially busy. First, the president had asked him to organize the second annual meeting of the Tri-College Conference on "Making Democracy Work." In late April, Dartmouth would welcome experts on national affairs and student delegates and faculty from Cornell and the University of Pennsylvania. It was up to Remington (and his assistants) to make the arrangements: select topics to be discussed and find people qualified to discuss them; locate living quarters for approximately fifty students, a dozen faculty advisors, and sixteen luminaries; and schedule the sessions and evening banquets. Such a complex job might have worried most seniors, but

Remington enjoyed the challenge immensely. The agenda reflected those issues that had long interested Remington: "Public vs. Private Enterprise in a Democratic Society"; "Are Our Civil Liberties Threatened?"; and "Economic Enterprise in a Democratic Society." Among the participants were Lewis Mumford, Roger Baldwin, Granville Hicks, Alexander Meikeljohn, and assorted scholars and government officials. The conference was a great success, attributable, in part, to what Professor Arthur M. Wilson called Remington's organizing genius. *The Dartmouth* later placed his name on its 1938–39 Honor Roll, a tribute to his achievement.[30]

The conflict between private enterprise and the public good was also the subject Remington focused on during his year as a Senior Fellow. In a series of reports titled "Problems of the Integrated Development of the Connecticut River Valley," he explored the area's economic and social inequalities and proposed solutions based on the model of TVA. He discovered that perhaps the greatest obstacle to progress was the continuing American commitment to rugged individualism, still so strong in an era of economic collapse. The answer, he thought, lay in the creation of "a collective consciousness of mutual dependence," that would "solve the problem of poverty in the midst of plenty."[31]

On Sunday, June 18, 1939, Remington received his bachelor's degree during ceremonies on the Dartmouth campus. He graduated "magna cum laude," 34th in a class of 514. His college career certainly appeared to be a remarkable success: star athlete, Phi Beta Kappa scholar, Senior Fellow, and Rhodes Scholarship nominee and regional runner-up.[32] But the cost of success came high in terms of personal relationships. President Hopkins resented Remington's habit of lecturing him and other Senior Fellows as if he had all the answers to the nation's problems, while Dean Neidlinger thought him "lacking in . . . self discipline."[33] Faculty member Russell Larmon thought him "intellectually arrogant and socially frustrated." On one occasion, he actually told Remington bluntly that he was too arrogant, and Remington became so angry that he stalked out of his office. (Some months later, while he was on his honeymoon in Mexico, he sent Larmon a short note in which he assured him that he was still arrogant and proud of it.) Philosopher Eugene Rosenstock-Huessy, who gave Remington the only C he ever received at Dartmouth, called him "a very cagey man. . . . He used to speak to me as if I were a poor little child who could never understand him." Yet, almost every professor who knew Remington could not help being impressed by his intelligence and determination, and they were usually willing to accept his difficult personality.[34]

His fellow students were less tolerant; some found him so irritating that they harassed him. One group that thought him unfriendly collected piles of snow that they shoveled through the transom into Remington and Bill Martin's room in Crosby Hall. Classmate Philip Thompson remembered that some in the dormitory disliked Remington doing his laundry in the communal bathroom sink, so they "decided to call on him and give him a little heat. . . . " A fistfight resulted in which Remington and another man were bloodied, but there were no serious injuries, except to Remington's reputation. Instead of using that incident as a way to resolve his differences with the men of Crosby Hall, he continued to irritate them.[35]

But there were a few, a precious few, who genuinely liked Remington and struggled to understand him. Sam Dix thought him "solitary but thoughtful, friendly, intelligent—always trying to look deeply into everything." Martin King, Class of '38, claimed that Bill Remington's kindness enabled him to graduate. King, a senior who was working his way through school, was unable to find a job until Bill hired him at the ASU Eating Club. He found his new boss a compassionate employer.[36]

"I liked [Remington] very much, but was eternally puzzled by him," said John Parke, whom Remington picked to be the "Best Man" at his wedding. "He was a very divided character. . . . For one thing, he was a star athlete. . . . Yet at the same time, he was very, very scornful of anything that smacked of bourgeois conventionality. . . . Here was a contradiction which he didn't even attempt to resolve and maybe he didn't even see." Often Parke and his friends would hear faculty discuss Remington's extraordinary potential, and they became convinced that he was destined for greatness. But as they watched him operate on campus, positioning himself for the Senior Fellowship by posing as a political moderate while also recruiting for the Young Communist League, their distrust grew. " . . . It eventually became a by-word among us all that he was a . . . habitual liar," Parke recalled. "After a while we began to see that he was on a course of self-destruction—either politically, or socially in the outside world."[37]

At the time, however, to Remington, the road ahead seemed bathed in a beautiful summer light. On June 23, 1939, Bill Remington "married" Ann Moos at her mother's Croton estate. The guests were a strange mix, representing the conventional and radical worlds in which Remington co-existed: Croton Communists, artists, philosophers; writers for *New Masses* and the *Daily Worker*; even a veteran of the Abraham Lincoln Brigade. There was his own family— Fred and Lillian Remington, the irascible Uncle Will and his wife, Arlene— probably feeling somewhat uncomfortable in this company. Present, too, were his friends and acquaintances from Dartmouth—men of the left like Bill Martin (their long friendship a casualty of campus politics and Remington's ambitions, but he was there, nevertheless); moderates like Charles Davis, who was almost not invited because he was black ("All our friends . . . can be carefully introduced to Charley . . . ," Bill told his parents in April. "Uncle Will and Aunt Arlene will be the . . . ones who must be sure to understand he is only a college friend."); and conservative Senior Fellows Louis Highmark and Rodger Harrison.[38]

Remington's friends were a little mystified at his choice of Ann Moos; Parke thought her unattractive and withdrawn and, like her mother, an open and avowed Communist. Lou Highmark recalled Ann's visits to Dartmouth, wearing cotton stockings to show that she was just an ordinary person and not the heir to a fortune. Some believed that it was a political union—Bill had decided to marry Ann as the way to advance himself within the Communist Party.[39]

The wedding was beautiful. The Reverend Charles Armstrong of the Ridgewood Episcopal Church presided, and later the guests walked around the grounds, chatting and sipping wine from tiny cups. For entertainment, a hillbilly band, complete with an expert caller, was imported from Tennessee. The only dissonant note was provided by Highmark and Harrison who, recognizing the political affiliations of most of the guests, took great delight in telling everyone they met just how much they admired Herbert Hoover. Eventually, Elizabeth Moos asked them to leave.[40]

Later that evening, Ann and Bill left Croton to begin their honeymoon: a cross-country drive that would ultimately take them to Mexico. Like most young people embarking on a new life, they were excited and expectant; so many happy things lay ahead—a regular, full-time marriage, Columbia University Graduate School, a new apartment in Manhattan, then a career in government and, when they were settled, a permanent home and children. So many reasons to rejoice.

In fact, Remington's happiest days were already behind him. Ten years later, in June 1949, his name in the headlines, Remington attended a party celebrating the fifteenth anniversary of Ridgewood High's Class of '34. One guest recalled Bill talking with an old friend whom he had not seen since graduation. "What have you been doing all these years?" he asked. The woman was embarrassed to admit that she had simply married a local boy and still lived in Ridgewood. "Aren't you fortunate that you never left," Bill said, his voice filled with sadness.[41]

6

Renegades

Their Mexican honeymoon was as unorthodox as their wedding, combining the two different worlds in which Remington loved to travel—the radical and the conventional.

For months prior to the wedding, he had worked on perfecting his Spanish, had poured over guidebooks noting the cleanest (and cheapest) hotels, and had even obtained from the American Automobile Association a list of the most reliable automobile mechanics in Mexico City. Stuart Chase, a veteran explorer of the Yucatán Jungle, assured him that there "simply weren't any more bandits in Mexico—with the exception of Generals in the Army . . . ," and that "the health problem isn't too terribly bad. With iron caution, one seldom gets sick."[1] From George Biddle and Joseph North, editor of the New Masses, and now Elizabeth Moos's closest friend, Remington received letters of introduction to Mexican artists, intellectuals, and Communists.

The couple's first destination was Chicago, where they spent a few days with Ann's grandparents, Joseph and Katherine Moos, who gave the newlyweds a check for four thousand dollars. On Sunday, July 9, 1939, they arrived in Mexico City, taking a room in a three-story fortress-like Spanish house. For the sake of both economy and safety, Remington put their car away; parking meters, he noted, cost ten centavos, while Mexican drivers raced through the city's streets ignoring red lights and pedestrians. Such iron caution must have pleased Fred Remington immensely.[2]

During that first week, Bill and Ann visited Communist Party headquarters in Mexico City, met with the New Masses correspondent, and learned about

Mexican politics. Bill also talked with other journalists and made arrangements to pass on any news he picked up during his visit. In return, he received press discounts at hotels and restaurants, free storage for his car, and favorable rates for the purchase of Mexican dollars.[3] Juan O'Gorman, a colorful old Trotskyite, bought them lunch and told them stories about his idol, Leon Trotsky, who fled the Soviet Union to settle finally in Mexico. (A year later he was assassinated there by one of Stalin's agents.)[4]

Politics was not the Remingtons' only interest. They spent an evening with composer Alex North (Joe's brother) and his companion Anna Sokolow, a well-known dancer who tried to incorporate social consciousness and class conflict into her musical repertoire. They went to the National Palace to see the magnificent frescos of Diego Rivera, the radical artist. Bill thought the murals, which depicted episodes of Mexico's revolutionary history, "startlingly good." They also saw the work of José Clemente Orozco, who, as a visiting professor of art at Dartmouth when Bill was a freshman, had painted portraits of Emiliano Zapata and Jesus Christ on the walls of Baker Library, examples of the "aesthetic adventurousness" admired by Remington.[5]

Despite his enjoyment of the city's art, culture, and exotic personalities, Remington longed to escape to the countryside. "This is a fascinatingly beautiful country," he told his parents, "and we don't want to bury ourselves in Mexico City. . . . It's hard to get anything done here. Get up at 9 A.M., leave the house at 11, back to eat at 1, siesta until 3, back to eat by 7 or 8, and then read a little or go out for a while and then to bed."[6] So, in late July, they traveled through the towns and villages of many of Mexico's thirty-one states. As an unofficial member of the press, Bill interviewed rural officials—seeking information about the country's leading politicians and how well they were governing. He sent his notes to fellow journalists in the capital. Eager to earn extra money, he sought out hotel managers and offered to write ads in English on local hotels and handicraft industries. Frequently he was hired and received gifts of pottery, blankets, and cheaper lodgings.[7]

He was greatly impressed by Mexico's political and economic systems and wrote his parents:

> [America] has so much to learn from some aspects of the Mexican social organization. They are experimenting with democracy in the control and planning of the economic machine on which all the people are dependent for their livelihood. They are trying to see whether or not a program of national economic planning and social responsibility may not increase rather than decrease the opportunities for individuals to use their initiative and to develop their capacities for leadership and to earn a fitting reward for successful work. It's a very exciting experiment.

He also loved the rugged grandeur of Mexico and the casual atmosphere that allowed him to wear a bright green and blue serape and a gigantic sombrero without being thought a bohemian. Peasant, economist, journalist, capitalist—Remington played all these roles during his honeymoon in Mexico.[8]

On their return to the United States in early September, the Remingtons stopped off in Knoxville, and Bill introduced his bride to the friends he had made during his year with TVA: Henry Hart, Mabel Abercrombie, and Muriel Speare. The pleasure of the reunion was dampened by two shocking events. On August 23, while they were traveling through Mexico, the unthinkable had occurred. Nazi Germany and Soviet Russia signed a nonaggression pact. Its eastern flank now protected, Germany swiftly invaded Poland, and, on September 1, Britain and France declared war on Germany. For many Communists and fellow travelers, this was the "nightmare season." Some who had slavishly supported Russian opposition to Hitler during the Popular Front era found it impossible to stomach Stalin's action and quit the Party. Others ignored the catastrophe and continued to follow the Soviet Union. The Remingtons found the Knoxville group deeply distressed by the Nazi–Soviet pact. Bill and Ann were also shocked. "We had an idea of Russia as the utopia . . . and [the pact] began to explode that," Ann later recalled. The next day Bill showed Ann Norris Dam; then they spent the night camping in the Great Smoky Mountains before driving to New York.[9]

After resting at Croton for a few days, they went into Manhattan to search for a place to live and found an apartment at 510 West 123rd Street, just a short walk from Columbia University. It was small, but since they had little furniture, it seemed spacious enough. Its spartan design was more a matter of choice than graduate-student economy. Typically, Bill had earlier decided just what they would need—a mattress, a dresser, a few lamps, two old desks, and a dining-room table and chairs. For entertaining, Bill asked his parents for a hand-woven linen tablecloth. A bare mattress and a linen tablecloth—an odd combination, but indicative of Remington's desire to unite the proletarian and the aristocratic.[10]

Once settled, Ann enrolled at the Pace Institute to pick up some secretarial skills, while Bill registered at Columbia, selecting the most advanced of the graduate courses in economics and public administration. He quickly established himself as a first-rate student. "Remington's scholastic record . . . can be fairly described as brilliant," noted Robert M. Haig, the chairman of the Economics Department, at the end of the academic year.[11]

He was especially close to Professor Arthur McMahon, who by chance lived in Croton and knew the Moos family. McMahon was also a trustee of the Hessian Hills School, where his children were educated, but by 1939 he was growing increasingly concerned about Elizabeth Moos's Communist associates. (She would be kicked out of the school a short time later.) McMahon was an outspoken anti-Communist and avoided contact with his Communist neighbors. He was therefore pleased to discover that Elizabeth's new son-in-law had apparently escaped being infected by the family's political virus. One day in

December, McMahon spoke emotionally to his class about Russia's brutal attack on Finland and noticed the smile on Bill's face.[12]

After class that day, and in the days following, Remington talked often with the professor about recent events, always stating his strong opposition to the Soviet Union. He also expressed such sentiments to others, including Bill Goodman, his liberal ally in the war against Dartmouth's pro-Communist ASU. That December, he sent Goodman a card wishing him "a Merry Christmas in this not-very-peaceful world," to which he added a postscript: "I wouldn't touch a Red with a ten foot pole these days—not after what Stalin is doing."[13]

Was this evidence, as Remington would later claim, that he had at last renounced his Communist sympathies? Perhaps—but it is also possible that Remington was again using anti-Communism to his personal advantage. McMahon was a prominent member of Columbia's faculty, who, through an old-boy network, was frequently successful in placing his students in government positions. Remington wanted such a job and knew that McMahon's help would be invaluable. Indeed, McMahon later admitted that had Remington shown "any tendency to follow the pro-Communist line . . . I [would] not have recommended him, as I did, . . . to friends in the public service."[14] Thus, an anti-Communist stand was likely to guarantee McMahon's support; as he had done at Dartmouth, Remington might again have been playing the role of the square character.

It is possible to question Remington's sincerity, because while he was assuring McMahon that he thought Russia guilty of a brutal invasion, he was also telling fellow graduate student (and Dartmouth alumnus) William Chamberlin that "the fault for the war did not lie with the Russians and that the Russians should not be censured for it." This conversation, according to Chamberlin's later testimony, occurred in either late December 1939 or early January 1940. He recalled talking with Remington on the steps leading up to Columbia's old library on 116th Street. Despite the chill in the air and snow on the ground, they talked for almost half an hour. "I [said that] Russia, of course, had committed aggression against Finland," Chamberlin recalled, "and that I didn't think anybody reasonably could justify such action. Mr. Remington stated . . . that he believed the first overt act had been made by the Finns and that Russia was entitled to protect its borders."[15] Another student also later remembered a similar conversation with Remington on the Columbia campus. "Remington," he said, "took the general attitude that Russia's activities at that time were beyond criticism. [He] was critical of preparations in the United States for its defense and was critical of Great Britain's part in the war, and described the war as being an Imperialist War."[16] If Chamberlin and the unidentified student are correct, then Remington was openly articulating the Communist Party line at the same time he was expressing the opposite viewpoint to Arthur McMahon. Which outlook truly reflected Remington's thinking is a mystery. What does seem clear is that he still enjoyed playing games—which seemed little more than ideological pranks. Later, however, this would have the most serious consequences.

Bill and Ann had other associations with Communists in the fall of 1939. They decided to take a course on Marxism offered by the Communist Party's Workers' School but did not stay in it for long. At the first meeting, as the lecturer began to discuss Marxist economic theory in what Bill thought was "a dogmatic way," Bill interrupted and challenged the instructor. Heckling him, the lecturer told him to shut up and sit down. Instead, Bill and Ann stormed out of the room and withdrew from the class. In October, when Communist Party boss Earl Browder sought a congressional seat for New York's 14th District, the Remingtons, according to Ann, were enthusiastic supporters. But Browder's defeat left them very disappointed with the candidate, who they thought had misled his followers. Bill later denied working in the campaign and said that he did not think that Ann had either. All that he could remember of that incident was Ann taking him to a Browder rally somewhere in New York.[17] It is not possible to resolve such conflicting testimony, but considering the Remingtons' prior actions, it seems likely that Ann did participate while Bill associated with the campaign without fully joining it.

Bill and Ann's closest institutional connection to the Communist movement came with their involvement with the American Youth Congress (AYC). This body, established in 1934, presumed to represent all American youth and, at the height of its influence, managed to bring under one roof some seventy organizations, including such disparate groups as the YWCA and the American League for Peace and Democracy. Its most distinguished patron was Eleanor Roosevelt. Although numerous non-Communist groups belonged to the AYC, by 1939 its driving force was the Communists. During the winter of 1939–40, Ann Remington was employed as a secretary in the AYC's New York office; her boss was Joseph Cadden, a member of the Communist Party, according to several congressional witnesses. Cadden's wife, Vivian, met Bill Remington at Columbia and told him about the group's desire to help unemployed youth, and Remington offered to compile information on government jobs. Ann did similar research, which was sent on to the Jobs for Youth panel of the Congress.[18]

Bill and Ann also attended the dramatic meeting of the American Youth Congress's Citizen Institute, in Washington, D.C., in early February 1940. The conference was expected to be contentious. The Nazi–Soviet pact and the Russian invasion of Finland had shaken the membership and had opened divisions between liberals and Stalinists, who wished to use the convention to promote Communist causes. Mrs. Roosevelt was troubled by the Congress's refusal to condemn Soviet actions but, nevertheless, helped members to find lodgings and arranged for administration officials to speak when the group gathered at the Labor Department Auditorium. She was also able to persuade an unsympathetic FDR to address the membership from the White Houses's rear portico.[19]

Saturday, February 3, was an unfortunate day for the AYC's pilgrimage along Constitution Avenue to the White House. It was cold and windy, with a hard rain falling on the Remingtons and the other five thousand marchers. The crowd gathered at the White House and received an equally chilly welcome from the President. He delivered a harsh speech. Those who believed in Soviet benevolence (most of the AYC's leadership) should remember that it was "a dic-tatorship as absolute as any other dictatorship in the world." As for the belea-guered Finns, they deserved American support; the view that a loan might drive the United States into an "Imperialist War" was "unadulterated twaddle . . . based on ninety percent ignorance." These remarks brought forth boos and hiss-es from an audience Walter Lippmann later called "shockingly ill-mannered, dis-respectful, conceited, ungenerous and spoiled."[20]

At the Labor Auditorium, the group had its revenge. They cheered CIO leader John L. Lewis, who attacked the President, and booed Mrs. Roosevelt, who accidentally tripped over Bill Remington's feet as she ascended the stage. Ann's boss, Joe Cadden, told the members that "all our social gains are threat-ened by the trend toward a war economy." Other AYC speeches followed suit, and a resolution supporting the Finns was defeated. This act was especially dis-turbing to the Remingtons. "The Youth Congress refused to pass the resolution and that made my wife and myself feel that the [AYC] was probably dominated by Communists because it took the CP line on Finland," Bill later said. They never attended another AYC meeting, Bill claimed, "because we completely lost sympathy with the organization at that time." In fact, this was not quite true. A year later, in February 1941, when the AYC—now firmly under Communist con-trol—met again in Washington, Ann assisted with the arrangements. Two men recorded her activities—a local policeman attached to the "Red Squad" and an FBI informant. The informant, observing a rally at the headquarters of the United Federal Workers of America on Sunday, February 2, 1941, later wrote: "A young woman, ANN REMINGTON, . . . a medium sized girl with dark brown wavy hair and very irregular lower teeth, took the floor and in a soft drawl made a plea for cooperation in housing the thousands expected to attend the meeting of the AYC. . . . "[21]

Five thousand members poured into Washington and received an even frosti-er reception from the Roosevelt administration. Mrs. Roosevelt refused to address the group, which was now lobbying against HR 1776, FDR's lend-lease bill to aid Britain. Joseph Lash, a former AYC activist turned anti-Communist critic, was given five minutes to speak on behalf of the legislation. "The hostili-ty of most of the audience was almost palpable," he later recalled. "Boos and hisses greeted my coming forward to speak my piece. Shouts of 'throw him out' interrupted me. . . . [A]s I came down the platform, one of the Youth Congress ushers, a college fraternity brother, came up behind me and hissed into my ear,'Judas!'" By this time, Remington's own connection with the AYC seems to have been peripheral, and he was apparently telling the truth when he later said that "Ann had been much closer to the Youth Congress than I. . . . "[22]

Socially, the Remingtons also gravitated toward those on the far left. Their closest friends were Bernard Redmont and his fiancée, Joan Rothenberg. Bill and Bernie had much in common. Redmont was a graduate of the City College of New York, where he was a radical, a member of the American Student Union, and editor of the school newspaper. When they were first introduced at the home of a mutual friend in the fall of 1939, Redmont, who was completing his graduate work at the Columbia University School of Journalism and was the recipient of a Pulitzer Traveling Scholarship, was about to leave for Mexico. Redmont was interested to learn that Bill had recently visited there, and the two spent the evening discussing Mexican politics and culture. Ann had a bit of a crush on Redmont because of his good looks and the fact that they were politically compatible. She also liked Joan, whom she later called "a charming girl and a loyal and flexible wife." Bernie and Joan were also Communists, according to Ann, although Bernie was more passionate. The women discussed politics frequently, and Ann thought Joan was aware of the disadvantages of life within the Communist Party. The Remingtons and their friends considered themselves renegades—believers in Communist philosophy but critics of Party activists and their overbearing methods.[23] In later interviews with the FBI and to a student of the Remington case, Redmont denied ever knowing that the Remingtons were Communists. In 1952, Redmont would give similar testimony, under oath, in court; he also denied that he or his wife had been Communists. Mrs. Redmont was at first reluctant to talk with the FBI about the Remingtons, but then she also "denied that [they] . . . revealed to her any Communist affiliation or sympathy. . . . "[24]

It is, of course, possible that Ann Remington was mistaken or lying about the political views and connections of the Redmonts. But it does not seem credible, as the Redmonts later argued, that Bill and Ann never expressed sympathy for Communism or discussed politics during a most politically charged decade. Such statements raise doubts about whether they answered FBI agents' questions truthfully. Furthermore, FBI records indicate that if they were not Communists, they were almost certainly fellow travelers. For example, an FBI wiretap on the Redmont telephone in 1946 recorded a conversation between Joan Redmont and a friend named Helen Scott in which Helen informed Joan of a rally in Baltimore where Communist Party official William Z. Foster would be present. Joan replied that she and her husband would like to attend; she also noted that her son, Dennis Foster Redmont, was "Bill Z's namesake." Other conversations also reveal Communist sympathy. What is at issue here is not the right of the Redmonts to be Communists or Soviet sympathizers; what is important is their failure to tell the truth, not just during the McCarthy era when to speak frankly was admittedly dangerous, but even forty years later, long after the end of the Cold War.[25]

The closest contacts the Remingtons had with members of the Communist Party occurred when Ann and Bill visited the Moos estate at Croton-on-Hudson. By 1939, Elizabeth Moos had turned to the Communist Party as an escape from the despair caused by the breakup of her second marriage. Robert Imandt had been replaced by two new men—Joseph North and Al Warren, who would have a profound influence on her political views and activities. North, a short, curly-haired bespectacled man of thirty-five, joined the Communist Party in the late 1920s and, in 1934, founded and edited the *New Masses*, a Communist weekly. Five years later, he met Elizabeth Moos and became, in Ann's words, "her protégé." She invited North to live in a converted garage on the Moos estate, and North reciprocated by introducing her to Al Warren and other friends in the Communist Party. Warren was a veteran of the Abraham Lincoln Brigade whom North had met while covering the Spanish Civil War for *New Masses*. Although Warren suffered poor health, Elizabeth was immediately attracted to him. They fell in love, though the relationship did not stop him from also flirting with Ann, which enraged her mother. Warren moved in with Elizabeth, and he and North persuaded her to join the Party. Ann also believed that her own prior Party membership at Columbia and Croton had influenced her mother. They "had always engaged in a sort of friendly rivalry," Ann recalled, "and her mother often patterned herself after [her] and did the same things."[26]

During their sojourn in New York City from the fall of 1939 to the spring of 1940, Ann and Bill would usually spend their weekends relaxing at the Moos estate. It was a relief to escape from their small apartment in Manhattan for the beautiful mansion at Croton, which Bill loved. Joe North was a frequent visitor, drinking and dining with Elizabeth and Al, and sometimes playing the piano and singing show tunes. Bill thought he was a pleasant and charming man. But North was also the type of Communist ideologue whom Bill loved to needle, and they would often argue, especially during the months following the Russian invasion of Finland.[27]

These squabbles did not prevent the Remingtons from helping North and the Communist *New Masses* at a critical moment in the spring of 1940 when the magazine was plagued by financial woes and the possible loss of mailing privileges. Bill and Ann joined Elizabeth and her friends in contributing money and holding a fund-raising party to save it. Ann drew one hundred dollars from their savings account and sent it to North, along with a letter Bill insisted on writing. "I wanted . . . to point out to North that . . . I was not capitulating in the discussions that he and I had been having." The letter was later published in a revised version under a pseudonym in *New Masses*.[28]

Such was the life Bill led within the Moos family circle, and he seems to have enjoyed it all—the lovely country home, good food and drink, the *Daily Worker* on the living room table, political debates with Communists and others Ann called screwballs. It could not have been more different from his cloistered existence at his parents' home.[29]

What do these activities and relationships—marital, social, or political—reveal about the Remingtons' view of the Communist Party in the late 1930s? First, Ann and Bill were philosophical rather than organizational Communists. Ann's experience with the Columbia University unit left her with a dislike for the orthodox arrangements of Party life. The regular Party members she met in New York (and later in Washington) were "a pretty unpleasant bunch." Attending Party meetings entailed endless, boring work, and for Ann, the ideology "didn't make sense at all." Bill understood better the body of ideas but, by 1939, believed that orthodox Marxism was nonsense. As a result, the Remingtons never joined a local Party unit in New York or Washington. Both were raised according to a strict code of behavior (one Victorian, the other bohemian) and were dominated by forceful mothers; now, they rejected the control that was part of Communist Party life. "We were not orthodox Communists in that sense of following all the rules," Ann later said. "We were Communists as much as we wanted to be Communists and not subject to a hierarchy." As independent Communists, they felt free to pick and choose those aspects of Communist life that interested them or served their own personal goals. Ironically, this position would lead them into a deeper and more troubled involvement than they ever anticipated.[30]

In May 1940, the Remingtons moved to Washington, D.C., where Bill took a part-time job as a junior economist with the National Resources Planning Board. He had earned his master's degree and was admitted to the doctoral program, which he planned to complete by commuting to Columbia once a week. His appointment was the result of his excellent standing in the Economics Department (he was awarded a University Fellowship for the 1940–41 academic year, even though he was not in residence most of the time) and a letter of recommendation Arthur McMahon sent to close friend and former colleague Thomas Blaisdell, now a director of the Planning Board. Blaisdell interviewed Bill on February 12 and later wrote, "After 15 minutes with this chap, I would stake my reputation on employing him. . . . He is the best material I have met in five years."[31]

The Remingtons rented an apartment at 5188 Fulton Street, N.W., and while Bill began work as Blaisdell's assistant (handling the budget and doing economic research), Ann searched for a job. She found nothing but secretarial work, which did not appeal to her. "She wanted to have responsibility and drama," Bill later said, so she turned again to politics. Through her contacts in the American Youth Congress, she became involved in the Washington peace movement. Hitler's armies were again on the march—Norway and Denmark fell that spring, and in June, France surrendered. In response, President Roosevelt, speaking at the University of Virginia, strongly attacked the doctrine of isolationism and held out the hope of aid to the victims of Nazi aggression. To American Communists who followed the Party line, Roosevelt's speech meant increased involvement in an "Imperialist War," and they tried to prevent it. Ann did her part. She helped to organize the Emergency Peace Mobilization Committee and was appointed executive secretary. She ran the office, answering the telephone, handling the mail, and arranging rallies at Turner's Arena on 14th Street. Sometimes Bill joined her. He decorated a hall prior to a meeting, compiled a mailing list of prospective members, sat in on executive committee meetings, and once wrote a leaflet, which the group later rejected. Their activities possibly cost them their apartment. Neighbors complained to the manager that the Remingtons made too many calls at night on the apartment's communal telephone (as many as twenty, one man claimed), so in August, they moved to an apartment on N Street, a building that attracted so many Communists and fellow travelers that it was called "The Little Kremlin." The incident must have reminded Bill of his days in Knoxville.[32]

By September, they had become disenchanted with the organization. For Ann, it was a question of personalities. Although she was not completely certain that her colleagues were Communists, they seemed to have all their worst qualities. Eventually, she concluded that she had been chosen executive secretary because the local Communists, desiring to dominate the chapter, wanted a fresh face without a Party record to lead the group. She was replaced early that month after members returned from a meeting in Chicago, having founded the American Peace Mobilization, an organization controlled by Communists. Bill's opposition was political. The group was now strongly isolationist, and he opposed that. Bill and Ann did attend the first meeting of the APM but, after their call for increased aid to Britain was rejected, quit.[33]

While Ann's ventures in politics ended in failure, Remington's career at the National Resources Planning Board prospered. At age twenty-two, he was Tom Blaisdell's chief assistant and admired by his colleagues on the staff. His first assignment was to help his boss compile a roster of scientific experts whom the government could call should there be a national emergency. Remington handled the initial research, conferred with scientists and other specialists, and acted as liaison with officials at the agency. He worked long hours and sometimes weekends during the blistering summer of 1940. "The Consulting Committee was meeting this weekend," he wrote his parents on July 21, "and somebody had to represent Blaisdell. The job fell to me. So Ann [went to Fire Island] and had a nice swim yesterday and today, and I've stewed through the two hottest days I ever remember. . . ."[34] When Blaisdell returned from a brief vacation, his secretary, Jane Herndon Smith, told him how well she thought his new aide was doing. Although young and barely on the job two months, Remington understood "deeply the importance of having such a roster of scientific people for the nation in time of need and . . . he was astute in the way he handled . . . Blaisdell's work with the other superior officers in the NRPB," Smith later recalled.[35]

At the same time, Remington prepared to take doctoral exams in economics at Columbia. The Planning Board allowed him to spend two days a week in New York, where he took courses in advanced economic theory, money and banking, economic history, and social psychology. His area of special concentration was the economics of national defense. He successfully passed his Ph.D. qualifying exams in April 1941, despite fatigue and a fever. He dismissed the symptoms merely as signs of overwork and pre-exam jitters, but a few days later he felt worse and was diagnosed as having typhoid fever. He convalesced for a few weeks at Croton, then returned to Washington.[36]

In mid-July, Remington was transferred to the Office of Price Administration, becoming a full-time associate industrial economist and assistant to the chief of the Standards Section, at a salary of thirty-two hundred dollars a year—a 100 percent increase over what he was earning at the NRPB. With Ann now pregnant with their first child, the extra income was welcomed. Blaisdell was especially sorry to see him go; losing Remington, he told statistician Ezra Glazer, was "like having my right arm cut off."[37]

Because OPA was then a part of the Office of Emergency Management—a national defense agency—Remington was required to undergo a loyalty check. The first of many he would experience during his career, it lasted more than a year and involved the Treasury Department's Bureau of Internal Revenue, the Civil Service Commission, and the FBI. The investigation began on August 20, 1941, when Remington was interviewed by D. F. Sloan, a special agent of the Treasury Department. He was asked a series of questions drawn from a standard four-page examination form, similar to applications he had filled out at the time of his original federal employment. Therefore, nearly all the questions were biographical—covering Remington's birth, education, employment history, and character references. Only one question bore directly on Remington's loyalty to the United States. Had he ever joined or associated with organizations that had connections or affiliations outside the United States? Remington replied that he and his wife had joined the Emergency Peace Mobilization in Washington the previous summer and had attended one or two meetings but had resigned in protest in September 1940. He also admitted to membership in the Cooperative League, Rochedale Stores, and the Washington Book Shop (where books could be bought at a discount). Although the latter had been called a Communist front by the House Committee on Un-American Activities, Remington said that neither he nor his wife had ever attended meetings of the group and assured Sloan that they never sympathized with Communism and were patriotic Americans.[38]

Given the superficial nature of the inquiry, it went quickly and easily. Sloan did ask for additional information regarding Remington's work at Dartmouth, with TVA, and during his Mexican honeymoon and was satisfied with Remington's responses. Asked to evaluate Remington, Sloan wrote, "[He] impressed me as being a high-class young man who is a loyal American citizen and suitable for Defense service. His frank explanation of his membership in the [various] organizations are [sic] quite satisfactory."[39]

In September and October, Sloan's colleagues contacted Dean Neidlinger at Dartmouth and Remington's former bosses at TVA and looked through the records of the House Committee on Un-American Activities but found no indication of disloyalty. Their brief report was sent to the Office of Emergency Management, where it was routed to examiner John E. Taylor in the Investigations Office. After quickly reading the two-page letter, he filled out an "Investigation Rating Form" and under "Action Contemplated" wrote just one word: "Unfavorable." Taylor was very unhappy with Sloan's brief interview with Remington. Where and when had the Remingtons joined the APM and the Washington Book Shop? What books had they purchased? It was true that Dean Neidlinger had recommended Remington for his new position, but the examiner was disturbed by the dean's comment that Bill was a rebel who might not function well in government. Similarly, his supervisor at TVA called Remington brilliant but somewhat unbalanced—what did that portend? All in all, there was real doubt in Taylor's mind that Remington was loyal. He recommended that Remington be called in for a hearing to resolve these uncertainties.[40]

Taylor's decision—endorsed by his boss—postponed Remington's clearance and led to the second stage of the investigation, this time conducted by agents of the Civil Service Commission. On February 21, 1942, the FBI was also authorized to check Remington, in response to a confidential informant's claim that Remington was still active in the American Peace Mobilization, an organization now considered a Communist front. If the accusation were true, then Remington had possibly violated the Hatch Act, a law designed, in part, to prevent federal employees from joining any party or group that advocated the violent overthrow of the government.[41]

Despite the fact that Remington had recently assumed an important position with the War Production Board Planning Committee, the FBI conducted a hurried and shallow investigation into his background and recent life. Agents from the Washington field office started first at 5188 Fulton Street, where the Remingtons had lived during their first two months in the capital. They interviewed two people who had vivid—if confused—memories of Ann and Bill. One claimed that Ann was either a Communist, fascist, or Nazi or a staunch sympathizer of one or all of them. Both Remingtons seemed to be extremely active in the Emergency Peace Mobilization Committee (the parent organization of the APM) and were observed organizing meetings and distributing peace literature. The informant also noted that "he disliked the activities of Remington and his wife especially because of the fact that Remington is on the government payroll. . . . " At 2325 N Street, agents spoke with Lena Montague, the apartment manager, whose major complaint was the way the Remingtons furnished their apartment. There were too many books and magazines strewn about to suit Mrs. Montague's taste. She also remembered that Bill was friendly with another tenant, Anna Goodman, who allegedly provided her apartment for what Mrs. Montague thought were Communist Party meetings. (Ann later told the FBI that Mrs. Goodman had indeed invited them to Party meetings, but because she and Bill disliked such groups, they never went.) Agents were instructed simply to record the information they received from informants, so the Remington file began to fill with a mixture of facts (they were active on the Emergency Peace Mobilization Committee) and fantasy (it is doubtful that the FBI thought Ann both a fascist and a Communist, but that characterization was accepted without editorial comment).[42]

Investigators did uncover a possible link between Remington and alleged Communists in TVA, but they did not pursue the lead or question Remington about that period during an interview on March 31, 1942. The focus of the conversation then was Remington's connection to two alleged subversive organizations—the American Youth Congress and the American Peace Mobilization. Remington's responses were terse and uninformative. He and his wife had been active briefly in both groups, he admitted, but quit when the APM turned isolationist and the Youth Congress failed to condemn the Soviet invasion of Finland. Agent R. F. Ryan did not question Remington about phone calls or meetings or any of the other more credible accusations made by their informants. He even seemed unaware that an investigation had been conducted, and a testy Remington quickly put him on the defensive. If malicious charges had been made, he demanded to know the details so that he could respond to each one.

No charges had been made, Ryan said, as if apologizing; in fact, no investigation had been conducted, just an inquiry that was now finished. The implication was that Remington had no reason to fear the FBI. "If you have nothing else to add for the record, we will conclude the interview," the agent said.

"All right," Remington replied, with the bravado that had frequently annoyed so many people. "Well, thanks very much, and my basic attitude is that if you have to get rid of a thousand of us who are innocent . . . in order to get hold of one person who might overthrow the Government, you may as well get rid of a thousand of us."

Did Remington wish to return to read a transcript of his interview?

"No," Bill said. "I don't wish to return."[43]

It was a poor performance on the part of the FBI. Later, with an air of embarrassment, the Bureau admitted privately that the inquiry was very limited, designed primarily to examine Remington's role in the APM.[44] Limited indeed—the typewritten transcript Remington dismissed barely fills four pages. Of the six questions asked that pertained to subversive organizations, none was more than one sentence long. Clearly, Ryan and the other agents had not studied their own files on the AYC and the APM and did not bother Remington for additional information. As far as the FBI was concerned, William Remington was an unexceptional employee with a perfectly conventional history; however, since the Civil Service Commission had not yet submitted its findings, the case was not closed.[45]

Because of bureaucratic inertia, it was not until late March that Civil Service Commission agent J. O. Hardesty began the third and final stage of the Remington investigation. Hardesty checked first with the local credit bureau and the Washington Police Department, but neither agency had any information on Remington. His personnel record was examined and letters sent again to Dean Neidlinger and four former professors, including Russell Larmon, whom Remington had taunted from Mexico but continued to list among his references. In early April, Hardesty began to interview Remington's superiors and colleagues in government, but, unlike the FBI, he allowed them to speak at length about his subject. "He is Ace-High as to character, habits, and morals," Tom Blaisdell told him. "I have never had a finer person work for me. . . . If Bill Remington is not loyal to our Government . . . there is not much hope for us." Herbert J. Goodman, an assistant economist who had worked with Remington, thought he was "one of the most clean-cut moral people I have ever known. I think he is a very loyal American and is entirely in sympathy for our form of government." Hardesty received similar reports from Remington's bosses at OPA and WPB.[46]

The most important part of the investigation occurred on the afternoon of June 29, 1942, when Remington appeared at Hardesty's office for a hearing. He was told that during the investigation, Hardesty had discovered information that might endanger his employment and that the Commission wanted to give him an opportunity to discuss these problems. An oath was then administered and the questions began, the majority focusing on Remington's association with the AYC and APM. For the most part, Remington gave an accurate description of his affiliations but tended to emphasize Ann's activities and said little about his own. Remington was more misleading about his year in Knoxville. Nothing was said about the possible presence of Communists in the group, and he described the Workers Education Committee as just a pro-New Deal lobby that spent most of its time supporting WPA appropriations and FDR's plan to add new members to the Supreme Court. He was the chief researcher and correspondent. Although Remington tried to characterize himself as both anti-fascist and anti-Communist, Hardesty asked him directly, "Are you now or have you ever been a member of the Communist Party or any affiliate?"

"No. I haven't been. Definitely not," Remington replied.

"And you are not at the present?"

"No, I am not. Definitely not."

Was his wife connected in any way with any organization since severing her connection with the APM?

"She belongs to the Red Cross and has been teaching First Aid . . . ," Remington said, "but that is the only organization which she belongs to. . . . "[47]

As the session drew to a close, Remington complimented Hardesty, telling him that he had had a fair, even pleasant, hearing. Hardesty must have agreed, because he later noted in his final report that Remington "created a favorable impression during the course of the hearing, makes a good appearance, is intelligent, cooperative . . . and displayed a good attitude." On July 14, 1942, he recommended an eligible rating. Remington received this happy news on August 4, 1942, nearly thirteen months after his initial appointment to OPA.[48]

Once again Remington had triumphed—he had managed to convince his professional colleagues and investigators from the Treasury Department, FBI, and Civil Service Commission that he was basically a conservative. In fact, he was a deeply divided man—attracted to the danger and adventure only the Communist world seemed to provide. For just at the moment that Remington received his loyalty clearance, he was involved in what would become the most controversial and—ultimately—destructive episode of his life.

7

Obliging a Lady

When the Remingtons first saw the area in the summer of 1940, it was just acres of lush, green trees, out in Fairfax County, Virginia. A cooperative corporation was formed, consisting of a Board of Directors and a manager who would supervise the construction of the first twenty homes. Tauxemont was the name given to the development, and the Remingtons arranged to build their first home there—for sixty-five hundred dollars they could have a house located on a half-acre lot. Construction began early in 1941, and by December, Ann and Bill were able to move in. It seemed ideal; close enough to the city so that Bill could easily commute, yet located in the country where they could experience the pleasures of rural life. Their neighbors were friendly; most were civil servants like Bill and some were leftists—members of the Washington Book Shop, the American League for Peace and Democracy, and other Communist Party front groups. They entertained one another, formed a riding club for those who drove to Washington, and during the Christmas holidays, went caroling through the neighborhood.[1]

Still, Bill and Ann were lonely and not entirely comfortable with their new life. Putting down roots in the conventional manner—buying a house, having a child (Ann was six months pregnant)—drove them back to the Communist Party. Croton was now too distant for regular weekend trips, and Joe North was unable to visit them in Alexandria as often as he had when they lived in Washington. Therefore, they sought a new connection with the Party, one that did not include the annoying requirements of membership. Moreover, an open, formal membership might threaten Bill's career with the government; better, a sub-rosa relationship through which they would receive Party literature and Bill could pass along information he picked up at the War Production Board, where he would start working in late February 1942. First, sometime in late 1941 or early 1942, Bill turned to his old friend Kit Buckles and asked her how he could establish a contact with the Party. She was not sure but would check with people she knew. One person she consulted was Franklin Folsom, formerly the executive secretary of the League of American Writers and still a Communist Party member. Tell Remington just to write a letter to Party headquarters, he joked. When she was unable to come up with anything further, the Remingtons turned to Joe North, who, after some prodding, asked them to come to New York, sometime in the early spring of 1942, to meet a friend who might be able to help them.[2]

They met at Schrafft's Restaurant at 4th Avenue and 31st Street. North's friend was a short, stocky, red-headed man wearing a worn brown suit. When he was introduced to Bill and Ann as John, he spoke with a foreign accent that Remington thought was Dutch. John was especially interested in knowing whether the War Production Board was sincerely advancing the war effort or was trying to make money. Bill thought he was dogmatic and uninformed, while Ann disliked him. "He was . . . an unpleasant character," she later recalled. "He had a sort of closed mind; he knew everything already." Although short on facts, Bill considered John very intelligent with the kind of closed mind he loved to pry open. When John asked if they could meet again, Bill quickly agreed.[3]

When the Remingtons returned to Schrafft's a few nights later, they found John sitting with a heavy-set, blond-haired woman in her late thirties, whom Bill assumed was John's wife; however, she was introduced only as Helen. While the two women talked, John told Bill that he was seeking specific information about the war production program. Remington, who had just joined the staff of the War Production Board Planning Committee, told John what he knew about the agency and its goals. John was very interested and wanted to talk with Bill again; unfortunately, he was rarely in Washington, but Helen would be going down and would call on him.[4]

As the weeks passed, Bill forgot about Helen and John. His work at the WPB kept him very busy, as did his new infant son, Bruce, born on March 15, 1942. Then, one morning later that spring, his office telephone rang and a soft, feminine voice said, "Bill? This is Helen Johnson."

Momentarily baffled, Bill answered, "Helen Johnson?"

"Yes, don't you remember . . . I met you in New York."

Of course, Helen and John, the evening at Schrafft's—it all came back to Bill in a flash. She was in Washington for a few days and wanted to meet for lunch. They arranged to meet at noon at Whelan's Drug Store on Pennsylvania Avenue.[5]

According to Remington, he saw Helen between six and perhaps ten times during the next two years. They would lunch together, meet for a late afternoon cup of tea or a milk shake, or just talk on a park bench near the Mellon Art Gallery. On these occasions, Bill would often give her airplane production data he extracted from the *Washington Post*, the *Kiplinger Newsletter*, and lesser-known trade journals; press releases describing WPB successes in meeting government deadlines; copies of his own memoranda on various issues; and once a formula for the making of synthetic rubber from garbage. Helen later claimed that Bill frequently said his information was secret or confidential but just as often denigrated it, arguing that it was of little importance. However the information might be classified, both Remingtons thought that they were helping to win the war. "We were allies with the Russians," Ann later said, "and it wasn't so dreadful perhaps in trying to give them secrets over the heads of the Government."[6]

Nevertheless, Bill was not happy about his relationship with Helen. Ann (who later claimed to have attended some of their meetings, at which time she paid their Party dues) described her husband as "very nervous about the whole affair." Helen agreed:

> He was one of the most frightened people with whom I had to deal. It was difficult to get him to bring out carbon copies of documents. Usually he would jot the information down on small scraps of paper, giving them to me furtively and with many admonitions about not letting them fall into the wrong hands. . . . [He] reminded me very strongly of a small boy trying to avoid mowing the lawn when he would much rather go fishing.

Nor was Ann very satisfied with the arrangement. She was unhappy with the literature that Helen brought and felt she did not receive the direction from the Party she desired. After the first few meetings, she remained at home. By mid-1943, Bill began to "regret the position in which he found himself," Ann said, and tried to break away. When Helen called, he would tell her he could not see her. "I got the very distinct impression that he didn't like what he was doing," Helen said later. "He became increasingly reluctant to give me information. I just couldn't get him out." In early 1944, while lunching together at the Mellon Art Gallery, Bill told Helen he would probably not be able to see her anymore, since he was expecting to go into the service. When Helen telephoned Bill in June, a secretary informed her that Mr. Remington had joined the Navy and was now at a language school in Boulder, Colorado.[7]

In later years, when his troubles began, William Remington would steadfastly insist that he neither knew that Helen represented the Communist Party nor that he gave her information that she was not entitled to receive. He claimed that she was a free-lance journalist for leftist newspapers as well as a researcher assisting John in the preparation of a book on war mobilization. Contradicting him was the not always reliable testimony of Ann and Helen that he knew that she belonged to the Party and had set up an arrangement by which there would be an exchange of information. Strong evidence exists that indicates that Remington did seek out such a relationship with the Party, knew whom she represented, and did provide information. First, there is Franklin Folsom's clear recollection of his talk with Kit Buckles about Remington's desire for a liaison with the Communists. Second, and more important, is a private document, in Remington's own handwriting, that contains an admission that he knew what he was doing. " . . . [W]hile I was a young employee of the War Production Board, I took it on myself to discuss information pertaining to war production with unauthorized persons on various occasions. . . . I knew personally that one of these persons was a dedicated Communist Party member. . . . " And, he would also say that he profoundly regretted what he had done and the "involvement with Communists that got me into trouble."[8] But this was many years later. By early 1944, his work for John and the Party had ended. Once again he had been able to cross over the line into dangerous territory and then return, without harm, to his other, safer life.

In February 1944, Draft Board Number 8 classified Remington I-A, eligible for military service, so he began to consider his options. He preferred enlisting to being drafted by the Army, and when he learned about the Naval School of Oriental Languages at the University of Colorado, he decided to join the Navy. Bill spoke to the official in charge and learned that two programs were presently available—a fourteen-month course in Japanese and a six-month course in Russian. For some time he had been interested in learning Russian, which would help him in researching his doctoral dissertation, so he enrolled in the program. On April 3, he flew to Boulder, Colorado, his status that of "Naval Agent"—a civilian in a Navy language school. Ann, again pregnant, would join him after the baby was born, which turned out to be sooner than they expected. Daughter Galeyn was born April 8, 1944.[9]

After moving into a dormitory on the University of Colorado campus, Remington formally applied for a commission in the U.S. Navy. Given his investigative history, he hoped to ensure his acceptance by offering a detailed personal history, which he attached to his application. He described his careers at Dartmouth, with TVA, at Columbia, and with the War Production Board, as well as both Remingtons' connections with those groups now considered Communist fronts. As in his previous statements, he was not completely honest about his past and even went so far as to proclaim that since 1934, "I have been an outspoken critic of totalitarianism in all countries (including Russia)." Although he stated that he was a fervent anti-Communist (reference was made to "my previous anti-Soviet college papers . . . "), if ordered "to cooperate with officials . . . of a country whose system I distrust and dislike, I will carry out these orders to the best of my ability . . . to help bring victory to America." This was not the Bill Remington most of his closest friends knew.[10]

His fellow students would have also been surprised to learn that he was a

Russophobe. One officer believed Bill more sympathetic toward Russia than other students were, because he helped to organize a fund-raising party for Russian Relief. When Ann arrived, with Elizabeth Moos as nanny for Bruce and Gale, the pro-Russia perception of him grew. Ann also studied Russian at the language school, worked for Russian Relief in her spare time, and generally developed the reputation of being pro-Communist. According to Ann, both Remingtons still possessed Communist ideas but found no one at Boulder who was politically compatible.[11]

Remington's final days in the language program were anxious ones. Although successful academically, he was the only civilian who had not yet received his formal commission. By late August, rumors began to circulate that Naval Intelligence had found evidence of loyalty problems. Tom Blaisdell had also informed Bill that he had been appointed Minister of Economic Affairs and was going to London to work on problems of postwar European reconstruction; he hoped that Bill might accompany him as staff assistant. Bill wanted very much to go—except for trips to Granville Ferry and Mexico, he had never left the United States. So he waited apprehensively for news from the Navy; once accepted, he planned to request a transfer, enabling him to accept Blaisdell's offer. Finally, on September 3, 1944, he received the news that he was now an ensign in the U.S. Navy. Immediately, he asked for a transfer but received no answer. As the days passed, he grew increasingly annoyed, so much so that he had a heated argument with Ensign George Perry, whose own transfer request had been quickly granted. "I am much more important to the country because of [my] abilities as an economist," Perry remembered an angry Remington telling him.[12]

It appears the Navy Department did not share Bill's view of his own importance, so, following graduation in November, he applied for a post with Naval Intelligence and was sent to New York City for further training. In December, Bill was ordered to Washington, D.C., where he joined the Office of Naval Intelligence Translation Unit.

During the next four months, while Blaisdell quietly lobbied the Navy Department and encouraged Bill to be patient, Remington, back in Tauxemont, followed a dreary routine. Each morning the riding club drove into the city dropping him off at the headquarters of ONI. In a musty and overheated office, he spent his days translating old Russian meteorological textbooks into English, a boring and unimportant assignment. Finally, in July 1945, he was ordered to report to the American embassy in London, to serve as a staff assistant to the Minister of Economic Affairs. On the evening of July 19, he took a cab to Washington's Metropolitan Airport and boarded a plane for Europe. Ann, pregnant with their third child, stayed behind, dividing her time between Tauxemont and Croton.[13]

As an assistant to Minister Blaisdell, Remington was introduced to what would soon become the important diplomatic questions of the decade. How could Europe—devastated by war—be rebuilt? What role should defeated Germany play in the postwar order? Should Germany, as Treasury Secretary Henry Morgenthau, Jr., recommended, be converted "into a country primarily agricultural and pastoral in its character" or, as Morgenthau's critics insisted, be revived to encourage East–West prosperity?[14] And, most important, would the Soviet–American alliance continue now that Hitler was dead, or would Russia, dominant in eastern Europe and part of Germany, pose a new threat to world peace?

Although Remington was a minor member of the American delegation, he was not shy about expressing himself on these subjects. He was critical of the Morgenthau plan for Germany and worried about Soviet expansion. Later he would say:

> Many of us in London felt strongly that the European continent, as well as western Europe, would not recover its strength needed to oppose Communism successfully, unless the German economy were built up . . . to supply tools and finished products to France, Great Britain, Belgium, and the Netherlands. So . . . we worked on memoranda designed to raise the problem of how much output would be necessary from Germany to help the recovery of the Allied powers and Italy. The Russians who participated in the early meetings . . . opposed policies leading to a revived Germany.

Remington later claimed that he fought them "every inch of the way. . . . "[15]

Remington's anti-Russian views were probably sincere. By the fall of 1945, he had grown skeptical of the Soviet experiment. Both he and Ann had been reading works by Soviet refugees, such as Kravchenko's *I Choose Freedom*, and began to realize that the Soviet system was undesirable. His own experiences in London and trips to Berlin intensified these feelings. And there were other factors also shaping his outlook. Opposition to Soviet expansion was now the chief objective of U.S. foreign policy, and Remington, an ambitious government official, no doubt saw anti-Communism as a way to serve his own professional interests.[16]

Remington's work abroad ended suddenly in November 1945, when he received the news that Ann had given birth but that the baby had been stillborn. The Navy quickly approved an emergency leave, and Bill flew to Washington. During that long flight, he must have thought about the major problem he would now have to resolve: his troubled relationship with Ann. The baby's death might have further strained her emotional stability, fragile for years before their marriage and no stronger afterwards. He had never truly accepted her original protests that she did not love him, could not even grow to love him, as he hoped. Colleagues at the WPB used to kid Remington about the frank and open way he talked about Ann—telling them how very much in love with her he was. But, by 1945, despite all his efforts to give her the love and reassurance she needed, the situation appeared hopeless. To a close friend, Bill said that Ann was a woman "who had never been happy," was "sexually unsatisfied," and seemed especially "unhappy in married life." In 1943, he had been able to convince her to seek help from Dr. Herbert P. Ramsay, a specialist in marital maladjustment, but she broke off treatment after only a few sessions. By the summer of 1945, Ann was again in therapy, this time with Dr. Douglas Noble, a Washington psychiatrist whom she saw twice a week. Later, Bill claimed that Noble told him that his wife was seriously ill.[17]

After seeing Ann and talking with her doctors, Bill could find no reason to challenge Noble's diagnosis. An autopsy performed on the body of his child revealed no organic cause of death, and Dr. Noble, who talked with Ann's obstetrician, told Bill that "his own hypothesis was that her own resentment and dislike of the expected child was sufficiently strong to have caused its death by one means or another." The explanation was bizarre, but it seemed consistent, Bill thought, with Ann's oft stated desire "to get rid of the responsibility for the children entirely." Ann resented Bill's discussions with her physicians, believing that he would try to control Dr. Noble's treatment and also use this opportunity to collect medical evidence proving that she was of unsound mind in order to lay the groundwork for a divorce.[18]

Ann's suspicions drove the couple further apart. "In December, 1945," Bill later wrote,

> she told me that above all else she wanted intense emotional relationships in her life [and] that she intended to seek them in sexual relationships outside of marriage. She told me if I wanted the marriage to continue I must do the same for two reasons: first, so that it would not only be herself who was guilty of adultery; and second, because only the challenge of making myself attractive to other women would overcome the dullness which made me unattractive to her. This doctrine was repeated earnestly and dogmatically against my protests.

If Bill would not cooperate, then perhaps divorce was the only answer. Often that month and later, Ann told him that "she would probably want a divorce," that "her mind was firmly made up. . . . "[19]

Bill opposed divorce, fearing that it would have a devastating effect on his children, to whom he was completely devoted. To protect them, he would agree to any reasonable request. When Ann asked him to consult a psychoanalyst, he did. While Bill considered himself neurotic, Dr. Benjamin Weiniger did not think that he required therapy. Of course, Ann had another explanation for her husband's refusal to enter therapy. Bill, she later claimed, did not like Dr. Weiniger and was not sincere in seeking help, which, according to her, the physician thought he required. Ann continued to insist that he see a psychiatrist, and eventually Bill met with Dr. Zigmond Lebensohn, who also felt that he did not need psychiatric treatment.[20]

The situation grew even more intolerable in 1946. Bill believed that Ann was abusing the children and encouraging them to hit each other. What the children needed most, Bill told Ann, was a mother who would love them. She allegedly replied, "Well, we'll be getting a divorce soon. If you want me to let you have the children you'll have to convince me you can find a woman who could bring them up better than you could yourself." By the summer of 1946, Bill concluded that divorce was the only answer and, encouraged by Ann, began to seek a possible new wife for himself and mother for his children.[21]

He soon found Jane Shepherd, an attractive divorcée, a pollster and journalist whose weekly column appeared in the *Washington Post*. She had met Bill first in late 1945 but did not see him again until they came together at a party in 1946. "I didn't really pay too much attention to him," she later recalled, "except to feel that—dressed in his naval uniform, he was almost impossibly handsome." Wounded by Ann and lonely, worried about his children's future and his own career (he had found work at the Office of War Mobilization and Reconversion), he thought Jane seemed the ideal woman to share his life with.

He called Jane a few weeks later and asked if they could have lunch. Officials at OWMR had asked him to conduct a study based on the kind of polling techniques she knew so well; would she mind meeting with him to discuss it? At the restaurant, Bill asked more questions about Jane than his project, so Jane suspected that he had really wanted a date. She knew for certain when he asked to see her again. Jane was hesitant; Bill was a very impressive man but not outwardly warm and friendly. He began "dogging my footsteps," Jane recalled. "He told me his marriage to Ann was really broken and they were . . . very unhappy. He wanted to see me and became quite obsessive about it." She relented, and they began meeting—at first, just occasionally for lunch or dinner; then by fall, several times a week. "I think he fell in love with me," Jane later said.[22]

Would Ann really agree to a divorce and grant him custody of the children? Or, perversely, would she find Bill more attractive now that he was involved with another woman and decide to continue the marriage? Surprisingly, Ann was willing to meet with Jane, to see how the children responded to her, so she invited her to Tauxemont for a weekend of discussion and observation. One can only speculate about what Ann must have been feeling. Did she remember her own childhood and the cruel way that her father chose to keep his sons and reject his only daughter? Now positions were reversed. No longer the helpless victim in her parents' game, she had become the central figure controlling others' destinies. Perhaps this partly explains the unusual way she chose to release her children to a man she obviously hated and a woman she barely knew.

Early that November 1946, Jane went to Tauxemont, but only for dinner and an evening; she saw no reason to prolong the agony of this audition for more than a few hours. The children liked Jane immediately, and later that night a final agreement was reached. There would be a quick divorce, after which Bill and Jane would marry and find a home where the new family would live.

The next day, Jane notified the *Washington Post* that she intended to resign, and she and Bill went house hunting. Then suddenly, Ann changed her mind. She telephoned Bill that evening and said that she needed more time to consider the deal. Jane thought that perhaps she had been too successful in winning the affections of the children, that this had caused Ann to reconsider her course. Bill was deeply disappointed by the delay and told a friend in December that he would remain with Ann for a while and then separate. By waiting, he hoped to improve his chances of winning custody of at least one of the children. Unfortunately, Ann learned of Bill's strategy and became furious, ending all negotiations. Finally, on January 1, 1947, at the suggestion of her psychoanalyst, she agreed to a trial separation.

Bill left Tauxemont and moved to the city, eventually renting a room at 1717 Riggs Street, the home of Maria and William Calfee. In April, Ann proposed a reconciliation but demanded that he have nothing to do with raising the children. As painful as this was, Bill said that he would consider it, hoping that this opening might lead to a better arrangement. Less than a week later, however, Ann withdrew her offer, and the stalemate continued for almost two more years.[23]

As if all this was not trouble enough, a new problem arose from a different, but not unfamiliar, source: the FBI. It was early on the evening of April 15, 1947, when Special Agents Kennerly R. Corbett, Oscar H. Sells, and William R. Cornelison arrived at the Calfee home, looking for William Remington.[24] Given his background, a visit from the FBI was never unexpected, but recent events made it likely, even inevitable. The Cold War abroad had created havoc at home, a "Red Scare," which politicians of all stripes, Republican as well as Democrat, tried to exploit for political advantage. But Cold War fears and postwar economic problems seemed to work best for the Grand Old Party, once tarnished by the Depression but now revived. In the congressional elections of 1946, the American people had elected Republicans overwhelmingly to the Congress, a powerful indication that the White House would soon be theirs, too. In response, President Harry S Truman struck out at his enemies abroad—the Russians—and his antagonists at home—the Republicans and, later, liberal Democrats who chose to follow former Vice President Henry Wallace into the Progressive Party. Against the background of Russian pressure on Greece and Turkey, the President, on March 12, 1947, proclaimed the Truman Doctrine. It would now be U.S. policy to assist countries resisting internal revolt and external threats from the Soviets. Just nine days later, Truman issued Executive Order 9835 establishing the Federal Employee Loyalty Program; the FBI was authorized to investigate all government employees (approximately three million) and those seeking government careers. The post–World War II "Red Scare" had officially begun.[25]

So when the FBI showed up that night in April 1947, it was like running into old friends, Remington thought, until he learned the exact purpose of their visit. It was far from routine, nor did it have anything to do with the new Loyalty Program. Espionage was the crime they were investigating, and Bill was possibly involved. They took him to their Washington office for an interview that lasted three and a half hours.[26]

The FBI had been interested in Remington for the past seventeen months. They had broken into his house, rifled his drawers looking for documents, intercepted his mail, tapped his telephone, and followed him around Washington and during trips he made to New York, New Hampshire, and Massachusetts. The reason for these violations of Remington's privacy was the testimony of Elizabeth Terrill Bentley, who had used many names during her career as a Communist and Soviet espionage agent—Sherman, Smith, Brown, and Jones. But to most of her contacts in what she said was an extensive Soviet spy network, she was known simply as Helen.[27]

Bentley first approached the FBI in August 1945. During a two-hour interview with Special Agent Edward J. Coady, she described her relationship with a man named Peter Heller, who, she said, claimed to be a government agent, possibly a member of the FBI. Coady did not quite know what to make of Miss Bentley. She seemed intelligent and coherent—but he thought the Heller story was phony and that she could be involved in illegal activities. It also occurred to him that she might be crazy. There was nothing he could tell her about Peter Heller (he had never heard of him), and he sent her on her way. Had her visit been just a "fishing expedition" to determine what the Bureau might know about her? Nevertheless, impersonating an agent was, to the FBI, an offense close to treason, so Coady sent a report to the New York office suggesting further investigation.[28]

She next turned up at the New York field office on October 17, 1945. Now she said that her friend Peter Heller was involved in Soviet espionage and implied that she was, too. But she gave no details and left Special Agent Frank C. Aldrich puzzled. He alerted the office's Soviet expert, Edward Buckley, who telephoned Bentley on November 6 and asked her to come into the office the next day. She was "upset and had a great deal on her mind," she told Buckley; she really was not sure that she could tell him anything. Buckley persisted. If she did have information regarding Un-American activities, the FBI should know about it.[29]

They met the following afternoon, and Bentley's story—which on this day took eight hours to tell—electrified the FBI and led to one of the longest, most expensive, and ultimately most fruitless investigations in the Bureau's history. Of her own past she said little, beyond the fact that she had been born in New

Milford, Connecticut, on January 1, 1908, and had spent her early life moving from one state to another. Nothing was said about her father, Charles Prentiss Bentley, the son of a Baptist minister, who ran a dry-goods store in Milford and edited a newspaper, which advocated temperance and other reforms; nor did she talk about her mother, Mary. When they eventually settled in Rochester, her father took over management of a department store, while her mother became an eighth-grade schoolteacher, a generous woman, it was said, who often gave shelter to lonely people. At East High School, Elizabeth was unpopular. Later, she would call her upbringing repressive and old-fashioned. Most of her life would be spent breaking the rules on which she had been reared.[30]

She entered Vassar College on scholarship in 1926, when she was eighteen. Angelica Gibbs, an acquaintance, thought she made enemies immediately when she arrived on campus escorted by Mary Bentley, who told all the other mothers how her daughter had been a prize-winning scholar and Girl Scout. Elizabeth's peers, many of whom came from more affluent families, tended to look down on her, calling her Bentley, as if she were a servant. Although she would claim membership in the French and Italian clubs, her college yearbook lists no such activities. She did show some interest in radical politics and briefly joined the League for Industrial Democracy, but she was nothing like the controversial figure Bill Remington would be at Dartmouth a decade later. After graduating in 1930 with a bachelor's degree in English, she taught Romance languages at Foxcroft, a finishing school for young women in Middleburg, Virginia. She made few friends and spent summer vacations touring Europe or taking courses at the Vermont Language School. In 1932, she quit her job, entered the Columbia University Graduate School to pursue a master's degree in Italian, and, in 1933, won a fellowship to attend the University of Florence.[31]

It was while studying in Italy that she first rebelled against all the conventions of her New England heritage. Joseph V. Lombardo, a young American also attending the university, remembered her as promiscuous and an alcoholic. She was often arrested for being drunk and disorderly, and Lombardo would frequently come to her rescue. Almost sixty years later, Lombardo would vividly recall a New Year's eve party at which Bentley, "so damned drunk she didn't know where she was," challenged the other women "to pull down your pants and have your partner take you right here on the floor." Her politics became equally unstable. Earlier she had been a mild socialist but now sympathized with the fascists. She joined the Gruppo Universitate Fascisti—not because membership allowed her to buy goods at a discount but, Lombardo believed, out of real conviction. As a result, her course work suffered, and when she was expelled from the university, she tried to kill herself. Lombardo again came to her aid, and she quickly recovered.[32]

Returning to New York in the summer of 1934, she presented her faculty advisor at Columbia with her master's thesis—"Il Bel Gherdino," which she claimed to have written while abroad. Professor Giuseppe Prezzolini was immediately suspicious; this was no graduate student essay but a treatise so sophisticated that it must surely have been produced by a mature scholar. (A private detective who later investigated Bentley's year in Florence believed the real author was one of Bentley's teachers, whom she had seduced.) Prezzolini accepted the thesis anyway, because there was no way to prove Bentley guilty of fraud or plagiarism.[33]

Unable to find a teaching job, she took business courses at Columbia and set her sights on becoming a secretary. But politics along with sex and liquor continued to be her major interests. Her political mentor was Lee Fuhr, a nurse, who was also a member of the Communist Party and active in the American League Against War and Fascism. Bentley, embittered by her experiences both in Florence and in a New York ravaged by the Depression, yearned to join Fuhr in her struggle against the fascists and the capitalists. Claiming to be distantly related to Roger Sherman, a signer of the Declaration of Independence, Bentley told Fuhr, "I'm a descendent of American revolutionaries, so don't you see that I must work for a Communist America." Suspicious of her sincerity and motives, Fuhr held her back but eventually introduced her into the league and, in 1935, joined a Columbia professor in sponsoring her membership in the Communist Party. Earlier, she had been isolated and alone; now as a Communist, she "felt suddenly very much at peace with the world." Like Ann Remington and her mother, who had similar backgrounds of turmoil, Bentley found a group of kindred spirits and a purpose to give meaning to an empty life.[34]

Reality was different from the dream. It was standing in picket lines, reading dull Party tracts, and paying dues. Then, on October 5, 1938, her life changed forever. On a New York street corner, she was introduced to a red-haired man in his forties named Timmy. She had been working for the Italian Library of Information and, discovering that it was only a front for the Italian Government's Ministry of Propaganda, had decided to become a "spy," collecting secret correspondence and waiting for the moment when she could "blow the whole works up and expose their machinations." But, Communist Party officials to whom she brought the information were indifferent, and when she complained, she was taken to see Timmy. He encouraged her to continue and informed her that she was now part of the Communist underground. "You must cut yourself off completely from all your old Communist friends," he told her. " . . . You will be completely alone except for me. Your fellow comrades may even think you are a traitor. But the Party would not ask this sacrifice of you if it were not vitally important." Bentley went home and experienced a sleepless night. "A wave of terror swept over me," she later wrote. "Without knowing quite why, I felt that I was entering a land from which there was no return."[35]

During the next few weeks, she brought information to Timmy and suddenly began to admire this odd man whom she first thought shabby and colorless.

"Strangely enough . . . , he reminded me of my New England parents. There was the same simple, plain way of life, the same capacity for hard work, the same unswerving loyalty to an ideal, the same shy kindness and generosity. . . . " By December she discovered that they were in love. "I've been afraid this would happen," he told her, after their first embrace. "Don't you know I've been in love with you since we first met?" Then he shocked her by saying it was all wrong; they belonged to the Communist underground, which forbade such intimacy between working partners. He should leave immediately or return her to the open Party. But his love was too strong, he said; so now their affair, like their work, must be secret. They would live apart, meet only occasionally, pretend theirs was only a professional relationship. "Do you think you would be able to do that?" he asked.

"I'll stick with you," she replied.[36]

Gradually over the next two years and in violation of the rules he had set, she learned more about her lover. His name was, of course, not Timmy but Jacob Raisin, and he was Ukrainian, born in Russia's Pale of Settlement in 1890. His parents fled to America in 1908, and he became a naturalized citizen seven years later. A printer and chemist by profession (although he also claimed to have studied medicine), he joined the Communist Party during World War I, edited Novy Mir, the Russian-language newspaper, and worked in both the secret and open branches of the Party. He operated out of a public front called World Tourists, a business established in 1927 with funds from the American Communist Party to assist those who wished to trade with and travel in the Soviet Union. Calling himself Jacob Golos, he became an important Party official, director of the Central Control Commission, "a post resembling that of the former inquisitor-general of Spain in theory and sometimes in practice." By the time he was forty-four, Golos was one of the most powerful Communist leaders and Soviet agents. Bentley later told the FBI that it was not until about 1940 that she discovered that Yasha (as she liked to call him) worked for Soviet intelligence and not just for the Party. That revelation did not concern her, nor did the fact that Golos had a wife and child and a mistress he continued to see.[37]

There was little time to worry about all this, for Golos now found himself under government scrutiny, and in March 1940, he was arrested for failing to register as a representative of a foreign power. He pled guilty but was given a suspended sentence. In December, the House Committee on Un-American Activities began to investigate him, as did the FBI, which put him under surveillance from May to September 1941. Agents staked out the office of U.S. Service and Shipping Corporation (another company established by Golos and funded by the Communists) as well as Bentley's apartment, since she was vice president and secretary of the firm. The agents were so obvious, however, that both Golos and Bentley immediately recognized them, let themselves be pursued, and lost them without much trouble. Bentley's first FBI statement of November 8, 1945, described these Keystone Cop charades, but her final report of November 30, considered by the Bureau to be her official confession, omits the embarrassing fact that agents had watched them, had examined their mail for four months, and then had terminated the surveillance in late September 1941.[38]

Had the FBI continued its investigation, it might well have uncovered Golos's most ambitious operation, which began at about the time it turned its attentions elsewhere. In August 1941, Golos began to receive information from Nathan Gregory Silvermaster, a 43-year-old Russian-born economist employed by the Farm Security Administration. According to Bentley, Silvermaster, either a Party member or a fellow traveler, was shocked by the German invasion of Russia that past June and visited Earl Browder, seeking a contact to whom he could give documents that might be of value to the Russians. With Browder's approval, Silvermaster organized a group of like-minded government employees, including William Ludwig Ullman, George Silverman, and others who had access to records from the Treasury Department and the Pentagon. That summer, Browder turned the group over to Golos. At first, he was primarily interested in political information—documents or just gossip that revealed the attitudes of American officials toward the Soviet Union. But after Pearl Harbor, when Ullman and Silverman moved into the Pentagon, Bentley claimed that they began to collect "a tremendous amount of military data; . . . almost every conceivable type of information relating to the Air Force's part in the war was included, aircraft production figures, allocation and deployment of aircraft . . . and reports on the efficiency of airplanes." Lud Ullman, whose hobby was photography, built a sophisticated laboratory in the Silvermasters' basement, where he photographed documents. Later, Bentley described a typical visit to the Silvermasters. Lud and Greg would "refresh their recollections . . . from small pieces of papers they would take out of their . . . pockets," then dictate the information to Bentley. Photographic material was in the form of rolls stuffed in a knitting bag that she would deliver to Golos, who would pass it along to his Soviet contact. Bentley only saw actual documents on a few occasions—most of the material she transported in her bi-monthly trips from New York to Washington and back was photographed. What such films contained she learned secondhand from Greg and Lud or, later, from Golos. She could never determine whether the military information was supplied by Ullman or Silverman.[39]

Bentley was also told by Silvermaster that others were assisting them, including Assistant Secretary of the Treasury Harry Dexter White; Solomon Adler, William Henry Taylor, and Sonia Gold, also of that department; presidential assistant Lauchlin B. Currie; Bela Gold, husband of Sonia and a member of the Federal Economic Administration; and Irving Kaplan of the War Production Board. However, Bentley later admitted that she never met White, Currie, Adler, Taylor, Kaplan, or Bela Gold (whom she misidentified) and his wife,

Sonia. All she knew of these individuals was what she heard from the Silvermasters.[40]

Bentley's work as a courier increased as time passed. (Golos had suffered a heart attack in April 1941 and was in poor health thereafter, so Bentley acted as contact and collector of information, both from those associated with the Silvermaster group and from those operating as individuals.) One source was Mary Price, Walter Lippmann's secretary; another, a young employee of the War Production Board named William Remington. According to Bentley, Remington gave her

> charts setting out airplane production and other matters concerning the aircraft industry that would, in the course of regular business, come through his hands as an employee of the War Production Board. He would also give me scraps of paper upon which he had scribbled information. . . . I also recall that he would verbally tell me about information that would come into his possession from his conversations with government officials and other individuals whom he would see in the normal course of his official duties.

She especially remembered the time Remington told her about "a new process that had been developed for the manufacturing of synthetic rubber. . . . However, he did not give me a verbatim report on this and the information was quite vague and probably of no value even to a chemist." Remington was also "a dues paying Communist Party member," she claimed, "and . . . on my visits to Washington I would attempt to obtain his regular dues." Through Remington, she was introduced to Bernard Redmont, a journalist working for the Coordinator of Inter-American Affairs, who provided her with information on Latin America that Golos thought was worthless.[41]

Toward the end of his life, Golos had as much trouble with the NKVD, the Soviet intelligence service, as he once had with the FBI. The Russians instructed him to separate his agents from the regular Party, but he often refused; he wanted his people to maintain their Communist affiliations, fearing that if they abandoned the Party it would weaken the Communist movement in the United States. He practiced what he preached, in violation of Moscow's directives. Instead of turning over all material he received from his contacts directly to the Soviets, he shared political information with Earl Browder. Thus it would appear that those Americans, like Remington, who were involved with Golos were, in fact, working (as Golos told them) "for John and the Party"; almost all of them (excepting Ullman and the Silvermasters) did not know they were connected to Soviet intelligence. Believing that Golos was running a dangerously inefficient operation, the Russians began to pressure him for control of Bentley and the Silvermaster group, but again he resisted. Bentley remembered him criticizing the Russians: "they were no good," he was supposed to have said, and "He told me the Russians tried to pry these people loose from him. He said no. He

said these are good American Communists who don't know what they are doing.
. . . I asked him whether Browder would stand by him. He said he didn't know.
He went to Washington to see this [important] Russian . . . [and] he came back
discouraged. He said he fought for Communism and now he was beginning to
wonder." Bentley later recalled that he was greatly agitated in the fall of 1943—
having to decide whether to give up his contacts or possibly leave the Party. On
Thanksgiving night, while at Bentley's apartment, he was stricken by a second
heart attack and died.[42]

Bentley now assumed all of Golos's duties, becoming case officer as well as
courier. Among her responsibilities was handling a new group, which originated
with Earl Browder. In the winter of 1944, she met them in the New York apartment of John J. Abt, general counsel of the Amalgamated Clothing Workers of
America. There were three members of the War Production Board—Victor
Perlo, Harry Magdoff, and Edward Fitzgerald—and an assistant to U.S. senator
Hardy Kilgore named Charles Kramer. Bentley later said that they talked about
paying Communist Party dues and the type of information each man could furnish. Perlo, Fitzgerald, and Magdoff would supply aircraft data from the WPB,
while Kramer would contribute Capitol Hill gossip. She was also informed that
there were others who could help, including a Communist named Hiss, who
worked for the State Department. (She had never met him, she told the FBI,
and since her information was vague, she was unwilling to say anything more
about him.)[43]

Bentley's new role also brought her closer to those agents who were the next
link in the espionage chain. First, there was a married couple known to her only
as Catherine and Bill. Bill was thirty-eight, a Ukrainian with dark eyes and a
turned up nose, who chased women. But he could be tough as well as romantic.
"I've been told to tell you to hand over all these people," he said to Bentley one
night; she resisted. The next time Bentley saw him, "he just smiled . . . like a cat
who swallowed the cream." He must have gone directly to Browder, because a
short time later Browder ordered her to release the group to the Russians.
Bentley's relationship with the Silvermaster group ended in September 1944.
"They didn't want to be turned over," she said. "They hated it."[44]

Bentley continued to handle the Perlo group and other individuals in New
York and Washington. She also received a new contact named Jack, a stocky
Lithuanian with kinky hair, blue eyes, and rotten teeth. Bentley told Jack that
she wanted to see someone in authority, a Russian. Jack seemed hurt but agreed
to arrange a meeting in October with a man called Al. "You could tell right
away he was different from the rest," she later noted about their first meeting.
His English was poor, spoken with an accent that Bentley thought was both
Russian and British. Short and fat, Al had a round face, wore glasses, and had
"two extra teeth jutting out, overlapping each other, like tiger teeth. . . . " "I
bring you greetings from Moscow," Al said. They spent the day walking.

Bentley complained about what might happen to the rest of her people. "I haven't got any power," Al told her, "but I'll listen." Bentley developed a dislike for him. "He is the kind of person that instinctively makes shivers run up and down your spine. . . . There is something slimy about the guy," she later told the FBI.

Nothing was accomplished that day, but when she next saw Al, around Thanksgiving 1944, he had a surprise for her. "A great honor has been bestowed upon you," he said. "The Supreme Presidium of the U.S.S.R. has just awarded you one of the highest medals of the Soviet Union—the Order of the Red Star." He then gave her a photograph of the decoration. That was the good news; the bad quickly followed. She would have to give up her remaining contacts by Christmas. "That just about finished me," she later said. "A wave of revulsion and nausea swept over me; I thought for a moment I was going to be violently ill." The Russians were trying to bribe her, she believed. It was at this moment, Bentley later claimed, that she first realized that Communism was just "a dirty racket." In December, she saw Al again, and they argued. She was through, she told him. "The trouble with you," Al said, "is that you need to get married." She thought that this time Al was offering himself, and she left.[45]

Then a new man entered Bentley's life, adding to her confusion and anxiety. His name was Peter Heller, a forty-year-old New Yorker she met in the lobby of the St. George Hotel in Brooklyn, where she was then living. Their first date— cocktails, dinner, and cocktails—was almost their last. "Bentley drank so heavily that she became very much intoxicated," Heller later recalled, and he was embarrassed by her behavior. But he continued to see her during the next six months, despite the fact that she continued to drink heavily and talk in a somewhat peculiar fashion. She told him of her relationship with a dead Russian and admitted that she had been involved with the Communists. Was he a Communist? she asked one evening.

No, a "rock-ribbed Republican," he said, and an investigator for the New York Executive Clemency Board.[46]

Befuddled by alcohol, Bentley came to believe that Heller might be an FBI agent. Al thought so, too. For insurance, he gave her an envelope filled with money—(two thousand dollars, she later found). This unnerved her further, and one night she confronted Heller directly. "I have this problem," she said. "What would you do if you were mixed up in . . . espionage, and all that sort of stuff?"

"I'd forget about it . . . ," Heller said, believing Bentley's tales the result of too much alcohol.[47]

But she could not forget it—Al's warnings, the shock of losing her people, Heller's true identity, and problems at U.S. Service (to which she returned only to find her Communist backers wanting their money back) propelled her back to the FBI, to whom on November 7, 1945, she began to tell everything. At 1:30 A.M. the next morning, a teletype containing Bentley's initial statement was rushed to headquarters, where the reaction was concern mixed with skepticism. After reading the message, Assistant Director Edward Tamm asked Agent Ed Conroy, one of those who debriefed her, whether he thought she was authentic. Conroy could not be sure but said she was "a Vassar graduate and had impressed the agents very much." More questions about Bentley arose as officials arrived at the office and studied the teletype. Who were these people working for? J. K. Mumford wondered. The NKVD? The Red Army? Conroy told him that Bentley said Earl Browder but believed that the information was going to Soviet intelligence. Mumford remarked that "it seems to make a big difference as to just who is getting the information." If it was the NKVD, then this was an espionage case; if it was Browder and the American Communist Party, it was not clear what laws had been broken. (Bentley had confessed passing information to Golos and then to her other contacts—Bill, Jack, and Al, but where the information went from there, she could not be sure, although she was fairly confident that it was the Soviet embassy, which would send it on to Moscow.) Headquarters wanted to see her seventy-page statement as soon as possible. It arrived by nightfall, personally delivered by an agent who flew down from New York.[48]

Reading the actual statement did not resolve their doubts. Mumford told Conroy that it was confusing and that Bentley had not signed it. It was a rush job, Conroy informed him. They wanted to get the statement typed up immediately. Furthermore, Bentley had not yet seen it; they expected to speak with her that afternoon, and she was planning to return to the office on November 10 to continue the interview.

Although the confession was incomplete, J. Edgar Hoover immediately alerted the White House that the Bureau had discovered that a number of government employees had been giving data to people working for the Soviets. Sixteen names were listed—about half of whom worked for Hoover's chief bureaucratic rival in the intelligence field, the OSS. The Director did admit, however, that he did not know "how many of these people had actual knowledge of the disposition of the information they were transmitting." Mumford's questions (for whom did Bentley work? How much did her contacts know about where their information was going? and where did the information actually go?) continued to plague the Bureau for years.[49]

On November 10, Bentley gave the FBI the names of ten other individuals said to be involved in Communist activities. Among them was William Remington. She spent all that day talking with agents and correcting her initial statement. Her interview on November 17 was especially memorable. Agents had arranged to meet her in a room at the St. George Hotel, and when she arrived, she opened her purse and removed an envelope and, with a dramatic flourish, tossed it on the bed. "Here's some Moscow Gold," she said. Special Agent Thomas G. Spencer picked it up and saw inside a wad of twenty dollar bills—Al's two thousand dollar gift. It ended up in an FBI safety deposit box, where it sat for seven years.[50]

The first test of Bentley's veracity came four days later, when she was scheduled to meet with Al. The New York office was confident that they had determined his true identity. Bentley had been shown a group of photographs and had positively identified him—but they could not be certain until he kept the appointment. On the morning of November 21, agents followed Al from his residence to the Washington National Airport. Those who trailed him after he arrived in New York concluded that Al was "hot"—alert to the possibility that he was being watched—so they broke off surveillance.

They picked him up again at 4:20 P.M. on the southeast corner of 8th Avenue and 23rd Street, where he met Elizabeth Bentley. The two walked a short distance, then abruptly entered Cavanaugh's Restaurant on 7th Avenue. Less than an hour later, they left the restaurant and went their separate ways. The FBI followed him until midnight, when he flew back to Washington. It was a long but important day for the FBI agents, now absolutely certain that Al was, in fact, Anatoli Borisovich Gromov, First Secretary of the Soviet embassy and the NKVD's principal agent in North America. (Gromov hurriedly left Washington a few weeks later.)[51]

Bentley's meeting with Gromov was less productive, however. The FBI had hoped to reactivate Bentley, planting her as a double-agent in the Soviet operation, but when she told Al that she was bored and wanted to go back to work, he failed to take the bait. He seemed friendly enough, she later told the FBI, but she thought he acted very cagy. While Gromov's reaction was disappointing, Bentley had proven that at least part of her story was true, so the interviewing went on until November 30, when a final 112-page statement was completed and typed. Bentley spent an hour carefully reviewing the document, initialing every page and then signing it. She did so reluctantly because she feared that her former contacts might go to jail, which was perhaps unfair. The Americans, she said, were "motivated by an ideology and . . . they felt that their information . . . was going to help an ally, who . . . was having great difficulty in fighting their war against Germany." But she did think that they should not be allowed to work for the government.[52]

During her month-long interview, Bentley gave the FBI more than a hundred fifty names; some, she claimed, were involved in Soviet espionage, while others were engaged in Communist activities. She was never entirely clear on how to specifically classify each and every one but considered Silvermaster and Ullman agents and the rest "good American Communists," who thought their contributions were going to Earl Browder. To the FBI, it made little difference (and indeed Browder, according to Bentley, was aware that the ultimate recipient of the information was the NKVD). In its view, it was "a staggering penetration by the Soviets" and one that began under the very eyes of its agents who had kept track of Golos and Bentley throughout the summer of 1941. Now, the job was to locate the spies to determine if the operation was continuing and, if so, stop it; if not, it would build a case that would put them in jail.[53]

To direct the investigation, Hoover chose 38-year-old Thomas Donegan, head of the Major Case Squad, which had hunted German and Japanese spies during World War II and now found itself with little to do. Donegan, a small, intense man, was known within the Bureau as "The Hat," because he focused so single-mindedly on his work that he often forgot to remove his fedora while in the office. During a meeting with officials on November 16, Donegan was informed that Hoover wanted the Bureau to devote all its energy to the investigation; there would be no limit on the number of agents Donegan would be supplied. (More than two hundred would eventually work on the case.) Physical surveillance of the suspects should be immediately started, and microphone and other technical tools would be used wherever necessary.[54]

Donegan and his aides began by separating the wheat from the chaff. Of the more than one hundred names mentioned by Bentley, fifty-one were considered important enough to receive close attention; twenty-seven of these still worked for the federal government, the majority in the Treasury and State departments. Those singled out for special treatment were Nathan Gregory Silvermaster, William Ludwig Ullman, Abraham George Silverman, Harry Dexter White, Victor Perlo, Lauchlin Currie, and Alger Hiss, among others.

William Remington was on Donegan's list of suspect government employees and was, therefore, the object of FBI surveillance. On November 17, 1945, Hoover recommended to the Attorney General that a wiretap be placed on Remington's telephone, because it was reported that he was "a member of an espionage ring working with . . . Soviet intelligence." After receiving authorization, agents secretly entered Remington's home and installed the device; by December 13, it was recording the conversations of the Remingtons and their friends, while agents listened from a nearby apartment.[55]

The only potentially important news uncovered by the tap was the evidence of the Remingtons' marital problems. On November 16, 1946, Ann received a telephone call from a physician and told him that she was considering a divorce because Bill "was ruthless where his interests are concerned." The tap also recorded a talk on January 7, 1947, in which Ann told a friend that Bill had left her. Although the Bureau faithfully kept a record of these calls, it ignored the opportunity they presented. The Remingtons' separation gave them a chance to question an obviously hostile Ann about Bill's relationship with Bentley, but the FBI ignored the opening and did not interview her.[56]

The FBI's investigation revealed nothing of a derogatory nature, but it soon began to affect Remington's civilian and military careers. In December 1946, John Steelman, Assistant to the President, considered appointing Remington to the White House staff until two FBI men told him that Bill was a principal figure in a Bureau investigation of Soviet espionage. That ended Remington's move to the White House. Steelman decided to leave him at the Office of War Mobilization and Reconversion, believing that he would be forced to leave government when that agency soon disbanded. This left the FBI with the incorrect impression that Remington's career was over. Later, the Bureau would discover that he had easily transferred to the staff of the President's Council of Economic Advisors. The Navy was more efficient in removing Remington from the Naval Reserve. When the Office of Naval Intelligence learned that Remington was allegedly a Russian espionage agent, he was given an honorable discharge; to do otherwise, might alert him to the ongoing investigation.[57]

Despite the fact that a year of the most intensive investigation revealed that none of Bentley's people were presently involved in espionage, the FBI believed that she had told the truth. A review of files plus mail covers and physical and technical surveillance first confirmed Bentley's claimed contact with a Russian agent. Second, the FBI was able to locate all one hundred fifty people mentioned in Bentley's statement, and they were, generally, as she described them. Third, she knew of several secret government operations that could only have been reported to her by those involved or someone who knew them. Fourth, Bentley had said that confidential documents were photographed in Silvermaster's basement. The FBI gained access to the basement and discovered there a sophisticated photographic laboratory. Fifth, extensive surveillance of the principal suspects revealed that they were well acquainted with one another—they talked on the telephone, lunched together, and visited each others' homes. "There appears little reason to doubt [Bentley's] statement that information and documents from Government records were supplied by Silvermaster, Perlo, et al. and that this material was turned over by [her] to a member or contact of the Soviet Intelligence Service," noted one FBI official in January 1947. But did they have the evidence to prove that espionage or other crimes had been committed? Beginning in late November 1946, the Bureau began a review of the case to answer that question.[58]

Hoover asked E. P. Morgan, one of the FBI's most able lawyers, to study the case to determine if prosecution was possible. His conclusions, submitted on January 14, 1947, were grim. Despite a massive undertaking, the Bureau had little more than the uncorroborated statement of one informant. An espionage network may have existed at one time, but it was no longer in operation. All that could be said about the many people the Bureau had investigated was that they socialized together. It would be their word against Bentley's, and they would probably be acquitted, which would be most embarrassing to the FBI. Furthermore, while there was little doubt Bentley had obtained information from many government departments, she could not testify as to where such information ultimately went—"there is a complete blank at the receiving end. . . . " This was only the beginning of the Bureau's problems. Could espionage be proved? Almost certainly not. Legally, the government would have to prove that Bentley's people intended or believed that their information would be used to injure the United States and benefit a foreign country. "We have no evidence from which 'intent or reason to believe' can be proved or reasonably inferred in the case of the Silvermaster or Perlo Groups," Morgan noted.

The Bureau also could not prove the existence of lesser crimes—failure of the subjects to register as agents of a foreign power, or defrauding the government by taking time from their duties to gather information for Bentley. "To my way of thinking, considering that a state of war existed, this case is one of Soviet espionage or it is nothing," Morgan concluded. "At this point the evidence very definitely is insufficient to sustain a successful prosecution under the espionage statutes."

Nevertheless, Morgan believed that something had to be done. "Had we been in contact with [Bentley] during the course of her courier activity, . . . evidence could have been developed sustaining prosecution for espionage. Coming in after the event as the Bureau did, we are now on the outside looking in, with the rather embarrassing responsibility of having a most serious case of espionage laid in our laps without a decent opportunity to make it stick." Still, several approaches offered possible success. Agents could contact one of the subjects, preferably "the weakest sister," and persuade the suspect to join Bentley as an informant. If this failed, Morgan recommended that all the principals be interviewed simultaneously "in the hope . . . that some of the lesser lights . . . would crack. . . . " Finding someone to corroborate Bentley was the main objective. If no one broke or chose voluntarily to cooperate, then the FBI could consider "exposing this lousy outfit and at least hounding them from the federal service." But a prosecution for espionage or lesser crimes seemed extremely unlikely.[59] Hoover agreed with Morgan. At this point he did not wish to humiliate the Bureau by going into court with a case doomed to fail. It is one of the unappreciated ironies of the postwar Red Scare that the man most opposed to prosecuting the alleged Soviet agents in the U.S. government was the nation's most celebrated Red hunter. The Attorney General shared Hoover's doubts and approved his plan to interview the subjects.[60]

The FBI agents who interviewed Bill Remington on the night of April 15, 1947, were extremely polite. While talk of espionage shocked Bill, the men put him at ease by first asking routine questions. Then they moved on to such familiar topics as TVA and his associations with the American Student Union, the American Youth Congress, and the American Peace Mobilization. He gave the now standard answers, except that he was more willing to provide the names of others who had worked with him in these organizations.

Another subject of discussion was his mother-in-law, Elizabeth Moos. "Always a sore spot in his life," he told the agents. He went on to say that he believed that Elizabeth was a member of the Communist Party, although he did not think she was when he married her daughter.

Was he acquainted with Joe North?

Yes, North lived next-door to Mrs. Moos, and was editor of the Communist *New Masses.* The man he once thought charming, he now called "a very dangerous person."[61]

Had North ever introduced him to any other people?

No, Remington said.

Had North ever introduced him to a man named John and a woman named Helen? Cornelison then showed Bill a photograph of a woman and asked if she were Helen.

"Yes, that's Helen," Bill replied. Remington suddenly became "visibly shaken and noticeably upset . . . ," the agents later noted. He "jerked his head back [and] got red in the face." Tell us about John and Helen.

Bill described them but could not recall precisely when he and his wife met the couple. He thought Helen was John's wife and a newspaper reporter for *PM.*[62]

Had he ever given Helen any information?

Just "bits and scraps of paper which contained the names of [WPB] officials . . . ," Remington said.

Was that all?

Yes, Bill said, then quickly changed that to no. He remembered giving her public press releases describing the WPB, which was being criticized by Helen's newspaper.

Did he ever give Helen any information about aircraft production?

No, but he did alert her to recent articles about how fast U.S. factories could manufacture aircraft; she was particularly interested in this subject.

Did he ever give Helen money—"payment of Communist Party dues"? Was he now or had he ever been a member of the Communist Party?

Bill strongly denied membership then, or ever, and said he had never paid Communist Party dues to anyone.

Had Bill ever introduced Helen to anyone?

Yes, his friend, Bernard Redmont, who he thought could answer Helen's questions about Latin America. But he could not recall precisely how the introduction occurred. He did know that Redmont saw Helen, although he had no knowledge of their discussions.

Where did Redmont stand politically? the agents asked.

"[I have] always considered [him] somewhat of a radical," Bill answered, but had never thought that he might be disloyal—until now.

Toward the end of the session, Remington confessed that the FBI "had every reason to suspect him of being a Communist" and that they were "entirely justified" in coming to him. But now—in 1947—he opposed Communism; in fact, he had just written a memorandum for the Secretary of State recommending aid to Greece and Turkey. He was very pessimistic about the future of Soviet–American relations; war seemed inevitable and he thought the United States should prepare for it. And if war came, it was his view that every American Communist should be considered "a potential agent for Soviet Russia. . . . " As the FBI men gathered their notes and prepared to return Remington to his home, Bill thanked them for their kindness, adding that "he did not deserve such good treatment."[63]

Frightened by his encounter with the FBI, he now attempted to convince the Bureau that he was innocent and, in doing so, became one of the FBI's many confidential informants. For the next year, he communicated with the Bureau in every possible way. He telephoned, he wrote letters, he came to the office. He saw Cornelison and Sills again on April 22, 1947, a meeting that lasted two and a half hours. He told them that he had been invited to apply for a position with the Atomic Energy Commission but had rejected the offer because he did not think he could pass FBI inspection. What did they think? The agents refused to advise him. He understood their position perfectly, he said; in fact, if he were an FBI agent he would reject his application. Bill Remington might be a loyal American but "if there were a hundred other people like him in the . . . Commission, some of them might do a great deal of damage." This was a most curious way to dispel their suspicions about him.[64]

The agents then offered to draft a statement describing his relationship with John and Helen, and he offered to help. As they worked, Cornelison asked him how he would characterize someone who associated with such people and belonged to organizations considered Communist fronts? Earlier in his life, he had joyfully challenged the prejudices of conservatives as well as Communists but now shrank from such combat. Exhausted by months of arguments with Ann and worried about his future, he could only say that "if he had to make a classification of himself, he would call himself a misguided liberal and possibly a Communist."[65]

How Remington thought that such statements could exonerate him is a mystery. But apparently he did, because he returned to the FBI's Washington field office the next morning. Only one act was required: that he read and sign the statement prepared the day before. He quickly went through the five-page document, made minor corrections—he did not wish to be held responsible for grammatical errors—then signed it. Sighing, he looked up at Cornelison and said that he made two mistakes that had led to this moment—a bad marriage and a rather absent-minded view of life. He expected "to pay for these mistakes . . . the rest of his life."[66]

Perhaps there was a way to make amends, however. With all the sincerity he could muster, Remington announced his willingness to become a secret agent for the FBI. He offered to contact Joe North, in the hope that he might introduce him to people still involved in espionage. And he also offered to spy on Bernard Redmont when his friend returned from Latin America where he was working for *U.S. News & World Report*. Cornelison told him that while they were not asking him to furnish information, they would receive anything he gave them. Remington interpreted this as a green light to proceed in his personal search for Communists in Washington, D.C.[67]

Despite efforts to cooperate with the FBI, it soon became clear that Remington's problems were not going to disappear. On the evening of September 2, 1947, he had another official visitor, who handed him a subpoena, requiring that he appear before a New York grand jury investigating alleged violations of the criminal code (the numbers meant nothing to him). He was directed to report to the U.S. Courthouse at Foley Square, where he should contact a Mr. Thomas Donegan, special assistant to the Attorney General. What specific crime he was accused of was a mystery, but he thought he knew where to go for help. Although it was after 9:00 P.M., he grabbed his coat and hurried down to the FBI field office, where he hoped to find someone who could explain what all this meant. Remington showed the subpoena to the agent at the duty desk and asked what crime was being investigated.

Espionage, the agent replied. This was a highly confidential matter, Remington was told. Grand jury proceedings were secret; its records sealed forever, unless otherwise ordered by the court.

The trip to New York would mean that he would miss work; what should he tell his superiors? Remington asked.

As little as possible, the agent instructed.

Leaving the Justice Department, Bill drove first to the Old State Department Building and then to the Commerce Department, where he left brief messages for his bosses, explaining only that he had been asked to testify at a trial and would be away a few days. Afterwards, he returned to Riggs Place, packed a bag, and tried to get some sleep. It did not come easily.[68]

He learned that he had good reason to be worried the next morning during a meeting with Thomas Donegan, who had been detailed from the FBI to supervise the work of the grand jury. In his office on the 14th floor of the U.S. Courthouse, Donegan explained that espionage was always a most heinous crime; but espionage committed while one's nation was at war was punishable by death. This grand jury, specially chosen to investigate Soviet espionage during World War II, was very interested in learning what Remington knew about a number of persons alleged to have been Soviet spies. If the speech was designed to frighten Remington, it succeeded, for Remington immediately asked Donegan if he should resign from government. The question seemed to be an admission of guilt and so surprised Donegan that he would later tell Remington that never before had a witness asked him such a question. Now all he said was that he could not advise him; only Remington himself could decide whether it was time to quit.[69]

Bill spent the rest of that afternoon and several hours of the next morning answering the grand jury's questions. Like the FBI agents the previous April, the jurors were primarily interested in his relationship with John and Helen. "Were they connected with the Communist Party?"

"They said nothing to indicate it," Remington answered. "It was my impression . . . that they were not."

What precisely had he given Helen? Had she collected his Communist Party dues? Was he now or had he ever been a member of the Communist Party?

He told them what he had told the FBI: he thought John and Helen were writers; he gave Helen only information available to the public; he was never a Communist.[70]

Remington left New York thinking that he had proven his innocence and, as the weeks passed without further word from the grand jury, became less worried about his future. In an attempt to provoke a more definitive answer, he wrote Thomas Donegan on September 28, 1947, that he thought it inconceivable that he could be indicted and that he had no intention of resigning. He must have therefore been disappointed when he received Donegan's terse reply just acknowledging receipt of his communication.[71]

To shore up his uncertain position, he continued feeding information to the FBI. On April 29, 1948, he wrote Cornelison about the presence of possible Communists on Washington's airways. One was a broadcast executive named Carter Barber, who, Remington claimed, followed the Party line when he selected topics for *Make Way For Freedom*, a Sunday afternoon news program on Radio Station WQQW. And there was another program the FBI should know about: *Americans All*, formerly on WQQW until the station manager fired its director, whom Remington described as a Negro who "seemed to be a radical [and] a nuisance." If the show's producers were not all Communists, they were "Negro nationalists who would probably . . . resist service in the Armed Forces because of segregation." In closing, Bill wrote,

> I am just as eager as you are to help rid this country of communists and their sympathizers (and I think my feelings on this matter may well be even more intense than yours, largely because of my experience with my wife which has been six hellish years ending up with the loss of everything I have loved and believed in).[72]

Remington's year-long career as FBI informer was one of the most shameful episodes of his life. He voluntarily testified about the alleged political affiliations of more than fifty people, only four of whom were connected with his case. He had never even met the majority of those named. Some he called Communists, isolationists, or Negro nationalists. One was "an extreme liberal who associates with questionable people"; another had a brother who "participates in front organizations"; a third was suspect because he had "no ethical compunctions against doing anything that pays him money." His evidence, as even he admitted, was based on hearsay or brief personal conversations that had occurred years before. He attacked his wife and mother-in-law, close friends, and their relatives, whom he barely knew. Nor did he spare himself—"the misguided liberal," who was "possibly a Communist," and a danger to his government. And despite all these efforts, there was still no guarantee that he would escape indictment by the grand jury.[73]

Elizabeth Bentley was also worried about the grand jury's continuing silence and, feeling nervous and distraught, sought out new friends and allies. On April 2, 1948, she visited the journalists Frederick Woltman and Nelson Frank at the *New York World-Telegram*. Like Bentley, both men had once been Communists who had left the Party and eventually joined conservative ranks, so she was hopeful that they would be able to advise her. Her day with Woltman and Frank was wonderful, and she felt much happier after seeing them. Woltman's reaction was different. "I never put too much faith in [her]," he later told fellow journalist Fred Cook. "Oh, she had belonged to the Party all right, and she knew some things. But I never knew how much she embroidered on the information that she had." Nelson Frank did not share these doubts and accepted Bentley's invitation to act as her agent and ghostwriter.[74]

The FBI's Joe Kelly was not happy that Bentley was wandering from the fold and shared his concern with Tom Donegan on April 5. Donegan warned him not to antagonize her and "drive her to some other ill-considered act. . . . Our chief concern," he said, "is to keep her quiet until the Grand Jury completed its considerations."[75]

The grand jury, like the FBI, was having difficulties with the Bentley case. After almost a year of taking testimony from most of the major characters (who took refuge in the Fifth Amendment), the panel was almost finished with its work. On April 6, they heard their final witness, and Donegan knew that he had again run into a stone wall. The grand jury would probably soon return a no bill, which would close the case without indicting anyone. Fearing the political consequences, Donegan asked them to wait while he prepared another case, this one against the top officials of the American Communist Party. The charge would be conspiracy to advocate the violent overthrow of the U.S. government, a violation of the Smith Act. Attorney General Tom Clark approved presenting the case and FBI agents were assigned to gather the evidence quickly. "The idea would be that upon the return of an indictment against the CP USA and its leaders the No Bill in the [Bentley] Case would become much less significant and the resultant publicity would not be unfavorable," Donegan told the FBI.[76]

While Remington waited for some word from New York, he faced another investigation, brought about by his appointment in the spring of 1948 as director of the Commerce Department's Export Program staff. In May, he learned from colleagues that the FBI was again examining his background. The FBI spent approximately thirty days—from May 6 to June 10, 1948—conducting an extensive full-field investigation. When Secretary of Commerce Charles Sawyer received the records, he gave them to his counsel to study over the weekend of June 19. Sawyer later claimed that he also reviewed the files, but if he had, it was quickly and casually, because on June 21 they were sent back to the Civil Service Commission. When Sawyer inquired what would happen next, he was told, "a hearing." Four days later, Sawyer notified Remington that he had been relieved of his duties until the loyalty board reached a decision.[77]

Meanwhile, Nelson Frank, Bentley's agent, was completing a five-part series of articles on her story for the *New York World–Telegram*. They began running on July 21 and had an immediate impact on Bentley's and Remington's fortunes. The next morning, Frank received a call from William Rogers, who asked if the mysterious blond spy discussed in Frank's articles would be a good witness to appear before the Ferguson Committee, which was launching its own investigation of Communist subversion.

Absolutely, Frank said, and arrangements were made for Bentley to testify, first in a closed-door executive session on July 27. The House Committee on Un-American Activities also contacted Bentley, and investigators gave her a subpoena to appear before the committee on July 31.[78]

Bentley's first Washington appearance before the Ferguson Committee on July 27 was a resounding success. "She is being treated very well . . . and is enjoying herself," Frank told Joe Kelly. Other secret sessions were scheduled, and it was announced that she would soon testify publicly.[79]

Only three of Bentley's original suspects were still in government, and just one had had extensive contact with her—William Remington.[80] So, after learning that Remington was vacationing in Vermont, Rogers sent him a telegram asking that he come to Washington. On July 29, while on a train bound for the capital, Remington discovered precisely why he had been so abruptly summoned. Reading a newspaper another traveler had left behind, he learned of events that had shocked Washington during his absence in rural Vermont. On July 21, the *New York World–Telegram*, its giant headline screaming, RED RING BARED BY ITS BLOND QUEEN, detailed the revelations of a "New England–born woman who headed one of the most intricate espionage systems ever established in this country." More than fifty Soviet agents—Communists all—the woman claimed, were present throughout FDR's government and in the White House itself. It was, said the *World-Telegram*, "a story so fantastic that even veteran FBI officials could not believe [it]. . . . but a year-and-a-half FBI probe convinced the agents that everything she said . . . was true." For more than a week, her tales had captured the attention of the nation, and now, Remington read, she would testify before committees of both the Senate and the House. "The paper had a picture of her,"

Remington said later, "but her name wasn't given. . . . The picture was blurred, but I thought she might be . . . Helen. . . . "[81]

His suspicions were confirmed the next morning, when, after testifying for two hours in secret session, he saw Helen near the Investigations Subcommittee's offices. He approached her and shook her hand saying, "I've just heard that you were a Soviet Spy but that you're now a patriotic American. I'm glad about that, but you have told some weird stories about me." He hoped that they could go over her statements together—surely she would then see that she had been mistaken about him. Bentley smiled and said that she would enjoy discussing it. Reporters began to gather, and the two posed for photographs. Then William Rogers called her away before they could resume their conversation. The next time he saw Helen, later that afternoon, she was being escorted into a crowded hearing room for another session before the Ferguson Committee.[82]

He took notes on Senate stationery as Bentley answered the senators' questions. She described her early life and education and how in 1935 she had joined the Communist Party. But it was her career as a courier collecting information from government employees, that was the focus of their attention.

"Why would they do it?" asked Nebraska senator Kenneth S. Wherry.

"In some cases they believed the information was going to Mr. Earl Browder for his use in writing books," Bentley said. " . . . They were a bunch of misguided idealists. They were doing it for something they believed was right. . . . As far as Communists are concerned, they felt very strongly that we were allies with Russia; that Russia was bearing the brunt of the war; that she must have every assistance. . . . " Her people did not believe they were being disloyal to the United States, nor did most of them know that they were connected to Soviet intelligence. " . . . [T]hose poor devils . . . were roped into Soviet espionage. . . . I don't think they knew what they were doing," Bentley insisted.

Toward the end of the session, Chairman Ferguson finally asked her, "Did you have a source in [WPB] . . . named Remington?"

"Yes, I did." She then discussed their meetings from 1942 to 1944, when Remington gave her what he claimed was secret information on aircraft production and also paid Communist Party dues for his wife and himself.

"Did Remington know the destination of the information he gave her?" asked Maryland senator Herbert O'Connor.

"We never discussed it," she said. " . . . I believe that in common with almost everyone else, he was told that this was for Browder [and] the Communist Party."

It was after 4:00 P.M. when Bentley finished testifying. Senator Ferguson announced that at ten o'clock the next morning, the committee would hear William Remington. "He will have a full hearing," Ferguson said. "We will give Mr. Remington his day in court."[83]

8

Fighting Back

"Don't you think someone should spend the night with you?" William Rogers asked Remington as he left the committee room following Bentley's testimony.

"Oh, nuts!," Remington replied. "I'm not going to commit suicide."[1]

Still, that next hour was "one of the blackest . . . of his life." He wandered aimlessly for a time, then decided to visit Jane, who provided both solace and good advice. " . . . I was stunned," he later recalled. "I saw my career ruined. Bentley's motives were obscure to me, but the Senators' motives weren't. Why this public hearing, with Senators Ferguson, McClellan and Ives trying to be district attorneys? Why didn't they let a loyalty board hear evidence in private?" Remington believed the answer was the political struggle between Republicans and Democrats in that election year. Truman had ordered the Republican-controlled 80th Congress back into session, and his antagonists countered with a special investigation of the Loyalty Program designed to embarrass the President. And he was caught in the middle. Remington wanted to resign immediately, but Jane encouraged him to stay and fight. "I'd been put in the position of being a cause, the last thing I ever wanted to be. . . . Other government officials were already under suspicion just for knowing me. If I quit under fire, they, too, might be out."[2]

Jane suggested that Bill give an exclusive statement to *Washington Post* reporter Mary Spargo, whom she thought fair and objective. Spargo was also a former investigator for the House Committee on Un-American Activities and might be able to offer suggestions on how he could handle his inquisitors. What

Jane did not know was that she was also a secret FBI informer, who would later report on her meeting with Remington to the Bureau.

When Spargo arrived for that evening's appointment with Bill, she found him in an angry mood. He had decided to hold a press conference that night at the Willard Hotel and would give her a preview of his opening remarks. It was, Spargo later told the FBI, "a harangue against Congress, a harangue against reactionaries and was typically along the Party line." He was certainly free to say anything, Spargo said, but if he repeated that speech "he would crucify himself." A heated discussion ensued, and, in the end, Remington chose to revise his statement, which in its final version expressed praise for both the committee and its star witness.[3]

At nine o'clock that evening, Remington met reporters in what the *Washington Post* later called an extraordinary press conference. He denied that he was ever a Communist Party member or sympathizer and claimed that Bentley was confused about their relationship. Nevertheless, he commended his accuser. "I have a very high regard for Miss Bentley," he told his audience, "and believe she is sincere. . . . I believe there were men in the Government who were thoroughly implicated in her Communist ring." But he was not one of them, Remington insisted. Bentley's confusion about him was the result of poor memory, or perhaps she was intentionally misled by her Soviet superiors. The Senate subcommittee was absolutely correct in pursuing its investigation, he also argued. So far, the committee had treated him fairly. America "must take steps to protect itself from the enemies within who would destroy it." His own involvement with the Bentley spy ring was accidental, the result of matrimonial connections. It was his former mother-in-law, Elizabeth Moos, who introduced him to its members. Through her best friend, Joseph North, editor of the Communist *New Masses*, Remington met Bentley and Jacob Golos, said to be the ring's leader and her lover. It was true that he had met Bentley in 1942 and 1943 but never gave her "one single scrap of confidential information" or paid her Communist Party dues. "I admit I was very gullible," he confessed. "I did things [at 24] I would not do now." But despite this minor lapse in judgment, he was and had long been staunchly anti-Communist. He was confident that he could prove his innocence when he met with the committee the next morning.

Remington was pleased with his performance and later chatted with reporters and posed for photographs. " . . . I was glad about that conference," he later said. "It made me feel I'd started fighting back."[4]

At the press conference and during his testimony before the committee the next morning, Remington revealed the strategy that would guide him during the days ahead: the sole reason for his involvement with Bentley was family relationships. " . . . I married a girl . . . whose family fell under the influence of

Communism," he told the senators. From this one, unfortunate event, all his problems derived.

"Give us your own family background . . . ," said New York senator Irving Ives.

"I am happy to say that all of my relatives . . . have never voted anything but Republican," Remington replied. " . . . And I am proud to say that I, too, have voted Republican. I was brought up as a Republican." But, he was quick to add, he had also voted Democratic.

As a Republican, he naturally detested Communists, although he was sometimes forced to associate with them in college and during his year with TVA. But by 1939, he was working against the Communists. Then came his fateful marriage. "There was no inkling that I was marrying into a family that was going Communist. Even I, in the emotional condition that most engaged youngsters are in, would have taken notice of that." He did not avoid those Communists he met through his new relatives; he tried to educate them. It was his mother-in-law who introduced him to Joseph North. Although they agreed on almost nothing "except that a particular bottle of wine was good," they did not argue; after all, he was Elizabeth Moos's closest friend, almost a member of the family.

"How did North happen to take you to meet Golos?" asked John McClellan, the senator from Arkansas.

"Sir, because he saw me at my mother-in-law's house and talked with me there . . . about Washington politics . . . and the war-production effort. . . . I tried to convince North that this government was not an appeasement government but was going to fight the war and win. . . . " And then North arranged the luncheon at which he met Golos, and the dinner followed with Helen. It was his feeling, he told the senators, that since North probably told Golos of Elizabeth Moos's Communist connections, Golos assumed that he, too, was a Party member. He had no idea that Golos and Helen were Communists (let alone spies). Was it so wrong for him to try to convince these critics that they were mistaken about the Roosevelt government? "Even if I had known Golos was a Communist, which I did not, I think I would have been making a contribution in trying to convince a Communist . . . that they should support a sincere war effort."

Not a word of it did the committee believe. "I actually think that your zeal for helping your country is most peculiar," said counsel William Rogers. "I don't think most young fellows [felt] . . . that the way to help the country was to try to convince the Russians. . . . If you were really so interested in persuading the Communist Party, why didn't you go up and see [Earl] Browder?"

"Sir, is that really a fair question?"

"I think it is," Rogers insisted.

Senator Ives could not understand how Remington failed to recognize that Golos and Bentley were Communists, since he met them through North, the

Communist who recruited his mother-in-law. " . . . [Y]ou must have seen that there was something dubious, and I cannot for the life of me understand . . . why you . . . [gave them] information before first demanding that they attempt to acquire [it] through regular channels."

But he had met Golos only twice, Remington asserted. If he was in fact a Communist, Golos was clever enough to hide it.

"I just do not comprehend it," Ives complained again. "It just does not make sense. . . . " Did he not think that his relationship with Bentley—the meetings in restaurants, on street corners and park benches—was not strange?

No. Other reporters had taken him to lunch. And one had also met him in the park.

"Look around you," Senator McClellan said, gesturing at the press who crowded the room. "Can you point out one of them that you ever met under such clandestine conditions . . . ?"

"No, Sir," Remington answered. Now even he admitted that "it was unusual and quite remarkable that I should have gone to a street corner or a park bench to meet Miss Bentley." But he did have an explanation. "I was . . . 24. I was not a high official. . . . I was silly enough not to realize that it was an unusual and preposterous procedure for me to go to those places. . . . My only defense is complete candor."

Finally, the committee lost patience. " . . . it just seems like a waste of time to further question this witness," Senator Thye complained to the chairman, " . . . he just turns these thoughts around to suit his convenience." To Remington, he said, "You get off on a rabbit track and none of us can follow you." And Senator Ives kept shaking his head, repeating, "it just does not make sense."

Again and again, Remington returned to his major contention—that his mother-in-law's Communist circle made it difficult for him to recognize a dangerous Communist, and Bentley certainly did not act like one. Even when he began to suspect her, he chose not to report her to his superiors because, first, there was nothing illegal about talking with Communists in 1943 at the height of the Soviet–American alliance; second, he had no concrete evidence that she was dangerous; and third, and most important, he had met Bentley through Elizabeth Moos's best friend. " . . . It isn't reasonable to ask a man to break off with his family when there is no ground for considering the Russians and the Communists active enemies." Now, of course, he had "broken with that side of the family, people whom I distrust and fear and whose policies and objectives I hate."[5]

After six exhausting hours, the hearing ended. It was not the triumph Remington had hoped for—the committee was openly hostile and the *Washington Post* called him "a boob . . . who was duped by clever Communist agents."[6]

"Candor is my only defense," he had proclaimed, but clearly he had failed to follow his own prescription. The Bill Remington who had once enthusiastically advocated Communism became, in his telling, a Republican who tolerated Communists and later had the misfortune to fall in love with a girl whose mother, unbeknownst to him, soon became one. Nothing could have been further from the truth, and the senators knew it. Earlier that morning, in executive session, he had described Ann as possessing a Communist mentality and wondered if she had been a Party member when he married her. In public session he had testified that his wife was not a Communist; it was no wonder that the committee did not know what to believe. Others also knew that he had lied—friends and enemies he had made over the years and in many places. Soon one would emerge from the past and publicly force him to identify the real Bill Remington.

There was no time to reconsider his course; in just two weeks he was scheduled to appear before an even more important tribunal—the Civil Service Commission's Fourth Region Loyalty Board. If they should conclude that reasonable grounds existed to doubt his loyalty, they would recommend to the Secretary of Commerce that he be dismissed from government service. Under the provisions of the President's Loyalty Program, he was allowed to submit affidavits and invite witnesses to testify in his behalf; so he quickly began to gather records and select those people who he hoped would accompany him. He also decided to seek legal assistance, but the men he contacted refused to represent him. Dean Acheson told him he could not help, because Alger Hiss, also accused of Communist Party membership that summer, was Acheson's friend, and Hiss's brother was a member of Acheson's law firm. After this and other rebuffs, Remington stopped looking. "It didn't bother me too much," he later noted. "I expected to win in a breeze. . . . To hell with lawyers, I thought—I'll take care of myself."[7]

Just a few days after his hearing ended, William Rogers ordered him to return to the Hill on Saturday, August 7, to face another accuser—someone (Rogers refused to identify him) he had known at Dartmouth. Who could it be? He spent hours Friday night going over a list of former students; at least fifty seemed likely prospects. Was it Bill Martin, whom he had recently met on a Washington street? They had argued during their brief time together. Martin was supporting Henry Wallace for President and was hopelessly biased. Martin thought Remington was a reactionary and the discussion had ended on a decidedly unhappy note. Or was it John Parke, who confessed to him in June that he had told the FBI that he thought Bill was a member of the Young Communist League at Dartmouth? Parke was another whom he had once counted among his handful of friends. Then there were his enemies—the many students he had snubbed, ridiculed, or shocked with his outrageous statements.[8]

Surprise became relief when he met the witness the next morning at the committee room. It was Robbins Barstow, Jr., the serious little freshman who wandered about the campus recording student views in his notebook. Remington was almost overjoyed to see him. "I thought there would be somebody here who could really embarrass me," he told the senators, "but he cannot."[9] He was wrong. Barstow's testimony proved to be extremely damaging, and the two-hour hearing was the roughest Remington had ever experienced.

Barstow, now twenty-eight and a teacher in Connecticut, had been following Remington's ordeal with great interest and some confusion. He remembered Bill as one of the most articulate Communists he had encountered at Dartmouth. But in his testimony before the Ferguson Committee, Remington had claimed that he was a Republican; had Barstow misunderstood him? The answer lay inside his college notebooks, which he had preserved among his personal papers. Consulting the first volume, which covered his freshman year, 1937–38, he discovered that his memory was correct. An entry dated January 5–6, 1938, read— "Communism . . . supported and striven for by Bill, and now working for CIO for immediate ends of workers' welfare." And there was more; much more. On August 4, Barstow had written Senator Irving Ives of his concern that Remington, now a government official, might still be a Communist; if so, he was a danger to American security. Two days later, the Ferguson Committee had invited Barstow to come to Washington.[10]

As Remington listened, Barstow read directly from his notebooks Bill's thoughts on Communism, the Russian constitution, the Spanish Civil War, and other subjects. For more damaging evidence, Barstow suggested that the committee examine back issues of *The Dartmouth*, where they would find Remington's pro-Communist articles and letters.[11]

When Barstow was excused, Counsel Rogers pounced on Remington. "You wanted to leave the impression that your connection with Communism was pretty much through your mother-in-law," he said. " . . . Mr. Barstow says—and I certainly believe him—that you were an active Communist before your mother-in-law in 1938 or 1937. What do you have to say about that?"

Remington's reply was confused and contradictory. "He is not telling the truth, and he is telling the truth as he understood it. . . . And I definitely espoused certain things . . . which I told you about." It was a question of definitions, Remington argued. "I advocated at college many . . . sweeping social reforms, [but] I was never an actual Communist, although I talked a great deal."

"What is the distinction in your mind between an actual Communist and what you did?" Rogers asked.

"The distinction is whether a person really believes in the Communist doctrines . . . revolution, dictatorship of the proletariat, and to say I was involved in that thing is sheer and utter nonsense."

During the Popular Front era, when Remington espoused, associated with, or perhaps joined the Communist Party, few Communists held such beliefs; Remington's characterization of a Communist as a wild-eyed bomb thrower committed to the violent overthrow of the American government hardly described the millions who followed or joined the Party. His definition was meaningless, and Rogers knew it. "I will tell you frankly, . . . that . . . I do not think that you made a full disclosure of your past," he said.

"I did, Sir," Remington insisted.

"You could have been very helpful to the Government if you wanted to be," Rogers continued. " . . . I think that you are a very clever fellow, . . . you succeed in giving the impression that you are being forthright and honest when you are not at all. . . . You beat around the bush as much as any witness that I have ever seen in my life."

There seemed to be nothing that Remington could do to alter the committee's view of him. He apologized for supporting FDR's "court-packing bill" in 1936; admitted that he was misled when he criticized capitalism at Dartmouth; and, finally, whipped and dejected, announced that he intended to resign from the Commerce Department. " . . . I don't expect to find a job except driving a taxi or something like that for quite a while. . . . [W]hen this thing simmers down, I may ask one of you gentlemen [for help]."

Rogers was not moved. "If you stand on your present position [and] do not tell the truth, you can never ask me for any help, because, frankly, I do not believe you."

Ferguson then asked Remington whether he would resign before his loyalty hearing.

"Oh, no, Sir," Remington said. "I am going through with the trial, . . . because I want some kind of clearance before I get out of the Federal Government. . . . "

Only at the end of the hearing was he briefly defiant, when he directly confronted Barstow about their days at Dartmouth. "I have been very restrained in dealing with Mr. Barstow," he said, "because I liked him at college . . . [but] there is an awful lot I can do to challenge his statement." Barstow claimed to have frequently visited Remington in his room. Describe the room, Remington demanded.

"It was, I believe, the second or third floor of Crosby Hall. . . . [I]t was an outside room, and I remember that you had a desk . . . in the southeast corner of the room and I believe there was a swivel chair and that you sat at that desk when I was talking with you and I can remember a typewriter with a paper in it that you were going to type . . . and you finally sent me home and went to work. . . . "

"I think you have described it," said an obviously pleased Senator Ferguson.

"And he is right on some things and not on others," Remington said, without elaboration. Could Barstow name his roommate?

At first, Barstow thought he was Chuck Livermore but then remembered that Livermore had been married. No other name came immediately to mind, but in earlier testimony he had mentioned Bill Martin, another campus Communist whom he admired.

"I want to point out that that is rather strange," Remington proclaimed. "I roomed with William Martin."

"I was just going to say that it might have been . . . Martin at one time," Barstow interjected.

"I think I have gone as far as necessary, along these lines," said Remington, abruptly concluding his interrogation. Barstow's memory was better than he had expected.

Remington's last refuge was the awards he had received at Dartmouth—proof, he claimed, that he had never been a Communist. His list of honors had no effect on the committee, which interrupted him and then adjourned.[12]

Barstow and Remington left the building together, and, incredibly, they decided to go to lunch. Later, they parted warmly that Saturday in August; Remington returned to his room on Riggs Street, while Barstow went sightseeing, looking for the monuments Remington told him no visitor to Washington should miss.[13]

For the next twelve days, Remington worked feverishly, preparing for the loyalty board hearing. He wrote more than seventy-five letters to friends, asking for affidavits and inviting them to testify on his behalf. August proved to be a poor time to locate people—many were on vacation in remote locations, where it was impossible to find a typist and notary public. Seven letters, including one from Ernest Hopkins, were handwritten and difficult to read. Using his own telephone to contact potential witnesses was also unexpectedly difficult. "Loyalty was in the wind and a wire-tapping panic was on." Those who received his calls would immediately say, "Bill, if you're not using a pay phone, will you please hang up and call me from one?" Therefore, much of his time was spent standing in oppressively warm phone booths, his pockets heavy with coins, making calls that now began, "This is Bill Remington. I'm in a public booth."[14]

A few friends refused to help. One was Albert Dickerson, Hopkins's former assistant, who had known Remington well at Dartmouth but now told him that he had "absolutely no direct personal knowledge whatsoever concerning your political convictions and associations as an undergraduate." The most he offered to do was certify that Remington had been a student, but even here he thought such a statement should come from the dean, not him. Although disappointed by Dickerson and a few others, Remington held no grudges, he later told journalist Daniel Lang; "but they don't mean as much to me as they once did."[15]

To those whom he wrote, Remington offered a spirited defense. Was he a Communist at Dartmouth? Definitely not, he argued. It was true that as a freshman and sophomore he had befriended many leftists, some of whom may have been YCLers, but he did not know who were formal members, and he was not among them. Primarily, he was involved in nonpolitical activities—track, debating, writing for *The Dartmouth*, working to pay his tuition, and trying to become Phi Beta Kappa.

He devoted only two sentences to his adventures in Tennessee, calling that period the "transition from sophomore foolishness to the dawn of reason" during his junior and senior years. By that time, he claimed to be a political moderate. "I was distinctly not one of the YCLers [nor] a fellow traveler. I was constantly bickering with those who . . . I think were. For anyone to think otherwise is sheer nonsense. . . . "

It was his family associations that led to his relationship with Bentley and Golos. He asserted that Joe North and Elizabeth Moos had arranged the first meeting with Golos. Bentley had seemed

> extremely New Dealish, but innocent enough—after all, 1943 was a period when the U.S. was trying to charm the U.S.S.R. out of concluding a separate peace, and pro-Soviet views were not subversive AT THAT TIME. So I was not suspicious. But this apparently innocent person seems to have been in the worst category of Communists.

Fortunately, he had never given Bentley any secret information. For the past eight years (even during his association with Bentley) he had been a staunch anti-Communist and this—he told his friends—had cost him "more than most people ever dare hope to find in life." He then lifted the veil that hid the history of his marriage:

> My wife had some fellow-traveler tendencies when we married. With the years they alternately waned and increased. When the U.S.S.R. and the U.S. were on the same side, life was livable. At other times it was not so easy. . . . Ann began to dominate our children—virulently. Three years ago she undertook psychoanalysis with an ultra-freudian, perhaps a Communist. . . . In secret she hired a lawyer and worked for perhaps a year planning a separation to which I agreed eighteen months ago because the children were going to pieces under the domestic tension. They are better now (less tension under her sole domination), but I fear for their futures. Her own behavior during this period has been little short of fantastic. The one thing which has enabled me to stand the loss of what was dear to me above all else was my work. If I'd been willing to play along with a Communist mentality I do not believe I would have lost what I would have died to save (if that could have saved anything). I'm not joking.

A reckless youth, dangerous in-laws, and persistent gullibility were the causes of his present crisis. He would fight the charges—not for himself but for those who believed in him, like his mentor Tom Blaisdell, "the closest to a saint I've ever known." Should "justice falter," he told his friends, "there will be no forwarding address here or at the alumni records office." With this vague threat of suicide, Remington ended his letter.[16]

Although Remington's story was filled with omissions, distortions, and lies, it was powerful enough to persuade more than forty people to write letters on his behalf, and an additional seventeen agreed to appear before the board to testify about his loyalty. Nearly all believed his central contention—that Ann and her mother were primarily responsible for his problems.[17] It remained to be seen whether the loyalty board would accept Remington's view that it was only fate and an unfortunate marriage that had led to the charges against him.

In selecting people to write for him, Remington was careful to choose men and women who were not only favorably disposed toward him but also had little knowledge of the radical past he was now denying. From Ridgewood came letters from an elderly neighbor and the widow of the rector of St. Elizabeth's Episcopal Church—who had seen him only occasionally over the past decades. He asked for an affidavit from only one childhood friend—Betsy Stokes, who had graduated from Ridgewood High when Remington was still a sophomore.[18]

Only two letters discussed his year in Tennessee. L. J. Van Mol, assistant to TVA's director of personnel, reviewed his record and stated that he found no evidence that Remington was a Communist. Lee S. Greene, a fellow employee whom Remington contacted, told the board that they were only casual acquaintances, so he had no knowledge of whether Remington was a Communist or not. No doubt his lack of knowledge was the reason Remington selected him; he could not have asked Henry Hart or Muriel Speare, both self-confessed former members of the Communist Party, for help or anyone else who remembered the disheveled young man in the black leather jacket.[19]

To describe him at Dartmouth, Remington asked only those men who remembered him best during what he called the "dawn of reason" from 1937 to 1939. Dean Neidlinger's affidavit was frank about Remington's earlier political activities, calling him "a rebel by inclination and a radical by preference," but was quick to add that before his senior year he had rejected such ideas and organizations. The dean was confident that Remington was "intellectually incapable of accepting the principles of communism or the doctrines of the Communist party." Unfortunately, Neidlinger's endorsement was undercut by an interview he had given to the FBI a few months earlier, which was now a part of Bill's loyalty file. Then, the dean had told agents that "he did not know whether Remington had ever actually been a member of the Communist party" and had mistakenly identified him as the head of the campus chapter of the American Student Union. Most damaging was Neidlinger's remark that given Remington's history at Dartmouth, his loyalty was in doubt. It was this interview and not the dean's affidavit that would attract the attention of the board.[20]

Those who truly knew Remington best at Dartmouth were his fellow students, but from the many he had known over the years, he selected only one to write the loyalty board, a star athlete and scholar named Stephen Bradley. Bradley was basically apolitical, which is probably why Remington chose him. He was never a campus activist or part of the radical circle that joined the ASU or YCL. Remington and Bradley became friendly in 1938, when Bill managed the Co-op Eating Club; it was this period that Bradley reported on to the board:

> . . . We had the pleasure of many discussions . . . on a great variety of subjects. I cannot recall that he ever attempted to promote Communistic doctrine. . . . Certainly my impression was that he was not a Communist nor a Communist camp follower. . . . I remember him then as a young man . . . with a keenness of intellect rarely found in college students.[21]

There is no reason to doubt Bradley's honesty, but his portrait of Remington was obviously incomplete; there is not the slightest hint of how controversial a figure Remington was in those days.

In the biography Remington was creating—through the letters and affidavits of his friends and teachers—the 1930s were years of youthful foolishness that eventually gave way to sobriety. The 1940s saw the emergence of the able economist, at least according to those he had asked to write the loyalty board. Willard Helburn, formerly of the War Production Board, thought Remington "cool and ambitious, well satisfied with the nature of the world in which he found himself and confident of making his way in it: excellent material for the business world, for which so many socialists and communists are handicapped by some quirk, grudge, or inferiority."[22]

Two letters were especially valuable to Remington, because they spoke to the charge that he had been a spy. Bertram Fox, director of the War Production Board's Military Division, had once possessed most of the secret records received from the War Department. "At no time," he wrote the board,

> did Remington ask to see any of these reports or documents, nor do I remember any discussions of them in his presence. . . . If he were engaged in any espionage activity, I would expect that he would have cultivated a closer contact with me to attain data. . . . There isn't a shred of doubt in my mind, that the charges against him are false.

Robert Nathan, chairman of the WPB's Planning Committee, supported Remington's position on press relations. "I never objected to my associates or subordinates talking with reporters and we often discussed the value of getting accurate unclassified material into the hands of the press," he stated. Nathan thus made Remington's relationship with Bentley seem more natural than the Ferguson Committee believed it was.[23]

The loyalty board also received letters from men and women who knew Remington in the immediate postwar years, when he served with the Office of War Mobilization and Reconversion, on the staffs of the President's Council of Economic Advisors and the President's Committee on Foreign Aid, and in the Department of Commerce's Office of International Trade. Friends and associates now characterized him as conservative, a man (said one) whose "political attitudes would be about as welcome to Communists or their sympathizers as would be a case of measles to a nursery school." His co-workers noted his vigorous support of the Truman Doctrine and Marshall Plan and his consistent criticism of Russia and American Communists.[24]

Remington was required to answer charges against him listed in a thirteen-page interrogatory, drafted by the board's three-man staff of examiners. Little is known about these men beyond their names: Cecil T. Dees, George St. Lawrence, and R. A. Loughton. But given the nature of their job and the biased report they produced, it is reasonable to assume that they were far more conservative politically than those they judged. The Loyalty Program's security officers, investigators, and examiners were generally former intelligence or FBI agents whose own personal histories were expected to be, as one scholar notes, "lily-white, . . . entirely devoid of derogatory information."[25] Their backgrounds made it almost inevitable that they would have little understanding or empathy for people, like Remington, who had associated with Communists. Their fifty-page analysis reflected hostility not only for Communism but also liberalism, which to them was evidence of disloyalty.

According to their report, the FBI had interviewed approximately a hundred individuals. Sixty provided either favorable information or knew nothing about alleged disloyalty, while forty questioned both Bill's and Ann's allegiance to their country. But of the latter group, only thirteen were willing to testify against them. Therefore, the results of the inquiry were, as even the examiners admitted, generally favorable, but they ignored their own conclusion and emphasized the unfavorable minority viewpoint. The most prominent hostile witness was Elizabeth Bentley, who repeated her charge that Remington was involved in Soviet espionage. The examiners ignored Remington's denial of her accusations, contained in his 1947 FBI interview, which was also in their files. Their analysis of the evidence led them to conclude that "there are reasonable grounds for belief that William Walter Remington is disloyal to the Government of the United States" and that he be "confronted with this information. . . ."[26]

The charges must have come as no surprise to Remington, since many were at least six years old. He was accused of membership in both the Young Communist League and the Communist Party, actions which, the board said, led him to associate frequently with known Communist Party members. No dates were given as to when he allegedly joined the YCL and the Party or consorted with Communists. He was also accused of membership in two organizations now considered subversive by the Attorney General: the American Youth Congress and the American Peace Mobilization. (Ann was similarly charged with membership in her own subversive groups: the Washington Book Shop and the National Federation of Constitutional Liberties.) Most serious was Bentley's charge. The board did not accuse him of espionage, but it did state that it had received information that as an employee of the War Production Board, he had frequently given secret data to unauthorized persons and that he had also introduced another government employee to these people.[27]

In an eleven-page response, Remington either denied or tried to explain his association with the various groups. "I am not, and have not been a member of the Communist Party or Communist Political Association," he wrote the board. "I have never paid dues to that organization. . . . I could never be a member or pay dues. I fear and, even though such a feeling is perhaps inconsistent with my religious faith, I hate Communism and its adherents." He also said he had never knowingly attended a Communist Party function, nor had he ever belonged to or associated with the Young Communist League. He did admit attending a Marxist study group at college but claimed it was simply an informal seminar that examined all political systems, including Marxism.[28]

In Tennessee, during 1936–37, he had associated with Communists, but he claimed that he was not then aware of their political affiliations. And once again, the "only significant association he ever had with Communists" was caused by his mother-in-law. Joining her family made some contact with these people unavoidable. He disagreed with them vigorously but accepted them for the sake of his marriage. But after the Cold War began, he left his wife because of their political differences.[29]

He also denied ever giving secret information to anyone and described his relationship with Bentley as he had to the Ferguson Committee. Neither Golos nor Bentley appeared to be Communists or spies, he repeated; the money he gave her was not Communist Party dues but contributions to a refugee fund that Golos had mentioned during their dinner at Schrafft's, although Bentley may have mistakenly thought it was dues; he met Bentley no more than ten times and gave her the kind of public information he would give to any reporter. The only government official he ever introduced to Bentley was Bernard Redmont, who, he learned from the FBI, "continued to see Miss Bentley long after my contact with her ended." Nevertheless, he did not believe that Redmont ever gave out state secrets.[30]

As far as the American Youth Congress and Peace Mobilization were concerned, he had never formally joined, although he associated with their members until it became clear to him that both groups were pro-Communist and isolationist. His wife may have continued her involvement after the fall of 1940, but if so, it was against both his will and desire.[31]

More important than these ancient associations was his current record in government: his opposition to the Morgenthau Plan and efforts on behalf of the European Recovery Program ("I worked up to 16 and 18 hours a day helping to stop Communism"). As director of the Export Program Staff, he worked eighty hours a week cutting off exports to Russia and its satellites.[32]

"I have told the complete truth," he concluded:

I am innocent. . . . [But] if I have learned anything from the shocking disclosures that Golos and Bentley were spies, it is that innocence is not enough. In times like these, with war threatening, persons with Communist relatives and associates must be screened with special care—out of fairness to them as well as the government.

Any federal servant with relatives such as my in-laws should, I believe, abandon association with them or . . . turn toward other employment. . . . Otherwise, the results for the government can be unfortunate, and the effects on him calamitous—even though his innocence may be sublime. My case certainly illustrates the dangers even for a man whose associations with Communists were innocent, and five years in the past; and who has broken with his in-laws, and who has lost his home and children partly because he would not bow to Communist sympathies in his wife.[33]

Like his selective choice of people to evaluate him, Remington's response to the interrogatory did not give the board a completely honest account of his past. He failed to tell the truth about his involvement in the Young Communist League at Dartmouth and the Communist Party unit in Knoxville. His description of the deterioration of his marriage was distorted. While it may be correct that Ann's commitment to Communist causes in the early 1940s was stronger than his, he exaggerated the extent to which political differences exacerbated marital tensions; for example, in an extraordinarily explicit essay about his relationship with Ann, which Remington later wrote for his attorneys, there is no reference to political disagreements as a major cause of their breakup—indeed, politics is not mentioned at all. It, therefore, seems more likely that Remington overstated political factors to indicate to his critics the depth of his anti-Communism and how it drove him to dissolve his marriage and lose his children. While this interpretation may have been inaccurate, it was the most powerful weapon at his command as he prepared to face the loyalty board. Who could not be moved by the plight of a man who chose loyalty to his government over devotion to his wife?[34]

9

Sorry about Everything

On the morning of August 18, 1948, in a conference room in Temporary Building R, Remington met the four men and one woman who would now decide his fate. "As I looked at them," he later said, "I couldn't help thinking any one of you and I could swap places."[1]

This was not likely, given the composition of the Fourth Region Loyalty Board. Its chairman was Robert Maurer, sixty-nine and a professor at Georgetown University, where he specialized in constitutional and administrative law. Joining him were three other lawyers: Russell E. Booker, forty-nine and treasurer of the Virginia state Bar Association; Fred E. Martin, fifty-three, who practiced corporate law in Norfolk and was a former state commander of the American Legion; Harry W. Blair, sixty-seven, a Missouri Democrat who served in FDR's Justice Department in the early 1930s; and finally, Marion Wade Doyle, fifty-three and president of the Washington, D.C., Board of Education. This was a group with which Remington had little in common—all were born in the late nineteenth century and were comfortably settled in careers when Remington was still at Dartmouth. None had been attracted to the radical politics of the early twentieth century or was affected by the ravages of the Depression. How could they understand Remington, who had rebelled against an economic and political order that they, as lawyers and civic leaders, had fought to maintain?[2]

Another important participant was R. A. Loughton, who drew up the charges against Remington; as the board's examiner, he would act as prosecutor, presenting the staff's findings and posing most of the questions. Even before the hearing commenced, Loughton had concluded that reasonable grounds existed to doubt

111

Remington's loyalty—a view shared by Harry Blair and Marion Doyle, who reviewed the evidence and approved the examiner's recommendation that the interrogatory be filed. The Loyalty Program had thus stood American jurisprudence on its head. Remington had no right to examine the records produced by the FBI for the board, nor could he cross-examine their witnesses, whose identities were secret. He was not allowed to challenge the staff's damning report, which was available to all board members but not to him. Presumed guilty at the start, Remington had to prove himself innocent to a tribunal of five, two already believing him disloyal.

By law, the board was required to examine Remington's current views and activities to determine whether he was loyal to his government. But it ignored this stricture and roamed freely throughout Remington's life, with long stopovers at Dartmouth, TVA, the War Production Board, and the Navy. He was also questioned about his relationships with his wife, mother-in-law, and the woman he knew as Helen Johnson.

After being sworn, Remington interrupted the examiner. "Sir," he said, "before the questions start I would like to emphasize that . . . I have been brought up in such a way in which an oath is very meaningful." Despite this declaration, however, Remington, during the five-hour hearing that day and the eight hours on August 19 and 27, distorted or denied his radical past, apologized for supporting the New Deal, and emphasized his anti-Communist convictions. For example, when asked about the American Student Union chapter at Dartmouth he replied, "I don't know anything about the . . . organization at Dartmouth. . . . I don't know whether it was named as subversive . . . by the Attorney General [it was not], but . . . I think it should be." Inexplicably, he said nothing about how he helped to destroy the ASU—perhaps his only authentic anti-Communist act while in college.

"While you were at TVA, did you meet with any left-of-center groups?" Loughton asked.

Only those associated with the CIO and the Workers Alliance, Remington replied, and he did not know if either group was Communist. " . . . I didn't know much about the Communists or Communism at that time," he said.

Have you ever participated in any labor disputes?

"No . . . and I never appeared in a picket line. . . . " The closest I ever came to such activity, he claimed, was organizing games for strikers' children, a favor for a friend, "a lady in the TVA [Christine Benson], I say a friend of mine [but] I didn't know her particularly well. . . . " And, as a teacher employed by the Workers Alliance, I supported FDR's packing of the Supreme Court, but now I think that I was completely mistaken about that issue.

The board expressed great interest in knowing more about his encounters with Helen Johnson. Did you not suspect that there was something very strange about her?

"It never occurred [to me] that she was a Communist," Remington replied. "If she had done something to really indicate that she was a Communist, I wouldn't have dreamed she was a spy for the U.S.S.R. or the Communist Party. I thought of her as a vague, rather pleasant lady," a social acquaintance who always inquired about my family, a kind of sad and aimless person I befriended for a brief time, but when I became suspicious, I stopped seeing her. And again he insisted that he had never given her secret information. Nevertheless, he was deeply ashamed about the entire incident. "The judgment I showed in dealing with Miss Bentley is thoroughly rotten. . . . It was a tragic thing to do and most unwise. . . . " But the board must understand that I was then only twenty-four and new to government service.

His closest connection with Communists was caused by his wife. "I don't want to say anything against my wife," he said, sadly, but then proceeded to tell them a somewhat twisted story of his marriage to Ann. According to Remington, it was politics that eventually destroyed their union. Since their wedding day in 1939, he found himself growing more and more conservative, while Ann, following her mother's example, moved further to the left. He tried to restrain her, but she rebelled; eventually, it became impossible for them to live together. Separation followed, and divorce seemed inevitable. Remington's emotional monologue brought him close to tears. " . . . I am sorry about everything. I . . . when I think of my kids I can't talk. I think perhaps I would like to stop now."

The second and most of the third day of hearings saw a parade of witnesses who testified about Remington's career in government since 1942. Dr. Edwin Nourse, chairman of the President's Council of Economic Advisors, described Remington's staff work as "sound conservative economic analysis." Others who knew him at the War Production Board, the Office of War Mobilization and Reconversion, the Council of Economic Advisors, the President's Committee on Foreign Aid, and the Commerce Department called him a good man and a capable, intelligent person.

His two most passionate defenders were his mentor, Tom Blaisdell, now the acting assistant secretary of commerce, and Richard M. Bissell, Jr., assistant administrator of the Economic Cooperation Administration (later a deputy director of the Central Intelligence Agency). From the outset, Remington had been a very diligent employee, Blaisdell told the board. When Remington joined the Commerce Department's Office of International Trade to chair the committee responsible for recommending exports to the Soviet Union and eastern Europe, he worked day and night. "If anyone ever took on a hard job and did it well, he did." In fact, he did it too well, according to State Department officials who complained about Remington's militant approach to Soviet–American relations.

Richard Bissell was also impressed by Remington. They first met in 1946 at the Office of War Mobilization and Reconversion. Bissell recalled for the board how Remington had strongly supported the continuation of wartime wage and price controls and had been especially critical of organized labor's attempts to eliminate them. Such positions, Bissell noted, were not supported by Communists, fellow travelers, or even liberal Democrats. When, in 1947, Bissell was appointed executive secretary of the President's Committee on Foreign Aid, which was charged with developing the Marshall Plan, he asked Bill to become his assistant. In that position, Remington called for increased aid to western Europe to block Soviet expansion and was again criticized for his extreme views. And recently, Bissell had heard that Remington's staff had gone too far in restricting trade with Russia; he was not surprised to learn this given his knowledge of Remington's conservative views.[3]

The board listened politely to Bissell, Blaisdell, and the others but seemed generally uninterested in their testimonies. A number of witnesses were never asked a single question, while other inquiries were brief and perfunctory. Marion Wade Doyle asked only seven questions of the eighteen witnesses, while Russell Booker was silent during the questioning of all but two. Chairman Maurer also asked few substantive questions and seemed to act primarily as expediter. "Make your statements just as brief as you can," he told Remington at one point, "we don't want to prolong the hearing unnecessarily." The most aggressive interrogators were Harry Blair and Fred Martin, whose main concern was that Remington's supporters were professional rather than social acquaintances. They could vouch for his daytime affairs, but what about his evenings and weekends, when he might be engaged in subversive activities?[4]

By the end of his hearing, on August 27, it was clear to Remington that he had not convinced the board that he was loyal. Although he had demonstrated that he was now rabidly anti-Communist, the members were still more worried about his past than his present activities—a violation of the requirement that only current acts were relevant in determining loyalty. Fred Martin could not understand why he had associated with Communists in the 1930s and 1940s.

"I have been raised from the cradle with the idea . . . that human beings although not perfect now could become perfect . . . ," he answered, in a final effort to explain the meaning of his early life. " . . . Those faiths were dominating me completely up until recent years. They don't any more. . . . The Communists that I knew . . . were certainly self-sacrificing and devoted to something. They too were willing to go out and spend hours helping get relief allotments for someone who deserved it and didn't have it. . . . I was willing to cooperate with these people on humanitarian grounds, but I want to emphasize that I did not cooperate with them consciously, knowing that they were Communists."[5]

Ultimately, it was life with his wife and her Communist mother that convinced him that he could not work with the Communists. "I know those people," he told the board, his voice, usually quiet, rising now with anger. "I know that they are not people you can live with. . . . I have had associations which are mighty suspicious, and I can't think of anybody who has been as badly burned by them as I." Today, the line between Communists and non-Communists is sharp; Communists are disloyal, and I would never associate with them. Looking back now, he castigated himself for his naive attitude toward the Reds and concluded that being a Communist Party member during World War II was disloyal.[6]

After more than thirteen hours of testimony, there seemed little more that Remington could say to persuade the board that he was not a Communist. He had expressed shame and regret; now he apologized for once having been liberal and pleaded with the group to acknowledge his anti-Communist record.

"[Can] you stop now?" Chairman Maurer interrupted. " . . . [H]ow much longer . . . ?"

"About five or ten minutes," Remington begged, frantic to burnish his anti-Communist credentials. Religion, he stammered—"the Communists are notoriously anti-religious and I am not. I was brought up in the Episcopal church, I was an acolyte, a choir boy and after that I was in the Oxford Group. . . . I was not an active churchgoer," he admitted, but would have been "if it had not been for . . . my wife."[7]

Maurer wanted to know if that was all.

Remington did not want to stop. "I am ignorant of your procedures. I don't know what you know." The interrogatory and the board's questions were based on statements made to the FBI by confidential informants. Who were these secret witnesses? Could he not cross-examine them?

"I explained that," Maurer snapped. FBI reports are secret.

That was exactly Remington's concern. What if those sources were mistaken? Or prejudiced? But he quickly withdrew his objections. "I understand . . . , I am not raising any question at all about the procedure. I know that it is . . . fair . . . and important."[8]

At the end of the hearing, the chairman explained that should the board reach an adverse decision, Remington had twenty days to appeal to the Civil Service Commission Loyalty Review Board, the Loyalty Program's Supreme Court.

"Would you like me to prepare a written brief . . . summarizing what I have said?" Remington offered, hoping to have the final word.

"It isn't necessary . . . ," Maurer said, bringing the hearing to a close.

"Good luck," Examiner Loughton wished him as he was leaving the room. He would need luck and more—his chances of clearance, he thought, were no better than fifty-fifty.[9]

Later, Remington looked back on his testimony with a mixture of anger, bitterness, and self-loathing. "The whole atmosphere at the hearing made you kick yourself for everything you'd ever done," he told Daniel Lang in 1949:

Why had I ever lectured to CIO workers in Tennessee? Why had I ever made donations to help the Loyalists in Spain? . . . What ever made me attend an American Youth Congress Meeting . . . ? What a pity I couldn't point to a model marriage! What made me blurt out to those strangers that I believed in God, that I'd been a choirboy and an acolyte in the Episcopal church? The board seemed to be comparing me with their idea of a loyal American—a composite character, a perfect mediocrity who never existed. If such a man did exist, I wouldn't care to meet him, because he wouldn't have a thought in his head or a beat in his heart. I don't think any of the board members could have filled the bill themselves.

If the board had indeed been looking for the person Remington described—the perfect mediocrity—it might have found him in Remington himself, the man who renounced his early idealism and political beliefs and who now believed only in anti-Communism.[10]

A few days later, he received more bad news. Although the board had not yet issued its decision, the Commerce Department had decided to change his employment status from leave with pay to leave without pay. This action was taken, he learned, because information indicated that he might be guilty of disloyalty or a crime for which he might be sent to prison; to retain him might also threaten national security.[11] What information? Had the FBI uncovered evidence overlooked in its earlier probe? Had Bentley accused him of some new treason? Had he been indicted by the grand jury? And what crime had he committed? Espionage during World War II, the penalty for which was death? It was now absolutely imperative that he find a lawyer to defend him against these mysterious charges.

He recalled the name of a young lawyer whom he had know casually when he had been with OWMR in 1946. Bill looked for him in the Washington telephone directory and found his office number. It was close to six o'clock, but Remington called anyway, not certain that the man would still be there. Surprisingly, the lawyer answered. "Come over, right away," Joe Rauh told him, and Remington left immediately for the office of Rauh and Levy at 1631 K Street, N.W.[12]

Joseph Louis Rauh, Jr., was thirty-seven years old in 1948 and had been in private practice just two years since returning from his wartime service in the South Pacific. But in that brief time, he had become one of Washington's most able and aggressive attorneys. Born in Cincinnati, Ohio, in 1911, the son of German immigrants who prospered in America, Rauh was educated at both Harvard College and the Harvard Law School. As a student, he so impressed his teachers that they recommended him to FDR's advisor Benjamin V. Cohen, who hired young Rauh to help draft legislation. After graduating first in his law school class in 1935, Rauh became an aide to the Supreme Court's Justice Benjamin Cardozo, and following Cardozo's death in 1937, he clerked for Justice Felix Frankfurter. Rauh returned to the executive branch in 1941, working first in several New Deal agencies and then, later that year, going back to the White

House. When A. Philip Randolph, president of the Brotherhood of Sleeping Car Porters, proposed a march on Washington to force Roosevelt to integrate the armed forces and allow black Americans to work in the defense industry, Joe Rauh was assigned to draft Executive Order 8802, which, when signed by the President, forbade discrimination in government and the defense establishment. Executive Order 8802 was "the government's most significant action on behalf of black citizens since Reconstruction," journalist Milton Viorst later observed, "and it would have no rival in the field of civil rights for another quarter of a century." Strongly committed to the cause of racial justice, Rauh and Minneapolis mayor Hubert H. Humphrey took the 1948 Democratic National Convention by storm, forcing it to adopt a strong civil rights plank that drove southern delegates to bolt and form the Dixiecrat Party; President Truman now vigorously courted black voters, many of whom turned to the Democratic Party as their champion.

Rauh was an activist as well as an advocate. In 1946, he helped to establish Americans for Democratic Action, an organization dedicated to liberal reform and anti-Communism. One of its goals was the destruction of the pro-Communist Progressive Party, which the ADA believed wanted to capture the liberal cause for Communist purposes. "I detest Communists and their fellow travelers," Rauh later told a friend, and he refused to defend them. He would remain an ADA official for the rest of his life.

Although the press often called him loud and unyielding in argument, he was remarkably warm and unpretentious. One of his trademarks was colorful bow ties, which he wore to show that he was not a stuffy, pinstriped attorney. He was also one of the few men whom Remington could actually look in the eye—at six feet two, he was as tall as his prospective client. The eyes were grey, enlarged slightly by glasses; the hair, brown and curly, framing a face writer Lillian Hellman (a future client) called crinkly and rugged and that "gives one confidence in the mind above it."[13]

Remington explained what had brought him to the office—Bentley's accusations, the loyalty board hearing, and his recent suspension with its intimation of even worse things to come. They talked for the next eight hours, the lawyer vigorously cross-examining him, covering his entire life from Ridgewood to Washington. "Every time I found the slightest inconsistency," Rauh said later, "I threw it in his face until I was satisfied that it had been an unintentional and minor misstatement." It was two o'clock in the morning when the interrogation ended.

Would he take his case? an exhausted Remington asked.

Not yet, Rauh replied—he wanted to do more checking, and during the week that followed, he called many who had worked with Remington. All told Rauh that Remington was a staunch anti-Communist. But Rauh was still uncertain and called Remington in for another long talk. He asked him directly if the charges were true. Had he been a Communist? Had he given Bentley secret wartime information?

No, Remington assured him; he was innocent. Finally, Rauh told him he would take the case.[14]

Although Remington claimed to be innocent, it is clear that he misled Rauh about his life. Kept secret were his youthful radicalism, his activities while with TVA, his role in the YCL, his life with Ann, and, most significant, the truth about his relationship with Elizabeth Bentley. Rauh sensed that he did not know the full story, noting later that Remington, like almost all clients, had shaded the truth. But despite the gaps in Remington's history, Rauh would fight for him. "Bill . . . is a strange combination of integrity and egotism, of reserve and brashness, of brilliance and gullibility," he wrote in 1949. "With it all, he is a decent boy and I like him." And beyond the imperfect client was the cause he represented. The Remington case was important, he argued, "because a man in a democracy has a right to make a mistake, even a bad mistake, without being crucified as disloyal." Even if, assuming the worst, Remington had joined the Communist Party in the desperate 1930s and had shared secrets with the Soviets when Russia was America's ally against fascism during World War II (neither of which Rauh believed), Remington's allegiance to his country was never in doubt.[15]

On Sunday, September 12, Bentley showed again her ability to injure Remington when she appeared on NBC Radio's *Meet the Press*.

"You've made charges . . . before a congressional committee naming several people as Communists," journalist Cecil Brown stated. "Now . . . here, Miss Bentley, you don't have congressional immunity, would you now identify William Remington as a Communist, or . . . anyone else that you've named, knowing that you might open your way to a libel suit?" After trying to avoid a direct answer, she finally said, "Yes, I would certainly do that. I testified before the committee that he was . . . a member of the Communist Party."[16]

Among those listening to the broadcast was Joe Rauh. He thought Bentley's statement libelous and told his client so the next day. Remington should sue everyone responsible for Bentley's appearance, NBC, the General Foods Corporation (the show's sponsor), and Elizabeth Bentley. They should also seek damages, a hundred thousand dollars or more. Bentley's statement could not go unchallenged—"We either sue or we quit," Rauh said. "If we accept [such statements on NBC], how can we deny it some place else?" Inaction might persuade the loyalty board that Bentley's accusations were true and contribute to a finding of disloyalty. Although not enthusiastic about the possibility of a lawsuit on top of his other problems, Remington could see that he had no choice but to proceed. Rauh said he would seek the best specialist in libel law, but first, they should give Bentley a chance to recant. Faced with a lawsuit, she might issue a retraction, which could end all of Remington's troubles. So, their first step was to draft a letter to Bentley, demanding a retraction and threatening a lawsuit; Rauh worked on it for several days, Remington approved it, and it was released to the press on September 23. Bentley did not reply.[17]

Privately, Remington was less contentious. The next day, without Rauh's knowledge, he telephoned the FBI and arranged to meet with them on September 30. His talk with D. M. Ladd, a top aide of Hoover's, lasted just eighteen minutes. He began by proclaiming his innocence and then asked "if the FBI wanted to see him out of government entirely or only not employed on classified . . . work." Ladd was typically unresponsive—the Bureau just collected information, he said; it made no recommendations in loyalty cases. Remington offered to drop his libel suit if Bentley issued either a public or private retraction. A legal confrontation would damage her credibility, he claimed, which would be unfortunate, since he believed Bentley's story, except as it applied to him. Ladd refused to bargain—Bentley had testified voluntarily, and the Bureau did not control her. Rising to leave, Remington remarked that he would have to attack Bentley's testimony.[18]

Five days later, on October 5, Remington followed Rauh's recommendation and formally retained the services of Richard G. Green, an expert on libel, who had recently won a noted victory in New York. Green also conferred with the celebrated attorney Arthur Greenfield Hays, who agreed to work with him if his busy schedule permitted.[19]

While Green drew up a complaint and spoke with the U.S. Marshal's Office about delivering it to Bentley, Remington and Rauh focused their energies on a more urgent problem. In late September, Remington was finally informed that the Fourth Region Loyalty Board had concluded that reasonable grounds existed to believe that he was disloyal to his government. Accordingly, his appointment as director of the Commerce Department's Export Program staff was cancelled. He had just twenty days to appeal this ruling to the Civil Service Commission Loyalty Review Board.[20] The letter from acting chairman Harry W. Blair said nothing about how the board had reached its decision, nor did it describe the evidence that convinced them that Remington was disloyal. All Remington received was a transcript of his hearing; the voluminous files containing FBI reports and staff memoranda remained secret.

The letter of notification may have been signed by Harry Blair, but it was actually Examiner R. A. Loughton and his two associates (Cecil T. Dees and George St. Lawrence) who had played the principal role in formulating the board's decision. Truman's Executive Order required the examiner to determine if Remington was now—in 1948—loyal to his government. Thus, the Memorandum of Decision, prepared for the board, should have analyzed Remington's reports and the testimonies of those who currently worked with him. It did not. Almost all of Remington's present activities were dismissed as self-serving, while the views of his colleagues were judged inadequate because the witnesses saw him only on the job.[21]   The seven-page memorandum said nothing about Remington's support of the Truman Doctrine and Marshall Plan and his energetic attempts to limit exports to Russia and eastern Europe.

It was Remington's past that monopolized the attention of the examiners, and their analysis revealed a hostility toward Communism and liberalism. Indeed, they described the young Remington as "saturated with 'liberal' or 'radical' idealism," which, after his marriage, developed into an enthusiasm for Communism. This is what led to his relationship with Golos and Bentley, to whom he intentionally gave secret information; that act, according to the Executive Order, constituted disloyalty. That these events allegedly occurred six years earlier was ignored by the examiners. As for Remington's explanation of the Bentley affair, they called it "strained and unsatisfactory. . . . The surreptitious manner and character of [their] meetings indicate conscious wrongdoing and a desire on the part of Remington that her identity remain secret. . . . We think he must have known that he was imparting non-public information to a person closely identified with communists."[22]   Loughton and the others also did not believe that Remington's postwar anti-Communism was authentic; rather, it was the result of his desire to prove his innocence after the FBI informed him in 1947 that he was suspected of espionage.[23]

Not knowing exactly how the board had reached its decision made mounting a defense difficult, but Rauh decided to strike directly at the Achilles' heel of the Loyalty Program: the inability of the accused to identify and confront the accusers. In Remington's case, the principal accuser was well known; therefore, on September 27, Remington wrote a letter to the Loyalty Review Board appealing the regional board's finding and asking that Elizabeth Bentley be called to testify so that she could be cross-examined by his lawyers. "The entire case against me depends on Miss Bentley's testimony," he said.[24]   If Bentley appeared (doubtful since the Review Board lacked subpoena power), Rauh could point out the contradictions in her previous testimony and thus destroy her credibility; if she refused to testify, this, too, could only favor him, since it would indicate that Bentley could not support her charges. For the moment, Remington allowed himself to hope that, perhaps, he might be cleared.

The regional board's decision had plunged him into a deep depression; at first, he thought he might resign, but Rauh's optimism encouraged him to appeal. Family and friends continued to be sympathetic, except for bitter Uncle Will who wanted desperately to campaign for his hero Thomas E. Dewey but felt it was unwise because his name was also William Remington. Nevertheless, he withdrew from the outside world during these days. "I didn't want to see my friends," he told Daniel Lang in 1949. "I might implicate more of them or they might implicate me further. Maybe some of them were Communists." He was especially uncomfortable with his new celebrity. A photographer who found him walking down a Washington street one day tried to take his picture, but an angry Remington shooed him away. Even going to the drugstore was no longer the anonymous act it once was:

> a salesgirl spotted me. She wanted to be sympathetic. "The way they run things in this country," she said, "sometimes I think maybe it would be better if the Russians took over." What was I supposed to do? Smile, because she was sympathetic? Glare, because she was disloyal—or maybe an FBI agent?

Most of his time was spent alone in his room. When invited to dine with Joe Rauh or the Calfees, he would decline; he refused to depend on the charity of friends, and besides, he could not afford a restaurant dinner. He was almost broke, his savings having been poured out in a steady stream to pay for long-distance telephone calls, stenographers, and a five hundred dollar bill for printing up a legal brief. Maria Calfee, an emotional Italian, considered Remington's reserve incomprehensible. "Why don't you go out and get drunk?" she asked one day.

"Don't care to," was Remington's brusk reply. Later, she confronted him again: "all right, don't get drunk. But would you mind punching this door for me?" Remington, stared at the door a moment, then punched it and returned to his room.[25]

His gloom lifted slightly in late October when Rauh informed him that the Loyalty Review Board had granted his request to call Bentley for questioning. But would she appear? After embarking on a highly publicized lecture tour during the summer, she now virtually had disappeared. Attorney Richard Green, who needed to serve her with Remington's complaint, had been unable to locate her, and none of her associates seemed to know her whereabouts. Given this uncertainty, Rauh asked Seth Richardson, chairman of the Loyalty Review Board, for a meeting on October 27. Rauh explained his dilemma. How could he adequately prepare for the hearing without knowing its focus—would it be the cross-examination of Elizabeth Bentley or in her absence merely a defense of Remington's record? Richardson had written Bentley in care of her friend Louis Budenz, another ex-Communist turned professional witness, and was confident the message would reach her. To make it more difficult for her to avoid appearing, Rauh agreed not to serve her at the hearing and also gave her immunity from further lawsuits for anything she said that day. This seemed more than fair to Richardson, but he found it necessary to make one demand: Rauh must proceed with the hearing even if Bentley agreed to appear and did not show up. Rauh agreed.

Rauh also informed Richardson of an important decision he had recently made. Because of the importance of the case, he had asked Bethuel M. Webster to act as senior counsel. A graduate of the Harvard Law School, the conservative 48-year-old Webster was a former assistant U.S. attorney in Manhattan and had worked for the Justice Department under Republican Presidents Coolidge and Hoover. Currently, he was the chairman of the Judiciary Committee of the New York City Bar Association and senior partner in the prestigious firm of Webster and Sheffield. If Webster agreed to represent Remington, he would be the lawyer defending him before the Board. Richardson knew Webster well; in fact, they had tangled in a courtroom earlier in their careers, but Rauh sensed no lingering anger. November 22 was selected as the possible hearing date, and Richardson promised to call Rauh as soon as he heard from Bentley.[26]

Less than a month remained until the hearing, and Rauh had not yet prepared his case or received a firm commitment from Webster that he would participate. The decision to seek a conservative senior counsel was made primarily "to take the liberal curse off me," Rauh later noted. Since President Truman had appointed Republicans (like Seth Richardson) to direct and staff the Loyalty Program (in the mistaken hope that this would end the Communist-in-government furor), Rauh felt that having a conservative lawyer plead the case would be extremely helpful to their cause.

It was lawyer Gardner Jackson, a friend of both Rauh and Webster, who had arranged for the two to meet earlier that October. Over dinner at New York's Harvard Club, Rauh had described the complex case and had assured Webster that Remington was innocent. Webster had been hesitant. A man with Remington's history and problems was not typical of his clientele. If Rauh could convince him of Remington's innocence, Webster had told him, he would take the case.

In early November, Rauh sent Webster a draft copy of the brief he planned to submit to the Board, and a few days later, Webster told Rauh that he would represent Bill *pro bono publico* (for the public good). One important question still remained. Would he be arguing against Bentley or for Remington? Would she appear and testify?[27]

She would not, Seth Richardson learned on November 15. In a hurriedly written letter, she informed the chairman that she had an important appointment far from Washington that would prevent her from appearing. Richardson immediately telephoned Rauh and reminded him of his earlier pledge; the hearing would go on as scheduled.[28]

In the week before the hearing, Remington's attorneys made one final effort to find Bentley and at the same time create some publicity about her disappearance. When federal marshals failed to locate her, Richard Green filed a deposition with the U.S. District Court in Manhattan, describing his fruitless attempts to locate her, and asked permission to personally serve the summons and complaint. When authorization was granted, Green leaked the news to the local press, which covered the story with these dramatic headlines: RED WITNESS "MISSING" AT 100-G SLANDER SUIT, and COURT BACKS BENTLEY HUNT BY REMINGTON.[29]

Word of Bentley finally surfaced on November 16. SPY QUEEN BENTLEY

EMBRACES CATHOLIC CHURCH AS A HAVEN, read the headline in that morning's *New York World-Telegram*, the newspaper that first published her story and, with reporter Nelson Frank's encouragement, remained her staunchest supporter. For the past two months, said the *World-Telegram*, Bentley had been receiving instruction on Catholic principles from the Right Reverend Fulton J. Sheen, who baptized and confirmed her on November 5. This was the reason for Bentley's disappearance, a friend told the newspaper. "A very eminent attorney will accept all papers for her within a day or so. She has nothing to fear." The anonymous friend also announced that on Sunday, November 21, she would make her first public appearance in months at the Rochester, New York, Aquinas Institute, where she planned to lecture on "The Communist Menace." This was the engagement that would prevent her from attending the Remington hearing, scheduled to begin the next day.[30]

The hearing before the Loyalty Review Board began at 9:45 A.M. on Monday, November 22. For Remington, the men seated across the table must have appeared identical to those who had judged him in July and August. Another panel of old, conservative lawyers: Seth W. Richardson, chairman, born in 1880, an associate U.S. attorney general when Remington was a child; George W. Alger, seventy-six, had graduated from the New York University Law School twenty-two years before Remington was born and had specialized in industrial and labor law for more than a half century; and Harry W. Colmery, of Topeka, Kansas, fifty-seven and currently chairman of the Republican Party's Veterans' League. How could they possibly understand the world of William Remington?[31]

Surprisingly, the hearing went very well, much better than Remington had anticipated, primarily because of the skill of Bethuel Webster. He took command from the outset, noting first how sorry he was that Elizabeth Bentley was not present.

"We share your disappointment," George Alger said.

"I am disappointed for professional reasons," Webster said. "I think Mr. Remington . . . is seriously prejudiced by her absence."

Remington was sworn in, and for the next half hour Webster questioned him about his views on world affairs, from the Nazi–Soviet pact to the Marshall Plan. This gave Remington the opportunity again to detail his consistent anti-Communist position from 1939 to the present. This time, his answers to Webster's questions were short, clear, and specific. When he sometimes began to wander into potentially dangerous areas, Webster steered him back on course.[32]

Then the Board questioned him for about forty-five minutes, primarily about Bentley. He repeated that he never suspected she was a spy or gave much thought to her political views and emphasized the casual and infrequent nature of their meetings.

"Do you think you did right in doing what you did?" Richardson asked.

"I think I was wrong in not evaluating Miss Bentley as a Communist, . . . but

I could not have done better with the information I had . . . from my contacts with her."

Did he not think he was "subject to criticism of the gravest type?"

"I definitely feel that I should not be subject to censor for what I did with Miss Bentley," Remington insisted. "I am embarrassed about it. I was not entirely alert in my perception, but I did nothing wrong."

At eleven o'clock, Webster began a formal presentation of his case. He again expressed his disappointment that he could not cross-examine the woman who had brought them together that morning. "Her testimony is just charged with inconsistencies and impressions and conclusions and superficialities which any trial lawyer would be eager to get at." He also felt hurt by not being able to examine FBI records or the findings of the lower board. "We lawyers are accustomed to drawing our attack against an objective and when we attack the decision of the regional board . . . it is like picking up a shock of hay with your hands; you just don't know where to take hold."

Because the lower board had spent so much time on his client's youth and young manhood, Webster felt it necessary to paint his own portrait of the life and times of William Remington. He described an idealistic young man, who, like so many in the 1930s, searched to find his "groove politically, philosophically, morally." Although he flirted with radicalism while at Dartmouth and with TVA, his flirtation was over by 1939. Radicalism was "like a case of measles," Webster noted. "It is a good thing to have it as a child and not . . . as an adult."

More significant were his years of government service, Webster argued, when from 1940 to 1948 he repeatedly took positions diametrically opposed to the Communist Party line. Webster's ninety-minute monologue was interrupted just three times, by Seth Richardson, who was still troubled about Remington's meetings with Bentley.

Webster responded by attacking Bentley's story. She said she had visited frequently with important Communist agents like Silvermaster and Ullman, stuffing her bag with microfilmed documents. They were her prize sources. But Remington she saw hardly at all—ten visits in twenty-four months—a lunch here, a milk shake there. "She wasn't getting anything," Webster said, "he was not a person of any importance at all." Moreover, Bentley had been educated in the Romance languages; how could she possibly understand the information she received? "To me it's incredible. It would be grotesque to hold [Remington] guilty of the highest form of crime on her testimony. . . ."

Remington was guilty only of inexperience and naivete, Webster argued. Twenty-four years old and new to government, he was seduced by what he thought were newspapermen. Flattered, he had tried to publicize his agency's programs, totally unaware that the sociable woman sitting next to him on a park bench was a spy.

And all this had occurred so long ago. As the chairman himself has noted, "under the Executive Order this panel must determine present disloyalty." Remington's present record shows him to be completely loyal. "It would be a very sad day for our country," Webster concluded, "if a man could be discharged and run out of office, disgraced for life, on any such flimsy record as we have got here. . . . I submit that it is this Board's duty to restore him to the position [he] held before this decision was made in September. Now, until one of my colleagues kicks me, I think I have said everything."

Turning to the usually outspoken Joseph Rauh, Richardson asked, "Are you going to remain silent?"

"I could never have made a statement as eloquent as Mr. Webster has made," Rauh said, "and I am delighted. . . . " At 12:30 P.M., less than three hours after it began, the hearing was over.[33]

Discouragement is what Remington felt, not delight. He was, of course, very proud of his lawyers but did not think vindication was inevitable. What if he were again found disloyal? How could he earn a living? No one would hire an economist suspected of espionage. Jane Shepherd's survey firm had given him a little work to do, canvassing neighborhoods and handing out a new brand of household cleanser, then later returning to ask housewives what they thought of it. The work was not so bad—perhaps there was even a future here. Construction was also a possibility. He had done a good deal of the work on his own house in Tauxemont and was still an able carpenter; when the Calfee's six-year-old son would no longer sit at the dinner table in a baby chair, Remington built him a new one. Seeing the child's obvious pleasure made him miss his own children all the more, and his depression deepened. Not even Webster's eloquence and Rauh's optimism could dispel it.[34]

Also unhappy about recent events was Republican senator Homer Ferguson, who had invested his prestige in Elizabeth Bentley and was now disappointed in her refusal to testify before the Board. Although its procedures were secret, Rauh made certain that the press was aware of these developments. MISS BENTLEY ABSENT AT REMINGTON HEARING read one headline in the liberal *New York Post*. For Ferguson, this was disturbing news. The senator feared that her absence would lead to Remington's clearance, victory in the libel suit, and the destruction of Bentley's credibility. So, in late November, he ordered his counsel, William Rogers, to confer with Richardson to see if some way could be found to force Bentley to testify.

The chairman told Rogers on November 29 that he would be willing to reopen the hearing but would not do so unless Bentley agreed definitely to appear. Perhaps her attorney, Raoul Desvernine, could persuade her. Rogers offered to act as a mediator between the Board and Bentley and phoned Desvernine the next morning. Richardson, Rogers told Desvernine, was disappointed that Bentley had not testified; could he produce her? Desvernine, a prominent Catholic who had agreed to act temporarily as Bentley's attorney at the request of Monseigneur Sheen, was reluctant to intervene. He thought the hearing was over and, besides, had never heard of Bill Rogers. Was this call some kind of a hoax perpetrated by Remington's attorneys? If Richardson wanted to talk to him, Desvernine asked, why didn't he call? Rogers apologized and assured him that he would have Richardson contact him.[35]

Desvernine and Richardson finally talked on November 30. The result was an agreement similar to that offered by Rauh in October: if Bentley appeared, her testimony would be privileged—nothing she said would be considered legally defamatory; nor would Rauh attempt to serve her with the complaint for twenty-four hours before, during, or after the hearing.[36]

Richardson telephoned Rauh on December 1, informing him of his discussions with Desvernine. After conferring with Webster, Rauh agreed to the conditions. Richardson was pleased. He felt certain that Bentley would approve the deal and set December 15 as the date for the hearing. Later that day, he spoke with Desvernine and Bentley, and the negotiations were successfully concluded.[37]

Or so Richardson thought until December 13, when he received a telegram from Desvernine: . . . MISS BENTLEY WILL BE IN NEW ORLEANS FROM 14th THROUGH 18th. THEREFORE IMPOSSIBLE ATTEND 15th.[38]

Once again, the calls went out—Richardson to Rauh: "It's off. Miss Bentley will not appear"; Rauh to Webster and Green: " . . . Bentley is stalling. Serving her won't hurt down there, if [Green] can find her. . . . "

He almost did, on December 15. With the help of two private detectives, Green discovered that Bentley had taken refuge at the Susan Devin Residence, a Catholic retreat in the Bronx. At a little past noon, Green and *New York Post* reporter Ted Poston were admitted by a maid but were informed that Bentley had already departed for New Orleans. Green was confident that Bentley would eventually be returning, because she had left something important behind: a handsome Turkish Angora cat he had spied on the premises, which looked remarkably like the animal he last saw sitting on Bentley's lap in a *World-Telegram* photograph. "We were in the right church," he told Rauh, "but we got there too late for Mass."[39]

Green tried the Susan Devin house again on Wednesday morning, December 29. Again, he was told that Bentley was not there. This time Green waited, and shortly after noon, the "blond Spy Queen" appeared—a stocky brunette who was surprised to see him.

"I would have been glad to accept service," she told Green.

He informed her that he had filed the papers on October 7 and had written to her in care of the U.S. Attorney's Office.

"I was too busy to answer it then," Bentley said. (A month earlier, when asked if she were evading Green's summons, she had told reporters, "I didn't even know Remington was looking for me until I saw it in the newspaper accounts.") Later that day, Green issued a statement to the press:

After a twelve weeks' chase we have finally caught up with Miss Bentley. . . . [She] must now prove her charges in a court of law. We hope that after the months of delay . . . Miss Bentley will now face the issue squarely and either back up her charges against Mr. Remington or retract them and clear his good name.

When reporters learned her whereabouts and called for a statement, she refused to comment. With Bentley served, her lawyers had twenty days to respond, which they undoubtedly would do with a motion to dismiss Remington's complaint on grounds of legal insufficiency. Green would file a countermotion and prepare answering briefs; it would be up to a federal judge to decide if the case should be dismissed or go to trial. All in all, December 29 had been a good day for Richard Green. He found the right church and was in time for the Mass.[40]

1949 began badly for Seth Richardson. On January 5, he was told by Raoul Desvernine that Bentley again was refusing to appear, and the next day, she dealt the chairman another embarrassing blow. In an interview for a New York paper, Bentley claimed that she had never been invited to testify before the Loyalty Review Board and did not even know that Remington had appealed the lower board's decision. This story caught Dick Green's eye, and he immediately sensed the opportunity for some major mischief. Have *New York Post* writer Jimmy Wechsler call Richardson for his reaction to Bentley's latest outrage, he suggested to Rauh. Rauh loved the idea and telephoned Wechsler to plot strategy. The reporter called Bentley first, and she not only confirmed the earlier story but embellished it. Now she stated that she had never conferred with any of the Board's members; how could she, she told Wechsler, "I don't even know who they are." Hardly able to contain himself, Wechsler telephoned Richardson and read him Bentley's remarks. She is "a liar!" Richardson yelled. "There is not the slightest truth in her statement. I have talked with her, myself. She agreed to come down here on two occasions and after the date was set she claimed to have previous engagements. . . . I have also communicated repeatedly with [her] attorneys. . . . I would still like very much to have her testify, . . . but we're going to decide this case in a week or ten days without her if she doesn't appear."[41] Wechsler wrote the story for the *Post*, which published it on January 10 under the headline, EX-SPY "QUEEN" DODGES QUIZ, SAYS REMINGTON APPEAL PANEL. Review Board member George Alger, also contacted by Wechsler, said that Richardson's account was entirely correct. SECOND LOYALTY REVIEWER SAYS SPY "QUEEN" LIED, led Wechsler's story on January 11, in which he detailed the Board's several attempts to bring Bentley to Washington.[42]

Angered over the delay in the Remington case, George Alger wrote Richardson: "It seems to me that we have waited as long as we can decently can trying to get this woman to appear. She is obviously insufficiently converted and seems to be a constitutional liar. . . . I feel that Remington has a real grievance that we have taken so long to dispose of this case. . . . " Richardson had continued the postponement because he had heard from several people (he did not

identify them) who promised to produce Bentley. Now he gave Bentley a specific deadline. If she did not appear by January 27, the Board would decide the case
without her. "I . . . feel it necessary to hear her," he wrote Alger in late January.
" . . . I do not think it wise to neglect any opportunity to have Miss Bentley
testify."[43]

This time, Bentley almost appeared because of pressure from Senator
Ferguson. On January 19 and 20, while most of official Washington was preparing to celebrate (or merely tolerate) the inauguration of Harry S Truman, the
senator frantically telephoned Bentley, but she refused to take his calls.
Ferguson also contacted her attorney, warning of the dire consequences if
Bentley did not testify: Remington would be found loyal and returned to government; the libel suit would undoubtedly be won; and, above all, no one would
believe anything she had said. As she often did in moments of stress, Bentley
looked to the FBI for comfort and advice. On inauguration night, she contacted
Joseph Kelly, a fellow Catholic and her favorite special agent in the New York
office. What should she do?

It was up to her, Kelly said, giving her the standard Bureau response. Bentley
chose not to appear.[44]

It was too late. By this time, the Board had unanimously decided to clear
Remington. The Memorandum of Decision was signed on January 27, 1949, but
could have been executed weeks before if Richardson had not waited so long for
Bentley to make up her mind. As early as December 1, George Alger had submitted a five-page opinion finding no reason for concluding that Remington is
or was disloyal. Richardson had also drafted a memo on December 13 (two days
before Bentley was supposed to appear), stating that he agreed with Alger.
Colmery's report had arrived last, on January 18, not because he disagreed with
his colleagues, but because of the delay caused by Bentley and Richardson. If a
majority of the Board had already reached a decision, why did Richardson go to
such lengths to hear her? In part, out of fairness to Bentley, who he felt had
been tried in absentia, and to Remington, whose attorneys desperately wanted to
cross-examine her. But politics also played a very important role. Since
Ferguson and other senators were constantly attacking Richardson for being soft
on Communists in government, the chairman felt it essential to placate them, at
almost any cost. "I don't want to get into controversy with a Congressional
Committee," he told a private meeting of the Loyalty Review Board on
September 30, 1948. "They have means to shoot us full of holes. . . . If, in the
Remington Case, we should . . . disagree with the Regional Board, and didn't call
Miss Bentley, then the arrows would fly. . . . [They would charge] we left out the
most important witness against Remington. . . . " To protect himself from
Ferguson's wrath, Richardson allowed Bentley to obstruct a final resolution of
the case, creating an unnecessary and time-consuming delay, which further
injured Remington.[45]

Nevertheless, it is a tribute to Richardson and his colleagues that they decided the case on its merits. The President's Executive Order required that the Board "must determine whether or not Remington is now—in the reasonably present period of time—disloyal," Harry Colmery noted. Therefore, Remington's activities while at Dartmouth and with TVA (which the lower board found sinister) occurred too distant in time to be relevant. But even if Remington was radical, the members found nothing subversive about it: "that was his right as a free, American citizen," Colmery insisted. " . . . So long as he followed the orderly democratic processes of discussion, reason and persuasion, and did not resort to nor advocate the use of force, or violence, or any unconstitutional means, to bring about . . . change, there would be no evidence of disloyalty."[46] Seth Richardson knew personally how it felt to be stigmatized by what strangers thought was a youthful indiscretion. While studying law at the University of Wisconsin in 1902, he had become a follower of Progressive governor Robert La Follette; twenty-eight years later his nomination to become assistant U.S. attorney general was held up because his prospective boss, Attorney General William D. Mitchell, thought Richardson was a Communist. He was eventually confirmed by the Senate, but he never forgot the incident. In 1948, as chairman of the Loyalty Review Board, he insisted that " . . . it would be unfair for our board to bind a man forever by what he did as a youth."[47]

The most serious charge against Remington was that he was a spy who gave secrets to Bentley. While the lower board consistently believed Bentley's story, Richardson and the others did not. " . . . The record here is the uncorroborated statement of a woman who refuses to submit herself to cross-examination," George Alger wrote in his opinion, " . . . a self-confessed spy as against a young man whose every action in public employment showed a distinct anti-Communist slant." To give information to a Communist today might surely be evidence of disloyalty, the members thought, but not during World War II, when America and Russia were allies. "Our government's attitude toward Russia in 1942 was such that giving the Russians information with respect to the progress of our war effort wouldn't necessarily spell disloyalty," Richardson argued. "We were certainly promising them as hard as we could that we were getting ready for a western front. . . . " "Russia was on our side," Colmery also noted. "We were in the process of encouraging her, and doing everything we could to keep her in the war, . . . to obtain with her a common victory. It was no more wrong under those circumstances to associate with a Russian or . . . to give [them] public information—than to have done either with or to, a Frenchman, or an Englishman or any other ally of the United States."[48]

If ever there was an example of a lower board committing procedural errors, the regional board's handling of the Remington case was certainly it. First, that board ignored the Executive Order's requirement that present disloyalty should be the only consideration. Second, it rejected all the views of those who submitted affidavits or testified for Remington. And third, the Maurer panel was guilty of what George Alger called "extreme and entirely questionable" thinking. "The whole report," he said, "is one of assumption based on unsupported suspicion."[49]

The Loyalty Review Board's conclusion was unanimous—there were no reasonable grounds to believe that Remington was disloyal. Richardson, while agreeing with the others, was the least enthusiastic. "I think that Remington knew he had no business to give out information," he told his colleagues. "I do not believe his story that he was doing it as part of his official permissive duty. I think the whole affair was . . . off-color. . . . However, . . . he was very young and immature, the times were different, and his work since has been above criticism." He therefore joined his associates in signing the Memorandum of Decision.[50]

Remington received the good news late on the afternoon of February 10. Rauh called and asked him to come immediately to the office; a clerk at the regional board office had notified him that a decision had just been delivered by special messenger, and Rauh had sent an associate to pick it up and telephone him. By the time Remington arrived, he found Rauh, and the office staff, waiting nervously for the phone to ring. Twenty minutes later, it did. Rauh listened and the room fell silent; then he smiled broadly. "New Year's eve broke out," Remington later observed. While his supporters cheered, Remington showed no emotion. "I sat down at a phone, just as I'd done when my kids were born and called a list of people that I'd prepared in advance—my parents, Blaisdell, the Calfees. . . . I've never been able to describe how I felt."

Rauh recommended that a press conference be held to announce Remington's vindication, so calls went out to reporters and a room was reserved at the Washington Hotel. Shortly after 5:00 P.M., Remington and his lawyers greeted representatives from the New York Times, the New York Herald-Tribune, and several Washington newspapers. Rauh read Richardson's letter, which said only that a panel of the Loyalty Review Board, after hearing testimony and considering the record, concluded that the finding of the Fourth Region Loyalty Board "was not supported by the evidence in the case and that their decision should not be sustained." The group from the office, now joined by Rauh's wife and Jane Shepherd, applauded, and Remington, this night, posed happily for photographers. To the press, Bill said simply that "he owed his clearance to the vigor of democracy" and the brilliance of two men—Joe Rauh and Bethuel Webster.

What effect would the Board's ruling have on the hundred thousand dollar libel suit? asked the Sunday Star's Miriam Ottenberg.

Three distinguished lawyers—Seth Richardson, Harry Colmery, and George Alger—have cleared Bill Remington, Rauh declared. "This decision demonstrates that Miss Bentley's charges . . . are false and libelous. Now that we have finally served her with papers, we have no doubt we can satisfy any court. . . . "

What would Remington do next, now that he was a loyal American again, someone asked.

Smiling, Remington said, "Tomorrow morning, I am reporting for work."[51]

10

A Marked Man

There was a new secretary in the anteroom, and his African violet was missing. These were the first two differences Remington noticed when he returned to the Office of International Trade on February 12.

"Where am I supposed to sit?" he asked the woman.

"That's still your office," she said. "We've been saving it for you." The plant would be returned, too—a colleague had been caring for it during his absence. "I was intensely eager to get it back," he later said. "I wanted to have a feeling of familiarity with my surroundings again."

At first, everything did seem familiar. His fellow employees welcomed him back and said that they were happy to see him again. One asked if he ever felt like Sacco and Vanzetti?

"No," Remington said, "The Count of Monte Cristo." Francis McIntyre, his supervisor, greeted him warmly and then took him to his first staff meeting in eight months. At day's end, he visited the accounting office, where he collected almost six thousand dollars in back pay; it vanished almost immediately—some went to his lawyer; the rest, to his mother, who had given him her life savings when he so desperately needed it.[1]

This pleasant homecoming did not last long. First to comment were his critics. His clearance was "a mistake," said Arkansas senator John McClellan. "It was pretty well established by Remington's own testimony that . . . he was careless and indiscreet. There is very strong evidence that he made a valuable contribution of information to a Communist who was passing on that information through spy channels to the Russian Government." New York Senator Irving

Ives, one of his most zealous interrogators on the Ferguson Committee, told the *New York Sun* that he thought Remington was "not qualified by temperament or attitude to occupy a position of responsibility." Elizabeth Bentley heard the news over the phone from her bête noir, the *New York Post*. "I'm sure he is very happy . . . ," she told reporter Walt Harrington.

Did she think the Board's decision would affect the libel suit?

"I haven't the slightest idea. . . . I would repeat my testimony against him if called upon again. You could hardly expect me to change it. Call my lawyer," she said, then hung up. "Mazel Tov!" Harrington wrote in a short memo to Jimmy Wechsler.[2]

The continuing publicity soon affected Remington's status at the Commerce Department. Immediately following his return, he still retained his old title as director of the Export Program staff, but within a few weeks, he was detailed to work on less important domestic issues. And to prove that the change was not just symbolic, Remington was physically moved to a shabby office on Constitution Avenue. To brighten his room, he brought along his African violet.[3]

Remington's troubles were shared by his mentor, Thomas Blaisdell. Since late May 1948, he had been serving as acting assistant secretary of commerce, and now, in March 1949, he was nominated to assume the position permanently. Before this could occur, he had to win the support of the Senate's Committee on Interstate and Foreign Commerce, which forced him to testify about his relationship with the controversial Remington. The committee was interested specifically in a conversation the two men had before Remington was appointed to his new post in 1948. Blaisdell, according to his later recollection, had asked Remington if there were any potential loyalty problems. Remington had said no, but Blaisdell should know that at his mother-in-law's request he had talked a number of times with a newspaperwoman but, not caring much for this relationship, had broken it off. "If you tell me that relationship was broken off, and there is nothing more, that is all I want to know," Blaisdell had replied. "Your work is good enough for me." Remington remembered the conversation differently. He claimed that he had told Blaisdell that the woman was a dangerous Communist and that he had been interviewed about their meetings by both the FBI and a grand jury. Blaisdell maintained that Remington had said nothing about the FBI and the grand jury. Their different recollections now threatened Blaisdell's nomination.[4]

Republican senators considering Blaisdell used the conflict in two ways: to re-open the Remington case and to embarrass Blaisdell (and the President) for first having placed Remington in an important position without adequately checking his background and then—worse—having returned to government someone they thought disloyal. Despite stiff Republican questioning, and more attacks on Remington, on April 13, 1949, the Senate unanimously confirmed

Thomas Blaisdell as assistant secretary of commerce.[5] "We have passed another hurdle," Rauh wrote Dick Green the next day, "and I should think Bill would be left alone for a while."[6]

For a while he was. In the months following his clearance, he received over one hundred congratulatory letters and telegrams, including one from a clergyman who wrote, "I feel that some priest of the church which Miss Bentley has joined with so much publicity should tell you that we are not a monolithic crowd of admirers of this lady."[7] And while the *New York Post*, *The Nation*, and *The New Republic* were generally supportive, the most sympathetic treatment of the Remington case appeared not in the leftist journals but in the sedate pages of the nation's most distinguished literary magazine, *The New Yorker*.

In March of 1949, Dick Green learned that journalist Daniel Lang was considering a profile of Remington. Green was receptive—Lang was a respected member of *The New Yorker* staff, known for his liberalism and "sharp *New Yorker* sense of humor." Lang is not interested in saying anything that might hurt Remington, Green told Rauh.[8]

Daniel Lang met Remington for a first interview on March 15, in a small, rented room near Arlington, Virginia, where Bill was now living. Lang observed:

> Remington is handsome enough to be a movie star. He is thirty-one, six feet two, slender, erect, blond and blue-eyed. His manner, however, would probably put a talent scout off. It is intellectual, earnest, and reflective. . . . He told me about his life during the seven months he was publicly suspected of being what amounted to a traitor. Except for two or three flashes of bitterness, he talked about his experience with relative detachment.

They met on two other occasions, and Lang also spent time with Dick Green and Joe Rauh and was given access to the records Remington submitted to the Loyalty Review Board.[9]

Six weeks later, the article was finished. The lawyers and Remington were given a chance to examine it prior to publication, and when Bill found parts that worried him, Lang removed them. Titled "The Days of Suspicion," Lang's piece is a powerful exposé of how the Loyalty Program crippled an able civil-servant's career. Although eventually cleared, Lang's Remington is a broken man. "Sometimes, I wish an FBI agent were assigned to watch me twenty-four hours a day," Lang quoted Remington at the end.[10]

Since "The Days of Suspicion" was a profile based on interviews with Remington and his lawyers, readers learned only about that part of Remington's life that he wanted revealed. Lang did not venture far from his major sources or the records they gave him. For example, Lang knew about Remington's radical record at Dartmouth and his role in the YCL from former member Walter Bernstein, now a fellow contributor to *The New Yorker*, but he devoted only three sentences to these years and chose to quote President Hopkins's statement that Remington was "mentally and morally incapable of the machinations and hypocrisies ascribed to him." Remington apparently told Lang that he had graduated first in his class—or Lang possibly picked this up elsewhere and Remington did not correct him—since that designation found its way into the article; actually, Remington ranked thirty-fourth.[11] Also, Lang barely mentioned Remington's activities while with TVA.

There are other more serious omissions in the article: that Remington had been under government scrutiny since 1940; that the FBI had questioned him in April 1947 about his possible involvement in Soviet espionage; that he had been called before a grand jury investigating that crime and that to protect himself he had become an active FBI informant accusing friends and strangers of pro-Communism and disloyalty. Nor did he tell Lang that after bravely challenging Bentley's testimony by suing her for libel, he had secretly met with the FBI to arrange a retraction in exchange for dropping the suit. Finally, he lied when he said to Lang, "I'd never known Bentley was [a Communist]." Content to rely on the information supplied by his subject, Lang produced an inaccurate account that omitted most of Remington's past.[12]

No doubt, this is why the article gave Remington such pleasure when he read an advance copy. "My gratitude to you is quite without bounds," he wrote Lang on May 19. " . . . For months, I have had reservations at the seashore so I could rush off the day the article appeared to bury my head for a while. When I saw the proof, I postponed my trip, and today I cancelled it with undiluted pleasure." Rauh was also very happy. "I see from the finished piece that you are not only a terrific writer but a kind-hearted soul," he told Lang. " . . . I noticed most of the things Bill asked for have been done."[13]

Remington and Rauh were not alone in praising the article. "The Days of Suspicion" was very well received and widely discussed following its publication on May 21, 1949. "A noble masterpiece," Walter Lippmann said; "it should be placed at once in all the anthologies of truly great journalism." From Washington, Eric Sevareid wrote Lang, "I am hearing about the article all over town. I think it will have a serious effect on official thinking here. . . . Can your office send a copy of it to every member of Congress?"[14]

Although Lang pictured Remington as a reluctant crusader, a number of readers found him a heroic figure. "I was heartened to learn that this nation has such courageous men as Remington," said Louis Baily of San Antonio, Texas; while Joseph G. Master, of Smithport, Pennsylvania, praised Remington for possessing the "moral stamina to fight on through to freedom."[15]

Hollywood agents were suddenly interested in bringing the Remington story to the screen, but Lang quickly realized that the chances of a film being produced were slim. Alan Jackson, of Paramount, thought Remington's ordeal an "unbelievable witch-hunt with a strange Kafka-esque quality" but doubted whether his studio would "ever touch this subject." Lang's friends in Hollywood explained the problem. "Such a picture would involve taking a political stand for or against something, whether it be Communism, Senate Investigating Committees, Loyalty checks, or even individual federal employees." In a Hollywood recently racked by HUAC's investigation of Communism in the film industry (which sent nine uncooperative writers and directors to jail and resulted in the blacklisting of others), few people were willing to risk their careers pursuing dangerous political crusades. There would be no film about the ordeal of William Remington.[16]

The events that followed Remington's clearance—the demotion, the struggle over the Blaisdell nomination, even Hollywood's refusal to seriously consider his story—were all evidence that he had not yet received the vindication he had hoped for. Perhaps a favorable verdict in the libel suit might end his troubles for good. If only the judge would make up his mind. On March 22, 1949, Green and the lawyers representing NBC and the General Foods Corporation, Alexis Coudert and Walter Barry, had argued their cases before federal judge Edward A. Conger. It was Green's view that Bentley's radio statements had libeled Remington—damaging him professionally and bringing him "into public odium and contempt." For the anguish that resulted, the defendants should be forced to pay a hundred thousand dollars. Coudert and Barry asked the judge to dismiss the complaint for two reasons. First, Bentley's remarks constituted slander, not libel, and, according to existing law, her words were not actionable because they did not fall into any of the accepted legal categories (accusing a person of a crime or having a "loathsome disease"; injuring a person's position "in a trade or profession"; or, when applied to women, "accusing them of unchastity"). And second, Bentley had merely repeated the privileged testimony she gave to the Ferguson Committee, which was protected from civil or criminal prosecution.[17]

In response, Green argued that whether Bentley's words were considered slander or libel they were actionable. "Nothing could be more disparaging of an economist in . . . government . . . than to say that he is a follower of totalitarian economics." Furthermore, if Remington was a Communist, as Bentley charged, he would be guilty of perjury, a crime punishable by a five-year prison term or a two thousand dollar fine or both. He would also be guilty of making false statements knowingly and willfully "in any matter within the jurisdiction of any department or agency of the United States" punishable by a fine of ten thousand dollars or imprisonment up to five years or both. Finally, Remington, the Communist, would also have violated both the Hatch and Smith acts, which forbade government employees from belonging to any party or organization calling for the violent overthrow of the government. Clearly, then, to call Remington a Communist was to accuse him of crimes and do injury to his profession; to Green, this meant that her charges were slanderous *per se*.[18]

Green also rejected the defendants' contention that Bentley's statement on

Meet the Press was privileged. To be considered such under Section 337 of the New York Civil Practice Act, it was required to be "a fair and true report" of the Ferguson Committee's full proceedings, which included Remington's denials that he was a Communist. "What . . . Bentley did," Green noted,

> was to repeat one fraction of what had been said before the Congressional Committee. This is neither a report, nor is it fair and true. . . . To allow the statutory privilege of fair and true report to cover a situation like this one . . . would permit all kinds of irresponsibles to make vicious charges before a legislative committee and then publish them at will with the added words: "That's what I told the Committee." That would not be privilege, it would be a license to defame, which the law does not give.[19]

Thus, the issues were joined—libel or slander; conduct actionable or insufficient to bring a lawsuit; privileged testimony or a fragmentary statement unprotected by congressional immunity. It was now up to Judge Conger to make his way through this legal thicket and decide whether the case should go to trial. Conger listened closely to the lawyers and at the conclusion of their arguments commented that he was inclined to reject the defendants' motion but would reserve decision. This remark did not encourage Remington's lawyers, who were not impressed by the judge. He was a Catholic, and they feared that he might favor his co-religionist, the recently converted Bentley. Also, he was noted for being slow to act and often avoided making difficult decisions. Still, Green hoped for an early resolution, since, given New York's crowded court calendar, it would probably be two years before the case could go to trial.[20]

There was no early decision. April and May passed without word from the court. Then on June 9, Green received a card from the court clerk, informing him that an order had been entered. Thinking this was Conger's decision, he hurried to Foley Square, only to discover that the order just approved new counsel for Bentley—Godfrey P. Schmidt of New York City had replaced the harried Raoul Desvernine. Green called Schmidt's office and talked about the case with an associate named Joseph Egan. Egan asked what he and Rauh would do about Bentley if NBC and General Foods should decide to settle out of court.

That was up to her, Green replied; "if we worked out a settlement, we would be willing to [deal] with all the defendants but that if she wanted a scrap, then we would simply slug it out with her alone; . . . If we went to bat, she was going to get hurt."

Egan fenced a little with Green. He doubted that they had anything derogatory on Bentley and asked how Remington's wife was, a sign that he knew of the continuing problems with Ann. "It would look very bad for Bill if he were to lose the libel suit after having been cleared by the Loyalty Review Board," Egan also said.

"We have no concern about this," Green countered; all he wondered was how large Remington's award would be.

All in all, Egan was a nasty piece of work, Green later told Rauh; "He talks like a member of the Un-American Activities Committee, or its Counsel."[21]

Egan was wrong. Rauh and Green had uncovered a good deal of new, derogatory information about Elizabeth Bentley. From two journalists who offered their help, they learned first about Bentley's problem with alcohol. Dr. Herbert Mann, house physician at the St. George Hotel, where Bentley had lived for several years after 1945, reported treating her regularly for what she called aches and pains. Mann's examination revealed nothing organic; the problems, he thought, were caused by severe hangovers. Bentley was a neurotic, who was drinking heavily in her room and at local bars. This corroborated the public testimony of two men, also accused by Bentley of being members of her spy group. Robert T. Miller had told the House Un-American Activities Committee in 1948 that when he knew Bentley during the war, she suffered from nervous tension and drank excessively. Duncan C. Lee had told a similar story. Her behavior eventually became so obnoxious that, when Lee informed her that he and his wife no longer wished to see her, Bentley reacted violently. Equally important was what the lawyers found out about Bentley's adventures in Italy in 1934–35. Private detective Frank Bielaski tracked down Joseph Lombardo, now a professor at Queens College, and he described Bentley's arrests, her sexual high jinks, the attempted suicide, the phony master's thesis, and her fascist activities. Most of this could also be supported by Columbia professor Giuseppe Prezzolini. He was ready to testify that he thought her thesis had been written by Mario Casella, her faculty advisor and lover. Rauh thought the new material was terrific.[22]

He tried to use it first at a pre-trial hearing on September 7. Did anyone help her write her master's thesis? Rauh asked Bentley.

No, she wrote it herself.

Did she ever know a man named Mario Casella?

"His name is very familiar," Bentley said, "but I can't place it."

Had she ever been expelled from the university?

"OBJECTION!" yelled Schmidt, before Bentley could answer.

Had she ever been suspended?

"Same objection," Schmidt said.

"Did Dr. Joseph Lombardo help you obtain reinstatement in the University of Florence?"

"Same objection."

"Did you take poison in Florence?"

"Same objection." And so it went for most of the day.[23]

"She is a pretty smooth lady," Rauh wrote of Bentley, after their first confrontation. "She can be pleasant and agreeable when she wants to and can lie without the slightest facial change. She is a worthy opponent . . . but I have the feeling that she is also deep down a very reckless liar who some day is going to destroy herself. . . . " It did not occur to Rauh that one could possibly say the same about his own client.[24]

The other woman in Remington's life was also causing him problems, which Rauh feared might affect the outcome of the lawsuit. That summer, Ann Remington filed for divorce, charging Bill with adultery. " . . . So far (knock on wood) there has been no publicity," Rauh told Green after learning of the action. "It can't get to trial for a long time, so if the complaint gets by without publicity we may be all right for some time." Green was less concerned and more militant. "I refuse to get upset . . . publicity or no. . . . This is New York City, and while divorce may be shocking to Catholics, you still can't call people Communists and traitors and get away with it just because they sleep with people other than their wives."[25]

Their client was both nervous and combative. He did not want this kind of lawsuit, he told a close friend, just at the moment when he was trying to rebuild his reputation, but if Ann wanted a fight, she would get one. It was just like her to attack him when he was so vulnerable.[26]

The separation had been as tumultuous as their marriage. One day, in 1947, Ann suddenly appeared at his parents' house in Ridgewood, bearing almost all of Bill's personal possessions. Fred and Lillian listened in horror as Ann described Bill's "extreme cruelty," "violent neurosis," "illicit love affairs" (she went back as far as Bill's adolescent relationship with Helen Martin), and "psychopathic deceitfulness." She was also cruel to the children, according to Bill. Once "she knocked Gale off a new Christmas tricycle so violently that the girl was thrown entirely across the living room." Ann's friend Alicia Lehman once told him that she had said to Ann, " . . . there must be a special place in Hell for mothers like you."[27]

Finally, there had occurred perhaps the most terrible event in their married life. On Sunday, June 8, 1947, Bill later recounted:

> I was preparing to leave the Tauxemont House where I had spent the day with the children. I had put both to bed, and shortly thereafter [five year old] Bruce began calling to me in his sleep not to go back to my room in Washington but to stay with him. I could not quiet him, and [Ann] was urging me every few minutes to go away and stop bothering the boy (which I was not doing). Finally, I called for her to come into his bedroom to quiet him while I departed. She came in the door say-ing something like this: "Shut up you damned little brat." As she got over to his bed she actually snarled at him, "Shut up, or I'll hit you!" She raised her hand, as if to strike, and I shouted, "Don't!" and slapped her a glancing blow with the flat of my hand that was aimed at her shoulder and hit the back of her head. The blow was strong enough to knock her down. She began to swear at me. I pulled her into the hall . . . and slapped her three or four more times with my open hand to avoid injuring her. After I stopped she called to [Bruce] to come protect her. When he appeared she told him to go back to bed, but I asked him to stay as a witness while I

apologized before she went over to a neighbor's house to complain about my conduct. Alicia Lehman told Jane Shepherd shortly after the incident that she thought my wife had been trying for a long time to provoke me into striking her.

Ann claimed that the attack was completely unprovoked. No act in his life caused Remington so much anguish. "He was filled with despair afterwards," Jane later recalled. "He had simply been driven nearly desperate with anxiety about the children. And, of course, he was severely conflicted by his own desire to stay and protect the children from Ann's influence and his own need to leave the situation." Despite this tragedy, he had again proposed reconciliation in August, and again she had refused.[28]

Ann seemed bent on Bill's destruction. Alicia Lehman recalled her saying that she wanted to ruin him. Her attorney, Carl Berueffy, remembered Ann telling him that she could always "fix Remington by saying that he had been a Communist."

Was it true? he asked.

"Oh, no," she said, "but I could always say that he had been one." She asked the attorney to hire a private detective to document Bill's affair with Jane Shepherd, a relationship she had initially encouraged but soon opposed. "She was nuts," Berueffy later said. Her "only motive [was] pure hostility—toward her mother, children, and Bill."[29]

Eventually, Ann met with Berueffy in May 1949 to draft a divorce complaint. Ann told him that Bill had come to her two years before to announce that he was in love with another woman, and then, later, he had moved out. Sometimes, he would return home to visit the children, and on one April night—she claimed—they made love at her request and in the hope that the marriage could be saved. But the effort failed, and her husband left again, returning now and then just to see the children. In June of 1947, she said, he had beaten her for no reason at all. Ann also charged that her husband was guilty of adultery with a woman she knew and that she had done nothing to further that relationship. Berueffy wrote up the complaint and filed it with the circuit court of Fairfax County, Virginia, on June 1.[30]

Ann's description of the events leading to her divorce differ significantly from Bill's, whose story is corroborated by Jane Shepherd and others, including—at one point—Ann's own statements to a close friend. Nothing was said to Berueffy about her initial support for Bill's relationship with Jane, his several offers of reconciliation, and the circumstances that led to her beating. As for her claim that she purposefully attempted to save the marriage by having sex with Bill in April 1947, she also told an intimate friend that Remington had tried to seduce her to prevent her from going ahead with the divorce. The evidence suggests that Ann probably lied when she swore to a notary public that the information contained in the complaint was true.[31]

With his career hanging in the balance and already facing one lawsuit, Bill decided not to contest the complaint and met with Ann in late June to negotiate the terms of their divorce. He agreed to pay her seventy-five dollars alimony and a hundred fifty dollars toward child support. She also received sole ownership of the house in Tauxemont and their 1940 Plymouth automobile. While retaining custody of the children, she allowed Bill to visit them on an occasional weekend and during their Easter, summer, and Christmas vacations. Bill was, of course, far from happy (the alimony and child support amounted to approximately 36 percent of his monthly income) but considered the settlement satisfactory. "The most important goal," he wrote a friend in July, "avoiding a spectacular and bitter clash which would injure the children most of all—seems to have been achieved." For once, Ann must have thought so, too, because in August, her attorney filed an amended bill of complaint that substituted desertion and abandonment for adultery and made no reference to battery. On December 5, 1949, Judge Paul E. Brown awarded Ann Remington a decree of divorce.[32]

One lawsuit closed, another opened. On that same day, Joe Rauh was notified that Judge Edward A. Conger would finally issue his opinion on December 7. Rauh was pessimistic—he interpreted the delay as meaning that Conger was going to grant Barry's motion and had used the time to write a statement explaining that decision. Yet, surprisingly, they won. In a sixteen-page opinion, Judge Conger dismissed the defendants' motion and ruled that Bentley's charge that Remington was a Communist was slanderous *per se* and cause for action. "I know of no accusation more discreditive of a United States government official with respect to the proper conduct of his office than that he is a Communist . . . ," Conger said. "Officers of our government and the public at large would distrust the honesty, the impartiality and the judgment of an economist in the employ of our government who was known as a Communist. His usefulness as a public servant would be ended." Conger's decision was significant. In a time of national hysteria, when a person's character and career could be destroyed by what Green called "the reckless tossing around of words," the ruling might give pause to anti-Communist demagogues who hurled charges so indiscriminately.[33]

Having finally won this important round, Green was eager to get on with the case. Putting their opponents on public notice that they planned to move ahead to trial, the lawyers next began to arrange for the resumption of Bentley's deposition and the examination of representatives of the network and sponsor. This flurry of activity was designed to provoke NBC into settling the case. Their strategy quickly bore fruit. By December 15, Green and Barry were negotiating. Green demanded ten thousand dollars, but Barry thought that much too high; twenty-five hundred was the usual sum of recovery in libel cases, but he would discuss the figure with his clients. Green held firm, warning him that henceforth the price of settling would climb. Perhaps a settlement was not really possible, Barry countered, trying a new tack; he was impressed by Bentley's story and wanted to try the case. Green thought Barry was probably bluffing and expected him to return with an offer of five thousand dollars—which he would push up to seventy-five hundred. He was confident that a settlement was near.[34]

Barry was not bluffing, and with luck, he might soon be defeating Green at trial. He had received what looked like an important lead in the Remington case and was about to leave town to pursue it. His source was a Knoxville attorney, who had written NBC in October 1948, offering to set up a meeting with a man who had once investigated Remington and could provide proof that he had been a Communist. So, in late December, Barry and Egan flew to Knoxville, where they were introduced to Josephus Remine, former under sheriff of Knox County, the man who had once shadowed Remington as he went about the city on behalf of the CIO and, probably, the local unit of the Communist Party. Remine was old and given to rambling conversation, the lawyers discovered. He described his pursuit of Communists and Remington's association with this "gang." There were many who could corroborate his story, he said: Ruby Cox, Remington's landlady, knew all about it, as did Jesse Reeve, who ran a Communist nudist camp where Remington and his friends ran around naked. And they should not go home without talking to Gay V. Valentine, the lawyer who worked for the mills having labor trouble.[35]

The next day, they met with Valentine in his palatial suite of offices in Knoxville's Empire Building. Valentine also claimed to know people knowledgeable of Remington's activities, and Egan thought he was the best man to supervise their investigation: there were eighteen witnesses to interview and Communist hangouts to photograph. Egan explained that Bentley had no money, and neither did they. He and Schmidt were defending Bentley without charge, as a service to the country. But they could not afford to pay for a full-scale investigation, which would probably cost ten thousand dollars. Egan appealed to Valentine's patriotism, but the lawyer refused his request. Later that afternoon, they returned to New York, their inquest barely begun.[36]

For Walter Barry, more pragmatic than the ideological Egan, the trip to Knoxville led to one conclusion: the case should be settled out of court. The cost of an investigation was prohibitive; his client, the Massachusetts Bonding and Insurance Company, which insured NBC, would never approve it. His assumption was correct—after reporting on the trip and making his recommendation, the insurance company authorized him to enter into settlement. Barry's first call went to Godfrey Schmidt, who was furious about the decision. "We've been double-crossed!" he cried. "We'll never issue a retraction and we'll never pay one penny towards settlement." Barry was sympathetic and just as patriotic as they were, but he had to think about his client's best interests. NBC's Lawrence Spivak was also opposed to the settlement, Schmidt claimed, but Barry ignored their pleas and called Green.[37]

At the end of a long, hard work day on February 7, 1950, Dick Green jotted one brief sentence in his diary: "Phs. w/ Barry and Rauh—OK on $9,000 but no release." It summed up perfectly the compromise reached by the two parties. The insurance company would pay Remington nine thousand dollars, while he and his lawyers would absolve them of any further liability and refrain from publicizing the settlement. Barry wanted a written guarantee, which Green sent him, after conferring with Rauh.[38]

Walter Barry publicly announced the settlement of the lawsuit on February 28 but gave no details. Lawrence Spivak was more forthcoming and a bit nasty. He told the *New York Herald-Tribune* that "We advised against settlement because we did not believe a libel had been committed. It was settled on the basis of the legal expenses involved, and the amount of the settlement indicates that it was based on expediency." Egan and Schmidt were not interviewed. Bentley's chief defender in the press, the *New York World-Telegram*, was the first to report that she had issued no retraction, while other newspapers were more interested that Remington was given only ten thousand dollars (*sic*)—100 G MATA HARI SUIT SETTLED AT 10 C ON A DOLLAR, said the *New York Sun*. As for the primary antagonists, Bentley could not be located and Remington had no comment. (He received his nine thousand dollar payment from the Massachusetts Bonding and Insurance Company on February 22. It "looked like a pretty nice vindication to me," he said later. "It's more money than I ever had." Most of it quickly disappeared. Green's fee amounted to two thousand dollars plus expenses; Rauh divided the rest with Remington, whose final share was thirty-five hundred dollars.)[39]

One of the last to learn of the settlement was Elizabeth Bentley. For the previous few months, she had been teaching at Mundelein College, a Catholic school in Chicago, and had been kept in the dark about recent developments. Schmidt had informed her of the efforts to reach an accord and of Spivak's opposition, but as late as February 27, the day before Barry's announcement, she was still unaware that the suit had been settled. She was so confident that a time-consuming trial was about to commence, she had told the FBI on February 23, that she was resigning from her position at Mundelein, fearing that negative publicity would embarrass the college. (The real reason for her resignation was allegedly moral laxity, according to a later investigation of Bentley's activities in Chicago. She was said to have been "living openly and notoriously with a man not her husband. . . . " When informed of her conduct, the college's president, Sister Mary Josephine, asked to meet with her, and they agreed that it would be best if Bentley left.) Schmidt telephoned her at the Hotel Commodore on the morning of February 28 to report that a settlement had been reached. Shortly afterwards, Bentley contacted Ed Scheidt, special agent in charge of the FBI's New York office. She did not know the precise amount of the settlement, she told Scheidt, but she thought it was five thousand dollars. Scheidt passed the news along to J. Edgar Hoover in a message marked "URGENT."[40]

Remington's victories in 1949–50—clearance by the Loyalty Review Board, *The New Yorker* article, Judge Conger's decision, and the settlement of the libel suit—did little to help him. In late October 1949, his government classification was reduced, without explanation, resulting in a loss of six hundred dollars a year in salary. Bernard Gladieux, Secretary Sawyer's chief assistant, openly called it a demotion and complained when Remington expressed his displeasure. Although the action was probably illegal, Rauh was unable to get him restored to his former rank or salary. Was Sawyer intentionally trying to force Remington to resign? The action and Gladieux's insulting public statements suggest that he was. Remington considered leaving and did a little job hunting but received no offers. With no place to go, he decided to remain in government, despite these humiliations. "Bill keeps talking about getting out of the Government but his job even now pays almost $10,000," Rauh told Green, "and I don't think he is quite ready to jump into the cold and uncertain waters outside. . . . "[41]

Life inside continued to be just as cold and uncertain in 1950. That March, reporter William S. Odlin, Jr., and a *Washington Times-Herald* photographer paid Remington a surprise visit to see how he was faring. They arrived at his office before he did; Odlin looked around while his colleague took pictures of Remington's old wooden desk and water-stained plaster walls. Resting on a window ledge was Remington's African violet. When Remington entered the room, he was startled to find two men waiting for him. Odlin noted Bill's "quick and successful struggle to maintain his composure. . . . " Identifying himself as a reporter, and not an FBI agent, did not cause Remington to relax. When asked about his specific duties, Remington told Odlin to see his superior. He was also unwilling to talk about his old job, Elizabeth Bentley, or the libel suit.

Was he anticipating additional income from other libel suits? Odlin wondered.

"I scan the papers every day, in the hope I'll run into something," Remington laughed. His only concern now, he said, was to remain anonymous.

Such was the fate of this former golden boy of the Truman administration, Odlin concluded, "pigeon-holed in a place where no harm could befall. He's a marked man and he knows it. . . . "[42]

11

No Peace

To the FBI's confidential informant in the Commerce Department (an economist named Acree), it must have been a remarkable moment. There, on the corner of 17th Street and Pennsylvania Avenue was William Remington talking to a mysterious woman. After a while, Remington took from his pocket a piece of paper that he gave to the woman, who then hailed a taxi and drove away. On February 6, 1950, Acree informed the FBI, and the next day Inspector Howard B. Fletcher recommended to Assistant Director D. M. Ladd that the Bureau reopen the Remington investigation. "Yes, do so at once," J. Edgar Hoover ordered; "cover carefully and DISCREETLY." It seemed to the FBI that William Remington was up to his old tricks, the woman obviously another Elizabeth Bentley. Bureau memoranda on Remington were again captioned, SUBJECT: ESPIONAGE. "I wish an FBI agent were assigned to watch me twenty-four hours a day," he had told Daniel Lang in 1949. In 1950, Remington's wish came true.[1]

The FBI moved quickly. On February 10, they interviewed Acree about what he had observed. He did not know the woman Remington was seeing but could give them a good description: about thirty-five years old, sharp features, medium height, medium build. Her hair was brown, cut in a masculine bob, and she wore brown horn-rimmed glasses with unusually thick lenses. She also dressed like the FBI's idea of a Brunette Spy Queen—her body was completely covered by an olive-green Army officer's military coat, belted and with a hood. Special Agent Lambert Zander, assigned to watch Remington, saw her for himself on March 2, when she and Remington entered the Tally-Ho Restaurant for lunch. Afterwards, other agents followed her cab, which dropped her off at the

Department of Agriculture. Another team picked up the surveillance from there, observing as she walked into Room 1429. Later that day, after checking his notes on the woman's appearance with Bureau files, Zander was able to iden-tify her. She was Jane A. Shepherd, Remington's fiancée and currently an employee of the Agriculture Department. Given these results—meetings and lunch with his fiancée, it might have been reasonable to expect the FBI to dis-continue its month-long investigation, but it did not.[2]

Hoover seemed more impatient than usual. "What progress are we making on the re-opening of the Remington Case?" he asked D. M. Ladd in early March.

Not much, Ladd reported; there had been no new developments.

"Press on it," Hoover ordered. Informant Acree had been busy befriending the suspect and told Zander that Remington was a staunch anti-Communist. He also carefully observed Remington's behavior at work—he rarely left the office before quitting time and usually lunched in the cafeteria. Zander wanted to be certain of this, so on March 10, he visited Remington's office, and there he was, hard at work. At noon, he saw Remington eating lunch—in the cafeteria. Zander returned for additional checks on March 13, March 14, and March 16, but Remington's routine remained the same.[3]

Others were also investigating Remington. William Rogers called assistant FBI director Louis Nichols in mid-February to report that he had learned that when Remington lived in Knoxville in 1937, he shared P.O. Box 1692 with lead-ers of the Communist Party. Rogers also had access to the March 1937 applica-tion for use of the box, which bore the signatures of four men: Horace Bryan, Harry (sic) Bridgman, Bernard Borah, and Merwin S. Todd. That the box was for official use was corroborated by Paul Crouch, former head of the Tennessee Communist Party. Remington, Rogers claimed, had listed P.O. Box 1692 as his mailing address when he applied for membership in the American Federation of Government Employees in Knoxville. The FBI checked its own files and found the same information, but agents were told to dig deeper for additional data. A month later, Father John Cronin, the anti-Communist priest who had earlier urged the FBI to force Bentley to cooperate with Seth Richardson's panel, also told the Bureau about Remington and Box 1692; Cronin's source was Donald Appell, an investigator for the House Un-American Activities Committee, who had been examining the Knoxville period to contradict Remington's testimony before the Loyalty Review Board. Cronin thought the Bureau might be interest-ed in this news.[4]

It was. If HUAC should somehow find a new witness and finally prove Remington had been a member of the Communist Party or guilty of espionage, it would be extremely damaging to the reputation of the FBI, which had spent years trying to develop evidence either to drive Remington from government or put him in jail. All members of the FBI, from lowly agents in remote outposts to the top officials in Washington, were familiar with their agency's most sacred commandment: "Thou Shalt Not Embarrass the Bureau." To prevent just this type of embarrassment, the FBI considered launching a loyalty investigation, which would run concurrently with the espionage inquest. But before a final decision was reached, the Bureau received news that made that investigation imperative. On April 4, Louis Nichols learned that the committee had at least one witness who would identify Remington as a Communist "and three others . . . whom they think they can secure to testify." The committee planned to hold hearings in about two weeks, so the FBI had little time to locate these people before they went on congressional display. He recommended that it complete its inquiry before HUAC returned. "Yes, and at once," Hoover wrote on Nichols's memorandum.[5]

On April 14, the FBI received an important tip that enabled it to narrow its search. Louis J. Russell, once an FBI agent and now HUAC's chief investigator, provided the names of those who would soon testify. They were Kenneth C. McConnell; Merwin S. (Pat) Todd and his wife, Elizabeth; and Howard A. Bridgman. McConnell was apparently the star witness, willing to testify that he knew Remington to have been a card-carrying member of the Communist Party while in Knoxville. Locate and interview the witnesses, Hoover telegraphed his troops; "Assign experienced personnel. . . . Handle immediately. . . . Expedite. . . . [The] Bureau cannot stress too strongly [the] urgency of interviews."[6]

Pat Todd was the first to be interviewed. The once fiery activist was now a 38-year-old electrician and the father of two children. His wife, Betty (once married to Kenneth McConnell), had surpassed him professionally. In 1950, she was assistant director of Network Operations for CBS Radio and director of the popular *Arthur Godfrey Show*. When the FBI arrived at their apartment on West 12th Street, they found Todd uncooperative. He did admit that he had briefly lived with Remington thirteen years earlier, and at that time, there was no doubt about his loyalty. When agents asked to see Mrs. Todd, they were informed that she did not wish to speak with them. The next day, the Todds were ordered to appear before HUAC on April 21.[7]

The FBI found Howard Bridgman in Medford, Massachusetts, where he was teaching economics at Tufts University. Agents Frederick M. Connors and Brenton S. Gordon interviewed him first on the evening of April 17. Bridgman was willing to talk but refused to sign a statement or appear before a loyalty board. "I did not want . . . this thing [to] come out," he said later. He told Connors and Gordon that he first came to Knoxville in 1936 and soon became part of a group of progressive young men and women. He discovered that a Communist Party branch was being organized and joined in December 1936, although he filled out no application, took no oath, and received no membership card or book. At first, the group consisted of only three other members: Pat Todd (his recruiter), Bill Remington, and a woman whose name he could not recall—it might have been Kit Buckles or her friend Christine Eversole or a Mrs. McLaughlin (he did not tell the agents that he had "grasped at the name McLaughlin but knew that wasn't right"). He most definitely remembered Remington—at work he was an enfant terrible, telling everyone what was wrong with the messenger service and then proposing how to improve it; in Party meetings, he was an active participant. The professor also informed the agents that he had left the Party in 1939 and was now a conservative.[8]

Agents Connors and Gordon returned to the Bridgman home on April 19, 21, and 22. By the time the last interview was completed, Bridgman had supplied most of the names of those, he claimed, who were members of the CP branch. He also agreed to testify before a loyalty board and permitted Agent Connors to draft a statement that described Remington as a Communist Party member in 1936 and 1937. Bridgman volunteered to type up the statement and then signed it.[9] The Bureau must have been pleased. Now they, too, had a witness who claimed that Remington was a Communist Party member, and he was on record a week before HUAC was scheduled to hear his testimony. They did not know that during the course of the four-day interview, Bridgman had committed an error so serious that it would later shake his faith in his ability to remember correctly both his own past and Remington's.

The FBI finally caught up with the last witness—Kenneth McConnell—on the evening of April 19, the night before he was to testify before HUAC. According to one confidential informant, McConnell was an alcoholic, so officials decided that only experienced agents should interview him and that everything should be handled carefully to avoid any later embarrassment to the Bureau. Veteran agents Julius S. Matson and Albert Solomon were selected to interview McConnell, a tall, outgoing man of fifty-two with bright blue eyes and a red mustache. He was friendly but also very reluctant to talk with them. He was under subpoena from the House Un-American Activities Committee, he loudly proclaimed; he had been brought to the Capital by HUAC and felt that he had a contractual obligation to give information only to the committee. The agents worked on him gently, until McConnell agreed to talk, but his story must have been a great disappointment.

Remington was a member of the Communist Party in Knoxville, McConnell claimed, but since he had no concrete evidence to support that assertion and was afraid of being sued for libel, he would not confess that to the committee. Furthermore, his contacts with Remington were limited to only two occasions in June 1937: a meeting that was either exclusively Communist or open to non-Communists, too (McConnell could not remember whether it was one or the other); and some other time when McConnell felt he had to criticize Remington's sloppy appearance, which he thought inappropriate for a Communist Party organizer. These incidents convinced McConnell that Remington was definitely a Communist and under Party control. That was all

McConnell could tell them. Matson and Solomon probably left the meeting feeling bewildered—this was HUAC's star witness?[10]

HUAC chairman John S. Wood must have wondered, too, after spending an hour with McConnell in executive session the next morning.

"What occupations have you followed in the past?" asked Chief Investigator Louis Russell, at the outset of the hearing.

"I am a seaman, and probably one of the finest jumping-horse trainers in America, and I want that on the record," McConnell said. " . . . I have got a three-year-old filly, Your Honor; . . . If I had the time and the patience which it requires to finish a jumping filly, I will bet you that I could make her the best jumper in the South. . . . "

"I will talk to you some more about that after the hearing," interjected Chairman Wood, no doubt hoping to regain control of the session.

"Have you ever been a member of the Communist Party?" asked Russell.

I have, McConnell said, and proceeded to describe his years as a Party organizer in Virginia, North Carolina, and Tennessee from 1935 to 1939.

Do you know if William Remington was a member of the Communist Party in Knoxville? asked committee investigator Donald T. Appell.

Although McConnell had told the FBI that he would not answer this question directly, he replied, "I do."

"Did you ever see William Remington's Communist Party card?"

"To my knowledge I cannot answer that other than by saying 'No.'"

"Did you ever discuss with William Remington the operations or actions which he should take as a member of the Communist Party?"

"That is a leading question," McConnell said, "and I can answer it in this wise, if this will satisfy you. I found it necessary . . . to call attention to the fact that his demeanor and behavior were uncommunistic."

Chairman Wood was confused. Is that what you meant when you said you discussed with Remington Communist Party activities?

The witness remained in a fog. "That is right. This is a psychic thing. Only a psychoanalyst can go into this for you. I will give you facts."

Did you ever see Remington at a meeting restricted to Party members?

"I can only answer that question equivocally," McConnell replied. He could remember just one Party meeting when Remington was present, and it might have included non-Communist union organizers as well as Communists. And he was not certain where the group met; first, he said Chattanooga, then Knoxville after Appell pointed out his error.

Did you ever discuss with Remington his return to Dartmouth?

Was it Dartmouth or Harvard? McConnell wondered aloud. Whatever, Remington's future was discussed. It was my ex-wife, Elizabeth, who urged Remington to return to school. We could only advise Remington, he said, because in 1937 he was under minimum Party discipline.[11]

McConnell's erratic testimony may be explained by a personal history that was marked by alcoholism and criminality. "I was the fledgling bird . . . who fell out of the nest and wandered off," he once said. The nest was Hicksville, Long Island, where he was born in 1898. Like a character in a Jack London novel, he left school at fourteen and ran off to sea. He fought in World War I (or claimed to have done so) and returned home to live a vagabond's life. In 1924, he embezzled seven hundred dollars from his employer and fled to California. He settled in Berkeley, where, in 1925, he was arrested for attempting to extort money from prominent homosexuals. His jail time was brief—the victims declined to press charges, and the city did not prosecute. During the decade that followed, he said he was a cow-puncher, a newspaper writer, a common laborer, and a cook. He also became a husband and father. In 1930, he married 22-year-old Elizabeth (Betty) Winston, and the next year they moved to Chapel Hill, North Carolina, where their son Jacob was born in 1932.

While Betty worked as a secretary, Ken's major preoccupations were radical politics and alcohol. He joined the Communist Party in 1935 and worked as an organizer in Norfolk, Chattanooga, and Chapel Hill; these activities did not stop him from drinking, however, because he was arrested frequently for public intoxication and disorderly conduct. The Malcolms (as they were known in Communist circles) arrived in Knoxville in mid-June 1937, Betty to work with TVA, Ken to work for the Party. A few months later, he drifted away, leaving behind his child and wife, who fell in love with Pat Todd. They divorced in October, and in November, Pat and Betty married. They soon moved to Washington and took up more conventional occupations, while Ken wandered and did Party work until he was expelled in 1939 because of alcoholism. Now, more than a decade after his Knoxville sojourn, McConnell came forward to denounce not just Remington but his ex-wife and the man who had become her husband and had adopted his son.[12]

On April 21, the Todds appeared before HUAC in executive session.

"Mr. Todd, have you ever been a member of the Communist Party?" Louis Russell asked.

"I don't wish to answer that question," Todd said, "on the grounds that [it] would tend to incriminate me."

Were you a Communist while with TVA? Did you know Remington to be a Communist Party member? To these and forty-nine other questions, Todd refused to give an answer, citing his constitutional protection under the Fifth Amendment. "There is no facetiousness in my attitude or in my refusal to answer these questions," Todd said. "I have been suspended from my job. I support two children. I am very much concerned, very much concerned, about this hearing."

Louis Russell intervened to protect HUAC's good name. "Mr. Chairman, if he has been suspended from his job, this Committee had nothing to do with that."

"I hope the Committee had nothing to do with it," Todd shot back. "I want to point out for seven years I have been associated with [the C. D. Electric Company of Glendale, Long Island], and my employer has known me and my family very well; and very suddenly, in much confusion, he suspends me."[13]

Perhaps Kenneth McConnell could induce Todd to talk, so he was brought back to the committee room to face his old friend. McConnell identified Todd as a Communist Party member and the man who had introduced him to William Remington. Todd admitted that he knew McConnell but continued to plead the Fifth Amendment.

Betty Todd came next. "She admitted name, rank, and serial number," her son later noted, "acting as though she were in the enemy camp and a prisoner of war. And she wasn't wrong." Like her husband, she consistently took the Fifth Amendment—forty-seven times.

McConnell's revenge was soon complete. Within hours of the Todds' return to New York, Betty learned that CBS had fired her. "They lost it all," Jacob Todd said.[14]

So far, HUAC's secret hearings had eluded the press and Joe Rauh, but on April 24, a friendly reporter informed Rauh that Chairman Wood had said privately that the committee had sensational new evidence on Remington. NBC was rumored to be especially bitter about settling the libel suit now that it appeared that it could have been won. Rauh wrote Dick Green, asking him to see if Walter Barry could explain these disturbing developments. Green's reply was typically blunt—he doubted that Barry knew anything and would have to handle him carefully so as not further to enflame NBC. "It still boils down to the same thing," he told Rauh. "Bill will have no peace until he gets himself a civilian job and forgets about working for Uncle Sam. He is one of the victims of our times. . . . I certainly would like to see Bill stay on and slug it out with these fellows, but I have no right to ask that he do so." If he learned anything, he would pass it on.[15]

Three days after Rauh learned of HUAC's secret proceedings, Wood made them public. He announced on April 27 that the committee had launched an investigation of Remington and, based on new information received from a highly confidential source, he was asking the Loyalty Review Board to consider re-opening the case. Remington was issued a subpoena to appear on May 11, but Wood said, hoping to heighten the drama, he might appear even sooner.[16]

HUAC's mysterious source was not Kenneth McConnell but Howard Bridgman, who had met with a committee investigator on April 25. That night, he learned of the testimonies of HUAC's three witnesses: McConnell, Todd, and Todd's wife, whom he remembered as Betty Malcolm. That small but important piece of information filled a gap in Bridgman's memory—the first female member of the Communist branch, whose name he could not remember but thought was something like McLaughlin, was, of course, Malcolm—Betty Malcolm. Everything had come together perfectly. The original four were Todd, Remington, Malcolm, and himself, or so he incorrectly believed.[17]

Bridgman's appearance before the committee on April 29 was a love feast. Unlike the Todds, Bridgman held nothing back. His friend, Pat Todd, a Communist Party organizer recruited him in December 1936, Bridgman testified, and Party meetings began about a month later.

"Who were the other members . . . ?" asked Tavenner.

The first named by Bridgman was William Remington.

Where were these meetings held?

At the home of Betty Malcolm, he said. It was the earliest meetings that he remembered best.

At the end of the session, Congressman Wood fulsomely praised his star witness. "Permit me, Mr. Bridgman, to . . . commend you for the . . . stand you have taken to denounce this cancerous growth to the free people of the world, and I hope that your appearance here will not mitigate against you."

"Thank you, Mr. Chairman," Bridgman replied, then hurriedly departed.[18]

On Thursday, May 4, Remington, wearing a somber blue suit and dark bow-tie, entered Committee Room 226, accompanied by his attorney Joe Rauh. He took his place at the long table provided for witnesses and their counsel and, as photographers' flash-bulbs popped, waited for the hearing to begin. The congressmen soon appeared, Remington was sworn in, and the now familiar questions began. Then, in mid-course, the hearing turned confrontational, as Tavenner read excerpts from McConnell's testimony. Looking hard at Remington from his elevated perch on the members' dais, the counsel said, " . . . Having heard that testimony, I ask you again: Were you at any time a member of the Communist Party while you were working for TVA or while you were in Knoxville? . . . "

"No, sir," Remington answered. " . . . It has been implied to me that some of the people with whom I worked most closely, people who were among my closest friends, were Communists. I was not."

"The question asked you was very simple," Chairman Wood snapped, "whether or not you were a member of the Communist Party."

"I said no," Remington replied. " . . . My views at that time would have made that utterly impossible, just as my views before that time and since that time make it utterly impossible. . . . I met Bridgman [at] labor union activities. If he was a secret Communist, if there were other secret Communists in that group . . . , he might have assumed from my association with the gang that I, too, was one of his ilk. I was not."

Suddenly, Remington recognized the flaw in Bridgman's testimony and said excitedly, "I want to point out something. . . . I know . . . that this Betty

Malcolm arrived in the summer of 1937, not at the time that Bridgman describes. . . . I can say categorically that I did not attend meetings in her place, over a period of time . . . because she wasn't there."

Tavenner shrugged off this contradiction, but Remington would not let it go. " . . . There has been testimony about when the Malcolms arrived in Knoxville. . . . It is impossible for us to have overlapped in Knoxville very much, if, indeed, we overlapped at all."[19]

Wood recognized that something was wrong, because he chose that moment to adjourn for the day. The questioning would continue the following morning.

The next session began with a request from Joe Rauh that he and Remington be permitted to examine McConnell's and Bridgman's testimonies, and after first denying the request, Wood agreed when the hearing stopped briefly so that members could answer a roll-call vote. The congressmen departed and the room was cleared, leaving Rauh and Remington alone to read quickly through McConnell's and Bridgman's transcripts. They had only a few minutes to cover approximately thirty-one pages. Nevertheless, Rauh was able to note immediately the weaknesses in each man's recollection of their days in Tennessee. First was the timing of McConnell's arrival in Knoxville. He claimed early June; Rauh thought it was later, perhaps after Remington left. But if they were there together, it was only for a matter of weeks—too brief a period, Rauh thought, for them to have established the relationship McConnell alleged. Furthermore, McConnell had no evidence that Remington was a bona fide, card-carrying Party member and could place him at only one meeting, the composition and location of which he could not precisely recall. One word of McConnell's instantly caught the attorney's eye—"equivocally." To him it neatly summed up McConnell's entire testimony. Bridgman's account was also preposterous; his most serious mistake was his contention that the early meetings he and Remington attended were held at Betty Malcolm's house—this was clearly impossible since she did not arrive in Knoxville until June 1937, six months after Bridgman said the meetings began.[20]

When the hearing resumed, Rauh told the chairman exactly what he had found. "Even a cursory glance at these two transcripts in the 20 minutes I have had shows gaps and holes you could drive a truck through. . . . I am convinced that these documents carry the seeds of their own destruction."

"The Committee is not interested in argument," Wood quickly responded, but he did grant Rauh's request to retain the records for closer examination, so long as this occurred under committee supervision.[21]

The questioning continued. If Remington was telling the truth, the committee asked at the end of the second day's hearing, why then were Bentley, McConnell and Bridgman lying?

For once, Remington was speechless and he asked to consult with his counsel. Apologizing for the delay, he answered that Bentley was a headline hunter, McConnell was a stranger, and Bridgman was guilty of mistaken identity.[22]

The Committee then stood in recess until the next day, May 6, when the witness would be Elizabeth Bentley.[23]

"Miserably petty" was how Dick Green described the hearings in a letter to Rauh. "It looks to me as if Wood—and whoever is pushing him—is simply going back to Bill's teens with the hope of building up a criminal prosecution for perjury. There is mighty little morality in the whole thing." Rauh soon learned again how petty the committee could be. The next morning, he appeared early at the committee's office, asking to see the McConnell–Bridgman transcripts, which Chairman Wood had promised he could study at his leisure. Instead of the records, he was handed a letter from Wood that restricted his use of the transcripts—he could study them to his heart's content, but only if he agreed not to release their contents without the committee's approval. Rauh told the startled clerk that this was completely unacceptable and walked away. How could he publicly defend his client without being able to quote from the witnesses' statements? But he did have notes from his quick examination and, using them, wrote a six-page report to Seth Richardson, hoping to convince the Loyalty Review Board not to re-open Remington's case. Richardson and the others saw nothing in the House committee's evidence to lead them to reconsider their findings.[24]

While Rauh spent that Saturday at the office, Elizabeth Bentley was testifying before HUAC. She was there less than ninety minutes, but she was able to regain some of the credibility she lost when Remington was cleared and the libel suit settled. The committee helped by allowing her to tell her side of the story. Neither she nor her attorney Godfrey Schmidt was a party to the settlement; in fact, she was "willing to fight to the end . . . even if it meant giving up my job. My attorney said the suit would come up right away, and I couldn't teach in Chicago and fight a lawsuit in New York. I asked Mundelein College to release me from my contract, and they reluctantly agreed. . . . " Then, suddenly, the suit was settled and she was left out in the cold, without a job or a permanent place to live. This was mostly fiction. No trial was imminent, and Bentley's hurried departure from Chicago had nothing to do with the lawsuit. But the committee accepted her version as the truth.[25]

Next, they questioned her about Remington, breathing new life into Bentley's old charges. In her previous congressional testimony, she had included Remington in the group of her contacts she called "misguided idealists," who thought the information they were providing was going to Earl Browder and the American Communist Party. Now, she testified that he was a Soviet agent, a spy who had left the open Party to go underground. But she did admit that he was one of her minor sources and may still have thought Earl Browder and not the NKVD was the recipient of his information. Bentley also provided new details about her relationship with Ann Remington. Heretofore, she had said almost nothing about her, but this time she described her as a more enthusiastic Communist than Bill and claimed to have met with her four times during her visits with Remington. Thus, Ann Remington now also stood accused of espionage.[26]

The HUAC hearings also had an impact on a man Remington had never met or heard of but who now played perhaps the most critical role in ending his career. He was John Gilland Brunini, a 51-year-old poet and essayist, executive director of the Catholic Poetry Society, and editor of its magazine, *Spirit*. Although the transplanted Mississippian was proud of his literary achievements, he was more excited about his present position as foreman of a special federal grand jury in New York City that was empowered to investigate Communist espionage.

"I felt as though someone had struck me over the head," Brunini recalled of his appointment as foreman on December 16, 1948. Little in his past had prepared him for this important role. Born in Vicksburg, Mississippi, in 1899, he was educated by the Brothers of the Sacred Heart and attended college at Georgetown University. His father, counsel for the Catholic Diocese of Natchez, insisted that he also pursue a career in law, but Brunini wanted to write, so after graduation in 1919, he moved to New York. The only work he could find was with the United Fruit Company, but he still yearned to be a writer. In 1923, he embarked on a four-year career in journalism and joined the staff of *Commonweal* in 1928. When he became director of the Catholic Poetry Society, he finally found a life that most pleasantly combined art and religion, his two great loves. He also devoted time to civic duties: organizing the Temple of Religion for the 1938 World's Fair and, during World War II, supervising Manhattan's Neighborhood Defense Councils.

Brunini recovered quickly from the shock of his selection as foreman of this most important grand jury and took command. It was Brunini who administered the sacred oath to witnesses, signed the subpoenas that forced them to appear, and ordered the grand jury room cleared of Justice Department lawyers when the 23-member body wanted to deliberate secretly or vote a true bill (an indictment that bound a person over for trial). He also discovered that he could make even the FBI do his bidding. Once, while visiting his family in Vicksburg, he was unable to secure passage east, so he telephoned local agents, demanding that they get him on a flight. Soon, he was back at the U.S. Court House at Foley Square, presiding over what he liked to call "my Grand Jury."

During the next months, he found himself involved in dramatic events. The previous grand jury had just indicted Alger Hiss for perjury, so initially, Brunini and his colleagues examined people connected with that controversial case. The experience convinced Brunini that few Americans recognized the peril posed by Communists and liberals, so he began a one-man crusade against them and their allies in government. When Truman was faced with the choice of either concealing or expelling subversives discovered by the FBI, or through the testimonies of ex-Communist patriots, the President, Brunini believed, "plumped for concealment." (He would have been shocked to learn that another official urging concealment was his hero, J. Edgar Hoover.)[27]

Given Brunini's worldview, he showed surprisingly little interest in the Remington case. The grand jury first heard Elizabeth Bentley in the winter of 1949, but she made no impression on the foreman. Then, in late January 1950, he received a telephone call from her. While teaching in Chicago, she had met an old friend of his, Miriam Rooney, who had asked her to phone and give him her best wishes. Brunini was pleased to receive a call from the famous Spy Queen. The grand jury had recessed and would probably remain inactive until it expired in June, so he had the time to cultivate a new friendship. The day Bentley phoned, he took her to lunch at the Hotel Commodore. She told him that she had been unhappy in Chicago and had decided to leave Mundelein College, chiefly because the government so often sought her services in New York or Washington. Her travel expenses were paid, but she was almost broke. In fact, she could not afford to pay her own hotel bill, and, were it not for the goodness of her new friend, Lady Armstrong, president of the Ladies of Charity, she would be homeless. Lady Armstrong was also a friend of Brunini's—part of the circle of New York Catholic anti-Communists in which he traveled—and knowing that she was not wealthy, Brunini suggested to Bentley that she write a book.

No, Bentley said; she did not know how to write and needed an income immediately. Brunini continued to encourage her in this regard, as did Lady Armstrong, whom they visited later that day. She would probably receive an advance, Brunini remarked, but first she would have to show a publisher an outline and a chapter. He would be happy to help, both as a favor to her and to ease Armstrong's financial burden.[28]

Collaborating with Elizabeth Bentley proved to be more difficult than Brunini had anticipated. "Knowing she had to relive her tragic love [for Golos] and its searing conclusion, she was reluctant to write one day, willing the next," he later observed. "Bitterly I once remarked she was like a pregnant woman, eager to have her baby yet dreading her confinement; and further, I filled the role of a doctor who must perform a Caesarian." Brunini would later claim that after Bentley received a contract and a two thousand dollar advance from Devin-Adair Publishers he had nothing more to do with the creation of her manuscript. However, FBI and other records indicate that Brunini continued to act as collaborator and, more often than not, actual ghostwriter, a job for which he expected to be paid.[29]

It was at this time that Brunini heard of new developments in the Remington case. At a dinner with Washington reporters in late April 1950, he learned that the FBI would soon present evidence to a grand jury and ask for Remington's indictment. But which grand jury—the one operating in Washington under the strict control of the administration, or his, which he believed had become unpopular at the Justice Department? Then came word that HUAC would soon hold hearings on the case. Convinced that there was real fire behind the smoke of rumors, Brunini, on May 2, wrote Alex Campbell, head of the Criminal Division, asking why the new evidence on Remington had not been presented to his grand jury and demanding that that be done. Campbell should telephone him immediately. The Justice Department did not feel such urgency. A few days later, Brunini was informed that the FBI's new evidence would be presented to a Washington grand jury. "Little boy go play with your marbles," was Brunini's interpretation of Justice's decision. Remington would appear before a grand jury totally unaware of his background; a few unimportant questions would be asked, then Washington would announce that the grand jury had declined to vote a true bill. The result, Brunini feared, would be another cover-up. (Indeed, Remington did appear before a Washington, D.C., grand jury in early May, and that body decided not to indict him.)[30]

Brunini spent two sleepless nights trying to decide what—if anything—he should do. But it soon became clear that indicting Remington would serve many purposes: it would begin criminal action against the last Bentley agent still in government; it would end the doubts of Bentley's credibility created by Remington's recent victories; it would reveal that the Truman Loyalty Program was fatally flawed and result in needed reforms; it would assist the enactment of new legislation against espionage that the grand jury had recommended; and, finally, it should certainly boost the sale of the book whose profits he was to share. Political extremism and personal gain led Brunini to choose action. On May 4, in secret session, he informed the grand jury members that their recess was over; he wanted them to investigate William Remington. After a brief discussion, all the members voted their approval.[31]

Traditionally, it was the Justice Department's prosecutor who developed the evidence produced by the FBI, selected the witnesses, and then brought them before the grand jury. But in the Remington case, it was Brunini who played this role. His first phone call was to his friend Godfrey Schmidt, who introduced him to Joe Egan, late of Knoxville. On May 5, while Remington was being questioned by HUAC, Brunini was conferring with Egan and Schmidt at their office on East 41st Street. Egan showed him the list of witnesses compiled during his talk with Josephus Remine and allowed him to listen to an hour-long tape recording of the old sheriff's recollections. Brunini invited Egan to be his first witness, and he agreed. They also discussed the settlement of the libel suit, Brunini noting that Remington's attorneys were interpreting it as vindication; he told Schmidt that it might be a good idea to issue a statement to correct these misunderstandings. Schmidt thought that was an excellent idea and later released such a statement to the press.[32]

Egan was a cooperative witness, but his appearance before the grand jury on May 9 was a comedy of errors. His testimony was a recitation of what he had learned from Remine about Knoxville's Communists, unionists, and nudists.

Was Remine "the type of fellow who would think that a nudist was necessarily a Communist?" asked one juror.

"Oh, no," said Egan.

"I don't think that question makes sense, Mr. Foreman," said a second juror.

"This is all ridiculous," a third fumed. Egan was quickly dismissed.[33]

Who should Brunini choose next? After the Egan fiasco, he needed someone who would impress the jury and silence those who appeared skeptical about the case. Above all, he needed a witness who could corroborate Bentley's testimony. During the next few days, he went "sleuthing." Reading Remington's congressional testimony, he noticed his contempt for Elizabeth Moos. What did Ann Remington think of her husband's malicious attacks on her mother? Suddenly remembering Lang's *New Yorker* piece, he quickly read it, looking for the answer. None was there, but he did learn that Ann had also met Golos and Bentley. What had she told congressional investigators about all this? Nothing, Brunini found. Returning again to the Ferguson Committee's published hearings, he saw that Ann Remington had never testified. He then examined the records of the old grand jury—only William Remington had been called. Surely the FBI must have interviewed her. They had not. It was incredible. No one had questioned Ann Remington. He discussed his discovery with Thomas Donegan, who confirmed it and appeared troubled by this serious oversight. Brunini said, "Subpoena Ann Remington" and signed the form when it was prepared.[34]

Ann was served on Monday, May 15; she immediately called Carl Beruffy and asked him to come to Tauxemont. Attorney Beruffy told her that she had the right not to testify and urged her to use it. If Remington lost his job or went to jail, there would be no more alimony or child support. There was nothing damaging about Bill that she could tell the grand jury, Beruffy later recalled her saying.

What about Elizabeth Bentley? asked the attorney.

Bentley was "a liar," Ann said.[35]

That evening, Bill called. He had purchased tickets for the circus and wanted to take Gale and Bruce; was that all right with Ann?

Yes, that was fine, she said, then told him that she had been subpoenaed by the New York grand jury. He was not surprised by the news. Bill was silent for a moment; he was still uneasy about talking on the phone. She would be flying to New York in the morning, she continued, and would be meeting with the grand jury in the early afternoon. Sensing his anxiety, she reassured him that he had nothing to worry about.[36]

▲ 1. The Executive
Committee of Dartmouth's
American Student Union
chapter. Bill Remington
(*back row, 2d from left*) and
Bill Martin (*front row, 2d
from left*) began as childhood friends and ended
their college days as bitter
enemies. Robbins
Barstow, Jr. (*front row,
right*) would later testify
against Remington before
a Senate subcommittee
investigating Communists
in government.
(Dartmouth Aegis, *1938*)

► 2. William Remington,
June 1939, was the most
controversial man on the
Dartmouth campus: liked
by only a few fellow stu-
dents, detested by many,
and a source of irritation
and wonder to college
authorities who could not
decide if he was "crazy" or
a "genius." (Dartmouth
Aegis, *1939*)

◀ 3. Remington met his future accuser Elizabeth Bentley on Capitol Hill, July 30, 1948, and protested, "You have told some weird stories about me." *(Library of Congress)*

▶ 4. William Remington, August 1948, defended himself against charges that he was a Communist and a spy before a hostile Senate committee. *(Library of Congress)*

◀ 5. Elizabeth Bentley, December 1948, ex-Communist and Soviet spy turned Catholic convert, government informant, and celebrity, was the principal witness against William Remington. *(Library of Congress)*

◄ 6. Remington with his principle champion, Attorney Joseph L. Rauh, Jr., February 1949. A fighter for justice and defender of civil liberties during the postwar Red Scare, Rauh struggled for six years to save Remington from his enemies. (*Library of Congress*)

► 7. Remington and Attorney William C. Chanler on the way to court, January 1951. Hired to take the "liberal onus" off of Joe Rauh, Chanler, a distinguished conservative, defended Remington at his first trial. (*Library of Congress*)

▼ 8. John McKim Minton, distinguished criminal lawyer, defended Remington during his second trial in 1953. His strategy caused Joe Rauh to withdraw from the case. (*Library of Congress*)

▲ 9. The prosecutors. Irving A.
Saypol (*left*) the government's chief
"Red Buster" tried the Remington
case in 1950–51. Myles Lane (*center*) succeeded Saypol as U.S. attorney and tried Remington in 1953.
Assistant U.S. attorney Roy Cohn,
called by Remington's attorney,
William Chanler, the "ever-present
genie," cross-examined witnesses
and plotted strategy that affected
the outcome of both Remington
trials. (*UPI/Bettmann*)

▶ 10. John Gilland Brunini—
poet, editor, theologian, and anti-
Communist zealot. Foreman of
the federal grand jury that indicted
Remington for perjury in June
1950, Brunini had his own secrets
that threatened to destroy the
prosecution's case against
Remington. (*Library of Congress*)

◀ 11. Thomas J. Donegan, FBI agent and government prosecutor, was obsessed with driving Remington from government service and putting him in jail. (*Library of Congress*)

▶ 12. The "Reluctant Witness." Ann Moos Remington prepared to testify against her ex-husband in January 1951. She was a woman of fragile emotional health, and her life was filled with bitterness, anger, and hatred, especially toward Bill. (*Library of Congress*)

◀ 13. Father and son go to court, January 1951. Frederick Remington, 81, testified on behalf of his son who had earlier called him "a stooge for the capitalists." (*Library of Congress*)

▼ 14. Bill Remington and his children—Bruce, age 9, and Galeyn, age 7. August 22, 1951, was a rare, happy day—the U.S. court of appeals had just reversed his conviction for perjury. (*Library of Congress*)

▼ 15. Bill and Jane Remington, 1953. Jane was lover, wife, and staunch supporter through the worst of times. (*courtesy of Jane Abramson*)

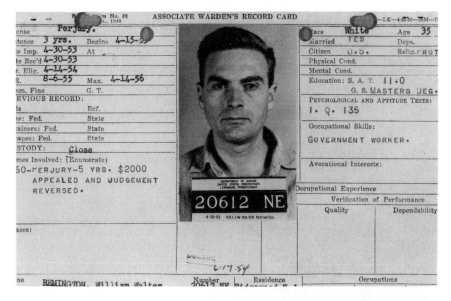

▲ 16. Remington's first prison photograph, April 1953. (*Federal Bureau of Prisons*)

▼ 17. This prison photograph was taken shortly before Remington was attacked on November 22, 1954—no longer the "New Deal glamour boy," the months in prison had taken their toll. (*Federal Bureau of Prisons*)

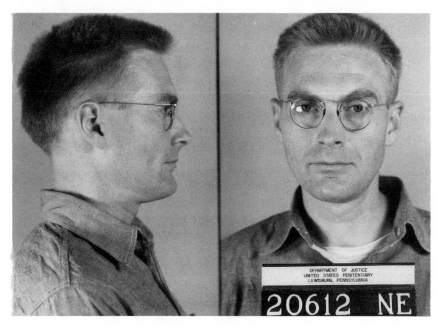

◄ 18. Lewis Cagle, Jr., was a 17-year-old juvenile delinquent with only days to go before his release from prison when he was persuaded to take part in an assault on William Remington. (*Library of Congress*)

▼ 19. Prison officials believed George McCoy to be a mild-mannered moron. Fellow inmates knew better. Although he had an I.Q. of 61, he was considered a killer, with an intense hatred for "Communists." (*Library of Congress*)

◄ 20. Robert Carl Parker, 21-year-old car thief, joined McCoy and Cagle for what he thought would be a simple burglary of Remington's dormitory room. McCoy and Cagle, armed with a sharpened bed rod and a brick-bat, had other plans. (*Library of Congress*)

12

Tool of Tyranny

How could Brunini have been so wrong? Here, sitting before him was Ann Moos Remington, whose ex-husband had insulted her publicly, had called her mother a Communist, and had deserted her to carry on an adulterous affair with another woman; if ever there was a woman scorned, it was Ann Moos Remington. But to his surprise and dismay, there was no bitterness or anger, just denials spoken so softly that he could barely hear her.[1]

On all the subjects of interest to Brunini and his colleagues, Ann Remington contributed little.

"Mrs. Remington," asked Thomas Donegan, "was your husband a member of the Communist Party?"

"Not to my knowledge," she replied, "and I think I would have known if he had been."

Again and again during the first hours of her hearing the question was asked, and always she said, "No I don't think so." Of course, as young people, they were interested in what the Communists were doing; everybody was. "The causes that they promoted seemed good and we got worked up about Spain and the unions and you met Communists in the course of working with these groups. . . . We were both kind of crazy in those days." But they were never more than sympathetic outsiders, and gradually their interest diminished.[2]

What can you tell us about that famous dinner at Schrafft's, when you met Helen and John and arrangements were made for Bill to give them information?

"It's a long time ago to remember a dinner," she replied.

Did you not know that Bill was going to give to Helen data that would then go to John, a Soviet agent?

"No, I don't remember any connection . . . between the woman and him. I must have missed something." Later, Helen came to Washington—"I can't remember much about it. . . . I'm not very clear as to what happened."

But Remington met with Helen or Elizabeth Bentley, as she was now known; even he admitted that. " . . . You must have wondered about this woman."

"No," Ann said. "I don't think so. People come [to] the Government all the time to get information. I never thought anything of it."[3]

Losing patience, Brunini began to probe personal "sore spots," no doubt hoping to provoke an outburst that would cause her to denounce Bill. "Were the difficulties between your husband and your mother because of Communist ideology?" he asked.

"What difficulties are you referring to?"

Brunini was incredulous. "His whole testimony before the Senate was apparently planned to leave the impression . . . that the basis of your original separation was due to an ideological conflict, you and your mother on one side, and him on the other. Now, is there any basis to that?"

"It would certainly not be a major cause."[4]

Surely, his next question would produce a reaction. "Are you aware that your husband testified before the Senate committee that your mother is a Communist?"

"Yes, I know that," Ann said, "and I am inclined to agree with him."[5]

Brunini dug deeper. "What were the terms of your divorce?" How much alimony and child support are you receiving? She told him the details in an emotionless tone and added, "it was hard to get that much out of him. He's Scotch."

Has Remington ever failed to pay his alimony?

Yes, when he was suspended by the Commerce Department, prior to his loyalty hearings.

"He paid you the back amount that was due, when he was reinstated?"

"No, I never got any money. . . . He is a penny-pincher, all right. . . . "

That was the worst thing she said about Bill during the early part of the hearing.[6]

Donegan asked for a five-minute recess, then the questions resumed.

"Have you had any discussions about . . . Bentley saying he was a Communist and that he was furnishing her with information . . . ?" Brunini asked.

"I can't remember," Ann said.

"You must be able to remember something about that," Brunini insisted. "Did he say 'It's all true' or 'It's all false' or 'this Bentley woman is a terrible woman' . . . ? He had become a prominent character. He even sued Bentley. . . . There must be something."

"Well, no," Ann replied. "I assume that he met her and he must have given her some information."

Donegan began to get angry. " . . . you say, 'He was not a Communist.' That is where it falls apart, right there. You must have some . . . very definite information that at one time he was a Communist. He had to be a Communist when he was contacting Bentley. . . . "

"Are you claiming that he is a Communist now?" Ann interjected. "That seems to me to be the important thing."

"Maybe he is not a Communist now," Donegan conceded. "Maybe . . . he changed . . . but nobody can ever convince me that he wasn't a Communist [when] he was in touch with Bentley. . . . "

Ann stuck to her story. "Well, I am sure he wasn't."

"Why are you so sure?" Donegan pressed.

" . . . It seemed more important to get ahead in the Government, and . . . we began to appreciate the American way more; and as we read more about Russia we became convinced that our way was better. . . . I am convinced that he is not [a Communist] and has not been . . . but he is a devious sort."[7]

From "penny-pincher" to "devious sort"; progress of a kind, so Donegan and Brunini continued, despite Ann's evasiveness—she said "I don't remember," or words to that effect, thirty-one times as the afternoon dragged on.[8] At one point, Donegan seemed to be on the verge of giving up.

"Does the Jury want to ask any more questions now? Let's excuse Mrs. Remington for a few minutes so we can discuss it."

She waited again in the witness room, throat parched, tired, hungry. There had been no recess for lunch, and she had not eaten since breakfast, hours ago. Surely, they would let her go now.

But Donegan brought her back to the jury room and treated her to a lecture on patriotism and civic duty.

" . . . You have expressed the thought, 'the present is important, not the past.' Maybe. . . . but the Grand Jury has the duty of considering the past and when your ex-husband was in contact with Bentley. There is no point in discussing whether Remington is a Communist now, . . . that is wasting time. It is the Bentley period that counts."

For the first time, Ann showed signs of weakening. "I'd like to point out that I am a very reluctant witness because if my husband is convicted, . . . I am going to be flat, without support. I think it is very unfair . . . to get me to say things which will convict him."

"You have given the impression of being a pretty honest-minded thinker," said Donegan, suddenly warm and friendly. " . . . I think if it were a matter of . . . support from Remington or whether you are . . . able to help your country, you would do the right thing."

"I don't think it is helping my country . . . to convict my husband. . . . I do not feel he is an enemy of the country. [I have] my two children, and since I have no job qualifications, I am concerned about support. . . . It is important."

"Would you wilfully withhold information because you feel that you are going to be in a financial jam? I don't think you would. . . . Nobody is desirous of causing you any personal hardship . . . but, after all, we have to do our duty no matter how embarrassing it is to us or how reluctant we are to cause somebody else some trouble."[9]

Ann continued to resist. "I would rather you get other witnesses."

Abruptly, Donegan switched from understanding friend to stern prosecutor. "You were subpoenaed here. . . . You are under obligation to testify. . . . You don't even have the freedom to tell white lies. . . . If we caught you in a white lie, we can prosecute you for perjury." He was misstating the law. She did not have to testify if such testimony degraded or incriminated her, but he was not about to tell her that now.

A juror suggested another nightmarish possibility and a way to avoid it. "Suppose eventually that your husband does confess that he was a Communist, and you knew it. Then look at the terrible position you would be in, your having tried to protect him might have involved you in having committed the crime of perjury." Those who "made a mistake early in life, admit it frankly and say, 'I am straightened out and now on the right road'; we don't have to bring an indictment." It was so simple: "Those who come in and help the Government . . . , they don't get indicted."[10]

They recessed again, and Ann waited in the witness room. When the hearing resumed, Brunini spoke about the significance of the Remington case.

"Elizabeth Bentley has told a story. In that story your former husband is a very minor figure. But because of certain circumstances, for which he himself is largely responsible afterwards, he has become an extraordinarily important person. . . . It is important for the simple reason that he has chosen to talk and . . . invent as he went along to cover up. . . . " He felt sorry for her, trapped between "personal considerations" and love of country. "We can live with ourselves much more comfortably if we face up to [conflicts] and make the right decision. This Grand Jury has been in existence for 17 months. . . . We have had one of the most important insights into what's been going on in this country. There are conditions which very definitely must be corrected, and they are only—unfortunately—going to be corrected by . . . following up . . . the case. That is why your husband ceased to be a cog and has become very important."

"I'm not clear on just how I would be helping my country," Ann said.

Brunini explained. America has been betrayed by Communists in the Government. Bentley has told them all about it, but she and other brave ex-Communists were being smeared. The American people must be awakened or "we are going to go under. That is the importance of it." In other words,

Remington has challenged Bentley, damaged her credibility, and threatened the crusade to rid America of the Red Menace.

" . . . Innocent people get trampled upon in such a search," Ann complained.

"How can any innocent people get trampled on with a jury such as this?" Donegan protested. " . . . If they haven't convinced you that they are trying to do an honest job, we might just as well give up. Nobody has been trying to brow-beat you, or trying to ask things for their own personal motives. Remington? Who is Remington? Even I never met him before he came in the grand jury room here [in 1947]."

"He's the father of my children," Ann reminded him.

"Don't you think, Mrs. Remington," Brunini asked, "that later, facing your children, it would be a happier situation if you could say to them, 'Yes, unfortunately, your father was thus and so.' . . . They are not going to be proud of their father, but you can make them proud of their mother."[11]

Donegan started in all over again. "Did Remington discuss with you the fact that he was furnishing information to Bentley?"

Now, instead of saying, "I don't remember," she murmured, "Hmm-mm." For Donegan it was a breakthrough. "Well, you see, you . . . are honest. You don't want to lie."

The cracks in Ann's façade were showing now, Donegan realized, and he searched for the means to shatter it. "Would it make it easier if I started off with Redmont because . . . he came into the picture, too . . . ?"

"I thought we were going to break off for today," Ann said.

"I don't think we should," Donegan said, afraid that he might lose her. "You don't want to wrestle with this. We have one foot over the threshold, and we might just as well go ahead."

" . . . I am getting fuzzy," Ann told him. "I haven't eaten since a long time ago, and I don't think I am going to be very coherent from now on. I would like to postpone the hearing. . . . I want to consult my lawyers and see how deep I am getting in."

They were very close now, so the prosecutor and the foreman continued their questioning, at times reassuring, then adversarial, and, eventually, threatening.

"Did you know why he was giving [money] to Bentley? You did, didn't you?" Donegan asked.

" . . . I don't want to answer any more questions now. . . . It's a deep responsibility, all this burden on myself, saying contradicting testimony that my husband has made. I don't like to do it."

Ignoring her protests, he asked, "Didn't he tell you he was giving that money to Bentley as Communist Party dues?"

"No."

"I know you are not lying," Donegan said, acting her friend again. "I know you won't lie to me. Now I can go through a long series of questions."

"No," she said. "I'm tired. I would rather stop."

" . . . Well, don't you think I have a duty to do? I have."

" . . . I'm hungry. I would like to get something to eat. Do I have to stay?"

" . . . I think this is the time to answer the question and let's get it over with today and get it out of the way. In 15 minutes we can break away. . . . "

"Is this the third degree, waiting until I get hungry, now?"

"Oh, no, I don't want you to accuse me of that, oh, no," he protested. Had he gone too far? "How about five minutes? . . . You . . . could answer some questions in five minutes. You couldn't say that was the third degree, waiting five minutes for your lunch. Now what was that money for. Why don't you say? . . . Was it money for the Communist Party?"

"I said I would rather not answer. . . . "

Was there a softening in her voice? Just a bit more. "Why not answer that question, and then we'll postpone it for another day. That isn't going to involve you, is it? It couldn't involve you. All you have to do is say yes or no as to whether that money was for the Communist Party."

"Well, I don't want to answer."

Had he lost her? Would she next invoke the Fifth Amendment or the doctrine of marital privilege? Donegan and Brunini had tried almost everything: appeals to country, vanity and motherhood, veiled promises of immunity and protection, warnings, threats; all had failed. Then the foreman, like some evil *deus ex machina*, stepped in and delivered the *coup de grâce*.

"Mrs. Remington," said John Gilland Brunini, "I think we have been very kind and considerate. We haven't raised our voices and we haven't shown our teeth. . . . Maybe you don't know about our teeth. A witness before a Grand Jury hasn't the privilege of refusing to answer a question. . . . When we get a witness who is contemptuous, who refuses to answer questions, [we] take them before a judge. . . . He will instruct the witness to answer the question. Then we come back here and put the question again. If the witness refuses to answer the question, we take him back to Court and the Judge will find him in contempt of Court and sentence him to jail until he has purged himself. 'Purging' is answering the question. . . . Did your husband or did he not give this money to the Communist Party? You have no privilege to refuse to answer the question. . . . I said show teeth. I don't want them to bite you." Turning to Donegan, he asked, "Do you want to put the question, again?" And while Donegan was asking Mrs. Gold, the reporter, "Can you find that question . . . ?" Ann Remington blurted out, "My answer is yes."

"I think you did the right thing, Mrs. Remington," Donegan said. "The Jury is impressed with your desire to cooperate with them."

"Well, frankly," Ann replied, "I didn't have the desire to cooperate, and I'm not at all happy."

" . . . Do you want to get something to eat? I think we ought to recess now . . . , in mercy to Mrs. Remington. . . . " But Donegan still had more to say. "You are not happy now, but I think you will be happy in the future; maybe not tomorrow or the next day, but eventually . . . I think you will be able to honestly reconcile in your mind that it was the only thing you could do." Within a few days he would send an FBI agent to talk with her, or if she preferred, they could wait until her next appearance before the grand jury.

She did not want to return but said she would. "If I go a little way, I might as well go all the way, I suppose. . . . "

"I think so," Donegan agreed, now afraid to let her step down, since she had just become his star witness. "Do you want to go all the way now? Do you want to go out and eat and come back again? I will probably get killed for that. Do you want to go out and eat and come back again?"

She wanted to eat, so at 3:16 P.M., a recess was called.[12]

A half hour later the hearing resumed.

" . . . Why don't you try and tell it in your own words," Donegan said.

She did, speaking quickly and without the evasions and loss of memory that had characterized her earlier testimony. "We were more interested than just sympathetic to the Party, and we didn't like local groups, so as I understood this, we were arranging for contact with a higher-up person, and Helen—Miss Bentley—was to be the contact. We wanted to help the Party . . . because we approved of [its] aims. . . . It did involve an interchange of information," but as far as espionage was concerned, "we—at least I—had no idea what we were getting into." Later, when I read about Bentley's activities, it produced "quite a jolt," and I am "sure" that Bill "had the same kind of jolt—we didn't realize what we were getting into. I also know once he was in, he wanted to get out," Ann said. "He wasn't happy about the whole situation. I don't know what he gave. That is it, I guess."[13]

The grand jury was not satisfied with this terse statement—they wanted to know more about the Remingtons' past lives. Why, for example, did Bill decide to seek a greater role than simply orthodox Party membership? "He must have been very strong in his Party ideas when he sought out that contact with Golos," Donegan probed.

"Yes," Ann said. She described him as an "idealist," a socialist when he was only twelve years old, his interest in Communism "a sort of rebellion against the family." And, to ensure his continued commitment to radicalism, she had forced him, prior to their marriage, to agree to remain on the left. She could not understand why they were so upset about his relationship with Bentley—"After all, we were allies with the Russians at that time, and it wasn't so dreadful, perhaps, in trying to give them secrets over the heads of the Governments."[14]

The jurors were especially interested in how Remington selected the information that he gave to Bentley, but Ann claimed that she knew almost nothing about it. "I remember only one thing . . . ," she said, a formula. "That was one meeting I went to, and he was very excited about this. It was some formula for something . . . "—a way to produce synthetic rubber, she thought—"and he was aware . . . that it was a secret and he was not supposed to be passing it on. . . ."[15]

Why did Remington lie about his past? Donegan asked.

It was the government application forms, she explained; each time he assumed a new position, he filled out a civil-service form requiring him to swear that he was not a member of any subversive group—"and, of course, he had filled them out in the negative, and he wanted to stick with it, and he got more and more involved, I guess. . . . He is not the villain that you paint him," she insisted, "he is merely a liar."

At the end, Brunini thanked her for cooperating, but she again expressed her unhappiness about what she had been forced to say. "I want to emphasize, in spite of my husband's refusal to admit an error, I'm positive that he has not been a Communist sympathizer for years. . . . "

"Mrs, Remington, you don't feel we tried to starve you out today?" Brunini asked.

"Yes," she said, "in a way." Trying to resolve her many conflicts had been "a damn difficult thing to do."[16]

It was almost 5:00 P.M. when Donegan released her. She left the courthouse and hurried to hail a cab for a ride to La Guardia Airport and the evening flight back to Washington.

"Is this the third degree . . . ?" Ann Remington had asked her inquisitors during her appearance before the grand jury. Many thought so when a portion of her testimony was later made public; among them, federal appeals court judge Learned B. Hand. "For myself," he wrote in 1953,

> the examination went beyond what I deem permissible. Pages on pages of lecturing repeatedly preceded a question; statements of what the prosecution already knew, and of how idle it was for the witness to hold back what she could contribute; occasional reminders that she could be punished for perjury; all were scattered throughout.

Harassment, threats, denying the witness the right to see her lawyer, pressuring her to answer after she complained of hunger and exhaustion—all this, Hand believed, was conduct typical of a medieval Star Chamber proceeding, which, historically, the grand jury system was created to prevent. "Especially important," Hand noted,

> is the fact that the examination was ex-parte and without the presence and control of a judge or any other impartial official, to . . . intervene . . . to protect the witness. . . . Save for torture, it would be hard to find a more effective tool of tyranny than the power of unlimited and unchecked ex-parte examination.[17]

Hand also accused Brunini of deceiving Ann Remington about her right, under both the Fifth Amendment and the doctrine of marital privilege, to refuse to answer his question. Perhaps Brunini was ignorant of the law, but Donegan, the Justice Department's lawyer, was not, and "he did not intervene to correct the mistake." In Hand's view, the foreman and the prosecutor were guilty of misconduct, coercion, and deceit.[18] Such criticisms seem accurate and fair.

The next witness, on May 18, was Elizabeth Bentley. Thomas Donegan handled the questioning; Brunini was less active than he had been when Ann Remington had testified—he asked only a few questions of the Spy Queen, perhaps because he already knew the answers. Bentley's story remained the same, but there were some refinements, particularly in her view of William Remington. In 1945, she had told the FBI that Jacob Golos was worried that Russian Intelligence was trying to take control of his group—"good American Communists who don't know what they are doing." Bentley had repeated that characterization in 1948. And, just two weeks earlier, testifying about Remington before HUAC, she had admitted that perhaps Bill thought that his information was going to Browder, not Stalin. Even Ann Remington was adamant that had they realized that they were committing espionage they would have stopped. But on this day, Bentley called Remington a conscious agent and described herself as his stern superior in the NKVD.[19]

Bentley's testimony also differed significantly from her earlier statements and from Ann Remington's. In her November 1945 FBI interview, she had said that Remington told her about a new way to produce synthetic rubber and his description was "quite vague and probably of no value even to a chemist." Now she said she had typed the formula and had passed it on to the Russians. Furthermore, Bentley had always maintained and stated again that she and Remington were alone when she learned about the formula; to the grand jury she said, " . . . I'm quite sure that Mrs. Remington wasn't there at the time. As a matter of fact, most of the information he gave me was when she wasn't around. . . . We tried very definitely not to have the wives around when the interchange of material went through. The fewer people who actually see it, in case somebody turned sour, the better." Yet Ann Remington had testified that she was present when the formula was passed. Finally, Bentley had told HUAC on May 6 that when Remington ceased being an agent it "wasn't too great a loss to us, because we had come to the conclusion that he was a hard man to deal with." On May 18 she told the grand jury that "we hated to let him go, because it was very difficult to get the type of agent he would be. . . . " If Brunini and Donegan were aware of the contradictions raised by Bentley's testimony, they did not confront her with them or ask her to resolve them. Donegan instead asked about Ann's health. "Did she seem a well person when you met her . . . ?"

"Yes, she seemed all right to me," Bentley replied. Bentley's examination was brief but satisfactory to the grand jury; she was excused after less than an hour's testimony.[20]

Remington's first chance to talk with Ann about her grand jury appearance came on Friday evening, May 19, when he dropped the children off at Tauxemont after taking them to the circus. "I was on edge and she was on edge," he said later, so the conversation that he remembered was brief and rambling.

"What happened?" he recalled asking her.

"Practically nothing."

"What were they interested in?"

"This Bentley business."

"Well, what did you say?"

"I told everything that I could remember. I told them things you won't like. I told the truth as I see it."

"Well, if you told the truth, that's fine."

"It is not," Ann had shot back. "You won't like it a bit. . . . You'll find out when you get there."

"I just don't think you realize what's going on. It is not only my job and reputation that are at stake but also Tom Blaisdell's."

"You ought to give up. They are going to get you anyway. . . . The Grand Jury want people to admit what they have done that's wrong."

"Golly knows, I have admitted it enough times. . . . "

"You better quit before it gets worse. . . . Just quit Government and forget about it."

"Your doctor can get you out of this," he had said as he was preparing to leave. "If you have done something . . . wrong, . . . why don't you consult your lawyer or your doctor. I think I can get you out of anything you have done wrong."[21] Ann had not replied.

Two days later, Remington and Rauh flew to New York for Bill's meeting with the grand jury.

13

Scene of the Crime

The grand jury was running behind schedule on Monday, May 22, 1950, when Remington was supposed to appear. He waited in the witness room with Joe Rauh and Bethuel Webster, who were permitted to accompany him this far but no farther; he would go into the jury room alone. They did not talk. Remington nervously thumbed through a newspaper or just stared at the wall. He did not look at the third man sitting in the room—Pat Todd. Next door, they could hear a witness talking loudly, a white-haired elderly man, who had been the first to be called that day. His name, Remington later learned, was Josephus Remine.[1]

The 78-year-old former sheriff told the grand jury that recently he had been ill and complained of fatigue, shortness of breath, impaired hearing, and poor vision. "But I am willing to testify and tell you what I know . . . ," he said. Despite the passage of time, he was still convinced that Remington had been a Communist. "I have stronger evidence than any card of Remington's. . . . You can stand up and hide a man near a hot doorway, with the doors open and the windows up and him under a bright light and see his lips working and saying . . . that we have to convince CIO members that the Communist Party is the coming party in this country . . . that's what he said. . . . He didn't do me any harm . . . [but] this Communist business is un-American. . . . "

Is there anyone else who can corroborate your testimony that Remington was a Communist?

No. My former colleagues are afraid to testify because they fear a lawsuit. So corroboration looked doubtful. After rambling on for a few more minutes, he was dismissed.[2]

Pat Todd was called next, but his appearance lasted less than ten minutes. When asked if he knew William Remington, he declined to answer because he thought it would incriminate him.

"Knowing Remington couldn't incriminate you, Mr. Todd," said Donegan. "I ask you again, have you ever met or talked with William Remington?" When Todd again refused to answer, Donegan threatened to take him before Judge Clancy to begin contempt proceedings. But first he wanted to discuss it with the jury. Todd returned to the witness room and then was told he could leave.[3]

A few minutes later, Remington entered the grand jury room and was sworn in by the foreman. For the first few minutes, nothing unusual happened. Remington was asked to discuss his background and answer a few questions about TVA and Helen and John. Then, he made a serious mistake, accidentally noting that he had talked with his ex-wife three days before about her appearance. Donegan and Brunini, spoiling for a fight, immediately demanded to know everything that had been said. Fearful that he might have violated some law of grand jury secrecy, Remington became evasive.

"What questions did you ask her?" Donegan inquired.

"I have forgotten specifically what they were," Remington answered, "some general questions about what kinds of things she had talked about, and she gave me some very noncommittal replies, and I realized that it was perhaps improper for me to ask further questions and I did not."

The prosecutor and the foreman spent the next ninety minutes badgering and insulting Remington, until he provided more details.[4]

Early in that exchange, Remington had made a second mistake. It suddenly occurred to him, he told the prosecutor, that a hidden microphone might have recorded his talk with Ann and that Donegan might possibly possess a complete transcription of their conversation. Therefore, he said, "I've got to be as precise as I can be."

At first, Donegan angrily stated, "Mr. Remington, I'm getting tired of your comments. . . . If you feel that you can't restrain yourself—"

I'm sorry," Remington interrupted.

Then, although there had been no microphone, Donegan played along and pretended that one had been placed at Tauxemont and warned Remington that if he lied he would be indicted for perjury. He asked for a two-minute recess so that Remington could review his memory. "You better think about that conversation," Donegan warned.

In the witness room, Remington quickly explained the situation to his lawyers and hurriedly jotted down on a pad all the topics he had discussed with Ann. The grand jury magnanimously gave him an extra three minutes, then Donegan returned him to the jury room.[5]

"I think I have covered it," Remington said, "although I say freely that I have been so wrought up over this that my reserves of strength and memory are not what they were two years ago. I am more on edge. I may be flubbing this recollection in some respect. I just don't know."

Go over it again, Donegan demanded, and remember "everything that you said and everything your wife said might have been recorded. . . . I want that whole conversation. . . . " Remington repeated what he had said before, but nothing seemed to satisfy them.

"Let us put it bluntly," Brunini said. "Did you threaten your wife?"

"Most emphatically not."

"I don't enjoy this a bit, Mr. Remington," Donegan added. " . . . You have a simple, clear issue here, and even you have to admit that you haven't handled it well so far."

"Yes, sir, I agree. I am doing the best I can, and I am being honest with this Grand Jury."

Donegan was unreachable. "I don't know whether to waste any more time of the Grand Jury. . . . You can't double-talk us. Now, just have a little respect for these people here, if you don't have any respect for me."[6]

Donegan's anger was authentic; he hated Remington, but his hostility was also an old prosecutor's trick—hammer the witness until he breaks. It had worked with Ann Remington, why not with her ex-husband? So the extended and pointless interrogation about the Remingtons' conversation was mostly a vehicle to weaken Remington, and given his admission about mental exhaustion, it now seemed the right time to focus on the truly important questions he was now supposedly too weak to evade.

"Were you a member of the Communist Party?"

"No, sir."

"Never at any time?"

"No, sir."

" . . . Did you hear the testimony of Bentley? She says that you were a Communist, under oath."

"That's what she said. But she is also—"

Donegan was not interested in his explanation. "Now either you or she is committing perjury. . . . I'm satisfied that the Grand Jury doesn't have to listen to you for another five minutes. . . . The example you just gave of conniving in your use of words, I think it's disgraceful; a conversation you had with your wife . . . and it took an hour and a half, at least, to get it out of you. . . . "

Remington could only repeat what he said many times that day, "I have done the best I can."

Now it was Brunini's turn to swing the hammer. " . . . You have an extraordinarily accurate memory, except when it comes to the truth. . . . You spend a tremendous amount of time in acquiring as many facts as you can in order to be able to give truths and half-truths and plain lies. . . . You are, despite your position in the Department of Commerce, a very small person and very small-fry.

You are important simply because you are mixed-up in a set of circumstances which lead to very many bigger things."

"Very tragic," Remington mumbled.

" . . . You have a chance here . . . to do something to reconstruct yourself. You testified before the Senate Committee that you had intended to resign. It is too bad that you did not do that. . . . But at the same time you can at this moment aid your Government by furthering this investigation and telling us the truth from TVA on."

Remington paused a minute, then responded. "You said some harsh things, some of them very wide of the mark. I am going to tell this group the truth." As far as leaving government is concerned, that is my intention, as soon as I can find another job.

Then Brunini resumed the formal questioning—about North, Golos, Helen, and the payment of Party dues. Remington repeated the now familiar story. He did not use North to contact the Party; he never paid dues to Bentley, or anyone; his information was not secret or confidential.

Donegan attacked. " . . . I will be perfectly frank, I will be brief, and I will sum it all up. . . . It doesn't make a bit of difference to me what position you take, but I am convinced . . . that you were affiliated with the Communist Party in Knoxville, and up to the time you went in the Navy . . . and anything else you say is just digging you deeper and deeper. . . . I don't think there is much more to be said or much more time to be wasted."

"What you have said hits me . . . hard," Remington said. "I am stunned. . . . I don't know anything I can say except to ask this jury to look at the facts."

Donegan was finished. " . . . There is no point in taking any more time of the Grand Jury." He wanted to excuse Remington, but Brunini wanted him to return the next day for more questioning.[7]

The inquisition, as Remington called it, continued through that week and on into the next. The prosecutor and the foreman could not have improved upon the methods of Torquemada. Once during the questioning, Donegan even seemed on the verge of a breakdown. "Answer my questions," he screamed. "Answer my questions. Answer my questions. . . . You might want to make fools out of the Grand Jury, but you are not going to make a fool out of me."[8]

The torrent of abuse had two goals: the vindication of Elizabeth Bentley and the destruction of William Remington. Brunini was especially interested in undoing Remington's victory in the libel suit. First, he demanded to know the details of the settlement with NBC and General Foods. Remington was unwilling to respond because of the agreement prohibiting public discussion of the case. Donegan reminded Remington that he had no right to refuse to answer the question unless he felt it might degrade or incriminate him; when Remington still held back, Donegan threatened to ask Judge Clancy to hold him in contempt. Finally, Remington told them everything they wanted to know.

Brunini emphasized that since Remington had received no retraction or payment from Bentley, there had been no vindication, whatever Remington chose to believe. By the time the exchange was over, history had been reversed: Remington had lost, and Bentley had won.[9]

Brunini probed deeper, hoping to discover information that would damage Remington's character. He asked if he had ever consulted a psychiatrist and what precisely had caused his divorce, and Remington described his unhappy relationship with his ex-wife. Donegan proceeded to complete this sad story by asking, "Did you strike your wife?"

"I did," Remington admitted. "And I'm thoroughly ashamed of it."[10] He was not given an opportunity to explain the circumstances that led to this unfortunate incident; the grand jury learned only that he had hit Ann. No one in the room ever questioned whether any of these subjects—psychiatry, adultery, divorce, and abuse—were relevant to the grand jury's investigation of Communist subversion. Clearly, they were not. They were discussed only because they served Donegan's and Brunini's personal agendas.

Remington frequently tried to describe his recent anti-Communist record, but Donegan forbade it.

"I am sorry you do not want to hear what I have done," said Remington.

"We want to hear the truth about what you have done . . . with Miss Bentley," Donegan said.[11]

Despite his horrific experience before the grand jury, Remington remained hopeful that he might escape indictment. While waiting to appear for a sixth day of questioning on June 1, the court reporter entered the witness room and smiled warmly at him. A federal marshal also suddenly became friendly and began chatting with him. Then Donegan appeared and told him that he had been released.

What does that mean? Remington asked.

He could return to Washington. Remington interpreted all this as a sign that he had been cleared.[12]

He could not have been more mistaken. On May 25, while Remington was in the process of testifying, Brunini had informed Donegan that the grand jury did not wish to question additional witnesses and ordered him to prepare an indictment charging Remington with perjury. Donegan needed little prodding but, later that day, informed the grand jury that certain problems had developed. FBI agents who were busy interviewing Ann Remington had reported that she did not wish to sign her statement or even testify publicly against her ex-husband. Without her cooperation, there was no one to corroborate Bentley, and the legal grounds for a perjury indictment disappeared. Furthermore, the testimonies of both Howard Bridgman and Kenneth McConnell (who had appeared before the grand jury on May 16 and 17, respectively) had been confused and contradictory. Donegan agreed to work on the indictment but recommended that both Ann Remington and Howard Bridgman be recalled before the grand jury reached a final decision. Brunini and the jury accepted his advice and arrangements were made to hear both witnesses again. So, Donegan knew that Remington had not been cleared when he inadvertently (or intentionally) gave Remington false hope by telling him he was released. In any event, Remington's euphoria did not last long. A *New York Post* reporter sent to interview Donegan on June 1 reported that the prosecutor said that Remington was only excused— the investigation was continuing. Later that night, Rauh telephoned Remington with the bad news.[13]

Tom Donegan must have been feeling as low as Remington. Having worked so hard to break Ann Remington, the reports of her new uncooperative attitude were very discouraging. FBI sources stated that she now regretted talking and was refusing to give additional information without first consulting her attorney. "The Government will have to build its case hereon without her assistance," the Bureau told Donegan on May 31. Donegan telephoned her the same day, and she explained her position. Remington should be fired and prosecuted, but she hoped that this would not happen immediately, since it would mean the loss of her alimony and child support. She had never held a full-time job or possessed any skills that made her employment likely, so she was very concerned about her future. She would not lead the case against her ex-husband or testify in court; if forced to do so, she would refuse to answer, claiming marital privilege or any other constitutional protection her lawyer recommended. Donegan did not try to dissuade her. They would talk further, he said, when she reappeared before the grand jury on June 2. That Friday morning, just before Donegan took her into the jury room, she told him again that she would not testify publicly or sign her FBI statement.[14]

Directing the questioning this day was John M. Kelley, Jr., a Justice Department attorney, and Clark M. Ryan, an assistant U.S. attorney in Manhattan. Brunini was suspicious of Kelley, who he thought was sent from Washington to block Remington's indictment, so he sat in sullen silence. As the prosecutors reviewed Ann Remington's FBI statement, discrepancies between her testimony to the agents and her present recollections were obvious. In her formal statement, she had claimed to have met Golos at lunch and Bentley at dinner, but she now said that she remembered only the evening affair. She also could not recall any conversation about the purpose of the meeting with John and Helen or any discussion of Communist Party dues or literature. Her memories of meeting Bentley in Washington were also vague. She saw her only twice, she said, and paid dues voluntarily but received no receipts. She also said that she saw Bill give Helen the secret formula but objected to the way that the FBI statement described the incident. Remington had been frightened, she said, not enthusiastic, as the statement read. Regarding the formula, she was uncertain if it was for explosives or some other substance. No matter, the FBI statement described the formula in a definitive fashion to which she now objected and had not been revised to reflect her doubts.[15]

When Donegan asked if she would now sign the document, she refused. "I do not want to be involved in any public trial," she told the grand jury, "[or] be in a position of testifying against the father of my children." Nevertheless, she was still willing to help off the record. Both Kelley and Donegan informed her that, in the event of a trial, she would undoubtedly be called by the government. She understood that, she said, but repeated that she would not testify publicly. Donegan tried to change her mind but failed, and when she left that day, it looked like the prosecutor had lost his most important witness.[16]

Howard Bridgman's appearance was also disappointing. Previously, on May 16, he had testified with confidence about Remington's active participation in the Knoxville Party meetings, especially the "early" ones at Betty Malcolm's house. John Kelley examined him closely, questioning him about joining the Party, and Bridgman again claimed to have entered in December 1936 a unit that had three members: Pat Todd, Bill Remington, and Betty Malcolm. He attended meetings until May 1937, when he left Knoxville briefly to look for a new job.

"Can you say positively that the five or six meetings that you . . . attended with Remington took place prior to your leaving Knoxville in May . . . ?" Kelley asked.

"To the best of my recollection, yes, sir," Bridgman replied.

"Do you have any hesitation in so saying?"

"No, sir."

Kelley now revealed to the grand jury the problem at the heart of the Bridgman testimony. TVA records indicated clearly that Betty Malcolm did not arrive in Knoxville until mid-June 1937, six months after Bridgman joined the Party and began attending meetings with Remington at her home. "We are not trying to trick you, sir," Kelley said, "[but] how can you reconcile those known facts with your testimony?"

Bridgman was stunned. "I can't reconcile it," he stammered. "I'm just floored. I have spoken according to my recollection, and my recollection may be faulty." He admitted that when he had first spoken to the FBI, he had difficulty remembering the original female member, then when Betty Malcolm's name surfaced at the HUAC hearings, he had just assumed she was the missing person.

Do you have any idea who the correct woman was? Kelley asked.

He did not, forgetting that initially he had claimed that the third woman was either Kit Buckles, Christine Benson, or a Mrs. McLaughlin. The Bureau had let him down. A quick check of TVA records would have revealed that Kit Buckles left Knoxville in November and Betty Malcolm arrived in June, leaving Chris Benson as the only possible female member at that time—a fact she later confirmed. But Bridgman's mistake, made first in April, then compounded in May, had now come back to haunt him in June. There were other inconsistencies, too, but Donegan interrupted Kelley's cross-examination to ask Bridgman his own questions.

"Is there any doubt in your mind that you attended Communist Party meetings with Remington?"

"No, sir," Bridgman said.

"And is it your testimony before this Grand Jury that . . . you knew Remington as a Communist in those meetings?"

"Yes, sir."

Kelley resumed his interrogation, but had asked Bridgman only three more questions when Brunini suddenly intervened and excused the witness.[17] It had certainly not been a good day for those who wanted to see Remington indicted.

While Remington waited for the grand jury's final decision, he struggled to hold on to his position at the Commerce Department. The HUAC and grand jury hearings had encouraged his enemies in the department to launch a new offensive. On May 15, it was announced that Secretary Charles Sawyer had ordered a new loyalty investigation, and later, Sawyer met privately with Remington and demanded that he leave voluntarily or be dismissed. Remington refused, arguing that it was unfair to be condemned without a hearing. He would stay on until the department's loyalty board reached a decision. Angered by Remington's resistance, Sawyer leaked the news of his ultimatum to the press, which covered the story prominently on May 27. Department officials were quoted as being "uncertain as to how to go about firing Remington," because he had been cleared by the Loyalty Review Board the year before, but they were searching for some kind of charges to file against him.[18]

It was a fight he had no chance of winning. On June 5, Bernard L. Gladieux informed him that due to the amount of time that he was devoting to his case, his continued employment was "administratively unfeasible and . . . detrimental to the efficiency of the Department." Therefore, he was being placed in a bureaucratic limbo, the first stage of which was separation with pay and then, after thirty days, suspension without pay until the department made a final determination. Even if he was again cleared—his present position was being abolished and there was no other work for which he was judged qualified. This decision, Secretary Sawyer said in making his announcement, was simply administrative and was not "intended to reflect in any way" on Remington's loyalty.[19]

That same day, the grand jury again asked Tom Donegan to prepare a perjury indictment, and after going into executive session, Brunini told him that he had just three days to complete it. Donegan and assistant U.S. attorney Clark Ryan considered four possible counts to the indictment (not included was Bentley's charge that he was a Soviet agent who gave her secret information) and finally selected Communist Party membership as the sole count, leaving it to the Justice Department to decide if there should be others. Not only was this accusation the most powerful, given the current political climate, but the act allegedly occurred prior to his marriage, so Ann Remington could be compelled to testify about a time not protected by marital privilege. Donegan and Ryan drafted the document hurriedly and sent it to Washington.[20]

Justice Department officials had been considering a perjury indictment against Remington for several weeks but were not yet convinced that enough reliable, admissible evidence existed to support it. When Kelley returned to Washington, James McInery, head of the Criminal Division, asked him to conduct an examination of the case, and after reviewing the files, Kelley reached two grim conclusions. First, Remington was guilty of perjury, and, second, it would be very difficult to prove. Ann Remington had supplied important information but was not willing to testify against her ex-husband. Bentley could contribute little to the proof that Remington was a bona fide Party member—she knew of no Communist Party meetings Remington attended and never saw his membership book. And the testimonies of McConnell and Bridgman were vague and contradictory. He recommended continuing the investigation rather than risk going into court with a weak case that might end with Remington's acquittal. McInery agreed with Kelley's conclusions. Thus, the Criminal Division did not call for Remington's immediate indictment in June 1950.[21]

Washington's news did not please Brunini, who was obsessed with indicting Remington before the grand jury's term expired on June 15, now just a week away. Brunini resented Justice Department attorneys, like Kelley and McInery, whose purpose, he believed, "was to thwart our indicting Remington." He must have thought the same of Donegan when he presented his view of the evidence to the grand jury on June 8. Heretofore, Donegan had always been Brunini's loyal partner in examining witnesses, but now he acted as the representative of the Justice Department and seemed unwilling to recommend indictment. The proof of Remington's perjury, Donegan said, rested on the testimony of McConnell, Ann Remington, Bentley, and Bridgman. Donegan pointed out McConnell's uncertainty about whether Remington was a formal Party member, one who attended meetings limited only to Communists, paid dues, and had a membership book. His credibility was also weakened by his background, which Donegan revealed for the first time to the grand jury; his arrests for extortion, disorderly conduct, and public intoxication spanned two decades and would make him a poor witness at trial. Ann Remington would not be helpful either. If called, she would refuse to testify, and most of what she knew might not be admissible in court. Donegan pointed out where her testimony differed from Bentley's, especially regarding the payment of dues—Ann said she never had received receipts while Bentley said that she had. He also noted that Ann had said that when they lived in Washington, Remington had never joined the Party. Bridgman could also contribute nothing to prove that charge. He had no evidence that Remington ever paid dues or received a membership book. Just as bad was his testimony regarding the meetings at Betty Malcolm's house. TVA records, obtained by the FBI, indicated conclusively that she was still living in North Carolina, when Bridgman said she was in Knoxville.[22]

There were others who could be interviewed, Donegan noted, including Betty Todd and Kit Buckles, but he remembered that the jurors had told him that they had heard enough. He could appreciate that they were tired—in less than a month, they had examined eleven witnesses, and the last four had wasted their time. Joseph North had declined to answer any questions about both Remingtons, because he thought that his answers might incriminate him. Horace Bryan, veteran Arkansas labor organizer and admitted Communist, had testified that when he knew Remington briefly in 1937, he did not think he was a Communist. Francis Martin, reputed to be the Communist Party organizer for Knox County in the late 1930s, had claimed that he had never met Remington. The final witness, on June 5, had been Louis Budenz, former managing editor of the *Daily Worker*, now an anti-Communist informer (and Elizabeth Bentley's Catholic God-father). All he could remember was that Joe North once told him Remington was a Communist involved in Washington work. (Was that underground work? Brunini had asked.

"He did not specifically say that, no . . . ," Budenz had replied.)

The jurors saw little point in continuing the investigation and were ready to hear Donegan's final conclusions. Summing up, Donegan explained that it was the Justice Department's position that "there is an uncertain and narrow basis on which an indictment would have to be predicated. I agree with that," he said. Had a stranger observed his performance that morning, he would not have recognized Donegan as the man who, for five years, had been trying to drive Remington from government and put him in jail.[23]

Some jurors must also have been confused. What had happened to Mr. Donegan? Just a few weeks earlier he had denounced Remington to his face, but now all he talked about was "sufficiency of the evidence," "federal law and the crime of perjury," and similar legal mumbo-jumbo. Brunini thought he understood Donegan's transformation from crusader to skeptic; at heart, he was with the Remington-haters, but at this time, he was forced to follow the orders of his Washington masters.

"You have put me in a bad hole," Donegan had supposedly told Brunini during the Remington investigation.

"I know I have, Tom," Brunini replied. "Your superiors expected you to control this Grand Jury and they'll not like it if you don't. But you cannot control this Grand Jury."

Following Donegan's address, Brunini excused him and invited Judge John W. Clancy to appear to answer any questions on points of law. Then the jury went into executive session for a meeting that lasted two hours. No record exists of the jurors' final deliberations, but shortly after noon, Donegan was summoned to the jury room. Brunini told him that the jury had voted unanimously to indict William Remington for committing perjury when he denied ever being a member of the Communist Party.[24]

Later, the grand jury investigation of Remington would become a subject of major controversy. Judge Learned Hand would attack Donegan and Brunini and accuse them of a host of judicial improprieties. Joe Rauh would call the mock courtroom where the hearing occurred the "scene of the crime"—the place where his client was more victim than villain. In addition to their cross-examination of Ann Remington, serious questions would be raised about the conduct of Thomas Donegan and John Brunini. Was it ethical for Brunini, given his personal and financial relationship with Elizabeth Bentley, to act as investigator and co-prosecutor and at the same time be foreman of a grand jury that was charged with objectively evaluating the evidence presented to it? Was it ethical for Thomas Donegan, who once was Bentley's personal attorney, to represent the Justice Department in a case in which Bentley was intimately involved? One does not have to be a member of the Remington defense team to conclude that the answer to these questions is no. Brunini's and Donegan's connections with Bentley; the improper, illegal, and abusive treatment of both Ann and William Remington; and the obsessive desire to win an indictment at any cost were disgraceful. Their conduct was also in violation of both the spirit and the letter of traditional American jurisprudence and an example of how excessive anti-Communism imitated totalitarian practices and poisoned American life during the postwar Red Scare.

Such misconduct, however, does not excuse Remington's own illegal behavior. Evidence indicates that Remington did commit perjury during his appearance before the grand jury, but, ironically, it occurred when he answered questions other than the one for which he was indicted. While it is likely that during his courtship Remington had told Ann that he was a Communist in Knoxville, no concrete evidence exists to prove that he formally joined the Communist Party. That he lived and worked within its orbit is unquestionable, but it would have been uncharacteristic of him to commit himself so irrevocably by joining. "Remington," a college friend once said, "was too smart to join anything." He enjoyed the danger of taking risks but always allowed himself a means of escape. It was, therefore, more likely that he associated with the Party in Knoxville but did not join.

It is possible to be more confident about Remington's answers to other questions. On May 22, 1950, he was asked if he sought a meeting with Communist Party officials in 1941 or 1942, and he answered no. Based on the evidence of his own later, written statement and the recollections of Franklin Folsom, that answer was false. On May 23, he was asked about his knowledge of Golos's and Bentley's Party affiliations, and he said that he had "nothing really definite, tangible, [or] ironclad," that pointed to such a connection. Again, according to his later confession, this answer, too, was false. Finally, on May 25, he was asked if he had any relationship with the Dartmouth Young Communist League, and he said no. While no evidence exists that Remington formally joined the Young Communist League, there is, according to those who did, little doubt that he was connected with it. Therefore, it is fair to conclude that Remington did commit perjury, but not when he answered the question that would now lead him to trial.[25]

At 12:30 P.M. on June 8, 1950, Brunini handed up the indictment to Judge Clancy. If convicted, Remington could receive a maximum prison term of five years and a two thousand dollar fine.[26]

Later that afternoon, the foreman and his colleagues accepted congratulations and fenced playfully with the press outside the courthouse. Asked if this was a runaway grand jury, Brunini laughed and said, "No comment." The jury acted "pleased over its indictment of Remington," conservative journalist Howard Rushmore observed. "They [were] smiling and some of them wink[ed] at reporters. The tension and strain of the past week seem lifted from their shoulders and some of them joked about 'earning a vacation' after next Thursday [June 15]." Brunini recalled that FBI officials were "jubilant. They had worked assiduously for several years to bring Remington to heel and effect his ouster from government. My back was vigorously slapped. . . . " J. Edgar Hoover later congratulated him on a job well done in a letter Brunini treasured, as he did the praise of Senator Karl Mundt, who told him, "your name will go down in history."[27]

While Brunini basked in his new-found glory, Judge John W. Clancy issued a warrant for Remington's arrest.[28]

14

Missionary Work

Joe Rauh later called it a dreadful week. It began on June 8 with the announcement that the special federal grand jury had indicted Remington for perjury. When Remington received the news, he hurried to Rauh's office to discuss strategy. Rauh recommended making a statement to the press.

"This is awfully risky," Remington said, worried about aggravating the government unnecessarily.

"It is only risky if you are guilty," Rauh replied. "I have to ask you once more, were you ever a member of the Communist Party? It is better to tell me now than later."

"I have never been a member of the Communist Party," he told Rauh again. Later that day, Remington appeared outside Rauh's office and again proclaimed his innocence to the waiting press. The U.S. attorney was also notified that Remington would surrender voluntarily on June 13, the day of the arraignment, so they could call off the U.S. marshals with the warrant for his arrest.[1]

The next day, Remington resigned from the Commerce Department. In a letter to Secretary Sawyer, he explained that he wished to devote all his time to proving his innocence. He felt no bitterness, just the deepest regret that he was leaving the government that he had served for his entire adult life. Sawyer never answered Remington's letter and accepted his resignation without official comment.[2]

On Monday, June 12, Remington's attorneys encountered a new and surprising obstacle. That morning, Henry Smith, an associate of Webster's, telephoned

the United States Fidelity and Guaranty Company to arrange for the five thousand dollar bail that would allow Remington to remain free to prepare for trial.

What is the charge contained in the indictment? asked a Fidelity official
named Bradbury.

Perjury, said Smith, regarding Communist Party membership.

"I'm very sorry," Bradbury said, "but Company policy forbids me from issuing
bonds for such offenses." He suggested that Smith contact one of the other companies. A bit annoyed, Smith took a cab to the office of Continental Casualty,
which generally issued bonds in criminal cases; not this time, however. Smith
was told to go to Hughes and Bates, located in the same building. Mr. Bates was
extremely belligerent, telling Smith that he thought Remington was guilty and
that he would never provide bond to a Communist. Angry now, Smith asked
him, "Wasn't it true that a bond would be written for a man charged with . . .
armed robbery?"

"Yes," Bates said, "but not in a case like this." No reputable New York surety
company will issue a bond for a Communist.

Smith discovered that Bates was right. He spent the rest of the day contacting ten other surety firms and was rejected by every one. Rauh was shocked to
learn of Smith's experience; Remington would never receive a fair trial in a city
polluted by such extremism. He offered his own home as collateral and made
calls, too, but was unsuccessful. They would have to ask Judge Clancy for a
reduction in bail and more time to raise it. If he refused or they failed to find the
money, Remington would go to jail, perhaps as soon as the next day, when he
was scheduled to be arraigned.[3]

To avoid the crowd of reporters milling around outside the courthouse,
Remington's lawyers brought him into the building through the subway entrance
and into Judge Clancy's courtroom for his 10:30 A.M. appearance. When John
Johnson, the clerk of the court, called Remington's name, Bill stepped up to the
bench briskly, flanked by Joe Rauh and Bethuel Webster.

"William Walter Remington," said Johnson, "this indictment charges you in
one count, on or about May 25, 1950, with committing perjury before a grand
jury. Are you guilty or not guilty?"

"Not guilty," Remington said, quietly but firmly; at the same moment, Rauh
was observed vigorously nodding his head, a gesture one journalist interpreted as
meaning, Amen! July 5 was set as the date for his next appearance, at which
time his lawyers would argue their motions.

When the government demanded that Remington's bail be set at five thousand dollars, Webster explained their predicament. His client was broke, and
since no surety company would assist him, he would have to raise the money
himself. Would the judge possibly reduce the sum to twenty-five hundred dollars?

He would not and gave Remington forty-eight hours to come up with the cash. Clancy did agree to permit Remington to live with his parents in Ridgewood, although it was outside the court's jurisdiction. Then, FBI agents came forward to take Remington to the Bureau's New York field office, on the building's sixth floor, where he was fingerprinted and photographed. When journalist Howard Rushmore later asked how Remington reacted, an agent allegedly replied, "Very cool—just like Hiss." A few hours later, Remington returned to the courthouse and paid his bail in five one-thousand-dollar bills, his mother's life savings.[4]

Rauh received more bad news the following day—Bethuel Webster was withdrawing from the case. There was another lawsuit coming up later that summer that his partners wanted him to handle, he explained to Rauh, and he doubted that he had the stamina to try both cases. Rauh urged him to think about it over the weekend, but the next day Webster told him that he was out. So, within one dreadful week, Remington was indicted, quit his job, barely made bail, and lost his principal attorney. "Bill was subjected to about every indignity humanly possible," Rauh later wrote Mary Robbins, a close friend of the Remington family. "He bore up bravely, . . . [but] is pretty discouraged. . . . "[5]

Rauh would stay on to the end, of course, but he immediately began a search for Webster's replacement. Hoping to repeat his earlier victories, he again searched for a distinguished conservative lawyer and eventually selected William C. Chanler, a corporate attorney and partner in one of New York's most prominent firms, Winthrop, Stimson, Putnam and Roberts, the founder of which was former Secretary of War Henry L. Stimson. Chanler was interested but wanted a week or two to review the case and to check with his associates before committing himself. (Among those he called was the Loyalty Review Board's George Alger, who told him that Remington was "as clean as a hound's tooth.")[6]

While Rauh waited for Chanler to decide, he focused on another major problem: raising the money to pay for Remington's defense. His client was broke and unemployed, and his parents were no longer in a position to provide more than room and board. Webster had told Rauh that a proper defense would cost over fifty thousand dollars. Where would the money come from? One possible source was a group of private benefactors, chief among them Mary Robbins, who proved to be Remington's most dedicated financial supporter. During June, she sent checks almost weekly—"I don't know what we would do without you," Rauh once told her. Rauh wrote candid letters to strangers in which he asked for contributions and described the challenges he faced and the importance of the case. " . . . I am . . . completely convinced of Bill's innocence," he wrote to one potential donor on June 19,

> but I am not naive enough to think that the odds are on our side. . . . The FBI has 200 agents ranging around the country looking for minor events that will color the jury's thinking about Remington. The Justice Department has anywhere from half a dozen to a dozen lawyers working on the case. I do not begrudge them this. I

simply want to get sufficient brain-power on our side to make a competent and thorough defense of a case which seems to me so extremely important to civil liberties. . . . If Bill is convicted, the McCarthyites will certainly re-double their efforts to make the Loyalty Program a method of ousting all non-conformists. An acquittal would help stop the trend that way.

The money did not exactly pour in, but Rauh proved to be a better fund-raiser than he anticipated. By the end of June, he had received almost ten thousand dollars. The money and letters of support were very encouraging and, as Rauh told one contributor, "compensated for a lot of pain."[7]

The greater sum, if Rauh were lucky, would come from the James Marshall Civil Liberties Trust, to which he applied for a grant in late June. "This is a civil liberties case of the highest import," he wrote James Marshall, the chairman of the trust, on June 24. Could a man accused of Communism or disloyalty obtain a fair trial? Was not Remington's indictment double jeopardy? His case had been thoroughly examined by the President's Loyalty Review Board; if this group of distinguished lawyers had believed Remington was a member of the Communist Party, he would not have been cleared. The government was also using perjury indictments as a vehicle to re-try a man already found innocent of pro-Communism. "Grave consideration for the future hinges on the outcome of this case," Rauh insisted.[8]

He was successful. On June 27, he learned that the Marshall trustees had voted him twenty thousand dollars, the largest grant the group had ever awarded. Shortly afterwards, Chanler agreed to represent Remington.[9]

On July 5, 1950, William Chanler made his first appearance as Remington's attorney in the courtroom of Judge T. Whitfield Davidson. This was the day when the defense was supposed to present motions and the judge was to set a trial date, but neither happened. Chanler asked for two weeks to study this complicated case, and Judge Davidson granted the delay and postponed the hearing until July 19. Among the courtroom observers was the FBI's Roger Tuohy, who informed Washington that Chanler was now Remington's attorney. "Search of Bufiles indicates William C. Chanler IS a particularly able and highly regarded attorney," one official notified Hoover later that day.[10]

He was, indeed. Born in England in 1896, William Chamberlain Chanler grew up in luxurious surroundings in New York, where his father served as lieutenant governor from 1906 to 1908, and was educated at both Harvard College and the Harvard Law School. After graduating and passing the bar exam in 1922, he joined the prestigious firm of Winthrop, Stimson, Putnam and Roberts at 40 Wall Street. Although he represented corporate clients and specialized in antitrust law, he was also drawn to public service. As counsel to the city's Seabury Commission, Chanler helped oust corrupt Mayor Jimmy Walker from office. His successor, Mayor Fiorello H. La Guardia, appointed him the city's corporation counsel in 1938. During the next four years, Chanler attempted to rid the city of corrupt businessmen and gamblers and reformed the way that members of the City Council were elected. In 1942, he joined the Army and was sent abroad as the chief legal officer for the Allied military government in Italy and Sicily. With the war's end, he returned to private practice. The Remington case would be his first venture in criminal law, but Rauh was satisfied that he had all the credentials he was searching for: conservative and anti-Communist, member of the New York establishment, and a litigator whose own skills were supported by a host of able young lawyers at Winthrop, Stimson. "I shall assist Mr. Chanler," Rauh told Mary Robbins, "but I am hopeful that he and his large firm will be able to bear the brunt of the battle. . . ."[11]

The battle would commence on July 18, so now Rauh and Chanler prepared their opening salvo. It was a motion for a bill of particulars, which Chanler would present to the court. The *Federal Rules of Criminal Procedure* and recent Supreme Court rulings required that a grand jury indictment "shall be a plain, concise and definite statement of the essential facts" of the crime. To Remington's lawyers, his indictment lacked all these qualities. Remington's bill of particulars asked the government to answer nine questions. When, where, and how did Remington join the Communist Party? When and where was Remington a Communist Party member and what duties did he perform? Which events of Remington's life was the government using to prove that he had committed perjury? And, most important, What did the government mean when it used the term "member of the Communist Party?" "The vagueness and indefiniteness of this term is one of the most confusing puzzles of our society today," Chanler wrote. "From the man on the street to the members of Congress the term 'member of the Communist Party' is bandied about without any concrete or definite meaning." Because of such confusion, "the Government should state whether it is relying on membership or affiliation with a student group, labor organization, fraternal group, learned society or political organization as proof of 'membership in the Communist Party.'" Here, too, the government should be held to rigid specificity—identify the exact Party unit of which it believed Remington was a member. Finally, if the government did not know the answers to these questions, it should be required to admit it, and if in the future such knowledge was obtained, the government should give it to the defense. On July 19, Chanler submitted to the court his intention to move for a bill of particulars (and the factual and legal memorandum supporting it). U.S. attorney Irving Saypol immediately stated that he would vigorously fight Chanler's request, during the oral argument that was scheduled for July 24.[12]

With Judge Stanley Sugarman presiding, William Chanler and Thomas Donegan squared off in the opening round of the Remington case. Chanler argued that given the great public turmoil caused by the Communist-in-government issue, Remington was entitled to all the legal safeguards provided by the Constitution. Here was a man who for the past five years had been investigated by every agency of the U.S. government—the FBI, committees of the Senate and the House of Representatives, and three grand juries, one of which indicted him on a vague and narrow charge. How could his attorneys properly defend him, if "we don't know what [the government] claims the essential facts are which constitute being a member of the Communist Party?"

Donegan rejected this view. The indictment was specific; to answer the questions posed by the defense would result in the disclosure of evidence vital to the government's case. That was what Remington's attorney was really seeking. He reminded the court that Chanler had described the long investigation of Remington, during which he was asked at least seven times whether he was or had been a member of the Communist Party, and Remington had answered no. Therefore, he must have known what it meant to be a Communist Party member.

Judge Sidney Sugarman found Donegan's position troubling. He recalled a time when a citizen could register to vote for a Communist Party candidate in New York. What if that voter was not a member of the Communist Party? Might that simple act be used by the government as proof that the person was a member?

"That is just what I would like to know," Chanler said.

It "could be one of the items of proof to be offered by the Government at the trial," Donegan replied.

This is what the judge feared, and he continued to explore Donegan's views. The Communist Party was now radically different from the Party of the past. "Isn't the defendant entitled to know in which category you claim he is placed?"

Donegan gave the same answer. If the government did have a voter registration card issued to William Remington, it would be considered evidence that should not be given to him before trial.

Sugarman became angry. " . . . I am not going to be victimized here because of the present unpopularity of the Communists; . . . We are concerned with the rights of defendants. . . . That is the . . . American view. . . . " Nevertheless, the judge would not issue an immediate opinion; he wanted to study the briefs before reaching a decision.

The last subject discussed was the trial date, and for the first time that morning, Donegan and Chanler were in agreement. Both preferred some time in mid-September, so the trial was postponed until that time, and the session ended.[13]

Chanler and Rauh left the courthouse pleased with the way the hearing had gone, but when the judge issued his decision on July 28, they found that they had won only a partial victory. Judge Sugarman ordered the government to answer the nine questions contained in the bill of particulars. If the government did not know, it must say so, and should it subsequently acquire that information, the defendant must be informed. But Sugarman also allowed the government to keep secret any documentary material it would later use as evidence to prove its charge. And, on the issue he had found so perplexing that day—how to define Communist Party membership—he was silent; it would be left to the jury to solve this riddle.

U.S. attorney Saypol complied with the order and, on August 17, issued an answer to the bill of particulars:

1. As to the time when and the place where the defendant became a member of the Communist Party:
   (a) Unknown.
2. As to the times when and the places where the defendant was a member of the Communist Party:
   (a) Hanover, New Hampshire—in or about the years 1934, 1935, 1936.
   (b) Knoxville, Tennessee—in or about the years 1937, 1938, 1939.
   (c) Washington, District of Columbia—in or about the years 1941, 1942, 1943, 1944.
3. As to the particular organization, fraction, cell or other subdivision within the Communist Party of which William Walter Remington is claimed to have been a member:
   (a). Unknown.

Saypol's response confirmed what Rauh had long believed; the government had no direct proof that Remington had ever joined the Communist Party "and simply planned to produce a large volume of damaging circumstantial evidence showing association with Communists and left-wing views" that would lead the jury to create its own definition of Communist Party membership. The burden of proof would be shifted from prosecution to defense—it would be up to Remington to convince the jury that he had never been a Communist. Adding to their difficulties was the time period they would have to explore—a decade from Remington's freshman year at Dartmouth (they "had the gall to say he was a Communist . . . when he was 16 years . . . old," Rauh fumed) to 1944, when he joined the Navy. (Inexplicably, they omitted 1939 and 1940, when Remington studied in New York and worked part-time in Washington.) There would be hundreds of potential witnesses to interview—college friends and enemies, TVA associates, government workers and ex-naval officers, by a staff numbering less than ten—Rauh; Chanler and two Winthrop, Stimson junior lawyers; a private detective; and friends who volunteered to help, like Remington's fiancée, Jane Shepherd, and Nancy Wechsler, wife of the *New York Post* editor. On the other side was the FBI, which had hundreds of agents covering the same ground.[14]

The FBI's perjury investigation was one of the most extensive and aggressive in recent Bureau history. "The case must be handled as 'special,'" J. Edgar Hoover told his troops on June 12. " . . . All possible leads . . . must be developed fully and handled promptly. This investigation must receive continuous attention looking towards successful prosecution." Over the next eight months, FBI agents conducted interviews and searched for evidence of Remington's

Communist Party membership in forty states, the District of Columbia, Hawaii, England, France, West Germany, Iran, Thailand, and Japan. The Bureau was also at the virtual disposal of Donegan and Saypol, who called upon it on an almost daily basis to seek out specific individuals or to evaluate fresh information.[15]

Like an invading army, FBI agents once again foraged around the Dartmouth campus, interviewing professors and administrators, and then spread out in search of former students who might know something about Remington. Of special interest were Bill Martin and Page Smith, Remington's former radical friends, who were now his foremost critics. Once they were fellow believers in "radical, Socialistic, . . . even Communistic ideas," Martin told the FBI, but after Remington returned from Knoxville in 1937, he was a changed man and rejected his old radical friends to "curry favor with college [administrators], business executives, and Government officials, in a constant effort to promote his personal career." Page Smith, Remington's former roommate and now in graduate school at Harvard, recalled that Remington participated in the activities of the Young Communist League but had no evidence that he was a formal member of the Party. Copies of the Martin and Smith interviews were sent to Thomas Donegan, who tagged them as likely government witnesses. Agents were ordered to locate other members of the YCL to determine if they would testify against Remington. But, despite all its efforts, the FBI never found concrete evidence that Remington was, as the government charged, a member of the YCL or the Communist Party while at Dartmouth.[16]

The Knoxville period proved a more fertile hunting ground. The FBI's most important breakthrough occurred on June 29, when Christine Benson telephoned the Knoxville office, seeking an appointment to talk with agents. When first contacted by the FBI on May 1, she had denied having been a member of the Communist Party. She had admitted to knowing Remington but had no knowledge that he was a Communist. The FBI had asked to talk with her again in mid-June, but, after consulting her attorney, she had declined to be interviewed. Local agents had kept the pressure on. One had telephoned on June 28 to say that his office had recently received a number of allegations that she had been a Communist. Perhaps Mrs. Benson might wish to join others who had previously refused to acknowledge their membership and give them a detailed statement. If she did, the agent strongly implied, she would probably save herself a trip to New York to testify at Remington's trial. This was a highly exaggerated account of the FBI's recent achievements. By that date, only two men had placed Christine in the unit—not the horde of former Communists the agent had suggested. The FBI had tried to trick Christine, and it worked. On June 29, she admitted her own past membership and also implicated Bill Remington.

She had joined the Party in October 1936, she told Agents Parker and McSwain during her seventy-minute interview but refused to name her recruiter or any other members of the group besides Remington and herself. She thought that Remington had also joined that fall and was certain that he had attended between six and eight Communist Party meetings, although she could not remember precisely where these meetings took place. (That they probably were held in her home on Churchwell Avenue may have had something to do with her inability to remember.) "She was under considerable emotional strain during the interview," Parker later noted, expressing great concern about how her involvement would affect her children and her husband's career with TVA (Forrest Benson was also being questioned about his loyalty). She was very reluctant to testify at the trial but would do so, if it was required. Over and over she said that she and her friends had done nothing wrong in joining the Communist Party; their activities were "carried out with a laudable purpose in mind and were particularly beneficial to organized labor." Although she had left the Party in 1938, she was still committed to the goals of economic and social justice she had fought for in the 1930s. "At this point," Parker observed, "Mrs. Benson broke into tears and the interview was terminated." The Knoxville office immediately informed Washington of its triumph, and Christine Benson's name was placed high on the government's list of potential witnesses.

While Benson seemed to corroborate the charge that Remington had been a member of the Party, there were weaknesses in her statement that the FBI ignored. She had said that she was given a membership book, paid dues, and received receipt stamps but had no evidence that Remington did. Nor did she know who recruited him or have any memory of his potential membership being discussed by the tiny group prior to his joining, as was the case with others. Moreover, Knoxville's initial reports, including the one sent to Assistant Attorney General James McInery, said nothing about the deceptive tactics employed to persuade her to talk. Later, McInery would ask FBI officials "whether any missionary work had been done" to persuade her to cooperate and to explain how the interview had come about. In the long run, this mattered less to the government than that they had acquired another person willing to testify that Remington had joined the Communist Party in Knoxville.[17]

Muriel Speare Williams also soon joined this group of cooperative witnesses. Years before, she had admitted to being a Communist Party member during appearances before congressional committees investigating Communism in the TVA but had not implicated her closest friends. She had also defended the Party and had refused to call it un-American. By the summer of 1950, however, she was ready to cooperate with the FBI, but not completely; she would only answer specific questions rather than volunteer information. On August 7, she told agents that it was her impression that Remington was a member of the Communist Party at Knoxville, although she was quick to add that she had no specific knowledge of his actual membership or attendance at Communist Party meetings. She still tried to protect her dearest friends: Christine Benson, who had encouraged her to join the Party in the spring of 1937, was not among those she named. As weak as her statement was regarding Remington, Williams nevertheless became another potential government witness.[18]

So did Henry Hart, who also had never called Remington a Party member. In 1948, he told the FBI that Remington was just "an energetic young man," but when agents visited Hart in October 1950, he had changed his mind. Howard Bridgman's testimony now led him to conclude that Remington probably was a member in 1937. Only Mabel Abercrombie Mansfield continued to insist that she had never joined the Communist Party and did not know Remington to be a member.[19] Everyone except Mansfield and Todd was willing to testify against their former friend.

Having corralled Benson, Williams, and Hart was not enough for the FBI. Agents also combed through Knoxville and the surrounding countryside searching for anyone who knew, saw, or heard of Bill Remington in 1936–37. They talked to policemen, landlords, TVA employees, textile workers, and postmen, among others, but found no evidence of Remington's Party membership, just opinions, impressions, and speculations.[20] So, the Bureau returned to its two original witnesses—Kenneth McConnell and Howard Bridgman, hoping that refreshed memories might produce something more concrete.

For a moment that summer, McConnell held out that possibility in the Remington case's version of the "pumpkin papers." McConnell recalled once owning a notebook filled with the names and addresses of many Communist Party members as well as detailed information on meetings and conferences, and, as he told agents that June, he thought Remington's name must be listed. Unfortunately, the notebook was lost, the result of a nasty domestic spat McConnell had had with a man named Kenneth, with whom he had lived in Washington in November and December 1945. McConnell had become ill and had returned to North Carolina, leaving Kenneth with a forty-dollar phone bill; in retaliation, Kenneth had refused to return his belongings. Pressed for more details, McConnell admitted that he could not remember Kenneth's last name or the address of their apartment. Perhaps a trip to the Capital might help his memory, so in late June, agents took him to Washington, where they drove around aimlessly until, by chance, McConnell recognized the building on Swann Street where they had lived. Kenneth was no longer there—the landlord had never heard of him—and others were now living in apartment 55. The notebook had disappeared, too. The FBI never found it. The incident was proof that chicken farmer McConnell could raise false hopes as well as poultry.[21]

Howard Bridgman also continued to be a difficult witness. Faced with the undeniable evidence that Betty Malcolm did not arrive in Knoxville until mid-June 1937, he finally eliminated her as one of the original members of the unit but could think of no one to replace her. Not even a trip to Knoxville in September could improve his memory; in fact, it probably created further confusion, because the one residence he identified immediately was the house on Forrest Avenue where Betty Malcolm had lived in the summer of 1937. (Had agents thought to drive him a bit further north, to 121 Churchwell Avenue, he might have recognized the old Victorian home where Christine Benson had lived in the winter of 1936–37, the most likely spot of the Communist Party meetings he had attended.) Nevertheless, the government still considered him an important witness.[22]

While agents in Boston, Charlotte, and Knoxville were hard at work, others interviewed Remington's former neighbors in New York and Washington, ex-colleagues with the War Production Board and former naval officers with whom he had studied in Colorado. Only a few potential witnesses were identified, those who could testify that Remington had access to information regarding air-plane production and knowledge of the formula to create rubber from garbage, although no one could testify that he had passed secret material to Bentley.[23]

At the same time, a special team from the Washington field office was assigned to Ann Remington in the hope that she could be persuaded to change her mind about testifying. Ann must "be handled with utmost discretion and treated with extreme care," Donegan advised headquarters in September, "so that she may be kept in a peaceful frame of mind and her status as a Government witness not jeopardized." She continued to cooperate but was extremely ambiva-lent about giving names. She did not want to become known as the "Spy Queen Informant," she told agents, by accusing people not directly connected with the case. To do so, she feared, might affect her ability to earn a living and also stig-matize her children. But she also wanted to help the FBI find people who would not only corroborate her testimony but legitimize it, to prove that Remington was wrong in treating her as if she were mentally incompetent. The FBI kept this fear alive by telling her that Remington's lawyers planned to focus on her emotional problems as a means of discrediting her. This approach, however, only increased her uncertainty—testifying would destroy her ex-husband but at the possible cost of the love and respect of her children and friends. The result was that Donegan and Saypol remained doubtful that she would appear.[24]

Bill Remington and his lawyers were also uncertain about what Ann was going to do. If she did not testify, the government's case would be severely weak-ened, perhaps fatally. If she did, then Remington's chance of acquittal was slim, at best. Bill tried to explore Ann's attitude in early September, when he visited Tauxemont to drop off his children after the court had allowed him to take Bruce and Gale on a brief vacation to Vermont. To break the ice, Bill talked first about their trip and how happy the children seemed, which pleased her. Then he became more serious.

"It would be a big help to me and my lawyers if you could . . . tell me what questions you were asked in New York, and what you are able to remember about your answers," he said.

"I won't talk to anyone. . . . That's final," Ann replied.

But just as swiftly, her mood could change.

"I'm going to win this trial," Bill said as he was leaving.

Ann's reply encouraged him, "I hope so," she said. Perhaps, she would not testify, and the trial he feared would never take place.[25]

15

Not in This Day and Time

William Chanler and Joe Rauh spent the summer and fall of 1950 searching for another William Remington—not the disciplined Communist Party member of the government's imagination but the rebel who challenged all political orthodoxies and was the prisoner of none. Like the FBI (although on a much smaller scale and without the coercive tactics), Remington's attorneys sought out those people who knew him between 1934 and 1944, hoping to find allies who would help them to refute the government's charges.

They, too, began with Remington's career at Dartmouth. The men they talked to were governed by one of two emotions—fear or a dislike of Remington that bordered on hatred. Donald Miller, the radical who befriended Remington during his freshman year, was very anxious to help, Rauh learned, but equally anxious not to be a witness. A founder of *Scientific American* and now its business manager, Miller felt that exposing his own radical past at the trial would damage his magazine. Rauh told him that they would not call him. Despite his anxiety, Miller recommended men whom Rauh should see: Fran Bartlett, a member of the Communist Party following his graduation in 1935, and Robert Boehm, a radical who had written for *Steeplejack*. They had been men of principle, fighters against privilege and the stuffy status-quo on the Dartmouth campus in the mid-1930s. Surely one of them would help Remington.[1]

Neither man would. When Chanler's assistant, James S. Rosenman, visited Robert Boehm, now comfortably situated in his law office at 60 Wall Street, he was reluctant to talk and frightened because the FBI had interviewed him about Marxist study groups and the Young Communist League. "He told me very frankly that he does not like the prospect of being dragged into the case," Rosenman later told Chanler and Rauh. Francis Bartlett and his ex-wife, Dorothy, also refused to testify for Remington—"not in this day and time," the former Mrs. Bartlett said.[2]

If fear inhibited the older Communists, it was animosity toward Remington that affected the younger radicals who had once been his closest friends. Charles Livermore, former president of the American Student Union in 1938, gave Rauh a warm welcome when he saw him in Buffalo on September 15, but it quickly became evident that Livermore detested Remington. What so annoyed him was Remington's habit of blaming his wife and mother-in-law for all his troubles. Rauh countered by arguing that Remington would never have met Bentley except for the family relationship, but this had no impact on Livermore. Still, he was willing to tell Rauh about his interview with the FBI and did have some interesting news about Bill Martin. A year ago, Livermore said, Martin told him that he and Remington were once members of the Young Communist League at Dartmouth but that Remington had been thrown out for "deviationist tendencies." When Rauh pressed for more details, Livermore was reticent. Later, however, he admitted that he was invited to join the YCL and signed a card with a fictitious name but could not remember whether Remington had been present.[3]

Rauh returned to upstate New York on September 26 to see Remington's oldest friend turned bitterest enemy, Bill Martin. The former Dartmouth Communist was now an untenured sociology instructor at Colgate University, located in the remote village of Hamilton, New York. Rauh drove down from Syracuse amidst the splendor of an eastern fall, the trees looking like they had burst into flame. He arrived at the Martins' apartment without prior notice, so Martin's wife was startled when he knocked on the door and introduced himself as Bill Remington's lawyer. During a seventy-five-minute conversation, Rauh and Martin discussed the two Bills, the Dartmouth YCL, and what Martin had told the FBI. "I told them I had been in the YCL at Dartmouth and that I did not know whether Remington had been," Martin said. (This was not completely true. Martin had said that Remington was a member but could not remember whether he had a card or paid dues.) To Rauh, Martin said that he assumed that Remington was a member but could not prove it. Nevertheless, he thought and spoke like a YCLer.

Can you name those who belonged or participated? the lawyer asked.

Walter Bernstein, Charles Livermore, Page Smith, and others, said Martin. It was an informal group—no one kept membership records, and people paid dues infrequently; I was the chief recruiter and organizer.

If it was as disorganized as you describe, is it accurate to call it a chapter?

Perhaps not, Martin said. Although he had told his friends that he had ejected Remington from the YCL, he now told Rauh (as he had the FBI) that he had just a hazy recollection of this period.

At the conclusion of their meeting, Martin said frankly that he did not want to get mixed up in the case. Perhaps, that is why his memory suddenly became so poor. Had he been willing to testify confidently that he had kicked Remington out of the YCL (as he had definitely told Livermore in 1949), he could have helped to refute the government's charge that Remington was a Party member. His refusal to come forward was a petty and cruel revenge, which seriously damaged his former friend.[4]

Walter Bernstein and Page Smith were also hostile toward Remington. When Rauh saw Bernstein in October, he had trouble remembering Remington—a javelin thrower and a romantic figure on campus was about all he could recall about him. He also told Rauh that he did not know anyone on campus who belonged to the YCL or the Party. Furthermore, he felt that Remington wrongfully turned on others, such as his wife. Unlike Remington, Bernstein was "not sorry for anything he'd done and . . . wasn't going to grovel. . . . " This bluster did not impress Rauh, who knew that Bernstein was lying about his own past. "I just don't know what he'd say [at trial]," Rauh concluded, eliminating Bernstein as a possible defense witness.[5]

There was no question as to where Page Smith stood. He told James Rosenman on October 6 that he expected to be a witness for the prosecution. Smith was absolutely certain that Remington had been a YCL member and was eager to testify. Rosenman told him that he was confused. Remington had been indicted for denying membership in the Communist Party, not in the YCL. Embarrassed by this news, Smith now said that he regretted talking to the FBI and went on to defend Remington. They had shared a small dormitory room in 1938–39, so Smith felt that he would certainly have known if Remington was a member. Remington, he said, was "too domineering not to have lorded it over him . . . by boasting of his CP connection. . . . " Despite his initial confusion and his strong feeling that Remington was not a Party member, Smith still considered himself a hostile witness. He recounted what another alumnus had told him recently: "Why should I perjure myself to help Bill Remington?"[6]

Remington made his own voyage into the past that October, going back to Dartmouth. It was not the traditional homecoming, where distinguished alumnus, his early promise fulfilled, revisits the scene of old triumphs. Remington went not with his wife and children but with his lawyer, who had had to ask the court's permission for his client to leave briefly its jurisdiction. The government had no objection, in fact it was an opportunity to discover what records the accused wanted and who might be asked to testify. From the FBI and other sources (including Dean Neidlinger), Donegan learned precisely when Remington and James Rosenman arrived in Hanover, how long they stayed, what back issues of The Dartmouth and college yearbooks Remington read (Donegan wanted his own copies), and which New Hampshire and Vermont residents were being considered as witnesses.[7]

It was not a pleasant visit. Professors Sidney Cox and Allan MacDonald, who once supported the campus Communists, were angry at Remington for denying his radical past and were, therefore, unwilling to help. No one could recall any anti-Communist acts or speeches by Remington during his years in Hanover; on the contrary, everyone remembered him as a radical. The only thing that the professors could testify to was the mood of the times—that there was no clear dividing line separating radicals and liberals from Communists—all favored the Spanish Loyalists and opposed war.[8]

Remington felt better after talking to Elba Chase Nelson at her farm in Hillsboro, Vermont. She did not recognize Remington, which was good news, because Elba Chase Nelson had been head of the New Hampshire Communist Party from 1934 to 1939 and was still a committed Communist. If Remington had been a member of the Party, she would have known, Mrs. Chase said. She was close to all the members and had never seen Remington until that afternoon. Just as important, she was willing to testify, if subpoenaed. At last, after months of interviews, they had found a person who seemed unafraid of going to court for Bill Remington.[9]

George Edson was willing, too. They met him at his bakery shop in West Lebanon, New Hampshire, the next day, and as customers shouted orders, Edson explained that he had been a member of both the YCL and the Communist Party when he was a student at the University of New Hampshire in the 1930s. He knew Remington only slightly but well enough to appreciate that he was too independent to ever accept Party discipline. Edson would testify, he said, if it would help Bill. Remington and Rosenman returned to New York a bit more optimistic than when they started—they had found two strangers brave enough to confront the government of the United States.[10]

Not every member of the Dartmouth community was unwilling to assist Remington. William Goodman and Charles Davis, his allies in the struggle against Bill Martin's ASU, offered to testify. Davis, the African American whom Remington had hesitated inviting to his wedding, was now an assistant professor of English at New York University. Although untenured and at risk in publicly supporting a man accused of being a Communist, Davis believed it was a matter of principle to testify about Bill's fighting the ASU. So did Bill Goodman, now a manufacturer of felt hats in Danbury, Connecticut. Ironically, he had a familial link to the prosecution. His wife's family had known the parents of government lawyer Roy Cohn, and Goodman's brother-in-law, Frank Karelsen, had gone to school with Saypol's young assistant. When Cohn learned that Goodman was going to appear for Remington, he telephoned Karelsen and said, "You better tell Bill Goodman, not to testify, or we'll get him!" Karelsen informed Goodman of Cohn's threat, and he just laughed it off. Both Davis and Goodman would make good witnesses, Rauh felt, a professor and a businessman, each with excellent war records and impeccable anti-Communist credentials, and they were not afraid.[11]

Next, Rauh focused his attention on Bill's years in Knoxville and with the help of Rosenman and William Hindman, another of Chanler's assistants, began to interview Remington's TVA friends.

They were not friendly anymore. An attempt was made to talk with Pat Todd, but it failed. "I have never seen anyone more frightened and nervous than Todd was during the few minutes we were with him," Rauh later told Chanler. On a swing through Knoxville, William Hindman spoke with Christine Benson. She was angry at Remington, blaming him for the trouble she and her husband now faced. On the TVA unit, she was very vague, remembering only that she and Remington had attended some party meetings at the home of Jim Persons, an African American. She did not recall the meetings at Betty Malcolm's house that Bridgman had described. (Later, during a trip to New York, she talked with Chanler and repeated the same story—that the only Communist Party meetings she had ever attended were at the Personses' house.) If she told this story on the stand, it might weaken Bridgman's credibility, but given her hatred for Remington, there was no way to predict what she might say.[12]

Henry Hart, now a political scientist at the University of Wisconsin, was also uncooperative. Although he had publicly testified three times about his life in the Communist Party and had never once implicated Remington, he refused to help. Learning that Rauh was planning a trip to Madison to speak at the law school (and see him), he wrote the lawyer that he did not wish to be called as a defense witness because he now thought that Remington was probably guilty. Howard Bridgman's testimony was generally accurate, he believed, and a long talk with Muriel Williams earlier that summer had convinced him that he had been ignorant of a great many things regarding the Communist Party in Knoxville. Hart kept FBI agents informed of everything he was doing—he gave them copies of his correspondence with Rauh, informed them of their future meeting, and assured them that he would not reveal the information about Remington he was giving the FBI.[13]

"The conversation started slowly, almost as if we were fencing with each other," Rauh later wrote of his meeting with Hart on October 14.

Have you talked to the FBI recently? Rauh asked.

"They come up here regularly," Hart said. (FBI records indicate that agents talked with Hart five times in September and twice in early October.)

Would you please tell me what you told them?

He would not.

Rauh explained that no matter what Remington had done in 1936, he was entitled to be defended by someone who knew the truth. Why are you so certain that I am wrong about Remington?

The Bridgman testimony and other incidents he had recently remembered.

One was the memory of Remington describing socialists as "mostly pedestrian people," while "poets and people who really manage things join the Communist Party." He also recalled that Bill once considered hanging pictures of Lenin and Stalin in their room.

I do not think that proves that Remington was a member of the Party.

It was the Bridgman testimony, Hart repeated. Rauh then took a copy of Bridgman's testimony from his briefcase, and together they went through it page by page, Rauh pointing out the errors. Hart nodded and even noted that there were more but still thought that, basically, Bridgman was correct. Why then did Rauh want him to testify?

Because three times you have given sworn testimony that contradicted Bridgman.

But now things are different, Hart claimed; I do not want to testify.

It all depends on Bridgman, Rauh said; if he will admit that he had been mistaken or confused, then it will not be necessary to call you. Joe Rauh, basically a warm-hearted, generous man, never forgave Hart for turning his back on Remington. " . . . I feel quite bitter and resentful for what he has done," he later told a friend. " . . . If there were less Henry Harts there would be less prosecutions of the vindictive kind that we are suffering now."[14]

The most candid member of the TVA group was Muriel Speare Williams, who met with William Hindman that October. Unfortunately, she was certain that Remington was guilty and expected to testify for the government. Williams said that she was convinced that Remington had been a Party member. For a decade, she had lied to congressional committees and felt fortunate that she was never held in contempt, but now she believed that honesty was the only way to protect herself.

Why are you so certain that Remington had been a Party member? Hindman asked.

Because the TVA cell was a close-knit organization, whose tiny membership constantly interacted with one another. Remington was part of the group, she insisted, a member; although under Hindman's cross-examination, she admitted that she had never seen his membership book, had never heard him state that he was a member, and could not recall any specific Party meeting he had attended. Nevertheless, she was convinced that Remington was a member.

Williams's testimony was potentially quite damaging, but at least the defense was prepared for it. As the lawyer prepared to leave, Muriel's husband remarked that the TVA episode was like "a very small ink spot in a very small puddle of water." Unfortunately, men were now drowning in such shallow waters.[15]

Perhaps Horace Bryan would be their lifeline. Of the men and women who knew Remington well in Knoxville, only Bryan had come forward to support him. Could he be believed? His story, told to Chanler over dinner at Childs's Restaurant, seemed improbable because Bryan had been a Communist-at-large in Arkansas, who claimed that when he lived in Knoxville in the spring of 1937 he saw no Party activity.

If his testimony made sense, a jury might like Bryan, a veteran unionist, descended from pioneers who blazed trails across the continent with Daniel Boone.

"How was it possible," Chanler asked him, "that someone who had been a Communist . . . should move into Knoxville and work with the TVA group, rooming with Pat Todd who was [allegedly] the chief Communist organizer . . . and not realize that they were Communists?"

It was perfectly simple, Bryan explained. CP membership was irrelevant—"they were all engaged in the same activity, trying to organize labor in the South; everybody was fighting for the same objectives. The interests and activities of the Communists were not distinct from those of other labor leaders and organizers." It had never occurred to him that Remington might be a Communist. He recalled Bill "as a wild young boy who wanted to . . . get into labor organizing activities." Had there been an active Communist Party recruiting effort going on in the spring of 1937, he would have known it.[16]

Perhaps Bryan was right, Rauh and Chanler eventually concluded. Muriel Williams did not join the Party until June; Henry Hart, not until August; while Bridgman could only recall attending meetings that could not have occurred until late June, barely a week before both Bryan and Remington left Knoxville. Apparently, the major push to sign up members came that summer. Furthermore, Bryan had been forced to run the government's gauntlet and had emerged unscathed. He had appeared in secret session before HUAC; the FBI had interviewed him a dozen times; and he had testified before Brunini's grand jury without being indicted. And he was tough. He liked to remind the lawyers that his great-grandmother was a full-blooded Cherokee Indian, and, although he knew he was risking his job with the New Jersey State Park Commission, he would not run from a fight. Remington was being persecuted; it was his duty to help him. Chanler and Rauh could not say no, although they were aware of Muriel Williams's comment: "If Bryan says that Remington is not a Communist . . . , he is lying. . . ."[17]

Finding witnesses to testify to Remington's patriotism during the war years proved to be the easiest task. Thomas Blaisdell, despite all the trouble Bill had caused him, remained faithful—"You can rest assured that I will not say anything that will hurt Bill," he told Rauh in November. Charles J. Hitch, who worked with Remington on developing the Controlled Materials plan at the War Production Board, was actually anxious to testify. He recalled that both the liberal and the Communist press denounced the plan, calling it pro–big business and a surrender of civilian control to the military. Although he could not remember any specific anti-Communist statement Bill made during that period, "he just never would have dreamed that Remington was a Communist." Daniel

Hopkinson remembered clearly Remington's opposition to the Morgenthau plan when both men were in London after the war. Hopkinson was also "lily white" (as he put it), "never belonged to anything or been a radical of any sort," which, in 1950, were the chief criteria in witness selection.[18]

Rauh also encountered difficulties. People who had worked closely with Remington in 1940 suddenly suffered memory lapses when asked about his call for aid to Britain and increased American preparedness—programs opposed by the Communists at that time. Oscar Altman, for example, told Rauh that while their entire office supported such efforts, he could remember nothing that Remington said or did. He recommended that Rauh contact Ezra Glazer. Glazer could not remember anything either. Call Paul Fisher, Spurgeon Bell, and Burke Horton, he said. Rauh spoke to all three, and they remembered nothing. Everyone seemed friendly and sympathetic, making it difficult for him to determine if they were unable to remember or simply unwilling.[19]

While investigating Remington's activities in the 1940s, Rauh and Chanler gave particular attention to the question of the formula that Bentley said she had received from Remington. Without access to Bentley's original FBI statement, they did not know how a meaningless oral report became magically transformed into a top secret document. Their own interviews indicated that Remington had correctly characterized the process as a joke, of value only to the man who invented it—William Jeans, a California scientist, who had been working on a means to convert garbage into low-grade gasoline and then to synthetic rubber. Ralph Austrian, a WPB official, learned of the project in the fall of 1942 and was ordered to evaluate it. A pilot plant was established on the back lot of Universal Studios, but it quickly became clear that the plan was worthless. Furthermore, no formula was ever sent to Washington—"There was just a lot of talk about it," said one official, Jim Newman, "and the whole idea exploded almost as soon as it came in." While the patent was secret, the process itself was widely discussed at the WPB and was never considered classified. Bentley's formula was just as much a fantasy as anything else produced by Universal Pictures in 1942.[20]

The man Rauh considered the most important defense witness was four thousand miles away, in Paris—Bernard S. Redmont, the journalist Remington introduced to Bentley in 1943. In 1948, Bentley had called him one of her agents but testified that Redmont, who had worked in the newsroom of the Coordinator of Inter-American Affairs, had given her no secret information. Redmont, then a correspondent for U.S. News & World Report, immediately issued a statement denying her accusations and described Bentley exactly as did Remington. He knew her as Helen Johnson, a researcher. They met just a few times and discussed material available to any journalist. He had asked to appear before HUAC to clear his name, but the committee did not call him. The FBI also interviewed him in August 1948, and he appeared before the grand jury in

September, but no indictment was voted. He was questioned again by the FBI in 1950. "Redmont's story is identical with Remington's insofar as Bentley is concerned," Rauh noted. "If Redmont's testimony stands up, it will greatly discredit Miss Bentley." It was therefore essential that Redmont testify, but Rauh doubted he would. Why should he, after what Remington had done to him?[21]

It was fear and FBI trickery, Remington said later, that explained why he said all those terrible things about Redmont and his family. Whatever the cause, the record was clear. When the FBI questioned him in April 1947, he said that he had always considered Redmont something of a radical, and, during his informer period, accused Redmont's brother-in-law of pro-Communism. Worse still was his secret testimony before the Ferguson Committee, which was published in July. He no longer considered his ex-friend (as he called him) a radical; now he thought he was a Communist. Rauh assumed that Redmont was aware of Remington's statements and wondered if it was still possible to persuade him to testify. To find out, he enlisted the help of his friend Arthur Schlesinger, Jr., the Harvard historian, who was planning a trip to Europe and agreed to seek out Redmont in Paris.

Schlesinger and Redmont met for coffee at a small café near his office on the Rue de la Paix in early September, and Schlesinger was able to obtain most of the information Rauh was seeking. In his judgment, Redmont was politically "OK, a PM liberal, decent and sentimental, easily frightened, and now alarmed over the possibility of jeopardizing his respectability in the journalistic world." Redmont did know of Remington's statement to the Ferguson Committee and was angry about it. He could not understand what had caused Remington to make such an outrageous charge. They had been friends during the early 1940s, and Redmont could not believe that the idealistic Remington had been a Communist. So, Redmont suspected nothing when Bill arranged an introduction to Helen Johnson.

While his version of events coincided exactly with Remington's, he did not want to become involved in the case, fearing the effect it would have on his conservative boss, publisher David Lawrence. Schlesinger thought Redmont's eventual decision would be influenced by what Lawrence recommended. Also, he sensed that Redmont was not all that upset to see Remington, who had recklessly called him a Communist, put on trial.[22]

Rauh and Chanler continued their effort to reach Redmont. On September 26, Remington wrote Joan and Bernie Redmont a letter of apology, claiming that when the FBI had interviewed him in 1947, they had implied that Redmont was a Communist and he had replied that perhaps he was. "That was a lot of damned nonsense," he now told them. He had repeated that statement before the Ferguson Committee because he had been badly frightened and had been desperate to extricate himself from the mess he was in. "I have a tough fight ahead," he told the Redmonts, "but I am confident that I am going to win it, and

I know I will never again hurt other people because of my being scared myself."
Inexplicably, Remington's letter also contained a blank sheet of paper and a buffalo nickel, which left Redmont baffled.[23]

Redmont was gratified to receive Remington's letter but sent no reply and
told David Lawrence that he planned no further contact with him. The presence of the coin and piece of paper allowed him to wound his ex-friend. "No
amount of idle speculation on my part can make the slightest bit of rhyme or
reason out of this enclosure, other than to wonder if I'm not being put into an E.
Phillips Oppenheim situation by somebody, or if there is some psycho-neurotic
element involved." This oddity provided Redmont another reason to maintain
his distance from Remington.[24]

When weeks passed without a response from Redmont, Remington's lawyers
assumed that this second attempt to win his help had failed. Next, they talked
with Lawrence, who Schlesinger thought (correctly) held the key to Redmont's
appearance. For two hours, on October 18, Chanler and Lawrence chatted
about Bernard Redmont and the Remington case. At the outset, Chanler said
that he might discuss confidential information, so he asked the publisher to consider their conversation in that light. Lawrence agreed. The publisher stated
firmly that he was opposed to Redmont testifying—it would damage Redmont's
career and his magazine. Redmont's association with Bentley, however innocent
it might have been, plus Remington's derogatory remarks had already hurt
Redmont badly. Recently, Lawrence had asked the Pentagon to give his reporter
military accreditation, but it had refused. If war broke out in Europe, Lawrence
said, Redmont would be fired.

The problem was Bentley, Chanler argued; she would probably repeat her
accusations against Redmont on the stand, and Redmont should be there to
deny them. If he hid, he would never receive a government clearance, and
Bentley's story would be believed. Chanler assured Lawrence that if Redmont
testified, "Remington would support Redmont's denials right down the line
and . . . that the result might well be that both would be cleared." Lawrence
promised to watch developments closely, and if Redmont was again attacked, he
would grant him the leave to return home. This pleased Chanler, and they parted amicably. Lawrence immediately contacted the FBI and told them everything
he had learned from Chanler. Long suspicious of Redmont and searching for a
way to get rid of him, Lawrence, over the next several months, continued to give
the Bureau information he acquired from Redmont and even advised on legal
strategy designed to ruin both Redmont and Remington.

Chanler finally received word of Redmont's plans, but it was disappointing.
On November 20, 1950, Redmont informed him that he was too busy to come to
New York; he would wait to see what Bentley did, then decide if he had to testify. Their three-month effort to persuade Redmont to join them had failed; if
they wanted him to appear for the defense, he would have to be subpoenaed.[25]

With the trial set to begin on December 18, both sides hurried to complete their final preparations. For Saypol and Donegan, this meant dealing with the special problems posed by their two star witnesses—Elizabeth Bentley and Ann Remington. Donegan had known Bentley since 1945, so he was accustomed to her fits of impatience, anger, and panic, but she seemed to grow worse as the trial date approached. In October, agents feared that Bentley was on the verge of a nervous breakdown. She heard odd noises on her telephone, which she thought were caused by a tap planted by Remington's private detectives. Then she began to suspect that she was being followed. Although friends informed her that Remington could not afford a team of investigators, she was not reassured. The noises continued, and she began to believe that the Communists were after her. Walking down the street one day, she pointed to two men who she thought were the culprits, but the FBI agents accompanying her saw nothing strange about them. In a memo to headquarters, Agent Thomas G. Spencer commented, "The writer has no claim of being omniscient but it definitely appears from conversations with Miss Bentley on recent dates that she may be bordering on some mental pitfall which, of course, would be almost disastrous to the prosecution of the . . . Remington case, as she is without doubt the principal witness."[26]

Bentley's jitters also infected her good friend and literary partner, John Brunini, who was living in Bentley's hotel while he was completing her manuscript. Fearing that Remington's detectives might have learned of their association, he telephoned Thomas Donegan on October 16 and asked for an immediate appointment. Brunini's news was extremely disturbing to the prosecutor. While foreman of the grand jury, he had helped Bentley find a publisher and then had gone on to collaborate with her on the book. No money had changed hands, Brunini claimed; in fact, Bentley and her publisher thought he should receive a collaborator's fee. Bentley had urged him to keep all this secret, but he wanted Donegan to know everything. Did Tom think it would be all right for him to accept the fee?

Tom did not. Under no circumstances should you receive any money from anybody, Donegan told him angrily; to do so would damage the government's case, if the story became public during the trial. Have you accepted anything else from Bentley? Are you sleeping together?

Absolutely not, a shocked Brunini replied. For now, Donegan ordered Brunini to write a report for Washington on his relationship with Bentley; he would also provide them with a record of this talk. If the Brunini–Bentley affair remained a secret, then no harm would be done. But if Chanler learned of it, accusations of judicial impropriety (and worse) would be raised; Chanler would ask for a mistrial; and the judge might grant it. Later that day (after first reporting all this to the FBI), Donegan informed Saypol, who must have been enraged. Plans were made to confer with Justice Department officials on how to proceed. (Donegan had his own skeleton in the closet—his representation of Bentley when she had successfully sued John Reynolds in 1947—but he said nothing of this potential bombshell, until three days had passed.)

Brunini's revelations sent shock waves that reverberated from New York to Washington. Even J. Edgar Hoover was angered by the foreman's lack of ethics, but he was more unhappy to learn that his own agents had been informed of the problem by Bentley five days earlier and, thinking little of it, had failed to inform him. They were reprimanded.[27]

At the Justice Department, on October 30, Saypol and Donegan met with Assistant Attorney General James McInery to discuss the crisis. Saypol recommended that a new indictment be brought against Remington, because Brunini's association with Bentley might prejudice the prosecution. Donegan and McInery disagreed. Quashing the first indictment would open up the whole affair to public scrutiny; it would be best just to proceed with the trial. Few people knew of these events, and plans were made to keep them secret. With the concurrence of the Attorney General, it was decided not to re-indict Remington.[28]

Ann Remington also caused the government considerable worry as the trial date approached. Although she continued to give information to the FBI, Saypol was still afraid that she would not testify. So, to keep her happy, he agreed to her every demand. Early in December, for example, the government began calling its witnesses to New York for pre-trial conferences, but Ann found it inconvenient to come because there was no one to watch her children. The only people she felt truly comfortable with were Bill's parents, but, under the circumstances, she was embarrassed to ask them to baby-sit. No problem. Saypol and Donegan would come to her. Saypol's fears were confirmed when he saw Ann on December 11. At first, she again seemed reluctant to testify, but by the end of the day, she said that she would. To ensure that she remained in a receptive mood, Saypol arranged for a nurse to watch Bruce and Gale while Ann was in New York and asked Hoover to allow her favorite FBI agent to accompany her. Hoover gave his permission, so Ann would come to trial with her own baby-sitter.[29]

More serious was Saypol's attempt to arm himself with derogatory information to discredit defense witnesses, an effort that even the FBI thought close to being unethical. They did agree, however, to run Saypol's names through the field-office indexes to check on criminal and credit records. Saypol took full advantage of the FBI's largess—he requested damaging information on approximately one hundred men and women—not just on those called to testify but also on many (like Remington's high-school English teacher, Alice W. Martin, and Dartmouth's Ernest Hopkins) who had submitted affidavits for Remington in 1948.[30]

Not only did Saypol have an army of FBI agents at his disposal and an almost unlimited fund of knowledge about whom Chanler might call, he also had an ally inside Chanler's office who provided information and insight into defense strategy. He was Albert W. Putnam, a senior partner and the uncle (by marriage) of Devin Garrity, Bentley's publisher. Putnam told Bentley of Chanler's plans, and she passed the information on to Saypol. Once again, Bentley had assumed her old role as a spy's courier.[31]

Saypol must have looked forward to the Remington trial with confidence. Elizabeth Bentley and Ann Remington were both under control; his other witnesses were well prepared (one had his teeth fixed for the occasion), and his intelligence and financial resources far outmatched the opposition's. The time was also right. On November 26, two hundred thousand Chinese troops crossed the Yalu River into North Korea surprising and badly mauling American forces that had been fighting the Korean Communists since June. As American casualties mounted, the country's anti-Communist feeling reached a fever pitch. What jury would acquit a man like Remington now? Only one government prosecutor seemed unhappy—Thomas Donegan. He and Saypol had worked uncomfortably together for the past six months. Frequently, Donegan complained about Saypol, blaming him for delaying the trial until he was free to lead the prosecution, a job Donegan himself coveted. "Saypol," he told one FBI agent, "would claim credit for the entire case if [the] prosecution is successful and will declaim responsibility" if the government loses. For his part, Saypol accused Donegan of leaking information to the conservative press and must have doubted his loyalty, which was pledged to the FBI. There was also Donegan's relationship with Bentley, which he kept secret from him until late October (as well as the Bentley–Brunini affair); both still threatened to rise up and possibly destroy their case. Therefore, Saypol decided that Donegan should play only a limited role at the trial. On December 15, Saypol informed Donegan that he himself would be handling the examination of Elizabeth Bentley and Ann Remington, the cross-examination of William Remington, and the opening and closing arguments. Roy Cohn would also participate. Then, with a cruel twist of the knife, he asked Donegan which witnesses he preferred to handle.

"There were no other witnesses in which he was particularly interested," he told Saypol, shaking his head. He would, of course, join the U.S. attorney and his assistants at the government's table, but, as he later reported to his beloved FBI, he "would be sitting in left field."[32]

The defense also experienced a number of surprises shortly before the start of the trial. On October 27, lawyer Gerald Gessell told Rauh that he had heard that the government had found Remington's Communist Party card.

"I don't believe [it]," Rauh said. "They were so anxious to get a confession . . . they would have thrown a Party card in Remington's face, if there had been one."

That was all Gessell knew, but his source was usually reliable. Rauh thought

the rumor was ridiculous but told Chanler that they should seek any documentary proof the government might have.[33]

Adding to the concern and the confusion, Saypol, on November 9, gave
Chanler an amended bill of particulars. This one now included New York in
1939–40 and Washington in 1940–41 as the places and times when Remington
was also a member of the Communist Party. But like the previous bill, the government admitted that it had no knowledge of the specific cell to which
Remington allegedly belonged. What was the government up to now? Rauh and
Chanler wondered. Whom had they overlooked? Then, on the eve of the trial,
they thought they found him. By chance, an aide of Chanler's was at the courthouse delivering papers when he overheard the clerk say, "get out subpoenas on
Mrs. Remington and Chamberlin." Who was Chamberlin? The only
Chamberlin Remington could recall was William Chamberlin, a Dartmouth
alumnus, whom he had known slightly in Hanover . . . and when they were both
students at Columbia! But to save his life, he could not remember what he
might have said to turn this acquaintance into an enemy. Chanler tried to find
out. He telephoned William Chamberlin, but Chamberlin would say only that
his testimony would hurt Remington. To counteract him, Chanler decided to
call Arthur McMahon, the Columbia University professor who despised the
Communists.[34]

Despite these last minute crises, Rauh was cautiously optimistic about the
impending trial. He felt certain that the government had no hard evidence, no
Communist Party application or membership book with Bill Remington's name
(or pseudonym) on or in it. And consider the opposition witnesses: a bitter ex-
wife, whose sole motive was to get even with a man she hated; a professional ex-
Communist and former spy, whose credibility was at stake; an alcoholic; and
assorted other TVA Communists who were caught lying by the government and
were now desperate to save themselves. With the right judge and jury and their
own team's legal skills, Bill Remington might yet win acquittal.[35]

16

Object of Hate, Engine of Destruction

This time, Remington's future would be decided not by a panel of prominent citizens but by twelve ordinary people, a jury of his peers. The selection of this group began with a mistake that Joe Rauh thought was serious. On December 18, 1950, the clerk of the court announced that potential jurors who were unable to participate in a trial that was expected to last thirty days or longer were automatically excused, without first informing them that the month would not begin until after Christmas. Forty-six people, the "best jurors," Rauh thought, left the courtroom. Then Judge Ryan declared that the case was assigned to the court of Judge Gregory F. Noonan, where on December 20, a jury would be impaneled and motions heard.[1]

Rauh and Chanler were not happy to learn that Noonan would be trying the case. An Irish Catholic and a graduate of the Fordham University Law School, like his good friend Godfrey Schmidt, Noonan, forty-four, was a prosecutor before being appointed to the federal bench by President Truman in 1949.[2] The Remington case would be his first important criminal trial, and his interpretation of the law would frequently clash with Chanler's, as it did on December 20.

The first order of business that morning was the voir dire—the examination and selection of twelve jurors and three alternates from a group numbering about a hundred. Chanler and Saypol had submitted a list of questions that the judge asked the prospective jurors. The first were personal—did they (or their families) know or have any relationship with the defendant and his lawyers? The prosecutors? Elizabeth Bentley? Had they ever been employed by the government or the courts? Were they ever jurors or witnesses in other trials?

Next came a series of political questions designed to identify those who might be either too liberal or conservative to render a fair and impartial verdict. Was anyone biased against the government's Loyalty Program? The U.S. Attorney's Office or any law enforcement agency? Did any juror support or belong to the Communist Party or any of the other hundred-odd subversive organizations on the Attorney General's list, which Noonan read one by one. Would they give Remington an objective hearing despite the fact that he was accused of Communist Party membership and association with a self-confessed Soviet spy?

Only two candidates admitted bias. "I am afraid I would be prejudiced . . . ," said William F. Gillenwater, who thought Remington's relationship with Bentley meant that he was guilty. Gillenwater was excused. So was Alfred Joffee, who disliked the CIA and sympathized with Remington. Others were challenged by Saypol or Chanler, and after two hours and ten minutes, the final panel was selected. It consisted of seven women and five men plus three alternates (all men). Among them were housewives (one a retired teacher), a power lineman for New York Telephone, a retiree, a hardware salesman, and a hospital attendant; the first juror selected automatically became the foreman—no poet, but a clerk at the Statler Hotel. It was not exactly a jury of his peers—no former radicals, government bureaucrats, or divorcées but, as Saypol put it, "twelve American citizens, representatives of this community, its everyday life and its everyday thinking. . . . " The jury was released after being sworn in and cautioned not to talk about the case to anyone; they would meet again on Tuesday, December 26, the first day of the trial.[3]

Later that afternoon, William Chanler moved for a dismissal of the indictment because it was fatally defective; the result was his first major argument with Judge Noonan. The problem again was the government's refusal to define Communist Party membership. The Bill of Rights and Supreme Court rulings required that the defendant must be informed of the precise nature of the accusation against him. This basic and fundamental right was being denied to his client, Chanler argued. "Here is a man indicted and brought to trial on the ground that he lied when he said, 'I don't belong to something.' 'But,' says the Government, 'we don't know what it is he didn't belong to. We can't explain it or define it, but he lied when he said he didn't belong to it. We will leave it to the jury to [decide] what it was.' How can a man possibly be indicted for perjury on any such preposterous statement as that?"

Judge Noonan quickly rejected the motion, noting that it was ingenious but without merit. "As a matter of cold logic . . . the defendant himself is the one who is best able to state whether he was or was not a member of the Communist Party and knows what that means."

Chanler was shocked by the judge's remark that Remington must have known the meaning of membership in the Communist Party—this seemed to imply that the judge presumed that he was guilty, and he told him so.

Noonan bristled and denied the implication. "If anybody asks me if I am a member of the Knights of Columbus, I certainly know whether I am or not."

"Yes, your Honor," Chanler agreed. "But what if somebody said that you were [and you] did not know what membership was? He knows he is not a member of what he considers to be the Communist Party. What we want to know is what did the Grand Jury mean and what does the Government mean, and they say they don't know. . . . If they don't know, how in the world can we know?"

Noonan did not wish to continue this debate; if Chanler had no other motions to make—he did not—then they were adjourned until Tuesday, December 26.[4]

The trial began the day after Christmas in Room 110 of the U.S. Courthouse at Foley Square. The oak-paneled courtroom was the largest in the federal building and second home to the government's chief prosecutor of Communists, Irving Howard Saypol, who stepped up to the lectern to deliver the government's opening statement. Saypol, rotund with steely blue eyes and the manner of an undertaker, was forty-five years old, the son of Russian immigrants, who had earned his law degree (at night) from Brooklyn College. He became a government prosecutor in 1945 and four years later was appointed U.S. attorney for the Southern District of New York. Speaking in a monotone so low that many reporters strained to catch his words, he said, "We will prove that William W. Remington was a member of the Communist Party, and we will prove that he lied when he denied it. . . . We will show his Communist Party membership from the mouths of witnesses who will take the stand before you, and from written documents which are immutable. . . . You will see . . . how, while drawing a high salary from the Government, he prostituted his position of trust . . . , for the benefit of his Communist Party to which he was attached. For that Party we will show that he took documents and vital information from the War Production Board and turned these over to a fellow member of the Communist Party, for ultimate delivery to Russia. It will be shown . . . that his adherence and his loyalty was [sic] primarily to the Russian Government. . . . I am confident that on the basis of the overwhelming and undisputed evidence which is about to be presented to you, you will find beyond any reasonable doubt that Remington lied to the grand jury, that he is guilty of . . . perjury."[5]

William Chanler walked to the lectern, "a lean distinguished-looking man," wrote one reporter, "with iron-grey hair, craggy New England features and a resonant courtroom style." The FBI had been investigating Remington for five years, Chanler said, but they had no proof that he was a Communist. In previous cases, the government had no problem producing evidence of membership, but here, they could find nothing. Remington was charged with being a member in five cities during a ten-year period. "Ladies and Gentlemen," Chanler cried, "if he was a member . . . he must have had at least 12 party cards, because every year you send in an application for a new card; he must have paid dues thousands of times. . . . There ought to be plenty of evidence available . . . if Remington had ever been a member of the Communist Party, really direct evidence, not loose talk." He begged the jury "to follow the mandate of the Constitution [and] presume that Remington is innocent; and if you will do that, I am quite sure you will find that there is no evidence here to overcome that presumption."[6]

The first witness called by the government was Hugh Doran, the grand jury secretary. Saypol asked if he recalled Remington's appearance on May 25, when he was asked if he had ever been a member of the Communist Party and had answered, "I never have been."

"I heard that answer," Doran said.

The government's charge of perjury having been formally presented, Chanler then asked if Doran knew precisely when the grand jury began to investigate Remington.

Doran could not recall.

Have you ever heard of a man named Joseph Egan, Bentley's attorney?

Saypol objected to the question and the judge cut Chanler off.

" . . . Surely we have not come to the time when a defendant may be brought into a secret chamber and brought out six days later and told he committed a crime and then not permitted to investigate the circumstances of the alleged crime," Chanler said. The judge stuck to his ruling, Chanler excepted, and Doran was excused.[7]

The most important witness of that day and the following two appeared next. "Ann Ruth Remington," the clerk called, and as she walked to the stand, the courtroom stirred. She wore a wine-colored suit and, with her hair swept to one side in a bob, looked like the college student she had been twelve years before. After being sworn in, she glanced quickly at her ex-husband, who donned a pair of gold wire-rimmed spectacles and stared intently at her as she began her testimony.[8]

First, Saypol took her through a brief personal history, making sure that the jury learned that she was no longer receiving alimony from her ex-husband and that her only means of support was a small inheritance from her grandparents and a meager salary earned as a part-time bookkeeper. Speaking softly, she described meeting Remington at a Dartmouth peace rally in 1938 and their courtship, which culminated late one night with the revelation that electrified the courtroom: "He told me that he was a member of the Communist Party and abjured me to secrecy on that." A smile quickly passed over her face, while Remington frowned. She also talked about attending a meeting of the YCL with Remington and visiting his dormitory room where she saw Communist literature. But a few months later, she said, he decided to end his YCL membership because he was seeking high academic honors.

What about his real attitude toward Communism? Saypol asked.

It did not change, she asserted.[9] A few minutes later, shortly after 5:00 P.M., Judge Noonan called a halt to the day's proceedings.

Ann was on the witness stand for only an hour, but her testimony filled newspaper headlines: EX-WIFE TESTIFIES HE TOLD HER HE WAS A COMMUNIST was the way the *New York Times* and other papers began their coverage of the day's events.[10] The headlines that followed the next day's session would be even worse.

Saypol built his case slowly and methodically, leaving the most dramatic revelations for last. On the morning of December 27, Ann Remington testified about the promise Bill allegedly made to her before their marriage in November 1938. "I was reluctant to marry Mr. Remington," she said, "and one of the requirements that I asked specifically, would he continue to be a member of the Communist Party, . . . and he said, yes, that I need not worry on that score. . . ." Even their honeymoon in 1939 was a political event, as they sought out Mexican Communists with letters of introduction supplied by Joe North. When they returned to New York, they enrolled at the Workers' School, where they briefly studied Marxist economics. Economics was Bill's chosen field of study at Columbia University, a decision that was approved by Communist Party officials, she claimed, because the Party needed good economists. And there were other Communist activities during the New York years: they campaigned for Earl Browder in the special congressional election of 1940 and helped the ailing *New Masses*. Finally, after moving to Washington in May 1940, Ann became executive secretary of the Emergency Peace Mobilization, which was dedicated to opposing the "Imperialist War" in Europe. And, of course, Bill assisted her by writing leaflets and regularly attending executive committee meetings.

Then came what the *Daily News* called "the sensational topper to her detailed story of Remington's consecrated Red Career." When they moved to Alexandria, Virginia, in 1941, she explained, they felt "out of touch . . . [and] wanted to . . . do more for the Party and for Russia." So they turned to Joe North, who arranged a dinner meeting with the man and woman she knew only as John and Helen. For a moment, Ann hesitated.

"Did you want to say something Mrs. Remington?" asked Judge Noonan.

"Well," she began, voice quivering, "I would like to say that I am a very reluctant witness. It is extremely hard for me to have to testify against the father of my children. I hold no malice toward him personally."

"I think that is evident," Saypol interjected.

"I have been compelled, subpoenaed by the Government and I am trying to tell the truth as I remember it," Ann insisted. "I don't like it."

Like it or not, she went on with her story, and it was devastating. In the most conventional of surroundings, a Schrafft's Restaurant, she and her husband embarked on a career in espionage. "We were told that she would go to Washington approximately at two-week intervals, she would call us when she arrived, giving her name as Helen. . . . Any information that they could use we would give her, and she was to bring us party literature."

"Was anything said [about] the nature of the information which you were to deliver to her?"

"It was information that would be usable to Russia," Ann said, "secret information . . . from government sources. . . . We were to pay our Communist dues to her also." About a month later, Helen arrived; Ann picked up Bill at his office, then stopped for Helen, who was waiting at 14th and Pennsylvania Avenue. They drove to a secluded spot on the Mall, where Bill gave Helen their Communist Party dues. Over the next two years, these meetings with Helen continued. Most were routine. They paid dues; Bill gave Helen notes he had written on cards; and occasionally, Helen would bring Ann literature, which later they destroyed. But one day was unforgettable. A very excited Bill Remington gave Helen a top secret formula on how to produce explosives from garbage and told her to send it immediately to Russia.

Ann also described their work as Communist Party recruiters. They invited their friends Bernard and Joan Redmont to establish a similar relationship with Helen, and they agreed to participate.[11]

Thus, by the time of the luncheon recess, Ann had portrayed her ex-husband as an ardent Communist, who followed the Party line religiously, recruited and worked for the Party, and stole secrets for the Soviets. Could William Chanler, on cross-examination, undermine such powerful testimony?

Chanler began by exploring her own history as a Communist, first in the Bennington YCL, then in Party units at Columbia and Croton. When you joined the Communist Party, did you believe that you were part of an organization dedicated to violent revolution?

"No," she said. "I felt . . . that the interests of humanity as a whole were furthered by the Communist principle. There was no conflict between what was good for the United States and good for Russia."

If there was no significant difference between a Communist and a liberal New Dealer, Chanler asked, how did you define Communist Party membership? (Earlier that morning she had told Saypol that "being Communist is largely a state of mind. . . . It is a way you talk and the way you thought." She now elaborated.)

" You carry out the Party program . . . and usually you pay them some money, too, but that isn't so important." These admissions, Chanler hoped, would weaken Saypol's description of the Popular Front Party as a group of sinister revolutionaries.

Next, Chanler bore in on the discrepancies in her earlier testimony. That class on Marxism at the Workers' School? Didn't your husband heckle the lecturer? "Yes," Ann said, "he tried to talk some real economics but they would not deviate from the written text. . . . "

Concerning your support for *New Masses*—were you aware of others, perhaps non-Communists, who contributed to the magazine in 1940?

"I don't remember the circumstances," was all Ann could say.[12] With that exchange, the day's proceedings ended.

Chanler's exposure of the holes in her testimony were minor compared to Ann's dramatic accusations, and it was these that captured the attention of the press and, no doubt, the jury. REMINGTON GAVE REDS EXPLOSIVE, EX SWEARS screamed newspaper headlines in New York and Washington. Besides being a spy, Remington, according to press accounts, was said to have entertained Communists in New York, Washington, and Mexico and had conducted a "dialectical romance" with his former wife. Ann's claim that she never loved Bill and had demanded that he continue to be a Communist before she would marry him reflected, said the *Daily Mirror*, "the traditional attitude of Reds toward love and marriage." The only newspaper that seemed to take Chanler's cross-examination seriously was *The Dartmouth*. Reporters were particularly fascinated by the tragic personal story that was also unfolding—two people who had once been close but now, as Max Lerner observed, regarding "each other on one side as an object of hate, on the other as an engine of destruction."[13]

When Chanler and Rauh returned to the offices of Winthrop, Stimson at the end of the day, they found a message awaiting them. A Boston attorney had telephoned and urgently wanted to speak to Rauh. What now? The lawyer's name was unfamiliar, but Rauh returned his call anyway, and the news he received was stunning. George Edson and Elba Chase Nelson, who had agreed to testify that Remington was not a member of the New Hampshire Communist Party, had now decided that they could not appear as defense witnesses. Arriving in Manhattan that morning, they had been met by FBI agents with subpoenas forcing them to meet with a grand jury. Their lawyer said that they would plead the Fifth Amendment and leave town as quickly as possible. Should Chanler subpoena them, they would do the same. Chanler and Rauh were enraged. Forcing potential defense witnesses to appear before a grand jury was both outrageous and illegal. They would inform Judge Noonan first thing next morning.[14]

"Preposterous!" Saypol yelled, when Rauh accused the government of threatening their witnesses, shortly before the trial resumed on December 28. "If there has been any attempt to sway witnesses, I suspect . . . that the fault lies on the other side."

Rauh asked the judge to quash the subpoenas requiring Edson and Nelson to appear before the grand jury that morning and also asked to examine the testimony of thirteen other witnesses, who had refused to speak to the defense because they said that they were under grand jury subpoena. Such government conduct was illegal, Rauh argued, a violation of the rules of criminal procedure.

The charges are "baseless and of whole cloth," Saypol responded. Noonan saw no evidence of improper conduct and denied Rauh's motion. Rauh then asked that the transcripts be sealed and made a part of the trial record.

"Perhaps counsel would like to take the grand jury and impound that too," Saypol angrily commented and continued his harangue until Noonan denied the motion.[15]

Rauh and Chanler had lost more than a legal argument. The jury would never hear Elba Chase Nelson testify that Remington was not, as the government charged, a member of the New Hampshire Communist Party.

A few minutes later, Ann Remington returned to the stand for the third and final day. Chanler reviewed her testimony, and a somewhat more accurate picture of her life with Remington emerged. Did I understand you correctly when you said that during your Mexican honeymoon you visited with a Trotskyite?

"We saw a good deal of him," Ann said.

"Wasn't that considered one of the worst offenses a Communist could engage in, to have anything to do with a Trotskyite?"

"That is quite right," Ann admitted.

"But you didn't care about that?"

"No. . . . We were always independent in our Communism."

You testified earlier about attending Communist Party meetings at Columbia and Croton, but when you and your new husband moved to New York City, you stopped. "Why didn't you attend . . . after that?" Chanler asked.

"Well, I never did enjoy the meetings, and we just decided that we would not join. . . . We followed the Communist position on our own more or less."

Mostly less, as Chanler now proved. Were you aware that the Communist Party Constitution required a member to attend branch meetings regularly?

"I probably heard that some time . . . ," Ann said.

"[But], as far as you know, Mr. Remington never attended any . . . Communist Party meetings during the time that you knew him . . . ?"

"Not during the time I knew him."

The Constitution also required prospective members to submit formal applications endorsed by at least two members of the branch to which they were applying for membership, he told her. Did you ever file such an application?

"No."

"Did Mr. Remington?"

"Not to my knowledge."

New members were also supposed to have a membership book. "To your knowledge, neither you nor Mr. Remington ever had a card, did you?"

"No."

Dues were also supposed to be paid on a regular monthly basis, but you testified earlier that you did not. And all payments had to be acknowledged by dues stamps pasted in the membership book.

"I never had one," Ann confessed.

" . . . Nor did Mr. Remington, did he?"

"Not to my knowledge."

"Then, Mrs. Remington," Chanler asked, "if these are the requirements of membership contained in the Constitution and by-laws of the Communist Party, neither you nor Mr. Remington were ever members of the Communist Party . . . ?"

"That is not the issue here, and I object," Saypol interrupted.

"Isn't membership in the Communist Party the issue we are trying in this case?" Chanler demanded.

Over Saypol's objection, Noonan permitted Ann to answer. "We were not orthodox Communists in that sense of following all the rules. . . . We were Communists as much as we wanted to be. . . . "

In his last few minutes with Ann, Chanler attempted to establish the motive for her becoming the principal witness against her ex-husband. It was hatred, he argued, caused by the breakup of their marriage, Bill's public attacks on her and Elizabeth Moos, and emotional problems. Responding to his questions, she did admit that after they separated she "had a great deal of trouble getting money out of him" and that their discussions regarding child custody were unfriendly. But when Chanler tried to get her to agree that Bill's remarks had made her angry, she denied it—saying only that "the unnecessary lies upset" her. Chanler was more successful in revealing her anger toward her mother.

"I don't like her," Ann admitted. "She can't seem to stop bossing me, and I don't care for her political views, either." This seemed the appropriate place to begin a discussion of her psychiatric history. She handled these questions fairly well—candidly explaining that she had been seeing a psychoanalyst twice weekly since 1945. Not wishing to probe too deeply and thereby turn her into a sympathetic figure, Chanler asked no further questions about her treatment and turned her over to Saypol.[16]

This would be Saypol's last chance to repair any damage done by Chanler. Since the psychiatric issue had been raised, Saypol asked whose idea it was that she receive such therapy.

It was her husband's, she claimed, and she consented, hoping that it would restore their marriage. This left the jury with the mistaken impression that Ann's problems were the result of a bad marriage rather than more serious emotional trauma. Saypol also brought out the fact that Remington, too, had consulted psychiatrists—two of them. More damaging was Ann's revelation that Bill "appeared anxious to avoid having me testify and suggested that I might ask my doctor to have me proved mentally incompetent. . . . "

"I take it you didn't accept that suggestion?" Saypol asked.

"No, I did not," she answered firmly.

Next, Saypol tried to revise Chanler's portrait of Ann as a vengeful ex-wife, who joyfully testified against her husband before the grand jury that indicted him. She explained that, at first, she tried to corroborate his version of events, but the foreman "threatened to take me to a judge and indicated that I had no privilege of refusing to answer that question. It took a good deal of inner turmoil . . . to answer . . . but I finally did. . . . "

Talk of threats was no good, so Saypol moved to correct it. "Was that said in a threatening or loud manner?"

"No," Ann said, "they were very nice to me."

Saypol was finished, but Chanler asked if the attorneys could approach the bench. Since Ann had discussed her appearance before the grand jury, he moved to inspect her testimony. When Judge Noonan refused, he asked him to examine the transcripts, and if Noonan found contradictions between what she had said then and her statements now, they should be made available to the defense and the witness recalled. For once, Noonan agreed and surprised Chanler further by offering to study the testimony of the fifteen witnesses Rauh claimed had been intimidated. The lawyers returned to their places; Noonan excused the witness and then adjourned the proceedings until January 2, 1951.[17]

Once again, it was Ann's dramatic testimony and not her admission that she and Bill had been unusual Communists that captured the newspaper headlines. Only the New York Times and the Washington Post led their coverage with the declaration REMINGTON NOT "ORTHODOX RED." The other newspapers in New York and Washington preferred EX SWEARS REMINGTON ATTEMPTED TO GAG HER. Reporters liked the exciting news Ann created more than the news maker. They described her as "sad-faced" and "sullen" as she answered questions "with the habit of not moving her mouth to form the words." She was more popular with the photographers, for whom she posed, tight-lipped and unsmiling. They thought she was sweet and called her "Mrs. Moose."[18]

If the press had had access to grand jury and FBI records, they might have used other words to describe Ann Remington—"confused," "mistaken," or "untruthful." For example, at trial, Ann Remington's story about what occurred during and after the dinner at Schrafft's could not have been more explicit. She testified under oath that Bentley, as planned at that dinner, would come to Washington every two weeks; they would give her secret information of value to the Soviets and pay their party dues.[19] But these statements are sharply different from those made earlier at her grand jury appearances and during pre-trial interviews with the FBI. Then, she had only the vaguest memory of the dinner, recalled nothing about receiving instructions, did not even know that Helen was their contact until she actually showed up, and said that she had never received dues receipts.[20] Six months later, she told a completely different story. How did this remarkable transformation occur? Possibly, during the summer and fall of

1950, her conversations with FBI agents and access to Bentley's more-detailed statements allowed her to remember events she had forgotten. Or, with little or no memory of these events, she had allowed the agents to create one for her. It was probably nothing so stark (and illegal) as having a story she did not believe forced upon her but rather her accepting information that seemed logical or probable. In her own mind, then, she might have believed that she was telling the truth and may not have intentionally misrepresented what actually happened. Or, she deliberately lied and committed perjury. One conclusion seems obvious—Ann's trial testimony detailing Bill's becoming a part of the Soviet underground during the dinner at Schrafft's was not true.

Just as disturbing is Judge Noonan's conduct regarding her grand jury testimony. He had promised that if he found contradictions, he would give her transcripts to Chanler and permit her to be re-examined. But when the trial resumed in January, Noonan told the lawyers that he had found no evidence of inconsistency between her grand jury and trial testimonies, so their request to inspect her minutes and those of the other thirteen witnesses was denied. It is impossible to understand Noonan's ruling; Ann Remington's trial testimony is riddled with contradictions, and one is forced to conclude that the judge did not read the transcripts or received a fraudulent copy from Saypol or did read the minutes and, given his pro-government sympathies ("Chanler's lost his case and he's desperately trying anything he can think of," Noonan was heard to remark to a reporter), ignored the inconsistencies. Whatever is the truth, Noonan apparently violated his oath to see that the law was fairly administered.[21]

The government's first witnesses of the new year were the TVA Communists Christine Benson, Muriel Williams, Kenneth McConnell, and Howard Bridgman. Benson testified that she had joined the Communist Party in October 1936 and admitted that she best remembered the meetings held at Betty Malcolm's apartment in June 1937, many of which Remington had attended. After brief questioning, assistant U.S. attorney Roy Cohn turned the witness over to William Chanler. He immediately attacked her testimony. Do you not remember your conversation with my associate William Hindman in Knoxville and our own talk in New York in which you stated that the only Communist Party meetings you recalled attending were at Jim Persons's home? Do you not remember sitting in my office at the end of the day, saying, "I wish I could find some other place where I could place those meetings?"

You must be mistaken, Benson said. It was the early period I was referring to, when we met at Persons's home; the later meetings were all at the Malcolms.

And do you not recall saying to me that "Howard Bridgman was wrong if he tried to place Mr. Remington at Mrs. Malcolm's house?"

I do not remember that conversation, either.

These meetings you attended, Chanler asked next, were they called to discuss the violent overthrow of the U.S. government?

"No", Benson said. "It was my chief interest, as I think it was of those who associated with me, . . . to work for those good things that we felt would make a real America. . . . "

Were the objectives of the Communists in Knoxville different from those of liberals who did not join the Party?

"Probably not," she answered.

Did you ever see Remington's Party card?

No.

Did you ever see him pay Party dues?

No.

And yet, Chanler noted, you insist that he was a Party member.

"I haven't stated definitely that I knew him to be a member," she said. "I stated definitely that I attended some meetings with him."[22]

Although Chanler had pretty much demolished her testimony, he nevertheless moved for inspection of her grand jury minutes and FBI statement on grounds of inconsistency. He also asked for her husband's loyalty file, because she had admitted that she had earlier lied to the Bureau to protect his TVA career. This request produced a torrent of invective from Saypol, and again Noonan rejected the motion on the grounds that no inconsistency had been shown by the defense.

Rauh, exasperated and angry, fought back. "We are hanged if we do and hanged if we don't," he said. "If . . . she admits she lied, then we don't get to see it because . . . your Honor says we have not proved it. What proof more . . . can we make? We do not have a counter-espionage agent inside the FBI. We have given your Honor everything a human being could."

Saypol quickly noted that there were no such agents, and Noonan added, "I am glad to hear that he [Rauh] has not got any pipelines in the FBI." Noonan did say that he would have been willing to let them see Benson's signed FBI statement, but, according to Saypol, no such document existed. (The FBI's interview with Christine Benson had ended when she broke down in tears, before agents could type up a record for her to sign.)

There must be reports, Rauh insisted, they would be sufficient for our purpose, but Noonan rejected this request, too.[23]

Of course there were reports, and Agents Parker and McSwain still had their original notes of the interview. Chanler and Rauh would have found these documents valuable. On the stand, Christine Benson testified that she definitely recalled meetings at Betty Malcolm's and that she had seen Remington there.[24] But on June 29, 1950, she had told the FBI that she remembered attending Communist Party meetings in Knoxville with Remington, but it had occurred so long ago that she could not remember when or where these meetings had been held. On other points as well, her trial testimony differed from her previous statements and from the accounts of others.[25] The witness's improved memory of meetings at the Malcolms' can only be explained in one or two ways—either a sudden remembrance or a willingness to give perjured testimony. In Christine Benson's case, with her husband's job at risk, the latter seems more likely.

The TVA witness the defense feared most—Muriel Williams—contributed almost nothing to the government's case. Although she also testified that she had attended Communist Party meetings at Betty Malcolm's, Roy Cohn never asked her if Remington had, and adhering to her philosophy of only answering specific questions, she did not volunteer information. Cohn was primarily interested in having her repeat what Remington had allegedly told her early in June 1937: "I am going back to college, but I am awfully glad to know that there is somebody who has come into town who can take over some of the work I have been doing." A few weeks later, she said, Knox County organizer Kenneth Malcolm arrived, and afterwards, she became a member of the Party.

Did you know that Remington had tried to organize a Workers Alliance chapter at Mascot, Tennessee? Chanler asked on cross-examination.

No, I did not.

Did you know that Kenneth Malcolm was also interested in organizing a Workers Alliance?

No.

It was this activity Remington was referring to, not Communist Party organizing, Chanler implied. He also brought out the fact that Muriel had testified previously about her Party membership and had said that she was "not completely frank and honest." She was still not testifying frankly. When asked who had recruited her, she said Betty Malcolm, when, in fact, it was Christine Benson. So far, every government witness had, intentionally or accidentally, given false or misleading testimony.[26]

So did the fourth witness, Kenneth McConnell, during his appearance on January 2, 1951. First, he testified about the Party meeting in Tyson Park that he had called to introduce himself to Knoxville's Communists. That event stood out in his mind because he remembered that Remington wanted to write a leaflet McConnell thought unwise. Then, he talked about the trip to Mascot, where he said Remington pointed out members of the Workers Alliance who he thought would make good Communists. He also spoke about once reprimanding young Remington for looking like a tramp. This produced laughter in the courtroom; even Remington broke into a smile. Finally, he described the time that he and his wife, Betty, had advised Remington to return to Dartmouth, because the Party needed an educated membership.

Since McConnell had already described these events before HUAC, Chanler was quick to point out the contradictions between that accounting and his present testimony. The Tyson Park meeting—was it a meeting attended by both Party members and interested observers, as you have told the committee? Or was it strictly a Party affair, as you just testified?

No, it was as I stated—an organizational meeting composed only of Party activists.

Chanler then read aloud what McConnell had said to the congressman who had asked him if he ever attended a Communist Party meeting with Remington: "I can only answer that question equivocally." It was this statement that Chanler hoped the jury would remember.

Your criticism of Remington for looking like a tramp—were those your precise words? Chanler asked.

I do not know—it was too long ago to remember. That was the admission Chanler hoped he would make.

It must be just as difficult recalling the conversation with Remington about returning to college. Were you aware that Remington had already made plans to go back to school, months before you supposedly urged him to?

"No," McConnell said.

Would this cause you to change your testimony?

"Nothing could cause me to change my testimony . . . ," he said indignantly, but then he suddenly did. "He might merely have been discussing plans which he had already made for corroboration. I don't know." That was the phrase Chanler especially liked: "I don't know."

McConnell had come to Knoxville as a Party organizer, so Chanler took advantage of his expertise to see how good a Party member Remington had been. Did you ever see Remington's membership book?

No.

Did you ever see Remington pay Party dues?

No.

Did you ever collect his dues?

No.

"Now," said Chanler, winding up, "if you never saw any Communist Party card belonging to Mr. Remington and never collected dues or issued dues stamps to him and never took any steps in regards to his transfer to New Hampshire, you can't state of your own knowledge, can you, that Remington was a member of the Communist Party?"

"Save by saying that my relations with Mr. Remington were those of a fellow Communist."

"That is all," Chanler said.[27]

The contradictions in McConnell's testimony were so obvious that Chanler did not bother to seek his grand jury transcripts. Had he read the minutes, he would have found additional discrepancies that would have further weakened McConnell's story. The most important concerned the Tyson Park meeting at which he said Remington had recommended drafting a leaflet. His grand jury transcript and FBI interviews reveal otherwise. Three times McConnell had been asked if he had spoken with Remington that evening, and each time he had answered no. With this in mind, it is reasonable to conclude that his sudden recollection of Remington speaking out was probably not true.[28]

To the jury, Howard Bridgman must have at first appeared an honest, straightforward witness. Under Roy Cohn's questioning, they learned that the tall, blond, 39-year-old was an assistant professor of economics at Tufts and, with four battle stars from the Pacific campaign and the Philippine liberation ribbon, a war hero, too. He had also been a Communist Party member at Knoxville in 1936–37 (although he then had no membership book—a fact Cohn emphasized) and had attended two or three meetings with Remington at the home of Betty Malcolm. His was simple, direct testimony—or so it seemed until William Chanler came to the lectern.

Cohn had not asked Bridgman one crucial question, and Chanler asked it now. When did those Communist Party meetings take place?

During 1937, the professor answered vaguely.

Could you please be a bit more specific?

I can recall only a few occasions. The first one was in March 1937 at Pat Todd's apartment and was attended by just three people—Todd, Horace Bryan, and me; the others were later, at Betty Malcolm's. Knowing that Bridgman had told HUAC that those meetings had occurred earlier, Rauh asked for access to his grand jury testimony, because of prior inconsistent statements. Cohn opposed the motion, and although Noonan tended to agree with him, the judge said he would examine Bridgman's testimony.

To everyone's surprise, Judge Noonan, on January 4, announced that Chanler could inspect Bridgman's grand jury transcripts because this time he had found inconsistencies. When Bridgman returned to the stand, Chanler interrogated him closely, pointing out that earlier he had confidently testified that he began to attend meetings at the Malcolm home in the fall of 1936 and that he best remembered the first five or six when he said Remington was present. Do you recall that during your appearance before the grand jury, Assistant Attorney General Kelley had noted that this was impossible since the Malcolms did not arrive until June 1937 and that you had been stunned by this news?

"I remember," Bridgman said. " . . . I was very upset by this information [about] Betty Malcolm. . . . I was floored by it."

"And you [have] been meeting with the FBI according to your testimony once a week or once every two weeks ever since? Trying to find some answer to it."

"Yes, sir."

" . . . But your mind is very clear about the meeting in March attended by Todd and Bryan . . . ?" Chanler asked.

"My memory is clear on that, . . . " Bridgman stuttered.

Then Chanler read from Bridgman's grand jury testimony: asked about

Horace Bryan you said you thought he was a Communist "but I can't put him at any meeting."

Bridgman was floored again. " . . . Those questions were coming thick and fast and I was trying to jump from one answer to another."

"Why was it necessary for the FBI to confer once a week . . . while you were attempting to refresh your recollections?" Chanler demanded.

Roy Cohn leaped to his feet. "I object to these implications that there is any impropriety in the FBI's refreshing that witness's recollection. . . . "

" . . . I want to know where he got those ideas . . . ," Chanler said.

From a variety of sources, HUAC investigators, congressional testimony; "I have done my best," a weary Bridgman concluded. "That is all."[29] A few minutes later, he was excused.

"Despite what you read in the newspapers, the case is going quite well," Joe Rauh wrote to a friend on January 4. "The Government's TVA case is hinged practically entirely upon a few meetings at Betty Malcolm's house . . . [during] a three-week period fourteen years ago. A few years ago the prosecutor would have been ashamed to present such a case, but now anything goes."[30] After the testimonies of Benson, Williams, McConnell and Bridgman, there was cause for a bit of optimism. That mood quickly changed later that day when a pleasant-looking man settled comfortably in the witness chair. His looks belied his reputation; his enemies called 47-year-old Paul Crouch "Mr. Stool Pigeon," among other less-printable names.

The son of a North Carolina Baptist preacher, Crouch became a Communist in 1925 and eventually served as district organizer in North and South Carolina and, in 1939, state secretary for Tennessee. He broke with the Party in 1942 and turned on his former comrades, becoming a government informer—or as he preferred to be known, an expert witness. By 1951, according to his own accounting, he had appeared before congressional investigating committees more than a dozen times, for which he was usually paid twenty-five dollars a day. His testimony was frequently unreliable. For example, in 1950 he told HUAC that although he knew union official Armand Scala, he did not know if he was a Communist. Then, a few days later, he called Scala the chief Communist courier in Latin America and suddenly became embroiled in a lawsuit that cost him five thousand dollars. As far as Remington was concerned, he had little to tell the FBI. In 1949, he thought he might have met him at some Party function in the 1930s but was unable to recognize his photograph. "He had received the impression," agents later wrote, "that Remington had been, at least, a Communist sympathizer" but "that his information was hearsay, and he knew nothing concerning Remington from his personal observation."[31]

Now, on the witness stand, he told a very different story. Asked by Chanler if he had ever seen the defendant before, Crouch said, "If it is the light-haired man seated at the end of the table, I recall having seen him several times, but I cannot recall the place or the circumstances." He also had more concrete evidence to link Remington to the Communist Party. As a member of the editorial board of *The Southern Worker*, a Party newspaper, and later editor of its successor, *The New South*, Crouch had access to the names of subscribers and, until recently, had forgotten that the records still existed in a cardboard box hidden at his mother's house. That box was now Government's Exhibit 13. Over Chanler's objection, Roy Cohn asked the witness, "Do you find a card under the name of Bill Remington?"

"I do," said Crouch, who passed it to the prosecutor. Remington's return address was P.O. Box 1692, which Crouch also said was Knoxville's official Party mailbox.

Chanler asked to examine the other subscription cards in the box, and his staff quickly thumbed through them, finally choosing three to use on cross-examination. One, he noted, belonged to Tennessee senator Kenneth McKellar. This was a complimentary copy, Crouch explained, sent to members of Congress and public libraries. Chanler saw the next card—Businessmen's Lunch Club—and broke into a smile. Cohn momentarily panicked, fearing that the name on the card was J. Edgar Hoover. Chanler showed the card to the witness, as Cohn looked on anxiously. Crouch noted the sick look on Cohn's face and winked at him. Chanler asked, "This one, the subscriber's the Businessman's Lunch . . . , Chattanooga, Tennessee. Do you know what the organization was?"

"I do very well," laughed Crouch.

"What was it?"

"It was a restaurant operated by a very active member of the Communist Party and was a favorite meeting place of the Communist leaders in Chattanooga. . . . "

While courtroom spectators howled with laughter, Chanler made a final attempt to salvage something from this humiliating exchange. He showed Crouch another card, bearing the name John W. Gunter, mistakenly believing it to be that of the popular journalist.

Cohn immediately pointed out his error. "Excuse me, I just caught a glance at the card. G-U-N-T-E-R. I believe the author is G-U-N-T-H-E-R."

"I am not sure," Chanler said.

Saypol added to his misery, "and he has no middle initial as far as I know."

Chanler stopped asking about other subscribers.

"We had scored decisively," Cohn concluded.

For the rest of the afternoon, Chanler questioned Crouch about his knowledge of the Communist Party in the 1930s, hoping that, like Benson, he would describe it as the vanguard of the New Deal. But this strategy failed, too. Crouch testified that Ted Wellman had been a very casual organizer and, since members worked in an environment that was hostile to Communists, rarely followed all the rules demanded by the Party constitution. In the end, Chanler was left with only one way to discredit Crouch—showing that he was a paid informant. While Saypol and Cohn cried out their objections, Crouch described his busy life, testifying before the California State Un-American Activities Committee, at the trial of labor leader Harry Bridges, and, most often, for the Immigration and Naturalization Service.

"In other words, Mr. Crouch," Chanler declared, "you are a professional witness."

"I am not a professional witness," Crouch insisted.

A friendly Judge Noonan interrupted. "Do you consider yourself an expert witness?"

"I do," said Crouch.

Finally, Chanler moved to have Crouch's testimony stricken from the record, because Crouch was not in Knoxville when Remington was and had no direct knowledge of what had occurred at that time.

"Motion denied," said Noonan, and Crouch left the stand.[32]

Next to appear was the first of the Dartmouth witnesses. Chanler had expected one of the ex-radicals who hated Remington—Bill Martin or Page Smith. Instead they were surprised by a man Remington knew only slightly, Roscoe Conkling Giles, Jr. The son of a prominent black surgeon, Giles entered Dartmouth in the fall of 1936 to prepare for a medical career. But he majored in sociology instead and became active in the American Student Union and, possibly, the Young Communist League. His years at Dartmouth were unsuccessful. He was suspended in June 1939, then readmitted in September 1940, only to leave again just before graduating, because of illness. Other records indicate that during his almost four years in Hanover, he was regularly treated by the Dartmouth psychiatrist.[33]

Giles never graduated and spent the 1940s wandering from job to job. When the FBI located him in October 1950, he was working as a stenographer for the Oakland, California, Police Department. Agents interviewed him several times that fall, and, initially, he seemed a most promising witness. He knew Bill Remington very well, he claimed, and recalled that he had "a comprehensive understanding of Communistic theory . . . and defended his views . . . with zeal and deep conviction." So impressed was Giles by Remington and his friend Bill Martin that he followed them into the American Student Union and the Young Communist League. Asked who had recruited him, Giles replied, the two Bills—Remington and Martin. He was certain that Remington was a member; why else would he have wanted to recruit him? But then problems developed. As the interview continued, Giles became confused. Although claiming that Remington was in the YCL, now he did not know definitely if he was a formal member. Then he said, "I never attended a meeting of the Young Communist League, and to my knowledge this organization never met on the Dartmouth campus, while I was there." The FBI men did not attempt to resolve the contradiction of how Giles became a member of a nonexistent organization; they just had him sign his statement and sent it to Washington.[34]

More interviews followed, each one as bizarre as the last. Three times in November and December, Giles repeated his contention that he had never attended a YCL meeting. Agents went over Giles's story again and again with no success. He remembered attending weekly meetings but was uncertain whether they were meetings of the YCL or of the ASU. And during his final interview on December 15, he told agents that his YCL recruiter might have been either Bill Remington or Rick Smith—he was not sure who it was. (Martin was not mentioned.) As for the meetings, he eventually described them as merely informal bull sessions. ASU and YCL literature had been available to the participants, but he had never been asked to join the Communist Party.[35]

FBI agents monitoring the trial must have cringed to see Roscoe Giles take the stand on January 5, 1951, repeat the oath, and begin to tell his story, until it became clear that it bore little resemblance to the waffling they had heard previously. During his sophomore year, 1937–38, he joined the Young Communist League, he said, recruited by William Remington, William Martin, and Rick Smith, who assured him that they were also members.

Did you attend any YCL meetings?

"Yes, I did," Giles said.

Was Remington present at the meetings?

"He was present at the majority of them."

Could you tell us what you discussed?

"Timely topics." . . . On one memorable occasion, there was a lively debate on the Russian Revolution, with Bill Martin supporting Trotsky and Remington siding with Lenin.

Was the Communist Party ever discussed?

Yes, said the cooperative witness. One member of the group had a girlfriend in New York who was a member, and after each time he saw her, he would encourage us to join the Party.

Was there Communist literature at the meetings?

There were *New Masses* and the *Daily Worker* and other brochures imported from New York.

Chanler had had enough. He moved to strike out Giles's testimony because it was "entirely incompetent, irrelevant, . . . and highly prejudicial," but the judge overruled him. Then he asked the judge to rule that YCL membership did not prove Communist Party membership—therefore, Giles's testimony about the YCL had no probative weight. On this point, Noonan agreed, and, over Saypol's objection, stated that any testimony on the YCL should be excluded. Chanler moved again to have it all stricken but was overruled. But, having second thoughts, Chanler asked for a moment to confer with Rauh and his staff. When he returned, he told the judge that since the jury had heard Giles's testimony, he had better cross-examine him, so he withdrew his first motion. He could not shake Giles's story. Everyone, but the defense, seemed to like Giles. Reporters thought him soft-spoken and confident, and his malapropisms brought humor to the otherwise grim proceedings. Asked if he was a student of Marx, he replied, "I was liberally exposed to it. . . . "

Does a YCL member, like you, ever attend church?

"Yes, [but] not religiously. . . . "

For Remington, however, the result of Giles's testimony was anything but humorous. Newspaper headlines later that evening and the following morning read along this line: REMINGTON LINKED TO RED RECRUITING.[36]

If Chanler had been able to interview Giles before the FBI, this fiasco might have been avoided. Between November 5 and January 5, Giles's story was completely transformed. Where did his new testimony come from? Not from the FBI, which, barring some supernatural strike of recollection, leaves only one possible person—Roy Cohn, the prosecutor assigned to prepare Giles for trial. Once again in its zeal to convict Remington, the government allowed a witness to deliver mistaken, or deliberately false, testimony.

On Monday, January 8, Elizabeth Bentley took her place in the witness chair. She did not look like an American Mata Hari, dressed as she was in a black suit and tailored pink blouse. For the next ninety minutes, she described her relationship with the Remingtons, and her story matched Ann's almost exactly.

"During dinner [at Schrafft's], Mr. Golos and Mr. Remington talked together and Mrs. Remington and I chatted about casual things. We sat for a while after we had finished the actual meal and then, as we were going out and putting our coats on, Mr. Golos turned to both Remingtons and said that he himself could not make trips to Washington to contact them and hence that in the future I would be considered their Communist contact, that I would go down and collect their Communist Party dues, that I would bring them Communist Party literature . . . and that I would collect from Mr. Remington any information he had been able to obtain in Washington."

Her memory of what followed was also clear and detailed—the trips to the Capital, calling Ann, arranging for an appointment, meeting with Bill. During their talks from 1942 to 1944, he discussed War Production Board affairs and often gave her secret information, written on scraps of paper because he was afraid to remove original documents. Golos thought his information was excellent and wanted him to produce as much of it as he could.

It was the formula that she particularly remembered. On one occasion, Remington told her about a process to convert garbage into synthetic rubber, but it was so secret that he did not think he could obtain it. Bentley reported this to Golos, who instructed her to tell Remington to deliver it. And one day, he brought it out. "He showed it to me and it was an extremely complicated thing. . . . He said to me that with war shortages going on that he thought that the Russians would need something very much like this. . . . "

Chanler's cross-examination took almost two full days. His goal was to destroy her credibility, but Bentley stood up to it quite well. There was, for example, her description of the now famous dinner at Schrafft's, which Chanler thought incredible.

"Now three times in that conversation while you were putting on your coat, Mr. Golos . . . used the words 'Communist' or 'Communist Party.' Do people in the underground talk to each other in public that way?"

"There was nobody around except for underground people," she snapped.

"And there was no [cloakroom] girl helping you on with your hat or coat?" Chanler asked.

Saypol interrupted. "Will the Court take judicial notice that at Schrafft's there are hangers and sometimes . . . the customers put their clothes on chairs."

"Any time Mr. Saypol cares to, I will take him around [to Schrafft's] and show him," Chanler said.

"Thank you for the invitation," said the prosecutor.

"Only after the case is over," joked Noonan.

How can you explain the differences between your earlier statements and your present testimony about meeting with the Remingtons? Never before have you said that you met them in their car. How have you suddenly remembered that? Chanler wondered.

" . . . Because I started thinking about it and because I back-tracked in my recollection to see if I could remember . . . and I found I was able to piece it together. . . . "

"You have no recollection of ever telling anyone the story until you took the stand?"

"I can't recollect either way. . . . It is impossible . . . for me to tell you." Saypol objected, but Bentley needed no one's help. As for this omission about the car, it really can be easily explained. "Nobody asked me whether I met him on foot or in an automobile, Mr. Chanler. I was asked location, not conveyance." Skillfully, she made fun of Chanler's obsession with "picayune things" with replies that began with "Oh, goodness, Mr. Chanler" or "Mercy, no."

Her last day on the stand was long and rancorous. Chanler attempted to show that Bentley had a financial interest in Remington's prosecution.

How are you presently earning a living?

Teaching, lecturing, and writing, she replied. (In fact, her living expenses through that month were being paid entirely by her publisher, Devin Garrity.)

Then Chanler got to the heart of the matter. The book you are writing, which would include your experiences with Remington—who is publishing it, and how did you come to select that particular house?

Devin-Adair, she replied, and it was her good friend Lady Armstrong who had suggested to Devin Garrity that she might write a book.

Did you receive any help with your writing?

"Nobody helped me at all. I wrote it all myself," she said.

"Do you know Mr. John Brunini?" he asked.

"Most certainly."

"Has he helped you with the book?"

" . . . [H]elp in the morale end. As far as writing, he did not do any writing, nor did he contribute to it," Bentley said.

" . . . You did not have any arrangement with Mr. Brunini that he was to be your literary agent at any time . . . ?"

"No. . . . "

"Mr. Brunini helped you with the writing of your book last spring?" Chanler asked again, despite her denials.

" . . . I wrote it myself," Bentley continued to insist.

"This Mr. Brunini . . . was the foreman of the grand jury that indicted Mr. Remington, was he not?"

Bentley answered calmly, "That is quite correct." Then Chanler showed her a copy of her contract with Devin-Adair, dated June 2, 1950 (six days prior to Remington's indictment), and she admitted that it looked authentic.

"There was no other contract that preceded this one?" he asked.

"No."

"You are quite sure of that?"

"Quite sure."

Did you ever discuss another contract for the book with Devin-Adair's publicity director?

"No. . . . There wasn't any previous contact."

"You are perfectly certain of that?"

"Well, certainly," Bentley said.

Having informed the court that Foreman Brunini had played a role in the creation of her book, Chanler then tried to reveal other improper features of the grand jury's investigation. Who was your attorney when you sued the U.S. Service and Shipping Corporation in 1947? he asked Bentley.

"I began with Mr. Thomas Donegan," Bentley answered.

From the last seat at the government's table, where Saypol had banished him, Thomas Donegan now arose and spoke for the first time during the trial, not as prosecutor but in his own defense. He admitted that, while in private practice in 1947, Bentley had retained him to begin a lawsuit and that some months later, when he returned to the Justice Department, he withdrew from the case. Another attorney helped her win an out-of-court settlement.

Even so, Chanler noted, was it not Mr. Donegan who had presented evidence to the grand jury, when you had first appeared there in 1947?

Bentley said she could not remember, but Donegan said that Chanler was correct.

Chanler was also able to bring out the fact that the first witness called by the Brunini grand jury was Joseph Egan, one of Bentley's attorneys in the libel suit. Saypol objected. This was all irrelevant; he did not know anything about Egan.

On redirect examination, Saypol attempted to restore Bentley to her former glory as ex-Communist patriot. Have you ever been paid for any of your many appearances before congressional committees, grand juries, and trials?

No, except for subpoena and per-diem fees.

Did you know, see, or speak to any of the other twenty-two members of the grand jury who unanimously voted Remington's indictment?

No, Bentley repeated.

"In the course of your appearance before the grand jury which voted this indictment, did you have any conversation of any kind, any place, anywhere outside of the domain of the grand jury with Mr. Brunini about the subject of your testimony . . . ?"

"No," Bentley said.

How much of your manuscript was devoted to Remington?

Just a few pages, she said, none of which discussed his indictment or prosecution.

You have testified that Brunini and publisher Garrity visited you to discuss the manuscript. Was that before or after the indictment was voted on June 8? Saypol asked.

After, she replied; they came sometime in late July or August (implying that Brunini's minor role as editor had occurred only after the grand jury had completed its work).

Saypol also questioned her about her relationship with her former lawyer Thomas Donegan. She claimed that chance had brought them together. Donegan had just resigned from the FBI to practice law, and, shopping for a lawyer, she learned from the Bureau that he was a very good one; so she hired him. Perhaps that was how Bentley understood it, but, of course, Donegan was hand-picked by the Bureau to act on Bentley's behalf and was still her lawyer when he resumed his work on the Silvermaster case. These details Donegan did not share with the court.

It was Chanler who got to ask Bentley the final questions, and for the first time in three days, she became agitated. Chanler demanded to see her manuscript, and she replied nervously, "it is not a complete book. . . . Some is chopped up and it is in no form to produce. . . . "

"Miss Bentley," Chanler said, "I am not asking you to produce it so that I can publish it. Can I have what you have?" When Bentley ignored the question, Chanler asked the judge to order Bentley to give it to the defense, and Noonan agreed. Bentley protested vehemently, but the judge reluctantly agreed to let

Chanler see it. Bentley was now on the edge of panic. " . . . it means that I am going to lose out on my contract with the publisher and my livelihood because Mr. Chanler wants to see it." Finally, she offered to produce just those pages on Remington, and the judge directed Saypol to help Chanler obtain them. There the issue stood, but later it would cause a major argument between the judge and Chanler.[37]

When Joe Rauh first tangled with Bentley in 1949, he noted that "she can be pleasant and agreeable when she wants to but can lie without the slightest facial tick." She certainly proved the accuracy of this evaluation during her three days of testimony. The evidence indicates that she definitely lied on several key issues. First, she lied about Golos giving instructions to the Remingtons that night at Schrafft's. Ann Remington, in her grand jury testimony and FBI interviews, recalled receiving no such detailed orders, and Bentley's own statements—to congressional committees, the grand jury, and the FBI—also indicate that that specific conversation never occurred. Second, she lied about the formula. In her original FBI interview in November 1945, she had described it as worthless. Now, the formula was so secret and vital that it had to be pried away from Remington. Furthermore, in 1945, she had told the FBI that Remington had given her charts detailing airplane production, but in late July 1950, she had said that "she could not recall the exact information Remington furnished her." This statement had so shocked Donegan that he had urged the Bureau to keep digging for more details about the formula, because it was the "only specific fact remembered by Bentley in connection with her contacts with Remington." At the trial, she somehow found the missing facts, and her account went further than any of her previous statements; her memory for specific detail had not been refreshed but invented.[38]

Despite Chanler's efforts to uncover Bentley's lies, the public perception of her appearance, as reflected by the press, was generally positive. Of the seven newspapers in New York and Washington that the defense considered the most influential, only the *New York Times* gave full coverage to Chanler's charge of grand jury impropriety. The others focused their attention on Bentley's shocking accusations: REMINGTON GAVE HER SECRET DATA, SAYS EX-COURIER, proclaimed the *Washington Times-Herald*, among others. The *Washington Post* neatly summed up Bentley's achievement in its headline, DEFENSE EXAMINATION FAILS TO SHAKE BENTLEY STORY. She had also succeeded in validating Ann Remington's testimony. Later, journalist Fred Cook commented on "this feat of legal legerdemain. Here was Remington's chief—and, indeed, for years his only—accuser appearing in a lesser role for the ex-wife who, in actuality, was her own corroborator!"[39]

"The Government now calls Robb Kelley . . . ," the clerk yelled out on the afternoon of January 10, and Saypol's last witness, a tall, heavy-set man with a face like a basset hound, lumbered to the witness chair. One reporter saw Remington change his glasses to get a better look at him.

"Do you have a recollection of attending a . . . convention at Ithaca, New York, with the defendant?"

I do. It was the annual tri-college conference on "Making Democracy Work," and I was a delegate who, by chance, shared a dormitory room with Remington. "We were visiting," Kelley testified, "and out of curiosity I asked him why he was a member of the Communist Party, and he told me that he was a member of the Communist Party because his father had always been a stooge for the Capitalists, and it was his hope that some day he would be able to do something better in order to improve the [world] situation. . . . "[40]

Joe Rauh later wondered how Kelley, after the passage of thirteen years, remembered the phrase "member of the Communist Party," during his conversation with Remington in 1938, instead of "Communist" or "radical," which he suspected were the actual words one or both men used. FBI records indicate that Rauh was right to be skeptical. According to Kelley's interviews with the Bureau in 1948 and 1950, he had asked Remington "why he was a Communist." Neither man had used the words "member of the Communist Party," and Remington never said he was a Communist. Again, a government witness gave testimony that differed significantly from previous statements given to authorities.[41]

As Kelley left the courtroom, Saypol rose and said, "the Government rests," and the first phase of the trial ended. During the preceding weeks, Saypol and Cohn had presented eleven witnesses and had taken almost fifteen hundred pages of testimony. Now Chanler would attempt to end the proceedings by presenting motions to the court. Two he had planned for, but the third was unexpected—the result of a nasty clash between himself and the judge.

At 2:00 P.M. on Thursday, January 11, Chanler approached the bench. He first renewed his original motion to dismiss the indictment on the grounds that the government not only had failed to define Communist Party membership but also had admitted that it was undefinable. The surest proof of membership was a Communist Party membership book, and none of the government's witnesses had testified that Remington ever had one. Second, Chanler moved for a directed verdict of acquittal—there was no direct testimony to indicate that Remington had lied; therefore, no *prima facie* case of perjury had been established. The government had offered nothing but circumstantial evidence, falling far short of the legal requirement of proof. Remington's alleged declaration to his future wife and his remarks to Robb Kelley at Cornell were just "boyhood badinage" Chanler claimed. To convict a defendant on such evidence would be a return to the practices of the Spanish Inquisition and the Salem Witch Trials.

In response, Saypol argued that Chanler was wrong to insist that possession of a membership book was the only way to prove Communist Party membership.

He quoted Supreme Court justice Robert H. Jackson's opinion in the *Marzani* case, where a man was found guilty of lying about Party membership even though the government produced no book: "If one is accused of falsely stating that he was not a member of, or affiliated with, the Communist Party, his conviction would depend upon proof of visible and knowable overt acts or courses of conduct sufficient to establish that relationship." Such visible and knowable acts had been presented to the court, Saypol said, "so . . . the motion for a judgment of acquittal should be denied."

Without so much as a pause to draw breath, Judge Noonan denied both of Chanler's motions.[42]

At this point, the proceedings grew heated. Chanler asked again to see Bentley's manuscript, but the judge, who had earlier told Saypol to help Chanler obtain it, now reversed himself, the result of having read a recent Supreme Court decision that relieved him of compelling Bentley to turn over the work. The book was vital to his defense, Chanler asserted. He had cut short his examination of Bentley, because he believed he would have a chance to see the book. If the judge was going to change his ruling, he wanted Bentley returned to the stand.

"Mr. Chanler, that is a gross misstatement," Noonan yelled. " . . . You did not stop your cross-examination on my statement or anybody else's statement that a book was going to be produced; you stopped your cross-examination period."

"I must protest your Honor's statement . . . ," Chanler said.

" . . . You didn't say a word, and you are now trying to throw the onus on me after consulting nine of your associates at the counsel table," Noonan countered.

Chanler continued to protest. "I either want the book or I want to question Miss Bentley," but the judge would not be moved, and Chanler asked for a mistrial.

"Motion denied," Noonan snapped and abruptly left the bench, ending that day's session.

Although Chanler knew his efforts would be futile, he returned the next morning to move for dismissal of the indictment on the grounds of grand jury impropriety. That motion denied, he asked for access to all grand jury testimony because of obvious irregularities. Again, he was denied, but Noonan permitted Chanler to renew the motion. He immediately did so, asking to inspect Remington's testimony. For the first time, the judge seemed sympathetic to Chanler's request, but after hearing Saypol argue that it would prejudice the government's case, the judge chose to reserve decision. Finally, Chanler asked to inspect the grand jury minutes of Joseph Egan—to determine whether his testimony had been relevant to the jury's purpose of investigating espionage or was another example of impropriety. That motion was also taken under advisement.[43]

Chanler's requests for dismissal of the indictment and a directed acquittal having been denied, the defense now prepared to call its first witnesses. Their evidence was so shocking that Chanler thought it might end the trial.

17

A Lot to Explain

It had been bothering Eileen Collins for more than six months. Something about the whole affair had been wrong, but what could she do about it now? She talked to her family and friends, who tried to reassure her, and she also told her story to Robert Brown, a student at the Yale University Law School. He thought it might be important, but he was only in his first year, not yet a real lawyer. He decided to contact the American Civil Liberties Union, which recommended that he talk to the judge. So, on Friday, December 29, 1950, Brown called Judge Gregory F. Noonan.

Judge Noonan is unavailable, his secretary said; could I take a message?

I have some information about Elizabeth Bentley and the Remington case, Brown said. The secretary took his name and number and promised to telephone him, after she found the judge. A few minutes later she called.

Judge Noonan said to contact the U.S. attorney or William Chanler, counsel for the defense. Brown tried Saypol's office first, but no one in authority was there; so he called William Chanler, who invited Eileen Collins to come to his office.

Chanler puffed slowly on his pipe while Mrs. Collins told him what she had observed.

Do others know?

They must, she said, it was an extremely small office. Leyla Sefa, the boss's assistant knew—they had talked about it.

Would you be willing to testify in court? It will not be pleasant; the U.S. attorney will give you a rough time on the stand. She was eight months pregnant and therefore reluctant. Chanler assured her that her appearance would be brief and that he would protect her during Saypol's cross-examination. Her information was extremely valuable to his client—she must testify. Finally, she agreed. After all, it was the right thing to do. She was confident that Leyla Sefa would also appear. So, two women whom William Remington never knew became the first witnesses for the defense.[1]

On Friday afternoon, January 12, Leyla Sefa, a slender, dark-haired woman, was called to the witness chair. Under Chanler's questioning, she explained that she had been publisher Devin Garrity's personal assistant from October 1949 to September 1950. She handled his manuscripts, typed up authors' contracts, and sometimes witnessed them. Chanler showed her just such a contract between Devin-Adair and Elizabeth Bentley, dated June 2, 1950. She recognized it.

"Did you ever see any other contract between Miss Bentley and Devin-Adair preceding this one?" Chanler asked.

Saypol objected, but was overruled.

"I saw two contracts. There was a contract prior to this one, which also included John Brunini."

"Was he, under the other contract that you saw, entitled to a percentage of the proceeds . . . ?"

Chanler barely finished the question before Saypol objected—he would object more than twenty-five times during Chanler's examination. Judge Noonan interrupted almost as frequently as Saypol. "What is the purpose of this, Mr. Chanler," he demanded at one point.

"Your Honor, I am trying to show motive. I have a right to show Miss Bentley's interest in this book. . . . "

"She is not on trial for writing a book," Noonan said.

" . . . I think the Jury are entitled to judge the credibility of Miss Bentley's testimony by the fact that she had an interest in this book [and] . . . I have a right to explore fully what happened in the Grand Jury in relation to this contract with the foreman," Chanler said.

"Wholly incompetent," Saypol insisted, and, although the judge thought it irrelevant, he allowed Chanler to proceed.

Eventually, Sefa testified that after seeing Bentley and Brunini at the office of Devin-Adair sometime prior to June 2, 1950, Devin Garrity instructed her to prepare a contract in which Brunini was to receive a percentage of the profits from Bentley's book.

Then, it was Saypol's turn. Sefa sat rigid, almost on the edge of the chair.

"Don't you want to sit back and make yourself comfortable," Saypol asked.

"I am comfortable," she replied.

The prosecutor "struck back hard," noted one reporter. During his cross-examination he brought out that Sefa never completed college or married and seemed to change jobs every few years.

Why did you leave Devin-Adair after eleven months? Saypol asked. Was your boss difficult to get along with? Did he ever yell at you?

"Once," she said.

"Didn't you say you hated Garrity?"

Perhaps, she admitted, but the remark was not to be taken seriously.

"You mean you indicated your admiration by expressing your hatred?" Saypol asked. "Is that the idea?"

"No, not at all," she replied.

Sefa ignored Saypol's sarcasm as well as his effort to confuse, embarrass, and discredit her. She calmly stuck to her story. She prepared a contract; Brunini was included for a percentage of the profits; but she did not know if it was ever signed. Later she learned that it was destroyed and another substituted.

Have you recently discussed the case with Mrs. Eileen Collins? Saypol asked.

Yes, we talked earlier today.

Saypol moved closer. "What did you say and what did she say? How much time were you together?"

We talked for about a half hour and both of us remembered that there had been two contracts, one with Brunini, one without.

"That is all," Saypol said, and the witness was excused.[2]

Eileen Collins appeared next, and Chanler's examination went smoothly, despite Saypol's ten interruptions. She testified that she first saw Elizabeth Bentley sometime in May 1950, when she was brought to Devin-Adair by John Brunini. "This is Elizabeth Bentley, who is going to do a book for us, and this is John Brunini who is helping her do it," Garrity had told Collins, who was the firm's publicity director. A contract was drawn up with Brunini and Bentley sharing the royalties; the two signed it, but later it was destroyed and a new one created.

Did you ever have a conversation with Miss Bentley about that first contract? asked Chanler.

"I asked her why the contract had been destroyed," Collins said. "To the best of my recollection these are her words—'. . . We just thought it would be best all around .' . . ."

She also remembered seeing Bentley in the office later that summer after Garrity had found her a home in Westport, Connecticut, where she could work closely with Thomas Sloane, the senior editor. On this day, Bentley had stormed in, loudly complaining that Sloane was a Communist and was ruining her book.

Although Mrs. Collins was obviously pregnant and uncomfortable, Saypol showed her no mercy. Do you know a woman named Sefa?

I do.

When did you last see her?

In the witness room, for about two minutes. Saypol remembered that Sefa had said that the two women discussed the case for half an hour, and he assumed it was in the witness room. Now Collins said it was two minutes. He thought that he had caught her in a lie and moved quickly to exploit it.

"You told us . . . that you saw Miss Sefa for about two and a half minutes. Is that right?" Saypol asked.

"That is right."

"Would you want to change your answer if I was to tell you that Miss Sefa said she . . . talked to you for about a half hour before you came in here?"

"I beg your pardon," Mrs. Collins said, "she never said I talked with her in the witness room. She could have said I talked with her earlier in the presence of . . . Mr. Chanler."

"You positively did not discuss this case with her outside?"

"I took a vow that I was telling the truth."

Suddenly, the judge began to harass Mrs Collins. "If Miss Sefa . . . testified this afternoon that she and you discussed this contract between Brunini and Bentley . . . for approximately thirty minutes, you would say she was telling the truth, or not?"

"Is this a question I am to answer now?" she asked, her voice choking with emotion.

"Yes, you answer it right now," Noonan demanded.

"Your Honor," cried Chanler, "we have the witness confused here."

Noonan looked down at the lawyer and said, "Now, Mr. Chanler, no explanations so that you can tip her off as to what the answer is."

Chanler was shocked; his face turned crimson, and he had difficulty speaking. Then he found his voice again. "I resent that statement very much and I move for a mistrial. Your Honor's question obviously indicates hostility towards this witness and disbelief."

"Overruled, Mr. Chanler, and sit down. The witness will answer the question."

Eileen Collins burst into tears.

"I advised your Honor before of this witness's condition," Chanler said. The judge leaned over and said softly, "Just take it easy, Mrs. Collins. . . . I am sorry."

On redirect, Chanler tried to set the record straight. Did you and Leyla Sefa talk about Bentley and Brunini this morning at my office?

"Yes, we did. . . . "

"That is all," Chanler said, then escorted her out of the courtroom.[3]

The day's proceedings continued.

"I have a motion, your Honor," Chanler said. The jury was excused and Chanler approached the bench. He moved for the dismissal of the indictment on the ground of gross impropriety in the grand jury room that had been proved by the testimonies of Sefa and Collins.

"I will deny the motion," Noonan ruled. "At the very least twelve men voted for the indictment, not one."

Chanler then renewed his motion to inspect all the grand jury transcripts. "I have reason to believe that [Foreman Brunini] was as much, if not more of a prosecutor than the prosecutor himself, and I think he was responsible for bringing about the indictment." That motion was also denied.

May I then have access to Remington's testimony? Chanler asked.

"I am going to reserve decision on that," the judge said. Years later, Chanler was still seething over Noonan's action. "I had a right to those minutes," he told journalist Fred Cook in 1957, "and . . . he had absolutely no right to refuse me. . . . If I had had access to them at the time . . . I would have blown this case right out of court." Thus ended what one newspaper called "the most dramatic day of the three-week-old trial."[4]

The next witness, on January 15, was Bernard Redmont, the 32-year-old journalist, whom Rauh thought was the most important defense witness. Redmont spent almost two full days on the witness stand. Chanler began by asking him about his relationship with Remington and Helen. He said that he had met Remington first in 1939, but they became good friends when he arrived in Washington in 1942. They would lunch together, and he and his wife, Joan, and young son, Dennis, often visited the Remingtons at Tauxemont. There was never any indication that the Remingtons were Communists.

" . . . If Mrs. Remington testified here that you and your wife told her in Remington's presence that you were both Communists, she was not telling the truth was she?" Chanler asked.

"That is complete imagination," Redmont replied. It is true that I lunched occasionally with Helen Johnson, a free-lance writer, who said she did research for PM and other leftist publications, but I never gave her secret or confidential information, paid her money, or met with John Golos.

Following a short recess, Saypol began his cross-examination, which immediately became a cruel and irresponsible attack. He noted that Chanler had asked the witness why, as a young journalism student, he had changed his name from Rothenberg to Redmont. " . . . You say Dean Ackerman [of Columbia University] advised you to do that? Tell us what he said to you and what you said to him."

" . . . I remember . . . saying that I was going into a career of journalism, and I felt that . . . anglicizing the name . . . would [mean] an effective and shorter byline. . . . His advice was that it was a good idea and he thought it should be done by court order, which we did. . . . I [also] remember discussing with him other questions which I will go into if your Honor thinks it is fitting, which are because of religious matters."

"What do you mean by that?" asked Saypol.

"Well," Redmont said, "there is a certain amount of anti-Semitism in the world, unfortunately."

Redmont had given Saypol the opportunity to make his point. "And you were going to hide under a phony name. Is that your idea?"

Chanler jumped up. "I object to that, your Honor. . . . Mr. Saypol has tried to bring religious prejudice into this case."

"Sustained," said Noonan, but Saypol continued to pursue that line anyway. "I take it you are of the Hebrew heritage?"

"That is correct."

"So you wanted to conceal that by taking this other name. Is that the idea?"

"It was not a question of concealment," Redmont insisted.

"That is your concept of good Americanism?" Saypol sneered. "As a matter of fact, it is the Communists who take the false names, isn't it?"

"It is not a false name, Sir," Redmont protested. "If it were . . . , I am sure the court would not have ordered it."

"I am sorry if I offended your sensibilities," said Irving Saypol (whose real name was Ike Sapolsky).[5]

Saypol was also obsessed with the name of another Redmont, Bernie and Joan's eight-year-old son, Dennis Foster Redmont. Since Redmont was a suspect in the Silvermaster case, the FBI had placed a tap on his telephone; in one conversation, recorded in February 1946, Joan was talking to their friend Helen Scott about attending a Communist Party rally in Baltimore, where Party leader William Z. Foster was to speak. Jokingly, Joan said that "Denny is Bill Z's namesake." Five years later, Saypol saw nothing funny about this, or the possibility that young Redmont might have also been named after another Party official, Eugene Dennis, who, along with Foster, Saypol had prosecuted the year before. Now he intended to skewer Redmont about these alleged Communist connections.

" . . . Did you have any admiration for [Foster]?"

"No, sir."

"Did you have any admiration for Dennis?"

"No, sir."

Saypol then placed a copy of Dennis Foster Redmont's birth certificate in evidence as Government's Exhibit 24. "And I take it you named him Dennis and you named him Foster in recognition of some ancestor or some outstanding American, is that right?"

"We named him Dennis because we liked the name," Redmont said. " . . . We named him Foster after . . . my grandfather. . . . In the old country his name was Fishel, which translated into English is Foster or other similar Anglicized names."

"After whom did you name Dennis?"

"After nobody."

"Just picked it out of the sky," Saypol mocked.

"Yes, that is right."

" . . . Didn't you tell some members of the Communist Party in Washington, D.C., . . . that you had named your son Dennis Foster in honor of these dignitaries . . . of the Communist Party?"

"I certainly did not," Redmont insisted.

"Don't you think you might want to change the boy's name now, Mr. Redmont?"

"That is absurd," Chanler yelled.

Saypol plunged ahead. "How do you spell Dennis."

"D-E-N-N-I-S."

"That is the way this Communist leader spells his name, isn't it?"

"I really don't know," Redmont said.

"As I remember it, the word 'Fishel' in yiddish means 'little fish,' doesn't it?" asked Saypol.

Redmont did not know.

"What you were doing was making a big fish of the child by naming him after William Z. Foster. Isn't that so?"

"No, it is not," Redmont said.

To further discredit Redmont, Saypol had only to draw upon the words of his friend Bill Remington and the file he had recently received from Redmont's boss, David Lawrence. "Let me read you [Remington's] testimony," Saypol announced, and the jury learned that Remington had told a Senate committee that he thought Redmont might be a Communist.

Redmont tried to help himself (and Remington) by informing the prosecutor that Remington had written him a letter of apology in which he called the accusations nonsense.

Tell me about that letter, Saypol asked, feigning ignorance (Lawrence had sent him a copy).

"He said it was one of the most difficult letters he ever had to write because he felt so badly about it, and that he was very frightened, and under this grilling which he had had, the FBI wanted him to say that there were certain names that they had given him who were Communists and that he yessed them, and that it was nonsense."

Did you reply to your friend?

No I did not, upon the advice of counsel and after informing Mr. Lawrence.

"Didn't you say . . . that you thought he was crazy?" Saypol asked, then walked to his table where Roy Cohn handed him a document. "This, Mr. Witness, is the letter . . . that you sent to your employer, isn't it?"

It was. Saypol read aloud Remington's letter, followed by Redmont's. "Mr. Witness, will you point out to me where in Mr. Remington's letter there is any retraction of the fact that he said that you were a Communist?" As Saypol read Redmont's letter, the jury learned that he had planned no further communication with Remington and that, mysteriously, Remington's letter had contained a

Buffalo nickel and a blank piece of paper, the product, Redmont had speculated, of "some psycho-neurotic element."

"You said 'psycho-neurotic,'" Saypol noted. "You thought maybe he was crazy?"

"I didn't know what to think," said Redmont.

On redirect examination, Chanler allowed Redmont to respond to Saypol's accusations that he was a Communist. "I believe in American democracy," Redmont said, "and I believe in all the freedoms that we enjoy here and I want us to continue to enjoy them. . . . I answered patiently all the questions . . . , [but] so far as I have known . . . the only places a man has been questioned on his opinions or on his religion . . . have been Nazi Germany, Fascist Italy and Soviet Russia, and I am dismayed that that should happen here."[6]

Redmont left the courtroom with his reputation all but shattered by Saypol's withering interrogation. Later, the United States Court of Appeals for the Second Circuit condemned Saypol for his handling of the witness: "The prosecutor continued his inquiry . . . long after it became clear that the change of name had no relevancy to any issue at the trial and could only serve to arouse possible racial prejudice on the part of the jury." (One of the judge's law clerks used less restrained language. Saypol's "attack," he wrote, "was inexcusably indecent . . . and should have been stopped.")[7]

The journalist's nightmare was far from over. Later that day, David Lawrence fired him. Redmont returned to Paris and for months was unemployed, until the British *Continental Daily Mail*, a conservative newspaper but opposed to McCarthyism, gave him a job. Years would pass, however, before his career recovered.

Though Saypol's conduct was outrageous, what about Redmont's? Did he tell the truth about his relationship with Elizabeth Bentley? The available evidence does not lead to a definitive conclusion. In fairness to Redmont, it should be remembered that he was the subject of an intense FBI investigation and testified twice before grand juries, which did not indict him for perjury or espionage. Nevertheless, some disturbing questions remain about his veracity. On the stand, he described Helen Johnson as just a researcher whom he knew slightly, but FBI records suggest a closer relationship. Furthermore, Remington knew Bentley's affiliation and had introduced her to Redmont, who met with her over the next two years. Is it likely that he would have deceived Redmont about Bentley? Redmont, like Remington, seems to have been close to the Party and became entrapped in something far more sinister than he realized; later, he found it too dangerous to reveal all that he knew.[8]

Saypol's reign of terror paused temporarily on the afternoon of January 16, when the defense called 81-year-old Frederick C. Remington to the stand. He was there for two reasons: to testify about his son's character and to produce evidence to contradict the government's contention that Bill spent most of the summer of 1937 attending Communist Party meetings at Betty Malcolm's home.

"Mr. Remington," Chanler asked, "have you complete confidence that your son was never a member of the Communist Party?"

"Oh, I know he wasn't," Fred replied. Fred Remington's more concrete evidence of his son's innocence was contained in a small, black leather notebook, which Chanler now showed him.

"Do you recall when your son returned from Knoxville, Tennessee?"

July 1 or July 2, he said; the proof is in that notebook. For the past twenty years, since buying his first new automobile, he had kept meticulous records about how well his cars performed during family vacations. That summer of 1937 he and his wife had planned a camping trip on the banks of the Houstamic River in northern Connecticut; Bill was expected to accompany them, but he did not return home until early July, so the trip was postponed. Instead, they celebrated Independence Day in Ridgewood. Therefore, Bill must have left Knoxville in late June, which narrowed considerably the period of time he could have spent with the Malcolms.

"Your witness," Chanler told Saypol.

The U.S. attorney glanced quickly through Fred's notebook, then said, "I have no questions." The judge thanked Mr. Remington, who walked back to the chair next to his wife's, from where he had watched almost every day of his son's trial. (Later, Lillian would give the same testimony about her son's character and his activities that summer.)[9]

The next witnesses testified about Remington's days in Knoxville. First was Horace Bryan, the 42-year-old former Arkansas Communist and veteran labor organizer. Under Chanler's questioning, Bryan described his colorful past—joining the Party and receiving a membership book in 1933; organizing the coal miners and being arrested and thrown into jail for his efforts; and, finally, deciding in March 1937 to accept the invitation of the TVA unionists to come to Knoxville to direct the Workers Education program.

When you assumed your duties, Chanler asked, did you apply for a local post office box?

"Well, it seems I did," Bryan replied, "although I don't remember originally. . . . " The lawyer showed him the application for the box, and Bryan admitted that his signature appeared on it.

Did you come to Knoxville to organize the Communist Party? Chanler asked.

"No," Bryan said.

"Did you apply for this box for any purpose other than the purposes of the Workers Education Committee?"

"I applied for it for the Workers Education Committee purposes, and that is all it was ever used for."

Bryan also denied Howard Bridgman's assertion that he had attended at least

one Communist Party meeting with him at Pat Todd's apartment; he had attended no Communist Party meetings in Knoxville. In fact, he recalled that state
secretary Ted Wellman had once asked him to consider organizing a TVA unit,
but he had declined.

Did you know the defendant in Knoxville?

Yes, I lived briefly with Remington from March to June 1937. Remington,
he said, was chiefly interested in the Workers Alliance and labor organizing; they
had never discussed the Communist Party. Bryan left Knoxville in June and in
1938, disillusioned with the Party's inability to help workers and farmers achieve
a better life, quit the Party. He did not hear of Remington again until 1950,
when the FBI visited him, and he was called to testify (in secret) before HUAC
and the grand jury.

With his categorical denials of the existence of a Communist Party unit in
Knoxville, Bryan posed the greatest threat so far to the government's TVA argument. Therefore, on cross-examination, Saypol set out to discredit Bryan but, at
first, found it tough going.

"Mr. Witness, you were a member of the Communist Party, weren't you?"

" . . . yes."

"An organization dedicated to the overthrow of the Government of the
United States by force and violence. . . . "

"Those are your words, not mine," said the feisty Bryan. "Mr. Saypol, my
people built the first Government and blazed the first trail across the . . . continent. . . . I am not here to tear it down but to build it up. I did nothing while I
was a Communist that violated my . . . good old Ozark conscience. . . . "

When that strategy failed to break down Bryan, Saypol tried another: comparing Bryan's previous statements to the grand jury with his current account
and noting where there were differences. One concerned Bryan's initial uncertainty about receiving a membership book from his recruiter. Bryan explained
that he had been given many cards over the years—by the Workers Alliance, the
Labor Non-Partisan League, the International Labor Defense—that were all very
similar to a Communist Party membership book, so when he gave that answer to
the grand jury, he had been honestly confused. Recently, however, after examining a Communist Party membership book in Chanler's office, Bryan was now
confident that he had received a book.

Saypol thought he was lying. "Was this answer that you gave to the grand
jury on June 2 [1950] true or false?"

"Part of it . . . was based on some confusion," Bryan admitted.

"Was it true or false?" Saypol repeated.

Bryan did not respond.

"Can't you answer that?"

"No, I can't. . . . "

"Answer that question," Noonan ordered.

This whipsaw questioning finally affected Bryan. Squirming in his chair, he said, "your Honor, this . . . is not a matter of being true and false. True and false implies that a person lies about a thing, and when I make an honest mistake and when my recollection fails me and I correct it again, it is not a matter of admitting later on that I told a lie."

Saypol had him now. "May the witness be directed to answer the question responsively?"

" . . . Answer the question yes or no," Noonan said again.

" . . . I could only answer the question by qualifying it. . . . "

"Yes or no, Mr. Bryan."

" . . . I will say no and qualify it by saying it is not the complete truth. I have been forced to tell a lie."

Saypol had achieved his goal. He raised doubts about Bryan's veracity and implied that the defense had coached the witness to give the answer their case required—that he always had a membership book. For the rest of his cross-examination, Saypol carried on in the same vein. When Bryan found it difficult to remember precisely what he had told the grand jury seven months before, Saypol, with obvious relish, listed subjects he failed to recall. Each time, Bryan replied that he could not isolate what he had told the grand jury from what he had told HUAC and the many FBI agents he had talked to since April 1950. Two important points were obscured by Saypol's verbal pyrotechnics—whether Bryan was testifying before the grand jury or at trial, he consistently denied that he knew Remington was a Communist Party member in Knoxville or that the post office box where he and Remington picked up their mail was an official Communist Party box. Newspaper headlines captured the confusion Saypol had cleverly created. At first they read, EX-RED DOUBTS THAT REMINGTON EVER BELONGED; then, on the final day of Bryan's testimony, REMINGTON WITNESS STORIES IN CONFLICT. Chalmers M. Roberts, reporting for the *Washington Post*, summed up Bryan's appearance astutely when he wrote, "Just what impression the jury . . . had when the witness finally was excused was anybody's guess."[10]

The government had a surprise ready for the next defense witness, David Stone Martin. When Roy Cohn had learned that the former TVA graphic artist was subpoenaed, he had asked the FBI to send him everything it had on Martin. When the files arrived at the Bureau's field office on the night of January 18, an FBI agent examined the records and hurried to Cohn with one document in hand—an old Civil Service questionnaire that Martin had filled out in 1943.

"Anything significant?" Cohn asked. The agent, stony-faced, thought there was one answer that might interest him. Cohn read the page and smiled broadly. It was unbelievable. For Cohn, Martin's appearance the next morning was "the most exciting moment at the trial."

At first, Martin's testimony on Friday, January 19, went so well that even Remington was openly beaming. He recalled nineteen-year-old Bill Remington only as a young man who liked to ride a motorcycle. He had no knowledge that he was a Communist.

"Do you know whether Mr. Remington was a member of the Communist Party?" asked Saypol on cross-examination.

" . . . [H]e was a very, very active union man," Martin said, "and he was interested in other current things . . . of a radical nature, but I certainly couldn't say on the basis of that the man is a Communist or not a Communist."

"Did he ever ask anybody to join the Party as far as you know?"

"Not that I know of."

Saypol approached the witness, an uncharacteristic smile on his face. Do you remember being questioned by the Civil Service Commission when you worked for the Office of War Information in 1943?

Yes, I do.

Saypol showed him Government's Exhibit 34, noting that Martin had sworn to tell the truth, just as he had that very morning when he took the stand. "Now will you follow me on this . . . , 'Question: The Commission has been informed that you were close to Bill Remington, who is known to have distributed Communist literature in Knoxville. [Answer:] . . . He was a young fellow who was fanatical in his political beliefs. I won't deny that he was a Communist as that was well known, because he approached everyone and asked them to join the Communist Party. . . . I knew him to say hello to on the street, but had no close association with him at all. In Knoxville, I never heard of a regular party, although people jumped to conclusions, and made irresponsible statements.'"

At the defense table, Remington grimaced and Chanler sat in stunned silence.

"You gave that answer . . . did you not?" Saypol asked the witness.

"Yes," said Martin.

Saypol turned smartly, walked over to Chanler, and handed him the document. Then court was recessed for lunch.

While Saypol and Cohn celebrated their victory, Chanler was closeted with his aides. At 2:30 P.M., when the trial resumed, he called Martin to the stand, showed him the Government's Exhibit 34, and asked if he had an explanation. Martin paused a moment, then said that he thought his statement was generally consistent with his testimony, which was that he did not know definitely if Remington had been a Communist. A witness should be sure of his facts before making such an accusation in court, and he had no such knowledge.

Chanler noted the final sentence in his answer: "In all Knoxville, I never heard of a regular party, although people jumped to conclusions, and made irresponsible statements."

"I think that possibly I myself have been guilty of that," Martin said.

It was too late for apologies and explanations. Cohn was right when he later observed: "As defense witness Martin's own words, naming the man for whom he was testifying as an active Communist, rang through the courtroom, I knew that we had scored a devastating point."[11]

Two stronger defense witnesses appeared next and performed admirably, but those reporters who had attended the early session were still talking about Martin's appearance. William Goodman and Charles Davis took the stand late that afternoon and testified about how they and Bill Remington had destroyed the pro-Communist ASU on the Dartmouth campus in 1938. Chanler informed them that their former classmate Roscoe Giles had testified that he had attended ASU meetings every Sunday in 1938 and 1939. Can that testimony be correct?

No, both men replied, Giles must be mistaken; no active ASU group existed that year.[12]

Goodman also had evidence to indicate that Remington's anti-Communism continued after graduation in 1939. That Christmas, against the background of the Russian invasion of Finland, Goodman remembered receiving a card from Remington, on which his friend commented on world events: "This proves that what we thought was right. I wouldn't touch a Russian with a ten-foot pole." But Goodman had misplaced the card and could offer only this anecdote.

On cross-examination, Saypol was less aggressive than usual, no doubt still feeling the glow of his earlier triumph. But he examined Goodman closely about the Christmas card. "Was it a single card or a folding card? Can you tell us what the message on the front of the card was? . . . Did he sign it 'Bill'? Did he put his wife's name on it? . . . What was the message that he inscribed on . . . this card? Will you tell us again?" Goodman answered each question clearly and confidently.

Unfortunately for Remington, it was the David Stone Martin incident that captured the attention of the press. The *New York Times* devoted fourteen paragraphs to Martin and only six to other witnesses that day, under a headline that read DEFENSE WITNESS TRIPS REMINGTON. Nearly all the Washington papers that the defense surveyed had followed suit.[13]

There was an air of expectation in the courtroom on Monday morning, January 22. For days, it had been rumored that the defendant would soon take the stand, and when he strode into the courtroom looking more dapper than usual in a brown suit, white shirt, and a scarlet tie, many thought that the moment had come. But instead of sitting down and studying notes, as a witness might do before testifying, he turned to a book, Vernon Parrington's *Main Currents in American Thought*, and began to read.

Another man was called to the stand when court opened at 10:30 A.M., Charles J. Hitch, the Rand Corporation economist, who had worked with Remington at the War Production Board during World War II. On direct examination, Hitch took the courtroom back to the desperate days following Pearl Harbor, when Washington was torn by a dozen controversies on how best to win the war. One was economic. Those on the political left (especially American

Communists) supported what Hitch called the horizontal plan for the allocation of material resources, while conservatives and big business generally favored the vertical plan by which the War Production Board allocated material to other government agencies for distribution to contractors. Writers in PM and other like-minded newspapers vigorously attacked the vertical plan, believing that it would lead to the dominance of what would later be called the military-industrial complex. As a member of the WPB's Planning Committee staff, Hitch said that he had worked closely with 26-year-old Bill Remington, who was enthusiastic about developing the Controlled Materials Plan (CMP), modeled on the centralized program. Hitch also remembered when an inventor proposed a scheme to manufacture rubber from garbage. "It was not regarded seriously by anyone that I knew," he testified. "I think most people regarded it as a crackpot scheme."

On cross, Hitch also proved to be a good witness for the defense. He argued that part of Remington's job was to promote the CMP to a skeptical Washington community, and this meant talking to the press. Like Remington, Hitch met with reporters for lunch or an after-hour's drink to discuss it. But, when pressed by Saypol, he did admit that he had never left his office in the middle of the day to meet a reporter at the Mellon Art Gallery or at a park bench on the Mall.

"It does seem rather odd, doesn't it," Saypol noted.[14]

Hitch's testimony was overshadowed by that of the next witness who followed him at 2:37 P.M. that afternoon—William Remington. His first three days on the stand were devoted to Chanler's direct examination, and because the government's bill of particulars charged that he was a Communist Party member from 1934 to 1944, he began his story at age sixteen. Speaking softly and calmly, he recounted how a young Republican became an ardent New Dealer and antifascist at Dartmouth. Asked by his lawyer if he had joined the Communist Party during his freshman or sophomore years, he answered "no"; nor had he joined the Young Communist League. In fact, he said that he had "no personal knowledge or recollection" that such a group existed on campus. Generally, he was a typical student—working hard in the classroom and on the athletic field, writing for the school newspaper, and selling stationery and football tickets to pay his tuition. After completing his first two years, he wanted to test his political and economic philosophy and also earn enough money to complete his education; so, in September 1936 he went south and was appointed a messenger with TVA. Tiring of this boring job, he spent most of his time in union work. The jury had already met some of the friends he had made in Knoxville—Christine Benson, Muriel Speare Williams, Howard Bridgman, and Horace Bryan. He did not recall that Bryan had rented a post office box, but when going through his records recently, he had discovered a letter he had sent his parents bearing the return address, P.O. Box 1692, so he must have used it. But he had no reason to believe that it was a Party mailbox. When he worked with Benson, Williams,

Bryan, or Pat Todd in the TVA union or the CIO organizing drive, he had no idea that they might be Communists. He certainly had never attended a Communist Party meeting with Benson or Bridgman and could not recall meeting McConnell. And the idea that he was supposedly encouraged to return to Dartmouth for the sake of the Communist Party was "just sheer nonsense."

Reporters were impressed by Remington's easy, unassuming manner and the way that he skillfully denied or explained differently the events described by government witnesses. When he returned to Dartmouth in 1937, he told the jury, he still considered himself a radical, but now getting an education was his chief objective, so he turned away from political involvement. He denied recruiting Roscoe Giles into the YCL and claimed, too, that he never told Robb Kelley that he had been a member of the Communist Party.

Were you ever asked at Dartmouth why you were a Bolshevik or Communist? Chanler asked.

"Oh, yes," Remington laughed.

What would you have said?

"I would answer depending on what I thought the motives of the asker were. If it were a serious question, I would talk perhaps of my own dreams about a better [world]; but if it were an unfriendly question, I would say, 'Well, I am a Bolshevik because I want to blow you up' or something like that."

Remington was comfortable discussing his early life but became angry when he was presented with Ann's story. "Did you ever tell her that you had been a member of the Communist Party at Knoxville?" Chanler asked.

"No, I did not," he said, shaking his head. He remembered that night; as he recalled, Ann and he had not talked much after being left alone in her car. And there had been no pre-marital agreement that he remain a Party member, Remington said, only a promise that he would never become a heartless businessman. The picture she painted of a Communist honeymoon and marriage was also distorted. Those letters of introduction to Mexican leftists had all come from Ann and her family, not from him. He never rang doorbells for Earl Browder in 1940; the truth was that he was coming more and more to hate the Communists. At a lecture on Marxism at the Workers' School, he had heckled the instructor and was thrown out. His contribution to *New Masses* was no endorsement of Joe North's Communist views but help for a family friend. The hundred dollars had come from Ann's savings account, not from his. Ann had also exaggerated his role in working with the Emergency Peace Mobilization after their move to Washington in 1940. She was the one who became executive secretary, while he just occasionally helped out. Once the group's isolationist and pro-Communist position became clear, they quit. His radical days were well behind him now, he argued. Nevertheless, that past came under close scrutiny once he became a federal employee; from 1941 to 1942, he was investigated by the Treasury Department, the Civil Service Commission, and the FBI, just at the time when he was supposedly spying for Elizabeth Bentley. What a ridiculous notion! That he would steal War Production Board secrets while he was being investigated by three government agencies!

"As you watch William Remington on the stand," wrote Max Lerner, "you know that on his performance the case will turn. The testimony against him thus far has been damaging and some of it has been deadly. But, at least in my own mind, the case has certainly not been closed and the verdict turned in. . . . He has a lot to explain, and he goes at it in so earnest and thoroughgoing a way that—guilt or no guilt—one can understand how he impressed his teachers at Dartmouth and Columbia, and his bosses . . . in Washington."[15]

Chanler interrupted Remington's testimony briefly on January 23 to put a new witness on the stand. Mildred Shelhorse for the past thirteen years had been the manager of the Schrafft's Restaurant, where the Remingtons had dined with Bentley and Golos. Earlier in the trial, Saypol had ridiculed Chanler for suggesting that Golos's parting instructions could not have occurred because of the presence of a hatcheck girl, who sat, Cerberus-like, near the restaurant's entrance. Even Judge Noonan poked fun at the idea. Now Chanler, with Mrs. Shelhorse's help, punched a rather large hole in Bentley's story. Schrafft's not only had a hatcheck girl, situated just to the right of the revolving door that brought customers inside, but also a cashier, who sat at a desk nearby, and a bartender, who served customers who chose to have a drink at the bar. Therefore, the area where Remington supposedly conspired to commit espionage was crowded with employees and customers.

There was not much that Saypol could do on cross-examination, but he tried. "It is not the policy of the employees of Schrafft's to eavesdrop on conversations of customers, is it?" he asked Mrs. Shelhorse.

"I think not," she said.

"I agree with you," said the prosecutor. " . . . That is all."[16]

Remington was cool and confident when he returned to the stand on January 24, the last and most important day of direct examination. This would be his final opportunity to explain fully how he came to meet Helen Johnson and what had occurred during their meetings, before Saypol attempted to destroy him. His purpose in seeing her, he told the court, was to defend the WPB against leftist attacks and to promote those programs he thought essential to the war effort.

Bentley has testified that you gave her detailed charts describing stages of aircraft production and the theaters of war to which they would be assigned, Chanler said. Is this true?

No, Remington claimed, the WPB did not have such information. There was a two-week period, in April 1943, when the Planning Committee had loaned him to the Air Force to do a statistical study of aircraft components, but he never showed it to Bentley. The only figures on airplane production and tanks and ships that he gave her were drawn from public sources.

What about that formula for making rubber from garbage that both your wife and Bentley said you stole from the government?

Remington laughed. There was never a formula, only a verbal description of a process that he had learned about from his colleagues. There was nothing secret about it; in fact, the whole thing began when a radio personality broadcast a story about a miraculous new way to make synthetic rubber. The board studied this invention, but it turned out to be a failure.

Why then tell Bentley about it?

Because she was complaining about the slowness of the synthetic rubber program, and I wanted to show her how carefully the board considered even the wildest ideas.

Did you ever give her any money?

Yes. He remembered one contribution to a refugee fund, a dollar for taxi fare, and a few quarters to repay her for copies of *PM* and the *Daily Worker* she once brought him. She wanted him to read these newspapers and report to her on their accuracy. They were usually wrong, and he told her so.

"Now you heard your wife testify here that . . . she drove to your office, picked you up in the car and Miss Bentley got in . . . and [you] drove to the Mall," Chanler said. Did this occur?

No, Remington said. In fact, this was the first time Bentley had ever publicly mentioned their car. And, he did not remember his wife ever being present during their meetings. By early 1943, he had begun to become suspicious of Helen, so he stopped seeing her.

During the first stage of the trial, nine government witnesses testified that Remington had been a Communist; now, Chanler presented evidence of Remington's most recent anti-Communist views and activities. Concluding, Chanler asked Remington seven questions. "Were you ever in the Communist underground?"

"No, I was not. . . . I also want to make it clear . . . that I had no idea that [Bentley] was representing the Communist Party and that anything I talked with her about went to the Communist Party [or to Russia]."

"Did you ever give Miss Bentley or anyone else any secret, classified information or any information to which they were not entitled?"

"I definitely did not."

"Have you ever been a member of any unit or branch of the Communist Party?"

"No."

"Have you ever to your knowledge attended Communist Party meetings?"

"No."

"Have you ever paid Communist Party dues?"

"I have not."

"Now, my final question: Mr Remington have you ever in your life been a member of the Communist Party?"

"I have not," Remington snapped.[17]

Now Saypol approached the witness. "Grueling," "intensive," a "relentless grilling session" was the way reporters described Saypol's three-day cross-examination of Remington. The prosecutor, said one newspaper, stalked the floor "like a cat trying to surprise a mouse." In preparation, Saypol's staff had examined every available record on Remington in search of derogatory information and contradictions between past statements and his present testimony. Then Saypol would play the true-false game: Mr. Witness, which was the truth, which the lie, don't explain, answer yes or no! It was not a very difficult task, since Remington's files contained an embarrassment of riches that Saypol exploited with relish.

"Now, there was a man by the name of Redmont; do you remember him?" asked Saypol. "That was the fellow that you said you thought might have been a Communist?"

"I once said that to my shame as well as my sorrow," Remington said.

"Do you still think he's a Communist?"

"No."

"You changed your mind since this trial, is that right?"

"Yes, because I know now where I got the impression [from the FBI]."

"Who told you? Who told you?" Saypol asked, advancing suddenly on Remington. "Who in the FBI told you . . . that Redmont might have been a Communist? . . . "

"I don't recall specifically. . . . That was a hectic interview, as you can imagine."

"They didn't attempt to beat you, did they?"

"No, no. Mr. Cornelison [of the FBI] . . . told me things about Mr. Redmont which gave me the impression that they knew he was a Communist; if they knew he was a Communist, I was certainly not going to contradict them. . . . "

"And so you say that you had a justifiable basis for concluding that he might have been a Communist?"

"They made me think he was."

Yet, Saypol noted, in September 1950, you wrote to Redmont, apologizing for your statements. "Why should you owe him an apology because of what some agent said about Redmont being a Communist?"

"Because I was ashamed of the way I had been bamboozled. . . . I was so shocked by the whole business I was ready to believe anything. . . . "

"Including the fact that you were a member of the Communist Party, were you ready to believe that, too?" Saypol taunted.

"I was not because I knew I was not."

" . . . Isn't it a fact that within a few days of the interview with the FBI in

1947 that you telephoned and asked for an appointment and saying that you . . . wanted to make a deal with them?"

"No," said Remington.

" . . . and that the terms of the deal were that you would become an informer on your friends Redmont, his brother-in-law, and your friend Joe North?"

"That is sheer nonsense and tommyrot," Remington insisted. But Saypol now forced him to discuss another embarrassing chapter in his life.

I never volunteered to become an informer, Remington claimed. The agents asked me to let them know if Joe North or anyone like Elizabeth Bentley ever contacted me, and I said I would.

Judge Noonan interrupted with a not very sympathetic question of his own. "How would you know it was somebody like Bentley if you did not know Bentley was a Communist spy when you were dealing with her?"

Remington slumped in the chair and said wearily, "Their request somewhat baffled me, but I made the promise nonetheless."

(J. Edgar Hoover, who was receiving daily summaries of the trial testimony, was enraged by Remington's comment that he was tricked by the FBI. William Cornelison, now employed by the CIA, was asked to review his notes of the interview, and he told officials that he was ready to publicly call Remington a "fanatical liar." That was exactly what Hoover wanted the record to show, and he asked Saypol to clear his agents of Remington's lies. Saypol gladly added Cornelison to the government's group of rebuttal witnesses who would testify after the defense concluded its case.)

When the most sensitive issues were raised, toward the end of Saypol's cross, Remington was ready and even coolly defiant. "Commencing at the beginning of 1946, did you carry on an illicit relationship in Washington with a woman whose name is Jane? Yes or no?"

"No."

Surprised, Saypol switched to another painful topic. "On June 8, 1947, did you assault your wife?"

"No. I slapped her in a disagreement over my son."

"Did you injure her?"

"Not that I know of," Remington said. "I was not living there at the time."

Saypol then offered into evidence a copy of the Remingtons' separation accord, which mentioned Bill's adultery. Chanler objected, but the judge allowed the questions that followed. "Do you now deny that you committed adultery with a woman by the name of Jane?"

"No."

"You do admit it . . . ?"

"Yes," Remington said, and he smiled at the prosecutor. "When you first asked, your question happened to be in error. That is why I said no to it before."

"In other words, . . . the adultery commenced at a later time. . . . But you were not divorced . . . ?"

"Not divorced."

"As a matter of fact, that was the cause of the separation, wasn't it?"

"It was not the cause," he replied confidently. No one knew how such testimony would affect the seven married women who sat on the jury, but it certainly could not have helped Remington.

For the most part, Remington displayed similar composure when confronted with Saypol's barrage of questions. He was examined on more than fifty specific topics, but nothing seemed to excite him. Saypol would point out minor differences between his previous statements and his current testimony, then ask him which was true. Remington calmly brushed away the questions with comments like: "That is not accurate. You left out [a] page"; "It's only half the picture"; or "both answers are true." Nor did Saypol's sarcastic insults faze him. He sat quietly while his testimony about John and Helen was called a "fantastic narrative"—"strange meetings in Washington, wasn't it strange?"

"Yes, in a way," he agreed. "It was not a normal experience for me."

"How many others did you do that with?"

"Nobody, I am happy to say," laughed Remington.

But when Saypol accused him of telling not just a fantastic story but "an untruth," then Remington became angry. Pounding his fist on the armrest of the witness chair, he yelled, "I am telling the truth." When the proceedings recessed briefly and Saypol and the jury left the room, Remington paced around, smacking his right fist into his left palm, while remarking angrily, "I'd like to do that to him!" It was the only time that he lost his poise during three days of relentless cross-examination. He finally left the stand on the afternoon of January 29, "unshaken in his claims that he never was a Communist and never gave secret government information to a Soviet agent," observed the *New York Post*.[18]

Had he told the truth? Not always. On at least three points, he definitely lied—when he said that he had no idea whom Bentley represented, that he did not give information to unauthorized persons, and that he had no knowledge of the Dartmouth YCL.

As the defense ended its case, Joe Rauh was subjected to a sudden and bitter attack by Judge Noonan. It had been building for weeks. As Rauh watched Saypol abuse defense witnesses, he could do nothing but grimace, sigh, and frequently groan. Noonan often complained to Chanler about Rauh's "audible expressions of dismay [and] disgust." Now Rauh approached the bench to offer motions and to ask the judge finally to rule on those he had deferred. Among them was the request to examine the grand jury testimony of Joseph Egan. "I will deny the motion," Noonan said. Then Rauh requested that all the grand jury testimony and the memorandum submitted by Brunini regarding his relationship with Bentley be sealed and made a part of the record. Rauh explained the reasons for his motion. Brunini and Donegan had violated their charge. Instead of investigating espionage, they had set out to indict Remington for perjury. Therefore, the question asked Remington and his alleged false answer were not legally relevant. Saypol exploded. "I never heard of anything like this," he told the judge. "It is wholly improper." The defense was creating "a straw man . . . to divert attention from the issue in the case, the perjury of the defendant. . . . " Noonan was skeptical but granted the motion to seal the grand jury records.

But he refused to include Brunini's memo. Rauh stated the grounds for his request. Brunini's account, he thought, flatly contradicted Bentley's testimony that the foreman had played only a minor role in preparing her manuscript; the document was also evidence that the U.S. attorney knew about the improper grand jury proceedings and illegally suppressed the information.

"Denied," said Noonan, but Saypol blasted Rauh's charges anyway, calling them "baseless" and "unfounded," "made of whole cloth."

Rauh tried again. He asked that the government either admit that its legion of informers never identified Remington as a member of the Communist Party or produce all their reports made between 1934 and 1944.

"I never heard anything like this," Saypol yelled. "It is getting to sound like one of the comrade's meetings. I submit the dignity of the Court is being affronted by this and ought to be stopped." The judge agreed. To Chanler, he said, "all of these things are entirely inappropriate at this time, as you should know."

"If your Honor is going to make a statement, we should be heard," Rauh interjected. "There is a basic principle that when the prosecution has evidence which will help the defendant, it is up to the prosecution to produce it, and that principle has not been properly preserved in this case."

Some dam of pent-up anger in the judge finally burst. "Are you accusing me, Mr. Rauh?"

"I am not accusing anybody. I am stating—"

Noonan cut him off. "From this point on, Mr. Rauh, any motions . . . will be made by counsel in chief. You may sit down."

Rauh protested. "Your Honor, I wish to say—"

"We will take a recess," Noonan yelled, then left the bench. Chanler leaped to his feet, crying, "I take exception to your Honor's comments about my associate."

"Perfectly well deserved," remarked Saypol.[19]

Later that afternoon, the defense rested. The trial was adjourned until the next day, January 31, when each side would present rebuttal witnesses, the beginning of the end.

Liar. Communist. Spy. Each of the government's final witnesses would attempt to prove Remington guilty of these charges. First to testify on January 31 was William Cornelison. He rejected Remington's claim that he had been mistreated by the FBI; on the contrary, even the defendant had admitted that agents had been kind and gracious.

The most embarrassing moment came when Cornelison testified about Remington's offer to spy on Joe North and other suspects. Saypol put Remington's letters to Cornelison into the record, and, by day's end, excerpts were running in newspapers throughout the country. If he did not call Remington a fanatical liar, Cornelison's testimony destroyed Remington's claim that the informer charge was just "tommyrot." There was not much Chanler could do to contradict such testimony and the evidence that accompanied it, but he tried to put a better face on it. The ex-FBI agent did admit, on cross-examination, that he never told Remington to stop sending him information. Overlooked in the exchange, was the irony that two government witnesses, Bentley and Crouch, professional informers, were treated as heroes, while Remington's amateur efforts were used to discredit him. Cornelison left the stand with the government's thanks, and, a few minutes later, the Bureau was notified that their former agent had done a "bang-up job."[20]

It was Remington's former Dartmouth and Columbia acquaintance William Chamberlin who implied that Remington was a Communist, because he followed the Party line in late 1939. Chamberlin was an effective witness, appearing in the uniform of a Marine Corps lieutenant colonel, a man who was both a soldier and a lawyer (since he was also assistant legal aid to the Marine Corps commandant). Remington's pro-Soviet views were obvious in 1939, Chamberlin testified, when they talked about the Russo-Finnish War. Chamberlin believed that Russia was guilty of naked aggression, while Remington supposedly had said that the Finns had attacked first and Russia was only defending its borders.

Chanler attempted to undermine Chamberlin's testimony by reminding the witness of Remington's habit of always taking the opposite side in a debate. So, if Chamberlin said he supported the Finns, then naturally Remington would have backed the Russians. "If you took a side, wasn't it customary for him to take a different side, and he would argue it with you?" Chanler asked.

"No, I wouldn't say that," Chamberlin insisted. His strategy having failed, Chanler thanked the witness and asked no further questions.[21]

The government's next witness was far more damaging. Rudolph F. Bertram was an official with the U.S. High Command in Germany, who, thirteen years before, had worked with Bill Remington while he was with TVA. "Did anybody ever ask you to join the Communist Party?" Saypol asked.

"Mr. Remington," the witness said.

"The defendant here?" said Saypol with artificial surprise.

"Yes, sir." Bertram testified about that afternoon in 1937 when Remington had allegedly invited the then TVA official to join the Communist Party.

Chanler, on cross-examination, suggested to Bertram that he had misunderstood the conversation that had occurred so long ago. It was a time of great unrest at TVA, when a group of labor activists, Remington among them, were trying to convince members of the local chapter of the American Federation of Government Employees to shift their allegiance from the AF of L to the new, dynamic CIO that many thought was Communist dominated. Bertram remembered. He had opposed the change.

"And I propose to you that that conversation originated out of a discussion over this burning issue that everybody was talking about between the CIO and the AF of L," Chanler said.

"No, sir," said Bertram. " . . . We were specifically discussing my joining the Communist Party."

Chanler took Bertram over the meeting again and again but failed to shake his story. "You say that Mr. Remington just walked into your office, . . . and said, 'Let's join the Communist Party.'"

"That is correct," Bertram insisted.

" . . . Are you positive of that?"

"I am positive."

A few more questions and Bertram was excused, leaving the jury with a greater impression that Remington had been a Party member at Knoxville.[22]

Finding witnesses to suggest that Remington might also have been a spy was a bit more difficult. FBI agents had interviewed more than forty former employees of the War Production Board and had found only three who were willing to put themselves in the government's hands. Ralph Austrian testified that, contrary to what Remington and Hitch had claimed, the rubber formula was both valuable and a national secret. He could say nothing less, since next to its inventor, no one had believed more in the process than he had. He had originally brought the idea to the WPB and was then placed in charge of making it work.

"Was this formula under serious consideration by the War Production Board . . . ?" asked Roy Cohn.

"Yes," Austrian said.

"Why . . . ?"

"Because at the time the country was suffering from a very acute shortage of both gasoline and rubber and the war effort was seriously hindered by that lack, and anything that could contribute toward its relief was always given serious consideration." Full reports on his activities were given to WPB official Thomas Blaisdell, who, Austrian said, informed the U.S. Patent Office in July 1942 that J. W. Jeans's application would henceforth be classified "secret." Austrian also told Cohn that he recalled seeing William Remington, Blaisdell's chief assistant, at the meetings he attended to explain personally his program.

On cross-examination, Chanler was able to deflate Austrian's balloon.

Austrian admitted that while their efforts did produce gasoline, Jeans's process was never used to manufacture it during World War II, when it was so desperately needed. Austrian was also aware that Jeans had first revealed his discovery to a California broadcaster, who had devoted an entire program to the inventor's plan. But he rejected Chanler's characterization of the whole affair as a joke and a crackpot scheme.[23]

To back up Austrian's claim of secrecy, the government called James L. Brewrink, of the U.S. Patent Office. He produced a letter from Thomas Blaisdell asking that the Commissioner of Patents keep Jeans's application secret. The Patent Office approved the request in August 1942. Chanler tried to stop what he thought was nonsensical testimony. "It has nothing whatever to do with secrecy in the War Production Board. It isn't binding on this defendant or anyone else. It is an order binding on the applicant for the patent . . . and has nothing to do with this case." But before Noonan could rule, Cohn noted that the Patent Office had informed the WPB of the secrecy order and that Austrian had mentioned it at a meeting attended by Blaisdell and Remington.

" . . . I will let the evidence stand," Noonan said. Despite Austrian's and Brewrink's testimonies, FBI interviews with top WPB officials indicate that most thought the formula "a comic opera affair," and none knew that its patent was secret, but the public perception now was that, next to the atomic bomb, it was the greatest secret of the war.[24]

A banker and a lawyer finally presented to the court the government's evidence that Remington was guilty of espionage. But neither man had had anything to do with the search for and discovery of the file that supposedly proved Bentley's charges. That assignment had gone to the FBI at Saypol's specific order, on the night of January 7—the eve of Bentley's dramatic testimony about receiving charts on aircraft production. Apparently, Saypol was skeptical because he told the Bureau "to determine whether Bentley's allegation is correct. . . . " It was very late to be still looking for such critical evidence, but he urged them on. "This information forms the crux of the case and it must be procured as soon as possible."

Agents visited New York, Miami, Oklahoma City, Chicago, and Baltimore, interviewing every WPB employee who might know something, from ex-director Donald Nelson to clerks and secretaries. At first, they learned only that since Remington was Tom Blaisdell's aide on the Planning Committee, he could probably have had access to any records on airplane production he desired, but these statements were worthless from an evidential standpoint. Interestingly, Donald Nelson and Lieutenant Colonel Robert J. Master noted that current information on aircraft allocations would have been available to Abraham George Silverman of the Army Air Force, said to be one of Bentley's most important sources. Adolph J. Goldenthal, who had worked in munitions production, told agents that Victor Perlo, another Bentley contact, would also have had access to classified aircraft data when he worked for the WPB's Progress Reporting Division. And, of course, the Bureau was aware that others named as members of the Perlo and Silvermaster groups worked for the board (like Harry Magdoff and Edward Fitzgerald), the Air Force (Silverman), or the Pentagon (Ullman). Thus, Bentley had at least five people who could have provided her with the material she had said came from Remington. In fact, in her original FBI statement in November 1945, her description of what she received from Silverman and Ullman was almost identical to that of what she claimed Remington gave her. But the FBI ignored these leads; after all, it was Remington who was on trial, not the others.

The evidence they were seeking was finally located at the National Archives, where War Production Board records were stored. One folder marked Planning Committee Staff—Weekly Summary of Activities March 1–6 [1943] Inclusive was thought to be especially important. It revealed that during that week in March, Remington had worked on aluminum supplies for airplane production and that one of the sources he might have consulted was an 8-L report containing monthly schedules of airplane production. The report was confidential and dissemination of its contents violated the Espionage Act. This was not exactly what Remington was supposed to have given Bentley—it was only a forecast of airplane production; final allocation to theaters of operations (which Bentley had said she received) was not listed—that decision was made later by the military. Indeed, four former members of the WPB told the FBI that "data regarding allocations of aircraft . . . to foreign countries was never set out in the specific manner described by Elizabeth Bentley." But the file would have to suffice—"it is," J. Edgar Hoover was informed, "the only information found in WPB files which definitely shows that Remington had reason to work with aircraft production figures and shows the exact document to which he had reason to refer."[25]

Whether or not the jury could be convinced that the 8-L was identical to Bentley's description of information received depended on how it was presented. Saypol gave that job to Roy Cohn, who handled it brilliantly. First, he read aloud from Remington's application for a naval commission that stated that his work at the WPB required him to know production goals and inventory of airplanes by type, companies, and plants. Then he put on the stand banker Edwin A. Locke, a former assistant to Donald Nelson, who was asked if he knew of any War Production Board document that contained such information.

The 8 Schedules, Locke said, "gave a very, very detailed breakdown [on] types of planes," the plants producing them, and the government agencies and foreign countries that had contracted for them. "These were all classified documents," Locke noted, "one of the most vital collections of strategic information that one could have . . . and therefore we were forbidden to share them with anyone outside the War Production Board." By 1943, the WPB was working from a schedule designated 8-L. Cohn produced a volume containing the document.

Chanler protested. "I object to this unless the witness can connect it up in some way with the defendant. . . . "

" . . . [T]he defendant has connected it up with himself," Cohn replied, "by his statement in his Navy application. . . . " Noonan overruled Chanler's objection.

Then, with a dramatic flourish, Cohn motioned to two aides who wheeled into the courtroom a large easel bearing photographic enlargements of an 8-L summary sheet and placed it before the jury box. Again, Chanler objected, but was overruled. Cohn invited Locke to take a stroll by the exhibit and point out each column of information to the jury: B for bomber, P for pursuit, and so forth.

And what do these words at the bottom of the page mean? Cohn asked the witness. "Will you read it?"

He did. "Confidential. This document contains information affecting the national defense of the United States within the meaning of the Espionage Act, . . . Its transmission or the revelation of its contents in any manner to an unauthorized person is prohibited by law."

"I have no further questions," Cohn said.

Did the WPB handle the allocation of aircraft to theaters of war? Chanler immediately asked Locke.

"No," Locke admitted, "our job was production. . . . "

"Do you have any knowledge whatever . . . whether [William Remington] ever saw any of these documents?"

"I did not know the defendant," Locke said, "never heard of him until this."

Turning again to the judge, Chanler asked that both Locke's testimony and the exhibit be stricken—"It is in no way connected with this defendant."

"Denied," said Noonan.

Chanler spent the rest of his cross-examination showing the witness articles from wartime issues of the *New York Times*, describing the numbers of bombers and other aircraft being produced, but they bore less resemblance to what Bentley had said she received than the huge exhibit that nearly dwarfed the defense counsel. To Chanler, the exhibit looked "as big as the side of a house," and it seems to have so intimidated him that he failed to ask two important questions: Could so much detailed information have been jotted down on little scraps of paper? and, more important, If Remington was the source of "one of the most vital collections of strategic information" in Washington, why did Bentley consider him one of her least important contacts? Instead of raising these questions, Chanler continued to argue that there was no evidence to connect the 8-L schedule to Remington, but his motions to suppress the testimony and exhibit were again denied.[26]

That connection was soon demonstrated. On February 5, the government presented its last rebuttal witness, William Coates Nemeth, a Virginia attorney, who was once in charge of compiling the weekly summary of activities for the board's Planning Committee. He identified the summary for March 1–6, 1943; then Roy Cohn was allowed to read it to the jury. "I call your attention particularly to page 3 under the heading Mr. Blaisdell's Office: We have . . . William Remington—Aluminum Supply in relation to 8-L requirements."

On cross, Chanler asked Nemeth if he knew what that entry signified.

Yes, " . . . it would be aluminum supply in relation to aircraft necessities, 8-L being your aircraft production report." And then he pointed to the exhibit, still resting grandly on its easel, evidence—the government believed—of William Remington's treason.[27]

To combat the government's seven hostile witnesses, the defense presented only three. Professor Arthur McMahon challenged Colonel Chamberlin's testimony that Remington supported the Soviet conquest of Finland. Bertram Fox, a WPB colleague, and Tom Blaisdell, Remington's battle-scarred mentor, were called to counteract Locke and Nemeth. Fox testified that, as far as he knew, Jeans's magic formula was never taken seriously by the War Production Board, nor was it classified. He also tried to help Remington by commenting on the 8-L schedule. It was less an actual statement of America's current military might than an estimate of future production. Furthermore, only the Munitions Assignment Board was authorized to make the final decision regarding allocations—"that was none of our business," Fox testified.[28]

Tom Blaisdell supported Fox's position on all these issues. Many WPB officials thought Jeans's formula was crazy, although he did admit that given the desperate need for rubber, he had agreed to the experiments, which eventually proved disappointing. "The process . . . was never classified," he also testified. "How can you shroud in secrecy a matter that was as widely discussed as this?" Asked about Remington's assignment in March 1943, Blaisdell said that it was not necessary for Remington to consult the 8-L schedule and that he could not recall ever having the documents in his office.

"Now, Mr. Blaisdell," asked Chanler in conclusion, "you . . . knew Mr. Remington when he worked either under you or in the same department on and off from about 1940 until about 1950. . . . Did he ever say anything or do anything in your presence that would lead you to believe he was a Communist or a member of the Communist Party?"

"No, sir," Blaisdell said.

To discredit both Blaisdell and Remington, Saypol probed the most vulnerable chapter in their long relationship—Remington's failure to give Blaisdell a complete report on his ongoing FBI and grand jury interviews about Bentley in 1948. The jury listened as Saypol read each man's testimony about the disputed conversation—Remington's claim that he generally told Blaisdell most of the facts; Blaisdell's denial that he had. Blaisdell had told Rauh that he would try not to say anything that would hurt Bill, but he could not avoid answering Saypol's final question about the incident.

" . . . As a man who is a responsible government official, is there any question at all that if it had been disclosed to you that a prospective employee . . . was under investigation by the FBI . . . or had testified before a grand jury considering him . . . , would there have been any doubt in your mind about proceeding with the appointment?"

"Not until it was cleared up, Mr. Saypol," Blaisdell said. There was no way for the jury to ignore Saypol's implication that Remington obtained his last position by deceiving his boss and oldest friend in government.[29]

Later that afternoon, Tuesday, February 6, 1951, Chanler rose and addressed the court. "Your Honor will be pleased to hear the defendant rests." After twenty-nine court days, thirty-seven witnesses, and the presentation of a hundred seven exhibits, the long trial was almost over. The remainder of the day would be devoted to final defense motions, all of which would be quickly denied. Now Noonan informed the jury that the final stage would begin the next day: summation by each counsel, the judge's instructions to the members of the jury, and the start—and perhaps the end—of their deliberations. It would be a very busy day, so he asked the jurors to arrive one hour earlier than was customary so that the proceedings could begin promptly at 9:30 A.M. One juror complained: "I come down 21 miles."

"Well, the trains will be running tomorrow," Noonan said. "I hope they will. I will be coming down, too. 9:30 tomorrow morning." He banged his gavel, and the jury was excused.[30]

18

The Only Verdict Possible

The jury finally received the Remington case on Wednesday afternoon, February 7, 1951, six hours after court opened. They had listened patiently but uncomfortably through the attorneys' five-hour summations and the judge's brief instructions on how to render a verdict. Now it was up to them to determine what constituted membership in the Communist Party and whether Remington was guilty of perjury.[1] At 4:20 P.M., the jury filed out of the courtroom to begin its deliberations.

Once they were settled in the small jury room, Foreman David L. Jones, the Statler Hotel room clerk, asked his colleagues for an informal vote, just to see where things stood. They were asked to fill out a paper ballot, writing guilty, not guilty, or undecided. These were passed down the table to Jones, who called them out one by one: undecided, guilty, guilty, undecided, undecided, not guilty, guilty, guilty, guilty, undecided, guilty, and undecided. Leonard Booker, the power lineman, was annoyed. They were wasting their time, he said; both Remington and Bentley should have been shot long ago. They talked for a while. John Connors, a hospital attendant, was absolutely certain about Remington's guilt; look at that statement by his own witness—David Stone Martin—everybody knew he was a Communist, or something like that. He asked the foreman to get the exhibit. Other jurors also wanted to see exhibits, and Jones made a list: the Remingtons' letter supporting *New Masses*; Horace Bryan's application for P.O. Box 1692; the 8-L schedule; the three issues of the *New York Times* that detailed airplane production statistics; the Patent Office file on Jeans's process; Remington's letter to his parents from Knoxville, which carried the post office box as return address; and his application for a naval commission, in which he described (and exaggerated) the WPB records to which he had access.

It was after 5:00 P.M. when the clerk brought the documents. Connors picked up Government's Exhibit 34. It was just as he remembered it, he said, reading it aloud: "I won't deny that he was a Communist as that was well known, because he approached everyone and asked them to join the Communist Party." That was proof enough for him. Mrs. Celia Friedman disagreed. She thought that Remington seemed merely a fellow traveler. And he was cleared by the President's Loyalty Review Board, Mrs. Evelyn Tracey added. How could they find him guilty after that?

At 6:00 P.M. they decided to break for dinner, and two U.S. marshals escorted them across the street to Caruso's Restaurant. By 7:30, they were back in the jury room. Jones called for an oral ballot, and they went around the table. Now it was nine for conviction, three undecided—Mrs. Mary Ward, Mrs. Pauline Brigandi, and Mrs. Tracey.

Shortly before 8:00 P.M., they asked the clerk for a copy of the indictment. More discussion followed. One juror mentioned the Bentley–Brunini connection, but they dismissed it because they thought it had occurred after the indictment was voted. They were also unimpressed by Chanler's insistence that a Communist Party member must have a book. The 8-L schedule was discussed— it appeared clear to all that Remington did have access to it, and it sounded almost exactly like the information Bentley had said she received from Remington. Of the thirty-seven witnesses who testified, it was Ann Remington who made the strongest impression. None of Remington's witnesses seemed to register at all. Jones asked for a second oral ballot. Mrs. Ward had changed her mind—"Guilty," she said; Mrs. Friedman and Mrs. Tracey remained uncertain.[2]

Meanwhile, the defendant and his lawyers waited in an almost empty courtroom. Remington sat comfortably at his counsel's table, eating chocolate cake and chatting happily with reporters who approached him. "I thought the trial had been won until the end," Remington later told Rauh, "because it seemed to me that every Saypol charge was demolished or otherwise countered with unassailable truth. On the law, the evidence, and, above all, the facts, I was sure of victory."[3]

At that moment, victory was out of reach—only two women stood between conviction and a possible hung jury. It was Mrs. Hirsh, a retired schoolteacher, who finally broke down the resistance of the holdouts. Two principal issues influenced the jurors, Mrs. Tracey later recalled: "Remington had access to the 8-L Schedule . . . in carrying out his duties," and since he knew Joe North was a Communist, "he must have known Bentley was one." Despite knowledge of Bentley's Communist affiliation, he gave her information. On the basis of such conduct, therefore, Remington must also have been a member of the Communist Party. At about 9:45 P.M., Jones called for another vote.[4]

Twenty minutes later, word reached the courtroom that the jury was coming in with a verdict, after four hours and twenty-five minutes of deliberation. The judge arrived, then Saypol and his assistants. Reporters took their places. Absent were Fred and Lillian Remington, who had grown weary and had returned to Ridgewood. When the jury finally entered at 10:10 P.M., Remington, who was calmly reading Vernon Parrington, put down his book and scanned the jurors' faces.

"Mr. Foreman, have you agreed upon a verdict?" the clerk asked David Jones.

"We have," he said, rising from his seat.

"How do you find?"

"Guilty as charged," Jones said in a husky voice.

Remington frowned, then gripped the table, as if he were suddenly dizzy. His face was ashen and he struggled to his feet.[5]

Ed Scully, Chanler's associate, asked that the jury be polled, and each number was called; all said guilty. Judge Noonan expressed his gratitude for their efforts and added, "I believe that the verdict you have arrived at is a fair one and based properly on the evidence produced in the case. Thank you very, very much. . . . " Saypol thanked them, too, and the jury departed.

For the lawyers, the night's business continued. Saypol requested that Remington be jailed immediately, before sentencing. Scully protested, but Noonan reminded him that it was his practice to remand the defendant before sentencing. The government's motion was harsh, Scully argued, and pleaded with the judge to continue Remington's bail, but he refused. Tomorrow Noonan would impose sentence, but for now Remington would have to go to jail.

"Need any cash, Bill?" Scully asked. Remington shook his head and, smiling weakly, picked up his book and was led away by two U.S. marshals. In a corridor outside the courtroom, he was handcuffed and taken to the basement garage, where he was placed in a van with barred windows and driven to the Federal House of Detention on West Street. He spent the next thirteen hours in a zoo-like cage, barred on all sides and above his head, sleep impossible because of the lights that burned day and night.[6]

At 2:00 P.M. the next day, he was back in his seat at the counsel's table in Courtroom 110, crowded again with journalists and spectators. Immediately after court convened, Chanler approached the bench to make one final, futile effort to erase all that had gone before. Under the *Federal Rules of Criminal Procedure*, he moved to set aside the judgment because the indictment did not charge an offense against the United States and also asked for a new trial on grounds of judicial error and prejudice to the defendant. The motions were quickly denied. Before pronouncing sentence, Noonan asked for Saypol's recommendation.

"William Walter Remington, step forward please," the clerk called out, and the defendant, his face grim, walked stiffly toward the bench. Remington's perjury was of the worst kind, Saypol stated, because it was committed so frequently, not only in the trial just ended but also before congressional committees and grand juries. "Intertwined is the terrible hurt that he has done to our country in betraying his trust by participating in the delivery to a foreign agent of important secrets of our Government." Therefore, he recommended the maximum sentence: five years imprisonment and a two thousand dollar fine. Remington listened quietly, showing no emotion.

Chanler protested the severity of that sentence. Remington had suffered enough, he insisted. His career and life were ruined. This was a case that did not warrant a maximum sentence. "There are other witnesses in this trial," Chanler reminded the court, " . . . who have been guilty of much worse crimes, who have not been punished at all," a not so veiled reference to the Blond Spy Queen who moved easily from espionage to celebrity. Chanler was particularly angry at Saypol's attempt to confuse the issue; Remington was indicted for perjury—if the government believed him guilty of espionage, it should have charged him with that crime.

Noonan imposed the maximum sentence. While the jury had convicted Remington only of perjury, his commission of the crime had involved disloyalty to his country, he said. He therefore believed that Saypol's recommendation was fair. Chanler had another request. Could the fine be set aside because Remington and his family were now penniless? Noonan refused and pointed out that one alternative to paying the fine was serving an additional month's prison time and then taking a pauper's oath. Despite rejecting every motion Chanler made that day (and almost all during the trial), Noonan congratulated him for ably defending his client. The U.S. Attorney's Office was also deserving of praise, and he expressed sympathy for the defendant's parents, if not for Remington himself.

"Your Honor, we ask for bail at this time," Ed Scully said, and another argument ensued. Following the sentence, the defense had notified the United States Court of Appeals for the Second Circuit that they intended to submit the trial record for review. Scully asked now that Remington's bail be continued so that he could remain free to assist in preparing the appeal. Noonan believed that no grounds existed for such an appeal, so he rejected Scully's request. They could, however, ask the court of appeals to rule on bail that very day.

That is our plan, Scully said. Could Remington wait in the courtroom until bail was fixed?

No, he cannot, Noonan said, turning Remington over to the custody of the marshals until the court of appeals acted. Remington's lawyers and Saypol then rushed off to the court of appeals, located upstairs, to begin the next chapter in Remington's long struggle for vindication.[7]

Representing the court that day was Learned Hand, one of America's most eminent jurists. Chanler explained to Hand that Judge Noonan had refused to continue Remington's bail because he did not believe that significant errors had been committed during the trial. Judge Hand, whose job it was to examine lower-court decisions that frequently contained some form of judicial error, must have found Noonan's arrogance annoying because when Saypol rose to comment he said sharply, "Sit down!" For now, he would continue Remington's bail until the full three-man court could meet the next day. "Any objections?" he asked Saypol.

"I certainly do," he said.

"Overnight? Nonsense," barked Hand, who then ended the proceedings.[8]

The hearing before the full court of appeals was déjà vu. Again Remington sat silently while Chanler and Saypol fought over the same ground covered during the seven-week trial. Also at issue was whether Remington's bail should be extended while his case awaited review. Chanler told Judges Thomas W. Swan, Augustus Hand, and his cousin Learned Hand that several judicial errors marred the trial. Prominent among them was the government's failure to define Communist Party membership and the Bentley–Brunini relationship. Chanler described the pair as parties to a contract in which the foreman of the indicting grand jury had a financial interest in Bentley's book, the success of which depended on Remington's conviction.

Saypol rejected Chanler's claims, arguing that there were no questions of law that needed review and that a convicted man had no absolute right to bail. He also dismissed the Brunini affair, calling it "nothing more serious than lacking in good taste" and essentially irrelevant because the indictment had been approved by all the grand jurors who were present that day. Then he surprised the court by threatening to collect from Remington's original five thousand dollar bail the two thousand dollar fine imposed by Judge Noonan when Remington was sentenced.

Of the various subjects discussed that day, it was the charge of grand jury impropriety that most troubled the judges.

"This is a very serious matter," one said to another, as Saypol and Chanler argued.

"Never heard anything like it," the third muttered. Reporters covering the hearing did not identify which judges made these comments, but the man from the Washington Times-Herald noted that "some persons within earshot said stronger language was used in the asides." Finally, the judges agreed to consider Remington's bail request and granted him another temporary extension.

Their decision came four days later, on Tuesday, February 14. In a terse statement, the court continued Remington's bail but demanded an additional two thousand dollars, apparently to cover Noonan's fine. Once again, Mary Robbins came to Remington's rescue; she gave Chanler the money, asking only that her name not be made public so that Remington and his parents would not feel obligated to repay the sum. That same afternoon, Chanler handed two thousand-dollar bills to Deputy Clerk Eugene Liehr, and Remington was temporarily a free man, at least until the court decided either to affirm his conviction or reverse it. Oral arguments between the government and the defense would take place during the summer, with a final opinion expected that fall.[9]

Seven months earlier, following Remington's indictment, Joe Rauh had predicted that a conviction would strengthen the anti-Communist extremists and weaken what few procedural safeguards existed in the President's Loyalty Program. Now, that prediction came true. First to exult in the jury's verdict was Remington's old enemy, Senator Homer Ferguson. On the morning of February 8, while Remington was incarcerated at the Federal House of Detention, Ferguson told his fellow senators that he and his former investigating subcommittee had been vindicated—Remington's conviction indicated that the Truman Loyalty Program was fatally flawed and required immediate reform. Above all, the standard of reasonable grounds to suspect disloyalty used to dismiss employees should be returned to the World War II standard of reasonable doubt, with the result, Ferguson believed, that Communists and fellow travelers still in government would be quickly expelled. Ferguson also praised the jury for establishing a new legal principle—"that to be a member of the Communist Party in the United States and part of its apparatus, one does not have to be a card-carrying member. . . . This is highly important as evidence of a realistic view of the nature of the Communist Conspiracy."

Conservative newspapers echoed Ferguson's views in stronger language and attacked not only Harry Truman but FDR. The *Washington Daily News*, in an editorial, declared that

> William W. Remington now joins the odiferous [sic] list of young Communist punks who wormed their way upward in the Government under the New Deal. He was sentenced to five years in prison, and he should serve every minute of it. In Russia, he would have been shot without trial.

In a class by himself, as usual, was Wisconsin senator Joseph R. McCarthy, who said, "No one will ever know how many American boys have died because William W. Remington was in charge of licensing exports of war materials to Communist countries." Such attacks in the Congress and in the press would lead President Truman, in April 1951, to restore the Loyalty Program dismissal standard to its wartime status.[10]

The best way to prevent the further erosion of civil liberties and help Remington, Joe Rauh believed, was to proceed as quickly as possible with his appeal. Of course, the jury verdict disappointed Rauh, but his natural buoyancy and the importance of the constitutional issues encouraged him to get on with the case. He tried to instill some of that fighting spirit in his client, who was bitter about the verdict and pessimistic about the future. As he had done during the loyalty crisis, Remington went into hibernation. Ignoring calls from friends, he spent his days making minor repairs around his parents' home. Saddest of all, Rauh thought, was Lillian Remington. She seemed so depressed, so dazed, by the outcome that her friends feared for her health. "It is very late to thank you and Mr. Chanler," she wrote him in March,

> but . . . the whole episode of the last year is so tragic and so out of scale with any-thing in our lives we can hardly comprehend it. . . . We do hope and pray that you will earn no discredit from handling so difficult and almost so lost a cause.

Rauh wrote her a comforting letter, while urging Bill to find some kind of job or begin work on his doctoral dissertation. But, above all, he should be careful, dis-creet, and circumspect. Any letters he wrote should first be checked by Chanler's office, and Rauh also vetoed any action that might draw public atten-tion or provoke the McCarthyites. Bill and Jane wanted to marry, but Rauh told them to wait, at least until after the court of appeals had decided the future of his case; unhappily, they consented. When Remington considered returning to Columbia under the GI Bill, Rauh strongly opposed it, as he did Remington's plan to deduct from his income tax expenses incurred during his loyalty case. "Your personal conduct throughout your entire battle has been exemplary," Rauh wrote Remington in March, "and I do not want to tarnish our fight with any petty actions."[11]

In May, Remington worked briefly at a medical supply warehouse in New Jersey. His salary was about sixty dollars a week. "He was without doubt the best employee we have ever had," noted his supervisor, Robert Dyer. When asked to comment on the fact that Remington was a convicted perjurer free on bail, he said, "We find it hard to believe."[12]

How to reverse that conviction was the task that Rauh and Chanler now undertook on almost a full-time basis. An appeal was a complicated and expen-sive project. A transcript of the entire proceeding, from Remington's arraign-ment in June 1950 through his trial and sentencing seven months later, had to be compiled for the court of appeals to examine. For appellants who could afford it, the record was printed; Remington could not, so a battery of Winthrop, Stimson secretaries prepared a typed copy from the original 4,100-page record. But it would have to be bound and indexed, and this, too, cost money. A major brief would have to be written, covering the history of the case and detailing those legal errors the defense believed Judge Noonan had made. Almost every sentence would be footnoted with citations to pages in the trial record or to legal authorities. The final product was a hundred thirteen pages long, and the price to print it came to almost two thousand dollars—a sum the defense did not have. Once again a letter was sent to the generous Mrs. Robbins, and a check for the full amount soon arrived. There would also be an oral argument before the court and the need to write a reply brief rebutting the government's response to their appeal.

Which point to emphasize in the brief and at the argument created a conflict between Chanler and Rauh. While Rauh never doubted that Communist Party membership was the most important question in the case, he nevertheless believed that grand jury impropriety and government misconduct in concealing the Bentley–Brunini affair from the defense provided the most likely reasons for reversal. Chanler disagreed, and in his first draft of the brief, stressed the government's and the judge's failures to define precisely what constituted Party membership. Rauh wrote him of his concern:

> My fear is that, if you argue the case as you briefed it, the Court of Appeals may find your basic position too theoretical and feel that the grand jury point, which you relegated to second fiddle, does not warrant a reversal by them of a seven week trial.

To ensure that this very important issue was not lost, Rauh twice offered to argue the point himself, but Chanler rejected the request, principally because he thought that he had more experience appearing before the court of appeals. Rauh complied. The outcome of their debate was that the question of grand jury misconduct became point five in the brief—"buried" (as Rauh put it)—and followed by three other points that were obviously less important.

Those who saw a copy of the brief were full of praise for Remington's lawyers. Roger Baldwin, founder of the American Civil Liberties Union, thought it very impressive but was skeptical that "anybody, even judges, can be convinced these days. . . . " Remington's trial reminded him of Sacco and Vanzetti's, and he recounted to Rauh the remark of one official involved in that tragic case: "It doesn't make any difference whether they are guilty of the crime; they are anarchists and wops and ought to be hung, on general principles." "Anyhow," Baldwin concluded, "every fight for sanity is worth making!" [13]

The fight resumed on June 15, 1951, when Chanler presented his case to the court of appeals. Appearing for the government was assistant U.S. attorney Bruno Schachner, who argued that it was unnecessary for the government to define Communist Party membership—a series of acts was sufficient proof. He also dismissed Chanler's charge that the indictment was the product of "political clamor" and "private malice." Even if one grand juror was biased, it would not invalidate an indictment voted by at least twelve jurors. Judge Learned Hand disagreed—the issue, he told Schachner, was whether that juror exerted undue influence over the others. That did not matter, either, Schachner claimed. All the jurors could be biased—an indictment was just an accusation that a jury would ultimately evaluate. Hand bridled at such disrespect for the grand jury system. "If that's the law," he angrily said, "there will be one vote to change it."

A room filled with prejudiced grand jurors would hardly care about the rights of the defendant.

Few judges were more distinguished than the three now considering Remington's appeal. Thomas Walter Swan, at seventy-four, was the youngest; a former professor and dean of the Yale Law School, he was appointed to the court in 1927 by President Calvin Coolidge. Augustus Noble Hand was eighty-one, the oldest. He also came to the court in 1927 after thirteen years as a federal judge. The most respected was Gus Hand's cousin, 79-year-old Learned Hand, a veteran of forty-two years on the federal bench. The author of more than two thousand opinions, it was said that Supreme Court justices quoted him more often than any other judge.

Following the oral argument in June, each of the judges drafted a memorandum on the Remington case that was then submitted to their brethren. Augustus Hand had initially believed that grounds existed for reversal but now thought differently. Only one of Chanler's arguments made any impression on him: Noonan's decision forbidding Remington's lawyers from examining his grand jury testimony. "They might disclose that the foreman browbeat the defendant and other witnesses," Hand wrote, "or they might disclose that when Remington denied that he had been a member of the Communist Party the context of the question would show that his answer was not a wilful lie" and therefore not perjury. But Hand was still not certain "that it was error for the judge not to allow examination." His conclusion—"Tentatively, I vote to affirm the conviction."

His colleagues disagreed. Thomas Swan was tentatively for reversal, primarily because he thought Judge Noonan's charge to the jury on what constituted Communist Party membership was inadequate. Without a clear definition, some jurors might have thought one act sufficient proof while others selected entirely different ones. "With the subject left at large," he noted, "I don't see how the jury could intelligently distinguish between 'direct proof' [required in perjury cases] and 'corroboration.'"

Learned Hand's memorandum was the longest and most thoughtful. He ranged widely over the defense's points. He also thought Noonan's failure to define clearly Party membership the most serious mistake. "The result of leaving the issue so vague was most unfair . . . because, as the case was tried, the accused did not know what he had to meet even at the end of the prosecution's case." He was quite confident that because of this error alone the conviction should be reversed.

Despite their public expressions of concern about the charge of grand jury impropriety, the three judges did not think it serious enough to warrant their own reading of the minutes. Swan's memorandum never mentioned Bentley or Brunini, while Gus Hand was willing to accept the government's denial that Brunini had an interest in finding Remington a Communist. Learned Hand did not want to take up the issue at all—to do so, he thought, would complicate matters by creating another trial just on how the indictment was procured. Should the full court decide to reverse, he recommended that Remington's lawyers be allowed to inspect his grand jury testimony, and if Brunini had abused his powers, the record should reveal it. He did admit that other abuses might not be disclosed but for now saw no reason to go further. No one took the time to examine the transcript, even though Leyla Sefa's and Eileen Collins's trial testimonies indicated that something was seriously amiss. For a group of men with such sterling reputations, this was a significant failure. Their thinking also revealed that Rauh was incorrect when he thought that the court would be so outraged by the evidence of grand jury misconduct that it would quash the indictment and either acquit Remington or order a new trial.

How the three judges resolved their differences and reached their eventual decision is unclear. Following the submission of their pre-conference memoranda, they met, deliberated, and Thomas Swan was assigned to write the court's opinion. Unfortunately, no record exists of those discussions, and all that can be stated is that regardless of his serious doubts Gus Hand was persuaded to change his mind, because on August 22, 1951, the court of appeals unanimously reversed Remington's conviction. Although Swan spoke for the court, most of the twelve-page decision was derived from Learned Hand's earlier memorandum. Swan wrote that the principal reason for the reversal was the inadequacy of Judge Noonan's charge to the jury, which was

> too vague and indefinite to constitute any definition at all of what facts the jury must find in order to convict the defendant. . . . The Court did not require the prosecution to specify what facts it would rely on to prove an act of joining or to justify an inference that the accused knew he was a member.

Then, borrowing Hand's words almost verbatim, Swan said that Noonan's vagueness prevented Remington from preparing a defense against the government's charges.

It was not a total victory for Remington, however. The court let the indictment stand and simply sent the case back to the district court for a new trial. But this time the judge would be required to issue a clearer charge to the jury. Overt acts proving Party membership would have to be described specifically and the jury instructed that unless they believed the testimony regarding these acts, they could not find the defendant guilty. The court also ruled that Remington's lawyers must be permitted to examine his grand jury testimony, so that they could adequately prepare his defense and determine if Foreman Brunini had abused his powers; in addition, they were given access to Ann Remington's testimony, to determine whether or not she had changed her story since her appearance before the grand jury.

Irving Saypol's conduct was also criticized. His frequent references to organizations on the Attorney General's list was called an error since the list was hearsay and had no probative value at the trial. More objectionable was Saypol's handling of Bernard Redmont ("the Jew who changed his name," Hand called him). "We wish to admonish counsel for the prosecution," said Swan,

> that in case of a re-trial there should be no repetition of the cross-examination attack upon defense witness Redmont. . . . Redmont testified that he had changed his name for professional reasons and that he had done so pursuant to Court order. On cross-examination the prosecutor continued his inquiry of this matter long after it became clear that the change of name had no relevancy to any issue at the trial, and could only serve to arouse possible racial prejudice on the part of the jury.[14]

It was not until that evening that Remington received the good news. He was vacationing with his mother and children at Mrs. Robbins's remote, hill-top lodge in Whittingham Township, Vermont, and Chanler phoned. Bill was, of course, very pleased to learn of the court's decision but, with Bruce and Gale pulling at his pant leg, could not really talk. He told Chanler that he would be home in a few days; they could discuss their next steps then. In fact, he was already thinking about how to avoid a new trial. The month before, he had casually mentioned to Chanler the possibility of making a deal with the government. It is not clear what he had in mind—both the conversation with Chanler and his report to Rauh about it were quite vague—but it involved Remington moving to Canada in exchange for the government dropping the case. "Chanler jumped at the idea," Remington told Rauh. "I rather felt he overbought it, but I do hope you will be agreeable to discussing . . . the pros and cons of trying to show the Justice Department that I'm not determined to be a thorn in their side." Rauh was not enthusiastic about Remington's scheme. " . . . if Chanler jumped at the proposal, either he didn't fully understand it or has lost his mind. . . . "

Remington also wanted to make overtures to his ex-wife, hoping that she might not testify at a second trial. What was going through her mind now that the conviction had been reversed? "If she should let the word get around that she wanted to back out, there could be no new trial," Remington told Rauh. "She is the keystone of the prosecution arch. . . . Everything depends on what she does." Somehow they had to reach Ann Remington. Bill thought of writing directly to her or having Rauh contact neighbors at Tauxemont who might be sympathetic to him. She had a cousin in Chicago, a lawyer named Leonard Rieser, who he thought was close to Ann. They had to try something. Rauh did speak with Rieser, but he could think of no way to help.[15]

Rauh had another plan in mind and presented it to Chanler in September. Since the court of appeals let the indictment stand, they would ask the Supreme Court to dismiss the indictment and acquit their client. It was, as Rauh himself admitted, unorthodox to petition the Court from a victory, and Chanler's lawyers were not certain it was even possible for them to seek a writ of certiorari because the matter had not been finally settled. Typically, Rauh saw the possibilities rather than the obstacles. Legal authorities may be divided on whether a victorious party could even go to the Supreme Court, but theirs was "only a partial victory," he told Chanler, so "there is always an outside chance that we could get cert." He thought it a chance well worth taking.

Chanler believed the attempt would be almost hopeless and might even damage their case, but Rauh continued to press him. His own research had uncovered cases in which the Supreme Court had reversed non-final judgments of the court of appeals, so there was precedent supporting their position. Furthermore, this time he wanted to play a more active role, if the Supreme Court agreed to hear the case. He had permitted Chanler to handle the oral argument before the court of appeals, but the Supreme Court was a different story—it was his bailiwick. He wanted to act as co-counsel—jointly writing the brief and making at least half of the oral argument. His mind was made up; they should go to the Supreme Court. Chanler remained unconvinced but eventually agreed, so on October 19, 1951, they formally petitioned the Supreme Court for a writ of certiorari and waited to see what the government would do.[16]

Like Remington's lawyers, the government had been considering a number of alternative actions, which also posed threats to their case. It, too, could appeal to the Supreme Court, asking that it overrule Swan's decision, but this might mean a review of the Brunini affair, and few in Saypol's office or the Criminal Division wanted that. Or it could retry Remington on the same questionable indictment and once again run afoul of the Communist Party membership question. It was Roy Cohn, the man Chanler called "the ever-active genie," who took credit for devising the government's ultimate choice. They would ignore the Brunini indictment, which raised the complicated issue of Communist Party membership and ask a new grand jury to indict Remington for other lies committed at the first trial.

Cohn received the Justice Department's authorization to proceed, and on October 24, 1951, after listening to the testimony of Ann Remington, Elizabeth Bentley, Howard Bridgman, Kenneth McConnell, and Lewis Holmes (a new witness who claimed that Remington participated in the Dartmouth YCL), a federal grand jury in New York indicted Remington on five counts of perjury. He was accused of having lied when he testified at his trial that he never knowingly attended Communist Party meetings; never gave classified or secret or any kind of information to Elizabeth Bentley for transmission to Russia or for any other reason; never paid Communist Party dues; never asked anyone to join the Communist Party; and had no knowledge of the existence of the Young Communist League. This time, Remington was not charged with lying about membership in the Communist Party. If convicted on each count, he could be sentenced to a maximum twenty-five years in prison and fined ten thousand dollars. The public announcement of the new indictment occurred the next day, October 25, Remington's thirty-fourth birthday.

There was little that the government could do to surprise or shock Joe Rauh, but the new indictment came close. It was a "transparent effort . . . to avoid Supreme Court review of prosecutorial action which cannot stand the light of day," he told reporters. "The Government now recognizes that they cannot prove Remington was ever a member of the Communist Party for they have not indicted him on that ground. They have vengefully sought to indict him on statements he made during his own defense during the last trial. We cannot believe that this attempt to avoid the time-honored rule against double-jeopardy will be sanctioned by the American people or the American courts." Others in the liberal community were equally outraged. The American Civil Liberties Union urged Attorney General J. Howard McGrath to quash the indictment. The *Nation* was even more outspoken. Its editor, Carey McWilliams, called the indictment a "subversive act . . . calculated to undermine basic precepts of Anglo-American justice."

Defending the government, newly appointed U.S. attorney Myles J. Lane (Saypol had resigned to seek election to the New York State Supreme Court) claimed that the new indictment would simplify matters and dismissed the charges of double jeopardy. Remington's alleged perjury was based on a new set of lies made at a different place and under different circumstances, he told the press. However, he did admit that the grand jury's action was unusual. Dismissing the first tainted indictment could not be done by administrative fiat, however; by law, the Justice Department had to win the approval of the Supreme Court before it could ask the district court to void the first indictment. Rauh opposed that application and now found himself facing two battles in the Supreme Court, plus a new trial. "Never a dull moment around here," he later said.[17]

A *New York Post* reporter who interviewed Remington on October 25 found him in a somber and reflective mood. "I'm 34," he told Fern Majura, his face twisted in a wry smile. "Perhaps I should calculate that—I don't want to be indicted on a new count of perjury." In the past, journalists had often described Remington as dapper, but now he wore grey work pants and a dark sweater, frayed at the elbows. He looked like a ghost of the former "New Deal glamour boy," as the right-wing press so often called him. The former director of the Export Program staff now described himself as an odd-jobs man, earning fifteen to twenty dollars a week digging ditches or building pantry shelves. When no work was available, he would visit the local chapter of the Red Cross, where he received five dollars for giving blood. Most of the time he worked in his mother's garden. But he wanted Majura to know that he was philosophical about his plight. "It is necessary for the United States . . . to assume a posture of defense, both physical and psychological, to prepare for war," he declared. "Because human beings are involved, there are bound to be excesses in that preparation. It's to be expected. That's why I can't get mad."[18]

Five days later, he returned to Foley Square for arraignment. Conservative journalist Howard Rushmore noted the change in Remington's appearance since the last time he had seen him at trial. "He was thin, pale, and his face showed deep worry lines." But his voice was strong when he pled not guilty to the five-count indictment. U.S. attorney Lane wanted an early trial date set, but Rauh objected vehemently. He asked the judge to wait until the Supreme Court acted on their petition for a writ of certiorari.

His request "was completely out of the question," Lane countered. "There is no connection between this particular indictment and the previous one," he told Judge Vincent L. Leibell.

Rauh explained the complex series of events and maneuvers that had led to Remington's trial, the reversal by the court of appeals, their decision to turn to the Supreme Court, and then the government's new indictment charging perjury at the trial Rauh wanted reviewed. "It is as related as two items could be," Rauh insisted.

Judge Leibell found Rauh's argument persuasive. "I think the defendant is entitled to know what the Supreme Court action would be on the first indictment before he makes motions on the second indictment . . . ," he said. "When you proceed in the administration of justice, you must be sure of the ground on which you . . . step. . . . " The judge also continued Remington's bail, and Bill returned home to await the decision of the Supreme Court.

The Court's first ruling came on December 11, and to Rauh's surprise and delight, it was an important defeat for the government. In a twenty-word statement, the Court blocked the Justice Department's effort to discard the Brunini indictment and ordered it to respond to Remington's petition. "We were all in Seventh Heaven," Rauh recalled later. "My God! We got four justices on the Supreme Court to think there's a pile of crap going on here." His fellow lawyers congratulated him, and one prominent Justice Department official told him privately that he expected the Supreme Court to grant cert. "This has the potential of a terrific victory for us," he wrote Remington that day. "While the Court hasn't passed on our petition . . . ,the balance of the probabilities now quite clearly favors their granting the petition."

William Chanler, who had opposed the move to the Supreme Court, was now grateful that he had listened to his colleague and told Rauh,

Whatever the Court may do with the petition, applying for certiorari has proven to be a master stroke of strategy, and of the utmost advantage to Bill. . . . Had it not been for your wise and effective persistence, over my strenuous objections, there would have been no petition, and no advantage to exploit. Bill would no doubt before now have been brought to trial under far less favorable circumstances than will now obtain. Here's hoping for good news . . . and no new trial at all![19]

The news was not good. On March 24, 1952, the Supreme Court, by a vote of eight to two, denied, without explanation, Remington's petition for a writ of certiorari. Only Justices William O. Douglas and Hugo Black thought it important to consider the defense's argument that the court of appeals should have quashed the indictment because of the Bentley–Brunini connection and the government's failure to reveal it to Remington's attorneys. "Governmental conduct here is abhorrent to a fair administration of justice," wrote Hugo Black for the minority. "It approaches the type of practice unanimously condemned by this Court as a violation of due process of law. . . . " At a press conference called that day, Myles Lane announced that he planned to go to trial as quickly as possible.

"I feel pretty disappointed and bitter," Rauh wrote Remington, "but there's no time to cry over the past." Money had to be raised and a new attorney found to represent him, for William Chanler, like Bethuel Webster before him, had decided that he could not try the case again. Having devoted almost two years of his life (and his law-firm's time) to the Remington case, he just could not continue. That last week in March 1952 must have reminded Rauh of the dreadful week in June 1950, when Remington was first indicted and lost both his job and lawyer. Now, the case had come full circle, and Remington was back where he had started—indicted and facing a second expensive trial without the money to pay for it or a lawyer to defend him.[20]

19

His Own Worst Enemy

High above Washington, D.C., on a flight bound for Manhattan, Joe Rauh jotted down legal strategy on the back of a postcard: 3 questions. 1) Basic Philosophy of Case; 2) Motions; 3) My Participation. The next day, April 18, 1952, he was to meet with the man whom William Chanler wanted to try the case—John McKim Minton, a distinguished criminal lawyer. But Rauh was not convinced that Minton was right for the job. A wide chasm separated Minton's views, as reported by Chanler, from his own, one that Rauh feared could not be bridged. He thought he might have to withdraw, a prospect Remington said "was too bitter to think about."

He had expected to work with Chanler's replacement, although the years of litigation were costing him time and money. For almost four years, he had turned down other cases to represent Remington without charge, paying even his own expenses—travel, accommodations, long-distance phone calls—that now amounted to over two thousand dollars. But, he believed that the legal principles were so important that he was prepared to go on; in fact, he had already drafted a series of motions calling for the dismissal of the indictment. He had no doubt that the court would reject them, but the effort was essential to keep alive the civil-liberties issues, should they again have to appeal. To Rauh, these were still the heart of the case. Could a man be accused of Communism or disloyalty and receive a fair trial? Should the government be allowed to abuse the law of perjury to convict a man cleared by the Loyalty Review Board? Even more important were the government's most recent actions: obtaining an indictment through "foul prosecutorial conduct" and then trying to take advantage of it by reindicting a man for what he had said in his own defense at trial. Rauh thought this totally without precedent, and his friends in the civil-liberties community agreed. One called Remington's reindictment "Hitlerism"; another, "the dirtiest thing that ever happened." What was required was a battle on civil-liberties issues, Rauh believed.

Jack Minton was also outraged by the government's action, Chanler had earlier told Rauh, but—and herein lay the source of their conflict—his concern now was which strategy would be best for the client. While Rauh wanted a battle, Minton preferred a polite contest, which would be decided on the merits and not because of some legal technicality. "He is . . . very anxious to avoid starting out with the atmosphere of personal bitterness between him and the Government," Chanler remarked. "He thinks that element hurt us a great deal in our trial, and believes if he does not go out of his way to stir up trouble, he can handle the situation. . . . " Nor did Minton think that the constitutional issues required dramatic motions; that would only further antagonize the government. He was willing to raise the question of government misconduct to preserve the points if an appeal became necessary, but it should be done quietly. Rauh, on the other hand, wanted a conflict that would take them again to the court of appeals, or perhaps the Supreme Court, the only place he thought Remington could be acquitted. Their strategies could not have been more different, and it was for that reason that Rauh requested the meeting toward which he was now heading.[1]

For two hours, the lawyers debated at Minton's Madison Avenue office. Present, besides the two antagonists, were William Chanler, acting as an outside adviser, and Bill Remington, who would ultimately decide which approach to follow. "Combat with the Government on legal issues [provided] the only real chance of success," Rauh argued. It would be hopeless trying to persuade a jury to find Remington innocent, given the continuing anti-Communist hysteria in America. No one charged with Communist activities, from Alger Hiss to the Rosenbergs, was acquitted by a panel of twelve ordinary citizens. Their best hope lay in a higher court, insulated from current passions.

Minton immediately agreed that a wide gulf existed between them. "I can't try [it] his way, because I am so anti-Communist," he said. "I just lost my nephew in Korea. . . . I will drop out."

At that point, Chanler strongly attacked Rauh's view. To emphasize constitutional issues at the trial, he said, "would enable the opposition to claim . . . that we were raising a red herring, because we had no defense on the merits." Remington was innocent and therefore entitled to victory on the merits. Furthermore, only a jury's verdict would free him from government harassment. A victory on the legal issues alone, imposed by the court of appeals, would be disastrous—the McCarthyites would never rest until Remington was either acquitted or jailed. A criminal lawyer as skillful as Minton had a fairly good chance to win, Chanler thought.

Remington agreed.

If that is your decision, Rauh said, I will not be able to represent you.[2]

Although Rauh would now only be observing from the sidelines, he could not resist giving Chanler a final warning. "I believe the path of least resistance which you, Bill and Minton have chosen is the road to defeat," he wrote the lawyer after returning to Washington. "I have done my damndest to make you three see the light and shall . . . sit quietly by, hoping and praying that I am totally wrong." Chanler was sorry that their radical differences on trial strategy had driven Rauh away but resented his charges. "I am quite confident that we have chosen the road that holds out the best hope of ultimate success for Bill," he replied, "[but] I fully realize that there is no certain road in this situation in any event." Despite their differences, they remained in contact over the next few weeks, exchanging papers formalizing Rauh's withdrawal and Minton's sub-stitution as lawyer of record—and Chanler kept Rauh informed of Minton's plans. In return, Rauh passed along any news that came his way, such as the rumor that Bentley was physically unable to appear at a recent congressional hearing. Had something happened to the Spy Queen?[3]

The rumor was true. In the spring of 1952, she was again entering what one friend called a "blue period," but it was much worse than that—an emotional slide that threatened her very sanity. The year following Remington's convic-tion had been uneventful for her. While Chanler and Rauh prepared their appeal and Remington hibernated, Bentley spent a month vacationing in Puerto Rico and the Bahamas. When she returned, she learned that *McCalls* magazine had purchased the serial rights to her book, and the first installment, "My Life as a Spy," appeared in the May 1951 issue amidst recipes for Hawaiian casseroles and romantic fiction.

That summer, she bought her first home, in Madison, Connecticut, and told one reporter that she was looking forward to a quieter life. But her duties as pro-fessional informer continued to occupy her time. FBI agents visited her fre-quently, asking endless questions about others she had named as spies in 1945, and she was often in Washington testifying before HUAC or the Senate Internal Security Subcommittee. So, she hired a local man named John Wright to act as her caretaker and chauffeur and to handle the chores she could not attend to.

In October 1951, her memoir *Out of Bondage* was published to mixed reviews. "This is a book . . . that exudes a smell of phoniness from its titled page, which does not tell you who did the actual writing, to its macabre conclusion," Joseph Alsop observed in *Commonweal*; but the *New Republic*'s H. W. Baehr thought it "an illuminating book," which revealed "the despair and spiritual loneliness which drove so many of the 'young professionals' of the depression years into Communism and the far worse degredations [sic] which drove them forth again."

Sales (at $3.50 per volume) were disappointing, and Bentley quickly spent what little royalties she earned. Fortunately, she was still in demand on the lecture circuit—in January and February 1952, she gave speeches (for each of which she charged a fee of three hundred dollars) in Pennsylvania, Illinois, Iowa, Missouri, Nebraska, and Colorado. In March, her income received a surprising boost when the FBI finally gave her the Moscow Gold, the two-thousand-dollar gift she had received from her last Russian spy master in 1945. From all outward appearances, she seemed to be doing fairly well as author, lecturer, and government witness.[4]

Her personal life, however, remained deeply troubled. She had lost none of her attraction to alcohol and bad companions. For example, there was John Wright, who she said was just her caretaker, while local gossips believed that they were actually lovers. She had hired the 52-year-old Wright in August 1951, apparently unaware of his criminal record—breaking and entering, assault, and two jail sentences. At first, there were no problems—Wright took care of her house and met her at the New Haven Railroad Station when she returned from trips to New York and Washington. Then in 1952, trouble developed. Some mornings, Wright would not appear or would arrive late and obviously drunk. In March, she discovered that he was charging liquor to her account at Jolly's Drug Store. Soon the bottles of scotch in her pantry began to disappear, and she decided to fire him. But she became ill and was bed-ridden and dependent on Wright to help her. When she recovered, Wright continued to spend most of his time at her home. He would also drive Bentley to New York, where Dr. Samuel Groopman treated her weekly for what she claimed was menopause. Groopman also examined Wright and concluded that he was below average mentally and a dangerous man. The doctor's diagnosis soon proved to be correct.

On the night of April 30, Bentley later claimed, Wright met her at the train station after a trip to Washington. Climbing into her 1939 La Salle, she immediately noticed that he was agitated and probably drunk. She ordered him into the passenger seat, while she changed places and drove away. Somewhere along the route, he grabbed the steering wheel. She slammed on the brakes, and when she turned to confront him, he struck her face with such force that she fainted. When she regained consciousness, she scrambled out of the car in an effort to run to the nearest residence for help, but he caught her, threw her back in the passenger seat, and drove home. She felt too dazed to do anything—call the police, order Wright away, or seek medical attention. Her major fear was bad publicity, she later told the FBI: "her credibility as a witness would probably be nullified and likewise she would probably lose any hope of further lectures, to which she looks . . . for a great part of her livelihood."

The next day, Wright drove Bentley to New York's St. George Hotel, and after checking in, she went immediately to Dr. Groopman. He was shocked by her appearance: "several teeth on the left side of her face were loosened, two of her lower teeth had gone completely through the lower part of her face, and the cuts on the inside of her mouth were badly infected." He cleaned the wounds with a topical solution and prescribed an antibiotic and a sedative for pain. She returned home the next day to find Wright lounging comfortably in her living room; he did not apologize or even acknowledge the attack. As the week passed, Bentley observed that a bottle of scotch was gone and feared that Wright was about to go on another bender. As a pretext, she asked him to drive her to New York for more treatment, planning to visit her oldest friend at the FBI, Tom Spencer. She related the story of Wright's assault and asked if he could arrange for a bodyguard to take her home, so that she could pick up some clothes and find another place to live. To her disappointment, Spencer said that it was not FBI policy to provide bodyguards. Next, she tried blackmail—surely the FBI could help her to solve this serious problem, to head off any adverse publicity that might affect her ability to testify at the second Remington trial. Spencer said that he could make no promises but would see if anything could be done.

To his colleagues, Spencer said that he thought Bentley's story "may be false and that actually she and her caretaker may have been drinking heavily together and became embroiled in an argument resulting in his beating her." Whatever the truth, Spencer told headquarters that something had to be done since her participation in the Remington trial was essential. Perhaps the U.S. Attorney's Office could help her.

This was the answer most acceptable to Hoover—let Roy Cohn handle Bentley, protecting the FBI from any possible embarrassment should word leak out of her latest misadventures. Cohn was willing to help; after all, she was a vital witness in the Remington case. After two meetings with Bentley, during which she sobbed uncontrollably and complained that the government was ignoring her, Cohn conceived of a plan to get rid of Wright. Bentley would ask the caretaker to come to New York, where he would be served with a subpoena and forced to meet with U.S. attorney Myles Lane. The plan worked perfectly. When Wright showed up at the St. George Hotel on May 14, he was whisked off to the U.S. Attorney's Office at Foley Square; there he was greeted coldly by Lane, Cohn, and FBI special agent John J. Danahy.

It has come to my attention that you have been harassing Miss Bentley and have even beaten her, Lane said to Wright. Explain.

Wright claimed that on the night of April 30, it was Bentley who had been drunk and had struck him. This was not the first time she had treated him this way, but he had had enough—momentarily losing his head, he had punched her.

Lane bluntly told Wright to leave Bentley alone. His subpoena was continuous; if he did not end their relationship, he would be brought before a grand jury and indicted for intimidating a government witness. Wright quickly agreed to follow Lane's orders, and a short time later, he disappeared. But Bentley's problems were far from over.[5]

On August 29, while driving her friend Lady Armstrong to the New Haven Railroad Station, Bentley sideswiped another automobile and failed to stop. Rosario Demaro, the other driver, took down Bentley's license-plate number and filed a complaint. Within the hour, the FBI's star witness was arrested by Connecticut State Troopers, charged with hit and run, and jailed. At first, she admitted hitting the other car, then denied it. Asked who her companion had been, she refused to say. Filled with indignation, she told her captors that she worked for the FBI and demanded that she be allowed to call the New Haven field office. She spoke with Joseph Casper, the special agent in charge, who told her that there was nothing he could do. Fortunately for Bentley, Casper also called New York and talked to Tom Spencer. Spencer called Roy Cohn and reported that Bentley, upset and very nervous, was in a Connecticut jail. Once again those familiar words rang out, this time from Cohn: "in view of the Remington case . . . some action should be taken." The Bureau could not intervene, Spencer said, so Cohn did. He contacted the Connecticut State Police Commissioner and informed him that they were holding an important witness in the Remington trial and demanded her immediate release. By 5:00 P.M., she was free without bond and back on the road to Madison.

Her next accident on September 15 was more serious and left her completely unhinged. While driving along Connecticut's Route 79, en route to a meeting with the lawyer handling her hit-and-run case, Bentley lost control of the car, struck a boulder and blacked out. Three bystanders took her home, but her beloved La Salle was damaged beyond repair. Six days later, she phoned the FBI, complaining of being seriously ill and ordering them to take her to Dr. Groopman in New York. Agents left for her home immediately, but Sunday traffic delayed them for three hours, and when they did arrive, they found Bentley furious and irrational. Agent Lester Gallaher later reported on their drive to Manhattan: "[She] engaged in backseat driving, weeping, sleeping, fingering a crucifix, chain-smoking, and was quarrlesome [sic] and demanding throughout the trip."[6]

After recovering from the accident, her demands continued. She wanted the FBI to pay off her debts and buy her a new car. If money was not immediately forthcoming, she might no longer cooperate with the Bureau or testify in court. The FBI and Roy Cohn eventually agreed to all her demands. Cohn obtained money from one of Bentley's many patrons so she could rent a car for as long as she needed it, while the Bureau (which had already arranged for Bentley to receive a weekly stipend of fifty dollars as well as an expert witness fee when she appeared in court), approved a one-time payment of five hundred fifty dollars.

But these victories did not help. On October 3, 1952, while having drinks at the Rochambeau Restaurant with Harvey Matusow, another ex-Communist FBI informant, she broke down and complained that she "had to keep finding things to testify about." It was Matusow's impression that Bentley had often lied during her years as a government witness.

"It just doesn't seem worth the struggle," Bentley told Ruth Matthews one day while walking to the Hotel Abbey. "Sometimes I think I should step out in front of a car and settle everything." Myles Lane and his aides who were preparing her for the Remington trial seemed unaware of just how close they were coming to losing their most important witness—from scandal, to a highway accident she could not walk away from, to emotional collapse or, perhaps, suicide.[7]

Less melodramatic but also troublesome was Ann Remington. Contacted by the FBI in March 1952 for more information on Bernard Redmont, she had refused to cooperate. The New York field office momentarily panicked—did this mean that she might not testify at the second Remington trial? Agents visited her and were assured that her desire not to hurt Redmont did not apply to her ex-husband. She was still willing to testify.[8]

The other government witnesses were more compliant. Christine Benson said she still supported the prosecution of Remington and would appear. Rudolph Bertram was also available. Kenneth McConnell wanted to study his previous testimony because, he told the FBI, "he has been interviewed so many times, testified before the Federal Grand Jury, as well as in the trial of Remington, that he is confused as to what is in the actual transcript. . . . " But he, too, was happy to go along, providing, of course, that the government reimbursed him for his expenses. Howard Bridgman would be returning, but when the FBI interviewed him again in December 1952, they found that his memory of Knoxville days was worse. Incredibly, the government still planned to call him, as well as Roscoe Giles, whose recollections were equally muddled. To testify about the formula and the 8-L report, Edwin Locke, Jr., Ralph Austrian, and William Nemeath would return.

To back up Giles's testimony on the YCL, Lane selected two new witnesses, a former Dartmouth student named Lewis Jack Holmes and Jack Wilgus, an ex-Communist who had worked as a janitor on campus during the 1930s. Holmes could place Remington at at least one YCL meeting, while Wilgus claimed that Remington attended a Communist Party meeting in Rutland, Vermont, during the 1936 marble strike. The FBI also approached Bill Martin, to see if his hatred for Remington was still strong enough to get him to testify against his old friend.

Martin's feelings had changed from hostility to pity. By chance, he had seen Remington at a Washington drug store in April 1952 and had been shocked by his appearance. He seemed "a very sick person, extremely upset, . . . worried over his [forthcoming] trial, and in very bad financial condition." So, when the FBI visited Martin on December 11, 1952, they found him unwilling to become a government witness. He really knew very little about the Dartmouth YCL, he told the agents—it was a very informal group, which met irregularly—no dues were paid, and no one had a membership card. In fact, the tiny, ineffectual

group was never officially known as the YCL, and while Remington had attended many of its meetings in 1935–36, he had stopped coming toward the end of
his college career. No one could prove those bull sessions were actually YCL
meetings, he claimed. There were also professional and personal reasons that
prevented him from testifying. His career as a professor at Colgate University
would be damaged, and he was very fond of Lillian Remington. Had not the
Remington family suffered enough? He begged them not to call him. A copy of
the FBI's interview was sent to the U.S. attorney, who still thought that he
might be able to use Martin.[9]

Jack Minton planned to call only five witnesses—Bill Goodman, Charles
Davis, Fred Remington, Bertram Fox, and the defendant. It would be a much
different trial than the first, Minton told Lane—shorter and more civil. He did
not intend to attack the government attorneys or the FBI as had Rauh and
Chanler. (In fact, Thomas Donegan was an old and dear friend.) The burden of
refuting the charges rested upon Remington. Three of the five counts in the
indictment dealt with the Knoxville period, yet Minton selected no one to contradict Benson, Bridgman, McConnell, and Bertram; nor was there anyone but
Remington who could challenge Elizabeth Bentley's and Ann Remington's testimonies about what he was alleged to have given Helen. Similarly, Goodman
and Davis could testify that they, like Remington, did not know of the existence
of a YCL chapter at Dartmouth, but, as strong as both men were, could they
weaken the accounts of three or possibly four government witnesses (Giles,
Holmes, Wilgus, and Martin)? Minton had decided not to call Horace Bryan,
who might have helped with the charge of Communist activities at Knoxville, or
Bernard Redmont, the only man other than Remington who knew Bentley as
Helen, because he felt (as he told Myles Lane) that both were better witnesses
for the government than for the defense. Minton would rely on Remington and
his own skills, honed in over forty years of criminal practice, to impeach the
credibility of more than a dozen government witnesses. It seemed that it would
be a most uneven contest.

On January 8, 1953, Jack Minton met with Myles Lane and Judge Vincent L.
Leibell in a pre-trial conference. Talking with Lane confirmed Minton's view
that the former Dartmouth All-American football player was not much of a
lawyer, certainly not in Saypol's league. Gone, too, was Roy Cohn, who had left
the U.S. Attorney's Office to become an aide to Senator Joseph McCarthy. His
replacement, James B. Kilsheimer, lacked both Cohn's skill and his ruthlessness.
Minton was also happy that Leibell, an experienced jurist, was going to preside.
He had known the 69-year-old judge for many years and respected him greatly.
Judge Leibell was friendly and "insisted that there should be good feeling
between the attorneys on both sides and no incident which would result in later
reversals. . . . "[10]

The voir dire (the selection of the twelve jurors and three alternates) went smoothly and quickly on January 13. Leibell, unlike Noonan, permitted the lawyers to question personally prospective jurors, which pleased Minton since he took pride in his ability to know what an individual was thinking after only a brief conversation. Thirteen New Yorkers readily admitted that they were unable to impartially evaluate the case because they hated Communists. They were excused. Minton searched for men and women in their fifties or older, who had experienced the Depression and World War II, when the Soviet government had seemed more benign. Most of the jurors eventually picked were in that approximate age group, while two were in their sixties. The twelve held a variety of occupations (unlike those in the first trial—eight were homemakers). There was a diamond appraiser, a stock clerk, a salesman, a messenger, a car foreman, a bookshop owner, an expediter for Shell Oil, an advertising man, a retired postal supervisor, a former insurance executive, and one housewife. There was also a somewhat broader racial and ethnic mix than before—two jurors were African Americans, while one was born in Russia. Although it was impossible to predict how a jury would vote, Minton was confident that the panel selected that day was at least as free of overt prejudice as any available at the time. Indeed, the FBI was concerned that the group might be too liberal; its examination of the pool from which the jurors were drawn indicated that it contained many it considered Communist sympathizers.[11]

The second Remington trial began on January 13, 1953, and differed significantly from the first. It was shorter, lasting just ten days, while the first had taken a month. It was held in a tiny courtroom on the seventh floor of the Federal Building, in contrast to the majestic walnut-paneled Courtroom 110, and went almost unnoticed by reporters. This time the government presented fourteen witnesses, compared to the previous twenty-five. Minton called five, while Chanler had presented seventeen.

The two principal government witnesses, Ann Remington and Elizabeth Bentley, repeated their earlier testimonies, almost without change, but Bentley showed the effects of her recent emotional crises (relatively unknown to the defense, because it lacked a budget sufficient to investigate fully her activities). Under Minton's cross-examination, Bentley was flustered, impatient, and quick to become angry. When Minton asked if anyone had helped her to write her memoir, she reacted as if she had been poked with a stick.

"Didn't you write a book . . . ?"

"I thought that would turn up sooner or later."

" . . . Who did you write the book in collaboration with?"

"I sat on a Manhattan telephone directory and wrote it myself."

" . . . Who is Mr. Brunini, with reference to the book?"

"Oh, again Mr. Brunini," she exclaimed.

" . . . Just what did Mr. Brunini do with you on the book?"

"Not a thing."

"You didn't testify [previously] that you collaborated with Brunini on that book?"

"I cannot possibly testify to a lie, Mr. Minton," she said, then did precisely that. "Mr. Brunini had nothing to do with my book."

While Chanler had been somewhat gentle with Bentley and Ann Remington, Minton cut and slashed. He got Bentley to admit that as a Communist she did not believe in the Ten Commandments or organized religion. Communism was her religion, she said, and to achieve its goals, she had not hesitated to lie. He was also rough on Ann Remington, getting her to express publicly her hatred toward her mother. Two of a kind, Minton implied, Elizabeth and Ann, Communists who believed in neither faith nor love.[12]

If the new defense lawyer behaved differently, so did his client. No longer the easygoing, confident defendant, Remington listened more intently to the testimony, made notes frequently, and often conferred quietly with Minton. He was also more candid about his past, admitting that as a young man he was not a Republican but a philosophical Communist. But while a believer in Communist principles, he was never an organizational Communist; he never joined the Party, had a membership book, or advocated the violent overthrow of the government. He was also more honest about his Dartmouth years. He said he was Communistic in viewpoint and part of a group other students called Communist, not because they were the only radicals on a conservative campus but because they thought of themselves that way. Yet, he still denied both knowledge of and membership in the Young Communist League, contradicting the testimony of Giles and the two new witnesses, Lewis Jack Holmes and Jack Wilgus. Since the YCL issue was count five of the indictment, he explained carefully what he meant by his denial. To him, knowledge meant direct evidence of its existence; he had heard rumors about such a group and may have known its members but insisted that he had no real knowledge of a Young Communist League at Dartmouth. On this point, he continued to lie.

His description of his year at Knoxville followed a similar pattern. He freely admitted that he would not have rejected socializing with a Communist but still denied that he knew that his friends were members or that he knowingly attended Communist Party meetings or attempted to recruit Rudolph Bertram or anyone else (the latter charges were counts one and four of the indictment).

He was also more contrite about his relationship with Elizabeth Bentley. Asked if he thought he had violated WPB security regulations, he said, "Not intentionally, [but] I may have been indiscreet. I know I was very indiscreet in the sense of having this contact at all. . . . I cannot in all honesty say that I knew I made no mistake." But that was as far as he would go. He did not change his basic story that Bentley was the PM researcher whom he had met to publicize WPB successes. He continued to insist that he did not believe that Golos or Bentley were Communists and denied paying Party dues—as charged in count three of the indictment. He certainly had no idea she was a spy; nor had he ever given her secret or confidential information to be sent to Russia or to be used for any other purpose—count two of the indictment. On all these points, he said, "I have been truthful." Not entirely—in denying that he knew that Bentley and Golos were Communists, he lied again.[13]

This time, Remington was able to tell more (if not all) of the truth, because there was a different judge on the bench. Vincent Leibell was almost seventy and close to retiring but was sharply observant and scrupulously fair. When U.S. attorney Myles Lane attempted to force Remington to discuss the beating of Ann Remington, Leibell, unlike Noonan, forbade it. Lane also tried to whipsaw Remington by asking questions and demanding only narrow yes or no answers, but the judge blocked this, too: "[I]t is a natural thing for a witness to say more than yes and no and to explain," Leibell lectured Lane. "If he rambles too far, I will bring him back to the subject. . . . " And, once, when Lane asked an especially sarcastic question—how could Remington recognize another spy, like Bentley, if he did not know she was one—Judge Leibell sustained Minton's objection, agreeing that the question was argumentative and speculative. He was unaware that Lane had borrowed the question from Judge Noonan.[14]

Under Leibell's watchful eye, the trial moved so swiftly that Minton and Lane were able to deliver their summations after only seven days. Neither man's closing argument was original or eloquent. Minton spoke for ninety minutes (half as long as Chanler) and employed a strategy Remington himself had often used during the past five years—the Pinocchio Defense—the tragic fable of a misguided, innocent youth who is befriended by evildoers, in this case his wife and the "Croton Gang"; unlike the original tale, he is not rescued but manipulated until eventually destroyed. Remington had been "a blasted fool," Minton admitted, but was guilty only of stupidity. U.S. attorney Myles Lane ridiculed Minton's portrait of Remington as a naive, gullible youngster duped by the Communists. This was no average youth, he reminded the jury, but a Phi Beta Kappa and Senior Fellow at Dartmouth, who had associated with Communists, had attended their meetings, and had spied for them. A "psychopathic liar," Remington deserved to be found guilty on every count.[15]

For three hours, Remington listened intently. He must have found it difficult recognizing the man described by both Minton and Lane—the real William Remington was no political puppet whose strings were pulled by his wife and mother-in-law; nor was he the committed Communist ideologue and Soviet agent. The truth was, of course, far more complex and not likely to be revealed in the courtroom.

Judge Leibell took center stage next, with a seventy-five minute charge to the jury. In contrast to Noonan's, Leibell's instructions were clear, straightforward, and carefully presented. He defined the rules governing the law of perjury (going over it twice to make certain the jurors understood) and went into each count, describing the testimony of each government and defense witness. At 2:40 P.M., the three alternates were excused, and the eleven men and one woman ate a quick lunch and then began their deliberations. The judge received a note from the jury at 5:30 P.M., requesting additional information. The jury was brought in at 6:00 P.M., and Leibell patiently addressed each question. He also re-read his instructions on counts one and five and discussed again the various testimonies involved. By 6:30, they had returned to the jury room. Two hours later, they went out for brief dinner, then Remington's waiting resumed. At 11:15, they had more questions.

An hour passed, then another. At 3:20 A.M., after almost twelve hours of deliberation, Judge Leibell called Lane and Minton together and expressed his concern. He thought he should consult the jurors; enough time had gone by for them to know if they could reach agreement. When the jurors were brought in, Foreman George Kempler, the diamond appraiser, gave Judge Leibell a note. He read it aloud to the almost empty courtroom: "The twelve jurors have reached a verdict on three counts after deliberating for more than six hours. It now appears to be impossible to reach a unanimous decision on the other two counts. May we have your advice?"

The judge said that he would accept their unanimous verdict on the three counts and directed them to return to the jury room to put their findings in writing. What could it mean? Remington wondered. Guilty on one to three counts and a possible fifteen-year prison sentence? Innocent on all three and a hung jury on the rest? Or some other mix? Ten minutes later he knew. After the jurors were again seated, the foreman rose and read the verdict: "We, the Jury, find the defendant Remington guilty on Counts Two and Five [giving Bentley information to which she was not entitled, and denying knowledge of the existence of the YCL]; not guilty on Count Four [that he asked anyone to join the Communist Party]; no decision on Counts One and Three [attending Communist Party meetings, and paying Party dues]." Remington's face turned crimson, and he rose unsteadily. Minton asked that the jury be polled, and all twelve repeated their verdict.

"You are discharged with the thanks of the Court," Judge Leibell told them, "and you can feel that you have conscientiously fulfilled your duties as jurors."[16]

It was now past 4:00 A.M. on the morning of January 28, 1953, but the trial was still not officially over.

Do you have any motions to make, Mr. Minton? asked the judge.

"I am not very bright right now," Minton said. Could I be permitted to wait until sentence is imposed?

Judge Leibell set January 29 as the day to present motions and to determine when Remington would be sentenced. He would be permitted to remain free on bail. The U.S. attorney objected; he asked that Remington be jailed immediately because of the seriousness of the charge—giving information to a Soviet agent.

"I know it is a serious charge," Leibell said, "but I do not see any reason to jail the defendant." Lane then proposed that Remington's bail be increased, which was merely another attempt to put him away since he knew that Remington was broke. Leibell rejected that request, too, and they finally adjourned.

The session on January 29 lasted only an hour. Minton moved that the verdict be set aside and a new trial granted on four grounds: that the court had erred in rejecting a motion of acquittal he had made when the government finished its case and then again at the trial's end; that no sufficient evidence had been presented by Lane to prove that the information Remington gave Bentley was secret or confidential; that the YCL count was not material since Judge Noonan had excluded it in his charge to the jury; and that Judge Leibell had improperly received into evidence information about Bentley's and Golos's Communist activities. Of course, the judge thought his rulings were correct, but unlike Noonan, he discussed his reasoning with Minton before denying his motions. All that remained was the sentencing, set for February 4.[17]

After returning home, Remington telephoned Joe Rauh to determine whether there was any point in continuing the struggle. Rauh was prepared to fight on to the court of appeals and, should it fail to reverse the conviction, seek a writ of certiorari from the Supreme Court. "Bill seemed pretty whipped," Rauh wrote Mrs. Robbins after their talk. "Minton and the others are discouraging him about his chances on appeal." Rauh was more optimistic.

Remington could not decide whether to appeal or not. He was still feeling very much let down by the outcome. "I have always had a blind feeling, . . . a faith more than anything else that justice could not miscarry twice," he later told Rauh. "When this jury and this judge went along with Bentley and Ann Remington, I felt overwhelmed." With a successful appeal so unlikely, he saw no reason to try. It would only prolong the agony and hurt the people he loved most—his children, his parents, and, most especially, Jane and the baby she was carrying. Seven months before, in June 1952, they had been married in a small church in Brooklyn. It had not been the easiest decision for Jane, given the uncertainties of the future, but she was deeply in love with a man she thought most people did not understand. "Behind the dignified, reserved, and somewhat cold front he presented to strangers," she later wrote, he was "gentle and humane, . . . exuberant . . . and somewhat quixotic. . . . He fit no molds. He was quite uniquely himself. . . . The delightful surprises of living with him were endless." For Jane, Bill's long ordeal had transformed him—there were now "few traces of bitterness, hatred, or ambition for personal success"; instead, he was "filled with love, and understanding. . . . " Four months after their wedding, she had become pregnant. Jane was almost thirty-five years old and the first months of her pregnancy had been difficult; her obstetrician had ordered bed rest for six

weeks, and Bill alone had cared for her. She was better now, but Bill feared that
further strain might damage her health and the baby's. So he was in no mood to
go charging off again; he wanted to serve his sentence so that he could put this
nightmare behind him. Nevertheless, he promised Rauh that he would think
carefully about an appeal.[18]

He returned to Foley Square on the morning of February 4 for sentencing.
Judge Leibell asked Myles Lane if he wished to make a recommendation. He
did. Remington had been convicted on two counts of perjury, he reminded the
judge: lying about giving Elizabeth Bentley information from the files of the War
Production Board, and falsely testifying that he had no knowledge of the YCL.
"The implications that flow from Count 2, in terms of national security, are very
serious," Lane said. " . . . [D]uring the war, he was transmitting information to a
representative of the Communist Party for transmittal to the Soviet Union, and
although we were allies of the Soviets, . . . we were very careful not to give the
Soviet Union this particular information, relating to airplane production. That
is something the Soviets wanted and wanted badly. . . . So they utilized their
Communist apparatus here in the United States for the purpose of obtaining
that information." He considered Remington's lying about the YCL almost as
serious, and although the jury could not agree about Remington's other alleged
Communist activities, he thought he was guilty on those counts, too.
Remington's offenses were no momentary aberration, he charged, but part of his
normal behavior. "This man has a pattern of perjury running all through his
life"; lying before congressional committees, grand juries, and courts threatened
American law and liberty. Therefore, the government recommended that the
court impose two five-year sentences (to run concurrently) and a two thousand
dollar fine.

Minton angrily rejected Lane's assertion that Remington was guilty of espionage. There was no showing that he knew the information he gave Bentley
was going to Russia—Bentley herself had said exactly that. Moreover, she considered him a minor figure—was it fair that only Remington should be sent to
jail while the more important suspects had managed to escape punishment? He
did not think so. Remington was "not a vicious figure, a criminal, an enemy to
society." He had "certainly shown complete and absolute contrition and peni-
tence for what he should not have done."

Does the defendant wish to speak? Leibell asked.

"The verdict in this case is not a just one," Remington told the court. "I
have told the truth as best I have been able to. . . . The problems of securing justice in a case like this [after] ten or fifteen years are difficult. I cannot remember
what was said, what was done, with utter precision over that length of time.
Moreover, there has been such a change in opinion: what was black is now
white, and vice versa. There is also a problem of semantics, definitions. This
case is just filled with it."

He talked about count five—the YCL. "The group at Dartmouth that was called Communist had no connection with the national organization . . . for example, no charter, no delegates to national conventions." What he knew of the YCL came only from research, he claimed—not personal experience.

"I never gave Miss Bentley secret or confidential information." He paused, his voice now shaking as he said, "I would like to make another comment, about the reasons why I have fought so hard over half a decade against exaggerated . . . zealous charges. . . . I remember, almost three years ago, about the time of the first indictment, my daughter was then six, asked me, 'Daddy, why don't you say it is true? . . . They will let you alone. It doesn't make any difference whether it is true or not, say it is, and they will let you alone.' There wasn't much I could say to help her," he told Leibell—his eyes filled with tears—"to keep her from growing up with . . . the view that it doesn't make any difference. To me, it made a difference. I have stood for what I know to be true as a matter of principle, long past the . . . end of my professional career, long past the point when all my resources were exhausted. And I continued, and I will continue throughout the rest of my life to stand for what I believe to be true."

He had nothing more to say and returned to his chair.

Now Leibell spoke. Having listened to the lawyers describe two sharply different Remingtons, the judge concluded that there was a third possessing the qualities of both. He perceived him as a youngster imbued with a naive idealism who, at college, "got the idea that the world was out of joint . . . and that it was going to be part of his mission in life to try and right the wrongs." Unfortunately, Remington's mission brought him into contact with Communists and "if you once fall into their toils, . . . you are their victim, and they try to keep a grip on you as long as they can." Many who believed in Communist principles eventually saw the light, destroyed their membership books, and left the Party forever, but Remington did not. And as he climbed through government ranks, the Communists continued to exploit him. " . . . I think he made the mistake of not renouncing them outright and promptly, breaking their grip upon him, and you know the old adage about 'what a tangled web we weave when first we practice to deceive.' So the defendant's troubles mounted as he . . . was investigated and examined by this board and that committee, and the Grand Jury, and at last the trials."

Leibell did not think Remington was any kind of super-spy. "Miss Bentley . . . didn't consider him too important . . . and I don't think he relished what they forced him to do in 1942, . . . but the jury has found this defendant guilty on these two counts, and I believe their verdict was justified from the evidence."

For a moment, Remington felt some small degree of hope—Leibell seemed sympathetic and understanding, perhaps his sentence would be light, and with time off for good behavior, he might be home within a year.

"The defendant will stand," the judge ordered. "The sentence of the Court . . . is as follows: On Count 2, he is sentenced to three years in the penitentiary. On Count 5, he is sentenced to three years in the penitentiary, to run concurrently with the jail sentence on Count 2."

It could have been far worse, Remington thought, but it was bad enough—there would be no early homecoming. Excepting the possibility of parole, he would have to serve over two years in prison.

The judge asked Jack Minton if he planned to appeal the conviction; if not, then Remington would be taken immediately into custody.

Minton replied that he had not yet decided or consulted with his client. Leibell did not believe that Minton had any substantial questions of law to appeal, but the lawyer respectfully disagreed. He thought there was a question of materiality on count five and the admissibility of certain testimony about what Remington may or may not have known about Golos's true activities. Minton then asked that bail be granted pending appeal. Lane objected—there were no substantial questions of law, as far as he was concerned, and, even if the court of appeals should hold that the YCL count was not material, Remington would still go to jail for three years on count two. Furthermore, the decision in the *Williams* case required that there must be evidence that substantial questions existed before bail could be granted, so he wondered if court could grant bail.

Leibell was convinced that he did have the power, but the question was, should he use it? Quickly, he decided yes. "I believe in appeals," he told the lawyers. " . . . Judges in the lower courts may commit errors. Judges in Appellate Courts . . . have the final say." Lane again expressed his opposition, but Leibell granted Remington bail and set it at ten thousand dollars. This was no good, Minton explained, since seven thousand dollars was already on deposit and it would be impossible for Remington to raise any more. Lane held out for the stated amount, but Leibell agreed to the lower sum and asked Lane if this was acceptable. It was not. "Your Honor, I am not satisfied, unless the defendant is committed." To Lane's disappointment, that would not occur immediately, and Remington returned home to make a final decision on whether to appeal or begin his sentence.[19]

When word reached Joe Rauh of Remington's sentence, he sent him a wire: PLEASE ACCEPT AND CONVEY TO JANE MY DEEPEST SYMPATHY CONCERNING SEVERITY OF SENTENCE. BELIEVE APPEAL ON CONSTITUTIONAL ISSUES WISEST COURSE. He received no answer that day or the next. "I don't know whether Bill plans to appeal or not," he wrote Mrs. Robbins on February 5,

> although I have constantly recommended it. . . . I suppose you have read in the newspapers that Judge Leibell gave Bill a three year sentence. Although I expected this, it does seem both severe and unjust. I gathered from Chanler that Bill is quite angry at Minton's failure to do better for him; but he really has little rational basis for this anger, as he chose Minton with his eyes open and over my vigorous protest

that just this would happen. Bill is his own worst enemy for many reasons, and for none more than his failure to recognize who his true friends are.

Rauh and Remington finally met for dinner in New York on February 13. Remington was still undecided about appealing the contrary court decision and had many questions. He had been told that if he again took on Bentley and Brunini, it would raise the ire of Catholic groups and give the impression that he was fighting the Church. What did Rauh think? Could he begin to serve his sentence and also appeal? If so, would the appeal destroy his chances of an early parole? Where would the money come from to pay the lawyers and other court costs? And did they have any chance at all to win? He asked Rauh to put his thoughts down on paper for him and Jane to study.

It took Rauh a week to write the memorandum Remington wanted. The first draft he tore up—"too preachy," he thought; he was still angry that Remington had chosen to follow Minton's advice and not his. The final version was seven pages long and was still likely to annoy Remington, but it was the best he could do. First, he quickly disposed of the various objections that had been raised by Minton and others. He rejected the idea that another assault on the Brunini–Bentley relationship would cause continued harassment. He knew of no effort by Catholic groups to affect the outcome of his case. Second, an appeal would not interfere with his serving his sentence, or prevent parole, which he thought unlikely. Money would not be a problem—he would handle the case without charge, and Dick Green and William Chanler had also offered to help. The Marshall Trust would probably provide the funds to print the record.

Could they win? Rauh did not know but thought it essential, not only for Remington but also for the country, that they try. Chances of success were less important than whether he still believed in his innocence and the righteousness of what Chanler called "the Great Cause." As for the basic legal questions at issue, Rauh had no doubts. "The legal principle is this," he explained, "The Government, having procured an unconstitutional indictment, cannot reindict a man for what he said on the witness stand. . . . " Unfortunately, there was no direct precedent to support their position, but the Supreme Court's ruling in the second *Nardone* case came close. Therein, the Court had declared that the government (which had illegally wiretapped a suspect later put on trial) could "not profit by its own wrongful doing." That ruling might apply to his case. Having procured the original indictment illegally, the government should be prevented from winning a conviction based on unconstitutional conduct.

Their legal principle might be sound, but their factual base was weak. To be sure, at the first trial, Leyla Sefa and Eileen Collins had revealed the connection between Bentley and Brunini, and although Saypol had called them liars, the government had called no witnesses to contradict them. But by not raising this issue vigorously in the second trial, Minton had cast doubt on their veracity.

Minton had also overlooked other opportunities that would have strengthened their position on appeal. For example, Bentley had flatly denied that Brunini had helped her write her book, and Minton had done nothing to attack her credibility by calling Sefa or Collins or even Brunini. Nor had he renewed an earlier request to inspect the minutes of the first grand jury to prove illegal conduct. Government attorneys, Rauh now feared, would exploit these factual weaknesses. Still, Rauh did not think such obstacles insurmountable. The record of the first trial as well as the second would be sent to the court of appeals, which should consider the scandal uncovered earlier by Chanler and Rauh. So Remington had every right to believe his cause was just.

There was also another important factor to consider: his innocence. "In a struggle for vindication of due process of law," Rauh told him, "not only the principal but the vehicle itself must be strong, and must be honest with those who seek to vindicate principal in his case." Did he still believe in his own innocence? He reminded him that at every step of the way during the past five years—when he took on the case in 1948, and when they hired Bethuel Webster in 1949 and William Chanler in 1950—"I asked you to assure me . . . that you had never been engaged in espionage, and had never been a member of the Communist Party. You assured me you had told me the whole truth; I believed you. . . . " Now he was asking Remington to renew that pledge:

> I have always felt that the Remington case was a cause to be proud of and that feeling was based on my belief in the principles involved and in your innocence which would one day lead to your ultimate vindication. If this possibility of your ultimate vindication has now gone, so be it. I shall not regret the efforts I put in the case, for they were expended in the honest belief that you were innocent, and that you were deprived of the processes of law, which have made our country great. But if that possibility is not gone, if you can honestly say, as you have said to me many times, "I knew Bentley as a newspaper woman; her charges of espionage are false; I never joined the Communist Party; I have told the truth as best I could"—if you can honestly say all that, I have no question in my own mind as to what course you should follow. Guilty men often appeal; innocent men always appeal.

Remington replied five days later, on February 25, but his letter did not contain the reaffirmation of his innocence that Rauh required. By March 4, he had decided. "I . . . want to keep on fighting . . . rather than . . . let the government get away with injustice." He hoped that they could work out the details soon, since the time period during which he could appeal would expire on March 16. But now it was Rauh who was having second thoughts. After a meeting with Rauh on March 13, Bill wrote him:

> In all my trial and other testimony I have told what I know to be the truth. While there are a few peripheral issues on which there are difficulties of definitions, concepts, etc., on the central issues, there is no possibility of confusion. If you do not

believe in my truthfulness at this stage, without requiring this kind of reiteration, I wonder about the question of your pursuing an appeal on my behalf.

Rauh also wondered, and while he told him on March 15 that he would probably handle the appeal, he still needed a few more days to make up his mind. Chanler would have to seek an extension of the deadline. Remington finally gave Rauh the declaration he had wanted the next day. It had taken three attempts to get it down on paper, and, in the end, Remington sent him all the drafts along with the final letter. He claimed that his hesitancy had nothing to do with doubts about his innocence, but only with the strain involved in continuing the struggle, and he thought that Rauh had shown "a lack of confidence in me, a lack of sensitivity to Jane's side of the problem" that touched them both "on the raw." In a separate statement, he said, "I am absolutely not guilty of the basic charge that I knowingly cooperated with a Communist courier. Nor was I ever a member of the Communist Party. I never joined it, never paid dues to it, never had a membership card or book, and never had any 'understanding' with it." This was satisfactory to Rauh, and on March 20, the U.S. Attorney's Office was formally notified that Joseph L. Rauh, Jr., was again William Remington's attorney.[20]

The government responded by creating a new obstacle. Assistant U.S. attorney James B. Kilsheimer, who had worked under Irving Saypol during the first trial, informed Rauh that he had less than a month to prepare the record and submit his brief. It was "a killing time schedule," Rauh told Dick Green. "Kilsheimer drew his pound of flesh on this, but I was in no position to fight back." In fact, it proved impossible, and when Rauh asked Kilsheimer for an extension, Kilsheimer offered a deal. If Remington would surrender now and begin to serve his sentence, he would give Rauh all the time he wanted. Rauh spoke with Remington, who agreed to the arrangement, but, of course, not happily. It would mean that he would miss the birth of his child—due in late May or early June, and he was very concerned about how Jane would fare without him. He was worried, too, about eleven-year-old Bruce and about Gale, almost nine, casualties, like himself, of the war with Ann. Over the years, he had tried to shield them from the publicity and provide comfort and reassurance, but they were separated by distance and his ex-wife's continuing animosity. On Tuesday morning, April 14, 1953, he wrote them to say goodbye:

Dear Gale and Bruce:

The time has come at last for some very sad news. . . . When you were here in March, I told you [about the] appeal. My lawyers find that they urgently need more time. The usual and courteous thing is for the time to be granted as a matter of course. But the prosecutor has decided to be quite nasty. . . . He won't grant the additional time unless I go off to jail tomorrow or Thursday. So, off I go.

I will not be able to see you two again for one year (if I am paroled as soon as the law permits) at least. It could be a bit longer . . . but I hope not. . . . I don't yet know how often I'll be allowed to write and receive letters. But I'll write you as often as I can.

. . . It's a nuisance to have a father in jail. (Rather more than that, as we all know). I suggest you not make an issue of it or mention it. . . . If someone mentions it to you, just say: "So what." And walk away. But just among us we can be very glad that this separation is not going to be a very long one. . . . And we can be glad that I'll be safe, and even cheerful—except for missing you, and Jane, and my parents, and friends. I know that I am doing what is right. I believe that I have told the truth . . . and behaved like a gentleman during the trials. If I have to go to jail for it, I can go with a clear conscience at least.

You can bid me farewell—a temporary farewell—with assurance that . . . I'll be home again SURE THING.

. . . You both have my very deepest love. I'll be thinking about you always and always, every hour of the day. I want you to have the best possible out of life. And the best things possible—the very best that a man or woman can have—are the courage, and the patience, the gentleness inside and the capacity to love other people, and the ability to perceive and enjoy beautiful things, and the capacity for friendship, and other qualities which make happiness possible under any circumstances. Money or freedom, without these qualities of mind and spirit, cannot bring happiness to anyone. So, until sometime later on, we'll have only letters for a bridge, and a very deep and exceedingly strong love as ties between me and you. And that is a very great deal.

Love,
Daddy.[21]

20

The Ends of Expediency

Surrendering to the government was not what he expected. "No crowing . . . no press conferences . . . no bothersome cameras and no reporters bothering me." He signed a few forms and it was off to jail. The whole procedure took less than an hour, and, surprisingly, "it was handled in quite a decent fashion."[1]

Jail was the Federal House of Detention on West Street—a depot where new prisoners were photographed, fingerprinted, examined, and interviewed until the Bureau of Prisons decided where to send them. Alger Hiss hated his brief stay there in 1951. "West Street was a scene of confusion and disorder, and a spirit of misery permeated this house of pandemonium," he observed. This was not Remington's experience. His quarters were not too uncomfortable, and he found his fellow inmates generally friendly and not too much different from him—"except for skewing on the downward side." Especially convivial were two Communists detained by the Immigration Service, but he strongly rejected their overtures. He missed Jane terribly but was not bored or lonesome. She visited him that first Sunday and again on April 29, when she was accompanied by his parents. Fred, now eighty-four, was pleased that he could be with Bill, even under these wretched circumstances, because he had been afraid that he would die before being able to see his son again.[2]

While Remington was adjusting to his temporary home, the Bureau of Prisons was deciding what to do with him. E. E. Thompson, warden of the Federal House of Detention, informed Washington of Remington's request that he not be sent to the same prison as Alger Hiss. James V. Bennett, director of the Federal Bureau of Prisons, rejected Remington's plea and ordered him sent to

Lewisburg Penitentiary, where Hiss and several other men accused of being Communists were now held. Nevertheless, Lewisburg's warden, G. W. Humphrey, was ordered to give Remington a job and living quarters where he would not be with Hiss and the others. On April 30, 1953, Remington boarded a bus with a dozen other inmates bound for Lewisburg.[3]

Joe Rauh hoped that his stay there would be short, if the court of appeals could be persuaded to reverse Remington's latest conviction. To Dick Green went the unenviable task of compiling and indexing the record and asking permission to appeal on the typewritten transcript instead of a printed version. If a federal judge allowed them to have it, part of that record would include the grand jury testimonies of Ann and William Remington. Those records had been denied to Chanler during the first trial; however, Judge Leibell, following the court of appeals's instructions, had ordered the government to make the transcripts of Remington's testimony available to Minton for the second trial and, given the furor surrounding alleged grand jury misconduct, had included Ann's testimony as well. (This now made it possible for Rauh and Green to seek the minutes, because they were no longer secret.) Unfortunately, however, Minton had not used them during his cross-examination of Ann Remington, nor had he made and renewed motions to dismiss the indictment on the grounds of impropriety. So, the government, sure to oppose the defense's request, could argue that no reason existed to allow Remington's lawyers to consult the records, since Minton had found no evidence of misconduct.

These issues could only be resolved by a judge; fortunately the task was assigned to Vincent Leibell, who, during a hearing on May 25, allowed Green and Rauh to examine the transcripts, despite the objections of assistant U.S. attorney Kilsheimer. As for the charge of grand jury misconduct, Leibell was "for laying the ghost once and for all," so he also ordered that a complete set of the minutes be made available to any appellate court that might consider the case. Later, he amended his ruling and imposed restrictions. The lawyers could keep no copy for their personal use and could only examine the records at either the U.S. Attorney's Office or at the Justice Department. More important, they were forbidden to quote directly from the documents—they could only paraphrase or summarize. Still, Rauh and Green were given their first opportunity to examine the scene of the crime on those days when Ann and Bill first testified. Would they find evidence of abuse of the grand jury system or just zealous, but not improper, interrogation?

Each lawyer reviewed the five-hundred-odd pages of the Remingtons' testimonies and were truly shocked by what they found. This was not an impartial investigation of Communist subversion but a witch hunt led by Brunini and Donegan, whose ultimate purpose was the rehabilitation of Elizabeth Bentley. The transcripts were filled with examples of abusive and improper tactics. Especially disgraceful were the questions about divorce, adultery, and battery.

"Brunini's influence is plenty," thought Chanler's associate John Tabor after reading Ann Remington's testimony. "He didn't merely threaten her on perjury or contempt or publicity on matters she [believed] would be secret. He misstated the law on the matter of her privilege after she had deliberately and repeatedly invoked it. His misstatement caused her to abandon her privilege . . . and go 'all the way.'" William Chanler was struck by

> Brunini's assertion that Remington was a very dangerous man, because he had contradicted Bentley. To me, this has implications that go far beyond Brunini's interest in the book. It means that our judicial process has been used by officers of the Court to punish people, who try to defend themselves against ideologically popular accusations. If you attack Bentley . . . , it is extremely important to the American people that you be punished.

The facts were now clear and well documented. The grand jury system had been misused; the Constitution's Fifth Amendment and Supreme Court rulings guaranteeing due process of law and other traditional judicial principles had been violated. Just as serious was the suppression of these facts by U.S. attorney Saypol. But would the court of appeals be less interested in these injustices than in precedent, especially the case of the *United States v. Williams*, in which the Supreme Court held that even if an indictment was technically flawed, a defendant had no right to commit perjury and could be prosecuted for it. Rauh's answer to this problem was the first and especially the second *Nardone* cases, in which the Court forbade the government from using illegally obtained evidence or information, and the *Silverthorne* case, which prevented the government from profiting from its own wrongdoing. Could the court of appeals be persuaded that *Nardone* and *Silverthorne* rather than *Williams* fit the facts of the Remington case? To achieve this would first require a powerful brief that would capture the busy judges' attention and an equally eloquent oral presentation. To Rauh, this was combat with the government for the highest stakes of all—not simply Remington's future but that of American civil liberties as well.

Jane kept Remington informed of his lawyers' activities, but he was more troubled than pleased. He was afraid that the appeal and the attendant publicity might cause the Justice Department to torment him further. The jury had been unable either to acquit or convict on two counts of the indictment; would he be indicted again once he left prison? And the Brunini indictment was itself still outstanding. Despite Rauh's gloomy prediction, he hoped to win an early parole in 1954 but thought it possible only if he received no publicity. He therefore wanted them to keep to a strict schedule: file the brief in June and present the case to the court in October, which, he was confident, would be followed in December by a decision affirming his conviction. In January, they would again apply to the Supreme Court for a writ of certiorari, and by March or April 1954, he would know what the Court planned to do, although he again expected defeat. Then, he wanted his lawyers to discuss with the authorities the dismissal of the remaining counts and the first indictment and meet with Judge Leibell, asking him to reconsider his sentence. If unsuccessful, he would apply for parole. The key to his ultimate success, he thought, was how the appeal was handled. It must be done quietly and politely, "so that nobody gets irritated to the point of keeping Count 1 and 3, and the first indictment, hanging over my head for the next decade or so."[4]

The other major concern on Remington's mind in late May 1953 was the impending birth of his child. "I am certainly with you absolutely every minute in every possible way . . . ," he wrote Jane on May 27. "You may be in the middle of things as I write this or things may be over. . . . I am hoping so hard and praying that things go well. We deserve a bit of good luck. Perhaps we'll have it. But if we don't there's lots more of life ahead."

Bill was a few days off schedule. On the afternoon of June 2, while reading in his dorm, a guard ran up the stairs and ordered him to report to the main floor. After arriving at the center, the duty officer gave him a telegram: SON BORN 2:10 PM JUNE 2. WEIGHT 8 LB 10 OZ AFTER BREECH DELIVERY. LABOR NORMAL. JANE AND NEIL FINE LOVE= JANE REMINGTON.

"Then I just took off inside," he later noted, "feet remaining entirely without ability to move. Tried to thank them. No voice. Pried feet lose and headed for the dorm. Someone noticed my face and asked what was wrong. All kinds of tears apparently look wet. I sat on the nearest bed and it took me several starts to break the news. Have been roundly congratulated since."

"What a terrific job!" he told Jane in a letter written that wonderful day. " . . . Too bad Neil has to start doing things backwards so early in life. We can't have him backing into trouble all HIS life (in my footsteps—only way to avoid that is to find him a wife like you . . .)."[5]

He had a voracious appetite for information about his new son and chafed at the prison's restrictions on how much mail he could receive. To compensate, Jane drew sketches of Neil on the margins of her letters, which he found charming. He was full of advice—he approved of her flexible feeding schedule but urged her to teach him that "the world is NOT Neil's oyster. He has to learn it. But in a gentle way. Gentleness and love come first." He desperately wanted to see them but was allowed only two hourly visits a month, and he did not want her to travel until she was completely recovered. The trip from Levittown to Lewisburg took nine hours and also required an overnight stay in a nearby motel, an added expense they could not afford.

As methodical as her husband and just as concerned not to alienate prison authorities, Jane carefully planned for Neil's first visit with his father. On August 31, she wrote Warden Humphrey, asking his permission to bring the three-month-old infant on a September visit to the penitentiary. She would bring the baby to morning visiting hours, then return alone in the afternoon to be with Bill, leaving Neil in the care of Lillian Remington, who would accompany her to Lewisburg. Acting warden M. S. Richmond granted her request and even encouraged her to bring the baby.

On the morning of September 16, 1953, Jane and her party entered the massive, brick-lined, two-story building, which always reminded Alger Hiss of Hampton Court Palace. They were taken to the visitors' quarters, where Jane filled out papers and showed identification. Then she and the baby were taken into a large lounge filled with casual furniture, where she saw her husband for the first time in nearly seven months. He looked well, considering the strain caused by recent events. He was dressed in a blue denim work shirt and matching pants; his face was care-worn, the forehead deeply lined; his hair, worn in a prison-style flat-top, was now flecked with grey. As guards watched, they talked excitedly, but Bill was not allowed to hold his son or touch Jane. But it was wonderful for all of them to be together, and the time passed quickly.[6]

That same week, Joe Rauh was preparing for his appearance before the court of appeals on October 15. He thought his brief was strong and effective but was uncharacteristically gloomy about the chances of success. Others echoed his pessimism. Bethuel Webster called the brief "a first class job, though I suppose not even the Brunini–Saypol business is likely to overcome judicial inertia at this late date." Chanler also thought it was terrific but feared that "no one will believe that what took place in the Grand Jury room was as bad as you say it is. . . . " He urged Rauh when making his oral argument "to shock the Court and get their attention away from the technical objections. . . . If you once get them listening, I am sure as the story unfolds they will become more and more deeply shocked."

By chance, Rauh faced the same three judges before whom Chanler had appeared in 1951—Thomas Swan and the Hand cousins. For close to an hour, Rauh presented the points argued at greater length in his brief: that the first indictment was invalid because of the financial collaboration of Brunini and Bentley as well as her previous association with Thomas Donegan; that Brunini and Donegan deceived Ann Remington regarding her legal rights and held her as a witness until she was dazed and incoherent, causing her to tell an entirely different story about her ex-husband, which eventually led to his indictment, trial, and conviction; that William Remington was subjected to a longer, even more intense grilling on questions unrelated to the crime for which he was indicted; that U.S. attorney Irving Saypol deliberately withheld information about the Brunini affair and, later at trial, denied that any irregularities existed. All these activities, Rauh argued, denied Remington due process of law and approached entrapment. Anticipating the government's response, he argued that the *Williams* decision did not apply to the Remington case. Remington was not the victim of a technical error in the indictment (as Williams had been) but of unconstitutional misconduct by high government officials.

James Kilsheimer spoke for the government. He brushed aside the so-called misconduct of Brunini, Donegan, and Saypol, calling it irrelevant because it had nothing to do with the second indictment, voted by an entirely different grand jury. Furthermore, the *Williams* case did apply. Remington was required to tell the truth, regardless of how the indictment was procured. Learned Hand interrupted Kilsheimer to say that Remington was not questioning the authority of the court to try him but was claiming that government officials were guilty of abuse and deliberate misconduct, and, if true, it was "much worse than procuring evidence by illegal means to convict a defendant." Kilsheimer reminded the court that when the case was before it in 1951 the judges had said nothing about alleged misconduct that might invalidate the first indictment. And, as Rauh had feared, he pointed out that during the second trial, when the defense had been able to examine the very records that it now claimed revealed impropriety—the grand jury minutes of the Remingtons' testimonies—no one had charged illegality. The best that Rauh could do was to note that motions to dismiss had been made several times—before and after the second trial and had been denied each time. The judges listened closely and, when the hearing ended, reserved decision; Kilsheimer later told the FBI that he thought Learned Hand appeared sympathetic to Rauh's argument.

Jane Remington was also encouraged by Rauh's performance, but when informed of this, Bill warned her against false optimism. "I hate to discourage you . . . ," he told her on November 5,

> but Judges Swan and A. Hand wouldn't go along with a decent verdict 3 years ago and it's a dead certainty in my mind that they will not this time either. They will delay another month or two finding the right words to slap the wrist of Saypol for withholding facts from the defense, but they will make jolly well sure that I stay right here. Really, they are not warm-hearted men, nor courageous except in a rather self-righteous way. L. Hand is different but he went along [before] and will again.[7]

Remington was wrong about Learned Hand. When the three judges submitted their pre-conference memoranda, there seemed a chance that Remington's conviction might again be reversed. Learned Hand felt quite strongly that the conviction should be reversed and the indictment dismissed; Thomas Swan's memorandum reveals that while he felt bound by the *Williams* decision, he did not think it directly applied to the Remington case. But he also thought that the facts did not support application of the second *Nardone* case, either:

> there is a logical difference between saying the prosecution cannot use evidence illegally obtained and saying that a defendant has a license to lie at a trial brought on by illegal procedure. It is not impossible that the Supreme Court will extend the *Nardone* doctrine or the entrapment doctrine to include a case like the present [but] I am disposed to think the Supreme Court should make the extension.

Thus, without even examining the grand jury records, Swan tentatively voted to affirm the conviction but did so "with some doubt and regret. . . . "

Augustus Hand had neither doubt nor regret in voting to sustain conviction. "I do not think the grand jury proceedings in the first case are relevant to the charges of perjury in the case before us," he told his colleagues. "It's a completely novel extension of any doctrine I know that Remington can come before the court and commit perjury under the last indictment, and be immune from prosecution. I feel sure that Judge Leibell was correct in his rulings and the judgment of conviction must be AFFIRMED." While Swan appears to have given the case at least some thought (his memorandum was two pages long), Gus Hand spat out his initial opinion in just three sentences.

No record exists of their final deliberations, but they were probably heated. Two years before, Gus Hand had also opposed reversal but then had changed his mind and had joined the majority. Now, however, nothing could cause him to reconsider—not even the strenuous efforts of his cousin Learned, who later told William Chanler how disappointed he was that he could not persuade Gus to change his vote. Perhaps because of his firm belief, it fell to Gus Hand to write the final decision.

In an eight-page opinion, Augustus Hand rejected the defense's arguments. Instead of alleging errors committed at the most recent trial, the defendant believed that because of grand jury misconduct and its concealment by the government, the original indictment should be dismissed and the first and second trials declared invalid. With a bit of sarcasm, Hand called this theory "new and novel" and could find no authority to support it. On the contrary, the *Williams* decision indicated otherwise—false testimony given at a trial on a flawed indictment was perjury and must be prosecuted. *Nardone* and the other cases cited by Remington did not apply, Hand argued, because they dealt with government misconduct committed during investigations, while Remington's perjury was a new crime that occurred after an alleged illegal inquiry. Hand also rejected the contention that Remington was a victim of government entrapment. "Remington has been entrapped," he concluded,

> not by devious means and methods employed by the government, but by his own acts. He is caught in a web of his own duplicity and zealous prosecution by the government. We should not overturn his conviction, where his guilt is clear and to do so would not serve to rigidly enforce a defendant's constitutional rights or prevent government misconduct in the future, but only to weaken our judicial process. Judgment of conviction affirmed.

Judge Swan added just two words to Hand's opinion: "I concur."

Learned Hand did not go along with the majority. For days, he worked on several drafts of a minority opinion until he was happy with the final one. Unlike his colleagues, Hand felt that the *Williams* decision was completely irrelevant to the Remington case. Instead, two questions were predominant. Did Brunini and Donegan do anything improper during the grand jury proceedings that would invalidate the first indictment? And, if so, could Remington then be convicted for testimony given in his own defense at that trial? The answer to the first question, he thought, was yes; to the second, no. Having examined Ann Remington's testimony, he found evidence of "oppression" and "deceit." "For myself," he wrote,

> the examination went beyond what I deem permissible. Pages on pages of lecturing repeatedly preceded a question; statements of what the prosecution already knew, and of how idle it was for the witness to hold back what she could contribute; occasional reminders that she could be punished for perjury; all were scattered throughout. Then, after complaining of hunger and fatigue, Brunini informed her that she must answer the question, because she had no privilege to remain silent.

As a result of pressure and intimidation, she made a full disclosure to the grand jury, giving information protected by both the Fifth Amendment and marital privilege. Brunini's statement was false, and Donegan, the Justice Department lawyer, "did not intervene to correct [it]." This failure alone, Hand insisted, would have "required the indictment to be quashed. . . . "

Relying upon *Silverthorne Lumber Co. v. United States* and *Sorrels v. United States*, Hand also argued that the government could not profit from its own wrongdoing; to him, an unlawful indictment was no different from evidence obtained illegally. Hand also believed that Remington had been entrapped by the government. "Having committed himself upon the grand jury proceeding to a denial of his membership in the Communist Party, Remington at the trial of the indictment based upon that denial, could not escape repeating what he had said. . . . Therefore, I do not see how it can be denied that the . . . first indictment was as direct a provocation of the perjury for which he has been convicted," as if government officials had incited Remington to commit perjury. Hand thought that the conviction should be reversed and the indictment dismissed. Despite his thoughtful analysis of Ann Remington's grand jury transcript, which Swan and Gus Hand did not even bother to read, the majority won, and on November 24, 1953, Remington's conviction was upheld.[8]

Anticipating total defeat, Learned Hand's remarkable dissent rejuvenated Rauh and his colleagues. "The decision is far from a loss," John Tabor wrote him. " . . . You have, I believe, a good chance for certiorari. You have [justices] Black and Douglas; there is a strong likelihood that Frankfurter will follow . . . Hand. The question is, can they persuade [Associate Justice Robert] Jackson?" Whatever their chances, Rauh could not turn back now. In December, he started work on a petition to the Supreme Court.[9]

As good as it was, it failed to convince the justices. On February 5, 1954, the

Supreme Court denied the writ of certiorari without comment. Joe Rauh was not the only one disappointed by the Court's action. On February 25, Learned Hand wrote his good friend Associate Justice Felix Frankfurter for an explanation. "I feel, shall I confess it? a sense of professional incapacity when your distinguished group would not even hear the Remington case. But it does serve as a warning, never to be forgotten, though never really learned, that what may seem [important] to oneself, may seem to others plain tosh."

"You should have no disquietude about Remington," Frankfurter replied on March 3. "The fact is that three of us voted to hear the case—and that the fourth didn't because of the extreme views expressed by that essentially lawless [Hugo] Black indicated the hopelessness of agreement even among those who were outraged by the Government's behavior. . . . I crave for talk."[10] Later, Joe Rauh, once Frankfurter's law clerk, learned from the justice a bit more about the incident. Apparently Justices Douglas, Black, and Frankfurter wanted to review the case and thought that Justice Robert H. Jackson would supply the fourth vote required to grant a writ of certiorari. At a conference called to discuss the question, Hugo Black remarked that the Remington case would provide the opportunity to overrule the *Williams* decision, in which both he and Frankfurter had dissented. Jackson, who disliked Black intensely, was so annoyed by this statement that he changed his mind and withdrew his support. Thus, Remington fell victim to the petty animosities that existed among the justices.[11]

With the Supreme Court's rejection of his petition, only two ways remained for Remington to win an early release from Lewisburg—a court-ordered reduction of sentence or parole. On March 4, 1954, Jane Remington, accompanied by John Minton, met with Judge Leibell to plead for the release of her husband. Leibell listened patiently but said that though he was sympathetic, an example had to be set to deter others who might violate the law. Therefore, the motion for a reduced sentence was denied.

A few weeks later, Remington decided to seek parole. The first step was the completion of a formal written application describing his plans for the future, his reasons why parole should be granted, and a brief explanation of what had led to his conviction. When released, he would live with his wife and baby on Long Island; he hoped to support them by selling real estate or managing a nursery, he wrote the board. He was applying for parole because of family need. His parents were ill and he had a wife and child to care for. In trying to explain his crime, Remington came closer than ever before to making a complete confession:

> When I was in my late teens and early twenties I associated with some Communists. In defending myself in recent years, I quibbled about some aspects of this association. I no longer believe that the semantic distinctions I used in my own defense have much significance alongside the paramount fact that, a dozen years ago when I was a young employee of the War Production Board, I took it on myself to discuss information pertaining to war production with unauthorized persons on various occasions. The fact I knew positively that one of those persons was

a dedicated Communist party member renders rather gratuitous the fine distinc-
tions I once drew on other related matters. . . . My involvement with Communists
that got me into trouble ended a decade ago before the collapse of wartime cooperation. Beginning in 1946 I worked against Communist goals and Russia's
policies. . . . After the wartime alliance with Russia broke down, and after the true
nature of the Communist conspiracy became obvious to everyone, I now believe I
should have regarded my earlier conduct as a bar sinister to further government
responsibilities—to protect public confidence in government if nothing else. The
mere fact that I regarded some of the charges against me as over-zealous did not justify over-zealousness in self-defense. . . . I profoundly regret the things I did which
ultimately brought me to Lewisburg. I feel a compelling obligation to avoid anything that smacks of self-justification. . . . My future will be as noncontroversial as
it is possible for me to make it. . . . By way of restitution I can do no more than
commit myself to live a loyal and useful life—both before and after my release.
Everyone has this obligation, but I should—and will—take it especially seriously.

After completing the forms on April 25, Remington submitted them to the
prison parole office and then met with the board on May 11, 1954. No records
of that conference or the deliberations of its members were retained, but it is
possible to speculate on how they reached their decision. The board would have
studied Remington's application and his exemplary prison record, which should
have weighed in his favor. Working against him were the views and recommendations of the U.S. attorney and Judge Leibell, contained in a report also submitted to the parole board—a biased document filled with serious factual and legal
errors. Although Remington was convicted of perjury, the government considered him a Soviet agent. U.S. attorney J. Edward Lumbard wrote,

> The defendant committed a crime which was in effect espionage. When confront-
> ed with the facts, the defendant did not cooperate in any way in an endeavor to
> uncover others who were engaged in such activities. . . . The defendant committed
> a most serious violation and has never admitted, but always attempted to brazen it
> out with explanations. In view of the serious nature of the crime and fact that the
> defendant has never yet showed any contrition or remorse for the wrongs which he
> committed, I would recommend that parole not be granted in this case.

Appended to the document was Judge Leibell's view. "The trial judge is opposed
to granting any parole in this case." Given these recommendations and the
political risks involved in lenient treatment of a man widely, if incorrectly, perceived to be a Communist spy, it is not surprising that the board voted on June
17, 1954, to deny parole to Remington.[12]

Now, there was nothing to do but wait. In April 1955, he could again apply
for parole; if rejected, he would serve out the rest of his sentence that, with time
off for good behavior, expired on August 6, 1955. "As the saying here goes,"
Remington once joked, "I've got the two best lawyers in the country working to
get my time reduced: Night and Day!" Mostly, he lived for Jane's monthly visits,
when she would also bring either Fred or Lillian or, four times in 1954, his son

Neil. Just as eagerly, he awaited her letters and replied as often as prison regulations allowed. Always, his thoughts turned to the future, when they would be together again. "Only 38 more to go," he wrote her on November 14. " . . . Am counting off the weeks with positive passion." Occasionally Dick Green would write to let him know that all his former lawyers were thinking of him and wondering if he needed anything. "Everything here is comfortable—even cozy," he replied. "It's hard to realize that in less than a year the hospitality I'm now enjoying will be terminated, and I'll have to start earning a living again. It may be difficult to adjust to life on the outside, where there is no wall to keep out the madding crowd, and no one watching through the night to make sure that all of us are safe. But I assure you, I can get used to it again."[13]

◆ ◆ ◆

There was no one watching on the morning of November 22, 1954, when George McCoy, Lewis Cagle, and Robert Parker rushed into his dormitory room; no one watching as Cagle and McCoy struck him with the brick-bat; no one watching when he dragged himself to the stairwell and inched his way down, leaving behind a trail of blood; no one watching, when, at 10:00 A.M., inmate Robert Hoosier found him clinging to the railing, then turned and ran for help.

Hoosier returned a few minutes later with another inmate, and they helped Remington back upstairs and into his room. There was blood everywhere—on the floor, the bed, splattered on the wall. A guard arrived at 10:30 and saw Remington lying on his back, his face and shoulders covered with blood. Leaning over him, he asked if he had been asleep when attacked, and Remington mumbled yes. He also said, "I have not told," a reference perhaps to the recent trouble with the men across the hall. Troy Jacobs, the chief medical technician, came next and, observing that Remington had a serious head injury, ordered the others not to move him. Remington complained of being cold and asked them to close a window, then mumbled something else, gritted his teeth, and began shaking. He was still bleeding from his ear, nose, and mouth and started to vomit. Dr. Leon Witkin, the chief medical officer, entered the room, and the men stepped aside while he quickly examined Remington. Jacobs brought a stretcher over to the bed, and they helped move him onto it. Then he was carried out into the hall and down the stairs to the prison hospital.

Remington was taken immediately into the operating room and prepared for minor surgery. Pushing aside his blood-matted hair, Dr. Witkin noticed five star-shaped lacerations, each about one inch long and several inches deep, in the left temple and parietal region of Remington's skull. These Witkin cleaned and sutured, and he also gave him an injection of penicillin. Twenty minutes later, Remington was moved to a bed in ward C. His bleeding had stopped and he was conscious, but he had difficulty speaking—his words sounded to Witkin like "gibberish." But his vital signs were stable: blood pressure at 11:00 A.M. was 122 over 70, his lungs were clear, and pulse and heart rhythm were normal. There seemed to be no serious neurological problem, except for the aphasia; so, he was taken for X rays, which proved unsatisfactory, Dr. Witkin later noted, because the patient was restless and they did not want to subject him to unnecessary movement. The films were developed by an inmate, under Jacobs's supervision, and they revealed "a linear fracture to the left parietal bone with suspicion of several additional fractures elsewhere."

By noon Remington was back in bed, but he thrashed about and was still unable to communicate. To calm him, Witkin injected two grains of sodium phenobarbital. Later in the afternoon, he was able to drink a little water and consume some warm soup, but he continued moving around trying but failing to speak. At 5:00 P.M., he was examined by Dr. Charles Tomlinson, an elderly general surgeon from nearby Milton, Pennsylvania, who saw no sign of increased cranial pressure and therefore recommended "a policy of watchful waiting."[14]

Seven hours after Remington was rushed to the hospital, his wife was informed of the assault. It was 6:00 P.M. when the telephone rang at the Remington home on Red Maple Drive. Acting warden Fred Wilkinson regretted telling Jane that her husband had been attacked by inmates and was in serious but not critical condition. "It was not a personal attack against Bill," the warden said, " . . . but just the actions of a couple of hoodlums who got all worked up by . . . the publicity about Communists." Bill's skull was possibly fractured, but the hospital staff and local consultants were doing everything they could. He would know more in a few days. Shocked and frightened, Jane immediately called Dick Green and, after describing Wilkinson's report, discussed having Bill moved to a hospital with more sophisticated facilities. Green recommended the medical center at the University of Pennsylvania and told Jane that he would call the chief of neurosurgery. Dr. George Austin persuaded Green that Pennsylvania was where Bill should be—a hospital with skilled physicians and an operating room designed for patients with serious head injuries. Dr. Austin said that if Bill's condition was stable, he should be moved immediately to Philadelphia—it could be done by ambulance at little risk.

A few minutes later, Green discussed his plan with Warden Wilkinson, who rejected it. He thought it was too dangerous to move Remington a hundred seventy-five miles to the University of Pennsylvania; besides, he was receiving good care at Lewisburg—they had brought in two specialists, a surgeon and a radiologist, and had talked with a physician in Philadelphia. Also, he lacked the authority to approve such a transfer.

Who does have the authority? asked Green.

Perhaps James Bennett, the director of the Federal Bureau of Prisons, Wilkinson said, or you might have to appeal directly to the Attorney General.

Green said he would call them both if necessary and hung up. Director Bennett refused to help—the most he would offer was to allow the Remington family to bring in their own physician to examine Bill. "Bennett was quite frank with me," Green recalled later. "He said, 'I understand, but in a case like this, with the political implications, if I said yes, and something happened to Remington, the roof would cave in.'" Green then called the Justice Department and was able to speak with Attorney General Herbert Brownell. He also said no. "We have adequate facilities at Lewisburg," he told Green.

No, they do not, Green insisted, but he could not change Brownell's mind. Next, he called William Chanler, a friend of Brownell's.

Of course, I will call, Chanler said, but he reminded Green that Brownell's chief deputy was William Rogers, former counsel to the Ferguson Committee and one of Remington's oldest enemies. Chanler spoke with the Attorney General later that evening, but he would not budge. Green reported his failure to Dr. Austin, explaining that the warden and the others did not think that Remington would survive the trip.

Ridiculous, Austin fumed. "Transporting him won't make it worse, and it may be the thing which saves him."

Would you consider going to Lewisburg? Green asked.

It would be pointless, the doctor said. Remington needed to be at a hospital that specialized in treating head injuries. If they could get him to the university hospital, he would take over the case. Years later, Green angrily recalled that long evening of heartbreaking telephone calls. "They were all scared to death that if Remington died in transit, the Attorney General would be blamed. Everyone, from Brownell on down, mishandled it."[15]

That night, Remington became progressively worse. At 8:00 P.M., a radiologist from Sunbury, Pennsylvania, examined his X rays and confirmed the presence of a mid-line skull fracture about five inches long, extending posteriorly from the mastoid region back to the temporal and parietal bone. There was also a fracture of the left malar bone and signs of hemorrhage in the sinuses. Remington began running a fever that fluctuated between 100° and 102°. His blood pressure was erratic—at 2:55 A.M., it was 148 over 62; an hour later, it shot up to 171 over 68, then by 8:00 A.M., it had fallen to 144 over 78. He sank into a coma. By the early morning hours of November 23, his pulse had become unsteady and his breathing shallow. When Dr. Witkin and his aide, Dr. Leonard Breslaw, examined him, there were unmistakable signs of neurological distress— both pupils were fixed to light and Remington was partially paralyzed. Dr. Tomlinson was called, and after he had checked Remington, he recommended immediate surgery to relieve intercranial pressure. At 1:10 P.M., the surgeon made an incision six centimeters long and five centimeters wide in Remington's skull, near the line of fracture. Cutting through the dura mater, the membrane that covers the brain, he found a "veritable lake of blood" and the brain itself lacerated and hemorrhaging. Using two penrose drains, he attempted to staunch the bleeding. A transfusion of whole blood was administered as the operation neared completion. The craniotomy lasted seventy-five minutes. "Patient's condition fair," Dr. Tomlinson wrote in his report. He was cautiously hopeful that Remington would survive, primarily because of his age—just three weeks before, he had turned thirty-seven.

Remington lingered in a deep coma for the next seventeen hours. Early on November 24, his blood pressure and pulse rose again, and he experienced difficulty breathing. "Patient emitting low moans," a nurse recorded at 4:30 A.M. At 7:10 A.M., medical technician Jacobs placed an oxygen mask over his face, but his breathing continued to be labored and his fingers were cyanotic. When his breathing stopped, Jacobs gave him a shot of adrenalin, then tried artificial respiration, but it failed to revive him. At 7:38 A.M., Bill Remington died.[16]

The full extent of Remington's injuries became more apparent later that day when county coroner Harry T. Beck ordered Drs. Tomlinson and Witkin to perform an autopsy. Cagle's and McCoy's blows had done frightful (and fatal) damage. There were multiple fractures on the left side of the skull, extending from the front to the base, and the entire left posterior of the brain was severely damaged and filled with blood. All the physicians agreed that Remington died of blows to the head that caused a fractured skull and massive brain damage and hemorrhaging.

On the night of November 24, the body was turned over to Glen Dornsife, a local funeral director, who embalmed and prepared it for travel to a mortuary in Midland, New Jersey, selected by the Remington family. Fearing a public incident, the warden announced the next morning that Remington's body would be moved by train later that night, then arranged for it to be driven in a special hearse that would leave Lewisburg at noon. Accompanying the body was George Dominick, the prison chaplain, who had befriended Bill during his nineteen months at Lewisburg and was the one who had informed Jane on Wednesday morning that her husband was dead.

The funeral took place on Saturday morning, November 26, at St. Elizabeth's Episcopal Church. While six policemen guarded the building (both the undertaker and the church rector had received threatening telephone calls), the Reverend Alexander M. Rodgers conducted a simple, twelve-minute service for the family and about forty friends and neighbors of the Remingtons'. (Missing were Ann Remington and her children as well as Bill's father, who was too weak to attend.) Rodgers quoted from Paul's letter to the Romans, "If God is for us who can be against us?" and led the assembly in singing the hymn "Dear Lord and Father of Mankind," which had been requested by Lillian Remington, who sat with Jane in the first pew. There was no eulogy. Afterwards, police set up a roadblock to prevent cars from following the hearse carrying Remington's casket (which was almost totally devoid of flowers) to North Bergen, the site of the New York–New Jersey crematorium. There, Remington's body was cremated.[17]

Word of the attack on Remington, and his death two days later, catapulted him again into America's newspapers. It was, proclaimed one tabloid, "the killing that shocked the nation." Reporters first rushed to the homes of his wife and parents, seeking comment. "Everything is all over as far as we are concerned," a grief-stricken Lillian Remington told the Associated Press. Her daughter-in-law gave a long interview to the *New York Post*'s Arthur Massolo on the night of Bill's death. "They killed him because they thought he was a Communist," Jane cried. "I know my husband was never a member of the Communist Party. He was a victim of his times. . . . It's a simple person's tragedy. It's the country's tragedy. There is so much fear about, it is frightening. The beating that Bill got could have happened to anyone."

Less willing to talk were the other important people in Remington's life. When asked about the tragedy, Elizabeth Bentley declined to comment. Ann Remington also refused to describe her feelings but did say that she was sorry to hear of his death. Years later, Ann told one writer that she thought that Bill had probably behaved foolishly in prison and had brought the violence on himself. He was "trying to be one of them when he wasn't at all . . . ," she said. "He'd try to be chummy and it didn't work. They knew he was different—a prig." No one sought comment from John Brunini, who no doubt would have been happy to give it. When he learned of Remington's murder, he had felt "saddened, if not regretful. After a night's brooding over my indirect responsibility for his death," he later wrote, "I decided I was being overly sensitive—a perennial fault of mine."[18]

For days, newspapers ran stories about the life and murder of William Remington and their meaning for America. DISHONORED DEATH COMES TO A REBEL, headlined one article in the still unfriendly *New York World-Telegram*. Editorials spoke of "The Shame at Lewisburg." "Apart from the other unfortunate aspects of the murder of William Remington," wrote an editor in the *Washington Post*,

> it will serve as a black mark against the United States in the eyes of critics abroad. Remington was convicted of a serious crime . . . and for that he was being punished. But he deserved a kind of protection which the Government did not give him. His death . . . will be grist for Communist propaganda. . . . "

Others focused on the story's final mystery. Who killed Remington, and why? When the answers were not immediately forthcoming from the Bureau of Prisons or the FBI, journalists wrote about the rumors they heard. Drew Pearson believed that Remington was killed while resisting homosexuals. Some claimed that inmates were incensed over the imminent release of Alger Hiss and searching for a Communist to attack chose Remington. Or Remington was killed for no other reason than that he was presumed to have been both a Communist and a spy. Dick Green gave reporters his version of the killing, based on the letters Remington wrote Jane describing his problems with the inmates living nearby. It was "illogical to say he was beat up by an anti-Communist fanatic," Green said. Remington's death was caused instead by the gangs who ran the prison. Green discussed with Jane the filing of a wrongful-death lawsuit, because of the prison's failure to protect her husband, but she decided against it. Devastated by Bill's death and stung by a "threatening visit" from FBI agents demanding Bill's letters (she said that she would destroy them rather than turn them over), she was "in no condition to withstand further prolonged pressures." She did agree to give James Wechsler five letters Bill wrote, in which he described the petty thefts, the burned mattress, and the rumors of possible violence against him or his roommates. The *New York Post* ran excerpts in a long article illustrating how little the warden knew about life at Lewisburg.

The Bureau of Prisons dismissed the charges and denied the rumors without releasing any information of its own. Director Bennett announced that he was launching a personal inquiry into Remington's murder and promised that his findings would be made public. His report was completed just six weeks later, and while noting the institutional problems that existed—an overcrowded, highly violent population, a small custodial staff guarding twelve hundred inmates, racial and political tensions, and housing arrangements that allowed many young, vicious convicts to roam throughout the prison—it concluded that Warden Wilkinson and other officials were not guilty of negligence or bad judgment. Fred Mullen, the Justice Department aide in charge of public relations, called the secret Bennett report "a whitewash." The FBI also refused to comment about the case, saying only: "We are investigating a murder."[19]

That investigation began a few hours after Remington was attacked on Monday, November 22. When Special Agents George Gamblin and Wayne Hunt arrived at the penitentiary, they were taken to I Dormitory, which had been sealed off by the warden that morning. They examined the stairwell where Remington was first found, then his dormitory room, which, because of its horrific condition, was obviously the scene of the crime. They asked to see Remington, but the doctors reported that he was only semiconscious and should not be disturbed. Instead, they interviewed those who were treating him and talked with other prison officials. Associate warden John C. Taylor knew nothing—he had talked to all the inmates present in the I wing at the time of the attack, he said, but had failed to learn who had attacked Remington. The agents made similar rounds but heard a different story. Remington had been generally well-liked, the convicts reported, except by the men in I-39, who often said that he was a "Communist and that all Communists should get hit on the head." One former roommate of these men said that "Remington was killed because he was a Communist and [because] he was convenient." As a result of this information, McCoy, Cagle, and Parker were moved to tiny cells that inmates called the "hole." Then, one by one, Agents Gamblin and Hunt began to interrogate them in the warden's office.

Robert Parker denied any knowledge of the assault. He neither saw nor heard anything unusual that morning, he claimed; however, the tall, lanky, car thief did admit going into I-32 at about 8:30 A.M. and taking several bathrobes and various commissary items. The agents thought that Parker was probably lying. His quarters were across from Remington's, so it would have been impossible for him not to have been aware of the attack. But they had no proof of this, and after only a twenty-minute interview, Parker was taken back to his cell.

George McCoy told a similar story. After work in the power plant, he returned to I-39 and went straight to bed. Everything was quiet. The first he heard of the trouble was later that morning when Robert Hoosier burst into their room crying that he had found Remington on the stairwell "all messed up."

Anything else? Hunt asked.

No, that was it, McCoy laughed.[20]

It was young Lewis Cagle who was the first to speak of the crime. Pale and frightened, he told the agents that he saw Parker and McCoy (who was carrying a white sock with something heavy inside it) go into Remington's room. Then he heard several thuds, and when they returned, McCoy's sock had blood on it, as did the brick that he pulled from the sock and washed off in the bathroom sink. Then McCoy flushed the sock down the toilet and told Parker to get rid of the brick. The agents had Cagle's statement typed, and he signed it. Telling the "truth" did not make him feel better, however. He now thought he was in terrible danger, because if McCoy and Parker found out he had talked, he would end up like Remington. But he was willing to testify against the two killers and reminded the agents that he was due to be released from Lewisburg on December 6. It was after midnight when they finished with Cagle, but they phoned Norman McCabe, the special agent in charge of the Philadelphia office, who immediately teletyped Cagle's statement to Washington.

There were other promising developments on November 23. At 8:20 A.M., a guard patrolling an area north of I Dormitory came across a large piece of brick and took it to Hunt and Gamblin. Unfortunately, they found no sign of blood on the brick or on the white sock that another officer found at the prison disposal plant a few hours later.

Special Agent McCabe arrived at the prison on November 24, shortly after Remington's death. He conferred with his agents and contacted the Bureau, reporting that they thought Cagle's statement sufficient to take to the U.S. attorney and would do so, if that was headquarter's wish. Later that day, Hoover gave his approval and plans were made to draft a statement announcing the break in the case. McCabe was told precisely what to say to the press, and should there be any questions about the alleged killers' motive or the government's evidence, he was to reply, "No comment." At 2:00 P.M., George McCoy and Robert Parker were formally charged with premeditated murder. No motive for the crime was mentioned. In its haste to solve the case, the FBI was prepared to accept only Cagle's version and charge McCoy and Parker (who never touched Remington) with murder, while one of the actual killers was now an informant whose identity had to be kept secret. It was like the Bentley affair all over again: the person who committed the crime becomes the government's chief witness and escapes punishment.[21]

Faced with the possibility of being sentenced to death for a murder he did not commit, Robert Parker now gave the FBI another account of what had happened on Monday morning. In a two and a half hour interview with the agents on the night of November 24, he described Cagle's and McCoy's beating of Remington but claimed that he had tried to stop them. His statement was drafted, typed, and signed. The agents thought it too self-serving and decided to call Cagle in for another interview shortly before midnight. Confronted with Parker's story, Cagle admitted his involvement in Remington's murder.[22]

News that the FBI's confidential informant was one of the killers reached Washington by teletype at 3:45 A.M., on the morning of November 25. Officials spent the day discussing the filing of charges against Cagle and the preparation of another public statement announcing his apprehension and hinting at the motive that caused the crime. From the beginning, the Bureau and the Justice Department were troubled by what Lou Nichols called the "wild speculative stories . . . and references to Remington as a Communist." The last thing the government wanted was anti-Communism identified as the cause of Remington's death; as Max Lerner noted in the *New York Post*, that motive "might prove embarrassing to a Justice Department that had so implacably pursued Remington. . . . I trust that the wall of silence the FBI has thrown around Remington's death will soon be broken," he wrote. "We have the right to know whether Remington was the victim of men crazed by political hates. . . ." Worse than embarrassing, it might make the government vulnerable to a lawsuit. "Confidentially, I think it is a mistake for anyone in authority to make [anti-Communism] the sole motive of the criminal act," U.S. attorney J. Julius Levy later told the Criminal Division. "If such a thing could be proven, it may be that Communists in the penitentiary are entitled to greater protection than the ordinary care that the law requires under such circumstances, . . . the United States may become liable to the widow or minor children of the victim." In Remington's case, it seemed to him that "there may be some liability and therefore . . . care should be taken in what is said . . . by [those] in authority. . . ." Cagle's confession thus posed both a danger and an opportunity for the FBI. While his statement was filled with evidence of the killers' hatred of Communists, it also provided an acceptable motive—robbery. Rejecting hysterical anti-Communism as the probable cause of the murder, Bureau officials carefully crafted a public statement in which McCabe would state that Remington's death occurred while he was being robbed. Without stating it explicitly, the FBI was subtly suggesting the reason for Remington's death. McCabe was instructed "to use that verbiage," Nichols told Clyde Tolson, " . . . to put a stop to the stories that focused on anti-Communism." The statement was also approved by Justice Department officials.[23]

McCabe's public announcement of Cagle's involvement and the circumstances surrounding the killing, created a heated argument between James Bennett, director of the Federal Bureau of Prisons, and Fred Mullen of the Justice Department. Bennett was convinced that there was a single motive—McCoy's desire to kill a Commie—and he told Mullen that he was upset by McCabe's remarks. Mullen "tied right into Bennett and blasted him," Nichols later wrote Tolson. "He told him that if nothing had been said about the motive, Bennett would be in the position of having to answer for speculative charges, not only made about retaliation against Communists in his own Prison Bureau, but also speculation which has been rampant about prisons being run by various gangs, which . . . could well lead to a congressional inquiry. . . . This shut Bennett up." J. Edgar Hoover also joined the argument by commenting, "If Bennett gave the same amount of energy to his job as he does to whining, such outrages as this would not occur." The government's internal disagreements over why Remington was murdered would continue for months and even affect the prosecution of the three inmates.

The FBI's strategy was successful—public interest in Remington's murder declined. Reporting McCabe's statement, newspapers throughout the country observed that at last the motive had been determined. "Just robbery," declared the *Washington News*, while the United Press stated "that the robbery motive ended speculation that Remington's death may have had a connection with Communism."[24]

Four days after McCabe's announcement, George McCoy finally confessed. For a week, he had held out against intensive interrogation by the FBI and prison authorities, but on November 30, he told the agents everything. Laughing and joking about the attack on Remington, McCoy said that he had been in many fights throughout his life and that his daddy had taught him that when in trouble, he should fight to win. Somebody had told him a few months ago that Remington was "a Communist . . . one of the Big Shots . . . and I hate Communists . . . ," he said. "I would like to line up a bunch of Communists and shoot them down, with a machine gun, just like cutting wheat." This had been no one-sided fight, McCoy also claimed. " . . . When I was in the mess hall eating supper, Remington was sitting at another table facing me, and said to the three inmates sitting at the same table, that if there is a prison riot, McCoy would be the first person that he would kill."

Could McCoy remember the names of the witnesses?

He could not. I "didn't mean to kill Remington," he told the agents; I just wanted "to mess up his head and straighten him out." But he did add that he "hated Remington bad enough to kill him because he had said . . . that he was going to take [his] life." When the agents read him Cagle's and Parker's statements, McCoy said that that was pretty much how it happened, except that he had no idea why Parker had joined them, because they were going to beat Remington and Parker did nothing.

Did Parker try to stop you and Cagle?

No, he did not, McCoy said. (Parker later admitted that contrary to his previous statement, he could not now recall pulling the men off Remington.) McCoy's statement was prepared for signature, but since he could barely write, the warden had to help him sign his name.[25]

On December 5, U.S. attorney J. Julius Levy presented the confessions and other evidence to a grand jury in Scranton. After deliberating less than three hours, the jurors voted a true bill, charging McCoy, Cagle, and Parker with murder on a government reservation, the site of the prison. Indictments were handed up to federal judge Albert L. Watson, and bench warrants were issued for the arrest of the three convicts; since they were already incarcerated, they would be held at Lewisburg. When Watson was informed that Cagle was only seventeen, the judge immediately appointed William Garvey, an ex-FBI agent and a graduate of the University of Pennsylvania Law School, as Cagle's counsel. December 13 was set for arraignment and defense motions. Judge Frederick V. Follmer would preside. (Later, the court also appointed lawyers for the others. Young Scranton attorneys Roger Mattes and Morey Meyers would represent Parker, while older, more experienced lawyers from Williamsport, Charles R. Bidelspacher, Jr., and Charles Szybist, would defend McCoy. William J. Conroy, of Scranton, was assigned to assist Garvey.)

Almost immediately, the six attorneys began a legal battle that would continue over the next six months. The arraignment scheduled for December 13 was postponed because the lawyers needed more time to draft their motions. Judge Follmer then set January 14, 1955, as the date, but it was put off again, as the lawyers argued a series of motions and exchanged angry words with U.S. attorney Levy. They charged that the indictments against the three were too vague and had been illegally procured because they had been voted by a Scranton grand jury rather than one convened in Lewisburg, where the crime had occurred. They asked to inspect the grand jury transcripts, the statements of the accused taken by the FBI, and other prison records. Bills of particulars were demanded, requiring the government to identify who actually struck the blows that killed Remington. (Three men could not have simultaneously clubbed Remington, Charles Bidelspacher argued.) When Levy criticized him, Counsel Bidelspacher snapped, "I don't need to learn the law from you!"

"There is no need for this bickering," Follmer said, but the lawyers disagreed, especially when he denied their motions, one by one. The suspects were finally arraigned on February 3. Each pled not guilty (Bidelspacher attempted also to plead McCoy not guilty by reason of insanity but was overruled by the judge). It was expected that the trial would not begin until June.[26]

While the lawyers fought, their clients were "cracking up." Parker threatened to kill himself and was moved from the hole to even smaller quarters, where he could be more closely watched. Cagle also began to panic, threatening escape and suicide. In March, he tried to hang himself. McCoy was the coolest of the group but was frightened that he would die in the electric chair. For their protection, the warden assigned officers to watch the three around the clock. Each man told anyone who would listen—the warden, the guards, their lawyers—that they would change their pleas to guilty if it meant avoiding a death sentence. U.S. attorney Levy rejected these overtures. He would not promise the defendants anything, the FBI learned, but stated confidentially that he had not yet decided whether to seek the death penalty and might accept a plea of second degree murder.[27]

Formal plea bargaining began in March. Charles Bidelspacher, authorized to speak for all the defendants, met first with Judge Follmer, and they arranged a conference with Levy on March 25 to see what the government might accept. Not murder 2, Levy told him. He was opposed to that plea, and so was the Justice Department. Bidelspacher asked if he could talk with officials in Washington. Levy had no objection, so five days later, Bidelspacher met with Alan Lindsay and Rex A. Collings, Jr., of the Criminal Division. Bidelspacher said that he and his five colleagues believed that it would be in the interest of justice to accept pleas of guilty to second degree murder from all the defendants; that this case did not involve premeditation; and that similar pleas were accepted in other murder cases that had occurred at Lewisburg. Lindsay and Collings rejected Bidelspacher's offer, but it began to look more attractive as time passed.

Although there was little doubt that Cagle and McCoy were responsible for Remington's death, the government found that it had almost no evidence to prove it. The FBI's laboratory found no traces of hair, tissue, or enough blood on the brick to connect it to either Remington or the killers. There was blood on McCoy's handkerchief and on the undershirt worn by Cagle on November 22, but it was insufficient to test. And there were other more serious problems facing the prosecution, Levy told Collings and Lindsay during a meeting in Washington on April 19. First, the government had no witnesses to the crime and would have to rely on the defendants' FBI statements, which Levy did not believe admissible in court. Parker and McCoy did not think that the sock recovered from the disposal plant was the one that held the brick—it was probably lost somewhere in the prison septic system. A brick without blood to type or a fingerprint to identify was also probably worthless, Levy thought. Finally, it was unlikely that a jury would find the defendants guilty of first degree murder, especially when that sentence meant the death penalty. Parker did not participate in the assault and would no doubt be found guilty of manslaughter. Cagle was seventeen at the time of the murder and was apparently dominated by McCoy, who was a moron. A jury might actually feel pity for these awful men.

And most important, there was "no jury appeal," when one inmate killed another, "particularly when the victim is considered by other inmates to be an alleged Communist." In other words, it might be impossible to persuade a jury to convict the men for killing a Communist, an act that some might consider patriotic. Therefore, Levy now recommended that the case "be disposed of by pleas of guilty to second degree murder, providing, of course, the defendants would be willing to enter such pleas." Levy told Lindsay and Collings that he had talked with Judge Follmer, who had agreed that this was the best possible course to follow. Lindsay and Collings were not entirely happy with Levy's proposed deal but instructed him to see whether the three would plead guilty after being assured that they would not receive the death penalty. Both Warden Wilkinson and Director Bennett supported the deal.

So did the defendants. On May 6, Cagle, McCoy, and Parker withdrew their earlier pleas and pled guilty to murder in the second degree. Judge Follmer asked each man if he understood what he was doing, and all said yes. "The ends of justice have been met," U.S. attorney Levy proclaimed. Sentence would be imposed on May 26, 1955. Only one minor newspaper expressed its dissatisfaction with the outcome. "The action of the Department of Justice, in arranging a quick and easy way out of a court trial that undoubtedly would have pin-pointed the glaring weaknesses of its Bureau of Prisons, is not at all unusual," noted an editorial in Pennsylvania's *Sunbury Daily Item*. "The ends of expediency have again been served, but the long-range effect of this deal upon conditions which led to the brutal killing of William Remington is a matter of real concern."[28]

When court opened at 10:38 A.M., on May 26, U.S. attorney Levy began with a review of the case. This was the first time that the government revealed fully its version of what had happened to William Remington on November 22, 1954, but it was not accurate. "The conviction of William Remington for perjury or any other crime had absolutely no connection with the crime," he said. " . . . [T]he mission that morning to Remington's room was not to satiate long-unsettled deadly hate or unfriendliness. It was simply to steal commissary . . . and only to prevent discovery did they so coolly put this man to death."

Follmer then imposed sentence. Ignoring the truth, he declared, "Communism and the notoriety of the victim have no part in this case. . . . It is my firm conviction that what should be done with these three is for the best interests of the government . . . , the public, [and] the defendants." Robert Parker received twenty years; McCoy and Cagle, life sentences. In early June, they were sent to their new homes—Cagle to the federal penitentiary at Leavenworth, Kansas; Parker to the prison at Terre Haute, Indiana; McCoy to Alcatraz in California.

The government had no further statement to make about the death of William Remington. That summer, a young reporter named Anthony Lewis telephoned Bureau of Prisons director Bennett, asking when he would be issuing his report. Bennett kept putting him off and eventually decided not to make the report public. To do so, he feared, might re-open the case. It would certainly have enraged the Remington family and might well have led to a lawsuit. While admitting that certain institutional problems existed at Lewisburg in 1954, the report noted that Remington never complained about the thefts and harassment; nor did Mrs. Remington, who was made aware of the situation through her husband's letters. "[I]f he had been more cooperative, or less naive about those with whom he was associated, and asked for protection, or given voice to his misgivings," Bennett concluded, "he would still be alive." Ignoring the system's culpability in housing Remington next to a group of dangerous inmates, Bennett chose instead to blame Remington for his own death. The report and Remington's prison records were sent to the Bureau of Prison archives in Suitland, Maryland, where they were placed with a special group bearing the classification "Notorious Offenders." The wall of silence the government had erected around Remington's death remained firmly intact.[29]

Epilogue

In Dubious and
Ambiguous Battle

Following the government's cover-up of his murder, Remington's name quickly vanished from the nation's newspapers. Other events soon captured the attention of the press and the public.

But the case did not entirely die. In 1957, a young reporter, Fred J. Cook, then writing for the *New York World-Telegram*, was invited to study the case for *Saga*, a pulp magazine. Cook first sought counsel from the paper's veteran red baiter, Frederick Woltman. "I don't know," Woltman said. "I think you've got a tough one. I'm not sure you'll be able to prove that Remington ever was a Communist, and I'm afraid the best you'll be able to do will be to leave it up in the air. Was he or wasn't he?"[1]

Nevertheless, Cook went ahead with his research—doggedly examining old congressional testimony and trial transcripts and interviewing Remington's lawyers. "That man was NEVER a Communist," John McKim Minton told him. "He was, intellectually, too arrogant and independent. . . . And the end! What a tragic waste of fine talent." Eventually, Cook reached the same conclusion; and his examination of Judge Noonan's and Prosecutor Saypol's behavior and the Bentley–Brunini connection sickened him. " . . . Nothing had prepared me for the high judicial connivance that had sent an innocent man to prison—and as it turned out, to his death." In April 1957, *Saga* published Cook's article, "An Overdose of Curiosity: William Remington's Tragic Search That Ended in Death," amidst advertisements offering cures for hemorrhoids and photos of

Hollywood starlets. Introducing the piece in breathless prose, the editors described Remington as "an animal at bay, stoned with every mistake he had ever made along the road. . . . The case is marked closed, but the lesson it teaches can never be forgotten. Was William Remington a deliberate traitor? Or was he a foolish victim of his own overactive curiosity?"[2]

For *The Nation's* Carey McWilliams, the case was not closed. In December 1957, he devoted an entire issue to Cook's article, now retitled, "The Remington Tragedy: A Study of Injustice." The editors wrote,

> There are some issues that never die until society makes amends for the injustice done. . . . Alger Hiss may yet be vindicated but Remington, whose violent and tragic death . . . was the result of the malice, prejudice and ambitions of cheap political opportunists, is beyond any meaningful vindication. Remington remains as a permanent, an irrevocable burden on the American conscience. . . . [I]t is only fitting that this Christmas issue . . . should be devoted to the proposition that he was cruelly, unjustly, and foully done to death.[3]

Those on the right had also not forgotten Remington. In a vigorous defense of Joe McCarthy published in 1977, Roy Cohn devoted a chapter to the Remington story in which he described him as a Russian spy, "more cunning" than Alger Hiss.[4]

While it certainly was true that Remington was "foully done to death" and that the conduct of the FBI, the Justice Department, a runaway grand jury, and the U.S. Attorney's Office was reprehensible and perhaps illegal, it is just as difficult for this historian to accept fully the portrait of Remington drawn by his partisans as the one sketched by his critics. Clearly, Remington was no political innocent duped by the Communists, and his conviction for perjury seems justified. Yet Remington was no pro-Soviet automaton, no slave to Party or ideology, and not even the FBI, at least privately, was willing to classify him as a Russian spy. Ultimately he remains a mystery—idealist and realist, radical and conservative, rebel and Cold War conformist. "William Remington died as he lived," Max Lerner observed in 1954,

> in dubious and ambiguous battle. He was a man who teetered on the edge of ideas, never a whole-hearted partisan of any cause. . . . He lived a life of bewildering mirror images. But while he was not a man to be admired, he did not deserve the vindictive pursuit he suffered, nor the hatreds he engendered among the unthinking and hysterical. Least of all did he deserve the brick in the sock wielded by two thugs who broke his skull in his prison cell.

"He was the least fortunate of men," journalist Murray Kempton also observed, " . . . the small sinner who paid capital penalties."[5]

Notes

1. Present in the Flesh

1. Memorandum for the Attorney General, January 5, 1955, 8–9, 10–11, 12, Bureau of Prison Records, Department of Justice, Washington, D.C. Hereafter cited as Memorandum for the Attorney General.

2. Ibid., 11.

3. *New York Herald-Tribune*, November 25, 1954, in FBI File Murder of William Walter Remington 70-22845A, FBI Records, Washington, D.C. Hereafter cited as FBI Murder File. . . .

4. Memorandum for the Attorney General, 12; see also ibid., 15–16.

5. "Letters From A Penitentiary" by William Remington, 5, 6, 11, in Remington Papers, Abramson possession. Hereafter cited as "Letters."

6. Memorandum, March 27, 1953, William W. Remington Bureau of Prisons File, Notorious Offenders Group Records, Bureau of Prisons, Suitland, Maryland. Hereafter cited as Remington File—Prison. See also Work Report, April 27, 1954, and G. W. Humphrey to the Director, April 27, 1953, ibid.; E. E. Thompson to the Director, April 17, 1953, 2, ibid.; see also J. V. Bennett to Warden Humphrey, April 22, 1952, ibid.; Alger Hiss to author, November 5, 1985, 1.

7. "Letters," 3.

8. Theodore W. Neumann, Jr., M.D., to Mr. Taylor, August 13, 1954, Remington File—Prison; Memorandum for the Attorney General, 3; William Remington to Jane Remington, November 14, 1953, Richard Green Papers, New York, New York.

9. On McCoy's attack, see FBI Murder File 70-22845-44, 8–9; Mr. Price to Mr. Rosen, December 2, 1954, ibid. 70-22845-27, 2.

10. Presentencing Report, October 9, 1953, 7, Records of the United States District Court for the Eastern District of Kentucky; see also Special Progress Report, September 14, 1956, George McCoy File, Bureau of Prisons, Department of Justice, Washington, D.C. Hereafter

cited as McCoy File—Prison; Presentencing Report, May, 16, 1955, 3, Records of the United States District Court for the Middle District of Pennsylvania; see also FBI Murder File 70-22845-44, 6; William F. Howland, Jr., to John W. Bolick, March 12, 1947, attachment with Presentencing Report, October 9, 1953.

11. Parole Progress Report, August 6, 1954, McCoy File—Prison.

12. Admissions Summary, Lewisburg, ibid.; see also Presentencing Report, October 9, 1953, 7; inmate interview (name redacted), November 25, 1954, FBI Murder File 70-22845-25, 1.

13. On Cagle, see U.S.A. vs. George Junior McCoy, Robert Carl Parker, Lewis Cagle, Jr., May 26, 1955, 29–30, Records, United States District Court for the Middle District of Pennsylvania. Hereafter cited as Transcript of Proceedings—McCoy. *Washington Post* and *Washington Times-Herald*, December 2, 1954, in FBI Murder File 70-22845-61, and ibid. 70-22845-75, 9.

14. Memorandum, November 28, 1954, 3–4, McCoy File—Prison; FBI Murder File 70-22845-44, 13.

15. FBI Murder File 70-22845-44; ibid. 70-22845-49, 2; on Hoosier, see Memorandum for the Attorney General, 5 ; on Parker, see FBI Murder File 70-22845-105, 1–2; 70-22845-109, 1–4; 70-22845-110, 1–2. See also profile in the *Sunbury Daily Item*, Sunbury, Pa., in ibid. 70-22845-A.

16. Notes of Reed Couzart, 7/28/56, 6–7, Office of the Pardon Attorney, Department of Justice, Washington, D.C.; author's interview with Mr. Stephan A. Teller, July 15, 1986. Mr. Teller was an assistant U.S. attorney in 1954 who interviewed Cagle, Parker, and McCoy.

17. McCoy is quoted in Record of Good Time Forfeiture Hearing in the Case of George McCoy, November 29, 1954, 3, McCoy File—Prison; see also Memorandum for the Attorney General, 12.

18. Memorandum for the Attorney General, 5; FBI Murder File 70-22845-75, 12–13; Memorandum Re: Death of William Remington, May 26, 1955, Bureau of Prison Records.

19. William Remington to Jane Remington, November 4, 1954, Green Papers; on Remington's "naivete," see Memorandum for the Attorney General, 18.

20. William Remington to Jane Remington, November 10, 1954, Green Papers.

21. William Remington to Jane Remington, November 14, 1954, ibid.

22. William Remington to Jane Remington, November 18 and 21, 1954, ibid.

23. Inmate Statement, November 25, 1954, FBI Murder File 70-22845-25, 2.

24. For Cagle and McCoy's discussion prior to the attack on Remington, see ibid. 70-22845-25, 21–22; Cagle Statement, November 25, 1954, in ibid., 20; McCoy Statement, date unreadable, ibid. 70-22485-44, 6.

25. Ibid. 70-22845-25, 21–22; Application for Executive Clemency, Lewis Cagle, Jr., March 15, 1963, 3, Office of the Pardon Attorney, Department of Justice, Washington, D.C.; Memorandum for the Attorney General, 6; FBI Murder File 70-22845-44; and Cagle Statement, November 25, 1954, ibid. 70-22485-25.

26. Memorandum for the Attorney General, 7; Interesting Case Write-Up, August 1, 1955, in FBI Murder File 70-22845, 3; Parole Report, 6/17/55 in ibid. 70-22845-117; A. Rosen to L. V. Boardman, 11/30/54, ibid. 70-22845-13; Mr. Price to Mr. Rosen, November 29, 1954, ibid. 70-22845-14, 1–2; Cagle Statement, November 25, 1954, ibid. 70-22845-24, 21; Robert Carl Parker Statement, November 24, 1954, ibid. 70-22845-25, 26–27; Robert Carl Parker Statement, November 25, 1954, ibid. 70-22845-26, 26–30.

27. Parker Statement, November 24, 1954, ibid. 70-22845-25, 27; McCoy Statement, date unreadable, ibid. 70-22845-44, 6.

28. Memorandum for the Attorney General, 7–8; Cagle Statement, November 25, 1954, FBI Murder File 70-22845-24, 21–22; Parker Statement, November 24, 1954, ibid. 70-22845-

25, 27–28; Parker Statement, November 25, 1954, ibid. 70-22845-26, 30; McCoy Statement, date unreadable, ibid. 70-22845-44, 7.

29. Interesting Case Write-Up, 1; Information Concerning Assault and Death of Victim—William Walter Remington, in FBI Murder File 70-22845-25, 12.

30. Fred J. Cook, *Maverick: Fifty Years of Investigative Reporting* (New York, 1984). Hereafter cited as Cook, *Maverick*.

31. *The Arrow*, 1934: "Some Of Us Seniors," unpaginated, received from confidential source, a Ridgewood High School alumnus who wished to remain anonymous.

32. Information on Fred and Lillian Remington came from Remington's second wife: Author's interview with Mrs. Edward Abramson, March 25, 1986, Victoria, British Columbia, Canada. Hereafter cited as Abramson interview. Information about Fred's career at Metropolitan Life came from ibid., and author's interview with Metropolitan's historian, Mr. Daniel May, July 18, 1986, New York, New York. Remington's view of his father is contained in a document provided to me by a confidential source who wished to remain anonymous. For Bill's view of his Uncle Will, see Bill Remington to Dean Lloyd K. Neidlinger, n.d., Special Collections, Dartmouth College, Hanover, New Hampshire.

33. Elizabeth Hunt Starks to author, June 7, 1986.

34. Admissions Summary, Lewisburg Penitentiary, Remington File—Prison.

35. William Remington testimony in United States vs. William Walter Remington, Cr. 132-344, 2369–70, National Archives and Record Center, Bayonne, New Jersey. Hereafter cited as Remington Testimony—First Trial; see also Cook, *Maverick*, 29.

36. Abramson interview; author's interview with Dr. Ann M. Remington, February 6, 1986. Hereafter cited as Ann Remington interview.

37. Author's interview with Mr. Donald H. Hammond, June 21, 1986; Abramson interview.

38. Abramson interview.

39. FBI interview with William A. Martin in FBI Summary Report, 8/27/51, Remington FBI File 101-1185-62, 391, FBI Records, Washington, D.C. Hereafter cited as FBI Summary Report, 1951.

40. Admissions Summary, May 28, 1953, unpaginated, Remington File—Prison. Comments on Remington's childhood were written by his mother as part of the summary.

41. Bill Remington to Bill Martin, June 14, 1930, Remington Papers.

42. Scholastic Records of William Remington, Ridgewood High School, Ridgewood, New Jersey; Bill Remington to Aunt Nan [Smith], July 6, 1932, Remington Papers.

43. Author's interview with Mrs. Elizabeth Hunt Starks, June 15, 1986; Bill Remington to Aunt Nan, November 3, 1933, Remington Papers.

44. Mrs. Albert Hildreth to Mrs. Elizabeth H. Starks, June 20, 1986; Mrs. Starks kindly let me see a portion of this letter describing their trip to Patterson, New Jersey.

45. Ralph Bergstrom to author, June 25, 1986.

46. Former classmates of William Remington who wish to remain anonymous.

47. Thelma Woltman to author, July 12, 1986; Bergstrom to author.

48. Author's interview with Elizabeth M. Trembecki, June 30, 1986; author's interview with Mrs. Margaret M. Conant, June 21, 1986.

49. Author's interview with Newell Gillem, February 12, 1986.

50. Alice W. Martin to George W. Norris, August 14, 1948, 3–4, William Remington File, Civil Service Commission Records, Record Group 146, National Archives, Washington, D.C. Hereafter cited as Remington File—Civil Service Commission.

51. Bergstrom to author; Trembecki interview; Hammond interview; James Coombs to author, July 21, 1986; Bill Remington to Aunt Nan, October 27 and November 3, 1933, Remington Papers.

52. Abramson interview; Ann Remington interview; Trembecki interview.

53. Abramson interview.

54. Author's interview with Col. Robert Davidson, July 10, 1986; Hammond interview; Abramson interview.

55. Bill Remington to Aunt Nan, November 3, 1933, Remington Papers; Trembecki interview.

56. On Remington's application to Dartmouth, see F. C. Remington to Robert O. Conant, January 2, 1934; William Remington to Director of Admissions, n.d.; William Remington to Office of Dean of Admissions, n.d., all in William Remington File, Special Collections, Dartmouth College, Hanover, New Hampshire. Hereafter cited as Remington File—Dartmouth.

57. *The Arrow*, 1934, 41, 58.

2. The New Student—Dartmouth, 1934–1936

1. *The Dartmouth*, December 2, 1954, Special Collections, Dartmouth College, Hanover, New Hampshire.

2. Hugh L. Elsbree to Prof. H. M. Bannerman, February 27, 1939; Malcolm Kier to Prof. H. M. Bannerman, February 25, 1939, both in Remington File—Dartmouth.

3. Eugene S. Waggaman (ed.), "Fiftieth Reunion," 9, unpublished booklet compiled by members of the Class of 1938, John Scotford, Jr., Papers, East Thetford, Vermont.

4. Author's interviews with Richard Sherwin, February 27, 1986, and June 9, 1990, Brattleboro, Vermont; author's interview with W. A. Fuller, June 4, 1990, Ellsworth, Maine; John R. Scotford, Jr., to Louis Highmark, February 24, 1986, 2, Scotford Papers; Affidavit, Richard Sherwin, May 15, 1950, Richard Sherwin Papers, Brattleboro, Vermont.

5. Fuller interview.

6. Remington Testimony—First Trial, 2372–73; Scholastic Record, William W. Remington, Remington File—Dartmouth.

7. Fuller interview.

8. Quoted in John R. Scotford, Jr., to Ellie Noyes, March 17, 1986, Scotford Papers.

9. Author's interview with Budd Schulberg, October 11, 1986, and Ellie Noyes to John R. Scotford, Jr., April 5, 1986, ibid.; Schulberg interview.

10. Author's interview with Donald Miller, June 1, 1990, Chappaqua, New York.

11. Quoted in Ralph Brax, *The First Student Movement: Student Activism in the United States During the 1930s* (Port Washington, 1981), 12–13. Hereafter cited as Brax.

12. Brax, 14.

13. Ibid., 42–43.

14. Quoted in ibid., 13.

15. Miller interviews June 1 and 15, 1990.

16. *Steeplejack*, December 3, 1933, 4, Miller Papers.

17. Brax, 30.

18. Miller interviews; author's interview with Asher Lans, August 12, 1990, New York, New York; Asher Lans to John Scotford, July 2, 1990, Scotford Papers; author's interview with Alan Rader, July 18, 1990, Los Angeles, California.

19. *Steeplejack*, March 8, 1934, 1, Miller Papers; see also issues of February 22, 1934; March 4, 1934; March 8, 1934; and March 26, 1934.

20. Remington Testimony—First Trial, 2374–76; William Remington Testimony in United States of America vs. William Walter Remington, Cr. 136-289, 615, 714–16, National Archives and Records Service, Bayonne, New Jersey. Hereafter cited as Remington Testimony—Second Trial.

21. William Martin to author, February 28, June 15, 1986, 4; John L. Steele to author,

September 25, 1986.

22. Author's interview with Stephen Bradley, March 8, 1986, Hanover, New Hampshire; the conservative is a former Dartmouth classmate of Remington's who wishes to remain anonymous; author's interview with William Bronk, June 6, 1990, Hudson Falls, New York.

23. Bill (Remington) to Dad, October 1935, Remington Papers.

24. Author's interview with Page Smith, February 14, 1986, Santa Cruz, California.

25. Miller interview, June 1, 1990.

26. Rader interview, 1986; Miller interview, June 1, 1990. See also Interview with Donald Miller, October 6, 1950, Joseph L Rauh, Jr., papers, author's possession. Hereafter cited as Rauh Papers.

27. Rader interview, 1990.

28. Quoted in *The Dartmouth*, February 14, 1953, 2; see also Harvey Klehr, *The Heyday of American Communism: The Depression Decade* (New York, 1984), 306. Klehr argues that the YCL "made no pretense of being independent from the Communist party." But this does not seem to be the case with the Dartmouth YCL. While registered with the Boston office, which sometimes sent officials to Hanover, the remoteness of the campus led to a group that can be fairly called independent.

29. A former member of the Dartmouth YCL who wishes to remain anonymous.

30. Miller and Rader interviews, 1990.

31. Interview with Hugh Elsbree, October 2, 1950, Rauh Papers; Interview with Budd Schulberg, October 5, 1950, ibid.; Interview with Nicholas Jacobson, October 15, 1950, 2, ibid.; Interview with Stearns Morse, October 18, 1950, 2, ibid.; Stearns Morse, "Hopkins of Dartmouth," the *American Scholar*, Volume 36, Number 1, 112, Miller Papers; author's interview with Schulberg.

32. According to Nicholas Jacobson, Class of 1934, Davis was a member of the Communist Party who tried to recruit Jacobson in 1937. Whether Remington and the other campus radicals knew of Davis's affiliation is unknown. Interview with Nicholas Jacobson, October 15, 1950, Rauh Papers. For Remington's participation in the study group, see Remington Testimony—First Trial, 2380–82; see also Memorandum of Conversation with Charles Davis, September 22, 1950, Rauh Papers. Information on the second study group was drawn from Prof. Jack J. Preiss to author, April 22, 1986, and author's interview with Preiss, June 22, 1986.

33. Author's interview with William Martin, September 7, 1986, Newark, Delaware; author's interview with Dexter Martin, May 4, 1986.

34. Fuller interview.

35. Author's interview with Page Smith, August 12, 1990.

36. Bill (Remington) to Ma and Aunt Nan, October 1935, Remington Papers.

37. FBI interview with Professor Allan MacDonald, July 13, 1948, in Remington FBI File 121-6159-45, 5. See also Page Smith, *Dissenting Opinions: Select Essays* (San Francisco, 1984), XI.

38. Bronk interview; Gobin Stair to John R. Scotford, May 13, 1986, 1, Scotford Papers; Budd Schulberg, "Looking Back From the 50th," 1, address to 50th reunion of Dartmouth Class of 1937, May 1987, Special Collections, Dartmouth College.

39. William Remington to Committee on Administration, October 15, 1935, 2, Remington File—Dartmouth.

40. Stair to Scotford, May 13, 1986; Lathrop is quoted in John R. Scotford, Jr., to author, May 10, 1986. For examples of Remington's articles, see "New Gallery Exhibit Shows Evolution of Genre Painting" by Bill Remington, *The Dartmouth*, November 12, 1935, 2; "Galleries Exhibit Van Goghs, Spanish-American Collection," ibid., November 26, 1935, 4; "Galleries Open Exhibition of Machine Art Frenzy," ibid., January 7, 1936; and "Local Art

Flows to Galleries," ibid., April 25, 1936, 1, all in Special Collections, Dartmouth College.

41. Quoted in *The Dartmouth*, December 3, 1935, 1, 4, ibid.

42. Ibid., 4.

43. *The Dartmouth*, December 4, 1935, 1; ibid., December 5, 1935, 1; see also ibid., December 6, 1935, 1; and Remington Testimony—First Trial, 2438.

44. Quoted in Budd Schulberg, "Dartmouth Rejects the Academic Mind," *Student Advocate*, April 1936, 13, reprinted in *Student Advocate* (American Student Union), Volumes 1-3, 1936–1938, (New York, 1968); see also *The Dartmouth*, December 9, 1935, 1, 4.

45. "Strike of Vermont Marble Company Workers—Verbatim Report of Public Hearing," Town Hall, West Rutland, Vermont, February 29, 1936, 22–23, Special Collections, Dartmouth College. Hereafter cited as Verbatim Report.

46. Bill (Remington) to Ma–Pa, n.d., probably mid-January 1936, Remington Papers.

47. Verbatim Report, 231.

48. William Remington to Office of the Dean, March 23, 1937, 1, Remington File—Dartmouth; William Remington to Office of the Registrar, September 22, 1936, ibid. See also Remington Testimony—First Trial, 2389–90, 2427–30.

49. Remington Testimony—First Trial, 2389–90, 2427–28; Background of Defendant at Knoxville, Tennessee, 1936–37, TVA File in Remington FBI File 74-1379-50, Sec. 4, 1–4.

50. Remington Testimony—First Trial, 2428–30; William Remington Testimony in U.S. vs. John Doe, Grand Jury Transcripts, 8281–82, author's possession. Hereafter cited as Remington (or other witness) Testimony—Grand Jury.

3. Enfant Terrible—Knoxville, 1936–1937

1. Alvin W. Stokes to Louis J. Russell, May 11, 1950, William Walter Remington—Investigation in Knoxville, Tennessee, May 4–10, 1950, inclusive, 9, attached to Frank S. Tavenner, Jr., to Honorable James McInery, May 18, 1950, Criminal Division Records, 146-200-5723, Department of Justice, Washington, D.C. Hereafter cited as Remington—Investigation Knoxville. Other documents from the Remington Criminal Division file are hereafter cited Remington—Criminal Division. See also Nellie Ogle statement, May 27, 1948, in Remington FBI File 121-1185-50, 10–11; Remington Testimony—Grand Jury, 8283; Bill (Remington) to family, n.d., Remington Papers.

2. Author's interview with Henry Hart, June 29, 1990, Madison, Wisconsin.

3. Bill (Remington) to Ma, Pa, and Aunt Clara, 10/36, Remington Papers; Remington Testimony—First Trial, 2459–61; Hart interview.

4. Remington Testimony—First Trial, 2445; FBI Summary Report, 1951, 479.

5. Bill (Remington) to Ma and Pa, enclosure Joseph L. Rauh, Jr., to James M. McInery, June 6, 1950, Remington—Criminal Division.

6. Burton Jack Zien statement, June 2, 1950, Remington FBI File 121-6159-1047, 7; author's interview with Franklin Folsom, July 6, 1990, Boulder, Colorado; Hart interview; Lucy Thornburg interview in Remington FBI File 121-6159-1047, 14; for more information on Buckles, see ibid. 74-1379-306, Sec. 11, 92–93; author's interview with Mrs. Mable A. Mansfield, July 17, 1990, Atlanta, Georgia. Remington is quoted in Remington—Investigation Knoxville, 7; FBI Summary Report, 1951, 476.

7. Author's interview with Muriel S. Mather, July 15, 1990, Cambridge, Mass.; on Muriel Speare's background and education, see her statements to the following congressional committees: "Investigation of Un-American Propaganda Activities in the United States," July 26, 1940, 899–900, 904, 912 in Exhibit 15, attached to U.S. Congress. 80th Cong., 1st Sess. Joint Committee on Atomic Energy. *Confirmation of Atomic Energy Commissioner and General Manager.* Washington, D.C., 1947. Hereafter cited as Joint Committee Hearing, 1947; her testimony before the latter committee is on 755–58; "FROM INTERVIEW WITH MURIEL

WILLIAMS MATHER" by Selma R. Williams, n.d., Papers of Selma R. Williams, private possession. Hereafter cited "FROM INTERVIEW WITH MURIEL MATHER." See also Selma R. Williams, *Red Listed: Haunted by the Washington Witch Hunt* (Reading, Mass., 1993), 104–24.

8. Mrs. Christine Benson declined to be interviewed about her days at TVA. For biographical information on Mrs. Benson, see "REPORT ON INTERVIEWS BY J. W. MACK WITH CATHERINE BUCKLES EGRI," n.d., 7–8, Rauh Papers; FBI Summary Report, 1951, 434, 437; Remington quote in Remington Testimony—First Trial, 2491.

9. Remington Testimony—Grand Jury, 8263–64; author interviews with Hart and Mather.

10. J. Gordon Reid statement, Remington FBI File 121-6159-50, 4; confidential informant statement in ibid., 5; anonymous informant in ibid. 74-1379-50, 52; Robert M. Howes statement in ibid. 121-6159-797, 4–5. Hereafter cited as Howes statement.

11. Bridgman Testimony—Second Trial, 65–66; Jerome Allen interview in Remington FBI File 121-6159-797, 2; Howes statement, 4; Interview with Horace Bryan, n.d., 7–8, Rauh Papers; Martin Testimony—First Trial, 2239.

12. Paul Crouch, "Broken Chains," chapter 19, p. 19, unpublished manuscript, Paul Crouch Papers, Hoover Institution on War, Revolution and Peace, Stanford, California.

13. John Jessup Howell interview in Remington FBI File 121-6159-958, 272–73.

14. FBI Summary Report, 1951, 494, 533–35; author interview with Hart.

15. Author's interview with Mather; INTERVIEW WITH MRS. MURIEL SPEARE BORAH WILLIAMS, October 6, 1950, 2, Rauh Papers; "FROM INTERVIEW WITH MURIEL MATHER," 3, 4.

16. Benson Testimony—First Trial, 470.

17. Bridgman Testimony, April 29, 1950, in U.S. Congress. House. 81st Cong., 2d Sess. Committee on Un-American Activities. *Hearings Regarding Communism in the U.S. Government—Part I.* Washington, D.C., 1950, 1755. Hereafter cited as Bridgman (or other witness) Testimony—HUAC, 1950; FBI Summary Report, 1951, 416.

18. INTERVIEW WITH MRS. MURIEL SPEARE BORAH WILLIAMS, October 6, 1950, 5–6, Rauh Papers.

19. FBI Summary Report, 1951, 444–45; see also Bertram Affidavit, ibid., 443; Bertram Testimony—First Trial, 3416–53.

20. Bertram Testimony—First Trial, 3429–52.

21. INTERVIEW WITH MRS. MURIEL SPEARE BORAH WILLIAMS, October 6, 1950, 3, Rauh Papers; Bridgman Testimony—HUAC, 1950, 1767.

22. "Report of Knox County Organizer, All Southern Conference Communist Party, September 11–12, 1937," 2, attachment Tavenner to McInery, Remington—Criminal Division. For recent scholarship on the Communist Party in the South, see Robin D. G. Kelly, *Hammer and Hoe: Alabama Communists during the Great Depression* (Chapel Hill, 1990); Kelly, "A New War in Dixie: Communists and the Unemployed in Birmingham, Alabama, 1930–1933," *Labor History* 30, 3 (1989), 367–84; for one Communist's account, see Nell Irvin Painter, *The Narrative of Hosea Hudson* (Cambridge, 1979).

23. Crouch, "Broken Chains," chapter 19, p. 20. The politics of the Popular Front era has produced a lively debate among ex-Communists and historians. See, for example, Theodore Draper, "American Communism Revisited," *The New York Review of Books*, May 9, 1985, 32–37 and "The Popular Front Revisited," ibid., May 30, 1985, 44–50, and "Revisiting American Communism: An Exchange," ibid., August 15, 1985; Maurice Isserman, "Three Generations: Historians View American Communism," *Labor History* 26 (1985). The experience of the tiny TVA unit suggests little Comintern control, a good deal of independence, and little impact on TVA employees or policy.

24. Benson Testimony—First Trial, 492; Benson Testimony—Second Trial, 98, 99.

25. INTERVIEW WITH MRS. MURIEL SPEARE BORAH WILLIAMS, October 6, 1950, 13, Rauh Papers; Remington Testimony—Grand Jury, 8294; Remington—Investigation Knoxville, 6.

26. Remington—Investigation Knoxville, 7, 9; author's interview with Hart.

27. Remington FBI File 121-6159-1047, 21, 22, 30–31; Remine Testimony—Grand Jury, 7935, 7944.

28. Remine Testimony—Grand Jury, 7931–32, 7943; Interview with Godfrey Schmidt by Robert Spivack, June 27, 1950, 3, Rauh Papers. Hereafter cited as Schmidt Interview— Spivack. See also Egan Testimony—Grand Jury, 7598.

29. Remington Testimony—HUAC, 1950, 1807; Remine Testimony—Grand Jury, 7962; Egan Testimony—Grand Jury, 7604.

30. Remington FBI File 121-6159-1047, 31, 32.

31. For Remington's resignation from TVA, see William Remington to Jerome Allen, May 10, 1937, 1–4, in Background of Defendant at Knoxville, Tennessee, 1936–1937, TVA File, in Remington FBI File 74-1379-50, Sec. 4; see also Summary Report, 9/8/50, 3, ibid. 74-1379-306, Sec. 11; Evaluation and Exit Interview, 5–6, in ibid. On the trip to Cookeville, see Remington Testimony—First Trial, 2467-70, 2479.

32. FBI, Knoxville, to Special Agent in Charge, Memphis, 6-15-50, Remington FBI File 121-6159-?; FBI Detroit to Director and SACs NY and Memphis, 6-9-50, ibid. 121-6159-814, Sec. 13; FBI interviews with Frank Pitts, Belle Weaver, and Alvin B. Winfree in FBI Summary Report, 1951, 280–81, 282–83, 284, respectively.

33. FBI interview with Mrs. Charles T. Massey in Remington FBI File 74-1379-663, Sec. 16. For Todd's account see "Transcript of Testimony of Merwin Todd Before NLRB, July 1937," 4–5, in Part VI, "Investigation Concerning Remington's Activities in Knoxville," ibid.

34. Transcript, ibid., 6–10.

35. For Todd and Remington's return to Cookeville, see summary and quotations from *Putnam County Herald* in Remington FBI File 121-6159-1029, 6–7; for Remington's view, see Remington Testimony—First Trial, 2479–80; Remington Testimony—Grand Jury, 8301.

36. Mrs. Lillian Remington Testimony—First Trial, 3060–62; Remington Testimony— Grand Jury, 8269.

37. Remington Testimony—Grand Jury, 2478–79; McConnell Testimony—Grand Jury, 7864–65; McConnell Testimony—First Trial, 586–93; McConnell Testimony—HUAC, 1950, 1703.

38. Remington Testimony—First Trial, 2474, 2475, 2476, 2495, 2774A; see also Remington Testimony—Grand Jury, 8311–16; INTERVIEW WITH MRS. MURIEL SPEARE BORAH WILLIAMS, October 6, 1950, 3, 8, Rauh Papers; McConnell Testimony—Grand Jury, 7866.

39. Remington Testimony—First Trial, 2484; author's interview with Page Smith.

40. Remington Testimony—Grand Jury, 8317.

4. A Square Character—Dartmouth 1937–1938

1. Bill Remington to Mrs. F. F. Smith, n.d., Remington Papers; Bill Remington to John Parke, June 8, 1948, 1–5, Remington File—Civil Service Commission; John V. Kelleher to John Scotford, June 20, 1986, 1, Scotford Papers.

2. Memorandum of Telephone Conversation with Edward Ryan, October 30, 1950, Rauh Papers; Charles G. Bolte to author, September 22, 1986.

3. Scholastic Records—Dartmouth; Eldridge's story is in John R. Scotford, Jr., to author, April 5, 1986.

4. Quoted in *The Dartmouth*, December 4, 1954, 4.

5. Allen MacDonald, October 17, 1950, 1, Rauh Papers; Memorandum on Conversation with William Martin, September 29, 1950, 5, ibid.

6. *The Dartmouth*, January 9, 1936, 1, 2.

7. For information on the establishment of the American Student Union at Dartmouth College, see the following issues of *The Dartmouth*: December 17, 1935, 1; December 18, 1935,

1; January 8, 1936, 1; January 9, 1936, 1; and January 11, 1936, 1, 4; for the ASU's early activities, see *The Dartmouth* for January 14, 1936, 1; January 15, 1936, 1; January 17, 1936, 1; February 21, 1936, 1; February 22, 1936, 1; March 7, 1936, 1; March 11, 1936, 1.

8. *The Dartmouth*, February 27, 1936, 1; March 13, 1936, 1; April 15, 1936, 4; April 16, 1936, 1; "Peace Activities at Dartmouth" by William Remington, n.d., 3, Remington File—Dartmouth. Hereafter cited as Peace Activities. On ASU activities under William Martin, see *The Dartmouth* for October 6, 1936, 1; March 22, 1937, 1, 6; April 10, 1937, 1; April 12, 1937, 1; April 14, 1937, 1; April 16, 1937, 1; May 4, 1937, 3; May 11, 1937, 4.

9. "Disagreements Between William Martin and Myself," by William Remington, n.d., Rauh Papers. Hereafter cited as Disagreements. See also Remington to Parke, June 8, 1948, 2, Remington Papers; Memorandum on Conversation with Charles Davis, September 20, 1950, 2, Rauh Papers; Memorandum of Conversation with Charles Livermore, September 15, 1950, 1, ibid. Hereafter cited as Conversation with Charles Livermore, 1950. Norris's statement is in FBI Summary Report, 1951, 395. For ASU activities in 1937–1938, when Charles Livermore became president, see *The Dartmouth*, October 21, 1937, 3; November 10, 1937, 1; November 17, 1937, 1; December 8, 1937, 6; December 9, 1937, 6; December 14, 1937, 6; January 5, 1938, 1; February 22, 1938, 4; March 10, 1938, 1; March 11, 1938, 1; April 11, 1938, 1; April 15, 1938, 1.

10. Disagreements, 2.

11. Ibid.; Bill (Remington) to Mom and Dad, 2/20/38, Remington Papers; Peace Activities; Bill Remington to Al Dickerson, n.d., 2, 3, and Al Dickerson to Bill Remington, 3/21/38, both in Remington File—Dartmouth.

12. E. M. Hopkins to Rev. Roy B. Chamberlin, November 15, 1937, ibid.

13. Author's interview with Samuel Dix, September 20, 1986; author's interview with Irving Paul, June 7, 1990.

14. Memorandum on Conversation with Arnold Childs, October 30, 1950, 1–2, Rauh Papers; Davis Testimony—First Trial, 2281–82; Davis Testimony—Second Trial, 823; Goodman Testimony—Second Trial, 646–47; see also Memorandum on Conversation with Charles Davis, September 20, 1950, 2, Rauh Papers; Affidavit of William Wolf Goodman, May 12, 1950, 2–3, Remington—Criminal Division; Affidavit of Charles T. Davis, May 25, 1950, 1–2, ibid.; author's interview with William W. Goodman, February 19, 1986; FBI Summary Report, 1951, 402–3 (Davis), 408–9 (Goodman).

15. *The Dartmouth*, May 14, 1938, 2, May 19, 1938, 1; "The ASU and The Dartmouth Liberal Club" by William W. Remington, October 27, 1950, 1–2, Rauh Papers. On White, see FBI, 4/28/50, Remington FBI File 121-6159-441, 1–3; on Childs, see FBI, April 27, 1950, ibid. Childs claimed that the Liberal Club had a membership of between 25 and 30 students and met infrequently.

16. Martin is quoted in J. Moreau Brown III to author, September 15, 1986, 2; on Smith, see Dissenting Opinions, XII; Paul interview; Memorandum on Conversation with William Martin, September 25, 1950, 4, Rauh Papers.

17. Conversation with Charles Livermore, 1950, 4, ibid.; Memorandum on Conversation with Robert Harvey, November 7, 1950, 1, ibid.; Interview with Charles Page Smith, October 6, 1950, 4, ibid.; Memorandum on Conversation with William Martin, 4, ibid.

18. Giles Testimony—First Trial, 1024. For the differences between Remington and Martin, see ibid., 984; FBI Summary Report, 1951, 376.

19. Author's interview with John Parke, August 30, 1990.

20. Conversation with Charles Livermore, 1950, 2–3, Rauh Papers; Memorandum on Conversation with Robert W. Harvey, 2, ibid.; see also Harvey statement to the FBI in Remington FBI File 74-1379-1212, 3.

21. Martin interview in FBI Summary Report, 1951, 391; Disagreements, 3; Remington

Testimony—HUAC, 1950, 192.

22. "New Myths in the Southland" by William Remington, *The Dart*, Vol. 10 (Winter 1938), 19–22, Remington File—Dartmouth. A copy of the essay can also be found in Remington FBI File 121-6159-660, Sec. 10; on the award, see Application For Fellowship, William W. Remington, 2, Remington File—Dartmouth; "If It's Good Enough For Pappy" by William Remington, *Pace*, Vol. 1, No. 1 (October 1938), 17–19, 38–39, ibid.

23. President Ernest M. Hopkins to William Walter Remington, March 21, 1938, Remington File—Dartmouth. See also *The Dartmouth*, March 23, 1938, 1, and editorial on 2. On Hopkins's role in creating the Senior Fellowship program, see Charles E. Widmeyer, *Hopkins of Dartmouth: The Story of Ernest Martin Hopkins and His Presidency of Dartmouth College* (Hanover, 1977), 98–100.

24. Author's interview with Page Smith, 1986; Parke interview.

5. Flirting with Danger—Dartmouth, 1938–1939

1. The senior is quoted in Daniel Lang, "The Days of Suspicion," *The New Yorker*, May 21, 1949, 42. Hereafter cited as Lang; Barstow's notebook references are quoted in his 1948 testimony before the U.S. Senate Investigations Subcommittee reprinted in U.S. Congress. House. 81st Cong., 2d Sess. Committee on Un-American Activities. *Hearings Regarding Communism in the U.S. Government—Part I.* Washington, D.C., 1950. Hereafter cited as Barstow (or other witness) Testimony—Investigations Subcommittee.

2. Barstow Testimony—Investigations Subcommittee, 1895; Robbins W. Barstow, Jr., Statement, June 15, 1950, in FBI Summary Report, 1951, 386.

3. Barstow Testimony—Investigations Subcommittee, 1896, 1900; FBI Summary Report, 1951, 386–87.

4. Barstow Testimony—Investigations Subcommittee, 1900; Barstow Statement, FBI Summary Report, 1951, 388.

5. Kelley Testimony—First Trial, 1429; Kelley Testimony—Second Trial, 891. See also Robb B. Kelley Statement, April 13, 1950, in FBI Summary Report, 1951, 405–6.

6. Elizabeth Bentley, *Out of Bondage: The Story of Elizabeth Bentley* (New York, 1988, paperback edition), 124. Hereafter cited as Bentley, *Bondage.*

7. Ann Remington interview, 2–3, 4–5. For information on her grandfather, Joseph Moos, see Elizabeth Moos FBI File 100-3072683-33, 3, FBI Records, Washington, D.C. Hereafter cited as Moos FBI File. . . . On Raymond Redheffer, see ibid. 100-307268-33, 2, 3; Elizabeth Moos, Security Matter C, December 2, 1963, ibid. 100-307268-104.

8. Ann Remington interview 2, 6; FBI Summary Report, 3/26/56, Moos FBI File 100-307268-33, 2; Report, Elizabeth Moos, Security Matter C, February 12, 1951, 2, ibid.

9. Ann Remington interview, 6–8; FBI Summary Report, February 12, 1951, Moos FBI File 100-307268-33, 2–3; Report, Elizabeth Moos—Hatch Act, 10-25-44, ibid. 100-307268-5, 2.

10. Ann Remington interview 8, 10; FBI Summary Report, 3/26/56, Moos FBI File 100-307268-33, 2, 6–7.

11. Ann Remington interview, 8–10, 11; Moos FBI File 100-307208-108, 45.

12. Ann Remington interview, 13; Result of Recent Interview with Ann Remington, n.d., in William Remington FBI File 74-1379-?, Sec. 15, 6.

13. Ann Remington interview, 14–16.

14. Ibid., 17; Report, 1956, Moos FBI File 100-307268-51, 7; for Ann's political activities at Bennington, see Remington FBI File 74-1379-?, Sec. 5, 42, and Ann Remington Statement, May 26, 1950, quoted in Ann Remington Testimony—Grand Jury, 8496; on Ann attending Party rallies, see Ann Remington Testimony—First Trial, 269–70 and FBI Summary Report, 1951, 35.

15. Ann Remington interview, 16–18; Ann Remington Testimony—Grand Jury, 8497;

Ann Remington Testimony—First Trial, 181–82, 263–68, 270–75, 282; see also FBI Summary Report, 1951, 36.

16. Remington Testimony—First Trial, 2503–5.

17. Ann Remington Testimony—First Trial, 304–7; Ann Remington interview, 24–25. In 1986, Ann commented on Remington's Cookeville story: ". . . a little idiot like him, he would have looked so out of place—to think he could persuade those hardened miners [sic] what was good for them." Ann Remington interview, 25.

18. Ann Remington interview, 26–27, 28; Ann Remington Testimony—Grand Jury, 8533.

19. Ann Remington interview, 27; Ann Remington Testimony—First Trial, 189, 196–200, 276, 282–83, 286, 289, 296–97, 298–303.

20. Ann Remington interview, 27–28; Ann Remington Testimony—First Trial, 289–90.

21. Ibid., 202.

22. Remington Testimony—First Trial, 2506.

23. Ann Remington interview, 28.

24. Bill (Remington) to Mom and Dad, n.d., Remington Papers.

25. Information on the Rhodes Scholarship was obtained by telephone from the Office of the American Secretary, Rhodes Scholarship, Pomona College, Claremont, California, August 3, 1990; John Kelleher to John R. Scotford, June 20, 1986, Scotford Papers.

26. Bill to Mother and Dad, n.d., Remington Papers.

27. Application For Fellowship, William Remington, n.d., Remington File—Dartmouth. For the letters supporting Remington, see Malcolm Kier to Prof. Harold Bannerman, February 25, 1939, ibid.; Russell Larmon to Prof. Harold Bannerman, February 24, 1939, 2, ibid.; Albert I. Dickerson to Harold Bannerman, February 20, 1939, ibid.; L. K. Neidlinger to Prof. Harold M. Bannerman, February 21, 1939, ibid.; George F. Theriault to Prof. Harold Bannerman, February 25, 1939, ibid.; Arthur M. Wilson to Prof. Harold Bannerman, February 21, 1939, ibid.; Joseph McDaniel to Prof. Harold Bannerman, February 21, 1939, ibid.

28. Albert I. Dickerson to William Walter Remington, March 16, 1939, ibid.; William Remington to Albert I. Dickerson, March 20, 1939, ibid.

29. Bill to Mom and Dad and Aunt Nan, n.d., Remington Papers; Ann Remington Testimony—Second Trial, 192–93, 207.

30. *The Dartmouth*, December 4, 1954; for Remington's preparations for the conference, see Remington correspondence with John T. Flynn, February 13, 1939; Alvin Hansen, February 27, 1939; Granville Hicks, February 10, 1939; Leo Huberman, April 12, 1939; John F. Tinsley, March 13, 1939; Hon. Peter Woodbury, February 28 and March 4, 1939—Remington also invited Eleanor Roosevelt, but she was unable to attend: M. C. Thompson to William Remington, February 9, 1939; Arthur M. Wilson to Prof. Harold Bannerman, February 21, 1939—all in Remington File—Dartmouth. For information on the conference, see the following issues of *The Dartmouth*: April 28, 1939, 1, 3; April 30, 1939, 1; May 2, 1939, 1.

31. Bill to Mom and Dad, n.d., Remington Papers.

32. Scholastic Records, Remington File—Dartmouth.

33. Ernest Hopkins to John P. Carlton, Esq., November 2, 1938, ibid.; L. K. Neidlinger to Rhodes Scholarship Committee of New Hampshire, October 19, 1938, ibid.

34. Russell Larmon interview in Remington FBI File 121-6159-45, 5; Theriault and Rosenstock-Hussey are quoted in *The Dartmouth*, December 2, 1954.

35. Author's interview with L. P. Baldwin, October 15, 1986; Philip Thompson to author, October 15, 1986.

36. Author's interview with Samuel Dix, October 12, 1986; Martin R. King to author, n.d., 1986.

37. Author's interview with John Parke, August 30, 1990.

38. Bill to folks, April 1939, Remington Papers; Parke interview.

39. Parke interview; Louis Highmark to John R. Scotford, March 7, 1986, Scotford Papers.

40. Highmark to Scotford, ibid.

41. Confidential source—a former Ridgewood High School classmate of Remington's who wished to remain anonymous.

6. Renegades

1. Bill to Mother and Dad, June 1939, Remington Papers.

2. Bill to Mother and Dad, July 12, 1939, ibid.

3. Supplemental Personal History, Application for Commission on Warrant, U.S. Naval Reserve, 34, Remington File—Civil Service Commission. Hereafter cited as Supplemental Personal History.

4. Diary of Ann Remington, quoted in FBI Summary Report, 1951, 59.

5. Diary, ibid.; for information on Orozoco's years at Dartmouth, see Hill, ed., *The College on the Hill*, 161–63.

6. Bill to Mother and Dad, July 12, 1939, Remington Papers.

7. Supplemental Personal History, 1–2; see also William W. Remington to D. A. Sloan, September 2, 1941, Remington Papers.

8. Bill to Mother and Dad, August 1939, ibid.

9. Remington Testimony—First Trial, 2510, 2511, 2516; Ann Remington Testimony—Grand Jury, 7764.

10. Bill to Mother and Dad and Aunt Nan, April 20, 1939; Bill to family, n.d., Remington Papers.

11. Remington Testimony—First Trial, 2516; Robert M. Haig to George M. Norris, August 15, 1948, 1–2, Remington File—Civil Service Commission.

12. McMahon Testimony—First Trial, 3472–90.

13. Bill and Ann Remington to William Goodman, n.d., in Remington FBI File 74-1379-2232. See also Director, FBI, to Assistant Attorney General William F. Tompkins, June 16, 1955, ibid. 74-1379-2233. For Remington's comment on this message, see Remington Testimony—First Trial, 2513, 2516. The postscript is in Remington's handwriting.

14. McMahon Testimony—First Trial, 3486.

15. Quoted in Report, Regional Loyalty Board, July 9, 1948, 32B, Remington File—Civil Service Commission. Hereafter cited as Report, Regional Loyalty Board; Chamberlin Testimony—First Trial, 3393–94.

16. Quoted in Report, Regional Loyalty Board, 32A.

17. Remington Testimony—First Trial, 2518, 2519, 2522; Ann Remington Testimony—First Trial, 212, 216.

18. On the American Youth Congress, see Walter Goodman, *The Committee: The Extraordinary Career of the House Committee on Un-American Activities* (New York, 1968), 81–85, and Harvey Khler, *The Heyday of American Communism*, 319–23, 468 n.39; FBI Summary Report, 1951, 28; Remington Testimony—First Trial, 2526.

19. Joseph Lash, *Eleanor and Franklin* (New York, 1971), 601–3.

20. Lash, ibid., 604–5; see also Page Smith, *Redeeming the Time* (New York, 1987), 901.

21. United States Civil Service Commission, Investigations Division, Report of Partial Interview and Special Hearing, July 23, 1942, 10–11, Remington File—Civil Service Commission. Hereafter cited as Report of Partial Interview; Report, Regional Loyalty Board, 41–42; Joseph Lash, *Eleanor Roosevelt: A Friend's Memoir* (New York, 1964), 231, 232.

22. REGIONAL LOYALTY BOARD HEARING in the case of WILLIAM WALTER REMINGTON, August 1948, 47, Remington File—Civil Service Commission. Hereafter cited as REGIONAL LOYALTY BOARD HEARING; for Remington's comments about Ann's activities, see Reply to Interrogatory directed to William W. Remington by the Fourth United States Civil Service

Regional office, n.d., 9, Remington File—Civil Service Commission.

23. Ann Remington Testimony—Grand Jury, 7814.

24. On the Redmonts, see FBI Summary Report, 1951, 108–18; Redmont Testimony—First Trial, 1646–47, 1659, 1660–61.

25. The conversations between Joan Redmont and Helen Scott can be found in Report, Nathan G. Silvermaster et al., FBI File 65-56402-1019, Sec. 45, 109–11, and in Silvermaster, ibid. 65-56402-450. In an author's interview with Bernard Redmont on August 14, 1991, he repeated his earlier statements regarding the Remingtons. Redmont discusses his involvement in the Remington case in a brief and superficial chapter in his memoir, *Risks Worth Taking: The Odyssey of a Foreign Correspondent* (Lanham, 1992), 57–66.

26. For information on Joseph North, see Remington FBI File 74-1379-?, Sec. 15; Remington Testimony—First Trial, 2519–20A; North Testimony—Grand Jury, 8035–83; *New York Times*, December 22, 1976; FBI Interview with Ann Remington, May 17, 19, 1950, Remington FBI File 101-1185-33, 15, 16.

27. Remington Testimony—First Trial, 2514, 2519.

28. Ibid., 2523–29; see also Ann Remington's FBI statement quoted in Ann Remington Testimony—Grand Jury, 8500. The letter to the *New Masses*, April 27, 1940, can be found in ibid., 8501–2.

29. Remington Testimony—First Trial, 2529–30; Ann Remington Testimony—First Trial, 219–20; Ann Remington Testimony—Grand Jury, 7755.

30. Ann Remington FBI Statement quoted in Ann Remington Testimony—Grand Jury, 7754, 7757, 7764, 8498, 8504; Ann Remington Testimony—First Trial, 442.

31. Application for Commission on Warrant, U.S. Naval Reserve, 10, Remington File—Civil Service Commission; Remington Testimony—First Trial, 2539; Blaisdell is quoted in United States Civil Service Commission, Investigations Division Report of Investigation and Special Hearing, July 14, 1942, 3, Remington File—Civil Service Commission. Hereafter cited as Report of Civil Service Commission Investigation. See also William W. Remington to Harold Merrill, December 12, 1939, Records of the National Resources Planning Board Control Office, Record Group 187, National Archives, Washington, D.C.

32. Remington Testimony—First Trial, 2531–32, 2540, 2541; Ann Remington FBI Statement quoted in Ann Remington Testimony—Grand Jury, 8503; Report, Regional Loyalty Board, 37A; Memorandum to File, August 21, 1950, Rauh Papers.

33. Ann Remington FBI Statement quoted in Ann Remington Testimony—Grand Jury, 8503, 8504; on the Communist role in the APM, see William L. O'Neill, *A Better World* (New York, 1982), 35–36; Remington Testimony—First Trial, 2543.

34. Bill to Mother and Dad, July 21, 1940, Remington Papers.

35. Jane Herndon Smith Deposition, quoted in First Trial Transcript, 3046–48, 3055–56.

36. Remington Testimony—First Trial, 2531–32.

37. Ibid., 2547; Glazer Statement, 5, Report of Civil Service Commission Investigation.

38. Leon Henderson to Matthew F. McGuire, August 19, 1941, Remington FBI File 101-1185-2; Examiner's Memorandum of Interview, 8/20/41, 1–4, Remington File—Civil Service Commission.

39. Examiner's Memorandum, 4, ibid. For Remington's supplemental statement describing his occupations from 1934–1939, see William W. Remington to D. A. Sloan, September 2, 1941, 1–3, Remington Papers.

40. Investigations Division, January 5, 1942, Remington File—Civil Service Commission; John E. Taylor to Chief, Investigations Division, January 10, 1942, ibid.

41. Associate Chief, Investigations Division to Senior Field Examiner, Civil Service Commission, January 19, 1942, ibid.; William H. McMillan to Vivian Carson, February 12, 1942, ibid.; on the FBI's authorization, see J. Edgar Hoover to Matthew F. McGuire, July 23,

1941, Remington FBI File 101-1185-1; Leon Henderson to Matthew F. McGuire, August 19, 1941, ibid. 101-1185-2; J. Edgar Hoover to Special Agent in Charge, Washington, D.C., February 21, 1942, ibid. 101-1185-3, 1–2; for the informant's report, see Office Investigator's Report, Department of Justice, New York, March 3, 1942, Remington File—Civil Service Commission.

42. Report of D. A. Hruska, April 1, 1942, Remington FBI File, 101-1185-4, 3–5, 6, 7. Hereafter cited as Hruska Report. For Mrs. Montague's complaints, see *Washington Times-Herald*, August 20, 1950, 1, Rauh Papers.

43. Hruska Report, 8, 10–12.

44. Lee W. Jones, "The William Remington Case," Ph.D. diss., City University of New York, 1989, 34.

45. J. Edgar Hoover to Wayne Coy, May 13, 1942, Remington FBI File 101-1185-4; Wayne Coy to J. Edgar Hoover, June 6, 1942, ibid. 101-1185-5.

46. Report of Civil Service Commission Investigation, 4–6, 8–9.

47. United States Civil Service Commission, Investigations Division, Report of Partial Interview and Special Hearing, 1, 2–4, 7, 8, 10–11, Remington File—Civil Service Commission. Hereafter cited as Report of Partial Interview.

48. Ibid., 11; Report of Civil Service Commission Investigation, 9, 10; United States Civil Service Commission to William Walter Remington, August 4, 1942, Remington File—Civil Service Commission.

7. Obliging a Lady

1. REGIONAL LOYALTY BOARD HEARING, 257–58; FBI Summary Report, 1951, 43, 45, 137; author's interview with Bernard S. Redmont; Remington Testimony—First Trial, 1645–46.

2. Author's interview with Franklin Folsom; Ann Remington Testimony—Grand Jury, 7831, 7832; Bentley Testimony—Grand Jury, 7904–5.

3. Bentley, *Bondage*, 64–65; Ann Remington FBI Statement quoted in Ann Remington Testimony—Grand Jury, 7719, 7756–7, 7780, 7883, 8505–6, 8507; Remington Testimony—First Trial, 2562–63, 2565; Remington is quoted in U.S. Congress. Senate. 80th Cong., 2d sess. Investigations Subcommittee of Committee on Expenditures in the Executive Department. *Export Policy and Loyalty*. Washington, D.C., 1948, 196. Hereafter cited as Remington (or other witness) Testimony—Export Policy Hearing, 1948.

4. Remington Testimony—Export Policy Hearing, 1948, 185.

5. Remington Testimony—First Trial, 2568–72; Bentley Testimony—Grand Jury, 7884–85; Bentley, *Bondage*, 124.

6. Bentley Testimony—Grand Jury, 7889; Hearing in the Appeal of MR. WILLIAM WALTER REMINGTON by a panel of the LOYALTY REVIEW BOARD, November 22, 1948, 19–20, 22, Remington File—Civil Service Commission. Hereafter cited as Loyalty Review Board Hearing. Remington Testimony—First Trial, 2576; "Is Congress Doing Its Job?" 4, Exhibit E, Remington File—Civil Service Commission. Ann Remington Testimony—Grand Jury, 7832.

7. Bentley, *Bondage*, 124–25; Ann Remington Testimony—Grand Jury, 7881, 7892, 8506, 8508, 8511–12. Remington Testimony—First Trial, 2577–81, 2583–84, 2586–88, 2632–34. See also Reply to Interrogatory Directed to William Walter Remington by the Fourth U.S. Civil Service Commission Regional Office, 6–7, Exhibit E, Remington File—Civil Service Commission; Bentley Testimony—Grand Jury, 7881, 7892, 7896–97; REGIONAL LOYALTY BOARD HEARING, 107, 110, 111, 118–19; Remington Testimony—Export Policy Hearing, 1948, 233–35.

8. Parole Application, 2, 3, Remington File—Prison.

9. REGIONAL LOYALTY BOARD HEARING, 60–62; Remington Testimony—First Trial, 2637–38; Application for Commission on Warrant, U.S. Naval Reserve, April 10, 1944, 1,

Remington File—Civil Service Commission.

10. Supplementary Personal History, 5.

11. For the views of Remington's classmates, see FBI interviews in Remington FBI Files 74-1379-131, 2; 74-1379-143, 3; 74-1379-312, 1; 74-1379-225, 1–2; 74-1379-256, 3; 74-1379-141, 2; 74-1379-101; 74-1379-235, 6; 74-1379-143; and 74-1379-256, 2; "Spy's 'Source' Gave No Hint of Communist Trend" by Earl Kirmser, n.d., 1948, *Minneapolis Tribune*, Remington File—Civil Service Commission.

12. Remington FBI Files 74-1379-96, 2, 4, and 74-1379-120, 2–3; Remington Testimony—First Trial, 2646; Loyalty Review Board Hearing, 37.

13. Remington Testimony—First Trial, 2639–40; Kirmser, "Spy's 'Source'"; Remington FBI File 74-1379-90, 4; REGIONAL LOYALTY BOARD HEARING, 62, 68–69, 131; Bill to Folks, July 24, 1945, 1–3, Remington Papers.

14. Quoted in Thomas Paterson et al., *American Foreign Policy: A History* (New York, 1977), 409.

15. Remington Testimony—First Trial, 2632. See also Thedore Geiger to Loyalty Board, September 13, 1948, 1, Remington File—Civil Service Commission; Testimony of Sigmund Timberg in REGIONAL LOYALTY BOARD HEARING, 185–86.

16. Ann Remington Testimony—Grand Jury, 7783; Ann Remington FBI Statement quoted in ibid., 8511.

17. Interview in FBI Summary Report, 1951, 67; confidential source; Notes on Ann Remington by Bill Remington, 1, Rauh Papers. Hereafter cited as Notes on Ann Remington.

18. Notes on Ann Remington, 4–5; Remington Testimony—First Trial, 2644; FBI interview with Ann Remington in FBI Summary Report, 1951, 67.

19. Notes on Ann Remington, 1.

20. REGIONAL LOYALTY BOARD HEARING, 117; confidential source; Notes on Ann Remington, 1–2; FBI Summary Report, 1951, 68.

21. Confidential source; Notes on Ann Remington, 3.

22. Abramson interview.

23. Ibid.; Notes on Ann Remington, 3, 7, 8; confidential source.

24. Cornelison Testimony—First Trial, 3246–47.

25. The literature on the Cold War and its impact on American domestic life is voluminous. The best introduction is Richard M. Fried, *Nightmare in Red: The McCarthy Era in Perspective* (New York, 1990).

26. FBI, Washington Field Office to New York Field Office, August 22, 1946, in Nathan G. Silvermaster FBI File 65-56402, Sec. 49, 3–4; Cornelison Testimony—First Trial, 3247.

27. J. D. Donehue to G. C. Callan, December 11, 1945, Silvermaster FBI File 65-56402-306; "Subject List," Silvermaster FBI File (New York Field Office) 65-14603-2998; Bentley testimony in U.S. Congress. House. 80th Cong., 2d sess. Committee on Un-American Activities. *Hearings Regarding Communist Espionage in the U.S. Government.* Washington, D.C., 1948, 717. Hereafter cited as Bentley (or other witness) Testimony—HUAC, 1948; Bentley Testimony—First Trial, 1259.

28. SAC, New Haven to Director, FBI, July 30, 1955, Elizabeth T. Bentley FBI File 134-435-177, 1–2, FBI Records, Washington, D.C. See also Peter F. Gleason to SAC, New York, August 29, 1945, Silvermaster FBI File 65-56402-3414, 1–2.

29. ASAC William G. Simon to SAC, New York, 7/28/55, Bentley FBI File 134-182-101, 1–3; Memo Re: Lieutenant Peter Heller, November 8, 1945, Silvermaster FBI File 65-56402-3466; Memo by Edward W. Buckley, November 13, 1946, Silvermaster FBI File (New York Field Office) 65-14603-40, 1–2.

30. Memorandum Re: Elizabeth T. Bentley et al., November 8, 1945, Silvermaster FBI File (New York Field Office) 65-14603-2; Elizabeth Terrill Bentley Statement, November 8, 1945,

1, unserialized, FBI Records. Hereafter cited as Bentley Statement, November 8, 1945. Richard G. Green to Joseph L. Rauh, Jr., October 28, 1949, 3–4, Green Papers. Hayden Peake, "Afterword" in Bentley, *Bondage*, 222–23.

31. Peake, ibid.; Green to Rauh, 4, Green Papers; Bentley Testimony—HUAC, 1948, 2–3.

32. Author's interview with Dr. Joseph V. Lombardo, 1991.

33. Green to Rauh, October 28, 1949, 2–3, Green Papers.

34. Bentley, *Bondage*, 19.

35. Ibid., 20–62, 66–67; see also Bentley Testimony—Export Policy Hearing, 1948, 4.

36. Bentley, *Bondage*, 68–70; Christopher Andrew and Oleg Gordievsky, *KGB: The Inside Story* (New York, 1990), 282.

37. Anthony Cave Brown and Charles B. MacDonald, *On A Field of Red: The Communist International and the Coming of World War 2* (New York, 1981), 34–341; Bentley, *Bondage*, 77; Elizabeth Terrill Bentley Statement, November 30, 1945, Silvermaster FBI File 65-56402-200, 12. Hereafter cited as Bentley Statement, November 30, 1945. See also Bentley Statement, November 8, 1945, 7.

38. Bentley Statement, November 30, 1945, 12–13, 14; Bentley Statement, November 8, 1945, 7, 8–9. On the FBI's first surveillance of Golos and Bentley in 1941, see Letter to the Director, January 31, 1947, in Silvermaster FBI File 65-56402-1976, 1–4; see also Bentley, *Bondage*, 94–98.

39. Bentley Statement, November 8, 1945, 24; Bentley Statement, November 30, 1945, 25–27.

40. "Subjects List" in Silvermaster FBI File (New York Field Office) 65-14603-2998.

41. Bentley Statement, November 30, 1945, 47–49. Bentley Testimony—Export Policy Hearing, 1948, 29.

42. Bentley Statement, November 30, 1945, 89, 91; Bentley Statement, November 8, 1945, 13; Bentley, *Bondage*, 147.

43. Bentley Statement, November 30, 1945, 50–57; on Hiss, see Teletype, NY to Director and SAC, 11/16/45, Silvermaster FBI File 65-56402-26, 3–4.

44. Bentley Statement, November 8, 1945, 13–16.

45. Ibid., 16–18, 19–20; Bentley, *Bondage*, 175–85; see also "Nathan Gregory Silvermaster," August 10, 1948, Silvermaster FBI File (Washington Field Office) 65-100-17483, Vol. 1, Sub. 1, 66–68. Hereafter cited as Silvermaster, August 10, 1948; Memo Re: Nathan Gregory Silvermaster, November 21, 1945, Silvermaster FBI File (New York Field Office) 65-14603-181, 3.

46. Civil Intelligence Report: Heller, December 28, 1950, 1, Rauh Papers; Civil Intelligence Report: Heller, January 9, 1951, 1–2, ibid.

47. Memo Re: Nathan Gregory Silvermaster, November 24, 1945, Silvermaster FBI File (New York Field Office) 65-14603-181, 3; Silvermaster, August 10, 1948, 67; Bentley Statement, November 8, 1945, 30.

48. Memorandum Re: Elizabeth T. Bentley et al., November 8, 1945, Silvermaster FBI File (New York Field Office) 65-14603-2; Memorandum Re: Elizabeth T. Bentley et al, November 8, 1945, in ibid. 65-14603-9; Memorandum Re: Elizabeth T. Bentley et al., November 8, 1945, in ibid. 65-14603-6.

49. Memorandum Re: Elizabeth T. Bentley et al., November 9, 1945, in ibid. 65-14603-15; David C. Martin, *Wilderness of Mirrors* (New York, 1980), 30; Hoover is quoted in Curt Gentry, *J. Edgar Hoover: The Man and the Secrets* (New York, 1991), 343. For Hoover's view of Bentley and the "Red Menace," see Athan G. Theoharis and John Stuart Cox, *The Boss: J. Edgar Hoover and the Great American Inquisition* (New York, 1990, paperback edition), 257–85, Richard Gid Powers, *Secrecy and Power: The Life of J. Edgar Hoover* (New York, 1987), 275–311. New York to Director and SAC, November 10, 1945, Silvermaster FBI File 65-

56402-13, 1. See also SAC, New York, to Director, November 14, 1945, ibid. 65-56402-20.

50. New York to Director and SAC, November 11, 1945, ibid. 65-56402-14. On "Moscow Gold," see Memo Re: Nathan Gregory Silvermaster, November 21, 1945, Silvermaster FBI File (New York Field Office) 65-14603-181, 2; Memo Re: Nathan Gregory Silvermaster, November 23, 1945, ibid. 65-14603-148; Memo Re: Gregory, August 18, 1948, ibid. 65-14603-3983; Memo Re: Gregory, August 18, 1948, ibid. 65-14603-3984; SAC, New York, to Director, FBI, January 4, 1951, ibid. 65-56402-3875, 1–3; SAC, New York, to Director, FBI, October 24, 1951, ibid. 65-56402-3923X; Director, FBI, to SAC, New York, November 5, 1951, ibid. 65-56402-3923X; SAC, New York, to Director, FBI, November 14, 1951, ibid. 65-56402-3932X; A. H. Belmont to Mr. Ladd, January 15, 1952, ibid. 65-56402-3944; L. H. Martin to A. H. Belmont, July 26, 1955, Elizabeth T. Bentley FBI File 134-435-?.

51. D. M. Ladd to E. A. Tamm, November 21, 1945, Silvermaster FBI File 65-56402-54; D. M. Ladd to E. A. Tamm, November 21, 1945, ibid. 65-56402-46; T. J. Donegan to D. M. Ladd, November 21, 1945, ibid. 65-56402-57, 1–2; Surveillance Log—Anatoli B. Gromov, November 21, 1945, ibid. (New York Field Office) 65-14603-Vol. B1, 1–2. On Gromov, see Silvermaster, August 10, 1948, 65–68.

52. On reactivating Bentley, see Memorandum Re: Gregory Silvermaster, November 16, 1945, Silvermaster FBI File (New York Field Office) 65-14603-56; New York to Director and SAC, 11/20/45, ibid. 65-56402-56, 1–3; K. C. Howe to Mr. Ladd, 11-22-45, ibid. 65-56402-58; Teletype, New York to Director and SAC, 11/30/45, ibid. 65-56402-432; D. M. Ladd to E. A. Tamm, December 3, 1945, ibid. 65-56402-? (number obscured); for Bentley signed statement, see Bentley Statement, November 30, 1945.

53. Silvermaster, August 10, 1948, 7; Robert J. Lamphere and Tom Shachtman, *The FBI–KGB War: A Special Agent's Story* (New York, 1986), 36.

54. Nelson Frank, "Special Assistant Donegan," the *American Mercury*, Vol. 77, 31 (August 1953). See also Memorandum Re: Gregory Silvermaster, November 15, 1945, Silvermaster FBI File (New York Field Office) 65-14603-53; Martin, *Wilderness of Mirrors*, 30; Memorandum Re: Gregory Silvermaster, November 16, 1945, Silvermaster FBI File (New York Field Office) 65-14603-56, 1; Silvermaster, August 10, 1948, 22–23.

55. "Underground Soviet Espionage Organization (NKVD) in Agencies of the United States Government," October 21, 1946, Silvermaster FBI File 65-56402-1862, XX1; Memorandum for the Attorney General, November 17, 1945, ibid. 65-56402-27X; Re: William Walter Remington in Nathan Gregory Silvermaster, 12/18/45, Remington FBI File 65-56402-237; Nathan Gregory Silvermaster, 12-21-45, Silvermaster FBI File 65-56402-262, 1–4; Teletype, Washington Field Office to Director, December 15, 1945, ibid. 65-56402-187, 1–2; "William Walter Remington," March 1–23, 1946, ibid. 65-56402-1019; "William Walter Remington," Nathan Gregory Silvermaster, 2/14/47, Remington FBI File 65-56402-2288; "William Walter Remington," 12/26/45, Silvermaster FBI File 65-56402-1981, 145; "William Walter Remington," 12/26/46, ibid. 65-56402-1980.

56. "William Walter Remington," ibid. 65-56402-1981, 145; "William Walter Remington," 2/14/47, ibid 65-56402-2294, 244.

57. Jones, "The William Remington Case," 73–74; J. C. Strickland to D. M. Ladd, 3/8/47, Silvermaster FBI File 65-56402-2136; E. G. Fitch to D. M. Ladd, 3/20/47, ibid. 65-56402-2282.

58. Re: Nathan Gregory Silvermaster, January 3, 1946, unserialized; E. P. Morgan to H. H. Clegg, 1/14/47, Silvermaster FBI File 65-56402-2077, 1.

59. Morgan to Clegg, ibid., 1–2, 3.

60. Edward A. Tamm to the Director, 1-23-47, ibid. 65-56402-20007, 1–3; Hoover's comment is on 3. For more on Hoover's reluctance to prosecute the Gregory case, see Memorandum for Mr. Tolson, 2/9/47, ibid. 65-56402-2057; Memorandum Re: Gregory, March 1, 1947, ibid. 65-56402-53; Memorandum Re: Gregory, March 7, 1947, ibid. 65-56402-2845.

61. Remington Testimony—Export Policy Hearing, 1948, 205, 207; FBI Summary Report, 1951, 77–79.

62. Cornelison Testimony—First Trial, 3167. See also FBI Summary Report, 1951, 79–80.

63. Cornelison Testimony—First Trial, 3169–70, 3170–73, 3190; FBI Summary Report, 1951, 80–83.

64. Remington Testimony—Export Policy Hearing, 1948, 205; FBI Summary Report, 1951, 83–84.

65. FBI Summary Report, 1951, 84–86.

66. Remington's FBI statement of April 23, 1947 can be found in ibid., 88–92. See also Cornelison Testimony—First Trial, 3176–86.

67. FBI Summary Report, 1951, 96, 97, 98.

68. The President of the United States of America to William Walter Remington, September 3, 1947, Remington—Criminal Division. Remington Testimony—Export Policy Hearing, 1948, 79; Remington Testimony—Grand Jury, 8100, 8074.

69. The Donegan–Remington exchange is discussed in ibid., 8088–89.

70. Remington's testimony before the grand jury in September 1947 is partially quoted in ibid., 8080–81, 8104–5, 8107, 8192–93, 8210–11.

71. William W. Remington to Mr. Donegan, September 28, 1947, quoted in ibid., 8071–73; Thomas Donegan to William W. Remington, October 2, 1947, quoted in ibid., 8073.

72. FBI Summary Report, 1951, 99, 100; William Remington to William Cornelison, April 29, 1948, quoted in Guy Hottel SAC, WFO to Director, FBI, June 1, 1948, Remington FBI File 65-56402-3253, 1.

73. William Remington to William Cornelison, March 16, 1948, quoted in Guy Hottel to Director, FBI, April 8, 1948, in Remington FBI File 65-56402-3249X; FBI Summary Report, 1951, 84, 93, 95, 96, 97, 98.

74. Bentley Testimony—First Trial, 1306–9; Woltman is quoted in Cook, *Maverick*, 27.

75. Memo Re: Gregory, April 5, 1948, Silvermaster FBI File (New York Field Office) 65-14603-3847, 1–2.

76. Memorandum Re: Gregory, March 20, 1948, ibid. 65-14603-3829; Memorandum Re: Gregory, March 31, 1948, ibid. 65-14603-3839; Memorandum Re: Gregory, April 16, 1948, ibid. 65-14603-3866; Memo Re: CP USA, June 11, 1948, ibid. 65-14603-3829. Donegan is quoted in Memorandum Re: Gregory, March 20, 1948, ibid.

77. H. B. Fletcher to D. M. Ladd, May 27, 1948; Charles E. Sawyer to Honorable J. Edgar Hoover, June 15, 1948; James E. Hatcher to the Commission, June 17, 1948; William Walter Remington, n.d., 1–2; Chief, Investigations Division to Executive Secretary, Loyalty Review Board, June 29, 1948; and Charles E. Sawyer to James E. Hatcher, June 21, 1948, all in Remington File—Civil Service Commission; Notification of Personnel Action, Office of International Trade, Department of Commerce, 1, ibid.; William W. Remington to Joseph C. McGanagy, July 28, 1948, 1–2, ibid.; Lang, 38.

78. Memorandum Re: Gregory, July 28, 1948, Silvermaster FBI File (New York Field Office) 65-14603-3939; Memo Re: Gregory, July 29, 1948, ibid. 65-14603-3934; Memorandum, July 23, 1948, ibid. 65-14603-3917; Memo Re: Gregory, July 26, 1948, ibid. 65-14603-3929.

79. Memo Re: Gregory, July 29, 1948, ibid. 65-14603-3934; Memo Re: Gregory, July 29, 1948, ibid. 65-14603-3936.

80. Besides Remington, the other two government employees were Solomon Adler of the Treasury Department and Irving Kaplan, assigned to the U.S. delegation to the United Nations. For Bentley's original charges against Adler, see Bentley Statement, November 30, 1945, 26; for Kaplan, see ibid., 2.

81. William Remington to Rex Anderson, n.d., in Remington FBI File 121-6159-K3, Sec. 14, 1; *New York World-Telegram*, July 21, 1948, 1, Rauh Papers.

82. Quoted in Lang, 38.

83. Elizabeth Bentley Testimony—Export Policy Hearing, 1948, 1–11, 12, 15, 24, 28–30, 31, 32, 38, 44, 45, 46, 47.

8. Fighting Back

1. Quoted in Lang, 39.

2. Ibid.

3. L. B. Nichols to Mr. [Clyde] Tolson, August 12, 1948, in Nathan G, Silvermaster et al., FBI File 65-56402-3478.

4. *Washington Post*, July 31, 1948, 1, 2; quoted in *New York Times*, July 31, 1948, 1; Lang, 40.

5. For Remington's appearance before the Ferguson subcommittee, see Remington Testimony—Export Policy Hearing, 1948, 90, 91, 180, 181, 189, 190, 196, 197, 207, 211, 213, 216, 217, 219, 221, 222, 230, 231, 236, 237, 238, 243, 246.

6. *Washington Post*, August 4, 1948, 1.

7. Lang, 40–42.

8. Ibid., 42; Bill Remington to John Parke, June 8, 1948, 4, Remington File—Civil Service Commission.

9. Remington Testimony—Export Policy Hearing, 1948, 1905.

10. Quoted in ibid., 1900; Barstow—Investigations Subcommittee, 1889, 1903. See also FBI interviews with Barstow on April 17 and June 15, 1950, in FBI Summary Report, 1951, 381–89.

11. Barstow—Investigations Subcommittee, 1894, 1903–4.

12. For the Remington–Barstow exchange, see ibid., 1906, 1909, 1913, 1916–17, 1921, 1922–23.

13. Remington discusses the luncheon with Barstow in REGIONAL LOYALTY BOARD HEARING, 260–61.

14. Lang, 40–42.

15. Albert Dickerson to William W. Remington, August 18, 1948, Remington File—Dartmouth; Lang, 42.

16. Remington to Parke, June 8, 1948, 1–5; Remington interview in "Is Congress Doing Its Job?" 2–3, attachment to Interrogatory in Exhibit E, both in Remington File—Civil Service Commission.

17. See, for example, Ernest M. Hopkins to Leslie H. Wiggins, August 18, 1948, 1, and Ernest M. Hopkins to ?, August 18, 1948, Remington File—Dartmouth; L. K. Neidlinger to William W. Remington, August 16, 1948, ibid.

18. D. O. Decker to George Norris, August 16, 1948; Lynette T. Armstrong to George Norris, August 16, 1948, and Elizabeth Hadley Hunt to George Norris, August 14, 1948, all in Remington File—Civil Service Commission.

19. L. J. Van Mol to William W. Remington, August 16, 1948; and Lee S. Greene to George Norris, August 26, 1948, both in ibid.

20. L. K. Neidlinger to George M. Norris, August 16, 1948, 1–2, ibid. Neidlinger's FBI interview is described in "Report," 11–13, Regional Loyalty Board, Fourth Region Office, July 9, 1948, ibid. Hereafter cited Report—Regional Loyalty Board.

21. Stephan J. Bradley to George M. Norris, August 13, 1948, 1–3, Remington File—Civil Service Commission.

22. See letters from Robert J. Francis to George Norris, August 14, 1948, 1–2; Irving I. Axelrad to George M. Norris, August 16, 1948; and Willard Helburn to George M. Norris, August 14, 1948, all in ibid.

23. Bertram Fox to George Norris, August 16, 1948, 5–6, ibid.; Robert R. Nathan to

George Norris, August 24, 1948, 2–3, ibid.

24. Dwight Chapman to George Norris, September 13, 1948, ibid.; Alicia H. Lehman and Robert S. Lehman to George M. Norris, September 13, 1948, 1–2, ibid.

25. Ralph S. Brown, Jr., *Loyalty and Security: Employment Tests in the United States* (New Haven, 1958), 28. For more information on the operations of the Federal Employee Loyalty Program, see Allan Barth, *The Loyalty of Free Men* (New York, 1952), 99–136; Eleanor Bontecou, *The Federal Loyalty-Security Program* (Ithaca, 1953), passim; John H. Schaar, *Loyalty in America* (Berkeley and Los Angeles, 1957), 130–74; Alan D. Harper, *The Politics of Loyalty: The White House and the Communist Issue* (Westport, 1969), 20–60; David Caute, *The Great Fear: The Anti-Communist Purge Under Truman and Eisenhower* (New York, 1978), 267–94. For the impact of the program on career diplomat John Carter Vincent, see Gary May, *China Scapegoat: The Diplomatic Ordeal of John Carter Vincent* (Washington, D.C., 1979), 167–280; for its impact on Beatrice Braude, see Stanley I. Kutler, *The American Inquisition: Justice and Injustice in the Cold War* (New York, 1982), 33–58.

26. See pp. 47, 50, Report—Regional Loyalty Board; Interrogatory, William Walter Remington, Fourth United States Civil Service Region Office, Washington, D.C., 1, Remington File—Civil Service Commission. Hereafter cited as Interrogatory. See also Joseph C. McGanaghy to William Walter Remington, July 19, 1948, ibid.; William W. Remington to Joseph C. McGanaghy, August 6, 1948, ibid.

27. Interrogatory, 3–12.

28. Reply to Interrogatory directed to William W. Remington by the Fourth United States Civil Service Region Office, 1, 4, ibid. Hereafter cited as Reply to Interrogatory.

29. Ibid., 2.

30. Ibid., 4–7.

31. Ibid., 8–9.

32. Ibid., 7, 9, 10–11.

33. Ibid., 11.

34. Notes on Ann Remington, 1–9.

9. Sorry about Everything

1. Quoted in Lang, 46.

2. For biographical information on Robert Maurer, see *Who Was Who in America with World Notables, 1974–1976* (New York, 1976); on Marion Wade Doyle, see *Who Was Who in America, 1980–1981* (New York, 1982), 96; Russell E. Booker information obtained from Virginia State Bar Association, Richmond, Virginia; on Fred E. Martin, see *Martindale–Hubbell Lawyers' Directory*, Vol. 3 (Summit, N.J., 1960), 2940; on Harry W. Blair, see May, *China Scapegoat*, 244.

3. REGIONAL LOYALTY BOARD HEARING, 3, 21, 23–26, 31–32, 97, 102, 103, 108–19, 135–38, 152–53, 207, 210–11, 218–20, 223–24.

4. Ibid., 203, 231–32; Maurer's comment is in ibid., 25. The examiner's comment is in Case of William Walter Remington, Fourth Region Loyalty Board, 51, Remington File—Civil Service Commission.

5. REGIONAL LOYALTY BOARD HEARING, 253.

6. Ibid., 210, 211, 236, 237, 254.

7. Ibid., 238–39.

8. Ibid., 260–61.

9. Ibid., 267–68; Lang, 48.

10. Lang, 46–48.

11. Notification of Personnel Action, Office of International Trade, Department of Commerce, September 5, 1948, Remington File—Civil Service Commission; Lang, 48.

12. Lang, 48.

13. For biographical information on Joseph L. Rauh, Jr., see Milton Viorst, *Fire in the Streets: America in the 1960s* (New York, 1979), 205, 237; Michael Kernan, "The Fighting Liberal: Joseph L. Rauh, the Voice of a Generation's Conscience," *Washington Post*, October 7, 1979, F1, F14; Rauh, Joseph Louis, Jr., entry in *Current Biography 1965* (New York, 1966), 331–33. For Rauh's obituary see the *Washington Post*, September 5, 1992, A1, A9; Lillian Hellman, *Scoundrel Time* (Boston, 1976), 60.

14. Lang, 48; Attachment, 4, enclosure in Joseph L. Rauh, Jr., to James Allen, July 6, 1949, Rauh Papers.

15. Joseph L. Rauh, Jr., to James Allen, July 21, 1948, 3, ibid.

16. Quoted in William W. Remington vs. Elizabeth T. Bentley et al., 4, Civ. 47-554, United States District Court, Southern District, New York, Green Papers.

17. Rauh is quoted in Jones, "The William Remington Case," 213; William Remington to Elizabeth Bentley, September 23, 1948, Green Papers (a copy is also in the Rauh Papers).

18. D. M. Ladd to Clyde Tolson, October 1, 1948, 1–2, in Silvermaster FBI File 65-56402-3618.

19. William W. Remington to Richard G. Green, October 5, 1948, Rauh Papers; Richard G. Green to Clerk, Appellate Division, Supreme Court, October 6, 1948, Green Papers; Richard G. Green to Joseph L. Rauh, Jr., January 10, 1949, ibid.

20. Harry W. Blair to William Walter Remington, September 22, 1948, Remington File—Civil Service Commission.

21. Case: William Walter Remington, Regional Loyalty Board, Fourth Regional Office, July 9, 1948, 51, ibid.; Decision of Fourth Region Loyalty Board, 6, ibid.

22. Decision, 3, 5.

23. Ibid., 6.

24. William W. Remington to the Loyalty Review Board, September 27, 1948, 1–22, Remington File—Civil Service Commission; see also L. V. Meloy to Robert A. Maurer, September 27, 1948; George M. Norris to Executive Secretary, Loyalty Review Board, September 28, 1948; and Memorandum by L. V. Meloy, September 28, 1948, all in ibid.

25. Remington is quoted in Lang, 40, 48, 49, 51, 52.

26. Richard G. Green to Joseph L. Rauh, Jr., October 7, 1948, Green Papers; Joseph L. Rauh, Jr., to Richard G. Green, October 7, 1948, Rauh Papers; Joseph L. Rauh, Jr., to Richard G. Green, October 8, 1948, Green Papers; Diary Entry, 10/12/48, ibid.; Richard G. Green to Joseph L. Rauh, Jr., October 13, 1948, Rauh Papers; Richard G. Green to Joseph L. Rauh, Jr., October 28, 1948, 1–2, Green Papers; Affidavit of Joseph L. Rauh, Jr., November 2, 1948, 1–2, Rauh Papers; Affidavit of Richard G. Green, November 8, 1948, 1–3, Green Papers; Joseph L. Rauh, Jr., to Bethuel M. Webster, October 27, 1948, Rauh Papers (copy also in Green Papers); Seth W. Richardson to George W. Alger, October 29, 1948, Remington File—Civil Service Commission; Seth W. Richardson to Harry W. Colmery, October 29, 1948, ibid.

27. Rauh is quoted in Attachment, 5, Rauh to Allen, July 9, 1948; Joseph L. Rauh, Jr., to William C. Chanler, March 25, 1952, 2, Rauh Papers; on Webster, see obituary in *New York Times*, April 2, 1989, 30, and Lang, 53.

28. Elizabeth T. Bentley to Seth W. Richardson, November 10, 1948, 1–2, Remington File—Civil Service Commission.

29. Deposition of Richard G. Green, 1–3, William W. Remington vs. Elizabeth T. Bentley et al., Civ. 47-554, Green Papers; headlines quoted are from the *Daily News*, November 13, 1948; *New York Post*, November 12, 1948; *New York Times*, November 13, 1948, respectively, all in Green Papers.

30. *New York World-Telegram*, November 16, 1948; see also *New York Daily Mirror*, November 16, 1948, both in ibid.

31. For biographical information on Seth W. Richardson, see *Who Was Who in America, 1951–1960* (New York, 1961), 726; on Alger, see *Who Was Who in America with World Notables, 1961–1968* (New York, 1969), 21; on Colmery, see the *New York Times Biographical Service* (New York, 1979), 1025.

32. Loyalty Review Board Hearing, 9–17.

33. Ibid., 17–24, 27–34, 38–39, 43–44, 45–49, 56–57, 60, 64, 67–69.

34. Lang, 52, 54.

35. *New York Post*, November 22, 1948, F4; for Ferguson's views, see memo, n.d., Elizabeth T. Bentley FBI File 134-435-9. The story of Rogers's role as mediator is found in Richard G. Green to Joseph L. Rauh, Jr., November 30, 1948, 1, Green Papers; see also Diary Entry, 11/30, ibid.

36. Seth W. Richardson to Joseph L. Rauh, Jr., December 1, 1948, Remington File—Civil Service Commission.

37. Richardson to Rauh, ibid.; Joseph L. Rauh, Jr., to Bethuel M. Webster, December 1, 1948, Rauh Papers (copy also in Green Papers); for the draft, see draft letter, Bethuel M. Webster to Seth W. Richardson, 12/1/48, Green Papers; Joseph L. Rauh, Jr., to Seth W. Richardson, December 3, 1948, Remington File—Civil Service Commission. This letter contains none of the objections stated in Rauh's draft of 12/1/48.

38. Telegram, R. E. Desvernine to L. V. Meloy, December 13, 1948, ibid.; Seth W. Richardson to George W. Alger, December 6, 1948, ibid.; Seth W. Richardson to Harry W. Colmery, December 6, 1948, ibid.; L. V. Meloy to R. E. Desvernine, December 7, 1948, ibid.

39. Diary Entry, 12/15, Green Papers; Richard G. Green to Joseph L. Rauh, Jr., December 15, 1948, 1–2, ibid. For the picture of Bentley and her cat, see *New York World-Telegram*, December 6, 1948, ibid.

40. Diary Entry, 12/29, Green Papers; see also *New York Star*, December 30, 1948, 1, 8, ibid.; *New York Herald-Tribune*, December 30, 1948, ibid.; Bentley is quoted in the *New York Post*, November 22, 1948, ibid.; Richard G. Green Statement, December 29, 1948, ibid.

41. R. E. Desvernine to Seth W. Richardson, January 3, 1949, Remington File—Civil Service Commission; Richard G. Green to Joseph L. Rauh, Jr., January 6, 1949, Green Papers; Richardson is quoted in *New York Herald-Tribune*, February 11, 1949, Green Papers; Attachment, 4–5, Rauh to Allen, July 6, 1949, Rauh Papers; Richardson is also quoted in draft letter Bethuel M. Webster to Seth W. Richardson, February 3, 1949, 5–6, Rauh Papers.

42. *New York Post*, January 10, 1949, Green Papers; *New York Post*, "Later Edition," January 10, 1949, 1, ibid.; Joseph L. Rauh, Jr., to Bethuel M. Webster, January 10, 1949, ibid.

43. George W. Alger to Seth W. Richardson, January 17, 1949, Remington File—Civil Service Commission; Seth W. Richardson to George W. Alger, January 25, 1949, ibid.

44. SAC, NY, to Director, January 20, 1949, Elizabeth T. Bentley FBI File 134-435-9; Hoover's opinion is scrawled in the margin of the memo.

45. George W. Alger to Seth W. Richardson, December 1, 1948, Remington File—Civil Service Commission (Alger's Memorandum is attached; "Memorandum in Remington Matter," 1). Hereafter cited as Alger. Seth W. Richardson, December 13, 1948, Remington File—Civil Service Commission. Hereafter cited as Richardson. For Richardson's comment about Bentley being tried "in absentia," see Loyalty Review Board Hearing, 10; on fairness to Remington, see Eighth Meeting of the Loyalty Review Board, U.S. Civil Service Commission, March 15–16, 1949, 17–18, Office of Personnel Management (OPM) Records, Washington, D.C.; on Richardson and congressional committees, see Seventh Meeting of the Loyalty Review Board, U.S. Civil Service Commission, September 30, 1948, 81–82, 91, and for LaRoe's comment, 82, OPM Records. Hereafter cited as Seventh Meeting.

46. Harry W. Colmery, Memorandum—In Re: William W. Remington, 1, 4, Remington File—Civil Service Commission. Hereafter cited as Colmery. See also Richardson, 1; Alger, 1.

47. Richardson tells this story in Seventh Meeting, 96–97, and in an interview in the *Washington "Evening" Star*, June 18, 1950, in Remington—Criminal Division.

48. Alger, 2, 3; Richardson, 2; Colmery, 3.

49. Alger, 4.

50. Richardson, 2; Memorandum of Decision, Loyalty Review Board, January 27, 1949, Remington File—Civil Service Commission; see also Seth W. Richardson to Bethuel M. Webster, February 9, 1949, ibid., Seth W. Richardson to William W. Remington, February 9, 1949, ibid., Seth W. Richardson to Joseph L. Rauh, Jr., February 9, 1949, ibid.

51. Lang, 55–56. Rauh is quoted in the *New York Sunday Star*, February 13, 1949; the *New York Daily News*, February 11, 1949; and the *New York Sun*, February 11, 1949; Remington is quoted in the *New York Times*, February 11, 1949; and the *New York Herald-Tribune*, all in Green Papers.

10. A Marked Man

1. Lang, 56, 57.

2. The senators are quoted in *New York Sun*, February 11, 1949; and *New York Times*, February 11, 1949, both in Green Papers; Bentley is quoted in Memo to Jimmy Wechsler, n.d., Rauh Papers. See also *New York Herald-Tribune*, February 17, 1949, and *New York Post*, February 10, 1949, both in Green Papers.

3. Attachment, 1, enclosure in Joseph L. Rauh, Jr., to James Allen, July 6, 1949, Rauh Papers; see also *New York Sun*, February 11, 1949, Green Papers.

4. REGIONAL LOYALTY BOARD HEARING, 39; Remington Testimony—Export Policy Hearing, 1948, 106; Richardson, 2; Colmery, 5.

5. U.S. Congress. Senate. 81st Cong., 1st Sess. Committee on Interstate and Foreign Commerce. *Nomination of Thomas C. Blaisdell to be Assistant Secretary of Commerce.* Washington, D.C., 1949, 17, 18, 23, 24, 26, 27, 30 31. Hereafter cited as Blaisdell hearing.

6. Joseph L. Rauh, Jr., to Richard G. Green, April 14, 1949, Green Papers; the *New York Sun*, March 22, 1949, ibid.; the *Washington "Evening" Star*, March 23, 1949, B-7, ibid.; the *Washington Post*, March 23, 1949, 7, ibid.

7. Quoted in Lang, 56.

8. Richard G. Green to A. J. Liebling, March 8, 1949, Green Papers; Richard G. Green to Joseph L. Rauh, Jr., March 8, 1949, ibid.; Joseph L. Rauh, Jr., to Richard G. Green, March 11, 1949, 2, Rauh Papers; Richard G. Green to Joseph L. Rauh, Jr., March 11, 1949, 3, Green Papers.

9. Lang, 37; Richard G. Green to Joseph L. Rauh, Jr., April 15, 1949, 2, Green Papers; Richard G. Green to Joseph L. Rauh, Jr., April 26, 1949, Rauh Papers; Joseph L. Rauh, Jr., to Richard G. Green, April 29, 1949, ibid; see also Remington Testimony—Grand Jury, 8227.

10. William Remington to Daniel Lang, May 19, 1949, Daniel Lang Papers, Muger Memorial Library, Boston University, Boston, Mass.; Joseph L. Rauh, Jr., to Daniel Lang, May 21, 1949, ibid.; Lang, 43.

11. Lang, 37. Rauh also thought Remington was "at the head of the Dartmouth class": see Blaisdell hearing, 32. See also Joseph L. Rauh, Jr., to James Allen, July 21, 1949, 2, for Rauh's statement that Remington was "the top fellow in his class. . . ." Fred J. Cook's *Maverick* also describes Remington as "top man in his graduating class," 30.

12. For Remington's inaccurate description of Bentley, see Lang, 40; he similarly called his contentious exchange with Barstow laughable—see Lang, 42.

13. Remington to Lang, Lang Papers; Rauh to Lang, ibid.

14. Walter Lippmann to Daniel Lang, May 24, 1949, ibid.; Eric Sevareid to Daniel Lang, May 27, 1949, ibid.

15. Louis Baily to the Editor, May 27, 1949, ibid.; Joseph G. Master to *The New Yorker*,

June 9, 1949, ibid.; for other comments, see also Edward Koenig to Dear Sirs, May 22, 1949, ibid.; Dr. Arthur M. Masters to Daniel Lang, June 1, 1949, ibid.

16. Ingo Preminger to Daniel Lang, June 6, 1949, ibid.; Helen Strauss to Daniel Lang, May 24, 1949, ibid.; Philip Dunne to Daniel Lang, June 21, 1949, ibid.; Daniel Lang to Joseph L. Rauh, Jr., October 28, 1949, Rauh Papers. Joe Rauh also explored the idea of a film with writer James Allen. For "Remington—The Movie," see Joseph L. Rauh, Jr., to James Allen, May 26, 1949, Rauh Papers; James Allen to Joseph L. Rauh, Jr., June 2, 1949, ibid.; James Allen to Joseph L. Rauh, Jr., June 8, 1949, ibid.; Joseph L. Rauh, Jr., to James Allen, June 10, 1949, ibid.; James Allen to Joseph L. Rauh, Jr., June 28, 1949, 1–2, ibid.; Joseph L. Rauh, Jr., to James Allen, July 6, 1949, ibid.; James Allen to Joseph L. Rauh, Jr., July 18, 1949, ibid.; Joseph L. Rauh, Jr., to James Allen, July 21, 1949, 3, ibid.; James Allen to Joseph L. Rauh, Jr., July 28, 1949, ibid.; Joseph L. Rauh, Jr., to James Allen, August 2, 1949, ibid.; William Remington to Madeline Brennan, September 2, 1949, ibid.; Joseph L. Rauh, Jr., to James Allen, September 3, 1949, ibid.; James Allen to Joseph L. Rauh, Jr., September 11, 1949, ibid.; William Remington to Madeline Brennan, September 17, 1949, ibid.; Madeline Brennan to William Remington, September 22, 1949, ibid.; Joseph L. Rauh, Jr., to James Allen, September 23, 1949, ibid.; James Allen to Joseph L. Rauh, Jr., November 3, 1949, ibid. For a discussion of the "Red Scare" in Hollywood, see Larry Ceplair and Steven Englund, *The Inquisition in Hollywood: Politics in the Film Community, 1930–1960* (New York, 1980) and Victor Navasky, *Naming Names* (New York, 1980).

17. For discussions of the case, see *New York Daily News*, March 23, 1949; and *The Billboard*, December 17, 1949, 9, both in Green Papers. See also Reply Memorandum in Support of Motion to Dismiss Complaint, Walter R. Barry and Alexis Coudert, Counsel, 1–12, William R. Remington vs. Elizabeth T. Bentley et al., Green Papers.

18. Plaintiff's Memorandum in Opposition to Defendant's Motion to Dismiss the Complaint for Failure to State a Claim on Which Relief May Be Granted, Richard G. Green, Attorney for the Plaintiff, 6–7, William R. Remington vs. Elizabeth T. Bentley et al., Civ. 47-554, District Court of the United States for the Southern District of New York, Green Papers; Joseph L. Rauh, Jr., to Richard G. Green, November 29, 1948, 1–2, ibid.; see also Plaintiff's Memorandum, 10–11, ibid.

19. Plaintiff's Memorandum, 22–27, ibid.; quotation from 24, 26; see also Plaintiff's Further Memorandum in Opposition to Motion to Dismiss Complaint, 1–12, and Richard G. Green, Attorney for the Plaintiff, William W. Remington vs. Elizabeth T. Bentley et al., Civ. 47-554, both in ibid.

20. Richard G. Green to Joseph L. Rauh, Jr., March 11, 1949, ibid.; Richard G. Green to Joseph L. Rauh, Jr., June 14, 1949, ibid.; Joseph L. Rauh, Jr., to Richard G. Green, November 18, 1949, ibid.

21. Richard G. Green to Joseph L. Rauh, Jr., June 9, 1949, 1–2, ibid.

22. Richard G. Green to Joseph L. Rauh, Jr., October 28, 1949, 2–3, ibid.; for Miller's statement, see Miller Testimony—HUAC, 1948, 785; for Lee's view of Bentley, see Lee Testimony—HUAC, 1948, 721, 737; see also Joseph L. Rauh, Jr., to Richard G. Green, October 26, 1949, Rauh Papers; and Memorandum of Conversation with Dr. Lombardo, October 6, 1950, 1–4, ibid.; Rauh to Green, October 26, 1949, ibid.

23. Examination of Elizabeth T. Bentley, William W. Remington vs. Elizabeth T. Bentley et al., Civ. 47-554, 2–6, 18, 19, 30–45, Green Papers.

24. Joseph L. Rauh, Jr., to James Allen, September 23, 1949, Rauh Papers.

25. Joseph L. Rauh, Jr., to Richard G. Green, June 9, 1949, Green Papers; Richard G. Green to Joseph L. Rauh, Jr., June 11, 1949, ibid.

26. Confidential source.

27. Notes on Ann Remington, 5, 6.

28. Ibid., 7, 8; Jane Abramson to author, November 28, 1985.

29. Notes on Ann Remington, 6; Memorandum on Conversation with Carl Berueffy, October 16, 1950, 2, Rauh Papers. Interview with Carl Berueffy by George Eddy, March 1, 1957, 1. I am grateful to Mr. Eddy for making his notes of this conversation available to me. See also Memorandum, 2, Rauh Papers.

30. Bill of Complaint, Ann Moos Remington vs. William Walter Remington, #7454, June 4, 1949, 1–2, Circuit Court Records, Fairfax County, Virginia. Hereafter cited as Bill of Complaint.

31. Confidential source; for the notary public's certification of Ann Remington's statements, see Bill of Complaint, 2–3.

32. "Agreement," June 27, 1949, 1–2, Circuit Court Records, Fairfax County, Virginia; William Remington to confidential source, July 8, 1949; Remington Testimony—Grand Jury, 8007; "Final Decree," 3, Ann Moos Remington vs. William Walter Remington, #7454, Circuit Court Records, Fairfax County, Virginia.

33. Joseph L. Rauh, Jr., to Richard G. Green, December 5, 1949, Rauh Papers; William W. Remington vs. Elizabeth T. Bentley, National Broadcasting Company, Inc., and General Foods Corporation, Civ. 4-554, Conger, D. J., United States District Court Southern District of New York, December 7, 1949, 1–16, Green Papers; Conger is quoted in ibid., 13–14; Green is quoted in Richard G. Green to Mrs. Ogden Reid, December 15, 1949, ibid.; see also Richard G. Green to Joseph L. Rauh, Jr., December 12, 1949, ibid. For Rauh's view of the Conger opinion, see Joseph L. Rauh, Jr., to James Allen, December 12, 1949, Rauh Papers.

34. Green Statement, December 8, 1949, ibid. See also *New York Post*, December 8, 1949, *New York World-Telegram*, December 8, 1949, *New York Herald-Tribune*, December 8, 1949, and *New York Times*, December 8, 1949, all in ibid.; see also Joseph L. Rauh, Jr., to Richard G. Green, December 13, 1949, ibid.; Richard G. Green to Joseph L. Rauh, Jr., December 16, 1949, Green Papers.

35. Patton's letter is quoted in Joseph Egan Testimony—Grand Jury, 7585; ibid., 7586, 7594–7601, 7604–5; on Remine's age and health, see Remine Testimony—Grand Jury, 7935.

36. Egan Testimony—Grand Jury, 7590–91, 7602, 7603, 7605–8.

37. Schmidt interview—Spivack; see also Egan Testimony—Grand Jury, 7615–21; see also Godfrey P. Schmidt to Elizabeth Bentley, May 5, 1950, quoted in Bentley Testimony—HUAC, 1950, 1851–52.

38. Diary Entry, February 7, 1950, Green Papers; Richard G. Green to Joseph L. Rauh, Jr., February 9, 1950, 1, ibid; Joseph L. Rauh, Jr., to Richard G. Green, February 10, 1950, Rauh Papers; Richard G. Green to Walter R. Barry, February 21, 1950, Green Papers.

39. For the announcement and Spivack's reaction see *New York Herald-Tribune*, March 1, 1950; *New York World-Telegram*, March 1, 1950; *New York Sun*, March 1, 1950; *New York Daily News*, March 1, 1950; and *Washington "Evening" Star*, March 1, 1950, all in Remington FBI File 101-1165-Sub A. The precise shares were Green, $2,094.61; Rauh, $3,404.39; Remington, $3,500. For Remington's reaction to the settlement, see Remington Testimony—Grand Jury, 8108, 8109, 8222, 8223–25. The quote is on 8225. See also Green to Rauh, February 23, 1949 and Statement of Account, Remington vs. Bentley, February 23, 1950, Green Papers.

40. Memorandum Re: Gregory, February 24, 1950, Silvermaster FBI File (New York Field Office) 65-14603-4270; Memo Re: Gregory, February 25, 1950, ibid. 65-14603-4269; Memorandum Re: Gregory, March 6, 1950, ibid. 65-14603-4275, 1–2. "Gregory" was Bentley's FBI code name; see also "Elizabeth Bentley," October 18, 1950, Rauh Papers. This information about Bentley was obtained by Washington attorney Thomas G. Corcoran; Teletype, NY to Wash. and Dir., February 28, 1950, Elizabeth Bentley FBI File 134-435-16; see also D. M. Ladd to the Director, February 28, 1950, ibid. 134-435-17.

41. Richard G. Green to Joseph L. Rauh, Jr., October, 25, 1949, Green Papers; Joseph L.

Rauh, Jr., to Richard G. Green, October 26, 1950, 2, ibid.

42. William S. Odlin, "Remington Gets New 'Non Sensitive' Job," in *Washington Times-Herald*, March 20, 1950, Remington FBI File 101-1165-Sub A.

11. No Peace

1. H. B. Fletcher to D. M. Ladd, February 6, 1950, William Remington FBI File 101-1185-25X, 1–2. See also Director, FBI, to SAC, Washington Field, February 11, 1950, ibid. 74-1379-?, Sec. 13; Lang, 57.

2. Guy Hottel, SAC, Washington Field, to Director, FBI, March 20, 1950, Remington FBI File 101-1135-31, 3; Guy Hottel, Washington Field, to Director, FBI, March 6, 1950, ibid. 101-1185-5, 1–2; Director, FBI, to SAC, Washington Field, March 1, 1950, ibid. 74-1379-?, Sec. 13.

3. Hoover is quoted in D. M. Ladd to the Director, March 6, 1950, ibid. 74-1379-?, Sec. 13; see also Ladd to Director, ibid., 2–4; Director to SAC, Washington Field, March 14, 1950, ibid.; Hottel to Director, March 20, 1950, ibid., 1–2; see also William W. Remington, Subject: Espionage Memorandum by Lambert Z. Zander, April 5, 1950, ibid., 8, 9.

4. William P. Rogers to Louis B. Nichols, February 15, 1950, ibid. 101-1165-27; A. H. Belmont to D. M. Ladd, March 24, 1950, ibid. 101-1165-34X, 6.

5. L. B. Nichols to Mr. Tolson, April 5, 1950, ibid. 121-6159-104X.

6. Hoover to SAC, New York and Knoxville, April 14, 1950, ibid. 121-6159-176; C. H. Stanley to A. H. Belmont, April 14, 1950, ibid. 121-6159-177. On Russell's role as informant, see A. H. Belmont to D. M. Ladd, April 28, 1950, ibid. 121-6159-342.

7. Author's interview with Jacob Todd, June 20, 1989, Raleigh, North Carolina; Report, April 11, 1950, Remington FBI File 121-6159-169. See also Todd Testimony—HUAC, 1950, 1707–8.

8. Teletype, Boston to Director, FBI, April 19, 1950, Remington FBI File 121-6159-232, 2; SAC, Boston, to Director, FBI, April 19, 1950, ibid. 121-6159-266; Bridgman Testimony—Grand Jury, 8605–6, 8580; Howard Bridgman Interview, April 17, 1950, Remington FBI File 121-6159-?, Sec. 5, 1–2.

9. For Bridgman's April 19, 1950, statement, see ibid. 121-6159-232; Bridgman's April 22, 1950, statement is quoted in Bridgman Testimony—Grand Jury, 7711–12; Bridgman's April 21, 1950, statement is in Remington FBI File 121-6159-248; his April 22, 1950, statement is in ibid. 121-6159-794.

10. Teletype, New York to Washington Field and Director, April 18, 1950, ibid. 121-6159-223, 2; L. L. Laughlin to A. H. Belmont, April 19, 1950, ibid. 121-6159-230; on McConnell's alcoholism, see Kenneth O'Reilly, *Hoover and the Un-Americans* (Philadelphia, 1983), 179, and author's interview with Jacob Todd; FBI Washington Field to Director, 4-20-50, Remington FBI File 121-6159-269, 1–2; FBI Washington Field to Director, ibid., 3; see also FBI Summary Report, 1951, 419–20.

11. McConnell Testimony—HUAC, 1950, 1697–98, 1699, 1700, 1701–3.

12. McConnell Testimony—Grand Jury, 7850; Elizabeth Winston Malcombre vs. Kenneth Malcombre, #A-5226, 1–2, William Remington File—Criminal Division; see also FBI Summary Report, 1951, 33, and Report Re: Paul Michael Crouch, May 19, 1949, Remington FBI File 121-6159-?, 3. Author's interview with Jacob Todd.

13. Todd Testimony—HUAC, 1950, 1708–12.

14. Ibid., 1717, 1718–23; author's interview with Jacob Todd.

15. Joseph L. Rauh, Jr., to Richard G. Green, April 24, 1950, Rauh Papers; Richard G. Green to Joseph L. Rauh, Jr., April 25, 1950, Green Papers.

16. *New York Times*, April 27, 1950, Green Papers. Louis Russell informed the FBI on April 26 of Wood's impending announcement and the HUAC investigator's meeting with

Bridgman—see Teletype, 4-26-50, Remington FBI File 121-6159-285.

17. Teletype, ibid.; Bridgman Testimony—Grand Jury, 8579–80.

18. Bridgman Testimony—HUAC, 1950, 1753–56, 1759, 1775. For Bridgman's treatment by HUAC, see SAC, Boston, to Director, FBI, 5-3-50, in Remington FBI File 121-6159-347, 2.

19. The questions and Remington's answers are in Remington Testimony—HUAC, 1950, 1783, 1785, 1788, 1793, 1795, 1796, 1797, 1799, 1812–13, 1813–14, 1814–16, 1817–18.

20. Joseph L. Rauh, Jr., to Seth W. Richardson, May 6, 1950, 2–6, Remington File—Civil Service Commission.

21. Rauh's comment is in Remington Testimony—HUAC, 1950, 1780–84, 1796, 1823, 1828, 1830, 1831–45. On P.O. box, see ibid., 1803, 1804–7.

22. Ibid., 1780–84, 1796, 1823, 1844, 1830, 1831–45, 1846–47 (Remington's answers on ASU, YCL, etc.).

23. Ibid., 1847–48.

24. Richard G. Green to Joseph L. Rauh, Jr., May 5, 1950, Green Papers; Rauh to Richardson, May 6, 1950, 2, ibid.

25. Bentley Testimony—HUAC, 1950, 1849–52.

26. Bentley Testimony—Export Policy, 1948, 14–15, 24, 31, 38; Bentley Testimony—HUAC, 1950, 1854–55, 1856, 1859–60.

27. For biographical information on John Gilland Brunini, see his self-portrait "John Gilland Brunini" in Walter Romig, ed., *The Book of Catholic Authors*, 4th Series (Grosse Pointe, n.d.), 40–47; see also Brunini's obituary in the *New York Times*, May 12, 1977; John Gilland Brunini, "Rolling Stone," chapter 13, pp. 2, 3, 4, 5, and chapter 14, pp. 1–2, unpublished manuscript, John Gilland Brunini Papers, Special Collections, Georgetown University, Washington, D.C. Edmund L. Brunini, Sr., brother of the late John G. Brunini, requested the author to note that "the autobiography was not completed prior to his death and probably not refined." Edmund L. Brunini to author, April 21, 1986. Brunini's views on the Red Menace can be found in John Gilland Brunini, "The '3 Spy Grand Juries,'" *Catholic World* (March 1953), 425; see also Brunini, "Has America Got the 'Red Jitters'?" *The Catholic Mind* (January 1950), 6.

28. "Rolling Stone," chapter 13, p. 23, and chapter 14, pp. 5, 6, 8–9.

29. Ibid., chapter 14, pp. 10, 11. On Brunini's role in arranging a contract for the publication of Bentley's book, see Memorandum by John Gilland Brunini, October 17, 1950, enclosure with Thomas J. Donegan to Hon. James M. McInery, October 18, 1950, Remington—Criminal Division, and Leyla Sefa Testimony—First Trial, 1539, 1540, 1550, 1580–81, 1582, 1589, 1600; on Brunini's collaboration with Bentley, see Teletype, New York Field to Director, October 16, 1950, Silvermaster–Bentley FBI File 65-56402-?, Sec. 151, 1–3.

30. John G. Brunini to Alex Campbell, May 2, 1950, quoted in L. L. Laughlin to A. H. Belmont, May 3, 1950, Remington FBI File 121-6159-111; Brunini, "The Three 'Spy Grand Juries,'" 422; "Rolling Stone," chapter 13, p. 13.

31. Brunini, "The Three 'Spy Grand Juries,'" 423.

32. Egan Testimony—Grand Jury, 7583–84; Schmidt's statement is in *New York Times*, May 8, 1950. For Brunini's role in the issuing of the Schmidt statement, see Schmidt interview—Spivack, 4.

33. Egan Testimony—Grand Jury, 7584, 7594–602, 7597–600, 7598, 7610.

34. "Rolling Stone," chapter 14, pp. 14–16.

35. Memorandum on Conversation with Carl Beruffy, October 10, 1950, Rauh Papers; Interview with Carl Beruffy by George Eddy, March 1, 1957.

36. Ann Remington Testimony—Grand Jury, 8551; see also 8546, 8547; on Remington's concern about speaking on the phone, see ibid., 8531.

12. Tool of Tyranny

1. Ann Remington Testimony—Grand Jury, 7742.
2. Ibid., 7747, 7764, 7766, 7782, 7783, 7784–85, 7795.
3. Ibid., 7757, 7758, 7759, 7768, 7791.
4. Ibid., 7766.
5. Ibid., 7755.
6. Ibid., 7767, 7775–76.
7. Ibid., 7778–79, 7782–83.
8. See, for example, Ann Remington's responses to questions in ibid., 7744, 7745, 7751, 7752, 7753, 7758, 7759, 7763, 7765, 7768, 7769, 7770, 7778, 7779, 7790, 7791.
9. Ann Remington Testimony—Grand Jury, 7794–97.
10. Ibid., 7799–804.
11. Ibid., 7805–11.
12. Ibid., 7811–13, 7817–30.
13. Ibid., 7831–33.
14. Ibid., 7834, 7836.
15. Ibid., 7841–42.
16. Ibid., 7835, 7844.
17. Judge Hand is quoted in Petition for Writ of Certiorari to the United States Court of Appeals for Second Circuit, October Term, 1953, 54, Rauh Papers; Brunini is quoted in ibid., 53 (footnote).
18. Ibid., 51, 52, 56. Quote is on 55.
19. Bentley Testimony—Grand Jury, 7876, 7881, 7895.
20. Bentley Statement, November 30, 1945, 48; Bentley Testimony—Grand Jury, 7881, 7906, 7908; Ann Remington Testimony—Grand Jury, 7842; Bentley Testimony—HUAC, 1950, 1859.
21. William Remington Testimony—Grand Jury, 7981–8018.

13. Scene of the Crime

1. Questions Asked Remington Before Grand Jury, May 22, 1950, By Joseph Rauh, August 24, 1950, 1, Rauh Papers. After each of Remington's grand jury appearances, he would describe the questions, and Rauh would record them for his files. Hereafter cited as Questions Asked Remington.
2. Remine Testimony—Grand Jury, 7923, 7927, 7928, 7930, 7932, 7934–35, 7940, 7947, 7956–57, 7958–61, 7963.
3. Todd Testimony—Grand Jury, 7966–67.
4. Remington Testimony—Grand Jury, 7981, 7997.
5. Ibid., 7999, 8000, 8002–3, 8008–9, 8010.
6. Ibid., 8010–11, 8012, 8013, 8014–16, 8017, 8018, 8019–21.
7. Ibid., 8021–22, 8024, 8025–28.
8. Ibid., 8005, 8061–62, 8179, 8209.
9. Ibid., 8067, 8095; Questions Asked Remington, 14–15; Remington Testimony—Grand Jury, 8230.
10. Ibid., 8227–28.
11. Ibid., 8182; see also 8014, 8032–33.
12. Questions Asked Remington, 12.
13. Presentation by Mr. Donegan, June 8, 1950, 8730, Grand Jury. Hereafter cited as Donegan Presentation—Grand Jury; Bridgman Testimony—Grand Jury, 7710–40; McConnell Testimony—Grand Jury, 7846–74; Questions Asked Remington, 12–13.

14. Ann Remington Testimony, June 2, 1950—Grand Jury, 8415.

15. Ibid., 8519, 8520–21, 8529–30; FBI Summary Report, 1951, 32.

16. Ann Remington Testimony, June 2, 1950—Grand Jury, 8513, 8514, 8515, 8554, 8555.

17. Bridgman Testimony—Grand Jury, 7721–22, 7727; Bridgman Testimony, June 2, 1950—Grand Jury, 8571–72, 8576–77, 8579, 8606, 8607.

18. *New York Herald-Tribune*, May 16, 1950, Rauh Papers; William W. Remington to Hon. Charles Sawyer, June 9, 1950, 1, Rauh Papers; *Washington Post*, June 10, 1950, ibid.

19. Bernard L. Gladieux to William Remington, June 5, 1950, Remington Papers; Sawyer is quoted in *Washington "Evening" Star*, June 6, 1950, Remington—Criminal Division.

20. Thomas J. Donegan to Hon. James M. McInery, June 5, 1950, 1, Remington—Criminal Division; see also Donegan Presentation—Grand Jury, 8730.

21. William E. Foley to James M. McInery, May 15, 1950, 1–2, Remington—Criminal Division; James M. McInery to Thomas J. Donegan, May 17, 1950, ibid.; John M. Kelley, Jr., to James M. McInery, June 7, 1950, 2, 3–6, ibid.; James M. McInery to John M. Kelley, Jr., June 15, 1950, ibid.

22. Brunini, "Rolling Stone," chapter 14, p. 15; Donegan Presentation—Grand Jury, 8733–35, 8741–42, 8743.

23. North Testimony—Grand Jury, 8036–38; Bryan Testimony—Grand Jury, 8483; Martin Testimony—Grand Jury, 8115, 8116, 8127, 8132; Budenz Testimony—Grand Jury, 8649; Donegan Presentation—Grand Jury, 8742.

24. Brunini, "Rolling Stone," chapter 14, p. 13; *New York World-Telegram*, June 9, 1950, Rauh Papers; Brunini, "Rolling Stone," chapter 14, p. 15.

25. Remington Testimony—Grand Jury, 8025, 8083, 8205.

26. The United States of America vs. William Walter Remington, Defendant, Indictment, Perjury Before A Grand Jury, 2, Rauh Papers.

27. *New York World-Telegram*, June 9, 1950, ibid.; Brunini, "Rolling Stone," chapter 13, p. 19, and chapter 14, pp. 15–16, 18; J. Edgar Hoover to John G. Brunini, June 28, 1950, John G. Brunini FBI File 94-42457-2; see also Memorandum For Mr. Tolson, June 26, 1950, ibid. 94-42457-1.

28. *New York Times*, June 9, 1950; *Washington Post*, June 9, 1950, and *New York Herald-Tribune*, June 9, 1950, all in Rauh Papers.

14. Missionary Work

1. Joseph L. Rauh, Jr., to Mrs. Mary L. Robbins, June 19, 1950, 1, Rauh Papers; for Remington's reassurance to Rauh, see Joseph L. Rauh, Jr., to William W. Remington, February 20, 1953, 6, ibid.

2. William W. Remington to Hon. Charles Sawyer, June 9, 1950, 1–4, Remington Papers. See also *New York Times*, June 10, 1950, and *New York Post*, June 11, 1950, both in Rauh Papers. Gladieux is quoted in "William Walter Remington," 4, enclosure with George T. Mooroe to Hon. Lloyd Wright, n.d. (May, 1958), Remington—Criminal Division.

3. Henry C. Smith, "My Conferences with Surety Companies and Their Agents with Respect to Obtaining an Appearance Bond for Client," June 12, 1950, 1, 2, 3–6, Rauh Papers; Rauh to Robbins, June 19, 1950, 1, ibid.; see also Joseph L. Rauh, Jr., to Mrs. Francis Brody, June 19, 1950, 1, ibid.

4. *New York Times*, June 14, 1950, 1; *New York Daily Mirror*, June 14, 1950, 2; and *Cincinnatian*, June 14, 1950, all in ibid.; Defendant's Plea and Admission to Bail, 22–25, in United States of America vs. William Walter Remington, Cr. 132-344. Hereafter cited First Trial Transcript; Rauh to Brody, June 19, 1950, 1, Rauh Papers; Rauh to Robbins, June 19, 1950, 1, ibid.

5. Memorandum to the File, June 16, 1950, 1, Rauh Papers; Rauh to Robbins, 2, ibid.; see

also Joseph L. Rauh, Jr., to Mrs. Mary L. Robbins, July 1, 1950, ibid.

6. Rauh to Robbins, June 19, 1950, 1–2, ibid.; Memorandum to the File, June 16, 1950, 1, ibid.; for Alger quote see Memorandum to the File, June 21, 1950, ibid.

7. Rauh to Brody, June 19, 1950, 1, 3, 4, ibid.; Rauh to Mrs. Robbins, July 27, 1950, ibid.; Joseph L. Rauh, Jr., to Mrs. William Scheft, June 28, 1950, ibid.; see also Joseph L. Rauh, Jr., to Joseph F. Ford, July 15, 1950, ibid.; Joseph L. Rauh, Jr., to James Marshall, July 3, 1950, ibid.

8. Joseph L. Rauh, Jr., to James Marshall, June 24, 1950, 3–4, ibid.

9. Rauh to Mrs. Robbins, July 1, 1950, ibid.

10. The July 5 proceedings are discussed in L. L. Laughlin to A. H. Belmont, July 5, 1950, Remington FBI File 74-1379-35; C. H. Stanley to A. H. Belmont, July 7, 1950, ibid. 74-1379-36. See also *New York Times*, July 6, 1950, *New York Post*, July 5, 1950, Rauh Papers; *New York Post*, July 12, 1950, ibid.; *New York Journal-American*, July 5, 1950, ibid.

11. Thomas Kessmer, *Fiorello La Guardia and the Making of Modern New York* (New York, 1989), 428; *New York Times Biographical Service* (New York, 1981), 915; Rauh to Mrs. Robbins, July 1, 1950, 2, Rauh Papers.

12. Quoted in Memorandum in Support of Defendant's Plea for a Bill of Particulars, 13, 16, United States of America vs. William Walter Remington, Rauh Papers. Hereafter cited as Memorandum in Support; Notice of Motion for a Bill of Particulars in Transcript of Record—First Trial, 25–26. Hereafter cited as Notice of Motion. See also Memorandum in Support, 9, 10, 11–12, 18–19; *Washington Post*, July 20, 1950; *Washington "Evening" Star*, July 20, 1950, Rauh Papers. For the government's argument, see Affidavit Opposing a Bill of Particulars, July 24, 1950, in First Trial Transcript, 34–36.

13. Affidavit Opposing a Bill of Particulars, 46–48, 52–60. *New York Times*, July 25, 1950, Rauh Papers; *New York Post*, July 24, 1950, *Washington Post*, July 25, 1950, ibid.

14. Order For a Bill of Particulars, August 3, 1950, in First Trial Transcript, 51–52. Sugarman's ruling was announced on July 28, 1950; see *New York Times*, July 29, 1950, and *Washington Post*, July 29, 1950, both in Rauh Papers; Bill of Particulars, August 17, 1950, in First Trial Transcript, 53–54; Joseph L. Rauh, Jr., "Report on the Remington Trial," n.d. (1951), 6–7, Rauh Papers; Joseph L. Rauh, Jr., to Mrs. Mary L. Robbins, August 21, 1950, ibid.

15. Hoover to SAC, NY, June 12, 1950, Remington FBI File 74-1379-8.

16. See, for example, FBI interviews with Hugh Elsbree in ibid. NY-121-1958, 339; Raymon Guthrie, ibid.; Stearns Morse, ibid.; Allan MacDonald, ibid., 362; Donald Michaeljohn, ibid., 354; Sidney Cox, ibid., 358–59; Rev. Roy B. Chamberlin, ibid.; Dean L. K. Neidlinger, ibid., 360–61; James Allen Carpenter, ibid., 332–33; Robert Fuller, ibid., 340–41; Alexander Jones, ibid., 344; W. A. Fuller, ibid., 351; Andrew Brown, ibid., 352. FBI interview with William A. Martin, April 20, 1950, Remington FBI File 212-6159-911, IA–3, and FBI Summary Report, 1951, 390–91; Charles Page Smith Statement, July 11, 1950, in "William Walter Remington," Remington FBI File 74-1379-52, 6–7; NY to Director and SAC, October 10, 1950, ibid. 74-1379-295.

17. A. H. Belmont to Mr. Ladd, January 3, 1951, Remington FBI File 74-1379-?, Sec. 28, 2, 4; FBI Summary Report, 1951, 432–39, 510–20, 521–27; FBI, Knoxville, to Director, FBI and SAC, NY, June 29, 1950, Remington FBI File 121-6159-992, 1; Benson Testimony—First Trial, 486; Bridgman Testimony—Grand Jury, 7728; B. J. Zien's June 2, 1950, FBI statement is in "William Walter Remington," June 9, 1950, Remington FBI File 121-6159-1041, 3–10; FBI, Knoxville, to Director, FBI, SAC, NY, June 29, 1950, ibid. 121-6159-993; "William Walter Remington," July 31, 1950, ibid. 121-6159-1047, 1–3, 4; for McInery's questions and the Knoxville office's explanation of how the Benson interview occurred, see Belmont to Ladd, January 3, 1951, Remington FBI File 74-1379-?, Sec. 28, 2, 4. On Benson as potential witness, see C. H. Stanley to A. H. Belmont, September 27, 1950, ibid. 74-1379-?, Sec. 9; Director, FBI, to SAC, Knoxville, September 27, 1950, ibid.; D. M. Ladd to the Director, October 12,

1951, ibid. 74-1379-341, 1.

18. Muriel Speare Testimony—Joint Committee Hearing, 1947, 904, 922–23, 925; Muriel Williams Interview in FBI Summary Report, 1951, 440–41, 472–73; Selma R. Williams, *Redlisted: Haunted by the Washington Witch Hunt* (Reading, 1993), 117–18.

19. For Henry Hart's FBI Statement, see FBI Summary Report, 1951, 492–93, 531; for Mabel Abercrombie Mansfield's FBI Statement, see ibid., 475–85.

20. FBI interviews with Lawrence Keeler in "William Walter Remington," July 31, 1950, Remington FBI File 121-6159-1047, 23–24; FBI interview with Homer Wilson in ibid., 25–26; FBI interview with Robert B. Weir, in ibid., 24; FBI interviews with Charles Thomas Love, Isaac Wiggs, and Mrs. Ann V. Hixson in ibid., 15.

21. On McConnell's missing notebook, see "William Walter Remington," July 11, 1950, in Remington FBI File 74-1379-65, 19–20; FBI Summary Report, 9/8/50, in ibid. 74-1379-306, 19–20. McConnell also visited Knoxville—see FBI Summary Report, 1951, 427–31.

22. C. H. Stanley to A. H. Belmont, June 22, 1950, Remington FBI File 74-1379-28; Hoover to SACs, Boston, et al., September 13, 1950, ibid. 74-1379-?, Sec. 10; "William Walter Remington," n.d., ibid. 74-1379-278, 2.

23. "William Walter Remington," August 22, 1950, ibid. 74-1379-256; "William Walter Remington," September 18, 1950, ibid. 74-1379-240, 2; "William Walter Remington," September 22, 1950, ibid. 74-1379-236, 2–3; "William Walter Remington," September 22, 1950, ibid. 74-1379-253; "William Walter Remington," October 2, 1950, ibid. 74-1379-266; Director to SAC, NY, October 6, 1950, ibid. 74-1379-249.

24. NY to Washington and Washington Field, September 25, 1950, ibid. 74-1379-260; Guy Hottel to Director, FBI, August 4, 1950, ibid. 74-1379-?, Sec. 6, 1–2.

25. "Discussion Between Ann Remington and Myself," by Bill Remington, September 3, 1950, 1–5, Rauh Papers.

15. Not in This Day and Time

1. Interview with Donald Miller, October 6, 1950, 1–3, Rauh Papers.

2. Interview with Robert Boehm, '35, October 11, 1950, ibid.; Re: Interview with Francis Bartlett, October 12, 1950, 1–2, ibid.; Interview with Dorothy Childs Bartlett, October 11, 1950, 1, ibid.

3. Memorandum of Conversation with Charles Livermore, September 15, 1950, 1–7, ibid.; see also Joseph L. Rauh, Jr., to Charles Livermore, September 18, 1950, and Second Conversation with Charles Livermore, September 20, 1950, ibid.

4. Memorandum on Conversation with William Martin, September 29, 1950, 1–7, ibid.; William A. Martin Statement in FBI Summary Report, 1951, 39.

5. Conversation with Walter Bernstein, October 27, 1950, Rauh Papers. For Bernstein's FBI interview, see "William Walter Remington," October 3, 1950, Remington FBI File 74-1379-278, 7–8.

6. Interview with Charles Page Smith, October 6, 1950, 1–2, 5, 7, Rauh Papers.

7. Boston to Director and SACs, October 14, 1950, Remington FBI File 74-1379-317; Boston to Director and SACs, October 18, 1950, ibid. 74-1379-342; Boston to Director and SAC, NY, December 19, 1950, ibid. 74-1379-821.

8. Interview with Sidney Cox, October 17, 1950, 1–2, Rauh Papers; Allan MacDonald, October 17, 1950, 1–2, ibid.; Robert Carr, October 14, 1950, ibid.; Mr. and Mrs. Hugh Morrison and Mr. and Mrs. Arthur Eugene Jensen, October 17, 1950, 1, ibid.

9. Interview with Elba Chase Nelson, Hillsboro, Upper Village, Vermont, October 16, 1950, 1–2, ibid.

10. Interview with George Edson, October 16, 1950, 1–2, ibid.

11. Charles Davis Testimony—First Trial, 2275–76; Affidavit of Charles T. Davis, May 25,

1950, 1–2, Remington File—Criminal Division. See also Memorandum of Conversation with Charles Davis, September 22, 1950, 1–2, Rauh Papers. Author's interview with William Goodman, March 15, 1986. See also Affidavit of William W. Goodman, May 12, 1950, 1–3, Remington File—Criminal Division.

12. Joseph L. Rauh, Jr., to William C. Chanler, Esq., August 12, 1950, 1, Rauh Papers; Christine Benson Testimony—First Trial, 470, 473, 474–75, 482–83, 489, 508, 527, 555.

13. Director, FBI, to Assistant Attorney General James M. McInery, October 10, 1950, Remington FBI File 74-1379-308; NY to Director, October 16, 1950, ibid. 74-1379-349.

14. "William Walter Remington," October 6, 1950, ibid. 74-1379-301; Memorandum of Conversation with Henry Hart, October 14, 1950, 1–2, 3, 6–8, Rauh Papers. For Rauh's comment on Hart, see Joseph L. Rauh, Jr., to Prof. Carl Auerbach, January 14, 1951, ibid.

15. INTERVIEW WITH MRS. MURIEL SPEARE BORAH WILLIAMS, October 6, 1950, 1–4, 12–15, Rauh Papers. Mr. Williams's comment is on 15.

16. US vs. Remington: Horace Bryan, n.d., 1–4, 7–8, ibid.

17. Ibid., 8–9; for Bryan's FBI Statement, see FBI Summary Report, 1951, 495–503; Horace Bryan Testimony, June 2, 1950—Grand Jury, 8458–94; Mrs. Williams is quoted in INTERVIEW WITH MRS. MURIEL SPEARE BORAH WILLIAMS, 10, Rauh Papers.

18. Memorandum on Conversation with Thomas Blaisdell, November 7, 1950, 1–2, ibid.; Memorandum on Conversation with Charles J. Hitch, September 15, 1950, 1–5, ibid.; Memorandum on Conversation with Daniel L. Hopkinson, November 6, 1950, 1–3, ibid.

19. Memorandum on Conversation with Oscar Altman, November 1, 1950, ibid.; Memorandum on Conversation with Ezra Glazer, November 8, 1950, ibid. The latter contains Rauh's comments on his other conversations.

20. Memorandum, December 28, 1950, 1–3, ibid. The latter contains Rauh's interviews with Fox, Austrian, Newman, Nathan, and Dickinson.

21. For Bentley's comments on Redmont, see Bentley Testimony—Export Policy Hearing, 1948, 532; Bernard Redmont's 1948 statement following Bentley's charges is in FBI Report, Remington FBI File 121-6159-516, 17–18; Bernard S. Redmont to Committee on Un-American Activities, August 30, 1948 in Appendix, HUAC Hearing, 1948, 136–61; for Redmont's 1948 FBI statements, see FBI Summary Report, 1951, 108–9; Redmont Testimony—First Trial, 1746, 1747–48, 1749; Memorandum, August 3, 1948, 2, Rauh Papers.

22. FBI Summary Report, 1951, 82; Memorandum, August 3, 1950, 4, Rauh Papers; Arthur Schlesinger, Jr., to Joseph L. Rauh, Jr., September 4, 1950, 1–3, Rauh Papers.

23. For Remington's letter to the Redmonts, see Redmont Testimony—First Trial, 1703–5.

24. Bernard S. Redmont to David Lawrence, November 1, 1950, read during Redmont Testimony—First Trial, 1706–11.

25. Memorandum of Conversation with David Lawrence, October 18, 1950, 1–13, Rauh Papers; L. B. Nichols to Mr. Tolson, 9/24/46, Silvermaster FBI File 65-56402-1579; L. B. Nichols to Mr. Tolson, 10/13/46, ibid. 65-56402-1634; L. B. Nichols to Mr. Tolson, October 21, 1950, ibid. 65-56402-?, Vol. 72; J. Edgar Hoover to Legal Attaché, October 28, 1950, ibid. 65-56402-411; Nichols to Tolson, October 21, 1950, ibid. 65-56402-?, Vol. 72; Director, FBI, to SAC, NY, October 28, 1950, Remington FBI File 74-1379-412; L. B. Nichols to Mr. Tolson, November 6, 1950, ibid. 74-1379-532; Director, FBI, to SAC, NY, November 14, 1950, ibid. 74-1379-532; L. L. Laughlin to A. H. Belmont, January 4, 1951, ibid. 74-1379-956, 1–2; Bernard S. Redmont to William Chanler, November 20, 1950, read during Redmont Testimony—First Trial, 1670–71.

26. NY to Washington and Washington Field, October 9, 1950, Remington FBI File 74-1379-268; NY to Director and SAC, November 8, 1950, ibid. 74-1379-490, 2; Teletype, 11/3/50, ibid. 74-1379-425; Memo Re: Gregory by Thomas G. Spencer, November 1, 1950, Silvermaster FBI File 65-56403-4320, Vol. 99, 1–2; Memorandum by Thomas G. Spencer,

October 31, 1950, ibid. (New York Field Office), 65-14603-4316, 2.

27. For information on the Brunini–Bentley affair, see Untitled Memorandum by John Gilland Brunini, October 17, 1950, 1–4, enclosure Thomas J. Donegan to Hon. James M. McInery, October 17, 1950, Remington—Criminal Division; and "John Brunini (Foreman of the Grand Jury) and Elizabeth Bentley," by Thomas J. Donegan, enclosure Thomas J. Donegan to Hon. James M. McInery, ibid. See also Memorandum from J. Donald McNamara to redacted, September 21, 1953, 4, U.S. Attorneys Records, National Archives, Bayonne, New Jersey; NY to Director, October 16, 1950, Silvermaster FBI File 65-56402-3854; Hoover's comments are written on the document; Director, FBI, to SAC, NY, October 17, 1950, ibid. 65-56402-3854.

28. NY to Director, October 31, 1950, Remington FBI File 74-1379-4587; on the Attorney General's approval to proceed on the original indictment, see Saypol's comment First Trial Transcript, 1527.

29. Director and Washington Field to NY, 12-4-50, Remington FBI File 74-1379-646. See also Hoover to SACs, NY and Washington Field, December 2, 1950, ibid. 74-1379-559; NY to Director and SAC, December 6, 1950, ibid. 74-1379-633; NY to Director and SAC, November 30, 1950, ibid. 74-1379-614; L. L. Laughlin to A. H. Belmont, December 21, 1950, ibid. 74-1379-825; Hoover to SAC, NY, December 21, 1950, ibid. 74-1379-825; Irving H. Saypol to S. A. Andretti, December 12, 1950, U.S. Attorneys Records.

30. For Saypol's request for derogatory information on Martin, see NY to Director and SAC, January 14, 1951, Remington FBI File 74-1379-143; on Hopkins, see Teletype, Boston to Director, December 27, 1950, ibid. 74-1379-843; for Saypol's request for derogatory information on others who signed a letter of support for Remington, which was sent to the Regional Loyalty Board, see NY to Director and SAC, January 15, ibid. 74-1379-1107.

31. Telephonic Communication from Miss Bentley, December 12, 1950, U.S. Attorney's Records.

32. For Donegan's criticisms of Saypol, see NY to Director, October 31, 1950, Remington FBI File 74-1379-4587, 2; A. H. Belmont to D. M. Ladd, November 9, 1950, ibid. 74-1379-526; A. H. Belmont to Mr. Ladd, November 27, 1950, ibid. 74-1379-580; Donegan is quoted in A. H. Belmont to D. M. Ladd, December 15, 1950, ibid. 74-1379-772.

33. Joseph L. Rauh, Jr., to William C. Chanler, October 31, 1950, 1–2, Rauh Papers.

34. Amended Bill of Particulars, November 9, 1950, First Trial Transcript, 55; Memorandum, November 10, 1950, Rauh Papers; Washington Field to Director and SAC, 1-3-51, Remington FBI File 74-1379-944.

35. Rauh, "Report on Remington Trial," 15, 17, 18, 19, Rauh Papers.

16. Object of Hate, Engine of Destruction

1. Memorandum, December 18, 1950, Rauh Papers; *Washington Post*, December 19, 1950, and *Washington "Evening" Star*, December 20, 1950, both in ibid.

2. Author's interview with Joseph L. Rauh, Jr., August 1990.

3. First Trial Transcript, 8, 9, 14, 15, 19, 22, 23, 25, 26, 28, 29, 32, 35, 36, 38, 53, 54. For Gillenwater and Joffee quotes, see 22 and 38, respectively; Saypol's comment is on 94. For the complete voir dire, see ibid., 7–53. For information on the jurors, see *New York World-Telegram* and *New York Sun*, December 20, 1950, Rauh Papers; *New York Daily Mirror*, December 21, 1950, ibid.; *New York Daily News*, December 21, 1950, ibid.; *Washington Post*, December 21, 1950, ibid.; *New York Times*, December 21, 1950, ibid.

4. First Trial Transcript, 57–70, 70–75. See also Memorandum in Support of Motion to Dismiss the Indictment, December 18, 1950, 1–35, Rauh Papers; on Noonan's anger, see Rauh, "Report on the Remington Case," 8, Rauh Papers; *Washington "Evening" Star*, December 21, 1950, ibid.; *New York Herald-Tribune*, December 21, 1950, ibid.

5. On Irving H. Saypol, see the *New York Times Biographical Service* (New York, 1977), 1017–18; *Who Was Who in America with World Notables, 1977*, 503; Ron Radosh and Joyce Milton, *The Rosenberg File: A Search for the Truth* (New York, 1983), 171–72; First Trial Transcript, 87–99.

6. *The Dartmouth*, January 18, 1951, Special Collections, Dartmouth College; First Trial Transcript, 99–124.

7. Doran Testimony—First Trial, 162, 164–70.

8. Max Lerner, "A Day with the Remingtons," *New York Post*, December 28, 1950, Rauh Papers. For another description of Ann Remington, see Frances Downing, "The Reluctant Witness," *The Commonweal*, January 26, 1951, 394, ibid.; and *The Dartmouth*, January 13, 1951.

9. Ann Remington Testimony—First Trial, 184, 187, 189.

10. *New York Times*, December 27, 1950, Rauh Papers; *New York Daily Mirror*, December 27, 1950, ibid.; *New York Daily News*, December 27, 1950, ibid.

11. Ann Remington Testimony—First Trial, 202, 207–9, 212–14, 215–26, 225, 227–28, 233–34, 236–37, 239–55, 273–74, 278–79; Fred J. Cook, "The Remington Tragedy: A Study in Injustice," *The Nation*, December 28, 1957, 486. Hereafter cited as Cook, "The Remington Tragedy." *New York Daily News*, December 28, 1950, Rauh Papers.

12. Ann Remington Testimony—First Trial, 285–86, 273–74, 283, 314–20.

13. *New York Daily News*, December 28, 1950; the *Washington "Evening" Star*, December 27, 1950; *New York Daily Mirror*, December 28, 1950; *New York Post*, December 27, 1950; and Lerner, "A Day with the Remingtons," all in Rauh Papers.

14. First Trial Transcript, 322–23, 334, 335.

15. Ibid., 324, 325, 328–36; see also the *Washington "Evening" Star*, December 28, 1950; the *New York Journal-American*, December 28, 1950; and *New York Post*, December 28, 1950, all in Rauh Papers.

16. Ann Remington Testimony—First Trial, 351, 356, 437–42, 443, 447, 449.

17. Ibid., 448–50, 451–56, 457–59.

18. *New York Times*, December 29, 1950, and *Washington Post*, December 29, 1950, both in Rauh Papers; *New York Daily Mirror*, December 29, 1950, ibid.; *Washington Daily News*, December 29, 1950, ibid.; see also the *Washington "Evening" Star*, December 29, 1950, ibid.; *Washington Times-Herald*, December 29, 1950, ibid.; *New York Daily News*, December 27, 1950, ibid.; *The Dartmouth*, January 13, 1951. For photographs of Ann Remington, see *New York Times*, December 28, 1950, *Washington Post*, December 28, 1950, *Washington Times-Herald*, December 28, 1950, *New York Daily News*, December 28, 1950, and *Washington Daily News*, December 29, 1950, all in Rauh Papers; comment on Ann Remington is from *The Dartmouth*, January 13, 1951.

19. Ann Remington Testimony—First Trial, 387–88.

20. For Ann Remington's statements that she could not recall any discussion regarding Bentley as their contact, exchanging information, paying dues, or receiving literature, see Ann Remington Testimony—Grand Jury, 8519–20, and Washington Field to Director and SACs, 8/17/50, Remington FBI File 74-1379-10, 1. Bentley's own statements to the grand jury contradict Ann's testimony. Asked by Donegan if they had discussed these matters, Bentley answered, "No. That had been arranged by Mr. Golos before." See Bentley Testimony—Grand Jury, 7884–85. There are other contradictions in Ann's testimony. At trial, she said that when she paid Communist Party dues, Bentley gave her receipts: Ann Remington Testimony—First Trial, 397. But when asked twice by John Kelley, and the FBI, whether she had received receipts, she replied emphatically, "no." See Ann Remington Testimony—Grand Jury, 8516, and Washington Field to Director and SACs, 8/17/50, Remington FBI File 74-1379-10, 1–2. At trial, she claimed that Remington brought home secret information to prepare for Helen. When asked about that by the grand jury, she said, "no." See Ann Remington Testimony—

Grand Jury, 7841. At trial, she testified that when Helen first called, she and Bill met her at 14th and Pennsylvania Avenue and drove to the Mall. But earlier, to the FBI, she had said that she could not remember where she met Bentley, or where they drove; quoted in ibid., 8508, 8542. At trial, she testified that Bill had promised to remain a member of the Party as a pre-condition to their marriage. To the grand jury, it was not Party membership but his radical views that she wanted him to retain; ibid., 7834. She made the same statement to the author during her 1986 interview.

21. First Trial Transcript (Noonan's statement), 634, 636; "January 7, 1951, Memo," Rauh Papers, has the judge's comment about Chanler.

22. Benson Testimony—First Trial, 465–67A, 468, 473–76, 481–82, 490, 491, 492, 492–92A, 496.

23. First Trial Transcript, 496–96A, 498, 510, 644, 645, 731.

24. Benson Testimony—First Trial, 465, 466; New York to Director and SAC, June 30, 1950, Remington FBI File 121-6159-989, 1–2; see also FBI Summary Report, 1951, 432.

25. Benson told the FBI that she had been recruited into the Party by a woman she had known prior to coming to Knoxville (Kit Buckles, the Bureau correctly surmised). At trial, she testified that it was state secretary Ted Wellman who recruited her: see Benson Testimony— First Trial, 464. When Chanler asked Benson if she had recruited Muriel Williams in 1937, she said "no." Williams told Bill Hindman that her recruiter was Christine Benson: INTERVIEW WITH MRS. MURIEL SPEARE BORAH WILLIAMS, October 6, 1950, 4, Rauh Papers. Muriel S. Mather repeated this statement during my interview with her in June 1990.

26. Williams Testimony—First Trial, 570, 572–73; INTERVIEW WITH MRS. MURIEL SPEARE BORAH WILLIAMS, Rauh Papers.

27. McConnell Testimony—First Trial, 586–88, 592–93, 595–617, 621–22, 672–73, 676–77, 684–87; Washington Post, January 3, 1951, Rauh Papers.

28. McConnell's FBI statement is in McConnell Testimony—Grand Jury, 7848, 7861; FBI, Charlotte to FBI and SACs, June 1, 1950, Remington FBI File 121-6159-?, 2.

29. Bridgman Testimony—First Trial, 687–97, 706, 723, 725, 731, 790–91, 945–53.

30. Joseph L. Rauh, Jr., to Prof. Carl Auerbach, January 4, 1951, Rauh Papers.

31. For biographical information on Paul Crouch, see David Caute, The Great Fear, 128, Richard H. Rovere, The American Establishment and Other Reports, Opinions, and Speculations (New York, 1962), 113–32, Willard Shelton, "Paul Crouch: Informer," New Republic, July 19, 1954, 7–9, and Crouch's unpublished memoir, "Broken Chains." For his initial lack of knowledge of Remington, see Remington FBI File 121-6159-432.

32. Crouch Testimony—First Trial, 841, 847–49, 850–53, 855, 858, 863–904, 928; Roy M. Cohn, McCarthy: The Answer to "Tail-Gunner Joe" (New York, 1977), 39–41. Hereafter cited as Cohn. See also Washington Post, January 5, 1951, and Washington Daily News, January 5, 1951, both in Rauh Papers.

33. For biographical information on Giles, see General Information, Dartmouth College Alumni Office; Matriculation Card, September 4, 1936, Special Collections, Dartmouth College; Questionnaire, 1/16/50, ibid.; Dartmouth Alumni Magazine, April 1985; Roy B. Friedman, "Bill Remington, '39," The Dartmouth, December 3, 1954; on Giles's health, see SAC, San Francisco, to Director, FBI, November 15, 1950, Remington FBI File 74-1379-517, 2.

34. William Walter Remington, November 5, 1950, ibid. 74-1379-464, 2–3.

35. SAC, San Francisco, to Director, FBI, November 15, 1950, ibid. 74-1379-517, 2; SAC, San Francisco, to Director, November 15, 1950, ibid. 74-1379-518; William Walter Remington, December 15, 1950, ibid. 74-1379-886, 3; Chicago to Director and SAC, December 15, 1950, ibid. 74-1379-712, 1; SAC, SF, to Dir., FBI, November 15, 1950, ibid. 74-1379-517, 1–2; William Walter Remington, December 15, 1950, ibid. 74-1379-886, 1–4.

36. Giles Testimony—First Trial, 980–81, 982–85, 992–94, 1021, 1022; *New York Journal-American*, January 5, 1951, Rauh Papers; the *Washington "Evening" Star*, January 6, 1951, ibid.; *New York Times*, January 6, 1951, ibid.; *Washington "Evening" Star*, January 6, 1951, ibid.; *New York World*, January 5, 1951, ibid.; *New York Post*, January 5, 1951, ibid.

37. *New York Times*, January 9, 1951, Rauh Papers; Max Lerner, "Portrait of a Lady," *New York Post*, January 10, 1951, Elizabeth Hunt Collection. I am grateful to Mrs. Hunt for sending me newspaper clippings on the Remington trial. See also Bentley Testimony—First Trial, 1044, 1058, 1063–64, 1065, 1073–79, 1163–66, 1185–89, 1198–99, 1211, 1215–18, 1224–25, 1233, 1235, 1237, 1240, 1243, 1387–94, 1407–8, 1411–15, 1417–21; Memorandum by T. G. Spencer, March 10, 1947, Silvermaster FBI File (New York Field Office) 65-14603-2854, 2.

38. Bentley Testimony—Grand Jury, 7906; Bentley Statement, November 30, 1945, 48; Bentley Testimony—Export Policy Hearing, 1948, 29, 31; Bentley Testimony—HUAC, 1950, 1859, 1861; Bentley Testimony—Grand Jury, 7878; New York to Director, SAC, December 12, 1950, Remington FBI File 74-1379-88. There are other major contradictions in Bentley's trial testimony. First, she testified that Jacob Golos thought Remington's information was excellent. Seven months earlier, she had told the grand jury that Golos was unhappy with Remington's information: Bentley Testimony—Grand Jury, 7915. Second, she lied about her relationship with Brunini. He was more than just an unofficial editor. He was her agent, collaborator, and ghostwriter: see Chapter 17.

39. *New York Times*, January 11, 1951, Rauh Papers; *Washington Times-Herald*, January 9, 1951, ibid.; *New York Times*, January 12, 1951, ibid.; *Washington Post*, January 10, 1951, ibid.; Cook, "The Remington Tragedy," 495.

40. *Washington "Evening" Star*, January 11, 1951, Rauh Papers. For a photograph of Robb B. Kelley, see *New York Herald-Tribune*, January 11, 1951, 12, Elizabeth Hunt Collection; Kelley Testimony—First Trial, 1432–33.

41. For Kelley's statements, see William Walter Remington, June 17, 1948, Remington FBI File 121-6159-59, 1–3; FBI, Richmond, to Director, FBI, and SACs, Washington Field and Chicago, April 26, 1950, ibid. 121-6159-298, 2.

42. First Trial Transcript, 1485–87, 1489.

43. Ibid., 1506–7, 1532–34.

17. A Lot to Explain

1. Collins Testimony—First Trial, 1607–9, 1627–29, 1635–36.

2. Sefa Testimony—First Trial, 1542–75, 1583–96.

3. Collins Testimony—First Trial, 1603, 1605–6, 1611–12, 1616–21; *New York Herald-Tribune*, January 13, 1951, Rauh Papers.

4. First Trial Transcript, 1624–27; Chanler is quoted in Cook, *Maverick*, 41; *Washington Post*, January 13, 1951, Rauh Papers; see also *New York Times*, January 13, 1951, ibid.

5. Redmont Testimony—First Trial, 1638–43, 1645–47, 1650–60, 1676–80; on Saypol's own name change, see author's interview with Joseph Rauh, August 1991.

6. Silvermaster FBI File 65-56402-450; Redmont Testimony—First Trial, 1688–89, 1694–99, 1702–6, 1720–23; 1809–15; 1706–11 (Redmont to Lawrence letter), 1870–71.

7. United States vs. Remington. 191 F. 2d 246 (2d Cir., 1951); R. F. Igl, "United States v. Remington," 2, Learned B. Hand Papers, Harvard Law School Library, Cambridge, Mass. Hereafter cited as Hand Papers.

8. Author's interview with Bernard S. Redmont, June 1992. Bentley's original FBI statement reveals a knowledge of Redmont's background that suggests an intimacy deeper than that described by Redmont on the stand. In November 1945, before her memory could be refreshed and revised, she described him (accurately) as New York born and a former student at Columbia University's School of Journalism, where he won a Pulitzer Traveling Scholarship.

(Bentley called it a "Pulitzer Prize.") She knew that he had traveled widely through Europe and Mexico and that when he returned home, he worked briefly for a small-town newspaper in Herkimer County, New York. Indeed, Redmont was briefly employed by the *Herkimer Evening Telegram*. She correctly identified his position at the Office of Inter-American Affairs, recalled that he had joined the Marines and was wounded, and then had returned to New York in the fall of 1945, eventually resuming his former job. It does not seem credible that a casual acquaintance would either know or remember so much detail about Redmont's history. Furthermore, Redmont seems disingenuous about the origins of his son's name. It was his wife who openly joked that young Dennis Foster was "Bill Z's namesake." Yet, in his memoir, he dismisses the affair as just "a 'Dennis the Menace' fantasy that could only have been fabricated by warped minds"; see Redmont, *Risks Worth Taking*, 65. Bentley Statement, November 30, 1945, 48–49.

9. Fred Remington Testimony—First Trial, 1886–96. Lillian Remington Testimony—First Trial, 3061–78.

10. Bryan Testimony—First Trial, 1897–912, 1916–20, 1922–29, 1942, 1945, 1947–48, 2004, 2034–35, 2067–68, 2101–9; *New York Herald-Tribune*, January 18, 1951, *Washington Post*, January 18, 1951, and *New York Times*, January 18, 1951, all in Rauh Papers.

11. Martin Testimony—First Trial, 2213–14, 2218–20, 2230–39A, 2244–46; on Remington's demeanor, see *New York Times*, January 20, 1951, Rauh Papers; Cohn, 41.

12. Davis Testimony—First Trial, 2225, 2275–90.

13. Goodman Testimony—First Trial, 2247–57, 2260–63, 2270–74; *New York Times*, January 20, 1951, *Washington Post*, January 20, 1951, *Washington Times-Herald*, January 20, 1951, and *Washington "Evening" Star*, January 20, 1951, all in Rauh Papers.

14. *Washington Post*, January 23, 1951, ibid.; Hitch Testimony—First Trial, 2295–315, 2331–35, 2349.

15. Remington Testimony—First Trial, 2325, 2342–45, 2349, 2350, 2374–76, 2388, 2392, 2396, 2401–2, 2406, 2408–11, 2417, 2447–53, 2491, 2496, 2504, 2506, 2508–9, 2516–17, 2523–43, 2547–57. On Remington's demeanor, see the *New York Times*, January 23, 1951, and the *Washington Post*, January 23, 1951, both in Rauh Papers. Lerner is quoted in the *New York Post*, January 23, 1951, 1B10.

16. Shelhorse Testimony—First Trial, 2418–26; exchange quoted is on 2425.

17. Remington Testimony—First Trial, 2558–63, 2571–76, 2580, 2581, 2583–84, 2591–97; on the formula, see 2600–609; 2610, 2611, 2612, 2613; on the refugee fund, see 2619–21, 2632–33, 2643–51, 2656–58, 2632, 2666–67. For press coverage of Remington's direct examination, see *New York Times*, January 23, 24, 25, 1951, Rauh Papers; *Washington Post*, January 23, 24, 25, 1951, ibid.; *Washington Times-Herald*, January 23, 24, 25, 1951, ibid.; *New York Post*, January 23, 26, 1951, ibid.; *Washington "Evening" Star*, January 24, 1951, ibid.; *New York Herald-Tribune*, January 25, 1951, ibid.

18. For Saypol's cross-examination, see Remington Testimony—First Trial, 2734, 2737, 2825, 2828–29, 2842–46, 2850–51, 2862–63, 2883, 2886–87, 2968–74; *Washington Times-Herald*, January 27, 1951, Rauh Papers; for FBI trial summaries, see, for example, Remington FBI Files 74-1379-1875 through 74-1379-1884; on Cornelison's appearance, see Washington to Director and SAC, New York, January 27, 1951, in ibid. 74-1379-1726; New York to Director, January 28, 1951, ibid. 74-1379-1760; L. L. Laughlin to A. H. Belmont, January 27, 1951, ibid. 74-1379-1759; for Cornelison's reaction to Remington's testimony, see William R. Cornelison, January 27, 1951, ibid. 74-1379-1880, 3; on Hoover's request, see Director, FBI, to the Attorney General, January 27, 1951, ibid. 74-1379-1882; *Washington Post*, January 26, 1951, Rauh Papers; *New York Post*, January 29, 1951, ibid. For press coverage of the cross-examination, see *New York Post*, January 23, 26, and 29, 1951, ibid.; *New York Times*, January 23, 24, and 25, 1951, ibid.; *Washington Times-Herald*, January 23, 24, 25, and 27, 1951, ibid.;

Washington Post, January 23, 24, 25, 26, and 27, 1951, ibid.; *Washington "Evening" Star*, January 23, 24, 25, 26, 27, and 29, 1951, ibid.

19. For Noonan's attack on Rauh, see First Trial Transcript, 1709, 2040, 2167, 2168, 2170, 2171, 3126–32, 3134–37; *Washington Post*, January 31, 1951, and *New York Herald- Tribune*, January 31, 1951, both in Rauh Papers.

20. Cornelison Testimony—First Trial, 3165–94, 3200–219, 3242–43; A. H. Belmont to D. M. Ladd, January 31, 1951, Remington FBI File 74-1379-1781. For press coverage, see *New York Times*, February 1, 1951, Rauh Papers; *Washington Times-Herald*, February 1, 1951, ibid.; *Washington Daily News*, February 1, 1951, ibid.; *Washington "Evening" Star*, February 1, 1951, ibid.

21. Chamberlin Testimony—First Trial, 3393–98, *Washington Times-Herald*, February 2, 1951, Rauh Papers; *New York Times*, February 2, 1951, ibid.; *Washington Post*, February 2, 1951, ibid.

22. Bertram Testimony—First Trial, 3415–17, 3432, 3542.

23. Austrian Testimony—First Trial, 3270–99.

24. Brewrink Testimony—First Trial, 3308, 3310, 3318, 3320, 3321. *Washington Post*, February 3, 1951, Rauh Papers; *New York Post*, February 2, 1951, ibid. For FBI interviews with Robert Nathan, former chairman of the WPB Planning Committee, see FBI Summary Report, 1951, 228; R. W. Goldsmith, ibid., 206; Edward T. Dickinson, former executive director of the WPB Planning Committee, ibid., 179. See also FBI comment on Donald Nelson's *Arsenal of Democracy*, ibid., 253–54. Matthew Fox, who supervised the experiments in California, also could not recall that the Jeans process was secret or had any other confidential classification, see ibid., 261.

25. FBI, Washington Field, to Director and SACs, January 7, 1951, Remington FBI File 74-1379-?; FBI Summary Report, 1951, 197, 231, 280, 287, 289; Bentley Statement, November 30, 1945, 27; Guy Hottel to Director, FBI, January 14, 1951, Remington FBI File 74-1379-1522, 2.

26. Locke Testimony—First Trial, 3350–53, 3359–61, 3363, 3387–88; Chanler's comment on the exhibit is in Cook, "The Remington Tragedy," 495.

27. Nemeth Testimony—First Trial, 3468, 3469; *Washington "Evening" Star*, February 5, 1951, Rauh Papers.

28. McMahon Testimony—First Trial, 3472–75; *Washington Times-Herald*, February 6, 1951, Rauh Papers; Fox Testimony—First Trial, 3514–15, 3536–37; *New York Times*, February 6, 1951, Rauh Papers; *New York Post*, February 6, 1951, ibid.; *Washington "Evening" Star*, February 6, 1951, ibid.

29. Blaisdell Testimony—First Trial, 3671, 3672, 3679, 3681, 3640–43, 3657–62, 3682–97; for Saypol's cross on the Blaisdell–Remington conversation, see ibid., 3657–62, 3682–97. For press coverage of Blaisdell, see the *Washington Times-Herald*, February 6, 1951, Rauh Papers; *New York Post*, February 6, 1951, ibid.; *Washington "Evening" Star*, February 6, 1951, ibid.; *Washington Post*, February 7, 1951, ibid. Daniel Hopkinson also testified for the defense on Remington's postwar anti-Communism; see Hopkinson Testimony—First Trial, 3087–88.

30. For Chanler's motions and each side's request to charge the jury, see First Trial Transcript, 3722–824.

18. The Only Verdict Possible

1. For Chanler's final summation, see First Trial Transcript, 3825–29; for Saypol's summation, see ibid., 3935–4002; for the judge's charge to the jury, see ibid., 4014-4022.

2. Memorandum by E. S. Scully, February 21, 1951, 1–2, Rauh Papers. My discussion of the jury's deliberations is based on Scully's interview with juror number 12, Mrs. Evelyn Tracey. Hereafter cited as Scully Memorandum. See also *Washington Post*, February 8, 1951, and *New*

York Times, February 8, 1951, both in Rauh Papers, for less informative comments by the jurors.

3. *New York Times*, February 8, 1951, Rauh Papers; William Remington to Joseph L. Rauh, Jr., April 9, 1951, ibid. See also William Remington to William C. Chanler, March 13, 1951, Remington Papers.

4. Scully Memorandum, 2.

5. First Trial Transcript, 4027; *Time*, February 19, 1951; *New York Post*, February 8, 1951, Rauh Papers.

6. First Trial Transcript, 4027–31; *New York Post*, February 8, 1951, Rauh Papers.

7. First Trial Transcript, 4033–45; *New York Herald-Tribune*, February 9, 1951, Rauh Papers; *Washington Post*, February 9, 1951, ibid.

8. Hand is quoted in *New York Times*, February 9, 1951, ibid.; see also *Washington Times-Herald*, February 9, 1951, and *Washington Post*, February 9, 1951, both in ibid.

9. Chanler is quoted in *Washington Post*, February 10, 1951, ibid. See also *New York Times*, February 10, 1951, ibid.; *Washington Times-Herald*, February 9, 1951, ibid. The judges are quoted in *Washington Times-Herald*, February 10, 1951, ibid. See also the *Washington "Evening" Star*, February 9, 1951, *Washington Post*, February 10, 1951, *New York Post*, February 13, 1951, *New York Times*, February 14, 1951, and *Washington Post*, February 14, 1951, all in ibid. On Mrs. Robbins's gift, see Joseph L. Rauh, Jr., to William C. Chanler, February 15, 1951, 2, ibid.; Joseph L. Rauh, Jr., to Mrs. Howard C. Robbins, February 15, 1951, ibid.; Joseph L. Rauh, Jr., to William W. Remington, February 15, 1951, ibid.

10. "United States Versus William Remington," reprint of speech by Sen. Homer Ferguson, 1, Congressional Record, 82d Cong., 1st Sess., copy in Rauh Papers; *Washington Times-Herald*, February 9, 1951, ibid.; *Washington Daily News*, February 9, 1951, ibid.; McCarthy is quoted in the *Washington "Evening" Star*, February 8, 1951, ibid. On changing the dismissal standard, see May, *China Scapegoat*, 240–41, 350 n.7.

11. Lillian Remington to Mr. and Mrs. Joseph L. Rauh, March 8, 1951, Rauh Papers; see also William Remington to Joseph L. Rauh, April 1951, ibid.; Bill Remington to Joseph L. Rauh, March 1, 1951, ibid.; Jane Shepherd to Joseph L. Rauh, February 8, 1951, ibid.; Joseph L. Rauh, Jr., to William Remington, March 7, 1951, ibid.; William Remington to John K. Tabor, February 20, 1951, 2, ibid.; William Remington to Joseph L. Rauh, May 2, 1951, ibid.; Joseph L. Rauh, Jr., to Mrs. Howard C. Robbins, June 18, 1951, ibid.

12. On Remington's employment from May through July 1951, see Admission Summary, 3, and Employment Questionnaire in Remington File—Prison.

13. On preparing the appeal, see Joseph L. Rauh, Jr., to William C. Chanler, March 10, 1951, Rauh Papers; John K. Tabor to Joseph L. Rauh, Jr., March 16, 1951, ibid.; Joseph L. Rauh, Jr., to John K. Tabor, March 19, 1951, ibid.; Joseph L. Rauh, Jr., to William C. Chanler, March 31, 1951, ibid.; William C. Chanler to Joseph L. Rauh, Jr., April 3, 1951, ibid.; John K. Tabor to Joseph L. Rauh, Jr., April 5, 1951, ibid.; Joseph L. Rauh, Jr., to John K. Tabor, April 7, 1951, ibid.; Joseph L. Rauh, Jr., to Mrs. Howard C. Robbins, May 29, 1951, ibid.; Joseph L. Rauh, Jr., to William C. Chanler, May 29, 1951, ibid.; Mrs. Howard C. Robbins to Mr. Joseph L. Rauh, Jr., June 2, 1951, ibid.; Joseph L. Rauh, Jr., to Mrs. Howard C. Robbins, June 5, 1951, ibid.; Joseph L. Rauh, Jr., to William C. Chanler, June 6, 1951, 1–2, ibid.; Joseph L. Rauh, Jr., to Mrs. Frances Brody, June 23, 1951, 1, ibid. "United States of America against William Walter Remington, Brief for the Appellant," U.S. Court of Appeals for the Second Circuit, 76–94, ibid. Hereafter cited as Appeal Brief 1; Roger Baldwin to Joseph L. Rauh, Jr., June 20, 1951, ibid.

14. Hand is quoted in *New York Times*, June 16, 1951, ibid.; Max Lerner, "The Keepers of the Conscience," in *New York Post*, August 27, 1951, ibid. For a sketch of Thomas Swan by Learned Hand, see "Thomas Walter Swan" in Irving Dillard, ed., *The Spirit of Liberty: Papers and Addresses of Learned Hand* (New York, 1953), 209–19; on Augustus N. Hand, see "Augustus

Noble Hand" by Charles E. Wyzanski, *Harvard Law Review*, Vol. LXI (April 1948): 573–91; on Learned Hand, see Irwin Ross, "The Legendary Learned Hand," *The Reader's Digest*, July 1951, 105. See also Dillard, *The Spirit of Liberty*, V–XXV. Augustus N. Hand, "United States v. Remington," July 5, 1951, 1–2, Hand Papers; Thomas W. Swan, "United States v. Remington," July 5, 1951, 1, ibid.; Learned Hand, "United States v. Remington," July 31, 1951, 1–5, ibid.; quote is from 5. United States Court of Appeals for the Second Circuit, No. 293, October Term, 1950, United States of America v. William Remington, 1958, 1860–66. See also United States vs. Remington, 191 F. 2d 246 (2d Cir., 1951). Hand's comment is in Hand, "United States v. Remington," 8. For the full text of the decision, see *New York Times*, August 23, 1951.

15. William Remington to Joseph L. Rauh, July 16, 1951, Rauh Papers; Joseph L. Rauh, Jr., to William Remington, July 17, 1951, ibid.; William Remington to Joseph L. Rauh, September 16, 1951, ibid. See also William Remington to Joseph Rauh, September 10, 1951, ibid.; Joseph L. Rauh, Jr., to William Remington, January 30, 1952, ibid.; William Remington to Joseph Rauh, February 1, 1952, ibid.

16. Joseph L. Rauh, Jr., to William C. Chanler, September 12, 1951, ibid.; William C. Chanler to Joseph L. Rauh, Jr., September 13, 1951, ibid.; Joseph L. Rauh, Jr., to William C. Chanler, September 22, 1951, ibid.; William C. Chanler to Joseph L. Rauh, Jr., September 25, 1951, 1–4, ibid.; Joseph L. Rauh, Jr., to James Marshall, October 22, 1951, 1, ibid.

17. Chanler's comment on Cohn is in Cook, "The Remington Tragedy," 497; on Cohn and reindictment, see Cohn, 42–43; United States District Court, United States of America vs. William Walter Remington, Cr. 132-344, 1–5, copy in Rauh Papers and enclosure SAC, New York, to Director, FBI, November 5, 1951, Remington FBI File 74-1379-1974. See also New York to Director, and SAC, October 24, 1951, ibid. 74-1379-1962; "Statement of Joseph L. Rauh, Jr.," October 25, 1951, Rauh Papers; ACLU News Release, October 25, 1951, ibid. See also Patrick Murphy Mullen and Arthur Garfield Hays to Hon. J. Howard McGrath, October 25, 1951, and Stanley Gewirtz to Editor, *Washington Post*, November 5, 1951, ibid.; *The Nation*, November 3, 1951, ibid. Lane is quoted in *New York Herald-Tribune*, October 26, 1951, ibid.; see also *Washington Post*, October 26, 1951, and *New York Times*, October 26, 1951, both in ibid. For Solicitor General Philip B. Pearlman's defense of the government's action, see Philip B. Pearlman to ACLU, November 14, 1951, ibid. In a similar view, see Editorial, *Washington Post*, October 31, 1951, 5, ibid. For response, see Stanley Gewirtz to Herbert Elliston, October 31, 1951, ibid.; author's interview with Joseph L. Rauh, Jr., August 1990, Washington, D.C.

18. Fern Majura, "Why I Can't Get Mad," in *New York Post*, October 26, 1951, Elizabeth Hunt Papers.

19. *New York Journal-American*, October 30, 1951, Rauh Papers; L. L. Laughlin to A. H. Belmont, October 30, 1951, Remington FBI File 74-1379-1970; United States of America vs. William Walter Remington, Cr. 136-289, 2–5, Rauh Papers; the ruling is quoted in *New York Times*, October 31, 1951, ibid.; Rauh's comment is in author's interview with Rauh; Joseph L. Rauh, Jr., to William Remington, December 11, 1951, Rauh Papers; see also Joseph L. Rauh, Jr., to Mrs. Thomas Lamont, December 19, 1951, ibid.; William C. Chanler to Joseph L. Rauh, Jr., January 28, 1952, ibid.

20. Supreme Court of the United States, No. 387, October Term, 1951, William Walter Remington v. The United States of America, on Petition for Writ of Certiorari to the U.S. Court of Appeals for the Second Circuit, March 24, 1952, 1–2, enclosure in Charles Elmore Cropley to Joseph L. Rauh, Jr., March 24, 1952, Rauh Papers. See also *Washington Post*, March 25, 1952, *New York Times*, March 25, 1952, and Editorial in *Washington Post*, March 27, 1951, all in ibid. For Remington's petition, see William Walter Remington, Petitioner v. United States of America on Petition for a Writ of Certiorari to the United States Court of Appeals for the Second Circuit, Supreme Court of the United States, October Term, 1951, No. 387, ibid. For the government's response, see Brief for The United States in Opposition, Rauh

Papers; Lane is quoted in *New York Times*, March 25, 1952, ibid.; Joseph L. Rauh, Jr., to William W. Remington, March 24, 1952, ibid.; author's interview with Rauh, 1990.

19. His Own Worst Enemy

1. "Notes On Meeting At Minton's Office, 10 AM, April 18, 1952," Rauh Papers. Hereafter cited as "Notes On Meeting." William W. Remington to Joseph L. Rauh, Jr., April 15, 1952, ibid.; Joseph L. Rauh, Jr., to William C. Chanler, March 25, 1951, ibid.; "Draft of First Motion To Dismiss Indictment," 1, ibid.; see also Affidavit in Support of First Motion to Dismiss Indictment, 1–4, ibid.; Second Motion to Dismiss Indictment, ibid.; Affidavit in Support of Second Motion to Dismiss Indictment, ibid.; Joseph L. Rauh, Jr., to Gardner Jackson, April 8, 1952, ibid.; Joseph L. Rauh, Jr., to William C. Chanler, March 25, 1951, 3, ibid.; Richard G. Green to Joseph L. Rauh, Jr., April 10, 1952, ibid.; William C. Chanler to Joseph L. Rauh, Jr., April 14, 1952, 2, ibid.; author's interview with Joseph L. Rauh, Jr., August 28, 1992.

2. Joseph L. Rauh, Jr., to William W. Remington, February 20, 1953, 4, Rauh Papers; William C. Chanler to Joseph L. Rauh, Jr., April 28, 1952, 2–3, ibid.; William Remington to Joseph L. Rauh, Jr., March 14, 1953, 1, ibid.; "Notes On Meeting."

3. Joseph L. Rauh, Jr., to William C. Chanler, April 21, 1952, Rauh Papers; William C. Chanler to Joseph L. Rauh, Jr., April 24, 1952, ibid.; William C. Chanler to Joseph L. Rauh, Jr., April 25, 1952, ibid.; see also Joseph L. Rauh, Jr., to William C. Chanler, April 26, 1952, ibid., and Joseph L. Rauh, Jr., to John K. Tabor, April 28, 1952, ibid.; Joseph L. Rauh, Jr., to William Remington, July 2, 1952, ibid.

4. SAC, New York, to Director, FBI, March 3, 1951, Silvermaster FBI File (New York Field Office) 65-14603-4344; SAC, New York, to Director, FBI, March 28, 1951, ibid. 65-14603-4350; "News Release," *McCall's* magazine, in Elizabeth T. Bentley FBI File 134-435-40; Tom Donnelly, "Capitalized, Televised, and Now Serialized" in *Washington News*, ibid. 134-435-41; see also Director, FBI, to SAC, New York, April 26, 1951, Silvermaster FBI File (New York Field Office) 65-14603-4357; SAC, New York, to Director, FBI, May 9, 1951, ibid. 65-14603-4359; Memorandum Re: Gregory, September 15, 1951, ibid. 65-14603-4380; Memorandum Re: Gregory, September 18, 1951, ibid. 65-14603-4381; SAC, New York, to Director, FBI, September 29, 1951, ibid. 65-14603-4383; Bentley is quoted in *New Haven Register*, October 6, 1951, Elizabeth Bentley FBI File 134-435-48; SAC, New Haven, to Director, FBI, October 16, 1951, Silvermaster FBI File (New York Field Office) 65-14603-4387; Elizabeth Bentley, n.d., ibid. 65-14603-4397; New York to Bureau, October 3, 1951, ibid. 65-14603-4393; New York to Bureau, October 13, 1951, ibid. 65-14603-4393. For reviews of *Out of Bondage*, see *Book Review Digest, 1951*, 75; Bentley called the book "amateurish"; see *New Haven Register*, October 6, 1951, Bentley FBI File 134-435-48; SAC, New York, to Director, FBI, January 23, 1952, ibid. 134-435-2; Memo Re: Gregory, March 17, 1952, Silvermaster FBI File (New York Field Office) 65-14603-4403; Director to SAC, New York, October 9, 1951, ibid. 65-14603-4386, 1–2; John B. Oakes, *New York Times Book Review*, September 23, 1951.

5. Memorandum Re: Gregory, May 7, 1951, Silvermaster FBI File (New York Field Office) 65-14603-4413, 1–3; on John Wright, see A. H. Belmont to D. M. Ladd, March 16, 1953, Bentley FBI File 134-435-74, 1; for Wright's version, see Memo Re: Gregory, May 14, 1952, Silvermaster FBI File (New York Field Office) 65-14603-4418, 1; see also Memo Re: Gregory, May 16, 1952, ibid. 65-14603-4420, 3–4; SAC, New York, to Director, FBI, May 16, 1952, ibid. 65-14603-4420; Memorandum Re: Gregory, May 7, 1951, ibid. 65-14603-4413, 3–4; for Spencer's view, see W. W. Cleveland to A. H. Belmont, May 8, 1952, ibid. 65-14603-4421, 1; Memorandum Re: Gregory, May 8, 1952, ibid. 65-14603-4414; Memorandum, May 9, 1952, ibid. 65-14603-4415; Memorandum Re: Gregory, May 12, 1952, ibid. 65-14603-4423, 1–2; on Wright's meeting with Lane, see Memo Re: Gregory, May 14, 1952, ibid. 65-14603-4418, 1–2;

A. H. Belmont to D. M. Ladd, May 15, 1952, Bentley FBI File 134-435-57; Memo Re: Elizabeth Bentley, May 15, 1952, Silvermaster FBI File (New York Field Office) 65-14603-4421. In 1953, Wright complained to J. Edgar Hoover about his treatment by Lane and Agent Danahy, forcing the Bureau to review its files on the incident. See John B. Wright to Hon. J. Edgar Hoover, March 9, 1953, Bentley FBI File 134-435-741; see also A. H. Belmont to D. M. Ladd, March 16, 1953, ibid. 134-435-74, 1–4; William M. Whelan to SAC, New York, March 16, 1953, Silvermaster FBI File (New York Field Office) 65-14603-4454, 1.

6. FBI, New Haven, to Director, FBI, and SAC, New York, August 29, 1952, ibid. 65-14603-44, 1–2; A. H. Belmont to D. M. Ladd, August 29, 1952, Bentley FBI File 134-435-61, 1–2; SAC, New York, to Director, FBI, September 4, 1952, ibid. 134-435-63; New York to Director, FBI, September 26, 1952, ibid. unserialized, 3–4.

7. SAC, New York, to Director, FBI, September 26, 1952, Silvermaster FBI File (New York Field Office) 65-14603-4439, 3–6; A. H. Belmont to D. M. Ladd, September 26, 1952, Bentley FBI File 134-435-67, 1–2; SAC, New York, to Director, FBI, March 24, 1955, ibid. 134-182-66; Bentley is quoted in "Unknown Subjects," Harvey Marshall Matusow, March 9, 1955, ibid. 134-182-74, 4–5, 6.

8. Washington Field to Director and SAC, March 22, 1952, Remington FBI File 74-1379-1997; New York to Director and SAC, March 24, 1952, ibid. 74-1379-1999; Director, FBI, to Assistant Attorney General James M. McInery, March 27, 1952, ibid. 74-1379-1998.

9. On the witnesses, see Teletype, New York to San Francisco, December 9, 1952, ibid. 74-1379-2038; William Walter Remington, December 9, 1951, ibid. 74-1379-2055, 1–2; Boston to Director, FBI, December 18, 1952, ibid. 74-1379-2065, 1–7; William Walter Remington, December 23, 1952, ibid. 74-1379-2073, 1; William Walter Remington, December 24, 1952, ibid. 74-1379-2073, 2–3; C. H. Stanley to A. H. Belmont, January 8, 1953, ibid. 74-1379-2099, 2; for the FBI's interviews with Lewis Jack Holmes, see FBI Summary Report, 1951, 372–74; on Wilgus, see Wilgus Testimony—Second Trial, 110–19; Teletype, Boardman to Bureau, December 4, 1952, Remington FBI File 74-1379-2099; William Walter Remington, December 23, 1952, ibid. 74-1379-2073, 2–3, 4–5; Stanley to Belmont, January 8, 1953, 2; Martin was placed last on the potential witness list.

10. Teletype, Boardman to Bureau, November 24, 1952, Remington FBI File 74-1379-2032; A. H. Belmont to D. M. Ladd, December 29, 1952, ibid. 74-1379-2085, 1–2; William C. Chanler to Joseph L. Rauh, Jr., February 9, 1953, Rauh Papers.

11. For the potential jurors' anti-Communist sentiments, see Second Trial Transcript, 20, 36, 93, 101, 102, 103; two alternates were "housewives," the third was a "maintenance supervisor." For the complete voir dire, see ibid., 2–111A; see also *New York Times*, January 14, 1953, for list of jurors' names, addresses and occupations; Teletype, FBI, New York, to Director, January 14, 1953, Remington FBI File 74-1379-2124, 1–2.

12. *New York Times*, January 14, 1953; Cook, *Maverick*, 46; Bentley Testimony—Second Trial, 272, 275–77, 292–93; Ann Remington Testimony—Second Trial, 211.

13. *New York Times*, January 14, 1953, Rauh Papers; Remington Testimony—Second Trial, 536, 543, 547, 572, 584, 626–27, 674–75, 708, 714, 716, 720, 734–36, 764–65, 771–72, 781, 798.

14. Leibell's view is in Second Trial Transcript, 665, 704–5, 707, 727–28, 777–80; see also *New York Times*, January 21, 1953, Rauh Papers.

15. For Minton's summation, see Second Trial Transcript, 942–65; for Lane's summation, see ibid., 974–1020.

16. For the government's requests to charge the jury, see Second Trial Transcript, 1021–24; for Minton's requests, see ibid., 1024–26A; *New York Times*, January 28, 1953, Rauh Papers; Second Trial Transcript, 1071–113.

17. Second Trial Transcript, 1114–18.

18. Joseph L. Rauh, Jr., to Mrs. Howard C. Robbins, January 30, 1953, Rauh Papers; William Remington to Joseph L. Rauh, Jr., February 25, 1953, ibid.; William Remington to Joe Rauh, June 27, 1952, ibid.; Joseph L. Rauh, Jr., to William Remington, July 2, 1952, ibid. For Jane's view of Bill, see Jane Remington to Cass Canfield, Dec. 12, 1954, Remington Papers.

19. Second Trial Transcript, 1124–45.

20. Joseph L. Rauh, Jr., to William W. Remington, February 4, 1953, Rauh Papers; see also Joseph L. Rauh, Jr., to William C. Chanler, February 5, 1953, ibid.; Joseph L. Rauh, Jr., to Mrs. Howard C. Robbins, February 5, 1953, ibid.; see also Joseph L. Rauh, Jr., to James A. Wechsler, February 5, 1953, ibid.; Joseph L. Rauh, Jr., to William W. Remington, February 20, 1953, 1–7, ibid.; William Remington to Joseph L. Rauh, Jr., February 23, 1953, ibid.; William Remington to Joseph L. Rauh, Jr., March 13, 1953, ibid.; Telegram, Joe Rauh to William Remington, March 15, 1953, ibid.; Bill Remington to Joseph Rauh, March 16, 1953, ibid.; Bill Remington to Joseph Rauh, March 16, 1953 ("Penn. Station letter"), ibid.; Bill Remington to Joseph Rauh, March 16, 1953 (final letter), ibid.; John K. Tabor to Joseph L. Rauh, Jr., March 20, 1953, ibid.; Telegram, Joe Rauh to John Tabor, March 24, 1953, ibid.

21. Joseph L. Rauh, Jr., to Richard G. Green, March 27, 1953, 2, ibid.; for Kilsheimer's demands, see John K. Tabor to Joseph L. Rauh, Jr., March 20, 1953, 1–2, ibid.; Daddy to Gale and Bruce, April 14, 1953, 1–6, Remington Papers.

20. The Ends of Expediency

1. William Remington to Jane Remington, April 16, 1953, 1, "Letters."

2. Hiss, *Recollections of a Life*, 165, 166; Remington to Remington, April 16, 1953, 2, "Letters"; E. E. Thompson to the Director, April 17, 1953, 2, Remington File—Prison; Visiting Record, Federal House of Detention, Remington, William, in ibid.; Jane Remington to E. E. Thompson, April 21, 1953, ibid.

3. E. E. Thompson to the Director, ibid.; James V. Bennett to Warden Thompson, April 22, 1953, ibid.; see also James V. Bennett to Warden Humphrey, April 22, 1953, ibid.; G. W. Humphrey to the Director, April 27, 1953, ibid.

4. United States District Court for the Southern District of New York, United States of America vs. William Walter Remington, May 25, 1953, 20, Rauh Papers. For Green and Kilsheimer's arguments, see 2–37; Judge Vincent L. Leibell to Richard G. Green, June 9, 1953, 1–2, Green Papers; Memo, John K. Tabor to Joe Rauh, n.d., Rauh Papers; William C. Chanler to Joseph L. Rauh, Jr., August 13, 1953, ibid. On the *Williams* case, see T. W. Swan, "U.S. v. Remington," 1, Preconference Memoranda in Hand Papers; William Remington to Richard G. Green, May 10, 1953, Green Papers.

5. William Remington to Jane Remington, May 27, 1953, 8–9, "Letters"; Telegram, Jane Remington to William Remington, June 2, 1953, Remington File—Prison; Bill Remington to Jane Remington, June 2, 1953, Remington Papers.

6. Bill Remington to Jane Remington, June 21, 1953, 13–14, ibid.; Jane Remington to G. W. Humphrey, August 31, 1953, Remington File—Prison; M. S. Richmond to Mrs. Jane Remington, September 3, 1953, ibid.; Visitor's Voucher, September 16, 1953, ibid.; Bill Remington to Jane Remington, September 17, 1953, 16–17, ibid. Remington's prison file contains copies of photographs taken of him at various times during his incarceration. Jane Abramson to author, September 17, 1993.

7. Joseph L. Rauh, Jr., to Mrs. Howard C. Robbins, July 31, 1953, Rauh Papers; Joseph L. Rauh, Jr., to William C. Chanler, July 31, 1953, ibid.; Bethuel M. Webster to Joseph L. Rauh, Jr., August 19, 1953, ibid.; see also John M. Minton to Joseph L. Rauh, Jr., August 10, 1953, ibid.; William C. Chanler to Joseph L. Rauh, Jr., October 13, 1953, ibid.; Brief For Appellant, 40, United States Court of Appeals for the Second Circuit, United States of America vs. William Walter Remington, ibid.; Teletype, New York to Director, October 15, 1953,

Remington FBI File 74-1379-2177, 1–3; Teletype, New York to the Director, October 16, 1953, ibid. 74-1379-2178, 1–3; Bill Remington to Jane Remington, November 5, 1953, 1–2, Green Papers.

8. Thomas W. Swan, "U.S. v. Remington," October 24, 1953, 1–3, Hand Papers; Augustus N. Hand, "United State vs. Remington," October 28, 1953, ibid.; Cook, *Maverick*, 47; United States of America v. William Walter Remington, United States Court of Appeals for the Second Circuit Before L. Hand, Swan and Augustus N. Hand, Circuit Judges, 108. Swan's concurrence is on 8; copy is in U.S. Attorneys Records. Citation for the decision is Remington v. United States, U.S. 208 F. 2d 567 (2d Cir., 1953); see also *New York Times*, November 25, 1953; on Hand's drafts, see Gunther to author, 2; L. Hand, dissenting, 1–6, 8–10, Remington v. United States, U.S. 208 F. 2d 567 (2d Cir., 1953); for Donegan's response to Hand's criticism, see Thomas J. Donegan to the Attorney General, November 30, 1953, Remington FBI File 74-1379-2188; United States Court of Appeals, United States v. William Walter Remington, November 24, 1953, Rauh Papers.

9. John K. Tabor to Joseph L. Rauh, Jr., December 3, 1953, ibid.; Joseph L. Rauh, Jr., to John K. Tabor, December 3, 1953, ibid.; Joseph L. Rauh, Jr., to Charles C. Burlingame, December 7, 1953, ibid.; see also Richard G. Green to Joseph L. Rauh, Jr., November 25, 1953, ibid.; Joseph L. Rauh, Jr., to Stanley M. Rosenblum, December 3, 1953, ibid.; Joseph L. Rauh, Jr., to James Marshall, December 7, 1953, ibid. For the writ, see William Walter Remington, Petitioner Against the United States of America, Petition for a Writ of Certiorari to the United States Court of Appeals for the Second Circuit, Supreme Court of the United States, October Term, 1953, No. 506, Rauh Papers. For Rauh's response to the government's Brief in Opposition, see Reply Brief For Petitioner, 1–2, William Walter Remington vs. United States of America, Supreme Court of the United States, October Term, 1953, No. 506, ibid.; see also *New York Times*, December 25, 1953.

10. Harold B. Wiley to Joseph L. Rauh, Jr., February 8, 1954, Rauh Papers; Harold B. Wiley to Richard G. Green, February 8, 1954, Green Papers. A copy of Wiley's letter to Remington's lawyers is also in Remington File—Prison; Learned Hand to Felix Frankfurter, February 25, 1954, 2, Hand Papers; Felix Frankfurter to B. [Learned Hand], March 3, 1954, 2, Hand Papers.

11. Joseph L. Rauh, Jr., "Felix Frankfurter: Civil Libertarian," *Harvard Civil Liberties Review*, Vol. 11, No. 3 (Summer 1976): 510–13, Rauh Papers; see also Joseph L. Rauh, Jr., "An Unabashed Liberal Looks at a Half Century of the Supreme Court," *North Carolina Law Review*, Vol. 69 (November 1990), ibid. On the Black–Jackson relationship, see Dennis Hutchinson, "The Black–Jackson Feud," in Kurland et al., eds., *The Supreme Court Review, 1988* (Chicago, 1989), 203–43, and Edwin M. Yoder, Jr., *The Un-Making of a Whig and Other Essays in Self-Definition* (Washington, D.C., 1990), 3–107.

12. For Jane's plea to Judge Leibell, see United States District Court for the Southern District of New York, United States of America v. William Walter Remington, 3–4, appended to Second Trial Transcript; Draft Application For Parole, n.d., 1–3, Remington File—Prison. The final draft is not in Remington's prison file; Report on Convicted Prisoner By United States Attorney, May 26, 1953, 2., ibid.; see also Rider attached. Notice of Action of Parole Board, June 17, 1954, ibid.; United States Board of Parole to Warden, June 17, 1954, ibid.; *Washington "Evening" Star*, June 25, 1954, Remington FBI File 101-1165-Sub A.

13. Supervision Card, Remington File—Prison; Bill Remington to Jane Remington, November 1, 1954, Green Papers; Visitor's Vouchers for February 18, March 25, May 13, June 16, September 8, October 6, and November 4, 1954, all in Remington File—Prison; William Remington to Jane Remington, November 18, 1954, 1, Green Papers; William Remington to Jane Remington, November 14, 1954, 2, ibid.; William Remington to Richard G. Green, October 18, 1954, ibid.

14. Information Concerning Assault and Death of Victim—William W. Remington, FBI Murder File 70-22845-25, 12; see also William Walter Remington, April 13, 1955, in ibid. 70-22845-108, 17, 19, 22; Information Concerning Assault and Death of Victim—William Walter Remington, ibid. 70-22845-25, 13; Nurses Notes, Remington File—Prison; Clinical Record, ibid.; Leon A. Witkin to Dr. H. M. Janney, November 26, 1954, ibid.

15. Jane Remington's conversation with Warden Wilkinson is quoted in *New York Post,* November 25, 1954, Green Papers. See also *New York Herald-Tribune,* November 25, 1954, ibid.; Notes, Green Papers; author's interviews with Richard G. Green, September 23, 1985, and September 3, 1992; Memorandum for the Attorney General, January 7, 1955, Bureau of Prison Records; Memorandum For Mr. Rogers by James V. Bennett, November 24, 1954, 2, ibid.

16. Witkin to Janney, November 26, 1954, 2, Remington File—Prison; Radiographic Report, November 22, 1954, ibid.; Clinical Record, 2, ibid.; Operation Report, November 23, 1954, ibid.; Dr. Leonard Breslaw to Dr. L. L. Ashburn, December 6, 1954, 1–2, ibid.; Dr. Charles Tomlinson Testimony, 7–11, Transcript of Proceedings—McCoy; Nurse Notes, November 24, 1954, Remington File—Prison.

17. Witkin to Janney, November 26, 1954, 3, ibid.; Dr. Ellsworth C. Alvord, Jr., to Chief Medical Officer in Charge, December 29, 1954, 1–3, ibid.; Death Certificate, William Walter Remington, November 24, 1954, ibid.; *Washington City News Service,* November 25, 1954, FBI Murder File 70-22845-A; on Remington's funeral, see *Washington News,* November 26, 1954, ibid.; the *Sunbury Daily Item,* November 27, 1954, ibid.; *Philadelphia Evening Bulletin,* November 29, 1954, ibid.

18. Lillian Remington is quoted in the *Philadelphia Evening Bulletin,* November 29, 1954, ibid.; Jane Remington in *New York Post,* November 24, 1954, ibid.; the tabloid is *Confidential,* May 1955, ibid.; for Bentley's comment, see Teletype, FBI, New Orleans, to Director, FBI, November 24, 1954, in Bentley FBI File 134-435-125. Ann Remington is quoted in unidentified newspaper, FBI Murder File 70-22845-A. Her later comments are in Ann Reminton interview; Brunini, "Rolling Stone," chapter 14, p. 18.

19. Jane Abramson to author, September 17, 1993; George Montgomery, "Dishonored Death Comes To A Rebel," *New York World-Telegram,* November 24, 1954, Green Papers; "The Shame At Lewisburg" in *New York Herald-Tribune,* November 27, 1954, FBI Murder File 70-22845-A; "Cowardly Attack" in the *Scranton Tribune,* November 26, 1954, ibid.; the *Scranton Times,* November 24, 1954, ibid.; "Murder at Lewisburg" in *Washington Post,* November 25, 1954, ibid.; Drew Pearson, "Ex-Inmate Bares Prison Vice," in the *Washington Merry-Go-Round,* December 4, 1954, ibid.; Green is quoted in *Washington City News Service,* November 24, 1954, ibid. See also *Newsweek,* December 6, 1954, 29. For a discussion of the various theories, see *New York Herald-Tribune,* November 25, 1954, and *Washington Daily News,* November 25, 1954, FBI Murder File 70-22845-A; *New York Post,* December 6, 1954, ibid. The letters excerpted were Bill Remington to Jane Remington, October 5, November 4, November 10, November 14, and November 18, 1954, all in Green Papers. Bennett is quoted in the *Scranton Times,* December 1, 1954, FBI Murder File 70-22845-A. For Fred Mullen's view, see L. B. Nichols to Mr. Tolson, June 1, 1955, ibid. 70-22845-16, 1–4; for Bennett's report, see Memorandum for the Attorney General, January 5, 1955, Bureau of Prison Files.

20. George J. McCoy et al., April 13, 1955, FBI Murder File 70-22845-108; Interview with Robert Carl Parker, November 22, 1954, in George J. McCoy et al., November 28, 1954, ibid. 70-22845-25, 22–23; Teletype, Philadelphia to Washington, November 23, 1954, ibid. 70-22845-10; SA to SAC, Philadelphia, January 27, 1955, ibid. 70-22845-90; Interview with George Junior McCoy, November 22, 1954, ibid. 70-22845-25, 31–32.

21. Interview with Lewis Cagle, Jr., November 22, 1954, ibid. 70-22845-25, 15–16; Teletype, Philadelphia to Washington, November 23, 1954, ibid. 70-22845-6; George J.

McCoy et al., November 28, 1954, ibid. 70-22845-25, 18; *Washington News*, November 23, 1954 (FBI comment on blood is typed on newspaper), in Prosecutive Summary Report, January 10, 1955, ibid. 70-22845-75, 34–35; Teletype, Philadelphia to Washington, November 23, 1954, ibid. 70-22845-10; A. Rosen to L. V. Boardman, November 25, 1953, ibid. 70-22845-5, 2–3; L. B. Nichols to Mr. Tolson, November 24, 1954, ibid. 70-22845-8; *Washington Post*, November 26, 1954, ibid. 70-22845-A; SA to SAC, January 27, 1955, ibid. 70-22845-70.

22. Interview with Robert Carl Parker, November 24, 1954, in George J. McCoy et al., November 28, 1954, ibid. 70-22845-25, 26–28; Interview with Lewis Cagle, Jr., November 24, 1954, ibid., 17–18.

23. Teletype, Philadelphia to Washington and Director, November 25, 1954, ibid. 70-22845-19; see also Mr. Price to Mr. Rosen, November 25, 1954, ibid. 70-22845-21; Mr. Price to Mr. Rosen, November 26, 1954, ibid. 70-22845-20; Mr. Price to Mr. Rosen, November 26, 1954, ibid. 70-22845-16, 1–3; Max Lerner, "Remington and Hiss," *New York Post*, Remington FBI File 101-1145-A; J. Julius Levy to Hon. Warren Olney III, May 27, 1955, 90-1-7-3786, Criminal Division Records—Remington Murder, Department of Justice, Washington, D.C. Hereafter cited as Murder File—Criminal Division. L. B. Nichols to Mr. Tolson, November 26, 1954, FBI Murder File 70-22845-9.

24. For Bennett's view, see Memorandum for Mr. Rogers, November 24, 1954, 2, Bureau of Prison Records; see also Memorandum for the Attorney General, January 5, 1955, 1, 12, ibid.; *Washington News*, November 26, 1954, FBI Murder File 70-22845-A; *Washington City News Service*, November 26, 1954, ibid.; *Bethleham Globe-Times*, November 26, 1954, ibid.; *Washington "Evening" Star*, December 1, 1954, ibid.; *Scranton Times*, December 1, 1954, ibid.; *Detroit News*, December 3, 1954, ibid.; *Philadelphia Evening Bulletin*, December 8, 1954, ibid.; Interviews with George Junior McCoy, November 23, 25, and 26, 1954, in George J. McCoy et al., ibid. 70-22845-25, 32; see also Record of Good Time Forfeiture Hearing in the Case of George McCoy, November 29, 1954, 1–5, McCoy File—Prison.

25. Interview with George Junior McCoy, November 30, 1945, in Prosecutive Summary Report, January 10, 1955, FBI Murder File 70-22845-75, 45–49; Interview with Robert Carl Parker, November 25, 28, 1954, in George J. McCoy et al., ibid. 70-22845-25, 44–45; Supplemental Statement, in George J. McCoy et al., December 6, 1954, ibid. 70-22845-44, 8; on the grand jury and Judge Watson's actions, see *Washington "Evening" Star*, December 1, 1954, in ibid. 70-22845-A; *Philadelphia Evening Bulletin*, December 1, 1954, ibid.; *Philadelphia Gazette*, December 1, 1954, ibid.; *Detroit Times*, December 1, 1954, ibid.; *Scranton Times*, December 1, 1954, ibid.; *Scranton Tribune*, December 2, 1954, ibid.; *Washington Post*, December 2, 1954, ibid.; *Philadelphia Evening Bulletin*, December 2, 1954, ibid.

26. *Washington Post*, December 12, 1954, ibid.; Teletype, Philadelphia to Director, FBI, January 25, 1955, ibid. 70-22845-83; SAC, Philadelphia, to Director, FBI, January 3, 1955, ibid. 70-22845-67; F. T. Wilkinson to C. H. Fleckinstein, March 21, 1955, Murder File—Criminal Division; *Washington Post*, December 14, 1954, *New York Mirror*, December 14, 1954, *New York Herald-Tribune*, December 14, 1954, *Washington "Evening" Star*, December 15, 1954, and *Washington Post*, January 15, 1955, all in ibid.

27. J. Julius Levy to Rex A. Collings, Jr., April 4, 1955, 1–3, Murder File—Criminal Division.

28. George J. McCoy et al., November 28, 1954, FBI Murder File 70-22845-25, 34–36; H. H. Helter to Files, April 19, 1955, 1–2, Murder File—Criminal Division; F. T. Wilkinson to James V. Bennett, April 26, 1955, 1–2, ibid.; Memorandum for Mr. Olney by James V. Bennett, April 19, 1955, 1–2, ibid.; *Washington City News Service*, May 6, 1955, and *Sunbury Daily Item*, May 7, 1955, both in FBI Murder File 70-22845-A; Editorial in *Sunbury Daily Item*, ibid.

29. See pp. 15–19, Transcript of Proceedings—McCoy; Follmer's remarks and the sentencing is quoted in ibid.; see also Teletype, Philadelphia to the Director, May 26, 1955, FBI

Murder File 70-22845-115; Memorandum for Mr. Mullen, June 9, 1955, Bureau of Prison Records; Memorandum for the Attorney General, January 5, 1955, 14, 18, ibid.

Epilogue. In Dubious and Ambiguous Battle

1. Cook tells the story of the Remington assignment in Cook, *Maverick*, 22–49. Woltman is quoted on 28.

2. Minton is quoted in Cook, "An Overdose of Curiosity: William Remington's Tragic Search That Ended in Death," *Saga*, April 1957, 86–87. Hereafter cited as Cook, "Overdose." Cook quote is in *Maverick*, 49; Cook, "Overdose," 8.

3. "Remington—and Hiss," editors' introduction to Cook, "The Remington Tragedy: A Study of Injustice," *The Nation*, December 28, 1957, 485.

4. Cohn, 31, 36.

5. Max Lerner, "Remington and Hiss," *New York Post*, Remington FBI File 101-1145-A; Murray Kempton, "The Victim," *New York Post*, November 26, 1954, Green Papers. Remington's experience with the Communist movement is so unusual that it contributes evidence to both historical schools focusing on American Communism in the postwar years. To the Theodore Draper*-Harvey Khler school of historians, which emphasizes the close connections between Moscow and the American Communist Party, Remington's activities partly suggest the contrary: that one could be an independent Communist, free to act as one wished without regard to the Party line or control from Moscow. But his activities also provide evidence that the Party was sometimes, if not always, used as a recruiting ground for Soviet espionage.

Bibliography

PRIMARY SOURCES

Personal Collections

John Gilland Brunini Papers, Special Collections, Georgetown University Library, Georgetown University, Washington, D.C.

Paul Crouch Papers, Hoover Institution on War, Revolution and Peace, Stanford, Calif.

Richard G. Green Papers, in the possession of Mr. Green, New York, N.Y.

Learned Hand Papers, Harvard Law School Library, Harvard University, Cambridge, Mass.

Daniel Lang Papers, Manuscripts Division, Muger Memorial Library, Boston University, Boston, Mass.

Donald H. Miller, Jr., Papers, in the possession of Mr. Miller, Chappaqua, N.Y.

Joseph L. Rauh, Jr., Papers, in author's possession.

William Walter Remington Files, Special Collections, Baker Library, Dartmouth College, Hanover, N.H.

William Walter Remington Papers, in the possession of Mrs. Edward Abramson, Victoria, British Columbia, Canada.

John R. Scotford, Jr., Papers, in the possession of Mr. Scotford, East Thetford, Vt.

Selma R. Williams Papers, in the possession of Ms. Williams, Boston, Mass.

Government Records

Department of Justice

Federal Bureau of Investigation Files: Elizabeth T. Bentley; John Gilland Brunini; Elizabeth Moos; William Walter Remington; Nathan G. Silvermaster case

U.S. Attorneys Files, National Archives and Records Center, Bayonne, N.J.

Criminal Division: William Remington File, 146–200–5723.

Bureau of Prison Files: William Walter Remington; George McCoy
Office of the Pardon Attorney: Lewis Cagle, Jr., File

Civil Service Commission
William Remington File, Record Group 46, National Archives, Washington, D.C.

National Resources Planning Board Control Office, Record Group 187, National Archives, Washington, D.C.

Office of Personnel Management Records, Washington, D.C.

Court Records

U.S. v. John Doe, Grand Jury Records, United States District Court for the Southern District of New York, May–June, 1950, in author's possession.
U.S. Court of Appeals for the Second Circuit, "United States vs. William Walter Remington," Transcripts of Record, (1950–1953), National Archives and Records Service, Bayonne, N.J. (cited as First Trial and Second Trial).
United States District Court for the Southern District of New York, "United States of America vs. William Walter Remington," Stenographer's Minutes (1953), National Archives and Records Service, Bayonne, N.J.
United States District Court for the Middle District of Pennsylvania, Transcript of Proceedings in case of George Junior McCoy, Lewis Cagle, Jr., Robert Carl Parker, May 26, 1954, court archives, Scranton, Pa.
Presentencing Report on George Junior McCoy, October 9, 1953, United States District Court for the Eastern District of Kentucky.
Presentencing Report on George Junior McCoy, May 16, 1955, United States District Court for the Middle District of Pennsylvania.
Trial Records of George McCoy, courthouse, Grundy, Va.
Lewis Cagle, Jr., v. United States of America, "Motion to Withdraw Plea of Guilty and Set Aside Judgment of Committal," April 17, 1973, Case No. 73-213, archives, U.S. district court, Scranton, Pa.
Ann M. Remington v. William Walter Remington, Case No. 7454, circuit court, Fairfax County, Va.

Government Publications

U.S. Congress. 80th Cong. 1st sess. Joint Committee on Atomic Energy. *Confirmation of Atomic Energy Commissioner and General Manager.* Washington, D.C., 1947.
U.S. Congress. House. 80th Cong. 2d sess. Committee on Un-American Activities. *Hearings Regarding Communist Espionage in the U.S. Government.* Washington, D.C., 1948.
U.S. Congress. Senate. 80th Cong. 2d sess. Investigations Subcommittee of Committee on Expenditures in the Executive Department. *Export Policy and Loyalty.* Washington, D.C., 1948.
U.S. Congress. Senate. 81st Cong. 1st sess. Committee on Interstate and Foreign Commerce. *Nomination of Thomas C. Blaisdell to be Assistant Secretary of Commerce.* Washington, D.C., 1949.
U.S. Congress. House. 81st Cong. 2d sess. Committee on Un-American Activities. *Hearings Regarding Communism in the U.S. Government—Part I.* Washington, D.C., 1950.

Author's Interviews

Mrs. Jane Remington Abramson, Mr. L. P. Baldwin, Mr. Stephen Bradley, Mr. David Bradley, Mr. William Bronk, Mrs. Margaret Conant, Col. Robert Davidson, Mr. Franklin Folsom, Mr. Samuel Dix, Mr. W. Atherton Fuller, Mr. George Eddy, Mr. William Goodman, Mr. Richard G. Green, Mr. Culver Griffin, Mr. Donald Hammond, Prof. Henry Hart, Mrs. Patricia Hatfield, Mrs. Elizabeth Starks Hunt, Mr. Nicholas Jacobson, Mr. Asher Lans, Mr. Robert S. Lehman, Mr. Charles Livermore, Prof. Joseph V. Lombardo, Mrs. Mabel Abercrombie Mansfield, Mr. Daniel May, Mr. Dexter Martin, Mr. William Martin, Mrs. Muriel Speare Williams Mather, Mr. Donald H. Miller, Jr., Mr. Willard Osborne, Mr. John Parke, Mr. Irving Paul, Prof. Jack Preiss, Mr. Alan Rader, Mr. Joseph L. Rauh, Jr., Mr. Bernard S. Redmont, Dr. Ann M. Remington, Mr. Bruce Remington, Mr. Storey Rise, Mr. John R. Scotford, Jr., Mr. Richard Sherwin, Dr. Page Smith, Mr. Budd Schulberg, Mr. Jacob Todd, Mr. Stephen Teller, Mrs. Elizabeth Trembecki, Mr. Gary Webb

SECONDARY SOURCES

Books, Articles, and Dissertations

Andrew, Christopher, and Oleg Gordievsky. *KGB: The Inside Story*. New York, 1990.

Barth, Allen. *The Loyalty of Free Men*. New York, 1952.

Belfrage, Cedric. *The American Inquisition, 1945–1960*. Indianapolis, 1973.

Belknap, Michael R. *Cold War Political Justice: The Smith Act, the Communist Party and American Civil Liberties*. Westport, Conn., 1977.

Bentley, Elizabeth. *Out of Bondage: The Story of Elizabeth Bentley*. New York, 1988 (paperback edition).

Bentley, Eric, ed. *Thirty Years of Treason: Excerpts from Hearings Before the House Committee on Un-American Activities, 1933–1968*. New York, 1971.

Bontecou, Eleanor. *The Federal Loyalty-Security Program*. Ithaca, N.Y., 1953.

Brax, Ralph. *The First Student Movement: Student Activism in the United States During the 1930s*. Port Washington, N.Y., 1981.

Brown, Anthony Cave, and Charles B. MacDonald. *On a Field of Red: The Communist International and the Coming of World War II*. New York, 1981.

Brown, Ralph S., Jr. *Loyalty and Security: Employment Tests in the United States*. New Haven, Conn., 1958.

Brunini, John G. "The Three 'Spy Grand Juries.'" *Catholic World*, March 1953.

Brunini, John G. "Has America Got The 'Red Jitters'?" *The Catholic Mind*, January 1950.

Caute, David. *The Great Fear: The Anti-Communist Purge Under Truman and Eisenhower*. New York, 1978.

Ceplair, Larry, and Steven Englund. *The Inquisition in Hollywood: Politics in the Film Community, 1930–1960*. New York, 1980.

Chamberlain, Lawrence H. *Loyalty and Legislative Action*. Ithaca, N.Y., 1951.

Cohn, Roy M. *McCarthy: The Answer to "Tail-Gunner Joe."* New York, 1977.

Cook, Fred J. *Maverick: Fifty Years of Investigative Reporting*. New York, 1984.

Cook, Fred J. *The Nightmare Decade: The Life and Times of Senator Joe McCarthy*. New York, 1971.

Cook, Fred J. *The F.B.I. Nobody Knows*. New York, 1964.

Cook, Fred J. "The Remington Tragedy: A Study of Injustice." *The Nation*, December 28, 1957.

Cook, Fred J. "An Overdose of Curiosity: William Remington's Tragic Search That Ended in Death." *Saga*, April 1957.

Dallin, David J. *Soviet Espionage*. New Haven, Conn., 1955.

Dillard, Irving, ed. *The Spirit of Liberty: Papers and Addresses of Learned Hand*. New York, 1953.

Downing, Francis. "The Reluctant Witness." *The Commonweal*, January 26, 1951.

Draper, Theodore. "The Popular Front Revisited." *The New York Review of Books*, May 30, 1985.

Draper, Theodore. "American Communism Revisited." *The New York Review of Books*, May 9, 1985.

Draper, Theodore. *Roots of American Communism*. New York, 1957.

Frank, Nelson. "Special Assistant Donegan." *The American Mercury*, August 1953.

Fried, Richard M. *Nightmare in Red: The McCarthy Era in Perspective*. New York, 1990.

Gentry, Curt. *J. Edgar Hoover: The Man and the Secrets*. New York, 1991.

Goodman, Walter. *The Committee: The Extraordinary Career of the House Committee on Un-American Activities*. New York, 1968.

Green, Gil. *Cold War Fugitive: A Personal Story of the McCarthy Years*. New York, 1984.

Griffith, Robert. *The Politics of Fear: Joseph R. McCarthy and the Senate*. Lexington, Ky., 1970.

Harper, Allan D. *The Politics of Loyalty: The White House and the Communist Issue*. Westport, Conn., 1969.

Hellman, Lillian. *Scoundrel Time*. Boston, 1976.

Hill, Ralph N., ed. *The College on the Hill: A Dartmouth Chronicle*. Hanover, N.H., 1964.

Hiss, Alger. *Recollections of a Life*. Boston, 1988.

Howe, Irving, and Lewis Coser. *The American Communist Party: A Critical History*. New York, 1957.

Isserman, Maurice. "Three Generations: Historians View American Communism." *Labor History*, 1985.

Isserman, Maurice. *Which Side Were You On?: The American Communist Party During the Second World War*. Wesleyan, Conn., 1982.

Jones, Lee W. "The William Remington Case." Ph.D. dissertation, City University of New York, 1989.

Kelly, Robin D. G. *Hammer and Hoe: Alabama Communists During the Great Depression*. Chapel Hill, 1990.

Kempton, Murray. *Part of Our Time: Some Monuments and Ruins of the Thirties*. New York, 1955.

Kessner, Thomas. *Fiorello La Guardia and the Making of Modern New York*. New York, 1989.

Klehr, Harvey. *The Heyday of American Communism: The Depression Decade*. New York, 1984.

Kraditor, Aileen. *"Jimmy Higgins": The Mental World of the American Rank and File Communist*. Westport, Conn., 1988.

Kutler, Stanley I. *The American Inquisition: Justice and Injustice in the Cold War*. New York, 1982.

Lamphere, Robert J., and Tom Shactman. *The FBI–KGB War: A Special Agent's Story*. New York, 1986.

Lang, Daniel. "The Days of Suspicion." *The New Yorker*, May 21, 1949.

Lash, Joseph. *Eleanor and Franklin*. New York, 1971.

Lash, Joseph. *Eleanor Roosevelt: A Friend's Memoir*. New York, 1964.

Latham, Earl. *The Communist Controversy in Washington from the New Deal to McCarthy*. Cambridge, Mass., 1966.

Martin, David C. *Wilderness of Mirrors*. New York, 1980.

May, Gary. *China Scapegoat: The Diplomatic Ordeal of John Carter Vincent*. Washington, 1979.

Morris, Roger. *Richard Milhous Nixon: The Rise of an American Politician*. New York, 1990.

Navasky, Victor. *Naming Names*. New York, 1980.

Newman, Robert P. *Owen Lattimore and the "Loss" of China*. Berkeley, 1992.

O'Neill, William L. *A Better World: The Great Schism: Stalinism and the American Intellectuals*. New York, 1982.

O'Reilly, Kenneth. *Hoover and the Un-Americans: The FBI, HUAC and the Red Menace*. Philadelphia, 1983.

Oshinsky, David M. *A Conspiracy So Immense: The World of Joe McCarthy*. New York, 1983.

Packer, Herbert L. *Ex-Communist Witnesses: Four Studies in Fact Finding*. Stanford, Calif., 1962.

Painter, Nell Irvin. *The Narrative of Hosea Hudson*. Cambridge, Mass., 1979.

Powers, Richard Gid. *Secrecy and Power: The Life of J. Edgar Hoover*. New York, 1987.

Radosh, Ron, and Joyce Milton. *The Rosenberg File: A Search for the Truth*. New York, 1983.

Redlich, Norman. "Spies in Government—the Bentley Story." *The Nation*, January 1954.

Redmont, Bernard S. *Risks Worth Taking: The Odyssey of a Foreign Correspondent*. Lanham, Md., 1992.

Reeves, Thomas C. *The Life and Times of Joe McCarthy*. New York, 1982.

Robins, Natalie. *Alien Ink: The FBI's War on Freedom of Expression*. New York, 1992.

Romig, Walter, ed. *The Book of Catholic Authorities*. Fourth Series. Grosse Point, Mich., n.d.

Rovere, Richard H. *The American Establishment and Other Reports, Opinions, and Speculations*. New York, 1962.

Shelton, Willard. "Paul Crouch: Informer." *New Republic*, July 19, 1954.

Schaar, John H. *Loyalty in America*. Berkeley, 1957.

Schlesinger, Arthur M., Jr. *The Politics of Upheaval*. Boston, 1960.

Smith, John Cabot. *Alger Hiss: The True Story*. New York, 1976.

Smith, Page. *Redeeming the Time: A People's History of the 1920s and the New Deal*. New York, 1987.

Smith, Page. *Dissenting Opinions: Select Essays*. San Francisco, 1984.

Steinberg, Peter L. *The Great "Red Menace": United States Prosecution of American Communists, 1947–1952*. Westport, Conn., 1984.

Summers, Anthony. *Official and Confidential: The Secret Life of J. Edgar Hoover*. New York, 1993.

Theoharis, Athan, and John Stuart Cox. *The Boss: J. Edgar Hoover and the Great American Inquisition*. Philadelphia, 1988.

Viorst, Milton. *Fire in the Streets: America in the 1960s*. New York, 1979.

Wechsler, James. "The Remington Affair." *The New Republic*, June 19, 1950.

Weinstein, Allen. *Perjury: The Hiss-Chambers Case*. New York, 1978.

Widmeyer, Charles E. *Hopkins of Dartmouth: The Story of Ernest Martin Hopkins and His Presidency of Dartmouth College*. Hanover, N.H., 1977.

Who Was Who in America With World Notables, Volume 3, *1951–1960*. New York, 1961.

Who Was Who in America With World Notables, Volume 4, *1961–1968*. New York, 1969.

Williams, Selma R. *Red-Listed: Haunted by the Washington Witch Hunt*. Reading, Mass., 1993.

Yoder, Edwin Y. *The Un-Making of a Whig and Other Essays in Self-Definition*. Washington, 1990.

Index

Export Program (U.S. Department of
Commerce), 94–95, 109, 119, 133, 176,
181

Federal Bureau of Investigation (FBI): and
the AYC, 58; and the Commerce
Department Export Program investiga-
tion, 94–95; designated to do investiga-
tion for Loyalty Program, 76–77; and the
Fourth Region Loyalty Board, 108, 115;
HUAC competes with, 146–47; and the
OPA loyalty check, 63, 64–66, 67; perjury
trial (1) investigations by the, 204–5, 218,
257; and perjury trial (2), 285. *See also*
Bentley, Elizabeth Terrill—and the FBI;
Federal Bureau of Investigation (FBI)—
and WR; *specific person investigated*
Federal Bureau of Investigation (FBI)—and
WR: and the Commerce Department
Export Program investigation, 94–95;
effect on WR's career of investigations by,
87–88; and espionage charges, 88–89,
145–47; and FBI breaks into WR's house,
77; FBI follows WR, 77, 145–46; and FBI
intercepts WR's mail, 77; and the FBI
interviews of WR, 89–91; and the FBI
loyalty investigation of WR, 147–48; and
FBI wiretap on WR's telephone, 77, 87;
and the libel suit, 119, 135; and the New
York grand jury, 92–93; and the perjury
indictment, 178, 180; and perjury trial
(1), 187–88, 251–52, 255; and the
Tennessee period, 178; and WR as an
informant, 91–92, 93–94, 135, 251–52,
255
Federal Employee Loyalty Program. *See*
Loyalty Program
Ferguson, Homer, 97, 103, 125, 128, 267
Ferguson Committee, 95–96, 97–100,
101–4, 158, 201
Fifth Amendment, 94, 150, 151, 166–67,
213, 299, 304
Finland, Soviet invasion of, 57, 58, 65, 246,
255, 260
Fisher, Paul, 200
Fitzgerald, Edward, 83, 258
Fletcher, Howard, B., 145
Follmer, Frederick V., 316, 317, 318
Folsom, Franklin, 69, 71, 179
Foster, William Z., 59, 239, 240

Fourth Region Loyalty Board: Bentley
charges considered by, 108; and the
Dartmouth College years, 104, 106–7,
108, 109, 110; and espionage/passing of
information, 105, 108, 120; FBI inter-
views/reports for the, 108, 115; interrogatory of the, 108–10; Memorandum of
Decision of the, 119–20; overturning
decision of the, 129–30; procedural errors
of the, 129–30; support letters for WR
sent to the, 105–8; and the Tennessee
period, 109, 110; witnesses for the, 104;
WR appeals decision of the, 120; and
WR's FBI interviews, 108; WR's prepara-
tions for the, 101, 104–8; WR's state-
ments to the, 109–10, 111–16
Fox, Bertram, 107, 260, 284
Frank, Jerome, 45
Frank, Nelson, 94, 95, 123
Frank, Waldo, 27
Frankfurter, Felix, 304, 305
Friedman, Celia, 263
Fuhr, Lee, 79
Fuller, W. Atherton "Athy," 16

Gallaher, Lester, 282
Gamblin, George, 312–13
Garrity, Devin, 205, 227–29, 235, 236
Garvey, William, 316
General Foods Corporation, 118–19,
136–39, 141–44, 172
Gerber, Serril, 38
Gessell, Gerald, 205–6
Gibbs, Angelica, 78
Giles, Roscoe Conkling, Jr., 224, 246, 248,
283, 284, 286
Gillem, Newell, 13
Gladieux, Bernard L., 144, 176
Glazer, Ezra, 63, 200
Gold, Bela, 81–82
Gold, Harry, 3
Gold, Sonia, 81–82
Goldenthal, Adolph J., 257
Golos, Jacob: and the appeal for perjury trial
(2), 292; and Bentley's book, 156;
Bentley's relationship with, 79–82; and
Browder, 82–83; FBI investigations of,
80–81; and the FBI Loyalty Program
investigation, 90, 91; and the Ferguson
Committee, 99–100; and the Fourth